GUANGDONG

Survey of a Province Undergoing Rapid Change

GUANGDONG

Survey of a Province Undergoing Rapid Change

Second Edition

Edited by

Y. M. Yeung and David K. Y. Chu

The Chinese University Press

ISBN 962–201–769–X

THE CHINESE UNIVERSITY PRESS
The Chinese University of Hong Kong
SHATIN, N.T., HONG KONG
Fax: +852 2603 6692
     +852 2603 7355
E-mail: cup@cuhk.edu.hk
Web-site: http://www.cuhk.edu.hk/cupress/w1.htm

Printed in Hong Kong

Contents

Figures and Tables

Tables

Preface to Second Edition

Rapid and widespread changes in Guangdong have made it necessary for us to revise and update many of the observations and data that were used in the first edition of this book. Many of the chapters of the original edition ended in 1992, when the paramount leader Deng Xiaoping made his historic tour of southern China. In February 1997, he died, an event that was received very stoically in a country he had opened up again for development and modernization. The five-year period 1992–1997 was, for Guangdong, one of exceptionally rapid growth followed by slowdown as macroeconomic adjustment policies originating from Beijing began to take hold. Meanwhile, other parts of China are rapidly catching up in economic growth; Guangdong must adjust its development strategies and plans in approaching its future.

The year 1997 is also historic in China's resumption of sovereignty over Hong Kong. Hong Kong has been a critical factor in launching China's trajectory of rapid growth and transformation since 1978, and its impact on Guangdong has been particularly far-reaching. The Hong Kong factor in Guangdong's development is even more important beyond 1997, as both administrative entities will have to cooperate and coordinate more closely for their shared future. How Hong Kong's integration with China will affect the nature and course of development in Guangdong remains to be seen.

In preparing this second and revised edition, considerable care has been taken to update all the tables and maps, as far as possible to 1995. Occasionally, some of the data and statistics go as far as 1997. Some chapters (Chapters 1, 2, 3, and 17) have been significantly rewritten, with the addition of new materials. Chapter 9 by Maurice Brosseau is completely rewritten, with even a new title. In all other chapters, new data and materials have been introduced to make this book as up-to-date as possible.

The completion of this book in its present form is the result of the efforts of many individuals, apart from the contributors themselves. We are indebted to the Lippo Group which has continued to support the Urban and Regional Development in Pacific Asia Programme. The Lippo Urban Fund has been its main source of research funding since 1993. Mr. J. P. Lee, OBE, MBE, JP, has been most supportive and caring of its research and for which we are most grateful. We wish to thank Joanna Lee, former research assistant of the programme, for her painstaking care and meticulous attention to detail. Polly Chui took up the work from Joanna recently and was largely responsible for reworking the indexes. Janet Wong was her dependable self and S. L. Too redrew some of the maps. We are grateful to the constructive comments on the manuscript of the updated and amended version by an anonymous reviewer; meeting these critical remarks has resulted in improvement of presentation and substance. We take responsibility for any possible lapses and oversights.

The editors
October 1997

Preface to First Edition

The acclaimed *The Other Hong Kong Report* and *China Review* launched by The Chinese University Press several years ago have now become eagerly awaited publications every year in Hong Kong and elsewhere for their shrewd insights and scholarly analysis. For some time, there has been a need felt for a volume that would straddle the immediacy of Hong Kong happenings and the macro trends of a vast country like China. Given Hong Kong's historical and rapidly growing links with Guangdong in innumerable ways, a comprehensive volume designed to take stock of the recent transformation of Guangdong is overdue. Its sparkling economic achievements attained under China's economic reforms and open policy have to be duly documented, elucidated and evaluated.

This volume has been undertaken as a project of the Urban and Regional Development in Pacific Asia Research Programme of the Hong Kong Institute of Asia-Pacific Studies at The Chinese University of Hong Kong. It has been one of the major projects of the programme since mid-1992, when a team of academics almost exclusively from Hong Kong was deployed to work on it. Not only the Institute but the Department of Geography of the University have lent their full support to this project, for which we are grateful.

For a project of this nature, many people have contributed to it directly or indirectly. In the first place, we must thank T. L. Tsim, director of The Chinese University Press, who most strongly suggested this project. While we unreservedly shared his enthusiasm, we could not readily respond to his invitation to prepare this volume for some time until 1992. At the Hong Kong Institute of Asia-Pacific Studies, Janet Wong and Irene Lai have never failed in their devotion and dedication to the project. Janet Wong oversaw many aspects of the project, including correspondence, liaison and typing, and Irene Lai was meticulous in research, proofreading and editorial assistance. Zhu Qing helped with the romanization of Chinese references in many chapters. Jane Wan and Yu Yuk-mui of the Department of Geography typed and retyped the manuscript. S. L. Too deserves all the credit in cartographic presentation, as he drew or redrew all the illustrations. Paul Kwong helped in strengthening this volume by compiling a comprehensive Index. This volume could not have been completed in its present form or within a relatively short time without the unstinting and professional support of The Chinese University Press. Last but surely not least, we reserve our sincerest appreciation to the contributors who share with us their expert knowledge in their respective fields and bore with our repeated demands with understanding and generosity. For any remaining errors and shortcomings, we are primarily responsible.

The editors
October 1993

Abbreviations

AIDS	acquired immunodeficiency syndrome
ASEAN	Association of South-East Asian Nations
CCP	Chinese Communist Party
CCPIT	China Council for the Promotion of International Trade
CERD	China Economic Research and Development
CIETAC	The China International Economic and Trade Arbitration Commission
CITIC	China International Trust and Investment Company
CLP	China Light and Power Company
COE	collective-owned enterprise
FBIS	Foreign Broadcasting Information Services
GATT	General Agreement on Tariffs and Trade
GDP	gross domestic product
GGPC	Guangdong General Power Company Limited
GITIC	Guangdong International Trust and Investment Company
GNP	gross national product
GVAO	gross value of agricultural output
GVIO	gross value of industrial output
HEP	hydroelectric power
HMSO	Her Majesty's Stationery Office
ICOR	incremental capital-output ratio
IDRC	International Development Research Centre
ISIC	International Standard Industrial Classification
MOFERT	Ministry of Foreign Economic Relations and Trade
NACE	Nomenclature des Activités Économiques dans les Communautées Européennes
NBFI	non-bank financial institution
NEPA	National Environmental Protection Agency
NIE	newly industrializing economy

NPC	National People's Congress
PAM	Province/Autonomous Regions/Central State-administered Municipalities
PRC	People's Republic of China
PWR	pressurized water reactor
R & D	research and development
R/C	Residential Committee
RMB	Renminbi (or *yuan*)
SEZ	Special Economic Zone
SOE	state-owned enterprise
SOEC	Statistical Office of the European Communities
STAQ	Securities Trading Automated Quotations System
TVE	township and village enterprise
TVRs	total value of retail sales

1

Introduction

Y. M. Yeung

Nineteen years after a historic decision attributable to Deng Xiaoping in 1978, China has made truly remarkable economic strides through its economic reforms and open (door) policy. World attention is once again focused on China's economic upsurge, to such an extent that a "China craze" reminiscent of the early 1970s appears to have resurfaced.[1] Leading China's bold and ambitious drive towards modernization and development has been Guangdong province, which has applied, with ingenuity and dexterity, a range of reform policies that have yielded astonishing and positive results across a broad front of economic and social life. The scope, pace and prospect of life in Guangdong have been so changed that its effect is being felt in many parts of the country.

Visitors and students of Guangdong cannot help but marvel at the breadth and depth of the change that has occurred in the province in recent years. Comparing the situation in 1978 with 1997, the transformation of Guangdong is almost complete, in which the physical landscape, the economic structure, institutions, the mindset of the people and, indeed, man and society, have undergone almost a complete reversal. Guiding socialist philosophy notwithstanding, signs of the market economy are everywhere. The rapidity of change in Guangdong is worthy of study in its own right, but the importance goes further. Not only are other open areas of China looking towards Guangdong as a barometer of change, but also overseas scholars and political leaders alike harbour no less interest in whether the largest remaining communist country has, in fact, succeeded in a smooth transition from a centrally planned to a market economy and whether the switch is durable.

This volume has stemmed from an abiding interest in and a neighbourly concern over the constantly shifting kaleidoscope of Guangdong that is unfolding across the border from Hong Kong. Consequently almost all the contributing authors to this project have been drawn from the academic community in Hong Kong. Its objective is to address the myriad of physical, economic and social changes in as encompassing a manner as possible.[2] The emphasis is emphatically placed on explicating and analyzing the evolving physical and human panorama in Guangdong over the past nineteen years, coinciding with the period of China's economic reforms. In setting the stage for each of the subsequent chapters to be better understood in an emerging context, this introductory chapter provides, firstly, a brief overview of Guangdong, drawing out some of its salient characteristics. Secondly, the main elements of its economic transformation are highlighted. Thirdly, how Guangdong is viewed in relation to a broader context in the neighbouring territories in Asia and what the future has in store for it are discussed. Finally, Guangdong's specific roles in the next century are addressed. In all these parts, reference to the chapters will be made as often as possible to strengthen the continuity and consistency of the volume. This approach will be echoed in the concluding synthesis (Chapter 20).

Overview of Guangdong[3]

With the exception of Hainan Island, which was separated from Guangdong into a new province and a Special Economic Zone (SEZ) in 1988, Guangdong is the most southerly of the 22 provinces and 5 autonomous regions in China. It has an area of 177,901 sq km, representing merely 1.85% of China's total area. However, its coastline is the longest of all provinces, amounting to 3,368 km, or 10.52% of the country's total. This is important for coastal and riverine shipping, as well as providing fishing and other marine resources. Guangdong's population in 1995 reached 68.68 million, accounting for 5.67% of China's population. This gives a population density of 382 persons per sq km, which is the ninth densest of all provinces in China.

The special character of Guangdong is manifested in many ways, in its physiography, climate, language, folklore and products. Topographically, it is separated from the rest of China by the east-west Nan Ling range. This factor, together with its long coastline, its contact with other countries through its overseas emigrants, and early exposure to Western influence through the port of Guangzhou, has the province historically associated with a degree of self-sufficiency and a tendency of separatism. Indeed, for a long time throughout Chinese history until the Song dynasty, Guangdong was viewed as nothing but a semicivilized frontier, to which disgraced officials were exiled as a punishment.

The geomorphology of Guangdong is diverse, being made up for the most part of rounded hills, cut by streams and rivers, and scattered and ribbon-like alluvial valleys (Chapter 18). Much of northern Guangdong consists of dissected uplands, but of the greatest economic value are alluvial and deltaic plains formed by the three major rivers of the Pearl River (Zhujiang) system — the West (Xi), the North (Bei) and the East (Dong) rivers. The Pearl River Delta, referring to the area of the West River beyond the confluence, is one of the fastest growing areas in China since 1978. Since 1984, the "Small Delta" and the "Large Delta" were differentiated, occupying, respectively, 11.1% and 21.7% of the provincial area.[4]

The Han River in eastern Guangdong is the most important river outside the Pearl River system.

Much of Guangdong lies south of the Tropic of Cancer and thus is the only province, along with Hainan, with tropical and subtropical climates (Chapter 4). What distinguishes Guangdong from most parts of East China is not its summer temperatures, which range from 28°C to 30°C in July in the West River valley, but its much higher winter temperatures, which range from 13°C to 16°C. Rainfall displays a pronounced summer maximum, with the rainy season lasting between mid-April to mid-October. Typhoons coincide with this rainy period when their occurrence can cause widespread human and material destruction. The mild winter means that two crops of rice can be grown everywhere in the province, and monsoon rains weave a pattern of agricultural land use that has been perfected for untold generations. Rain-fed rivers are not only a major source of water supply for the burgeoning population, but also a means of cheap and common means of transport.

The administrative system in Guangdong has undergone many changes since 1949. However, since 1978 there has been a tendency for many counties (*xian*) to upgrade themselves to cities. Many city-administered counties thus came into being. In Guangdong there are at present 75 counties which are administratively under 21 cities, forming what might be viewed as city regions. An idea of the administrative hierarchy *circa* 1997 may be gained in Figure 1.1. At the apex of this hierarchy is Guangzhou, which is the provincial capital. Guangzhou used to be the unrivalled metropolis in Guangdong, dominating its economic and cultural life to a very large extent. Since 1978, because of the rapid rise of secondary cities in the delta area through their economic growth and population influx, Guangzhou's relative importance has declined. Edward Woo has depicted divergent paths in the transformation of major cities, but they have tended to converge in the diversified functions they perform in trade and the tertiary sector. Urban regions in their inchoate forms are also being established (Chapter 15).

Beginning in the seventeenth century, a deteriorating man-land ratio and a weakening Manchu rule gradually led Guangdong to become an area of emigration. Emigrants from the province went far and wide and have since settled in many parts of the world. Despite the long physical and temporal separation, these emigrants have never forgotten their roots and have actually forged enduring links with their places of origin. The importance of this factor of life in Guangdong itself can be appreciated by the

Figure 1.1 Administrative Divisions of Guangdong, c. 1997

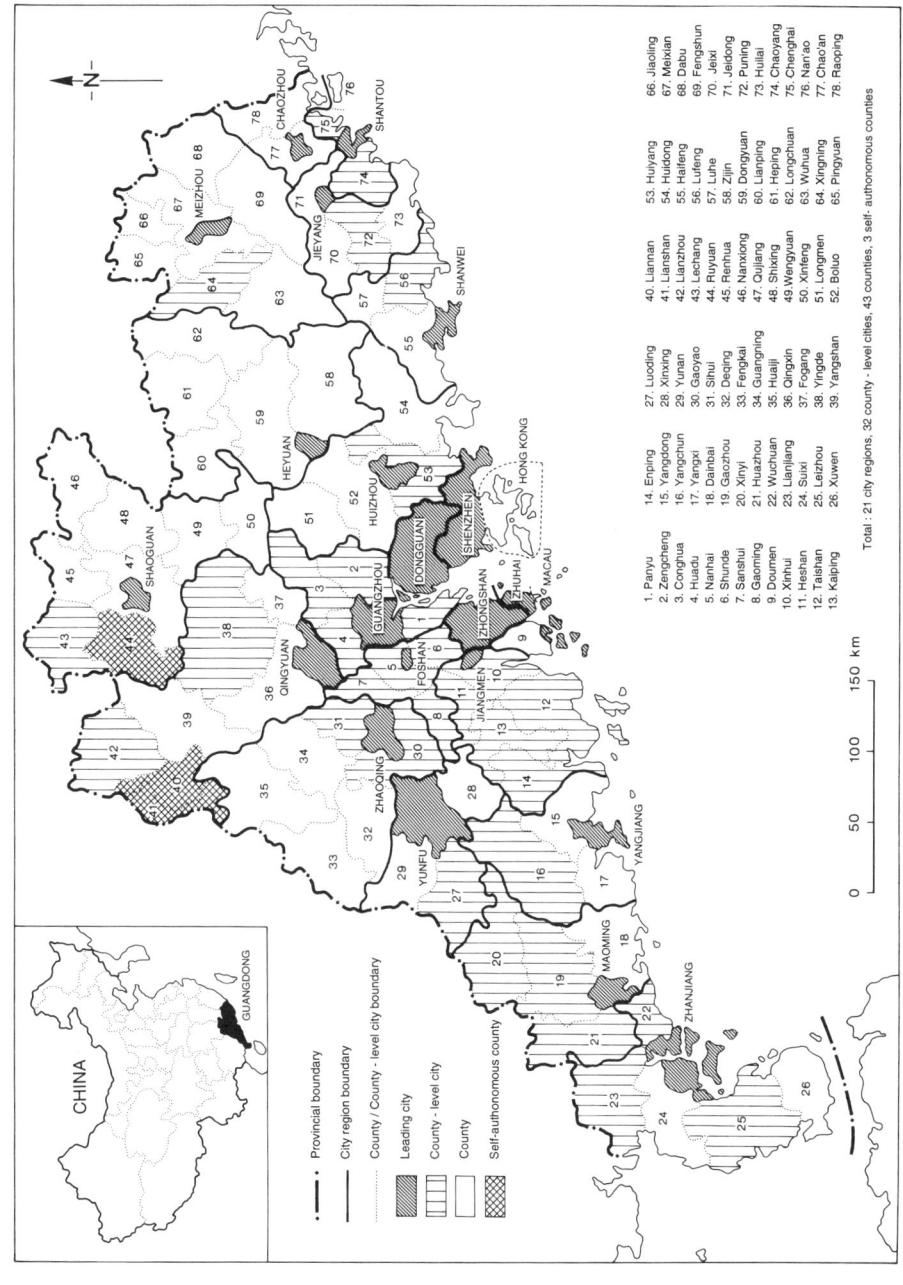

Total : 21 city regions, 32 county-level cities, 43 counties, 3 self-authonomous counties

1. Panyu
2. Zengcheng
3. Conghua
4. Huadu
5. Nanhai
6. Shunde
7. Sanshui
8. Gaoming
9. Doumen
10. Xinhui
11. Heshan
12. Taishan
13. Kaiping
14. Enping
15. Yangdong
16. Yangchun
17. Yangxi
18. Dainbai
19. Gaozhou
20. Xinyi
21. Huazhou
22. Wuchuan
23. Lianjiang
24. Suixi
25. Leizhou
26. Xuwen
27. Luoding
28. Xinxing
29. Yunan
30. Gaoyao
31. Sihui
32. Deqing
33. Fengkai
34. Guangning
35. Huaiji
36. Qingxin
37. Fogang
38. Yingde
39. Yangshan
40. Liannan
41. Lianshan
42. Lianzhou
43. Lechang
44. Ruyuan
45. Renhua
46. Nanxiong
47. Qujiang
48. Shixing
49. Wengyuan
50. Xinfeng
51. Longmen
52. Boluo
53. Huiyang
54. Hudong
55. Haifeng
56. Lufeng
57. Luhe
58. Zijin
59. Dongyuan
60. Lianping
61. Heping
62. Longchuan
63. Wuhua
64. Xingning
65. Pingyuan
66. Jiaoling
67. Meixian
68. Dabu
69. Fengshun
70. Jiebi
71. Jieidong
72. Puning
73. Huilai
74. Chaoyang
75. Chenghai
76. Nan'ao
77. Chao'an
78. Raoping

fact that returned overseas Chinese totalled approximately 10 million in the mid-1980s, or about 15% of the total population.[5] The vital links overseas Chinese provide in technology transfer, capital accumulation and information access have been emphasized in many of the chapters. In this connection, Hong Kong Chinese have been playing, since 1978, the role of Guangdong's window to the world exceedingly well.

The early exposure to Western influence with Guangzhou as the only port of external trade for one hundred years prior to the Opium War (1839–1842), coupled with the overseas Chinese link, has traditionally facilitated Guangdong to nurture political and cultural leaders whose thinking was ahead of their times. Prominent leaders of political movements include Hong Xiuquan, Kang Youwei, Liang Qichao and Sun Yat-sen (Sun Yixian). They have left indelible marks in the history of modern China. Lau Yee-cheung traces the historical development of Guangdong from an economic perspective. The rise of Guangzhou and Foshan owed largely to the flourishing commerce and trade that the province experienced as a result of the single-port policy and the use of the Meiguan Pass as the sole north-south conduit for movement of goods between Guangdong and other parts of China (Chapter 19).

A Profile of Societal Transformation

Over the past nineteen years since China adopted an open policy, Guangdong has become a transfigured land. Hardly any facet of society has not been touched by the people's passion for change, so much so that a societal transformation has occurred in the province. From the abyss of stagnation in the late 1970s that was the bitter legacy of the Cultural Revolution, Guangdong has dramatically turned the corner and, by the mid-1990s, can proudly show its face of modernity and breathtaking economic gains in its SEZs, in the bustling cities in the Pearl River Delta and elsewhere. All this has been achieved amid such a climate of experimentation, trial and hesitation, with the rules of the game hardly delineated, that China's economic boom has been likened to a "modern gold rush." Chinese businessmen's enthusiasm for change has been compared with the gold-rush fever that opened up the West Coast of North America in the 1800s.[6]

The best way to bring home Guangdong's startling economic progress in recent years is to cite some comparative statistics. Between 1991 and 1995, real economic growth in Guangdong averaged 19.1% per year, as opposed to 12% per year for China, i.e., 7.1 percentage points above the national rate for five years (see comparable figures in Chapters 3 and 8). In the period 1985–1995, Guangdong's gross domestic product (GDP) multiplied 9.73 times.[7] Toyojiro Maruya further marshals other data to show the much enhanced relative position of Guangdong in China over time. In 1980, Guangdong's gross national product (GNP) per capita was lower than the national average, but by 1995, it was 67.6% above it. Whereas Guangdong had ranked seventh in its contribution to China's GDP in 1978, it soared to the top rank by 1995 (beginning in 1989). Guangdong is now the foremost province in foreign capital utilizations, exports, investment in fixed social output and agricultural production. The share of Guangdong in China's production of consumer durable goods has similarly soared. Guangdong's share in the country's camera production has increased by many orders of magnitude, from 10% in 1978 to 82% in 1995. Likewise, Guangdong was responsible for producing a sizeable proportion of China's refrigerators (23.2%), washing machines (19.7%) and television sets (25.3%) in 1995.

One primary factor which enabled Guangdong to grow as rapidly as it did was the decisive policy adopted at the Third Plenum of the Party's Eleventh Central Committee in December 1978, whereby economic reforms and an open policy would be pursued. Guangdong, through the three Special Economic Zones of Shenzhen, Zhuhai and Shantou, was allowed "special policies and flexible measures." As Peter Cheung (Chapter 2) documents, the relationship between Guangdong and the central government has had its ups and downs, buffeted by the jostle for political power between the pro-reform and conservatives groups in Beijing. There are many dimensions to the fascinating tussle for political power and economic concessions. One breakthrough which permitted Guangdong to achieve a greater measure of fiscal autonomy was the agreement, in 1980, of a five-year fixed-amount quota system, whereby Guangdong would pay the central government RMB1 billion annually. Since 1985, the fixed-amount system has been replaced by one of "steadily increasing responsibility." There are many other facets of central-provincial relations, touching on foreign trade, taxation power and economic policy-making power.[8]

In proceeding with its economic transformation, Guangdong initially focused its attention on the rural sector between 1979 to 1983. Chau Kwai-cheong (Chapter 4) has revealed that agricultural production reached a record in the mid-1980s, with diversification and specialization.

Production since then has tended to be stagnant. Forestry productivity is, however, low by national and world standards. Its development has been hampered by backward technology. The rural landscape has witnessed drastic changes as a consequence of land disturbances and technological breakthroughs. Most disconcerting is the rapid loss of cultivated land, which amounted to 3.3 million *mu* in the period 1980–1990.[9] In the early 1990s Guangdong had only 0.61 *mu* of arable land per person, the second lowest of all provinces in China. In 1994 this further decreased to 0.51 *mu*.

In the period 1984–1988, after successful economic reforms in the rural sector with the adoption of a responsibility system, development was concentrated in the urban sector. This was the beginning of what may be described as an economic take-off. From the mid-1980s, all economic indicators began to show a sharp upward swing. Lau Pui-king (Chapter 6) ascribes advances in industry and trade to the stimulus that came with marketization and the emergence of a free enterprise system. Collectively or privately-owned enterprises grew phenomenally, at the expense of state-owned enterprises. In the period 1983–1988, the value of industrial products from state-owned enterprises consistently declined, losing 19 percentage points to less than 50% of the total. The proportion of state-owned industrial enterprises decreased from 59.3% to 41.2% from 1983 to 1988.[10] In the explosive growth of Guangdong's industrial capacity, the vital role played by township and rural enterprises is clearly shown in their staggering increase from 80,000 in 1978 to about 1.2 million in 1989, a 25.2% increase per year over 11 years.[11]

In fact, in the heart of the Pearl River Delta, Maurice Brosseau (Chapter 9) has detected a new entrepreneurial spirit — a delta spirit — that has propelled the exceptionally fast growth in the area. In the "Four Small Tigers" — Shunde, Nanhai, Zhongshan and Dongguan — the growth in GDP in the period since 1978 averaged over 20% per year, considerably above the provincial average. They are certainly in the forefront of economic reforms, as the examples of Panyu and Shunde have shown that incremental reform through private enterprises has achieved effective developmental change and positive results. To make up for previous neglect and to be in step with the recent economic renewal, service industries, Wong Kwan-yiu (Chapter 7) observes, have boomed in a variety of forms. There has been a structural shift of the economy towards services, which at present accounts for one-third of the GDP of the province. The nascent consumer market in Guangdong is the envy of many transnational corporations which have diverse goods and services to sell. It has been suggested that domestic consumption will likely replace exports as the motor of China's development.[12] Tourism has also become an important income-earner. In the midst of economic prosperity, there is a real need for Guangdong to evolve new ways to manage banking and finance. Tsang Shu-ki (Chapter 8) argues that Guangdong is "above average" in money and banking in China. It is evolving new forms of financial intermediation, for example, by developing in Shenzhen one of China's two stock markets. As a matter of fact, both Shenzhen and Zhuhai are pioneers in financial reforms in China. Financial reform is a critical component on which the sustainability of economic reforms at large depends.

As the delta region prospered economically, the wage differentials between that area and other counties in Guangdong and other provinces increased. While the wage differentials between Guangdong and its neighbouring provinces were only 10% in 1978, the gap was magnified to between 35% and 70% by 1990. This induced intra-provincial and inter-provincial labour migration into the delta region in search of work and economic opportunities. In fact, most of the farming in the prosperous delta region is undertaken by outside workers.[13] As Li Si-ming and Siu Yat-ming (Chapter 17) have demonstrated, the scale of migration has been massive and unprecedented. Understandably, most migrants move for economic reasons. There is also a sizeable mobile or temporary population in many of the cities in the delta region. In Guangzhou alone, the mobile population totalled 0.91 million in 1989, or about 25% of the city population. It has been estimated that Guangzhou's mobile population increased annually at 12.9% in the period 1979–1989.[14]

In order to keep pace with the spurt of development, Guangdong has found it hard to provide the necessary supporting infrastructure. As Luk Chiu-ming (Chapter 14) has illustrated, considerable progress has been made in improving all modes of transport and communication. Construction of highways, airports and seaports, in particular, has been ambitious, but coordination of such mega-projects at the provincial level or within the delta region itself is seriously lacking. Similarly, energy shortages prove to be a bottleneck which has the effect of holding back development. Hung Wing-tat and Peter Hills (Chapter 5) show that demand for energy has been increasing rapidly and, despite foreign investment and participation, will remain insatiable for some time.[15] Often viewed as a component of infrastructure, housing has been rapidly evolving, as Rebecca Chiu (Chapter 13) has documented, from being a welfare provision to a tradable commodity in the market. Guangdong is, however, still a long way from the full commodification of housing, but the beginning of housing reforms has been made, with the SEZs leading in such reforms and the development of housing markets. Teething problems are yet to be overcome.

Guangdong's headlong economic development has also spilled over into domains not directly involved in income generation. In education, Grace Mak (Chapter 10) has concluded that a rudimentary take-off in education has occurred, with the early signs of market forces already at play. However, economic opportunities as a result of the open policy have lured many teachers away from schools, resulting in a crisis in the teaching profession. A related problem is the alarming wastage of some 1.12 million students in the period 1985–1989, lost to the job market. The more material orientation of society has likewise caused a change in the content of education, with vocational education being given greater emphasis. Higher education, too, is changing in fundamental ways and even the meaning of education is a subject of debate. With respect to health, Wong Tze-wai and others (Chapter 11) have called attention to one negative side-effect of rapid industrialization. This is the question of occupational health problems associated with township and rural enterprises, which are omnipresent while health services are poorly provided for or not provided for at all. Migrant workers, especially those engaged in "dirty jobs," are also prone to occupational health problems. The health system as a whole has undergone radical changes and, with the ageing of Guangdong's population, the health of the elderly is a subject requiring special attention. Eva Li (Chapter 12) has outlined several important changes in social provisions, divided into social insurance, social relief, social welfare and privileged security. A situation of shared responsibility with the government has arisen as new enterprises are established. As well, new social problems emerge as Guangdong moves towards a market economy, such as the reappearance of prostitution, another deleterious by-product of opening the province, for which there is no ready solution.

Guangdong in a Wider Context

The success of Guangdong's economic reforms is probably beyond the expectations of the original proponents of the open policy. By the early 1990s, there were plenty of signs of prosperity in the province and the future path of development in Guangdong will be keenly watched, in China as well as abroad.[16] The meaning of Guangdong's economic leap may perhaps be grasped at three levels.

At the first level, within Guangdong itself the impulse of economic growth has been spatially differentiated, with the Pearl River Delta viewed by some as a marvel of the open policy but many of the outlying mountainous counties scantily affected in material ways. The huge and widening personal income gap between the delta and the mountainous regions has been emphasized by Guangdong officials. However, the provincial government as well as the cities which have developed the fastest have faced up to the responsibility of assisting the laggard counties to catch up and narrow the difference in several ways.[17] There are also other ways in which the economic reforms have impacted Guangdong society.

Before the reforms will have a good likelihood of sustaining themselves, two particular sectors require urgent attention. One is related to the legal system, which is at present chaotic and arbitrary, leaving little recourse to the wronged investor and trader.[18] Susan Finder (Chapter 16) reveals slow progress in legislative reforms, although Shenzhen has been allowed freedom in enacting local regulations. As economic development has accelerated, the Guangdong courts are faced with a skyrocketing increase in the number and variety of commercial litigation cases. An interim solution is for many of the economic disputes to be settled in mediation centres that have been established. A disturbing concern appears to be that even the judiciary is not above corruption, a phenomenon that is widespread and undermining the administrative and social systems. Equally deserving of immediate remedial measures is environmental degradation in many forms that R. J. Neller and K. C. Lam (Chapter 18) have highlighted. The pollution that comes especially with industrialization has become a serious problem. Despite the existence of environmental legislation and standards, their weak enforcement and the decentralized pattern of polluting industries have been chronic difficulties. Environmental control is more relaxed outside the major cities of the delta, and the main threat has originated from industrial development in small- and medium-sized cities and towns and rural industrialization.[19] However, Guangdong plans to spend up to RMB14.4 billion during the Ninth Five-year Plan (1996–2000) on environmental protection in the Pearl River Delta, with 14 large projects to be implemented.[20]

At the second level, Guangdong's experimentation with economic reforms is part of the national design to bring China out of its previous self-imposed isolation from the world community and economy. As Ezra Vogel has aptly put it, Guangdong's attempt at modernization and development is merely one step ahead in China.[21] What is indisputable are the impressive gains economic reforms and the open policy have brought to Guangdong, in particular to the three SEZs which all started from very humble foundations (see Chapter 20). Shenzhen is the epitome of what the open policy has created. It grew at an average of 500% per year during the 1980s and is now the city with the highest standard of living and wages in China. In 1995, it had a population of 3.45 million, of which 2.46 million consisted of temporary population.[22] Consequently, Guangdong, especially the SEZs, has been a major destination for migration of skilled and un-skilled labour from many parts of China. In fact, it has been observed that since 1978 there has been a relative shift of China's centre of gravity, involving the movement of capital, talent, technology and labour to the south.[23]

Indeed, the substantive and symbolic meaning of what happens in Guangdong is viewed seriously across China, other open areas in par-ticular. Thus the visits of top political leaders to the SEZs in Guangdong in 1984–1985, 1987–1988, 1990 and 1992 were targeted to assess certain critical stages of the open policy, requiring the messages to be fully aired to the nation (see Chapter 9). These visits contributed in no small way to formulating the "socialist market economy" policy that culminated in Deng Xiaoping's visit to the south in January 1992.

With the passing of time and as other open areas succeeded in obtain-ing the same special status as the SEZs and open cities in Guangdong to pursue their economic development, the Special Economic Zones are no longer actually that special. While the development of other areas of China is needed and fully justified, there has been a problem of duplication and redundancy among the coastal cities in the choice of their development policy and direction. What had succeeded in Guangdong tended in some cases to be blindly replicated, without taking into account the local cir-cumstances or comparative advantage.[24]

Whatever the role of Guangdong as a pace-setter is in China's transi-tion to a market economy, the decision in 1990 to set up Pudong in Shang-hai as a free-trade zone, with policies similar to the SEZs, was inspired by Guangdong's scintillating achievements in the 1980s. In part, the Pudong plan was conceived of as a counter-magnet to the economic pull of Guang-dong and a "major economic base" from which to launch an economic rejuvenation of Shanghai and its surrounding region. From the signs that are emerging to date, it will likely be another centre of economic growth for China in the 1990s and beyond.[25]

At the third level, Guangdong's recent development must be viewed against the background of the neighbouring territories, Asia and the world. The original choice of Shenzhen and Zhuhai as SEZs was surely predicated upon their advantage of geographical proximity to Hong Kong and Macau, two colonial territories that are due to return to Chinese sovereignty in 1997 and 1999, respectively. At least for Hong Kong, its lucrative symbiosis with Guangdong that began hesitantly in 1978, has flowered into massive trade flows, two-way investments and all-round explosive growth since 1984. Hong Kong has fully utilized the cheap land and labour costs in the delta region and relocated *en masse* the bulk of its industrial capacity north of the border. Guangdong has essentially become Hong Kong's workshop, employing around 3 million workers in factories owned by Hong Kong investors. Hong Kong capital accounts for Guangdong's overwhelming share of external economic activity, amounting to 80.9% in trade and 70.0% in investment.[26] Hong Kong investors are involved in more than 10,000 joint ventures, as well as deriving their products from 20,000 processing factories in the province. Guangdong-processed goods offer a 70% profit margin, against 20% in Hong Kong, providing a strong economic motivation to Hong Kong firms to effect their industrial relocation.[27] In turn, Hong Kong's advanced transport, communication, financial and service sectors serve Guangdong well to market its products overseas and to gain access to the latest market information. Hong Kong investors' willingness to take a chance in the face of uncertainty to provide capital for Guangdong development in the 1980s provided the critical initial momentum that was later sustained as other investors also joined in.

The obvious and substantial mutual benefit that Guangdong and Hong Kong reaped from the open policy has given rise to other conceptual designs for "Greater Hong Kong," "Southern China" and other permutations. The Southern China proposition involves the broader area of Guangdong, Fujian, Taiwan and Hong Kong, capitalizing on the Hong Kong–Guangdong link and the close Taiwan–Fujian linguistic and geographical relations. In fact, it is one of several existing and potential growth triangles in the Asia-Pacific region, in which several contiguous countries are anxious for economic cooperation across national boundaries for the common object of accelerating development.[28] A variant of the same theme is a Cantonese newly industrializing economy, involving Hong Kong, Macau, the neighbouring SEZs, Guangzhou and the Inner Delta, as Vogel has envisaged.[29]

Irrespective of which extended territorial design is more appropriate, the development of Guangdong being linked to a wider region means the fortune of the province is subject to the vicissitudes of the world economy. By leading China in the open policy, Guangdong has already been partially integrated with the world economy. China's openness has coincided with a period of globalization of production and more open economies since the 1980s. A recent Australian study has perceived propitious opportunities for economic change in Northeast Asia, including China, which has shown signs of greater openness and integration into the regional economy.[30] China is anxious to rejoin the General Agreement on Tariffs and Trade (GATT), which has been replaced by the World Trade Organization (WTO), but must further its economic reforms in trade, currency and other spheres before it can succeed.

Looking towards the future, Deng Xiaoping in his tour of Guangdong in January 1992 called on the province to become another Little Dragon of Asia in twenty years. This was translated at the Fourteenth National Party Congress held in October 1992 into development objectives, requiring Guangdong to realize modernization goals in two decades. Concrete development targets have been set, in two stages, to 2000 and 2010 (see also Chapter 3). Guangdong has since adopted 17 ways to open more areas to the outside, including declaring Meizhou, Shaoguan and Heyuan as part of the coastal open areas.[31] Guangdong's recent record of growth is any government's envy as it has become one of the most rapidly developing regions of the world. It has already successfully translated, ahead of schedule, an early development goal set by central planners in China to quadruple GDP between 1980 and 2000. However, to be on par with the Four Little Dragons is a different proposition. A recent assessment has it that in twenty years, Guangdong can realistically catch up with Taiwan and South Korea, but to reach the level of Hong Kong and Singapore would be a different matter.[32] In any event, it is an admirable development goal which, even if not entirely attained, will be an inspiring target towards which forces of energy and enterprise should be purposefully directed, as they have been in the recent past.

Towards the Twenty-first Century

During the Eighth Five-year Plan (1991–1995) period, Guangdong achieved tremendous growth, with GDP annual growth averaging at 19%, 6.5% higher than the previous Plan period and 7.3% higher than the national average. It marked the period of the most rapid growth in Guangdong since 1949. The delta area grew even more phenomenally, averaging at 26.2% during the period 1991–1994. However, beginning in late 1993, macroeconomic adjustment began to be implemented and growth began to be moderated. The year 1995 marked the last year of rapid growth, with the annual growth of GDP at 15%.[33]

However, for the Ninth Five-year Plan (1996–2000) period, Guangdong has set for itself more subdued rates of growth, with GDP annual growth projected at 10–13%. Per capita GDP is projected to increase from RMB5,166 in 1995 to RMB8,610 in 2000. In addition, the Plan has set specific goals for the province to achieve slightly faster growth in heavy industry versus light industry, to lean more towards export growth than economic growth, to emphasize technology upgrade and to co-ordinate development among regions, specifically to minimize disparity between development in the two flanks of the delta area and between the northern hilly region and the rest of the province.[34]

Indeed, on the theme of technology upgrade, state-owned enterprises (SOEs) will form an obvious target. Guangdong's SOEs had the highest asset value among all provinces, estimated at RMB260 billion in 1997, with an indebted rate at 76.9%. Most of these SOEs are scattered and inefficient, with a high degree of duplication.[35] Guangdong has been reported to have lagged behind Shanghai and Shandong in SOE reform during the past few years.[36] This should thus form a major focus of the current Plan period. A total of 250 SOEs have been identified for experimental reform, so that smaller enterprises will come first and all enterprises will eventually have to adjust to the demands of the market economy.[37]

One of the key factors in furthering Guangdong's development in the years ahead is the return of Hong Kong to Chinese sovereignty in 1997. Closer integration across a broad front can be anticipated. In fact, the Guangdong authorities have plans to stitch Hong Kong and Macau into the infrastructure of southern China. By 2010, more than 25 expressways, crisscrossing Guangdong, are expected to be completed, providing better access not only to Hong Kong and Macau but to neighbouring provinces. Just in the current Plan period, some RMB90 billion is earmarked for the construction of 16 expressways.[38] These include the Tiger Gate (Humen) and Lingdingyang bridges. The latter bridge will connect Hong Kong and Macau over a distance of 37.9 km at an estimated cost of HK$13 billion. A business consortium is reported to be actively pursuing the project to a completion date of 1999.[39] It is therefore certain that by the twenty-first century, Guangdong will be much better provided in terms of infrastructure and other facilities for it to play a leading role in China's development and modernization.

A recent study making a comparison of Guangdong and Shanghai reveals that by 1994, Guangdong had increasingly outdistanced Shanghai when measured in terms of their share of national importance. For instance, in the share of GDP Shanghai accounted for China's 7.5% in 1978, but it decreased progressively to 4.4% in 1994. Conversely, Guangdong's share of the national GDP total progressively increased from 5.1% in 1978 to 9.4% in 1994. Similar statistics have been assembled for exports, utilized foreign capital and trade over time. While details of their relative importance in the national picture might differ in the selected indicators, the trend is unmistakable that Guangdong has gradually garnered a greater national share in all the dimensions under review.[40] Despite the special policy and resources allowed for Pudong, the recent rapid growth of Shanghai has, surprisingly, not changed the general tendency. It is thus clear that Guangdong is already in a commanding position to lead China to a period of sustained growth and development, now and in the next century. A reflection of Guangdong's success in economic transformation is the fact that in 1996, it provided a quarter of China's individual income tax revenue, at RMB1.53 billion.[41]

The future outlook for Guangdong is distinctly robust, but its planners and policy-makers must be fully aware of the possibility of its being a victim of its own success. As Guangdong will become more saturated with foreign and domestic investment, competition for land and labour will become more intense. Higher costs could price Guangdong out of the international market, much analogous to what Hong Kong and the other Little Dragons have experienced, triggering their economic restructuring. Already Hong Kong firms have been looking beyond Guangdong to Wuhan, Shanghai and elsewhere, for expansion and long-term investment.[42]

With the rise of Pudong, Sichuan and other open areas in China, Guangdong has essentially lost its previous special advantages in terms of favourable policy. What it must now create for itself are new comparative advantages related to generative mechanisms and economic development to supplant its former privileged position bestowed on it by the central government. Deng Xiaoping's death in February 1997 has not in any way made any negative impact on China's open policy. To be sure, this is reassuring to Guangdong and other open areas, as it has resulted from careful planning of top decision-makers including Deng himself. As

China's open policy further unfolds, China's development and modernization in the twenty-first century will be spatially more diffuse and substantively more broad-based. There is little doubt that in this process Guangdong will continue to play a critical role in advancing China's development goals and modernization programme.

Notes

1. A proximate indication of the general interest on China is the recent publication of a number of special or cover feature articles on China in several popular magazines. These include *Asiaweek* (27 January 1993), *Asia Magazine* (12–14 February 1993), *Newsweek* (15 February 1993), *Time* (10 May 1993), and *Maclean's* (10 May 1993).

2. A conscious attempt was made to cover in this volume as many important subjects as possible. Two key topics are nonetheless missing from it, namely, customs and culture, and Guangdong–Hong Kong relations, resulting from two contributors failing to complete their work. These drawbacks are largely rectified by two recent publications: David Faure, "History and Culture," in *Guangdong: China's Promised Land*, edited by Brian Hook (Hong Kong: Oxford University Press, 1996), pp. 1–29; and Reginald Yin-Wang Kwok and Alvin Y. So (eds.), *The Hong Kong–Guangdong Link: Partnership in Flux* (Armonk, NY: M.E. Sharpe, 1995).

3. The best bird's-eye view of Guangdong is still our joint contribution completed in the early 1970s. See Y. M. Yeung and C. T. Chang, "Kwangtung," in *The New Encyclopaedia Britannica* (15th ed.; Chicago: Helen Hemingway Benton, 1974), Vol. 10, pp. 553–58. Despite sweeping changes since 1978, much of the general description remains valid.

4. The "Large Delta" refers to eight cities (Guangzhou, Foshan, Zhongshan, Jiangmen, Huizhou, Zhaoqing, Shenzhen and Zhuhai) and 24 countries. The "Small Delta" includes six cities (Guangzhou, Foshan, Jiangmen, Zhongshan, Shenzhen and Zhuhai) and 13 counties. See A. G. O. Yeh, K. C. Lam, S. M. Li and K. Y. Wong, "Spatial Development in the Pearl River Delta: Development Issues and Research Agenda," *Asian Geographer*, Vol. 8, No. 1 (1989), p. 1.

5. See Wu Yuwen (ed.), *Guangdongsheng jingji dili* (Economic Geography of Guangdong) (Beijing: Xinhua chubanshe, 1986), p. 81.

6. The frontier atmosphere of economic change in China has been highlighted in, for example, Brenda Dalgish, "The Chinese: Will They Be Capitalists?" *Maclean's*, 10 May 1993, pp. 24–28.

7. Guangdong's GDP in 1985 was RMB55.31 billion and leaped to RMB538.17 billion in 1995. See *Guangdong tongji nianjian 1996*.

8. Apart from Chapter 2 which deals with most of these issues, see also Zhu Jia Jian, "Guangdong's Economic Relationships with Central Government and with Other Provinces/Municipalities," in *Guangdong: "Open Door" Economic Development Strategy*, ASEDP No. 19, edited by Toyojiro Maruya (Tokyo: Institute of Developing Economies, 1992), pp. 98–125. For another relevant article that provides a wealth of empirical data, see Toyojiro Maruya, "The Development of the Guangdong Economy and Its Ties with Beijing," *Jetro China Newsletter*, No. 96 (1992), pp. 2–10.

9. One *mu* is equivalent to 0.06 ha or 0.165 acre. The other side of the coin in the loss of agricultural land is the rapid increase of built-up areas in the Pearl River Delta. In the period 1978–1984, there was an increase of 40.3% of built-up area, but the explosive increase was really to come later. See Yeh et al., "Spatial Development in the Pearl River Delta" (see note 4), pp. 1–9.

10. See Zhang Xiangrong, "Jingji tizhi gaige yu duiwai kaifang de jincheng" (Economic Structural Reform and the Degree of Openness), in *Guangdong: "Open Door" Economic Development Strategy* (see note 8), pp. 1–17.

11. See Wen Simei and Zhang Yue Hue, "Rural Economic Development and Social Changes in Guangdong Province," in *Guangdong: "Open Door" Economic Development Strategy* (see note 8), pp. 49–78.

12. Elizabeth Cheng and Michael Taylor, "Delta Force: Pearl River Cities in Partnership with Hong Kong," *Far Eastern Economic Review*, 16 May 1991, pp. 64–66. See also, J. Cheng and S. MacPherson (eds.), *Development in Southern China: A Report on the Pearl River Delta Region* (Hong Kong: Longman, 1995).

13. For a useful discussion of labour supply in the Pearl River Delta, see Yun-wing Sung et al., *The Fifth Dragon: The Emergence of the Pearl River Delta* (Singapore: Addison Wesley, 1995), pp. 109–32.

14. Li Mengbai and Hu Xin (eds.), *Liudong renkou dui dachengshi fazhan de yingxiang ji duice* (Impact of the Floating Population on Large Cities and Relevant Strategies) (Beijing: Jingji ribao chubanshe, 1991), p. 192.

15. An analysis of the infrastructure development of Guangdong and Fujian, particularly in its relation to Hong Kong and Taiwan and the involvement of international assistance agencies may be found in Yue-man Yeung, "Infrastructure Development in the Southern China Growth Triangle," in *Growth Triangles in Asia: A New Approach to Regional Economic Cooperation*, edited by Myo Thant, Min Tang and Hiroshi Kakazu (Hong Kong: Oxford University Press, 1994), pp. 114–50. In this paper, both transport and energy issues are tackled, pointing to important recent innovations in funding infrastructure projects in Guangdong as well as Hong Kong capital as a key external factor in accelerating development.

16. As an example of growing prosperity, 90% of households in Guangzhou owned a colour television in 1990, compared with 40% in 1986, and families

which owned refrigerators increased from 40% to 76% over the same period. See Cheng and Taylor, "Delta Force" (see note 12). In 1994 the proportion of households owning a colour television further increased to 98%.

17. Measures include the provincial government allocating RMB200 million in subsidies every year to the poor mountainous counties; construction of infrastructure to improve linkage of these parts to the more developed parts; and assistance provided for workers from the poor counties to work in thriving cities in the delta. See Yukari Sawada, "Guangdong's Reforms and Their Impact on Society," *Jetro China Newsletter*, No. 97 (1992), pp. 6–12. It was estimated that by century-end, another 600,000 more people have to lift above the poverty line. In 1996 alone, 400,000 were helped out of poverty. See Jasper Becker, "Guangdong Vows to Stay on Fast Track," *South China Morning Post*, 14 March 1997.

18. See Cheng and Taylor, "Delta Force" (see note 12).

19. Yeh et al., "Spatial Development in the Pearl River Delta" (see note 4).

20. Daniel Kwan, "$13.4b Earmarked for Anti-Pollution Drive," *South China Morning Post*, 6 August 1996.

21. Ezra F. Vogel, *One Step Ahead in China: Guangdong under Reform* (Cambridge: Harvard University Press, 1989).

22. Barry Porter, "A Tale of Two Cities — Shenzhen and Guangzhou," *South China Morning Post*, 11 January 1993. See also *Shenzhen tongji nianjian 1996*.

23. See Yue-man Yeung (ed.), *Zhongguo chengshi yu quyu fazhan: Zhanwang ershiyi shiji* (Urban and Regional Development in China: Towards the 21st Century), Monograph No. 14 (Hong Kong: Hong Kong Institute of Asia-Pacific Studies, The Chinese University of Hong Kong, 1993), p. viii.

24. For a full discussion of the role of China's coastal cities in its recent development, see Yue-man Yeung and Xu-wei Hu (eds.), *China's Coastal Cities: Catalysts for Modernization* (Honolulu: University of Hawaii Press, 1992). As an illustration of the mindless duplication of successful projects, it was reported in a South China seminar co-hosted by the Hong Kong Institute of Asia-Pacific Studies in February 1993 that, as many as ten applications had been received for folk villages to be established in Chinese cities, following the acclaimed China Folk Culture Village that was opened in 1991 in Shenzhen.

25. For a discussion of the emergence of Pudong and its impact on the coastal region in China, see Yeung and Hu, *China's Coastal Cities* (see note 24), pp. 316–21. See also *Shanghai: Transformation and Modernization under China's Open Policy*, edited by Y. M. Yeung and Sung Yun-wing (Hong Kong: The Chinese University Press, 1996).

26. Sawada, "Guangdong's Reforms" (see note 17), p. 6.

27. Cheng and Taylor, "Delta Force" (see note 12), p. 66. See also Kwok and So (eds.), *The Hong Kong–Guangdong Link* (see note 2).

28. For an excellent statement on the recent economic development of the Southern China Growth Triangle, see Edward K. Y. Chen and Anna Ho, "Southern China Growth Triangle: An Overview," in *Growth Triangles in Asia*, edited by Thant et al. (see note 15), pp. 29–72. For an account of the infrastructure in a paper at the same workshop, see Yeung, "Infrastructure Development in the Southern China Growth Triangle" (see note 15).

29. See Vogel, *One Step Ahead in China* (see note 21), p. 385. For an indigenous Chinese perspective of the emerging economic relations of Guangdong in the Asian region, see Zheng Tianxiang et al., *Yi Sui–Gang–Ao wei zhongxin de Zhujiang sanjiaozhou jingji dili wangluo* (Networks in the Economic Geography of the Pearl River Delta Centred Around Guangzhou, Hong Kong and Macau) (Guangzhou: Zhongshan daxue xuebao bianjibu, 1991), pp. 9–21.

30. See East Asia Analytical Unit, Department of Foreign Affairs and Trade, *Australia and North-East Asia in the 1990s: Accelerating Change* (Canberra: Australian Government Printing Service, 1992), pp. 1–36.

31. A full account of how Guangdong will reach modernization in 20 years may be found in an interview report with Zhu Senlin, Governor of Guangdong, "Guangdong to Achieve Goal of Modernization in 20 Years," *China Trade and Investment*, Vol. 7, Nos. 11–12 (30 December 1992), pp. 7–9.

32. See Sung et al., *The Fifth Dragon* (note 13), pp. 214–17.

33. See Chen Mingjin, Chen Chunhua and Su Huahong, "'Bawu' shiqi: Guangdong jingji de huigu yu sikao (shang)" (The Eighth Five Period: Review and Contemplation of Guangdong Economy I), *Nanfang jingji*, No. 12 (1995), pp. 5–7.

34. See Chen Mingjin, Chen Chunhua and Su Huahong, "'Bawu' shiqi: Guangdong jingji de huigu yu sikao (xia)" (The Eighth Five Period: Review and Contemplation of Guangdong Economy II), *Nanfang jingji*, No. 1 (1996), pp. 7–9.

35. "Yue guoyou zichan erqian liubai yi" (Guangdong's State-owned Enterprises Asset 260 Billion), *Wen Wei Pao*, 27 February 1997.

36. Meng Yan, "Guangdong jingji dadie" (The Great Fall of Guangdong Economy), *Hong Kong Economic Daily*, 4 February 1997.

37. Lin Shusen, "Guangdongsheng yijiujiuwu nian guomin jingji he shehui fazhan jihua zhixing qingkuang yu yijiujiuliu nian jihua anpai cao'an de baogao" (Report on the National Economy and Social Development of Guangdong 1995 and Proposal for 1996), *Guangdong fazhan daokan*, No. 1 (1996), pp. 7–14.

38. Keith Wallis, "Expressways Uniting with Motherland," *South China Morning Post*, 27 April 1997.

39. Emma Batha, "Businessmen Aim to Build 37.9-km HK–Macau Bridge," *South China Morning Post*, 2 May 1997.
40. See Sung Yun-wing, "'Dragon Head' of China's Economy?" in *Shanghai*, edited by Yeung and Sung (see note 25), pp. 171–98.
41. The Economist Intelligence Unit, *Economic Outlook Guangdong*, February 1996.
42. Carl Goldstein, "Ties That Bind: Hongkong Firms Seek Closer China Links," *Far Eastern Economic Review*, 30 July 1992, pp. 61–62.

2

Changing Relations between the Central Government and Guangdong

Peter T. Y. Cheung

The relationship between the central government and Guangdong is a crucial factor in understanding the province's rapid economic growth in the post-Mao period.[1] This chapter is a preliminary analysis of this relationship since 1978.[2] It is organized into four parts. Part one is an overview of central–Guangdong relations from 1949 to 1978. Part two discusses the key dimensions and characteristics of this relationship in the post-Mao era. Part three analyzes the evolution of this relationship from 1979 to 1992, focusing on the interactions between the central government and the province over the granting of "special policies, flexible measures."[3] Part four explores the prospects of the relationship in the 1990s.

Relations between the Central Government and Guangdong from 1949 to 1978

Beijing had tightly controlled Guangdong in the first three decades after 1949. The province's distinctive sub-culture, its history as a trading centre and treaty port, its distance from the capital and its proximity to Hong Kong and Macau not only inspired a local spirit and identity but also aroused central suspicion. Furthermore, the Communist guerrillas in south China had developed strong local identities and organizations in order to survive during their struggle against the Nationalists. Demands for greater power for local cadres and resistance to central policies, which were considered manifestations of "localism," had caused great concern for the central authorities in Beijing. For instance, the moderation of Guangdong's local cadres during the Land Reform Campaign (1951–1953) had led to their decline and replacement by outside cadres who had few local ties, such as Tao Zhu and Zhao Ziyang. The contradiction between outside and local cadres culminated in the rebellion of officials in Hainan Island and its subsequent suppression in 1958.[4] Since 1949, the central government aimed to establish a centralized state that could implement national

This is a revised and updated version of the original chapter. Since some of the empirical data are already well documented in the original version, they will be condensed here in order to make room for new materials. The author would like to acknowledge the financial support provided by a CRCG grant from the University of Hong Kong which funded his continuing research on economic reform and development in Guangdong.

policies effectively rather than to accommodate any substantial provincial autonomy.[5]

Often dubbed the "Southern Gate" of China, Guangdong had evolved as a leading ground for political contest in modern China. Even before the Communist took power, the province was the base from which the Nationalists launched campaigns against the warlords in the late 1920s. Since 1949, the provincial leadership was often in the hands of officials trusted by the power-holders in Beijing. As the former Party leader in Guangdong, Tao Zhu had used the province as a springboard to establish himself as a powerful regional leader from the early 1950s by closely following central policies. When he was promoted to Beijing in mid-1966, his close associate, Zhao Ziyang, was put in charge of the province. During the Cultural Revolution, Tao was attacked by the Red Guards and died miserably while Zhao also disappeared in 1967.[6]

The beneficiaries of the Cultural Revolution tried to use their influence in the province to campaign for political power as well. Lin Biao allegedly planned to establish a separate Party centre in Guangdong if his ill-fated coup against Chairman Mao failed because his close follower, General Huang Yongsheng, was the head of the Guangzhou Military Region.[7] After the downfall of Lin Biao and the subsequent liquidation of his lieutenants, Liu Xingyuan and Ding Sheng, two military officials favoured by Mao, were appointed as Guangdong's leaders. Zhao resumed his duties as a Party Secretary in 1972 and later became First Party Secretary in 1974, but he failed to achieve any breakthroughs during his tenure in the period 1972–1975 because of the prevailing radicalism. His vacancy was filled by Wei Guoqing, a military leader from Guangxi, who was close to Deng Xiaoping.[8] During his tenure in Guangdong from 1975 to 1978, Wei and Xu Shiyou, Guangzhou Military Region's Commander, reputedly protected Deng when he was persecuted by the "Gang of Four." After the fall of the Maoists and Deng's full comeback in December 1978, Deng sent two trusted associates, Xi Zhongxun and Yang Shangkun, to Guangdong in order to eradicate the legacies of the "Gang" and introduce reform.

In the first three decades of Communist rule, Guangdong often suffered from Mao's radical policies, and provincial interests were subordinated to national priorities. Owing to the containment policy of the United States after the Korean War, Beijing shifted industrial development from the coastal areas to the interior and allocated little investment to the province. National economic policies, especially after the Cultural Revolution, also did not favour Guangdong. For instance, national policies emphasizing grain production and heavy industry failed to tap the province's comparative advantage in many other spheres. Guangdong's economy grew rather slowly during the period 1966–1975. Its agricultural output of 2.55% lagged behind the national average of 4.0% while its industrial output of 9.7% was also lower than the national average of 10.7%.[9] While the Guangzhou Export Fair provided a vital conduit for China to maintain external economic relations with the outside world after 1957, the restriction over domestic and foreign trade failed to revive the province's past role as a hub of commerce in pre-1949 China. The striking contrast between the vibrant capitalist Hong Kong and the economically backward socialist Guangdong inevitably generated a strong impulse for change in the province in the late 1970s.

Characteristics of the Relationship between the Central Government and Guangdong

This chapter mainly deals with the interactions between the central government and Guangdong over economic policy, but three key dimensions of the linkage between the central government and Guangdong, namely (a) constitutional relations, (b) political relations, and (c) economic relations, will be briefly examined here in order to provide a broader framework for understanding their relationship.[10]

Constitutional Relations

Constitutionally, the Chinese political system is a centralized, unitary state. Guangdong is only a province inside the People's Republic. The relationship between the central government and Guangdong remains one between a superior and a subordinate, hence the provincial government is responsible for implementing central policies. Since 1979, the central government has delegated a package of economic powers, i.e. the so-called "special policies, flexible measures," to Guangdong and Fujian, which substantially enlarged their authority over economic management. However, this new relationship is not enshrined in the constitution. Instead, it is based upon three Central Documents, one State Council Document, and one State Council Correspondence. Since this relationship is defined by political rather than constitutional decisions, changes in policy preference or the composition of the central leadership, as happened in 1989, would mean a reversal of fortune for the province. In order to deal with the uncertainty of central policy towards the province and to protect its special status, Guangdong's leaders have devised several coping strategies. Three examples serve to illustrate this point. Firstly, the province might further delegate its newly acquired economic power and resources to sub-provincial levels in order to stimulate local initiative and development and to forge a coalition of local governments with vested interests in reform. Besides, a sense of urgency in taking advantage of its new-found autonomy is generated among Guangdong's leaders because such powers could be stripped away, depending upon the political winds at the central level. Last but not least, the province may interpret central policies in a flexible manner in order to maximize its room for manoeuvre.

Political Relations

Politically, the Communist party-state organs and their cadres in Guangdong are subject to the same ideological and organizational discipline as in other parts of China. The central government has not offered any political privilege to Guangdong. Of the various powers granted to the province, political reform was conspicuously not on the agenda until 1988 when the nation already moved slowly towards that direction. While the province has more leverage in staffing sub-provincial positions, the appointment of provincial leaders is still firmly in the hands of the central government. In the pre-1978 as well as the post-1978 period, the central leadership has used its control over personnel appointment to guarantee that its desired policy orientation would be followed. In the pre-reform era, with the exceptions of Ye Jianying (1949–1955) and Chen Yu (1957–1967), none of Guangdong's party secretaries and governors were Cantonese.[11] Since Deng Xiaoping came to power in late 1978, Guangdong natives were not appointed to these top positions until 1985 (see Table 2.1). If Tao Zhu faithfully implemented national policies in the 1950s and the early 1960s, Xi Zhongxun and Yang Shangkun, too, were sent to the province in order to ensure a smooth transition to the post-Mao era. As soon as they had proved to be less adept in the task of introducing reform, they were transferred back to the capital. In particular, the appointments of provincial leaders like Ren Zhongyi and Liang Lingguang in 1981 and later Lin Ruo and Ye Xuanping in 1985, had proved to be crucial steps by Deng Xiaoping in maintaining the course of reform. Furthermore, the special relationship between the central government and Guangdong since 1979 owed a great deal to the support of the radical, market-oriented reformers at the central level. The province was sensitive towards its role as a pioneer of reform because its achievements and failures would have considerable impact on national policies as well as on the central leaders who supported its reforms. For instance, the conflicts within the central leadership had injected uncertainties into the relationship because the radical reformers and their conservative counterparts tried in turn to protect and oppose Guangdong's reforms, as occurred in 1982, 1985 and 1989.[12]

Table 2.1 Guangdong's Party Secretaries and Governors since 1949

Provincial Party Secretaries	Governors
Ye Jianying (1949.8–1955.5)	Ye Jianying (1949.11–1953.9)
Tao Zhu (1955.6–1965.2)	Tao Zhu (1953.9–1957.6)
Zhao Ziyang (1965.2–Cultural Rev.)	Chen Yu (1957.6–Cultural Rev.)
Liu Xingyuan (1970.12–1972.3)	Huang Yongsheng (1968.2–1969.6)
Ding Sheng (1972.3–1973.12)	Liu Xingyuan (1969.6–1972.3)
Zhao Ziyang (1974.4–1975.10)	Ding Sheng (1972.3–1973.12)
Wei Guoqing (1975.10–1978.12)	Zhao Ziyang (1974.4–1975.10)
Xi Zhongxun (1978.12–1980.11)	Wei Guoqing (1975.10–1978.12)
Ren Zhongyi (1980.11–1985.7)	Xi Zhongxun (1978.12–1981.2)
Lin Ruo (1985.7–1991.1)	Liu Tianfu (1981.3–1983.4)
Xie Fei (1991.1–)	Liang Lingguang (1983.5–1985.7)
	Ye Xuanping (1985.8–1991.5)
	Zhu Senlin (1991.5–1996.2)
	Lui Ruihua (1996.2–)

Sources: Guangdong Yearbook Editorial Committee (ed.), *Guangdong nianjian 1987* (Guangdong Yearbook 1987) (Guangzhou: Guangdong renmin chubanshe, 1987), pp. 83–85 & 89–90; Ma Qibin et al. (eds.), *Zhongguo Gongchandang zhizheng sishinian* (The Chinese Communist Party in Power for Forty Years) (Beijing: Zhonggong dangshi ziliao chubanshe, 1991), p. 611; *China Directory* (Tokyo: Radio Press, various years).

Economic Relations

Of the changes in the relations between the central government and Guangdong, none was more important than the decentralization of economic powers from the central government to the provincial government. This decentralization has several salient features. First, while the special policies have defined the broad parameters of Guangdong's new economic powers, both the central government and the province would still make demands on one another in order to maximize their interests. Just as the province could creatively interpret central decisions, the central government could also exact concessions from the province through irregular means, such as the requisition of more revenue in addition to the contracted lump sum. Hence the economic relations between these two levels of government reflected the results of mutual adjustments, bargaining and compromises.

Second, the relationship between the central government and Guangdong has evolved gradually over time rather than being totally recast in a brief period. Instead of granting all the economic powers that the province might have wanted once and for all, the central authorities delegated power only gradually in the 1980s. Again, these changes reflected the results of interactions between these two levels of government. Such an incremental process had significant repercussions for the undertaking of reform as Guangdong's reforms could only be partial rather than comprehensive. The province could not demand more comprehensive reforms until the late 1980s.

Third, the new relationship between the central government and Guangdong since 1979 was predicated upon the principle of preferential treatment. As early as the late 1970s, several provinces like Shanghai or Jiangsu had contended for Guangdong's privileges. In the 1980s, the coastal areas, especially Guangdong and Fujian, received special treatment by the central government which would be denied to other regions. However, the central government would have growing difficulties in decentralizing more power to Guangdong over time because one province after another have been demanding similar treatment and Guangdong had already benefited tremendously from the special policies. Not only did this competition for more power cut into the central government's own position, but it also allowed many other areas to share Guangdong's once monopolized privileges by the early 1990s and become its keen competitors. Finally, this new phase of central–provincial relations since 1979 has taken place with the simultaneous launching of an open policy which enabled the province to take advantage of economic opportunities overseas and shore up its bargaining position with the central government by soliciting more foreign investment.[13]

Relations between the Central Government and Guangdong since 1979

After examining the different dimensions of central–provincial relations, the following analysis of this changing relationship since 1979 will focus on their interactions over a critical issue, namely the granting of special policies to Guangdong. The evolution of the relationship can be roughly divided into four phases: (a) 1979–1984, (b) 1985–1986, (c) 1987–1989, and (d) since 1989.

A New Era in Central–Provincial Relations, 1979–1984

The Genesis of "Special Policies, Flexible Measures" in 1979

The evolution of central–Guangdong relations in the post-1978 period can best be examined with reference to the legacies of the first three decades of Communist rule. Since the central government had exercised effective control over the province since 1949, the yearnings for a better living standard and faster economic growth among Guangdong's officials and people had unleashed a strong impetus for taking radical measures in reform and opening up. An apt reflection of such sentiments was a statement by the provincial party secretary, Xi Zhongxun, who remarked that Guangdong would develop much faster if it were an independent nation.[14] The province's quest for greater autonomy, however, would not materialize if not for the convergence of its goals with that of the central government, or at least some of its key leaders. That golden opportunity came after Deng Xiaoping made his full political comeback in late 1978. Not only did Deng encourage some areas to pioneer reform and get rich first, but he also tried to step up the development of Guangdong and Fujian in order to prepare for the future unification of Hong Kong, Macau and Taiwan with the mainland. Such ideas were already discussed in the April 1979 Central Work Conference that led to the creation of the Special Economic Zones and the decentralization of foreign trade power to the localities and enterprises.[15] Deng Xiaoping himself was responsible for approving the special treatment of Guangdong and Fujian.

A new relationship with the central government began, however, only with the adoption of the influential Central Document No. 50 in July 1979.[16] As the first of a series of key central documents on Guangdong, the document helped to redefine the relationship between the central government and the province with a number of *ad hoc* contracts and by decentralizing mainly economic powers, rather than funds or resources, in eight areas. This new framework, which was later expanded and refined, provided the basis of the "special policies, flexible measures." It should be noted that this decentralization took place when the central government was tightening its own belt during readjustment in the early 1980s.[17] Exactly because the whole country was following a deflationary policy,

Guangdong was allowed more autonomy in economic policy because, unlike areas such as Shanghai, the province's economic position was not yet critical in the national economy.

The first and foremost element of the new central–Guangdong relationship was a five-year fiscal contract under which Guangdong was obliged to transfer a lump sum of only RMB1.2 billion (later reduced to 1 billion) of revenue to the central government.[18] This lump sum transfer fiscal regime had become the foundation of Guangdong's reform in the 1980s because it enabled the province to garner more resources in sub-sidizing reform and enjoy greater autonomy in setting its own budgetary priorities. Since the province would be mainly responsible for its own surplus or shortfall after remitting the lump sum, this provision also motivated its leadership to raise more revenue or seek outside investment. Furthermore, except for customs duties and income from centrally managed units, all revenues would be designated as local revenues in order to expand the sources of provincial income. Nonetheless, the province would have to rely upon itself for capital investment.[19] Similarly, a favourable arrangement in sharing foreign exchange income was made in order to stimulate the province's export.

Second, Guangdong had also been granted more powers in formulat-ing its own socio-economic development plans. Enterprises and business units that were under central control (except in certain public utilities) would be transferred to and managed by the province.[20]

Third, the province's authority over foreign trade and investment had also been substantially enlarged. While some products and export quotas were still under central control, the province was granted more authority to manage existing branches of foreign trade companies, create provincial foreign trade corporations, use its own foreign exchange to import, and manage the foreign trade of locally produced goods. Instead of referring to ministries in Beijing, the province would also have the power to approve foreign investment projects in export processing, compensation trade and joint-venture that did not involve national balances (e.g. in funds and materials). Together with Fujian, the province would establish special export zones (later renamed Special Economic Zones; hereafter SEZs) in Shenzhen, Zhuhai and Shantou, which would serve as sites for even bolder reforms.

Fourth, the province would also enjoy more freedom and privilege in financial matters, including greater discretion over foreign exchange loans and the power to set up its own financial corporation in order to absorb foreign capital for its own development.

Fifth, a contract between the province and the related ministries over material allocation would be established. The material allocation system would be mainly under the control of the province so that it would have more latitude in distributing centrally and ministerially managed materials.

Sixth, decentralization of the commercial sector was also approved so that the central government's commercial units would be put under provincial management. The delegation of power in this respect enabled the province to reduce planning over purchase and sales of commodities.

Seventh, the power of the province over labour management was increased because it no longer had to be restricted by national targets over labour allocation and it could also raise bonuses above the national level. Consequently, the province would have much greater freedom in reforming labour management through the use of material incentives.

Eighth, the province was also allowed much greater autonomy in price management and price reform, such as enlarging the scope of locally set prices and increasing the prices of locally produced products.

Taken as a whole, this unprecedented package helped to relax the macro-economic enivronment for Guangdong and build up a new framework of central–provincial relations within which the province could have much greater freedom in managing the provincial economy, speeding up market-oriented economic reform and reducing central planning, as well as establishing links with the world economy.

In order to translate the above general principles into more concrete measures and obtain co-operation from central ministries, the second of the key central policies, Central Document (1980) No. 41, was promulgated in mid-May, 1980.[21] This document further extended Guangdong's powers and privileges in several areas, such as the power to utilize overseas capital in infrastructural development, more flexible treatment in foreign exchange management, the reduction of the province's revenue remittance from RMB1.2 billion to RMB1 billion, and the exemption of remittance of enterprise depreciation funds. Other key reform measures in opening, such as adopting the market mechanism in the SEZs and setting the income tax rates at 15%, had also been ratified. In order to counter the persistence of bureaucratic inertia and ideological opposition in some units inside the national government, the document also asked central ministries to be more co-operative towards Guangdong in implementing this bold programme. Hence this document clearly advanced and further consolidated the special treatment enjoyed by Guangdong.

Contending Orientations Towards the Province in the Central Leadership

Neither Deng Xiaoping's endorsement of the special policies towards Guangdong and Fujian nor the promulgation of the two central documents in the period 1979–1980 had entirely settled the emerging difficulties in central–provincial relations. Although the two documents did lay out a framework for decentralizing economic powers to the two provinces, they were still subject to interpretation. If problems arose, the attitudes of the central authorities would still influence the pattern of central–provincial relations. As soon as the special policies were formulated, two broad orientations towards the special status of Guangdong could be identified within the central leadership.[22]

One orientation that favoured these special policies as a means to champion faster reform and opening was supported by more liberal and market-oriented reformers, among them included Hu Yaobang, Zhao Ziyang, Wan Li and Gu Mu. Feeling impatient with the pace of reform in the two provinces in the early 1980s, they were generally more accommodating to the demands and more lenient towards the mistakes committed by Guangdong.[23] For instance, the initial fiscal contract proposed by Gu Mu, the central official in charge of open policy, was supposed to last only three years, yet he later agreed with Guangdong's request to extend it to five years.[24] Another orientation to Guangdong shared mainly by conservative central leaders, including Chen Yun and Yao Yilin, was that they had far more reservations about a faster pace of reform and the special policies. Consequently, they were generally more critical of Guangdong. For example, Vice-Premier Yao Yilin was reluctant to grant too much power to the province because he believed that it should solve its own problems without always asking for more concessions from the central government.[25] These two orientations towards reform and Guangdong differed most sharply about the political and ideological consequences of reform and opening. Unlike their more liberal colleagues, the conservatives were much more critical of the unintended consequences of reform, such as the deterioration of social norms and economic irregularities, which were of course most conspicuous in Guangdong.

In line with his own political style in forging a consensus among the top leadership in the 1980s, Deng Xiaoping had tried to strike a balance between the two alternative orientations. Nonetheless, he often favoured the radical reformers. Together with the support of radical reformers,

Deng's favourable attitude towards granting more autonomy to the province was a key factor that explained its special treatment during economic retrenchment in the early 1980s. The radical reformers had become ever more concerned with the slow progress in implementing special policies when national economic policy turned towards centralization since late 1980. Guangdong's leaders took advantage of this opportunity to make more demands on the central government, such as asking for more grain transfer, more power over tariffs, and more import of profitable goods such as fertilizers and pesticides, although not all of these demands were satisfied.[26] While maintaining that the province should deal with its problems independently without asking for more concessions from the central government, a party secretariat meeting held in December 1980 even suggested that:

> The central government has delegated power to Guangdong province to adopt a flexible method in dealing with the directives and demands of various departments at the central level by implementing measures that are appropriate and not implementing those that are inappropriate or handling them in a flexible manner.[27]

The persistent concern over Guangdong among the radical reformers and Deng was reflected in a central move that was later proved to be crucial: the reshuffling of Guangdong's leadership. Since Xi Zhongxun and Yang Shangkun failed to accelerate reform in the province, they were transferred back to the central level. Two reform-minded officials, Ren Zhongyi and Liang Lingguang, respectively first party secretary of Liaoning Province and minister of light industry, were appointed Guangdong's first party secretary and governor in order to bring about a breakthrough.[28] Ren later became the key motivating force behind the province's drive for reform and opening.[29]

Consolidating the Reform Initiative in 1981

The convergence of policy objectives between central and provincial leaders was a critical factor behind the decentralization of economic power in the post-Mao era. The granting of special policies to Guangdong served not only the interest of the province, but also that of the radical reformers at the central level because they wanted to maintain the initiative of reform by local experiments when central policy emphasized planning and readjustment.[30] The growing differences between the two contending orientations to the province became more evident when unintended consequences of reform and opening began to emerge. A party secretariat meeting convened in late December 1980 warned Guangdong about the deterioration of social norms, the influence of Western ideology, as well as the need for increasing foreign earnings.[31] The meeting also pointedly stated that the SEZs were only special economic zones, not special political zones. When the province did not seem to bring about a breakthrough in reform in 1980, the radical reformists in the central government encouraged both Guangdong and Fujian to be more "special" in economic affairs, to overcome the obstructions from central units, and most importantly, to keep reform alive during readjustment.[32]

The third major document on Guangdong and Fujian in three years — Central Document (1981) No. 27 — was promulgated in July 1981 in order to consolidate the reform initiative.[33] This document unambiguously summarized the essence of "special policies, flexible measures" as "further opening to the outside," "further relaxation in domestic policies," and "further expanding the powers of the two provinces." Further, the SEZs, Deng's pet project, were considered a "significant content" of special policies whereas accusations of the zones as concessions or colonies by conservative leaders were rebutted.[34] The further extension of autonomy to Guangdong in this document should be interpreted as a victory for the new provincial leadership under Ren's energetic guidance and for the radical reformers in the central government.

In the midst of growing doubts among conservative leaders on reform and the open policy, this document not only consolidated the new yet precarious central–provincial relationship, but also pinpointed economic system reform as a key aspect of Guangdong's special policies. Earlier measures had been reaffirmed while important new measures were also initiated in order to allay provincial fears over unpredictable changes and to counter obstruction from central government departments. First and foremost, the fiscal contract would remain in place from 1980 to 1985. Production and construction projects which did not affect national balances would also be co-ordinated and managed by the province. Aside from securing central support and foreign investment, the province was allowed tax exemption and withholding of profit remittance from enterprises in infrastructural projects in order to develop its energy and transport sectors.

The province had also been successful in seeking more power in finance. The Guangdong Branch of People's Bank would gain more autonomy, as exemplified by its new power to issue short or medium term loans. By reducing central control over the availability of investment funds, this new arrangement would greatly enhance Guangdong's ability to stimulate economic growth. Taxation power was delegated to the province for the first time. The central government would still be in control of promulgating national tax laws and international tax matters; however, the two provinces would be allowed to levy and exempt taxes for enterprises and products (except liquor, tobacco, sugar and watches) as well as adjust all local taxes. Such powers would give Guangdong greater latitude in stimulating its industries because it could relieve the burden on enterprises by tax reduction or exemption.

The promotion of export and acquisition of foreign capital remained a key concern of this document. The province would maintain the power to formulate its own export plan (except for products that were nationally controlled) and its own import plan (which would be paid for by its retained foreign exchange). Export to Hong Kong and Macau would be managed by Guangdong and Fujian and their units stationed in these territories. Although the income from tariffs and the power to reduce or exempt tariffs would still be centrally controlled, imported raw materials and spare parts used for making export goods would be tax-free. The province could also freely use its retained foreign exchange and have the freedom to set up foreign exchange accounts in Bank of China at home or abroad, or in Chinese banks in Hong Kong and Macau. Policies on the SEZs were further elaborated as well.

The Crises in Early 1982 and the Central Government's Response

The first major central intervention in Guangdong's economic affairs in the post-Mao era came when new opportunities offered by the special policies led to economic irregularities that were seized upon by the conservative wing of the Party. Even in the 1980 No. 41 document, central attention on illegal economic activities in Guangdong was already obvious.[35] The document specifically warned the two provinces not to procure products from other provinces at higher prices or to import and resell goods which might imperil domestic industries. The new powers approved in Central Document No. 27 in 1981 might give the province a freer hand in economic affairs, yet the emergence of economic crimes led to the first important central intervention since 1979. Despite repeated warnings from the central government in 1980–1981, localities in Guangdong continued to purchase cheaper products from neighbouring areas at higher prices for export and to import consumer goods with their locally retained foreign exchange, especially through the SEZs, and resell them to the interior for handsome profits. Yet the provincial leadership failed to effectively stop these activities, probably because it was encouraging more local initiatives at that time. Furthermore, owing to the rising export procurement prices of agricultural produce, the increasing domestic demand, the over-valued exchange rate and other problems of the foreign trade system, the province failed to reduce export costs, which would be imperative as it had a foreign trade contract with the central government. Hence the above-mentioned illegal profiteering might have helped the province to cover its foreign trade losses by earning more foreign exchange.

Such problems led conservative Party elder, Chen Yun, to try to apply the brake on the special policies in December 1981. Instead of tolerating further experimentation, he argued that the number one task for the SEZs was to sum up their experience and complained that the zones had not yet done so. He warned that provinces like Jiangsu could not establish SEZs and these zones had already brought about undesirable effects, such as its impact on RMB.[36] In late January and early February 1982, an urgent central-level meeting was called in order to deal with the widespread economic crimes in the two provinces, especially Guangdong.[37] This meeting reflected not only the seriousness of the situation, but also a compromise among the radical and conservative wings of the leadership over the pace of reform and opening.[38] Since these problems had national implications, the radical reformers were careful not to let their reform programme derail. Unlike the conservatives, the radical reformers regarded these problems mainly as the unintended consequences of reform, not ideological issues or class struggle.[39] On the contrary, the lack of planning, the exceeding of planned capital investment, the excessive issuance of bonuses and the reselling of expensive consumer goods to other areas by Guangdong were seriously criticized by conservatives like Yao Yilin.[40]

This incident of central intervention almost resulted in the abolition of Guangdong's special status, yet the province survived this crisis because of the staunch support of radical reformers and its tough measures to rectify the situation. The province also accepted several restrictions imposed by the central government, such as incorporating all important economic activities into the national plan, prohibiting the use of higher prices to procure agricultural products for export and the import of consumer goods for sale in the interior, or the reselling of foreign exchange.[41] Other measures which aimed at stabilizing Guangdong's rising prices (which also affected neighbouring areas), such as restricting the scale of capital investment and limiting the issuance of bonuses, had also been ratified. In August 1982, the State Council forbade Guangdong to use its foreign exchange to import seventeen kinds of commodities, such as cars and electrical appliances.[42] Owing to a variety of internal and external economic changes mentioned earlier, the severe costs of subsidizing export spelled the death of the foreign trade contract in 1984. The use of locally retained foreign exchange had been restricted as well.[43]

Guangdong's Economic Boom after Implementing Special Policies

The economic powers given to Guangdong had enabled the province to take reforms one step ahead of the nation, e.g. launching bold price reforms for agricultural and other products, relaxing control over domestic trade, decentralizing economic management, and attracting foreign capital. In particular, Guangdong achieved rapid economic growth during the period 1979–1984 as its total social output registered an annual growth of over 11%. During this period, Guangdong's industrial output grew at an annual rate of 11.1%, of which light industry rose at 13.6% and heavy industry only 7.1%.[44] Its agricultural output had also grown rapidly at an annual rate of 8.5%.[45] The share of farming in agricultural output had fallen from 61% in 1978 to 50.4% in 1984 whereas the share of animal husbandry, sidelines and fishery rose from 28.7% to 40.2%.[46] Its actual acquisition of foreign capital (mostly from Hong Kong) had skyrocketed during this period. While the worldwide recession and the 1982 anti-economic crime campaign were apparently not conducive to foreign investment, foreign capital actually invested in Guangdong jumped more than 15 times to reach US$653.7 million in 1984.[47] In the 1979–1984 period, foreign direct investment reached US$1.29 billion and other forms of foreign investment amounted to US$590 million, respectively 42% and 56% of the national figures.[48] After a drop in the preceding two years, its exports in 1984 also recovered and increased to US$2.5 billion.[49] By the time the first contract with the central government ended in 1985, Guangdong had already surpassed the economic targets in the 1979 document. During the period 1979–1984, the province's economic growth rates were ahead of the nation, except in exports, agriculture and revenue.[50]

Guangdong's Precarious Quest for More Autonomy, 1985–1986

The reform process in socialist countries is full of twists and turns because the interests of different sectors are often affected. Whether the reformers can seize the right moment in pushing reform is thus of critical importance. In China, in the winter of 1983, the conservative wing of the party initiated a campaign against "bourgeois liberalization" and the SEZs again became a target of attack, even though such an initiative failed to derail the province from its course of reform.[51] Hence Deng pushed for faster reform by personally endorsing the SEZs and other coastal areas during his tour there in early 1984 while other provinces that envied Guangdong's privileges had campaigned hard for similar special treatment.[52] These combined efforts cumulated in the opening of the fourteen coastal cities (including Guangzhou), hence extending open policy to China's most economically vibrant areas and making the rolling back of such a policy more difficult.[53] With the adoption of the comprehensive reform programme in October 1984, the national political and economic environments seemed to be favourable for Guangdong to pioneer reform again. Nonetheless, the uncontrollable import drive led to the dwindling of foreign exchange reserves. Moreover, the Hainan automobile smuggling scandal revealed some undesirable outcomes of special policies, and the growing problems of the SEZs further exposed the perils of reform and opening.

The emergence of these social and economic problems nonetheless presented another opportunity for Guangdong. Since the province and the SEZs had been so identified with the reform programme of the radical reformers in the central government, they were particularly unwilling to see their reform-minded allies in the localities become targets for their conservative critics. Hence, not only was the provincial leadership able to keep Guangdong's special policies on track despite these difficulties, but it was also able to exploit the new situation to press for more autonomy. Another opportunity emerged when Zhao Ziyang toured the Pearl River Delta and the SEZs in late November 1984. During his trip, Zhao proposed that the SEZs and the coastal areas digest advanced management techniques and technology before spreading them inland.[54] He specifically recommended the province to focus on developing export-oriented light industries by adopting the commerce–industry–agriculture strategy which would gear agricultural production and industrial processing towards global market demands.[55] In mid-February 1985, three of the China's major deltas, including the Pearl River Delta, were granted SEZ-styled special policies.[56] Consequently, the size of Guangdong's localities that enjoyed such privileges had expanded considerably to cover its most economically active areas.

Guangdong's quest for more autonomy seemed to be secured, at least for the moment, by the promulgation of State Council Document (1985) No. 46 in March 1985. This key document extended another five years of special policies and granted new powers to Guangdong and Fujian.[57] Most importantly, although the amount of remittance was adjusted, the lump sum transfer fiscal contract would be in place from 1985 to 1989. The province could approve construction of production projects invested with its own funds or foreign capital under RMB200 million as well as foreign-invested production projects under US$10 million that did not involve national balances and export quotas. Like other open cities, it could decide on all non-productive projects, without any restriction on investment scale. Various favourable measures promoting technical renovation had also been espoused while other measures delegated more financial power to the province, including the power to set up its financial institutions, handle foreign exchange account business and issue bonds abroad. Together with the growing surpluses from saving accounts available for bank loans, the above measures had greatly enhanced Guangdong's access to capital.

Even more preferential treatment over foreign economic relations was also approved, such as raising Guangdong's retention of foreign exchange income from 25% to 30%, i.e. 5% higher than other provinces, and delegating more power over the issuance of export quotas and licenses from the Ministry of Foreign Economic Relations and Trade (MOFERT) to the province.[58] Following Zhao's recommendations, the province would have more power in exporting fresh produce (except live pigs and cows) to Hong Kong and Macau. Guangdong and Fujian were also allowed to approve business and foreign trade enterprises operating abroad.[59] Further-more, the attack on economic crimes and bourgeois ideology was only mentioned briefly in the last paragraph, reflecting the victory of the radical reformers and the province. Having weathered earlier difficulties, developed a penchant for experimentation, and now armed with these new provisions, the province attained faster economic growth rates and under-took bolder reforms since the mid-1980s.

However, Guangdong's special policies, especially the SEZs, had be-come targets of conservative criticism again in early 1985. Conservative critics attacked the SEZs as a menace to national sovereignty and a hotbed of economic problems such as the dependence on state subsidies, the failure to earn foreign exchange through export, and the continuing import of expensive goods for resale in the interior.[60] The Hainan Island automobile smuggling scandal caused the central authorities to intervene in early 1985. These problems threatened policy consensus at the central level and clearly put the radical reformers in the central leadership on the defensive. In late June, even Deng Xiaoping had to admit that, "the success of Shenzhen has yet to be proved," and in early July, the opening of the coastal cities was limited to only four (including Guangzhou).[61] Further exposing the differences between the conservative and radical reformers, party elders, Chen Yun and Li Xiannian, respectively criticized the economic and political problems caused by reform during the party conference held in September 1985. Since the radical reformers had tried audaciously to prevent the province from becoming a trophy for their opponents, Guangdong and Hainan officials who committed errors received relatively lenient punishment. However, the State Council had again imposed various restrictions on the import of twenty-four kinds of commodities (including automobiles and consumer durables) and the reselling of such products to the interior in December 1986.[62] Policies towards the SEZs were also tightened. In other words, despite the recurring attacks by those critical of the province, Guangdong's quest for more autonomy in the 1985–1986 period achieved what was politically possible at that time because of the national trend towards more systematic reform and the support of the radical reformers at the top.

Guangdong's Unfulfilled Goal as a Comprehensive Reform Area, 1987–1989

Since 1984, Guangdong's economy has grown dramatically because of its privileged position as well as its skills in taking advantage of the unsaturated domestic market and foreign economic opportunities. Compared with 1985, both the exports and foreign capital it acquired in 1988 were more than doubled, reaching, respectively, US$7.48 billion and US$2.4 billion.[63] Its industrial output also doubled between 1985 and 1988 because of the rapid growth of light industry and the booming of rural industries which contributed one-third of such output.[64] During the period 1979–1988, the annual growth rate of its total social output reached 15.2%, gross domestic product 12.9% and gross output value of industry and agriculture 15.5%.[65] While agriculture, especially grain production, experienced slower growth since 1984, Guangdong's economic growth rates during 1979–1988 had surpassed that of the nation as well as that of the East Asian newly industrializing economies in the 1960s and 1970s.

The central government, still dominated by Deng and his allies, continued to shape Guangdong's affairs through its control over personnel appointment in a way that also served its policy objectives. The promotion of two Guangdong natives, Lin Ruo, a veteran local cadre, and Ye Xuanping, the eldest son of the powerful Marshal Ye Jianying and a vice-governor of Guangdong, respectively to the posts of party secretary and governor in 1985, ensured the continuation of the path of reform and opening. Reminiscent of the period 1979–1981 and the year 1985, the initiative of the radical reformers for more comprehensive reform and opening had created another opportunity for Guangdong in the period 1987–1988. The purge of Hu Yaobang in early 1987 undoubtedly weakened the liberal wing of the party, but Zhao Ziyang still managed to take over as general secretary of the party and later set forth the theory of the primary stage of socialism and the goal of building a socialist commodity economy at the Thirteenth Party Congress in late October 1987. As Zhao attempted to implement his coastal development strategy, which envisioned closer integration between China's coastal areas and the world economy, Guangdong took advantage of this new "policy window" and demanded further decentralization of economic power by presenting a brief request to the central government in mid-October 1987.[66]

In this request, the province asked for nothing less than an open-ended reaffirmation of "special policies, flexible measures," especially a provision in the minutes of the December 1980 Party Secretariat meeting that suggested the province had the perogative to implement only those central directives that it considered appropriate.[67] The request specifically called for expanding the area of the existing Pearl River Delta Open Economic Area, enlarging its power in getting foreign loans and approving foreign investment, decentralizing to the province the power to approve productive construction projects under RMB100 million, further relaxing policy over overseas Chinese investment, and continuing the lump sum transfer fiscal regime. Such a bold request was made only two weeks before the convening of the Thirteenth National Party Congress and Zhao Ziyang quickly gave his personal imprimatur to most of these demands.[68] The convergence of central and provincial objectives was again critical for the approval of greater autonomy to the province. The State Council Correspondence No. 25 issued in February 1988 was based on a second, more extensive proposal presented by Guangdong in early January 1988.[69] This document expanded the powers of the province in ten areas and designated it as a comprehensive reform area, hence a pacesetter for Zhao Ziyang's reform initiative. Though never fully implemented, this document deserved a closer scrutiny not only becuase it suggested the kind of autonomy that the province demanded but also because it pointed out the extent of provincial freedom that the central government would accommodate during the heyday of the radical reformers.

First, Guangdong's new powers in finance would allow the province a sharp edge over other areas in acquiring funds at home or abroad to support reform and development. For example, it was granted authority not only in developing an emerging stocks and securities market, but also in setting up foreign exchange adjustment centres in its cities and formulating its own plans for foreign borrowing, subject to central approval. The creation of a local, share-holding commercial bank — the Guangdong Development Bank — was approved and later incorporated in 1988.

Second, in tandem with similar national reforms, foreign trade reforms were proposed in this document. Guangdong's powers over direct foreign investment were further increased. It could approve projects that did not involve export quotas and licenses or national balances under US$30 million, or three times higher than the existing limit. In addition to the power to approve wholly-funded foreign investment, Guangdong could approve other export-oriented or import-substitution projects, and its export power was also expanded.

Third, the province would be granted unrivalled autonomy in price management. Not only would the national government stop setting mandatory price control targets for Guangdong, but the province could also determine when and how to introduce price reform. With only several exceptions, the management of most prices and fees controlled by the central government would be decentralized to the province.

Fourth, major reforms in labour management were approved. The contract system would be applied to all enterprises while increases in the province's total wage would be linked with the growth of various economic indicators. Enterprises would be given greater power to adjust wages and a social security system would be designed together with the above reforms.

Fifth, the lump sum transfer fiscal regime would, however, be modified, which reflected a bargaining between the central and provincial governments. Rather than handing over a lump sum to the central government, the province would remit an additional 9% annual increment during a three-year period starting from 1988.[70] The future incremental rate after the three-year period would have to be renegotiated. The province was also allowed for the first time to levy new kinds of local taxes (fees) and set such tax (fee) rates. Since the province had become much richer and wanted to acquire more freedom in reform, the central government was now able to demand more contribution and the province would find it difficult to resist.

Sixth, important enterprise reforms such as the contracting system and the director/manager responsibility system were endorsed. Guangdong was authorized not only to try the share-holding system in big- and medium-sized state-owned enterprises, but also to auction or lease small enterprises. Bankruptcy would be allowed, excepted for a few large enterprises and public utilities. Other reforms, such as the promotion of large-scale and export-oriented agriculture, would be continued.

Seventh, reforms in education and science and technology were suggested. Eighth, the privatization of housing would be pioneered as well. Ninth, Guangdong's autonomy in planning would be maintained. The province could also decide on its own scale of fixed capital investment within the range of RMB200 million. Finally, limited political reform was for the first time mentioned, including "democratization" of the policy-making process, the establishment of a civil service system, an administrative redress system, as well as the improvement of consultation between the government and the people.

Compared with previous ones, this 1988 document was much bolder and more comprehensive in promoting market-oriented reform. While some provinces had taken similar reforms such as in housing, only Guangdong could introduce reforms on so many fronts. As the province seemed ready to take a giant step in the 1990s, the runaway inflation and panic buying in the summer of 1988 jeopardized the consensus at the top level. With the grave economic situation and the subsequent ascent of more conservative leaders like Li Peng and Yao Yilin, a programme of economic austerity was introduced in the fall of that year. While the province was able to extend the Pearl River Delta Open Economic Area to cover twenty-eight cities and counties, about one quarter of the total area and close to 30% of the province's population, and establish other open zones in western and eastern Guangdong in the summer, it was not able to fully implement the 1988 document because of political and economic difficulties that loomed in the second half of 1988.[71] Some reforms that had been approved such as the commercialization of housing and the creation of the regional bank had been introduced, but the whole package was basically shelved.[72]

Difficulties and Opportunities in Central-provincial Relations since 1989

The Tian'anmen Incident in June 1989 not only shook the course of China's reform and opening, but also exacerbated the tensions between the central government and the provinces. Guangdong's reaction towards the martial law declared on 19 May and the suppression on 4 June was understandably lukewarm because the violent suppression of dissidents would ruin its investment environment.[73] The downfall of the radical reformers such as Zhao Ziyang who were sympathetic towards Guangdong's special role in the midst of the crisis cast another dark shadow over its future. Bold economic reform had been largely overtaken by economic retrenchment since the fall of 1988. The growing pre-eminence of planning-oriented leaders like Premier Li Peng and Vice-Premier Yao Yilin, reoriented economic policy from preferential treatment of the coastal areas to the basic industries and towards large- and medium-sized state-owned enterprises.[74] The tightening of the ideological and political atmosphere further made initiatives in reform and opening risky if not impossible.

Personnel appointment and economic policy had become two outstanding issues in central–Guangdong relations since 1989. First, the central government, now dominated by the conservatives, had attempted to reshuffle those among Guangdong's leadership who were close to Zhao Ziyang, yet the province's leaders had been quite successful in resisting such efforts. Having reached retirement age, Lin Ruo, then provincial party secretary, stepped down in January 1991, but his vacancy was filled by Xie Fei, another Guangdong native and veteran cadre. While Liang Xiang, the governor of Hainan, was dismissed for corruption, the widely watched central effort in transferring the more liberal governor, Ye Xuanping, from the province to a central post was a noted failure partly because of his background as the son of Marshal Ye Jianying (who played a key role in arresting the "Gang of Four") and partly because of his popularity as a staunch reformer at home and abroad.[75] It was not until early March 1991 that he had agreed to become a vice-chairman of the Chinese People's Political Consultative Conference, but he still stayed in the province.[76] The appointment of Zhu Senlin, a former mayor of Guangzhou, as the new governor in mid-January 1992, seemed to reflect Guangdong's influence even over personnel matters.[77]

Second, while not abandoning reform and the open policy, the central leadership since 1989 emphasized central co-ordination and management rather than local initiative and experimentation. One of the most serious challenges to Guangdong's special status centred on central efforts to overhaul the fiscal regime. In late 1990, Premier Li Peng attempted to abolish the lump-sum transfer regime to a tax-sharing one in order to raise central revenue and he maintained that the richer areas should contribute more to the central government. The lump-sum transfer regime had been subject to increasing stress since the mid-1980s because the central government had resorted to various measures to get money out of Guangdong on top of the contracted lump sum. As mentioned earlier, the regime was changed in 1988 when the province had to pay an annual 9% increment on top of the 1987 baseline of RMB1.4 billion.[78] In addition, the central government earned other revenues from the province, including profits and taxes from centrally run enterprises, customs duties collected by customs units, and banks, as well as various kinds of bonds and funds (such as the state budget adjustment fund and the transport and communication construction fund). In fact, the net remittance of Guangdong to the central government (after deducting central transfers) amounted to RMB19.22 billion in the period 1980–1989. In 1990, the sum of provincial remittance was over RMB5 billion, or already 40% of total provincial revenue, but the central government further redefined the Industrial and Commercial Tax collected by customs as a central revenue to reduce provincial income![79] Moreover, the central government borrowed money (*yazhi shangjiao*) and demanded extra contribution (*duozuo gongxian*) from the province whenever it was facing economic hardship. The acquisition of such extra funds from Guangdong had increased enormously since the mid-1980s and its amount in 1990 was a sizeable RMB1 billion.[80] The central government also asked the provinces to issue several billions of RMB's worth of state bonds in the 1980s. Hence, in an article published simultaneously in *Nanfang ribao* and *Renmin ribao*, on 11 March 1991, Lin Ruo tried to dispel suggestions that Guangdong merely benefited from central concessions and reiterated the contributions made by the province:

> From 1979 to 1990, Guangdong's net financial contributions to the central government increased from more than RMB800 million to over RMB5.2

billion (including customs duties collected by Guangdong), or multiplied by 6.5 times. The enterprises, customs institutions, and banks subordinated to the central government increased their tax-profit contributions to the state from less than RMB500 million to more than RMB10 billion, or multiplied by 21 times. In the 11 years up to 1989, Guangdong turned over a total of more than US$17.4 billion in foreign exchange to the central government.[81]

In sum, the actual remittance to the central government had greatly exceeded the contracted fee since the mid-1980s and had become a burden on the province.

Economic policy changes since 1989 had not only eroded Guangdong's special status, but also made the full implementation of the 1988 State Council document on the province impossible. For instance, in late 1990, Premier Li Peng rejected the request by "some localities" to subdivide credits to branch offices of the People's Bank so that they would have more autonomy in allocating these funds.[82] While this measure was already approved in the 1988 document, Li said that this idea was "unacceptable" because it would be "unfavourable to macro-economic regulation and control."[83] Since raising funds by issuing stocks and bonds had become important means of financing Guangdong's rapid economic growth, these restrictions would circumscribe its development. Other policies that once stimulated Guangdong's rapid growth, such as the repayment of loans before tax by enterprises, had also been criticized. The shift of central attention from Guangdong and its SEZs to the development of Shanghai and its Pudong area since 1990 reflected a strategic change in China's regional development strategy.[84] Inevitably, the competition between the province and other areas for foreign capital would only be keener. Given the personnel and policy changes at the top since 4 June 1989, the relationship between the central government and Guangdong was hardly amicable.

Provincial Responses to the Retrenchment

Responding to the growing concentration of economic power at the central level, Guangdong's leadership had defended reform and the special status of the province since mid-1989. In an article published in the 16 September 1989 issue of *Qiushi*, Lin Ruo argued that the province developed not merely because of central concessions.[85] As he put it, "Guangdong's construction funds have changed from depending upon central appropriation to mainly depending upon the province's own acquisition." During the period 1979–1988, "the proportion of central investment was very small" in Guangdong's fixed capital investment: 6% in the building of bridges, 13.6% in electricity supply, and 0.7% in education.[86] On the contrary, one-quarter of Guangdong's gross domestic product (hereafter GDP) was realized in the international market while one-quarter of its national income and one-third of its construction funds came from the world market by 1989.[87]

Guangdong's leaders also criticized the slow pace of reform and opening under Li Peng's retrenchment programme since 1988. For instance, the 11 March 1991 article by Lin Ruo praised the effectiveness of commodity economy. Most interestingly, even the former party secretary, Ren Zhongyi, published an article in *Nanfang ribao* on 3 April 1991 complaining that the special policies approved in 1988 "have not yet been fully implemented" and implicitly criticized the economic austerity programme.[88] The then Governor Ye Xuanping had also allegedly confronted Li Peng over economic policy issues in the meeting of governors held in fall 1990.[89]

The strength of Guangdong's response can be at least partly explained by the makeup of its leadership. Most positions of power in the province were held by local cadres who were either Guangdong native or veteran cadres who favoured market-oriented reform. The party secretary, Xie Fei, is a Guangdong native as well as a long-time local official while the Governor, Zhu Senlin, is a Shanghainese who made his career in the province. The failure of Li Peng and his associates to reshuffle Guangdong's leadership might be a good indicator of the new assertiveness of the more affluent provinces.

Deng's Tour to the South in Early 1992

Dissatisfied with the impasse of reform and confronted by the collapse of communism in Eastern Europe and the Soviet Union in the period 1989–1990, Deng Xiaoping toured southern China from late January to late February 1992 in order to stir up another wave of reform and opening. Following his strategy of "playing to the provinces" and reminiscent of his 1984 tour to the south, he encouraged local officials in these areas, especially Guangdong and Shenzhen, to step up reform and spend twenty years catching up with the "Four Little Dragons" in East Asia. In other words, Guangdong would again have to play a critical role in China's modernization in the 1990s.[90]

Guangdong's leadership was quick to take advantage of Deng's opening of another "policy window." Responding to Deng's call, Governor Zhu Senlin suggested in March that the province would be able to achieve double digit economic growth rate in the 1990s. Emboldened by this new situation, Zhu made four demands to the central government at the National People's Congress in late March.[91] He suggested the central government apply open policy to the mountainous areas in Guangdong (i.e. extending coastal area policy to the entire province), re-share the customs taxes collected by its ports for the central government, resume the implementation of the 1988 document (i.e. State Council Correspondence No. 25), and further accelerate financial reform.[92] At the same time, while discussing Li Peng's Government Work Report, the former party secretary Ren Zhongyi reiterated similar points by criticizing officials for focusing more on dealing with "peaceful evolution" than on economic construction. He also pointedly requested the abrogation of various economic austerity policies issued by Premier Li Peng which also applied to Guangdong and urged the State Council to reaffirm the 1988 document on the province.[93] While Guangdong could take advantage of the new political atmosphere to push for further reform and faster growth rates, the 1988 document was still not fully implemented. Nevertheless, with the inclusion of three of its cities as part of the coastal open zone in August, the entire province is now enjoying various kinds of special policies modelled after those of the SEZs.[94]

Deng's audacious rally for bolder and faster reform cumulated in the Fourteenth National Party Congress held in mid-October, which could be interpreted as a major effort in consolidating Deng Xiaoping's reform policy and a key event in the development of Guangdong's relations with the central government. For the first time since 1949, Guangdong's incumbent party leader had entered the Politburo and seven of its party and state officials had been elected members of the new Central Committee.[95] The addition of party leaders from Beijing, Shanghai, Tianjin and Shandong in the Politburo as well as the greater representation of the provinces in the Central Committee testified to the growing political prominence of the more affluent coastal provinces in the Chinese political scene. The report made by the general secretary, Jiang Zemin, which essentially repeated what Deng said in early 1992, also pinpointed the significance of Guangdong and Shanghai. Whether the presence of its party leader in the central government did lead to favourable treatment of the province remained to be further explored, but given the overall orientation of national policy, it was clear that the province would have more direct access to the central government and might play a key role in Deng's rally for building a socialist market economy.

Developments after 1992

As the Central Committee decided to establish a socialist market economy in November 1993, the role of Guangdong seemed to be further emphasized because it was already a pioneer in market-oriented reform. However, a number of developments soon revealed Guangdong's precarious political and economic position since the conclusion of the fourteenth party Congress in October 1992.[96] First, the central government introduced various economic policies and reforms that aimed at recentralizing macroeconomic power into its own hands. These included, for instance, the macro-economic adjustment programme introduced in the summer of 1993, the revenue-sharing reform in 1994 and reform of the banking sector in recent years. For instance, the revenue-sharing system replaced the lump-sum transfer regime from which Guangdong had benefited significantly in the 1980s with a more standardized revenue-sharing system aimed at increasing the share of central revenue.[97] Furthermore, the priorities of the central government in regional development strategy also experienced important shifts. Although the economic significance of the three main economic regions (Yangzi Delta, South China, and Bohai) was recognized in the Ninth Five-year Plan (1996–2000), the central government had already tried to address the issue of regional disparities between the coastal and inland regions through the establishment of a system of intergovernmental revenue transfers, the provision of preferential policies and the support given by the more affluent coastal areas to the poorer areas. The central government's emphasis on Shanghai and the Yangzi Delta region has become increasingly apparent as commercial and financial reform would be mainly spearheaded by Shanghai rather than Guangdong. While General Secretary Jiang Zemin has given regular assurances on the continuity of the SEZs in Guangdong since he came to power in 1989, a major debate about the fate of the zones erupted in 1995 between policy researchers with close connections with the central government and officials in the SEZs.[98] Furthermore, after more than seventeen years of rapid economic growth, Guangdong has to face a wide range of social and economic problems, including intra-provincial disparities, deterioration of public and social order, as well as rampant corruption.[99]

Second, the pattern of Chinese politics and central–provincial relations are also changing rapidly in the 1990s. Strengthening the power and resources of the central government was a key theme in Jiang Zemin's effort to consolidate his control over the political succession. In the Politburo elected after the fourteenth party Congress, party leaders from Beijing, Tianjin, Shanghai, Shandong and Guangdong were represented. By December 1996, however, only Shanghai and Guangdong remained in the Politburo as the death of Tianjin's party secretary, Tan Xiaowen, resulted in the lost of the city's "seat," while Beijing's former party secretary, Chen Xitong, was relieved of his position in the Central Committee and Politburo in September 1995.[100] Most importantly, Chen's downfall not only reflected a victory of the central government under Jiang Zemin in dealing with corrupt officials, but also sent a strong signal to non-compliant provincial leaders. In fact, the fortunes of Guangdong since 1978 are clearly tied to the political fate of a pro-reform wing in the top echelon. If one of the province's most valuable assets in the 1980s was its special relations with top officials like Deng Xiaoping and Zhao Ziyang, the elevation of Xie Fei to a Politburo member in 1992 means that the province can now directly make its case at the highest policy-making body. However, should Xie Fei step down as Guangdong's party secretary in the near future, then it is unclear whether his successor will still keep a seat in the Politburo after the fifteenth party Congress to be held in the fall of 1997. Furthermore, it is clear that General Secretary Jiang Zemin is building up support not only among the military and other groups in the central party and state apparatus, but also among provinces like Shandong and especially Shanghai in the past few years. With the probable exception of Qiao Shi, who is not likely to become an active force in Chinese politics because of his age and other reasons, no potential contenders for power seem to enjoy a close relationship with Guangdong. As Shanghai is tapping the advantages of being the gateway to the booming Yangzi Delta and is developing as China's premier commerical and financial centre, it is apparent that Guangdong will no longer be the sole star of reform as it once was.

Last but not least, a new generation of provincial leaders was also emerging in Guangdong.[101] Not only were they much younger, better educated, and professionally more qualified, but they were also mostly natives and veteran Guangdong cadres. A comparison of the fifth standing committee and the seventh standing committee of the Guangdong Provincial Party Committee (GPPCSC) is most instructive. When the fifth GPPCSC was formed in March 1983, none of the fourteen members were in their 40s; however, by the seventh GPPCSC elected in March 1993, six of the fifteen members of the seventh GPPCSC were in their mid- and late forties and another seven were in their 50s. Only the two most senior members (Xie Fei and Zhu Senlin) were in their early 60s. Furthermore, half of the members of the GPPCSC in 1983 only had secondary (or below) level education; but by 1993, over 93% of the members had a university degree or an equivalent level of education. One of the recent key personnel changes was the stepping down of Governor Zhu Senlin in February 1996, who took up the chairmanship of the Guangdong Provincial People's Congress. His successor, Lu Ruihua, is a Cantonese and a former executive vice-governor who made his early career in Foshan. The selection of Lu as Governor is good news to Guangdong because he is a popular official who has extensive experience in economic management and local administration. However, it is still unclear who will succeed Xie Fei, the party secretary, who is likely to retire or move to another post as he turns 65 by the fall of 1997. While this group of new Guangdong leaders is pragmatic and sensitive to the province's interests, the lack of a batch of senior cadres among the current provincial leadership might not be that favourable to the province in handling its relations with the central government, at least in the short run.

Conclusion

The past seventeen years is undoubtedly Guangdong's golden era. Given the special policies granted by the central government, the presence of an entrepreneurial provincial leadership, and its favourable geographical location and socio-economic ties to Hong Kong, Guangdong was able to take many steps ahead of other areas by taking advantage of the new opportunities in the reform era. The economic and political environment in the late 1990s is, however, radically different from the 1980s when Guangdong began its economic take-off. On the one hand, the interests of the province are still served by further reform and opening not only because it has accumulated considerable experience in market-oriented reform, but also because it is in a better position to capture the domestic market, attract foreign investment and export to other countries. On the other hand, the opening up of China and the progress of economic reform across the nation inevitably mean keener competition among the provinces for the domestic market as well as for foreign capital in the longer run. Guangdong's comparative advantage in export processing and light industry will likely enable it to maintain an edge over others in these sectors for some time to come. However, many provinces ranging from Fujian to Sichuan are also entering the competition as there are few barriers to entrants in the consumer goods market. Furthermore, although the province is already undergoing a process of industrial restructuring and trying to move up the technological ladder, it might not yet enjoy a strong advantage in the manufacturing of technology-intensive products such as automobiles, computers, telecommunication equipment, and so on, which are becoming increasingly in demand as China modernizes. In fact, the provincial government has already scaled down its GDP growth target from the actual annual growth rate of 19% in the period 1991–1995 to an estimate of only 11% in 1996–2000.[102]

Guangdong's economic resources and the political influence that entails, together with the province's special ties with Hong Kong, will be the most important capital for it to play a significant role in Chinese politics in the post-Deng era. Guangdong has already established itself as an economic powerhouse in China. With only 67.8 million people (about 5.6% of China's population) and less than 2% of the nation's land area, it contributed about 10% of the nation's GDP.[103] In 1995, the province ranked not only first in GDP, total retail sales, and revenue, but also second in industrial output and fourth in agricultural output among the provinces. As the recipient of more than one-fifth of China's total foreign investment, Guangdong has been the number one exporting province since 1986, accounting for about 40% of China's export.[104] In sharp contrast to most other provinces, Guangdong enjoys extensive external socio-economic ties through its network of overseas Chinese in Hong Kong, Southeast Asia, North America and elsewhere. Such ties have brought about numerous tangible and intangible benefits to the province through cultural exchange, tourism, trade and investment, networking, as well as donations which registered RMB3.3 billion in official accounts in 1995 alone.[105]

In particular, Guangdong's special links with Hong Kong will become even more critical assets for its economic future and its relations with the central government. In 1995, an estimated four million workers in Guangdong were directly or indirectly employed by Hong Kong companies.[106] Hong Kong accounted for about 74% of total foreign investment and 80% of foreign direct investment in the province.[107] Extensive transportation and telecommunications links between the province and Hong Kong have already been established. Economic interdependence between the two areas is widely expected to grow further after Hong Kong's return to Chinese sovereignty on 1 July 1997. Especially in the first few years after 1997, major economic and social instability in Guangdong would introduce great risks and problems for the Hong Kong Special Administrative Region. Hence the central government will handle its relations with the province very carefully. If the province becomes unstable socially, economically or politically, it might fare very badly for China's foreign economic relations, as well as trigger withdrawal of overseas capital, unemployment, and unpredictable political shocks to Hong Kong and Macau. To be sure, how the province manages its relations with the central government after a new central leadership takes the helm in the fifteenth party Congress in late 1997 depends not only upon its overall economic position in the national economy and the orientation of the central government, but also upon the visions, skills and strategies of its future leadership. If Deng Xiaoping had to ally with the provinces in order to protect his course of reform, his successors will probably also depend on important provinces like Guangdong for support in consolidating their authority and in maintaining social and political stability. As long as Guangdong remains an important economic powerhouse in China, which is likely at least in the short run, it will continue to enjoy considerable influence in Beijing and play a critical role in China's modernization.

Notes

1. The most comprehensive study of the province under reform in English is: Ezra Vogel, *One Step Ahead in China: Guangdong under Reform* (Cambridge: Harvard University Press, 1989). For a sample of recent studies in English, see Joseph Y. S. Cheng and Stewart MacPherson (eds.), *Development in Southern China: A Report on the Pearl River Delta Region* (Hong Kong: Longman, 1995); David S. G. Goodman and Feng Chongyi, "Guangdong: Greater Hong Kong and the New Regional Future," in *China Deconstructs: Politics, Trade and Regionalism*, edited by David S. G. Goodman and Gerald Segal (London: Routledge, 1994), pp. 177–201; Reginald Yin-Wang Kwok and Alvin So (eds.), *The Hong Kong–Guangdong Link: Partnership in Flux* (Armonk, N.Y.: M.E. Sharpe, 1995); Stewart MacPherson and Joseph Y. S. Cheng (eds.), *Economic and Social Development in South China* (Cheltenham: Edward Elgar, 1996); Toyojiro Maruya (ed.), *Guangdong: "Open Door" Economic Development Strategy* (Hong Kong: Centre of Asian Studies, University of Hong Kong, and Institute of Developing Economies, 1992); Yun-wing Sung et al., *The Fifth Dragon: The Emergence of the Pearl River Delta* (Singapore: Addison Wesley, 1995). For a select bibliography of Guangdong under reform, see my bibliography in

    Provincial China, No. 1 (March 1997), pp. 50–63. Studies of Guangdong in Chinese are too numerous to cite. One of the best fact-finding sources in Chinese is: Guangdong baikequanshu bianzuan weiyuanhui (ed.), *Guangdong baikequanshu* (An Encyclopaedia of Guangdong) (Beijing: Zhongguo daibaikequanshu chubanshe, 1995).

2. The "centre" (*zhongyang*) in central–provincial relations refers to the "State Council and its commissions, ministries, and leadership small groups in Beijing as well as the Party Politburo, Secretariat, and the organs of the Central Committee." However, the term "central government" will be used in lieu of the "centre" in this chapter for the sake of simplicity. See Kenneth Lieberthal and Michael Oksenberg, *Policy Making in China* (Princeton, N.J.: Princeton University Press, 1988), p. 138. Similarly, the term "provincial government" will be used to refer to provincial party and state authorities.

3. Since the focus of this chapter is on the interactions between the central and provincial governments, I can only briefly discuss the implementation and outcomes of special policies, which is an important topic that demands a separate analysis.

4. Ezra Vogel, *Canton under Communism* (Cambridge: Harvard University Press, 1969), pp. 211–16.

5. This is one of the themes of *Canton Under Communism* (see note 4).

6. Ibid., p. 21.

7. Vogel, *One Step Ahead in China* (see note 1), p. 31.

8. David Shambaugh, *The Making of a Premier: Zhao Ziyang's Provincial Career* (Boulder: Westview, 1984), chapter 5.

9. Guangdong figures are calculated from Guangdongsheng tongjiju (ed.), *Guangdong tongji nianjian* (hereafter *GTN*) *1986* (Guangdong Statistical Yearbook 1986) (Guangzhou: Guangdongsheng tongjiju, 1986), p. 87, and national figures are from Carl Riskin, *China's Political Economy* (New York: Oxford University Press, 1988), p. 185.

10. A more indepth analysis of the relations between the centre and Guangdong from a multi-dimensional perspective is: Peter T. Y. Cheung, "The Case of Guangdong in Central–Provincial Relations," in *Changing Central–Local Relations in China: Reform and State Capacity*, edited by Jia Hao and Lin Zhimin (Boulder: Westview, 199), pp. 207–37. For recent and forthcoming studies that deal with central–provincial relations, see, e.g., Shaun Breslin, *China in the 1980s: Centre–Province Relations in a Reforming Socialist State* (London: Macmillan, 1996); David S. G. Goodman and Gerald Segal (eds.), *China Deconstructs: Politics, Trade and Regionalism* (London: Routledge, 1994); Huang Yasheng, *Inflation and Investment Controls in China* (Cambridge: Cambridge University Press, 1996); Linda Chelan Li, *Shifting Central–Provincial Relations in China: The Politics of Investment*

in Shanghai and Guangdong, 1978–1993 (Oxford: Oxford University Press, forthcoming). Detailed bibliographic information on central–provincial relations can be found in Jae Ho Chung, "Studies on Central–Provincial Relations in the People's Republic of China: A Mid-Term Appraisal," *China Quarterly*, No. 142 (June 1995), pp. 407–508. A study that examines provincial leadership and reform strategy as well as central–provincial relations is: Peter T. Y. Cheung, Jae Ho Chung and Zhimin Lin (eds.), *Provincial Strategies of Economic Reform in Post-Mao China: Leadership, Politics and Implementation* (Armonk, N.Y.: M.E. Sharpe, forthcoming).

11. It should be noted that Ye actually expressed a continuing interest to serve in south China in 1953, but he was transferred back to Beijing in October 1953. Hence Tao Zhu became the *de facto* leader in Guangdong since October 1953, although Ye was not officially replaced by Tao until 1955. See Yu Yongbo and Xu Caihou (eds.), *Ye Jianying zhuan (A Biography of Ye Jianying)* (Beijing: Dangdai Zhongguo chubanshe, 1995), p. 757. Chen Yu reappeared after the Cultural Revolution, but he served only as one of the vice directors of the Guangdong Provincial Revolutionary Committee until his death in March 1974.

12. This chapter mainly follows the differentiation of the central leadership into the moderate and radical reformers as analyzed in Harry Harding, *China's Second Revolution* (Washington, D.C.: Brookings, 1987), chapter 4. Since I think the term "conservatives" is more appropriate to describe the moderate reformers, it will be used throughout this chapter.

13. On this issue, see, e.g., Linda Chelan Li, "Guangdong Playing the 'Foreign Card' in Central–Provincial Relations and Economic Development, 1978–95" (paper presented at the conference, "Subregionalism in East Asia: Comparative Approaches," City University of Hong Kong, 6–7 December 1996).

14. See Zhonggong Guangdongshengwei bangongting (ed.), *Zhongyang dui Guangdong gongzuo zhishi huibian* (hereafter *ZDGGZH*) *(1979–1982)* (A Collection of Central Directives on Guangdong's Work (1979–1982)), p. 53. Gu Mu referred to this statement by Xi.

15. One key document on foreign trade was approved in this conference and promulgated as State Council Document (1979) No. 202. *ZDGGZH (1979–1982)*, pp. 1–8.

16. Text of the report can be found in *ZDGGZH (1979–1982)*, pp. 20–30.

17. The following provides only a summary of the most important provisions of "special policies, flexible measures." Ibid., pp. 24–27.

18. Ibid., pp. 19 and 23–24.

19. For a discussion of Guangdong's fiscal relations with the central government, please refer to my earlier study, "The Case of Guangdong in Central–Provincial Relations" (see note 10), pp. 225–28. For a more detailed analysis

of Guangdong's fiscal policy, see my chapter "Guangdong's Provincial Leadership and Policy toward Resource Allocation" in *Provincial Strategies of Economic Reform in Post-Mao China* (see note 10).

20. Enterprises still under central control included railways, ports, postal service and telecommunications, civil aviation units, banks, as well as national defense and research units.

21. *ZDGGZH (1979–1982)*, pp. 61–71.

22. For studies of the contending perspectives towards China's reform and open policy, see Carol Lee Hamrin, *China and the Challenge of the Future* (Boulder: Westview, 1990); Jude Howell, *China Opens Its Door: The Politics of Economic Transition* (Boulder: Lynne Rienner, 1993); Ruan Ming, *Deng Xiaoping: Chronicle of an Empire* (Boulder: Westview, 1994). For other recent studies of the politics of economic reform, see, e.g. Richard Baum, *Burying Mao: Chinese Politics in the Age of Deng Xiaoping* (Princeton: Princeton University Press, 1996); Joseph Fewsmith, *Dilemmas of Reform in China: Political Conflict and Economic Debate* (Armonk, N.Y.: Sharpe, 1994); Susan Shirk, *The Political Logic of Economic Reform in China* (Berkeley: University of California Press, 1993); Gordon White, *Riding the Tiger: The Politics of Economic Reform in Post-Mao China* (London: Macmillan, 1993).

23. In April 1981, Wan Li said he and Zhao still maintained that reform should be implemented during readjustment. *ZDGGZH (1979–1982)*, pp. 42 and 50–53.

24. Ibid., p. 102.

25. See his comments in a Party Secretariat Meeting held on 24–25 September 1980, ibid., pp. 94–108.

26. Ibid.

27. Ibid., p. 110.

28. Vogel, *One Step Ahead in China* (note 1), p. 88.

29. Ibid., pp. 316–17.

30. See Susan Shirk, "Playing to the Provinces: Deng Xiaoping's Political Strategy of Economic Reform," *Studies in Comparative Communism*, 23 (Autumn/Winter 1990), pp. 227–58.

31. The communiqué of the meeting was promulgated as Central Document 1981, No. 5, in *ZDGGZH (1979–1982)*, pp. 128–31

32. The two speeches by Gu Mu on 27 May 1981 and 12 June 1981 made it amply clear that he and Zhao Ziyang wanted to allow more flexibility to the two provinces. *ZDGGZH (1979–1982)*, pp. 152–60.

33. Ibid., pp. 163–79.

34. In fact, the provisions regarding the SEZs occupied the major part of the document, ibid., p. 166.

35. *ZDGGZH (1979–1982)*, p. 71. This document stated that all policies

involving external economic activities had to be cleared with the central government before they were promulgated, foreign exchange had to be centrally managed, reduction or exemption of import tariff had to be approved by the central government, and the SEZs had to strictly follow national laws.

36. Ibid., pp. 243–45.
37. Ibid., pp. 245–46.
38. Ibid., p. 250.
39. See Hu Qiaomu's speech, ibid., pp. 253–58.
40. Ibid., pp. 287–88.
41. Ibid., pp. 308–309.
42. Ibid., pp. 361–64.
43. Ibid., p. 310.
44. *GTN 1985*, pp. 33 and 35.
45. Ibid., pp. 33 and 106.
46. Ibid., p. 106.
47. Ibid., pp. 276–77. The 1979 figure of US$40.15 million was reported in Guangdongsheng tongjiju (ed.), *Guangdongsheng tongji ziliao tiyao 1978–82* (Guangzhou: Guangdongsheng tongjiju, 1983), p. 71.
48. *GTN 1985*, p. 276 and Guojia tongjiju (ed.), *Zhongguo tongji nianjian* (hereafter *ZTN*) *1989* (Chinese Statistical Yearbook 1989) (Beijing: Zhongguo tongji chubanshe, 1989), p. 645.
49. *GTN 1985*, p. 267.
50. *GTN 1986*, pp. 33–35 and *ZTN 1985*, pp. 16–17.
51. Chen Yizhi, *Zhongguo: Shinian gaige yu bajiu minyun* (China: Ten Years of Reform and Democratic Movement in 1989) (Taipei: Lianjing chubanshiye gongsi, 1990), pp. 63–64.
52. Ibid., p. 83.
53. See Deng's comments in *ZDGGZH (1983–1985)*, pp. 123–27.
54. For a transcript of Zhao's talks during the tour, see ibid., pp. 192–213.
55. Ibid., pp. 158 and 200–202.
56. Ibid., pp. 341–54.
57. Ibid., pp. 378–91.
58. Since all above-baseline surplus of foreign exchange from the growing business of export processing would still be retained, the resulting increases of foreign exchange accrued to the province's income would be quite substantial.
59. Those enterprises that wanted to operate in Hong Kong and Macau, however, still had to receive approval from MOFERT.
60. Carol Lee Hamrin, *China and the Challenge of the Future* (note 22), pp. 171–73.
61. Ibid.

62. Dangdai Zhongguo de jingji guanli bianjibu (ed.), *Zhonghua renmin gong-heguo jingji guanli dashiji* (A Chronology of Economic Management in the People's Republic of China) (Beijing: Zhongguo jingji chubanshe, 1987), pp. 659–60.
63. *GTN 1989*, pp. 331 and 342.
64. Ibid., p. 139.
65. Wu Yixing, *Guangdong shinian jingji tizhi gaige yanjiu* (A Study of Ten Years of Economic System Reform in Guangdong) (Guangzhou: Zhongshan daixue chubanshe, 1990), p. 6.
66. The text is in *ZDGGZH (1986–1987)*, Vol. II, pp. 370–75.
67. *ZDGGZH (1979–1982)*, p. 110.
68. *ZDGGZH (1986–1987)*, Vol. II, pp. 384–86.
69. *ZDGGZH (1986–1987)*, Vol. II, pp. 426–44. According to Yang Xiaohui, when Lin Ruo proposed such ideas to Zhao, the party's General Secretary was so interested that he called the province to produce a report, the October Document. See Yang Xiaohui, *Shengji zhengfu de zhizhu xingwei — Kaifang gaige shiqi de Guangdong zhengfu* (The Autonomous Behaviour of Provincial Government — Guangdong's Government in the Era of Reform and Opening) (M.A. thesis, The Chinese University of Hong Kong, 1990).
70. *GTN 1989*, p. 205.
71. The figures are from Wan Zuoxin et al. (eds.), *Guangdong touzi zhinan* (A Guide to Investment in Guangdong Province) (Tianjin: Tianjin kexue jishu chubanshe, 1992), p. 43.
72. Yang Xiaohui, *Shengji zhengfu de zhizhu xingwei* (see note 69), p. 45.
73. Ibid., pp. 53–54.
74. See *Far Eastern Economic Review*, 4 April 1991, pp. 21–29.
75. Talks of removing Ye from Guangdong surfaced in the Hong Kong press in the fall of 1989. See, e.g. *South China Morning Post* (Hong Kong), 2 September 1989, p. 10.
76. *Hong Kong Standard*, 11 February 1991, p. 1, in Foreign Broadcasting Information Services, *Daily Report: China (FBIS)*, FBIS-CHI-91-028, 11 February 1991, p. 57.
77. *Nanfang ribao*, 17 January 1992, p. 1.
78. *ZDGGZH (1986–1987)*, Vol. II, p. 435.
79. Wang Zuo et al. (eds.), *Guangdong gaige kaifang pingshuo* (Comments on Guangdong's Reform and Opening) (Guangzhou: Guangdong gaodeng jiaoyu chubanshe, 1992), p. 62.
80. Guangdong Yearbook Editorial Committee (ed.), *Guangdong nianjian* (hereafter *GN*) *1990* (Guangdong Yearbook 1990) (Guangzhou: Guangdong renmin chubanshe, 1990), p. 308.
81. Lin Ruo, "Several Points of Understanding on Developing the Socialist

Commodity Economy" (in Chinese), *Nanfang ribao*, 11 March 1991, p. 3, in FBIS-CHI-91-054, 20 March 1991, p. 35.

82. Li Peng, "Make Great Efforts to Adjust the Economic Structure and Improve Enterprises' Economic Results." Beijing Xinhua Domestic Service, 2106 GMT, 31 December 1990, in FBIS-CHI-91-001, 2 January 1991, p. 27.

83. Ibid., p. 27.

84. *Far Eastern Economic Review*, 9 October 1990, pp. 68–69.

85. All quotations are my own translation, see Lin Ruo, "Gaige kaifang yu Guangdong jingji de fazhan," *Qiushi* (Seeking Truth), No. 18 (16 September 1989), p. 27. However, another article critical of Guangdong's economic situation was published in the 6 November 1989 issue of *Liaowang* (Outlook) magazine.

86. Lin Ruo, "Gaige kaifang yu Guangdong jingji de fazhan" (see note 85), p. 29.

87. Ibid., p. 30.

88. See Ren Zhongyi, "Reform, Opening up, and Taking Economic Construction as Center" (in Chinese), *Nanfang ribao*, 3 April 1991, p. 123, in FBIS-CHI-91-071, 12 April 1991, pp. 54–55.

89. *Pai Shing Monthly* (Hong Kong), 1 December 1990, p. 4 and 1 April 1991, p. 9.

90. Zhonggong Shenzhen shiwei xuanchuanbu (ed.), *Deng Xiaoping yu Shenzhen* (Deng Xiaoping and Shenzhen) (Shenzhen: Haitian chubanshe, 1992), pp. 6–7.

91. *Nanfang ribao*, 25 March 1992, p. 1.

92. On the issue of financial reform, Zhu suggested that a fixed percentage of savings be allowed as credits, a fixed percentage of national income be issued as bonds, and a fixed amount of foreign exchange bonds be issued, see *Nanfang ribao*, 25 March 1992, p. 1.

93. *Nanfang ribao*, 28 March 1992, pp. 1–2.

94. Hainan was hived off in 1988 as a separate province with SEZ-styled privileges.

95. *Ming Pao Daily News* (Hong Kong), 19 October 1992, p. 6.

96. Since a detailed analysis of this period is not possible within the confines of several paragraphs, the following discussion only identifies some of the salient issues that are closely connected to the development of central–provincial relations in this period.

97. For a study of this reform and its application to Guangdong, please see my chapter "Guangdong's Provincial Leadership and Policy toward Resource Allocation," in *Provincial Strategies of Economic Reform in Post-Mao China* (see note 10). For a study of this reform and its impact on central–provincial relations, see Jae Ho Chung, "Beijing Confronting the Provinces: The 1994 Tax-sharing Reform and Its Implications for Central–Provincial

Relations," *China Information*, Vol. 9, No. 2/3 (Winter 1994/95), pp. 1–23, and his "Central–Provincial Relations," in *China Review 1995*, edited by Lo Chi Kin, Suzanne Pepper and Tsui Kai Yuen (Hong Kong: The Chinese University Press, 1995), pp. 3.1–3.45.

  98. For analyses of this debate, see *The Nineties*, October 1995, pp. 45–51 and *South China Morning Post*, 20 September 1995, p. 21.

  99. For a preliminary analysis of the social and political consequences of Guangdong's rapid economic growth, see my "Prosperity and Politics: Guangdong" (paper presented to the 92nd annual meeting of the American Political Science Association, San Francisco, 29 August–1 September 1996).

100. *Hong Kong Economic Times*, 30 September 1995, p. A11; *South China Morning Post*, 3 October 1995, p. 8.

101. The following data draw from my paper "Prosperity and Politics: Guangdong" (see note 99) and *Far Eastern Economic Review*, 22 February 1996, p. 20.

102. *Hong Kong Economic Times*, 3 April 1996, p. A23.

103. The following statistics draws from *GTN 1996*, pp. 89 and 551–57.

104. *ZTN 1996*, pp. 595 and 600.

105. *GTN 1996*, p. 374.

106. Hong Kong Government, *Hong Kong 1996* (Hong Kong: Government Printer, 1996), p. 54.

107. *GTN 1996*, pp. 366 and 370.

3

The Economy

Toyojiro Maruya

Introduction

Ever since China adopted the policy of reform and opening to the outside
world in the late 1970s, Guangdong has experienced tremendous economic
growth due to its special policy and flexible measures and to its proximity
to Hong Kong. The national income of Guangdong posted a low annual
5.3% growth between 1952 and 1978, compared to the national average of
6.0% for the same period. However, between 1979 and 1994, when the
policy of reform and opening up was introduced, the provincial income
grew at an annual average of 14.2%, more than twice the figures posted
before the reforms. Moreover, the rate well exceeded the national average
of 9.8%. The rapid economic growth in Guangdong after the reforms is
largely attributed to the development of the market economy as well as the
establishment of export-led industrialization.[1]

The purpose of this chapter is to survey the Guangdong economy.
First, in order to clearly bring out the dynamism of the Guangdong
economy after 1978, the performance of the Guangdong economy before
and after the adoption of reforms and open policy will be reviewed.
Second, the factors which enabled the economic growth and structural
changes will be analyzed. Finally, prospects of the future Guangdong
economy based on its long-term economic plans will be evaluated.

Guangdong Economy before the Reforms (1952–1978)

The Guangdong economy was a highly centralized one. Such a centralized
system operated successfully in the founding years of the People's
Republic of China (PRC) when the people's living standard was extremely
low, because it allowed China to concentrate its limited resources on
certain fields and areas to overcome the lack of savings and investment.
The Guangdong economy grew rapidly in the founding years of the PRC.
However, the speed of growth gradually decelerated after the second half
of the 1960s, when the negative effects of the planned economy became
visible and political failures occurred repeatedly due to the unstable political atmosphere.

The Guangdong economy posted a relatively good growth during the
First Five-year Plan (1953–1957), a period in which China began to establish a socialist economy after recovering from the confusion of the founding years of the country. Agriculture was emphasized in the economic
development of Guangdong, because the province was selected as the

national defence front line after the foundation of the PRC, as well as its close proximity to Hong Kong and Macau. Moreover, its subtropical climate is favourable for agriculture.[2] With this emphasis, agriculture and light industry using agricultural products as its raw materials became the locomotives of the province for this period, while heavy industry also showed a high growth supported by improvement of the mining industry. Consequently, as a whole, a well-balanced economic growth was achieved during this period.

However, soon after the Second Five-year Plan (1958–1962) was introduced, the Great Leap Forward policy was employed to put production factors such as land and labourers into heavy industries, particularly steel production. As a result, production of light industries decreased considerably, destabilizing the total balance of the economy, and inflation emerged as money supply was increased to finance the huge basic construction investment. The Guangdong economy suffered much damage.[3] During the Second Five-year Plan period, investment for basic construction allotted to heavy industries increased 9.1 times as much as the amount for the first period to RMB1.89 billion, of which 82% was appropriated for the Great Leap Forward of 1958 to 1960. As a result, the share of heavy industries in all basic construction investment rose from 16.5% during the first period to 49.4% during the second period.[4] This biased policy, which ignored the principle of economy, was a sheer failure, and the Guangdong economy experienced a great setback.

During the following adjustment period (1963–1965), measures contrary to those during the Great Leap Forward were devised to recover and develop agricultural production, stabilize commodity prices by restraining basic construction investment, and recover industrial balance by reducing the importance of heavy industries. Agriculture thus showed an annual growth rate of over 14% on average, and Guangdong's gross domestic product (GDP) posted a high growth rate of 13.2% during this period.

However, the Cultural Revolution promoted by Mao Zedong in the second half of the 1960s and the political activities of the "Gang of Four" in the middle of the 1970s confused economic management. Around the same period "three line construction" started to develop, and again heavy industries became the focus of the economy for the Third (1966–1970) and Fourth Five-year Plan (1971–1975) periods. During these periods, consumption was restrained to accumulate capital, and production goods were blindly given priority and promotion without considering the demand of agriculture and light industry for such goods. Consequently, investment in heavy industries increased, while little was allocated to light industries, with an obvious decrease in investment in the agricultural sector. The production of agriculture and light industries thus stagnated, while heavy industries, which focused only on production without considering economic efficiency, did not record a remarkable production growth relative to its large-scale investment.[5] Economic growth slowed down and the economic efficiency of Guangdong decreased rapidly. The incremental capital-output ratio (ICOR) as shown in Table 3.1 demonstrates a sharp increase after the second half of the 1960s, reducing the amount of value-added products by a unit of investment from one-third to one-fourth. The centralized planned system lost its economic dynamism gradually in the late 1960s, because of political confusion and the negative effects of this system, such as the lack of incentives for enterprises and labourers.

The characteristics of the Guangdong economy before the reforms

Table 3.1   Growth Rates of GDP, Agricultural and Industrial Output, Investment Share and ICOR, 1952–1994

(Unit: %)

	GDP	Investment shares	ICOR	Annual growth rates of industry		
				Agricultural	Light	Heavy
1953–1957	8.7	16.2	1.9	6.0	14.9	25.2
1958–1962	−1.2	22.9	—	−3.4	3.0	10.1
1963–1965	13.2	15.6	1.2	14.4	14.7	25.5
1966–1970	3.5	16.4	4.7	2.9	8.1	15.0
1971–1975	6.0	22.5	3.8	1.4	6.6	13.5
1976–1980	7.1	25.1	3.5	5.0	9.1	7.1
1976–1978	(4.1)	(27.0)	(6.6)	(5.1)	(6.2)	(11.3)
1979–1980	(11.8)	(23.1)	(2.0)	(5.0)	(13.6)	(1.0)
1981–1985	12.2	27.9	2.3	7.4	18.1	13.2
1986–1990	12.5	28.9	2.3	7.7	24.5	20.1
1991–1994	20.1	44.8	2.2	5.1	32.9	37.2

Sources: *Guangdong tongji nianjian*, various years; and Chen Kexuan (ed.), *Guang-dong — One Step Ahead in China* (Hong Kong: Hong Kong Daido Culture Ltd., 1989).

Notes: 1. Growth rate means annual average real growth in these periods.
2. Investment shares of income are the ratio of accumulation of national income from 1952 to 1980, while from 1980 to 1994 the ratio of investment in fixed assets to GDP are used.
3. Incremental capital-output ratio (ICOR) = Investment share ÷ GDP growth rate.

may be summarized in three ways. First, Guangdong demonstrated constant growth, particularly in agriculture and light industries in the founding years of the PRC because Guangdong satisfied the necessary factors for development. However, after the late 1960s, inefficient allocation of resources with the biased strategy that favoured heavy industries caused a stagnant economy.

Second, economic growth was very unsteady, especially after the Great Leap Forward, when the Guangdong economy began to change extensively in the cycles of three to five years. This is largely because the economic policies were politicized.

Third, the economic performance of Guangdong was always below the performance of China as a whole. Guangdong's economic growth was recorded as 7.1% in the 1950s, 3.5% in the 1960s and 5.4% in the early 1970s.[6] These figures were 1.9, 0.5 and 0.1 percentage points lower than the figures for China as a whole during the corresponding periods. Behind Guangdong's slow economic growth was the fact that the province is located on China's southern periphery, facing Southeast Asia, and was not one of the regions which the state prioritized for construction because the province was under the threat of military invasion.[7] In particular, in the late 1960s, when the world political situation became very tense, the Chinese government concentrated its energies into constructing in "safe" areas and therefore stressed capital construction in the inland regions, reducing investment in Guangdong.

Guangdong Economy after the Reforms (1979–1994)

At the end of 1978, China switched to the policy of reform and opening, and Guangdong along with Fujian were given "special policies and flexible measures" ahead of other provinces in China.[8] In addition, Guangdong's close proximity to Hong Kong was an advantageous factor in realizing the policy of reform and opening. Consequently, the speed of structural change well exceeded that of other regions. First, price reform developed rapidly: in the middle of the 1980s, the market-determined prices exceeded 50% of all prices, and in 1991, the percentage further reached 90%.[9] The importance of state-owned enterprises decreased sharply and diversified ownership emerged. While in 1980, the share of state-owned enterprises to total industrial production output was 63%, this figure fell to 39% in 1990 and to 18% in 1994, allowing rural enterprises, private enterprises and foreign affiliated firms to flourish. As the market-ization of Guangdong developed rapidly, the production system in Guangdong shifted markedly from the conventional planning type of production to market-oriented production. Guangdong's favourable economic environment allowed the province to attain a remarkable development of foreign economic relationships. With a rapid inflow of direct investment from Hong Kong, the province gradually increased its export of light industry products and processing and assembly products. In the late 1980s, the Guangdong economy established export-led in-dustrialization with a focus on labour-intensive industries.[10]

The Guangdong economy, which established a market-oriented mechanism, promoted light industries and agriculture again. As shown in Table 3.1, after 1979, light industries and agriculture demonstrated a remarkable growth. In the case of light industries, the average annual growth was 18.1% in the early 1980s and 24.5% in the late 1980s, while agriculture grew at an annual rate of around 7.5% throughout the 1980s. At the same time, due to a demand derived from developing agriculture and light industries, heavy industries also showed a remarkable growth. This new economic mechanism strengthened economic activities, improved economic efficiency and contributed to overall economic development. In spite of the sharp increase in investment after the reforms, ICOR remained low, showing a remarkable improvement in capital efficiency. Behind this was an improvement in labour productivity. The Guangdong economy, pushed by the improvement in investment ratio and economic efficiency, saw a rapid increase in its economic growth rate.

The Guangdong economy, which always hovered below the national average before the reforms, changed completely to outperform the national average (Table 3.2). The province enjoyed an economic growth rate from 1978 to 1994 of an average of 14.2%. This figure exceeded the national growth rate of 9.8% by 4.4% annually, and registered the highest among the 30 provinces and autonomous regions of China. As a result, Guang-dong, which in 1978 ranked seventh in the country in terms of GDP, rose to the top position by 1989. Indeed, many of the macroeconomic indicators of the province moved to top or close-to-top positions in the country. Guangdong was first, of course, in the amount of foreign capital utilized and also in exports, investment in fixed social assets and retail sales of social commodities; and, in spite of possible ecological negative feedback, third in industrial output as well as in agricultural output. These raised Guangdong's share in the macroeconomic indicators of the country such as GDP and total social output from roughly 5% in 1978 to 10% in 1994. The

Table 3.2 Trends in Macroeconomic Indicators

(Unit: %)

| | Average annual rates of increase | | | | | | Share of Guangdong in nation | | |
| | Guangdong province | | | China as a whole | | | | | |
	6th Plan	8th Plan	1978–1994	6th Plan	8th Plan	1978–1994	1978	1985	1994
Population	1.6	1.7	1.8	1.3	1.2	1.4	5.3	5.4	5.6
Area	—	—	—	—	—	—	2.2	2.2	1.9
No. of workers	2.9	2.9	2.7	3.3	2.0	2.4	5.7	5.5	5.7
GDP	12.2	20.2	14.2	10.1	12.2	9.8	5.1	6.2	9.4
(per capita GDP in RMB)	(365)	(2,356)	(6,337)	(373)	(1,621)	(3,755)	(0.98)	(1.15)	(1.69)
Agricultural output	7.4	5.1	6.6	8.1	6.6	6.2	6.1	6.8	7.3
Industrial output	16.4	34.4	21.7	12.0	24.0	14.9	4.7	5.5	9.5
Investment in fixed assets	37.0	54.8	31.4	22.8	38.5	22.9	4.2	7.3	13.1
Retail sales	18.5	29.1	22.0	15.0	22.4	17.3	6.1	7.6	11.4
Export	6.1	35.4	22.5	8.6	21.4	15.9	14.2	10.8	38.8
Foreign capital (utilized)	33.8	54.2	32.9	—	66.9	28.4	—	19.8	26.5
Price index	5.3	10.6	8.7	3.5	10.6	7.3	1.0	—	—
Average annual wages	12.0	24.9	16.5	8.5	20.7	13.3	—	1.2	1.6

Sources: *Guangdong tongji nianjian* and *Zhongguo tongji nianjian*, various years.

Notes: 1. Average annual rates of increase are in nominal terms except GDP, agricultural output and industrial output, which are in real terms.

2. 8th Plan is for 1991–1994.

3. Figures in parentheses for per capita GDP are for the years 1978, 1985 and 1994. Those for Guangdong's shares are ratios of per capita GDP of Guangdong with respect to China as a whole.

per capita GDP of Guangdong was lower than the national average until 1978, but jumped to 68.8% above the national average in 1994, reflecting tremendous progress in the local economy.

Structural Change in Demand: "Beneficial Cycle of Exports and Investment"[11]

The rapid development of the Guangdong economy since the reforms was naturally accompanied by changes in its industrial structure. The structural changes of the Guangdong economy strongly reflected the influence of the economic reforms. The economic reforms in China can be divided into five stages, and the Guangdong economy also shows corresponding structural changes. Reviewing the process of development of the Guangdong economy from the demand side, one might note that private consumption expenditure led the Guangdong economy between 1979 and 1980 just after the reforms. The consumption boom swept not only Guangdong but also throughout China as consumption was liberalized after 30 years of restraint. As shown in Table 3.3, Guangdong achieved 11.8% of annual growth in GDP for these two years, out of which 10.3% was realized through the growth of private consumption. After these years, private consumption maintained a relatively high growth and thus contributed to economic growth. However, in the 1980s, private consumption was replaced by investment and exports as locomotives of the provincial economy. The average annual real wage increased by 6.7% in the early 1980s, and by 4.0% in the late 1980s. These figures were considerably lower than the economic growth rates in these two periods: 12.2% and 12.5%, respectively (Table 3.1). These trends have not changed much in the first half of the 1990s in spite of the upward tendency of real wage increase. As a result, the share of private consumption in GDP began its downturn trend after 1980, and instead, investment and exports were capturing larger shares. The Guangdong economy in the 1980s and the early 1990s reflected a policy of providing much of the fruit of economic growth to capital accumulation rather than to labourers.

In the first half of the 1980s, private consumption slowed down and investment increased sharply. Between 1980 and 1984, Guangdong's fixed asset investment increased by an annual average of 36% compared to each previous year, although this tendency slowed down in 1989 and 1990 due to a policy of economic improvement and rectification. Since 1991 the amount of domestic fixed capital has been on an uphill path

Table 3.3 Composition of and Contribution to GDP, 1978–1994   (Unit: %)

	Private consumption expenditure	Public consumption expenditure	Gross domestic fixed capital formation	Inventory investment	Trade balance	Exports	Imports	GDP
Guangdong								
			Composition of GDP: nominal					
1978	53.6	3.6	14.7	9.1	10.8	12.6	1.9	100.0
1980	61.8	4.2	15.6	4.8	11.2	13.4	2.2	100.0
1984	52.3	4.9	29.5	2.9	7.2	13.1	5.9	100.0
1988	46.8	5.4	32.2	10.7	8.0	25.4	17.3	100.0
1990	40.6	6.2	25.3	8.0	15.7	34.6	18.8	100.0
1994	36.6	8.5	50.5	8.0	25.8	95.5	69.6	100.0
			Contribution to GDP: real					
1978–1980	10.3	0.7	2.1	-1.0	1.5	1.8	0.4	11.8
1981–1984	4.1	0.6	4.8	0.3	0.2	1.3	1.1	10.3
1985–1988	7.0	0.9	5.5	4.6	1.4	5.4	4.0	16.1
1989–1990	1.9	0.8	0.5	0.0	3.5	5.6	2.1	9.1
1991–1994	6.9	2.0	12.9	1.6	6.3	25.8	19.5	20.1

Table 3.3 (continued)

China as a whole

	Private consumption expenditure	Public consumption expenditure	Gross domestic fixed capital formation	Inventory investment	Trade balance	Exports	Imports	GDP
	Composition of GDP: nominal							
1978	48.5	13.2	21.8	8.4	-0.5	4.6	5.2	100.0
1980	51.3	14.6	20.2	6.0	-0.6	6.0	6.6	100.0
1984	51.2	14.2	26.3	4.8	-0.6	8.1	8.7	100.0
1988	51.1	11.6	32.0	5.8	-1.9	11.8	13.8	100.0
1990	49.2	12.2	24.0	9.2	2.2	16.1	13.9	100.0
1994	46.0	13.2	36.4	3.5	1.0	23.2	22.1	100.0
	Contribution to GDP: real							
1978–1980	4.8	1.5	1.0	-0.3	-0.1	0.9	1.0	7.7
1981–1984	5.1	1.4	3.6	0.3	0.0	1.2	1.2	10.0
1985–1988	5.8	1.0	4.0	0.8	-0.4	1.7	2.1	11.3
1989–1990	1.6	0.6	0.9	0.9	0.8	1.3	0.6	3.9
1991–1994	5.3	1.7	5.5	-0.1	0.0	3.4	3.4	12.2

Sources: *Guangdong tongji nianjian* and *Zhongguo tongji nianjian*, various years and Chen Kexuan (ed.), *Guangdong — One Step Ahead in China*.

Notes: 1. Nominal GDP is calculated by using the following figures:
   a. Private consumption expenditure and public consumption expenditure are from private consumption and public consumption in national income.
   b. Gross domestic fixed capital formation is from total investment in fixed assets.
   c. Inventory investment is from current assets in accumulation.
   d. Trade figures are shown in RMB exchanged from US dollars by official rates at the time.
   2. Contribution to GDP is calculated by multiplying real GDP growth and nominal contribution by GDP.

again. Consequently, the rate of investment in GDP, which was about 15% until 1980, rose to almost 30% in 1984, and exceeded 50% in 1994. Also, the rates of contribution to GDP growth by investment were extremely high at 4.8%, 5.5% and 12.9% for the periods 1981–1984, 1985–1988 and 1991–1994, respectively. It is therefore clearly shown that investment played a part in the "engine of growth."

The fact that Guangdong was slow in establishing the infrastructure of economic development and that enterprises maintained many old machines and equipment caused a strong investment boom. Such strong investment demand was mainly served by self-procured funds. Fixed asset investment in Guangdong was mainly served by the national budget before the reforms, but in the 1980s, retained profits of company and domestic loans became important sources of funds. In the late 1980s, with the introduction of foreign funds, sources of investment funds were becoming more diversified.

Another factor which supported the sharp growth of Guangdong was the rapid growth of the export sector. From 1979 to 1994, exports of the province increased by an annual average of 25% in US dollars, or 38% in RMB, achieving a 39% share in China's overall export value. Consequently, the share of exports in GDP rose from 13% in 1978 to 95% in 1994. In particular, exports played an important role in the late 1980s and the early 1990s. Reviewing the rate of annual export increase of the first and second half of the 1980s and 1991–1994, Guangdong's exports increased by 6%, 29% and 35%, respectively, for the three five-year periods (Table 3.2). In 1984, the foreign trade planning system and the foreign currency reserve system were changed, and control of foreign trade management became less strict.[12] This resulted in a sharp increase of exports in the late 1980s. Yet another feature of the Guangdong trade structure is that exports have consistently been higher than imports in value. In addition, the amount of trade surplus has been very large. The trade figures include intermediate processing commissioned by Hong Kong companies, but even leaving this out, the trade balance is basically a surplus. Further, the trade surplus of Guangdong hovered mostly in the range of 7–11% of the GDP throughout the 1980s and increased to 16–35% after 1990. Thus, the contribution of exports to the economic growth has increased steadily after the late 1980s.

The trade structure of Guangdong characterized by a large surplus draws even more attention compared to the national average. The trade of China has also been increasing remarkably, but the country has suffered from continued deficits. After the late 1980s, these deficits expanded, hindering sustained economic growth. Since 1990, the national trade structure has been improved with the nationwide spread of the Guangdong model. However, one can perceive a "ceiling of international balance of payments" in the national trade structure.

These differences between the trade structures of Guangdong *vis-à-vis* the nation mainly arose from the differences in the composition of export products. As to the export items of Guangdong in 1991, 73% of the export products consisted of labour-intensive products such as light industrial products, garments and processed goods, while the rate of agricultural products including processed goods decreased to as little as 25%.[13] In contrast, for China as a whole, agricultural and heavy and mineral products count, even today, for about half of the exports. Guangdong exports industrial products with a high income elasticity of export, while the country as a whole exports mostly primary products with a low income elasticity of export. This has much effect on the two trade structures. We also have to consider the extent of the opening, the relative progress in reforming the foreign trade systems and the influence of the Hong Kong economy. In particular, since Guangdong adjoins Hong Kong, it can easily access the information on export markets, new products, designs and technology.

From the expenditure side, then, the Guangdong economy in the 1980s achieved growth through expansion of investment and exports. This fact clearly demonstrates that the "beneficial cycle of exports and investment" found in the highly developing states of NIEs and ASEAN countries, was realized in Guangdong, too. Also, the export-led industrialization supported by the "beneficial cycle of exports and investment" was established, fully utilizing the advantages of the international and the huge domestic markets. Soon after the reforms and opening, Guangdong procured foreign currency through the export of agricultural products and labour-intensive traditional industrial products, and imported raw material, parts and technology. This promoted a development of newly-established industries mainly involving consumer durable goods. These consumer durable goods were first sold in the domestic market, and the accumulated profits funded economic growth, thus ensuring the balance of funds between foreign currency and RMB in export companies. In the establishment of the export-led industrialization, intermediate processing also played an important role. In the garments and consumer durable industries, processing technology designs and management know-how were transferred from Hong Kong. At the same time, foreign currency required for introducing technology was procured. As the consumer durable industries matured, Guangdong enterprises entered the international market. After the late 1980s, productivity was improved through the importation of machinery and equipment with the money generated from the increasing export of labour-intensive industrial products. With improved productivity, Guangdong has been upgrading its industries. Goods produced by these upgraded industries are again sold in the domestic market, then exported to foreign markets where they are sufficiently competitive, creating the beneficial cycle of domestic sales, exports and investment.[14]

As a result, Guangdong's share in the national consumer durable production rapidly increased. The share of Guangdong-made cameras, which was about 10% in 1978, increased to 80% of China's total production in 1994, while the shares of cassette tape recorders and electric fans rose to 86% and 65%, respectively, dominating more than half of the market. Refrigerators, washing machines, colour TV sets, which Guangdong did not produce or produced only few of them in 1978, captured a share of around 25% in 1994. The production of consumer durable goods accelerated in the late 1980s. When we look at Guangdong's shares of the increased portion of products of the country as a whole from 1986 to 1992, the ratio of colour TV sets and refrigerators was about 30%, while watches and electric fans were about 80%, and washing machines, radios, cassette tape recorders and cameras exceeded 100%. The products which recorded figures over 100% indicate that provinces other than Guangdong were forced to produce even less than their previous volume due to the expansion of Guangdong-made products. It is clear that Guangdong enterprises increased production not only in the export market but also in the domestic market.

Structural Change in Supply: Progress of the Non-State-Owned Sector

The economic development of Guangdong also changed the supply structure. The change is characterized by, first, the industrial sector playing the leading role, and second, the shift in the principal contributors of the economy from state-owned enterprises to rural and private enterprises as well as foreign-affiliated enterprises.

If one classifies industries into three categories, namely, agriculture, industry, and service, and compares their ratio of contribution to GDP, which shows the degree of contribution of these industries towards economic growth (Table 3.4), one finds that the industrial sector is the highest, at 70%, from 1978 to 1994, followed by the service sector at 24% and agriculture at 6%. Consequently, the production ratio of agriculture, industry, and the service sector changed from 30:46:24 in 1978 to 9:67:24 in 1994.[15] It is no exaggeration to say that the economic development of Guangdong after the reforms was realized by industrialization. However, the Guangdong economy after the reforms was not consistently pulled by the industrial sector. Agriculture contributed at a relatively high rate until the early 1980s, and after the middle of 1980s, the industrial sector developed remarkably. This trend may be seen in the country as a whole, and reflects well the way in which the reforms of China's economic system were pushed forward.

Led by industry, then, Guangdong's industrial structure has changed dramatically. Traditionally, Guangdong's industrial structure had been based on the light industries compared with the national average, but since the middle of the 1960s the province consistently pursued a policy of heavy industrialization. In 1978, however, Guangdong's industrial structure shifted again from its emphasis on heavy industries towards light industries. The ratio of heavy to light industries in Guangdong in 1978 was 42:58, but changed to 32:68 in 1991, with a 10 points growth in light industries. Consumer durable goods such as colour TV sets and refrigerators, which developed remarkably among the Guangdong industries, are statistically included in heavy industries as manufacturing and processing industries in China. The share of these manufacturing and processing industries on the whole increased from 50% in 1978 to 60% in 1991. Altogether, light and manufacturing and processing industries accounted for 89% of the total industrial output of Guangdong.[16]

Another characteristic of the supply side is the fact that rural, private, and foreign-affiliated companies had replaced the position of the state-owned enterprises as agencies contributing to the growth of the Guangdong economy. Particularly, rural enterprises progressed remarkably. The rural enterprises means a complex of township and village enterprises in the rural area which operate manufacturing and service business, absorbing surplus labour in the country. The government of Guangdong established the household responsibility system and employed a policy of *litu bu lixiang* (not engaged in agriculture, but not leaving the village), which utilizes agricultural groups and individual economy to develop industrial and service sectors in order to solve the employment problem of surplus labour in agricultural areas. As a result, the 81,000 rural enterprises in

Table 3.4 Trends in Industrial and Employment Structures by Sectors

(Unit: %)

	Guangdong province				China			
	Agriculture	Industry	Service	Total	Agriculture	Industry	Service	Total
Industrial structure								
Share: 1978 fixed prices								
1978	29.9	46.4	23.7	100.0	28.1	48.2	23.7	100.0
1984	26.6	49.0	24.4	100.0	25.3	47.3	27.4	100.0
1990	17.3	53.5	29.3	100.0	18.7	51.2	30.1	100.0
1994	9.0	67.0	24.1	100.0	13.2	60.4	26.4	100.0
Contribution: Real								
1978–1994	6.4	69.5	24.1	100.0	9.2	63.7	27.1	100.0
1978–1984	22.7	52.1	25.2	100.0	21.2	46.1	32.7	100.0
1984–1990	9.4	57.2	33.4	100.0	9.2	56.9	33.9	100.0
1991–1994	2.4	77.6	20.0	100.0	4.8	74.4	20.8	100.0
Employment structure								
Share:								
1978	73.7	14.2	12.1	100.0	70.5	17.4	12.1	100.0
1984	63.7	18.9	17.4	100.0	64.0	20.0	16.0	100.0
1990	53.0	27.2	19.8	100.0	60.0	21.4	18.6	100.0
1994	42.3	33.6	24.1	100.0	54.3	22.7	23.0	100.0
Average annual increase								
1978–1994	-0.8	8.4	7.3	2.7	1.0	4.4	6.9	2.7
1978–1984	0.0	7.5	9.0	2.5	1.4	5.5	8.0	3.1
1984–1990	-0.3	9.3	5.1	2.8	1.7	4.0	5.3	2.8
1991–1994	-2.7	8.4	8.0	2.9	-0.5	3.5	7.6	2.0

Sources: *Guangdong tongji nianjian 1995* and *Zhongguo tongji nianjian 1995.*

Guangdong with 1.95 million workers and RMB3.05 billion of production in 1978, increased to 1.46 million enterprises with 10.17 million workers and RMB355.8 billion of production in 1994. These figures demonstrate that during the past 16 years, rural enterprises in Guangdong increased by 20% in number, 11% in workers, and 35% in production on an annual basis. In particular, the number of rural enterprises involved with industry sharply increased. As a result, the rate of rural enterprises in industrial production rapidly increased. The share of rural enterprises which accounted for 18% of workers and 7% of production in 1978, increased to 60% of workers and 30% of production in 1994.

The first reason why rural enterprises developed so rapidly is that unlike the state-owned enterprises, there was no intervention from the administration. Management of rural enterprises was relatively flexible and decisions were made based on market conditions. Therefore, unlike state-owned enterprises which did not consider the needs of consumers, rural enterprises which excelled in service and sold marketable products, expanded their market share. The second reason is that their close proximity to Hong Kong allowed rural enterprises in Guangdong to have many business opportunities and easy access to overseas markets. To be more specific, after 1978, the establishment of Hong Kong enterprises in Guangdong provided business opportunities such as commissioned intermediate processing and related businesses, and at the same time, the inflow of funds and technology from abroad along with foreign market information facilitated the formation, continuation and development of enterprises in Guangdong. These reasons are attested to by the fact that in Guangdong, rural enterprises developed, particularly in the Pearl River Delta which is close to Hong Kong and Macau.

Along with rural enterprises, individual and private enterprises and foreign-affiliated companies continued to grow rapidly. Industrial output of individual and village-run enterprises increased from RMB1.2 billion in 1978 to RMB162.4 billion in 1994, thus, exhibiting an average increase of 33% on an annual basis, expanding the share in industrial output from 6% to 26%. Industrial output by foreign-affiliated enterprises, which were non-existent since they were prohibited before the reforms, began to increase in the late 1980s, when direct investment from foreign companies to the manufacturing sector increased. Foreign-affiliated industrial output sharply increased especially after 1988, when direct overseas investments rapidly grew due to the change in the international economic environment caused by global structural adjustment after the Plaza Agreement as well as the accelerated pace of reforms in China in 1992. The share of the foreign-affiliated companies in the industrial output increased from a mere 5% in 1985 to 12% in 1988. From 1989 to 1990, the fact that local enterprises in Guangdong made little progress during the economic rectification period favourably allowed the share of foreign-affiliated companies to increase sharply; the share reached 22% in 1990. Then, in the early 1990s, the share soared to 37% in 1994.

As export is the main purpose of foreign-affiliated companies established in Guangdong, these companies contribute notably to Guangdong's export performance. The rate of *sanzi qiye* (enterprises with foreign investment) in the exports of Guangdong increased sharply after the late 1980s as in the case of industrial output. These enterprises expanded to capture 40% of all exports in Guangdong in 1994, and this share rises to 68% if *sanlai yibu* (commissioned intermediate processing plus compensation trade) is included. These figures prove that, like the rural enterprises, foreign-affiliated companies have recently played an important role in Guangdong's economy. As of the end of the 1980s, the number of enterprises with foreign investment registered at the Guangdong Province Industry and Commerce Management Department reached 55,632 companies, accounting for 25% of the national total. The contracted amount of direct investment after the reforms totalled US$98.4 billion, out of which US$28.8 billion was actually utilized. These figures represent 32% and 30%, respectively, of the national totals. In addition, there are about 98,000 projects engaged in intermediate processing. The actual investment amounted to US$1.955 billion, accounting for 46% of the total national investment.[17]

As is clear from the above, the recent production structure in Guangdong has changed in fundamental ways. While export-led industrialization was established, state-owned enterprises, which are based on the conventional command economy, were replaced by non-state-owned enterprises such as rural, private and foreign-affiliated enterprises, which decide their production activities according to the market principles. Such an industrial structure is reflected in the employment structure of Guangdong as well. Since the reforms, industry has displayed the strongest capacity in absorbing labour, followed by services. Not only was the agricultural sector unable to absorb the natural increase in the labour force but the absolute number of workers engaged in agriculture dropped. In fact, agriculture fell 32 percentage points in the share of labour from 74% in 1978 to 42% in 1994 as can be seen in Table 3.4. By contrast, the industrial and services sectors rose by 19 percentage points and 12 percentage points, respectively. Compared with the national trend, the change in the employment structure of Guangdong is different in terms of both the extent and the direction of change. Firstly, the changes in the employment structure of Guangdong were more intense. Secondly, there was a difference in the sector the surplus agricultural labour force moved to. In Guangdong, the industrial sector absorbed more labour than the services sector, while at the national level, the services sector absorbed more. In addition, there was a difference in the relationship between the speed of economic growth and the changes in the employment structure. In Guangdong, there were major changes in the employment structure in the later years of the reforms, when economic growth accelerated. The reverse was true in the case of China as a whole.

Reviewing the changes in the industrial and employment structures, it is evident that in Guangdong the industrial sector exhibited a strong labour absorption capacity because of its labour intensive industrialization. At the national level, however, despite the fact that industry was leading economic growth, the industrial sector showed a weak capacity to absorb labour because the industrial structure of the national economy continued to be dominated by capital intensive industries. Therefore, the structural changes in Guangdong went along with more efficient allocation of factor resources than the nation as a whole.

Long-term Plans and Prospects

Since the reform and open policy was initiated, Guangdong's economy has been growing rapidly. In particular, the pace of economic growth in Guangdong quickened in the early 1990s, so that the average annual growth rate of GDP reached 19% in the Eighth Five-year Plan (1991–1995).[18] Now in Guangdong, economic growth is centred on industry which has planted its roots deeply and the sophistication of the industrial structure has also progressed. The Pearl River Delta has achieved startling economic growth and is taking the lead in all fields of economic activity in Guangdong. Therefore, Guangdong in having quadrupled its per capita GDP in 1993 compared with 1980, had realized the national target of quadrupling China's GDP between 1980 and 2000, almost eight years ahead of time.[19]

Guangdong entered a new stage since the lunar new year of 1992, when Deng Xiaoping, the paramount leader, visited there. He praised the remarkable economic development of Guangdong after China's reforms and open policy, and then put forward in his "Speech in the Southern Tour"[20] that Guangdong must catch up with the economic level of the Four Little Dragons in Asia. Taking instructions from Deng, Guangdong made the Plan for Catching up with the Asian NIEs in Twenty Years in May 1992.[21] This plan was revised broadly, basing on inputs from both domestic and overseas specialists, and was superseded by a new Twenty-year Economic and Social Development Programme (1990–2010).[22] This Twenty-year Development Programme was tabled and adopted in the People's Congress of Guangdong in July 1994.

The Twenty-year Development Programme is a development strategy for Guangdong to catch up with the level of the Asian NIEs in terms of per capita GDP. It targets specifically on Korea, which has a relatively large area and economy among the Asian NIEs, and has set as a macroeconomic target the level of GDP and per capita GDP in the coming twenty years of RMB1.67 trillion and RMB20.8 thousand in the 1990 fixed prices, respectively. In order to achieve the target in the Twenty-year Development Programme, Guangdong's economy must continue to grow by an average annual rate of 12.9% for twenty years until 2010.

The Twenty-year Development Programme was also divided into two periods with different targets. The target of the first period (1990–2000) is to upgrade the level of Guangdong's economy to those of Asian NIEs by the year 1990, while Guangdong has to catch up with the economic level of the Asian NIEs in the second period (2000–2010). In order to achieve these targets, Guangdong's economy has to grow at an average annual rate of 13.4% in the first period and 12.4% in the second period. The Twenty-year Development Programme also set its policy target in the first period to be making an effort to the improvement of the infrastructure and the development of human resources to provide for a more sophisticated industrial structure after 2000, its target in the second period to be introducing high-technology and building up a technology-intensive industrial structure, taking energy-saving and environmental protection into consideration.

In February 1996, the Guangdong government also adopted the Ninth Five-year Plan (1996–2000),[23] based on a comprehensive study of the experience of the Eighth Five-year Plan, in order to achieve the target of the first period of the Twenty-year Development Programme. Guangdong aims at a real economic annual growth rate of around 11% and an export annual growth rate of 12% in the Ninth Five-year Plan period. Guangdong would rather seek a stable growth path, however. The growth rate of its fixed asset investment is set at around 33% annually in the Ninth Five-year Plan period and the amount of utilized foreign capital is estimated at a total of US$48.5 billion for the coming five years. As for policy targets, Guangdong upholds ten targets, such as the change from an extensive economy to an intensive economy, strengthening of the basic standing of agriculture, acceleration of state-owned enterprises reform and so on. However, the aims of the Guangdong government seems to be that of strengthening the competitiveness of Guangdong enterprises, both in the domestic market and overseas, and in promoting structural adjustments by developing the service industry.

Guangdong's long-term plans have been mentioned above. Can the Guangdong government realize the macroeconomic target, namely the continuous growth of Guangdong's economy at an average annual rate of more than 12% in the coming 15 years in the Twenty-year Development Programme? If so, Guangdong's economy will have been growing at an average annual rate of more than 12% for thirty years from 1980 to 2010. Many difficulties would be encountered in putting the programme into reality, however. Three main problems may be raised as follows.

The biggest problem is Guangdong's dependence on the future international and domestic economic environments. Guangdong's economy has expanded rapidly, having attracted a large amount of foreign capital and expanded export markets without much difficulty as a developing economy. However, in the early 1990s, neighbouring countries and regions, including China itself, had also adopted an outward-oriented development strategy relying on foreign direct investments (FDI). The period in which Guangdong can get the lion's share of FDI and expand its export market continuously, will therefore be limited by the emergence of new competitors. In fact, by 1996, exports and domestic sales of Guangdong reached a plateau and Guangdong economy slipped into a recession.[24] Behind this was the catching up of neighbouring countries and other parts of China which have worsened the competitiveness of Guangdong. In order to continue the growth at an average annual rate of more than 12% in the coming five years, let alone the coming fifteen years, Guangdong cannot avoid seeking greater sophistication of its industrial structure.

The second problem is one of finance. Guangdong province expects that the introduction of foreign capital will amount to US$190 billion in the Twenty-year Development Programme period, of which US$40.6 billion was already utilized in the Eighth Five-year Plan and US$48.5 billion will be used in the Ninth Five-year Plan.[25] Judging from these amounts, Guangdong will have to procure foreign capital of US$100 billion in the second half of the Twenty-year Development Programme. How can Guangdong province attract the amount of foreign capital of more than those utilized in the early 1990s — the boom period of business in China — in the next fifteen years? The competition for the introduction of foreign capital is getting stronger with neighbouring countries and China's other coastal areas adopting the same policy as Guangdong.

Difficulties can be predicted for the plan of investment in fixed assets as well. Guangdong province estimates the growth rate of investment in fixed assets at 29% annually in the Twenty-year Development Programme, almost the same level of investment in fixed assets for the last eighteen years since the reforms and opening. The Guangdong government has to rely solely on funds from the provincial treasury, provincial savings tapped through the floatation of bonds and foreign capital, rather than on Beijing. Moreover, the Guangdong government is obliged to supply Beijing with increasing amounts of funds. In this regard, the latter half of the Twenty-year Programme and the Ninth Five-year Plan may be somewhat shaky.

The third problem is the imbalance of the macroeconomy. In Guangdong, reflecting the progress in price reform, the price mechanism functions well in the goods market. However, it does not operate completely in the production factors market such as labour, capital and land, because the conventional system still operates in these sectors. Under these circumstances, if Guangdong speeds up its economic development, production cannot catch up with demand, both in terms of quantity and quality, thus leading possibly to inflation again. Therefore, it is essential that Guangdong not only aims at economic growth but also proceeds further in social and institutional reforms to achieve balanced economic development.

Notes

1. For a more detailed discussion of economic development in Guangdong, see T. Maruya, "Guangdong as a Model of National Economic Development for China," in *A Decade of "Open-Door" Economic Development in China 1979–1989*, edited by Edward K. Y. Chen and T. Maruya (Hong Kong: Centre of Asian Studies, University of Hong Kong, 1992), pp. 153–83; and *Guangdong: "Open Door" Economic Development Strategy*, edited by

T. Maruya (Hong Kong: Centre of Asian Studies, University of Hong Kong, 1992).

2. *Dangdai Zhongguo* congshu bianjibu (ed.), *Dangdai Zhongguo de Guangdong* (China Today: Guangdong) (Beijing: Dangdai Zhongguo chubanshe, 1991), pp. 58–59.

3. Ibid., pp. 93–95.

4. *Guangdongsheng guomin jingji he shehui fazhan tongji ziliao 1949–1988 nian — Guding zichan touzi bufen* (Statistics of National Economy and Social Development in Guangdong Province 1949–1988 — Investment in Fixed Assets) (Guangzhou: Guangdongsheng tongjiju, 1989), pp. 93–95.

5. See note 2, pp. 124–31.

6. Statistics on the national income have been released since 1952. The average annual growth rate in the 1950s was obtained from figures between 1952 to 1960.

7. Liang Rong (ed.), *Lun Guangdong 150 nian* (Discussing 150 Years of Guangdong) (Guangzhou: Guangdong renmin chubanshe, 1990), pp. 233–35.

8. See note 2, pp. 145–48.

9. Personal communication from the System Reform Office, Government of Guangdong Province in May 1991. For recent and comprehensive work on the economic reform in Guangdong, see Wu Yixin (ed.), *Guangdong shinian jingji tizhi gaige yanjiu* (A Decade of Economic System Reform in Guangdong) (Guangzhou: Zhongshan daxue chubanshe, 1990) and Lin Ruo (ed.), *Gaige kaifang zai Guangdong* (The Reforms and Opening in Guangdong) (Guangzhou: Guangdong gaodeng jiaoyu chubanshe, 1992).

10. For a more detailed discussion of the export-led industrialization in Guangdong, see *Guangdong: "Open Door" Economic Development Strategy* (note 1).

11. Institute of Developing Economies, *Asian Economy in 2001* (Tokyo: Tokyo Keizai Shinposha, 1989), pp. 6–10.

12. Zhu Jia Jian, "Guangdong's Economic Relationships with Central Government and with Other Provinces/Municipalities," in *Guangdong: "Open Door" Economic Development Strategy* (see note 1), pp. 104–107.

13. Calculated from *Guangdong tongji nianjian 1992* (Statistical Yearbook of Guangdong, 1992) (Beijing: Zhongguo tongji chubanshe, 1992).

14. Wang Xue Ming, "Guangdong: Economic Growth and Structural Changes in 1980's," in *Guangdong: "Open Door" Economic Development Strategy* (see note 1), p. 26.

15. Figures are calculated at 1978 constant price.

16. See note 14.

17. "The Development and Effect of Utilizing Foreign Capital in Guangdong

Province," in *The Role of Japanese Direct Investment in China*, edited by T. Maruya (Tokyo: Institute of Developing Economies, 1993).

18. "Guangdongsheng guomin jingji he shehui fanzhan dijiuge wunian jihua gangyao" (Ninth Five-year Plan of Economic and Social Development in Guangdong), *Nanfang ribao*, 16 March 1996.

19. Ibid.

20. "Nanxun jianghua" (Speech in the Southern Tour) by Deng Xiaoping is summarized in *Zhonggong zhongyang er hao wenjian*, 28 February 1992.

21. "Guangdong lizheng ershinian ganshang Yazhou sixiaolong de gouxiang" (Design for Catching up with the Asian NIEs in Twenty Years), in *2010 nian de Guangdong*, edited by Wang Dingchang (Guangzhou: Guangdong renmin chubanshe, 1994), pp. 443–50.

22. "Guangdong ershinian jingji shehui fazhan jihua gangyao" (The Twenty-year Economic and Social Development Programme), ibid., pp. 474–93.

23. See note 19.

24. Personal communication from the Economic Development Research Centre of Guangdong Government in August 1996.

25. See note 19.

4

Agriculture and Forestry

Chau Kwai-cheong

Introduction

Guangdong has an area of 178,100 km^2, representing 1.9% of the nation's total area. Land may be roughly divided into mountainous terrain, undulating hills and flatland, representing, respectively, 62%, 13% and 25%. The dominant red soil group, consisting of latosol, lateritic krasnozem, red soil and yellow earth, blankets 70% of the total land area. These soils are strongly acidic, deficient in potassium, nitrogen, phosphorus, organic matter and boron. Paddy soil occupies 13% of the province, mainly in valley bottoms, river plains and the delta areas. The rest of the province (17%) is made up of limestone, hydromorphic and saline soils.

Climatically, Guangdong lies in the sub-tropical to tropical zone with an annual temperature of 19°–23.5°C and a total rainfall of 1,400–2,200 mm per year. The province is frost-free, cumulative heat reaching the ground being 4,180–5,430 MJ/m^2/year. With a surface flow of 1,800 billion m^3 water, equivalent to 70,425 m^3/ha, the province has abundant water for agriculture and forestry.

In 1994, 71% of Guangdong's population of 66.91 million was engaged in agriculture and average cultivated land was only 0.52 *mu* per capita.

Up to 70% of the cultivated area is devoted to the growing of staple crops including predominantly rice, sweet potatoes and wheat. Rice production accounted for 86% of the total grains produced in 1994, and Guangdong is the fourth largest grower in China.[1] Intensive cropping is practised throughout the province taking advantage of the favourable climatic conditions.

In terms of development rate since 1952, agriculture in Guangdong (including forestry) lagged behind industry, construction, transport and commerce.[2]

Progress Since 1978

Profound changes of agricultural policy have occurred since 1978. The problem of egalitarianism in distribution was redressed, resulting in evolution of the responsibility systems, as well as contracts and family farming.[3] This was supplemented with a restructuring of the rural economy through an extension of market and price regulation.[4] Retention of private land was allowed. State farm procurement prices were raised by an average of 25%, thus giving more incentives to farmers. All these changes are hailed as the beginning of a new era in China's recent economic history.

With no exception, Guangdong benefited from these policy changes. Agricultural production was seriously affected during the turbulent years of the Great Leap Forward and the Cultural Revolution. The then political slogan, "grains as the key link in agriculture," was translated into nation-wide policy in which forests were converted into grain fields, and lakes, rivers and the coast were likewise reclaimed for grain production. This bold attempt resulted in soil deterioration and land degradation.[5] The agricultural reform brought a halt to this "leftist" policy with remarkable success. In 1984, for instance, although the grain producing area was reduced by 17.5% against that of 1978, the yield increased by 20.7%, representing a steady increase of 3.2% per annum throughout the period.[6] The increased productivity can be ascribed to crop intensification and increased fertilizer input.[7] The latter is of paramount importance because up to the late 1970s Guangdong's fertilizer use, albeit small in quantity, was confined to the ammoniacal type. To supplement crop intensification, more potassium and phosphorus fertilizers were used following soil tests, thus improving the nutrient balance of the soil.

An integrated pest management programme was introduced to contain the outbreaks of crop diseases and insects. Biological control is becoming popular, thus reducing the reliance on chemicals. The use of high yielding hybrid varieties, especially rice, was continued and expanded throughout the 1980s.[8] In 1987, for instance, hybrid rice varieties constituted 27.6% of the total paddy field. The yield was 10–15% higher than that of the ordinary varieties. Some hybrids possess the property of cold hardiness making them suitable for growth as a second crop in northern Guangdong.

Crop intensification was complemented with increased crop diversity and rotations. The double cropping of paddies was changed in area to rotation with peanuts in an attempt to avoid soil gleying and to improve the soil physical properties. Species were reorganized to optimize the use of light, space and soil. Typical examples are the expansion of the "mulberry bund — fish pond" agroecosystem[9] and the so-called three-dimensional planting involving different combinations of forest species, rubber, tea and peanuts. These practices are examples of sustainable agriculture with the objective of improving productivity through a more efficient transfer of nutrients and energy within the respective agroecosystems.

With a shift of agricultural policy, farmers are freed from the self-reliance principle, resulting in the emergence of specialized households and commercial agriculture. Some of the least productive farmlands are converted into forest and pasture.[10] Large expanses of paddy fields are changed to the growth of sugar cane, high-quality fruits, vegetables and flowers. Poultry rearing and fish farming are becoming important in the Zhujiang Delta region including Shenzhen,[11] Dongguan,[12] Zhuhai,[13] Guangzhou,[14] and Foshan.[15] Parallel to the expansion of commodity agriculture, nodal points of food processing are also established. The remarkable achievement in rural specialization is owing partly to investments at the provincial, city, township and departmental levels as well as by individual farmers.[16] Foreign investment from Hong Kong and Macau accounts for 10% of the total agricultural investment in Dongguan since 1978. Equally important, of course, is a high demand for fresh vegetables, fruits and poultry by Hong Kong and Macau.[17]

As a result of diversification in the rural economies, the reliance on agriculture also declines. For the first time in the history of Guangdong, the gross productivity of forestry, pastoral rearing, fishery and other related economic activities climbed from 49.5% of the total agricultural production in 1985 to 52.3% in 1994.[18] The importance of fishery, in particular, recorded a sharp increase from 8.3% to 17.6% during the same period. Similarly, non-agricultural production jumped from 43.8% to 72.8%, whereas township enterprises constituted as much as 69.0% of the total rural production in 1994.

Problems

Despite the implementation of agricultural reforms since 1978, Guangdong is still confronted with numerous problems in agricultural development, viz. low productivity, shrinkage of cultivated land, backward technology and low capital input. Many of these problems are deep-rooted and are inherent to the physical environment, while others have stemmed from economic reforms during the last decade. Equally notable and of concern to the authorities are remnant ecological backlashes arising from mismanagement of the environment during the Great Leap Forward and the Cultural Revolution. The net results are that productivity per unit area as well as per capita cultivated land are lower than that of the national average. Agricultural production lags behind gross domestic product (GDP) increase and rise in living standard. This necessitates the import or subsidy of staple foods from the central government.

Low Productivity

Low productivity is a common problem in South China including

Guangdong, the agricultural landscape of which suffers from low soil fertility, pollution, ecological backlashes, natural hazards and meagre capital input. The problem eased slightly in the mid- to late seventies when fertilizer input increased drastically parallel to the introduction of high yielding rice varieties. Boom harvests of grains were recorded for 1984 and 1989 despite a continuing shrinkage of cultivated land. Other than these two years, however, production slackened in the 1980s due to the aforesaid reasons.

The red soils of Guangdong are subjected to intensive leaching and podzolization effect. Over 80% of the soil is strongly acidic with pH values below 5.5. Under this condition, aluminium, iron and manganese toxicity are reported alongside deficiencies in soil organic matter, phosphate, nitrogen, potassium and boron.[19] A low organic matter and nitrogen content results in destabilization of soil aggregates rendering the soil vulnerable to erosion. Phosphorus deficiency reduces root vigour and the lack of potassium is detrimental to fruit growth. Worse still, the problem has intensified due to crop intensification and insufficient fertilizer input.[20]

Agriculture in Guangdong also suffers from acid rain and aerosols laden with mercury, lead and cadmium[21] as a result of rapid economic growth. Township enterprises are characterized by simple and backward set-ups and discharge of untreated pollutants like wastewater, sulphur dioxide and fluoride further aggravates the soil environment. Soil crusting, structural breakdown and suppressed microbial activities are thus conducive to declining productivity. In addition, the location of these enterprises are haphazard, rendering control difficult.[22]

Anyway, 29% of the cultivated area in Guangdong records an annual productivity in the region of <1,500–2,250 kg/ha, which is extremely low by world standards. It is an arduous task to raise the productivity of these unproductive farmlands.

Ecological Backlashes

Agricultural development in Guangdong since 1949 did not deviate much from that of China with regard to resource perception and policy implementation. As discussed earlier, agriculture has been perceived as a process of grain production only and as such agricultural resource is also equated, albeit wrongly, to arable land management. Disastrous impacts on the countryside occurred when large expanses of forests, lakes, river banks and coastal flat lands were converted to grain fields. Not only is the converted land marred with low productivity, but also the problem of soil erosion has significant repercussions on the environment. Erosion removes organic matter from the soil surface, and also, by a preferential transport process, removes the clay fraction from the mineral soil component. Fertility was depleted due to insufficient protective measures, and leaching and removal of the top soil, especially on steep slopes. Dry paddy and dry bed farming account for 40% of the total cultivated land in Guangdong, a majority of which is found on steep slopes where the soil is thin and deficient in nutrient reserves. Coupled with few inputs, inadequate irrigation provisions, monoculture and continuous cropping, erosion has intensified and reduces overall productivity. Indeed, the areas under erosion have increased by 38–76% since the 1950s notwithstanding a massive reforestation programme.[23] In 1985, eroded lands at the upper reaches of the Hanjiang, Beijiang and Dongjiang amounted to 12,000 km², representing 6.7% of the total provincial area. Annually, 870 km² of cultivated land is affected by sediments eroded from the upland regions.[24]

Natural Hazards

Guangdong is prone to attack by floods and typhoons which inflict heavy losses to agriculture. Floods occur not only in the low-lying deltaic area but also in valleys every two to three years. Waterlogging and soil gleying affect spring sowing of paddy rice in northern Guangdong as much as drought in the early spring season.[25] Foggy weather and intermittent cold spells in February likewise cause spring dieback of the rice seedlings. Disease and insect outbreaks are recurrent problems, too.

Capital Input and Drainage Provisions

Guangdong's agriculture is traditionally labour-intensive due to a shortage of capital input for mechanization, agro-chemicals and irrigation. Since 1949 a total of RMB4.6 billion had been spent on pasture improvement, which is equivalent to only RMB0.5/ha/year.[26] The meagre capital input shrank further during the Seventh Five-year Plan and the hardest hit sector coincided with drainage improvement schemes. As of 1990 some 7,330 km² of cultivated land (29% total) was not irrigated.[27]

Shrinkage of Cultivated Land

Perhaps the most acute agricultural problem facing Guangdong is the rapid shrinkage of cultivated land since 1980. During the period 1949–1980, the area of cultivated land declined gradually, yet the acreage remained at around 41 million *mu* (Table 4.1). During the period 1980–1994, however, there was a rapid decrease of 6.4 million *mu* as a result of urbanization, industrialization, farm households construction and highways development.[28] Cultivated land continues to diminish at a rate of approximately 1% a year. The present per capita cultivated land is 0.52 *mu*, which is less than half that of the national average and the second lowest among all

Table 4.1   Cultivated Land in Guangdong

Year	Cultivated land (10^4 *mu*)	Per capita acreage (*mu*)	Year	Cultivated land (10^4 *mu*)	Per capita acreage (*mu*)
1949	4,515.2	1.62	1972	4,172.6	0.91
1950	4,538.2	1.59	1973	4,172.9	0.91
1951	4,929.5	1.72	1974	4,176.9	0.87
1952	4,447.2	1.53	1975	4,187.3	0.86
1953	4,553.3	1.53	1976	4,185.5	0.87
1954	4,589.6	1.49	1977	4,182.8	0.84
1955	4,619.6	1.50	1978	4,168.3	0.82
1956	4,624.1	1.44	1979	4,150.7	0.81
1957	4,585.6	1.39	1980	4,123.0	0.79
1958	4,337.0	1.29	1981	4,099.0	0.77
1959	4,170.6	1.20	1982	4,073.4	0.75
1960	4,136.5	1.19	1983	4,056.9	0.74
1961	4,166.8	1.19	1984	3,999.2	0.72
1962	4,177.6	1.17	1985	3,897.9	0.69
1963	4,149.6	1.13	1986	3,839.7	0.67
1964	4,188.6	1.10	1987	3,797.4	0.65
1965	4,122.1	1.07	1988	3,777.7	0.64
1966	4,131.9	1.04	1989	3,787.0	0.63
1967	4,118.6	1.01	1990	3,793.3	0.61
1968	4,086.7	0.98	1991	3,768.2	0.59
1969	4,118.4	0.95	1992	3,650.5	0.56
1970	4,163.7	0.95	1993	3,525.6	0.54
1971	4,182.0	0.93	1994	3,487.1	0.52

Sources: X. H. Chen and X. J. Zhong, "2000 nian Guangdong gengdi ziyuan de bianhua qushi ji qi duice" (see note 22 below).
Guangdong nianjian 1995 (see note 18 below), pp. 639–40.
Note: 1 *mu* = 667 m².

provinces in China. This landuse conflict is surely a blow to Guangdong which is at the crossroads of modernization. Productivity will be reduced because most of the lost lands are fertile and productive. To compensate for the loss, marginal lands can be developed or greater capital inputs be made available to boost the productivity of existing lands. There is, however, a limit to land productivity unless there is a breakthrough in genetic engineering typical of yet another Green Revolution.[29]

Problems Arising from the Responsibility System

The agricultural reform in Guangdong province has been criticized for scratching the surface so that problems still exist in the areas of procurement price, finance, service and technology back-up. Conversely, the reform of "contracting output to the household" creates new problems. Very often contracts are difficult to honour; farmers switch over to non-agricultural activities without having to surrender the land. Loopholes in the reform programme and legislation are fully exploited. The contracted land is either not fully utilized for crop production, misused for illegal building of households or abandoned entirely.[30] As much as 30% of the rural labour force is freed from the reform, thus adding pressure to the unemployment situation. Moreover, "family farming" undermines the collective, resulting in negligence of irrigation and drainage work, agricultural machinery maintenance and repair, and disease control.

Sustainable Agriculture

Agriculture is a process by which man tries to maximize net community productivity at the cost of stability.[31] Net community productivity refers to crop yield which, in modern agriculture, can be boosted with auxiliary energy subsidies, including fertilizers, irrigation, pesticides, mechanization, and so on. This is, of course, complemented with technology to increase gross production, including genetic engineering and the selection of high yielding varieties. Very often, excessive energy subsidies result in a wide range of environmental problems, including soil acidification, erosion, eutrophication, food chain contamination and a wastage of energy. These problems are common in the developed industrialized countries where the practice of high energy subsidy agriculture is criticized as being non-sustainable.

The nature and scope of the agricultural problems in Guangdong province is, however, different from those of the industrialized countries.

Soil acidification and lake eutrophication are not necessarily caused by excessive fertilizer usage which is in fact a limiting factor to crop productivity. Apart from continuous cropping without adequate rotations, soil erosion in Guangdong is also enhanced by deforestation as well as the combustion loss of animal dung and crop residues, a problem which does not apply to industrialized agriculture either. Since capital inputs are small and mechanization is in its infancy, large-scale energy wastage (except manual labour) does not happen with Guangdong's agriculture. As the province is at the crossroads of modernization, such environmental problems associated with highly developed agriculture might one day occur in Guangdong when energy inputs become excessive. In short, the sustainable development of agriculture in Guangdong province is suffering from too few inputs in contrast to excessive energy subsidies received by its Western counterparts.

Goals

With a rising population and an increasing demand for food and raw materials, the imminent task of sustainable agriculture in Guangdong is to boost land productivity through technological, institutional and financial support. Despite favourable climatic conditions, the productivity is greatly impaired by low and diminishing per capita acreage of cultivated land, inherent soil problems, low capital inputs and loopholes in the agricultural policy.

As sustainable agriculture encompasses an ethical value of meeting the needs of future generations, it is essential that any measure adopted today will not cause irrevocable deterioration of the environment, as is happening with industrialized agriculture. Because the land source is finite, it is also non-renewable. The objective of sustainable agriculture in Guangdong, therefore, lies in improving and preserving the land in productivity while maintaining biological diversity, environmental quality and ecological stability.

Practices

Agricultural productivity in Guangdong can be sustained and improved by arresting the shrinkage and misuse of cultivated land, and improving current productivity as well as the development of marginal lands. The success of these measures hinges on legislation and the implementation of integrated crop management.

As cultivated land is diminishing at an alarming speed, being lost to urban encroachment and infrastructure development as a result of economic reforms, abuses are not uncommon. Very often lands are reclaimed more than is necessary, and prematurely, before any final decision is made about their development. This happens at nearly all levels (city, township, department and individual) as a result of the race towards competitive developments. The loss of cultivated land is also accompanied by waterlogging and pollution problems due to poor planning. Legislation on landuse development is either weak or simply ignored under the existing political atmosphere. More stringent landuse control must be enforced, especially when productive lands are under threat. Surveillance teams should be set up and in the event of discovering a misuse of land, heavy penalty and tax should be imposed.[32]

Under the "family farming" system, peasants are given permission to buy and sell the rights to use land resulting, too, in the misuse of collective land. Arable lands are either not properly cultivated, or abandoned or even used for illegal building of farm households. While remedial measures are necessary for plugging loopholes in the responsibility system, heavy penalty should also be imposed.

The surprisingly low productivity per unit area owes as much to inherent characteristics of the soil as to poor crop management. The red soils are noted for their strong acidity, low organic matter and nutrient contents as well as poor physical properties. These problems are not evident in undisturbed forest or grassland ecosystems in which stability is maintained by intricate flows of energy and transfer of nutrients. For agroecosystems, however, they are severely stressed due to continuous cropping and the removal of nutrients from the soil. This "minable" activity and the problems thus caused are particularly serious in monoculture, as in double cropping of rice and non-rotational use of the land.

As Guangdong is endowed with plentiful water and heat, agricultural productivity can be improved by measures designed to conserve the soil and to restore soil fertility. Both engineering and biological measures are needed for soil conservation. It is certainly undesirable to cultivate crops alone on slopes >25° in a humid environment even with the most sophisticated ploughing and terracing techniques. Mechanical methods such as the construction of check dams and earth berms are necessary to stop sheet erosion, rilling and gullying on eroded granitic areas in Wuhua and Deqing. This engineering structure will not only help stabilize the soils upstream, but also protect cultivated lands downstream from being buried by sediments.

Agroforestry is a powerful tool in soil conservation.[33] Shelterbelts and windbreaks incorporating the use of fast growing species provide natural barriers to typhoon damage and soil erosion. The inclusion of woody legumes, for instance *Acacia confusa* and *Leucaena leucocephala*, also enriches soil nitrogen and provides fuel for the villagers. Animal dung and crop residues previously combusted for energy supply can then be returned to the farm, thus improving the soil structure and nutrient-holding capacity. As organic matter is a key factor in sustaining soil productivity, it can also be added with the inclusion of green manure (e.g. *Astragalus spp.*) in mixed cropping or of legumes (e.g. peanuts, beans) in crop rotations. It is essential that soil organic matter be maintained at around 3% for optimal crop growth otherwise the effectiveness of chemical fertilizers and other technologies will be reduced. Despite the importance of interplanting crops with woody and pasture legumes, the practice is frequently overlooked in Guangdong.

As a result of crop diversification, the growing of cash crops including sugar cane is indeed very profitable to peasants. Sugar cane is extremely efficient in assimilating photosynthetic energy and because of this, it depletes soil fertility rapidly. Prolonged planting of sugar cane will there-fore result in soil nutrient imbalances, which can only be rectified with sensible crop management techniques. In addition, the continuous crop-ping of rice also disrupts the soil redox potential resulting in the release of manganese and ferrous iron that are toxic to crop growth. Thus, the con-tinuous growth of cash crops aggravates the soil environment as much as staple crops do. Crop rotation will eliminate this problem. In short, the problem of low productivity can be rectified by improving the soil organic matter through agroforestry, recycling wastes, crop rotation and the use of green manures. This integrated crop management is applicable to alluvial soil, red soil and acid sulfate soil. Though easier said than done, there is no short-cut to render the soil sustainable.

The loss of cultivated land can perhaps be compensated for by the development of marginal lands in Guangdong. No attempt is made here to review the different definitions of marginal land. In the broadest sense, marginal lands are those with physical limitations for the sustained ap-plication of a given land use. Adverse physical conditions that cause the low productivity of marginal land in Guangdong include soil acidity, drought, excess water, winter chill, steep slopes, and shallow or stony soils. At present marginal land constitutes 65% of the total land area in Guangdong. Fifty-eight counties are found on this vast expanse of unproductive land accounting for 40% of the total population. Owing to the harsh biophysical environment and meagre capital input, the productivity of these lands is the lowest in Guangdong. Erosion is an acute problem inherited at least partly from the conversion of forest into grain fields during the Great Leap Forward. Any attempt to expand staple crop growth on these lands is unrealistic and disastrous. Instead, poverty can be alleviated and soil productivity sustained via a massive reforestation programme to check erosion plus integrated farming incorporating forestry, orchard plantation, pastoral rearing, and perhaps crop growth on gentler slopes.

Forestry

A wide range of biophysical attributes enhance the development of forest and forestry activities in Guangdong. Mountainous terrain and hills constitute approximately 75% of the total area. These upland areas are dominated by the red soil group, the parent materials of which are intensively weathered and develop into deep soil profile. Located in a tropical to sub-tropical environment, the province is endowed with plentiful rainfall and high enough temperatures to sustain a luxurious forest growth all year round. Maximum species diversity, indigenous and exotic, is made possible by the presence of varied habitats, thus adding value to forest resource development. Not only are these elements favourable to forest growth in Guangdong, but also the stability of the biophysical environment, notably soil and water conservation, hinges greatly on the sustainable development of forestry. A holistic review of the current status and problems of forestry development will be examined in later sections, followed by a comprehensive analysis of sustainable forestry in the province.

Forest Area

Prior to 1949 the forest resource of Guangdong suffered from excessive cutting by warlords, Japanese invaders and local villagers. Very little planting was carried out during the same period, resulting in only 17.6% of the area being under forest cover in 1949 (Table 4.2).

A massive reforestation programme was launched after 1949 in an attempt to control soil erosion, conserve water and provide fuel for the

Table 4.2   Forest Area of Guangdong

Year	Area (10^6 ha)	% cover
1949	3.72	17.6
1985	5.35	26.8
1987	7.18	38.8
1991	8.47	51.5
1993	8.80	53.6
1994	8.88	54.7
1996	—	56.3

Sources: *Guangdong nianjian*, 1991–1995 (see note 42 and 18 below).
Guangdongsheng tongjiju (ed.), *Guangdong tongji nianjian 1997* (Statistical
Yearbook of Guangdong 1997) (Beijing: Zhongguo tongji chubanshe, 1997).

people. This gradual improvement in the forest environment was brought
to an abrupt end during the period 1958–1976, when a large expanse of the
countryside, as discussed previously, was deforested and turned into grain
fields regardless of ecological constraints.

The reforestation programme was revived after 1979. A responsibility
system similar to agriculture was introduced in an attempt to increase
people's incentive and to guarantee people's ownership right of forests.[34]
This was complemented with reorganization of the marketing system
and network, a policy most welcome to the people engaged in forestry
activities.

Also for the first time revegetation of the country was not considered
an end in itself; instead the programme formed an integral part of a central
policy to alleviate poverty and to speed up economic development of
upland regions. All institutional hurdles were removed and full support
from the authority at different levels was forthcoming. These efforts paid
off handsomely in 1986 when, for the first time in Guangdong's history,
the forest logging rate and the productivity rate levelled off. In 1992 the
forested area increased to and levelled off at 53.6% of the total area.

Despite the remarkable increase in forested area since the early 1990s,
the achievement is quite deceptive with regard to spatial distribution and
ecological benefits of new forests. Most of the revegetated areas are confined to the mountainous terrain, offering protection to major river catch-
ments of the province. Little attention has been paid to the practice of
agroforestry and the planting of windbreaks and shelterbelts for the protection of agriculture against storms, floods and typhoons. The forested
area of 38 lowland counties remained at below 10% in 1993. Also, to date

the per capita forest area of Guangdong stays at 0.12 hectare as against 0.97 hectare by world standards.[35] In addition, urban forestry is neglected notwithstanding the rapid urbanization process and the necessity to improve the urban environment. In short, the ecological and social benefits of forests are overlooked.

Revenues derived from forest activities have fluctuated greatly since 1949. The percentage of revenue increase becomes steady after 1976 (Table 4.3), which is clearly a remarkable achievement after the last two decades. Total revenue in 1994 amounted to RMB4.1 billion, as against RMB0.7 billion in 1980. However, forest products and services contribute less than 10% of the GDP.

Table 4.3   Average Percentage Increase in Forest Revenues

Year	%
1953–1957	38.3
1958–1962	5.2
1963–1965	14.8
1966–1970	5.2
1971–1975	0.4
1976–1980	6.5
1981–1985	7.4
1986–1990	6.9

Source: *Guangdong nianjian 1991* (see note 42 below), p. 129.

Age and Species Composition

The success of forestry development is indeed remarkable for the last decade with regard to policy reform, reforestation and income improvement. A closer analysis, however, reveals that a large proportion of the existing forests are at their youthful stage of growth (Table 4.4). Approximately 73.6% of the existing species has a diameter at breast height (dbh) of <12 cm.[36] As seen from the table, mature forest constitutes only a small percentage of the total, indicating that harvestable products in the immediate future are limited. It normally takes 25–30 years for pine and fir forests to mature.[37] Similarly, a large percentage of young to medium-aged stands (88.3%) necessitates input and silvicultural practices to assist growth in the years ahead. Not only will there be a delay in economic return, but the social and ecological benefits derived from massive reforestation are also limited.

Table 4.4   Forest Area by Age

Age class	Area (10^4 ha)	%
Young	287.7	47.8
Medium-aged	243.7	40.5
Near mature	50.6	8.4
Mature	19.9	3.3
Total	601.9	100.0

Source: Kuang Ji (ed.), *Dangdai Zhongguo de Guangdong* (see note 1 below), Vol. 1,
p. 382.

In addition to the dominance of young forests, the species composition of forests in Guangdong is relatively simple notwithstanding a rich local flora and diversified habitats. Evergreen conifers constitute 75% of the total forest area.[38] Worse still, *Pinus massoniana* is the dominant reforestation species which constitutes 37.5% and 42.3% of the mature and young stands respectively. The fast growing pine is indigenous to South China and tolerable of harsh biophysical conditions. As a softwood, the timber is harvested for use in furniture manufacturing and the paper pulp industry. Resin is a valuable product too, while the fallen needles and branches are valuable fuel for the villagers.

Despite these advantages, however, the ecological benefits of pines and other conifers have been challenged recently. Numerous studies suggest that rainfall is exceedingly acidified upon contact with the needles. The acidified leachate not only enhances the loss of the alkali elements, potassium, calcium, magnesium and sodium from the soil profile, it also solubilizes iron, manganese and aluminium.[39] The net result is increased soil acidity and nutrient deprivation, which ultimately lead to soil deterioration and land degradation. Indeed, stunted growth of *P. massoniana* has been reported on eroded granitic areas in Wuhua of Guangdong.[40] *P. elliottii*, becoming popular in Guangdong, is believed to have similar effects on the environment.

Forest Types

Apart from a simplified species composition and the dominance of conifers, Guangdong's forestry is also confronted with the problem of unbalanced type composition. As seen from Table 4.5, 76.5% of the existing forests are planted for timber production while conservation and fuel planting is neglected. To the Chinese, forest development is considered

Table 4.5   Forest Area by Type

Type	Area (10^4 ha)	% total
Timber	549.2	76.5
Conservation	31.6	4.4
Fuel	28.0	3.9
Foodstuff, oil, fruit	104.8	14.6
Special use	4.3	0.6
Total	717.9	100.0

Sources: Kuang Ji (ed.), *Dangdai Zhongguo de Guangdong* (see note 1 below), Vol. 1,
            p. 382.
            Q. Liu and Q. Q. Wei, *Guangdongsheng dili* (see note 36 below), pp. 161–64.

analogous to the harvests of timber, wood chips, paper pulp and resin products. Likewise, forest resource is equated, albeit incorrectly, with the acreage of forest cover. The multi-faceted values of a forest including ecological, social and economic benefits are overlooked. This is dangerous, if not disastrous, as reflected in the uneven composition of forest types. As discussed before, forests designated for timber and resin production are dominated by conifers which have been proven deleterious to the edaphic environment. Moreover, the forest is susceptible to insect attack (e.g. *Dendrolimus punctatus* is widespread in the pine forests of Guangdong) and fire damage. Indeed, insect damage accounted for the annual loss of 570 km^2, 1,500 km^2 and 2,700 km^2 of forests in the 1950s, 1960s and 1970s, respectively.[41] Although insect damage has since been minimized with the introduction of integrated pest management technique including biological control, the infected area remained at 1,000 km^2 in 1990.[42]

Conservation and fuel planting constitute less than 10% of the total forests in Guangdong. This is inadequate in the light of the rapid transformation of the countryside. Encroachment on fertile cultivated land necessitates the development of marginal lands where water conservation and soil protection works pose great challenges to the authorities. Conservation planting incorporating the use of fast-growing legumes is no doubt essential to stabilizing the biophysical environment of these upland areas. Lowland areas and their productivity also benefit from conservation forests upstream, which will conserve water, help binding particles into stable aggregates and reduce surface runoff. Thus forests with a conservation goal should be increased in the immediate future.

Similarly, forests planted for fuel supply are few in Guangdong despite the shortage, as in other parts of China, of rural energy. Fuel supply is a nationwide problem in China and according to an estimate made in the late 1980s, about 60% of the household energy consumed in rural areas came from crop residues and animal dung.[43] Under ideal circumstances, crop residues and animal dung should be returned to the soil and re-cycled for crop growth. Owing to the rural energy shortage, however, these organic farm wastes are combusted and because of the immense rural population, energy is also supplemented with litter and ground fern. To solve the energy problem, many UN- and CAB-funded projects recom-mend the extensive planting of trees for fuel in the rural areas amongst which *L. leucocephala* and casuarinas are popular species.[44] The situation in rural Guangdong is no better as wood fuel forest constitutes only 3.9% of the total. People have to cut ferns and collect surface litter as supplementary fuels, resulting in accelerated erosion and soil loss. As fuel becomes scarce, villagers spend longer time in fuel collection thus increasing the opportunity cost.[45]

Forest Productivity

With adequate water and heat, vascular plants in Guangdong can grow all the year round. Fir grows rapidly in northern Guangdong, annual timber production being 22.5 m^3/ha as against 33.8 m^3/ha for *P. massoniana*. Similarly, *P. elliottii* grown in Yangjiang records annually a height growth of 0.8 m, dbh 1.46 cm and timber volume 10.9 m^3/ha.[46]

Notwithstanding a favourable biophysical environment for forest growth in Guangdong, the productivity is exceedingly low owing to the poor quality of the forests and harsh site conditions in some places. A large proportion of the forests is comprised of young and immature stands dominated by conifers. More important still, many of the mature forests appear to decay considerably in quality due to pest attack, fire damage and illegal cutting resulting in decreased productivity. The average annual timber increment is only 2.88 m^3/ha. Consequently, the average timber volume of 39 m^3/ha is less than 50% that of the nation's total. Where the soil is strongly acidic and contains a toxic level of aluminium, pine forests are stunted, too.

The emphasis on timber production results in the declining importance of forests designated for raw materials production. *Paulownia sp.,* for instance, is a valuable species for oil production. Owing to repeated cutting and conversion to grain fields in the 1960s, however, a large percentage of the forest has disappeared, leaving behind nowadays only fragmented patches of the species. Under these circumstances production is not cost-effective and therefore not appealing to the upland populace.[47]

Survival Rate

Forests in Guangdong are established by means of direct seed sowing, plane broadcasting and pit planting. Reports of the survival rate have been conflicting, ranging from less than 50% to 85%.[48] In his assessment of the reforestation programme in China and using a remote sensing technique, Smil estimated that the average survival rate is only 1%.[49] While the different results reflect different assessment techniques employed, there exists the possibility that local officials habitually exaggerate the survival rate in order to obtain support and rewards from the authority. Survival rate is dependent on species, capital inputs and post-planting care. Naturally, quality is as important as quantity, particularly when not all "forestable" areas have been planted. Measures must also be taken to improve the productivity of low-quality forests that exhibit simplified structures and stunted growth patterns.

Sustainable Forestry

Since 1949 but still more apparent since 1979, forestry in Guangdong has undergone rapid changes in legislation, policy, coverage, planting objectives, capital input and marketing network. To date, more than 50% of the province is under forest cover, a majority of which consists of young stands dominated by a few popular species including *P. massoniana*, *P. elliottii* and *Cunninghamia lanceolata*. Regional disparity in forest cover has been intensified; reforestation of the mountainous terrain was accorded top priority and relatively little attention was paid to agroforestry and coastal planting. Planting is geared towards the production of timber whereas forests earmarked for the supply of raw materials and fuel, and conservation purposes are overlooked. Productivity is low by national and world standards, as are per capita forest acreage and standing timber volume. The quality of many forests, including the environment, exhibits signs of decline due to a lack of silvicultural practice, mediocre capital input, unbalanced species and forest composition, as well as successive plantations without rotation.

Since 1978, rapid economic growth, industrialization and associated activities result in a rising demand of the so-called four materials including fertilizer, fuel, animal feed and raw materials. Although many of these non-timber materials originate from the forests, the demand is never taken care of seriously in Guangdong's forestry policy as reflected in the preferential planting of timber species.

Owing to urban encroachment, cultivated land in Guangdong has witnessed a rapid shrinkage. To compensate for the loss of agricultural productivity, fertilizers must be used together with the development of marginal lands comprising of grassy slopes, undulating terrains and some upland areas which would otherwise be devoted to forests. The opening up of newly cultivated areas necessitates supportive measures to conserve water and soil which can best be met by forest planting. Thus, forestry also plays a vital ecological role in sustaining soil productivity. In short, conservation planting and agroforestry are challenges to the provincial planners. Guangdong simply cannot survive without trees.

In the 1980s ecologists and conservationists called for the preservation of species diversity in ecosystem management. This appeal culminated in part in the UN Conference in Rio de Janeiro in 1992. Guangdong has a rich flora although floristic composition of the existing forests is simplified. Undoubtedly, the species diversity of existing forests should be improved in order to enrich wildlife and to spruce up ecosystem productivity. The task ahead is how to implement this long-awaited objective.

Guangdong province is now at the crossroads of modernization. The success of agricultural and industrial development hinges on the sustained growth of forests which, unfortunately, are marred by deep-rooted anthropogenic problems. Sustainable forestry development is no longer an ideal; it is an imminent task for the policy makers.

Goals

The sustained productivity of forests includes not only timber and raw-materials, but also the hidden and yet important values of genetic diversity as well as ecological and social benefits to the environment. Also embodied in this important concept is the ethical value of taking into consideration the well-being of future generations.[50]

Practices

The successful development of sustainable forestry in Guangdong depends primarily on the restructuring of criteria or guidelines on forest policy. One most important step is to recognize the varied functions of a forest.

Traditionally, forest in China is viewed as a resource for timber production and because of this preoccupation, it is an exploitable and harvestable commodity. This is reflected in the biased species and type composition of the existing forests. In essence a forest performs different functions; it conserves water, protects the soil against erosion, provides fuel and a wide variety of raw materials, and so on. The ecological and social benefits of a forest are at least as important as its being a source of fuel, energy and foodstuff. With a revamped understanding of the values of forest, the selection of species and the choice of management strategy would lead to a different outcome.

Until 1994, too much emphasis had been placed on the overall increase in forest area without adequate consideration for a balanced spatial distribution of the resource. Irrespective of the revegetation techniques, sustainable forestry must give balanced emphasis on the collective benefits of forests. Upland terrain, lowland cultivated areas, coastal zones and urban settings must be treated alike in order to optimize the benefits of forests and improve environmental quality. Agriculture deprived of forestry support would sooner or later suffer from drought, flood, storm, silting and the burial of fertile soil.

Another important principle is that logging must be compensated for by replacement planting, otherwise there will be a net loss of timber volume and forest cover. However, the successful implementation of this principle again hinges on the composition of forest types. The more diversified the forest type, the more easily this goal will be achieved; otherwise young and immature stands would still dominate at any one time.

The preservation of species diversity is imperative to the quality of an ecosystem. Other factors being equal, a forest characterized by high species diversity has a higher recuperative potential against the perturbations of fire, insects and illegal logging. While the resource inventory of Guangdong is everybody's guess, it is essential that a forest count be made soon in order to substantiate research needs and planning work. Equally important is the need to broaden the choice of local and fast growing leguminous species that are more acceptable and familiar to the local people. Although eucalypts are popular exotic species in Guangdong, they have recently been found to deplete soil fertility quickly. Thus, their suitability must be reviewed.

Guangdong accounts for 30% of the nation's total resin production as a result of the dominance of *P. massoniana* in the existing forests. Annual production has increased from 6,000 tons in 1950 to 22,500 tons in 1987 due to a concurrent increase in pine acreage.[51] Pines exhibit a strong podzolization effect on the soil, resulting in increased soil acidity and solubilization of aluminium, manganese and iron. Successive planting of pine will therefore result in soil deterioration and land degradation. It is certainly impracticable to do away with the pine forests, otherwise a large number of factories and workers engaged in the resin industry would suffer. As a remedy, new forestry products and industries must be expanded so as to reduce the reliance on pines. The existing area under pine cover should not be increased; instead every measure must be taken to improve the site conditions under pine. Very promising results have been reported in underplanting the pine forest with pasture and woody legumes.[52] Not only will this practice improve the growth of pines, the soil will also benefit from nitrogen fixation by the legume. Through a modification of the pH and organic matter status of the forest floor, the solubilization of metals by acidified leachate could also be reduced.

No drastic measures can be employed to change the species and type composition of existing forests. The best approach is to diversify planting (species and forest type) once existing forests mature and are harvested. Rotation with legumes and between conifer and broadleaved species would have the dual benefits of increasing species diversity and improving site quality conditions.[53] Apart from the use of indigenous legumes, more emphasis should be placed on the planting of forests that will provide a wide range of raw materials, wood fuel and specialty products.

A. confusa, A. mangium and *A. auriculiformis* have been used with considerable success in checking gully erosion on granitic areas in Deqing.[54] On the other hand, the acreage of timber species should be scaled down and confined to the more accessible upland regions. Conservation planting should also be expanded to valley bottoms, river banks, urban areas and along the coast.

The low productivity problem is typical of the red soils in South China, which are strongly acidic and deficient in nutrients. The deficiency in phosphorus is detrimental to the growth of a wide range of broadleaved species in Guangdong province.[55] Lime will out-compete phosphorus for adsorption sites on the soil mineral colloids, thus releasing the element for normal root uptake. Indeed, the supply of lime in Guangdong is plentiful. Together with an extensive use of nitrogen-fixing legumes, the site conditions can be improved in the long run which, in turn, favour the growth of broadleaved forests.

Forestry development in Guangdong is very much hindered by

backward technology, as exemplified in fire fighting, communication and pest control. Capital investment in these aspects must be increased parallel to a change in the planting strategy and species choice. Equally critical are the research needs and the necessity to import foreign techniques to optimize resource use. Under the present situation, only 9% of the timber material is utilized, resulting in the wastage of valuable materials.[56] Technology should either be expanded or imported to optimize the manufacturing of wood products from chips and sawdust which would otherwise be wasted.

Forestry law standards are stringent in China and Guangdong is no exception. Very often these standards are not enforceable due to a lack of surveillance teams as well as a critical shortage of fuel in the countryside. Devoid of fossil fuel, hydroelectric power (HEP) or other sources of energy, people have no choice but to defy the law by illegal cutting of the forests. Apart from the expansion of wood fuel forests, demand must be supplemented where possible with biogas, small HEP stations and fossil fuel.

Conclusion

Agriculture and forestry are inseparable primary activities in Guangdong province, the development of which during the period 1949–1978 was subjected to the combined influence of vigorous land disturbances and technological breakthrough, resulting in drastic changes in the rural landscape, and fluctuations in productivity with time and environmental degradation problems, with far-reaching implications. Production responsibility systems were introduced since 1978 in an attempt to increase peasant incentives and enthusiasm. Coupled with crop diversification and specialization, and increased fertilizer input, agricultural production reached a record high in the mid-1980s. Unfortunately, this trend of improvement is not consistent with the policy change because production became stagnant again thereafter. Similarly, a massive reforestation programme was launched during the last decade in an attempt to rehabilitate the countryside and supply varied forest products. The percentage of forest cover increased significantly, yet the province is confronted as ever with the problems of poor site quality, unbalanced species composition and forest type, dominance of young stands, production inefficiency and illegal logging.

Guangdong has to date a population of approximately 67 million. With an increasing demand for food, timber, fuel and raw materials, the sustainable development of agriculture and forestry is all the more essential. For agriculture and forestry to be sustainable, they must maintain productivity and environmental conservation for many generations. Despite the fact that Guangdong is endowed with plentiful heat and water, both agricultural and forest production lags behind many of its sister provinces, resulting in staple food import and subsidies from the central government. The problem of low productivity is owing partly to ecological backlashes from the past, inherent limitations of the edaphic environment, and to low capital inputs. It can be solved with greater capital inputs, integrated crop management and development of the marginal lands. Forest productivity can be enhanced gradually with a recognition of the ecological benefits of trees. A step-wise restructuring of the forest species and forest type composition is the long-term objective, while improving the site quality through rotation and interplanting with legumes are the short-term ones.

In short, agriculture and forestry play an important role in the modernization of Guangdong. A sustainable development of these activities will provide an ecologically stable environment for the people.

Notes

1. Kuang Ji (ed.), *Dangdai Zhongguo de Guangdong* (Contemporary China: Guangdong) (Beijing: Dangdai Zhongguo chubanshe, 1991), Vol. 1, pp. 332–75.
2. Guojia tongjiju zonghesi (ed.), *Quanguo gesheng zizhiqu zhixiashi lishi tongji ziliao huibian, 1949–1989* (Historical Statistics of All Provinces, Autonomous Regions and Municipal Cities of China, 1949–1989) (Beijing: Zhongguo tongji chubanshe, 1990), p. 624.
3. T. Cannon and A. Jenkins (eds.), *The Geography of Contemporary China* (London: Routledge, 1990), pp. 146–48.
4. R. F. Ash, "The Evolution of Agricultural Policy," *The China Quarterly*, No. 116 (1988), pp. 529–55.
5. X. Y. Hou, *Shengtaixue yu nongye fazhan* (Ecology and Agricultural Development) (Anhui: Anhui kexue jishu chubanshe, 1984), pp. 21–25.
6. See note 1.
7. Anonymous, "Sustainable Agriculture in the Asian Context," *Agrochemicals News in Brief*, Vol. XV, No. 1 (January–March 1992), pp. 12–21.
8. The extensive growth of hybrid variety rice in Guangdong started in 1977 in the Pearl River Delta area.

9. Guojia huanjingbaohuju (ed.), *Zhongguo de shengtai nongye* (Ecological Agriculture of China) (Beijing: Zhongguo huanjing kexue chubanshe, 1991), pp. 21–59.

10. The productivity of the "least productive" farmland is in the region of <1,500–2,259 kg/ha/year.

11. J. Z. Xu and Z. H. Lu, *Shenzhen* (Guangzhou: Zhongguo haiyang chubanshe, 1985), pp. 65–67.

12. Z. J. Wang et al. (eds.), *Guangdong si xiaohu* (The Four Little Tigers of Guangdong) (Guangzhou: Guangdong gaodeng jiaoyu chubanshe, 1989), pp. 199–233.

13. G. Ku, *Zhuhai tequ jingji yu jinrong* (Economy and Finance of Zhuhai Special Economic Zone) (Guangzhou: Zhongshan daxue chubanshe, 1988), pp. 234–44.

14. Guangzhou City Committee Research Unit and Guangzhou Socio-economic Development Research Centre (eds.), *Jiushi niandai Guangzhou fazhan qianjing yu duice* (The Development, Prospect and Strategies of Guangzhou in the 1990s) (Guangzhou: Huanan ligong daxue chubanshe, 1991), pp. 72–78.

15. Foshan Local History Editorial Unit, *Foshan shihua* (History of Foshan), (Nanhai: Zhongshan daxue chubanshe, 1990), pp. 325–29.

16. See note 12.

17. According to the 1990 Hong Kong Agriculture and Fisheries Department Statistics, 60.5%, 37.5%, 82.8% and 15.7% of the live poultry, fresh vegetables, fresh water fish and fresh fruits consumed by the local population were imported from South China, principally Guangdong.

18. Guangdong nianjian bianzuan weiyuanhui (ed.), *Guangdong nianjian 1995* (Guangdong Yearbook 1995) (Guangzhou: Guangdong nianjianshe, 1995), p. 654.

19. Nanjing turang yanjiusuo (ed.), *Zhongguo turang* (Soils of China) (Beijing: kexue chubanshe, 1978), pp. 50–71.

20. R. K. Lu, "Shilun woguo turang yangfeng pinjihua de weixie" (On the Threat of Soil Nutrient Depletion in China), in *Zhongguo tudi tuihua fangzhi yanjiu* (Research on the Prevention of Land Degradation in China) (Beijing: Zhongguo kexue jishu chubanshe, 1990), pp. 25–31.

21. W. Z. Yang, "Woguo nongye tudi tuihua xianzhuang, yuanyin ji qi duice" (On the Status, Cause and Amelioration of Land Degradation in China), in *Zhongguo tudi tuihua fangzhi yanjiu* (see note 20), pp. 21–25.

22. X. H. Chen and X. J. Zhong, "2000 nian Guangdong gengdi ziyuan de bianhua qushi ji qi duice" (The Varying Tendency of Cultivated Land in Guangdong Province by 2000), *Redai dili* (Tropical Geography), Vol. 12, No. 1 (1992), pp. 9–14.

23. D. H. Jiang, Y. G. Zhang, L. Yang and S. F. Hou, "Zhongguo pinkun diqu

leixing huafen ji kaifa yanjiu tiyao baogao" (Researches on the Classification and Development of Poor Area in China), *Dili yanjiu* (Geographical Research), Vol. 7, No. 3 (1988), pp. 1–16.

24. See note 22.

25. Z. F. Jiang, "Woguo tudi ziyuan shengchanli sangshi yu fangzhi duice" (On the Preventive Measures for Declining Land Productivity in China), in *Zhongguo tudi tuihua fangzhi yanjiu* (see note 20), pp. 35–39.

26. See note 21.

27. See note 22.

28. M. Liu, Z. J. Tang and C. L. Zhi, "Gengdi jianshao shige burong hushi de yanzhong wenti" (On the Critical Problem of Cultivated Land Shrinkage), *Jingji dili* (Economic Geography), Vol. 9, No. 3, (1989), pp. 194–98.

29. See note 7.

30. See note 22.

31. R. Lal, *Tropical Ecology and Physical Edaphology* (West Sussex: Wiley, 1987), pp. 618–85.

32. See note 28.

33. Agroforestry refers to land-use systems in which trees or shrubs are grown in association with agricultural crops, pastures, livestock or fishery, and in which there are both ecological and economic interactions between the trees and other components.

34. Kuang Ji (ed.), *Dangdai Zhongguo de Guangdong* (see note 1), Vol. 1, pp. 375–93.

35. The per capita forest area of China is 0.11 hectare.

36. Q. Liu and Q. Q. Wei, *Guangdongsheng dili* (The Geography of Guangdong Province) (Guangzhou: Guangdong renmin chubanshe, 1988), pp. 160–73.

37. Y. M. Liu, "Shamu yinglin yu tudi tuihua" (Fir Plantations and Land Degradation), in *Zhongguo tudi tuihua fangzhi yanjiu* (see note 20), pp. 471–74.

38. Y. W. Wu (ed.), *Guangdongsheng jingji dili* (Economic Geography of Guangdong Province (Beijing: Xinhua chubanshe, 1985), pp. 171–86.

39. W. T. Cheng, "Prevention of Soil Deterioration in Forest Plantations," in *Zhongguo tudi tuihua fangzhi yanjiu* (see note 20), pp. 153–56; K. C. Chau, "Aqueous Leaf Extracts of *Pinus massoniana* and *Acacia confusa* and Its Effects on the Leaching of Cations in Soils of Hong Kong" (paper presented at the 27th International Geographical Congress held in Washington, D.C., 9–14 August 1992); H. T. Liu and R. S. Tian, "Relationship Between Decline of a Masson Pine Forest and Aluminium Activation in Nanshan, Chongqing," *Acta Scientiae Circumstantiae*, Vol. 12, No. 3 (1992), pp. 297–305.

40. G. H. Zeng and H. X. Chen, "Huagangyan qiuling qinshiqu maweisong canlin gaizao tujing chutan" (On the Improvement of *Pinus massoniana*

Plantations in Eroded Granitic Areas), _Zhongguo shuitu baochi_ (China Soil and Water Conservation), No. 12 (1992), pp. 50–51.

41. See note 38.
42. Guangdong nianjian bianzuan weiyuanhui (ed.), _Guangdong nianjian 1991_ (Guangdong Yearbook 1991) (Guangzhou: Guangdong renmin chubanshe, 1991), pp. 233–34.
43. V. Smil, _China Environmental Crisis—An Inquiry into the Limits of National Development_ (London: Sharpe, 1993), p. 102.
44. A. Young, _Agroforestry for Soil Conservation_ (Wallingford, Oxon: CAB International, 1989), pp. 105–28; K. E. Giller and K. J. Wilson, _Nitrogen Fixation in Tropical Cropping Systems_ (Wallingford, Oxon: CAB International, 1991), p. 185.
45. J. Whitney and C. H. Choi, "An Economic Optimization Model of Soil Erosion Control Measures, Deqing County, Guangdong Province," in _Soil Erosion China Project, IDRC Report_ (Ottawa: International Development Research Centre, 1989), pp. 89–94.
46. See note 34.
47. See note 38.
48. See note 42.
49. V. Smil, "Deforestation in China," _Ambio_, Vol. 12, No. 5 (1983), pp. 226–31.
50. World Commission on Environment and Development, _Our Common Future_ (Oxford: Oxford University Press, 1987), p. 383.
51. See note 34.
52. See note 40.
53. See note 39.
54. Q. Y. Yao, "Huanan huagangyan diqu rengong shengtai xitong de yanjiu" (Man-made Ecosystems of Granitic Areas in South China), in _Guangdong-sheng shuitu baochi yanjiu_ (Soil and Water Conservation Research in Guangdong Province), edited by China–Canada Soil and Water Conservation Group (Beijing: Kexue chubanshe, 1989), pp. 117–30.
55. Phosphorus deficiency will have no adverse effects on pines and casuarinas because mycorrhizae present on the root systems help to absorb soil phosphorus.
56. See note 38.
57. Guangdong nianjian bianzuan weiyuanhui (ed.), _Guangdong nianjian 1993_ (Guangdong Yearbook 1993) (Guangzhou: Guangdong nianjianshe, 1993), p. 246.
58. Guangdong nianjian bianzuan weiyuanhui (ed.), _Guangdong nianjian 1994_ (Guangdong Yearbook 1994) (Guangzhou: Guangdong nianjianshe, 1994), p. 229.

5

Energy Resources

Hung Wing-tat and Peter Hills

Guangdong has grown rapidly since 1978. The growth rates might have been even higher had sufficient energy supplies been available in the province. Electrical supply cuts have been commonplace, often occurring twice a week. As a result, many factories have had to work at well below capacity with obvious negative impacts on industrial output. Unless measures are taken to improve the energy supply situation and to use energy more efficiently then the situation is likely to deteriorate further and future growth will be restricted.

The problem is not the result of an absolute lack of energy resources within the country. China is endowed with virtually all forms of conventional energy resources: coal, oil, natural gas and hydropower. Table 5.1 shows China's energy production in the last decade.

Table 5.1   Energy Production in China, 1984–1994

Year	Total energy (Mtce*)	Coal (%)	Oil (%)	Natural gas (%)	Hydropower (%)
1984	778.55	72.4	21.0	2.1	4.5
1985	855.46	72.8	20.9	2.0	4.3
1986	881.24	72.4	21.2	2.1	4.3
1987	912.66	72.6	21.0	2.0	4.4
1988	958.01	73.1	20.4	2.0	4.5
1989	1,016.39	74.1	19.3	2.0	4.6
1990	1,039.22	74.2	19.0	2.0	4.8
1991	1,048.44	74.1	19.2	2.0	4.7
1992	1,072.56	74.3	18.9	2.0	4.8
1993	1,069.95	76.8	19.4	2.1	1.7
1994	1,140.09	77.7	18.3	2.0	2.0

Source: State Statistical Bureau, *China Statistical Yearbook 1995* (Beijing: China Statistical Information and Consultancy Service Centre, 1995), p. 199.
* Mtce stands for million tonnes of coal equivalent.

In many respects, China is one of the best endowed countries in the world in terms of energy resources. This is particularly so in the case of coal. Furthermore, substantial reserves of oil and natural gas probably remain to be found in the far west of the country and possibly in offshore areas as well. The basic problem, however, is that energy resources are distributed unevenly. To complicate matters, the areas rich in energy resources are typically remote from the major centres of demand. Table 5.2 shows the regional distribution of energy resources in 1980.

Table 5.2   Regional Distribution of Energy Resources in China, 1980

Region	Distribution (%)	Composition (%)		
		Coal	Hydropower	Petroleum & gas
North	43.9	98.2	1.3	0.5
Northeast	3.8	54.6	14.2	31.2
East	6.0	72.9	22.5	4.6
South	5.6	44.5	51.8	3.7
Southwest	28.6	25.2	74.7	0.1
Northwest	12.1	66.7	31.3	2.0

Source: Liu Bao and Guo Gongsong, *Nengyuan xitong gongcheng* (Energy System Engineering) (Beijing: Jixie gongye chubanshe, 1991), p. 7.

Clearly, the northern, southwestern and northwestern regions contain over 80% of the total national energy resource endowment. The southern region, including Guangdong, contains only 5.6% of total energy resources. Transportation of energy resources, particularly coal, from other regions into Guangdong to support its growth has imposed a heavy burden on the transportation system, especially the railways.

The lack of indigenous energy resources in Guangdong is just one of the problems. Lack of effective energy planning and consequent shortcomings in the management of energy supply and demand is an equally significant issue. Energy wastage is common and has aggravated the supply situation. Most of China's industries rely on low levels of technology and the production equipment is out-of-date.[1] Alternative forms of energy such as biogas, solar, wind and nuclear have high development potential in Guangdong but this has not been realized, largely because conventional energy sources are inappropriately priced. Centrally controlled and subsidized energy prices provide no incentive for consumers to use energy more efficiently. Furthermore, the energy industries themselves have long been unprofitable. Changes in energy pricing policy are a recent development and have only come with the growing success of the economic reform programme and China's involvement with Hong Kong in collaborative projects, notably the Daya Bay nuclear power plant (in conjunction with China Light and Power), thermal power plants at Shajiao (in conjunction with Hopewell Company) and Hainan natural gas purchase and sale contract.[2] The formulation of an energy policy based on free market principles and on the experience of these new collaborative projects is crucial to the future development of Guangdong.

Another important dimension of energy resource development in Guangdong is the continuing exploration for offshore oil in the South China Sea. Although billions of RMB had been spent over the past decade by both Chinese and international oil corporations on this exercise, it provided few successes, at least until the beginning of the 1990s.

Energy Demand and Development in Guangdong

Energy consumption in Guangdong had been increasing steadily before 1978, when the open policy was adopted, and thereafter the rate of increase has been very sharp. Table 5.3 shows energy consumption trends in the province since 1952. Coal and oil are the major energy sources, constituting more than 80% of the total consumption.

Taking into account the consumption of hydropower, total energy consumption since 1985 is as shown in Table 5.4.

A significant part of coal consumption is in the power sector (i.e. to generate electricity). Final consumption in the form of electricity accounts for approximately 30% of total consumption and has changed little over the past ten years.

Table 5.3   Energy Consumption Trends in Guangdong, 1952–1993

(Unit: 1,000 tonnes)

Year	Coal	Charcoal	Oil	Fuel oil	Petrol	Diesel	Coal oil	Lub oil
1952	247	—	—	—	2	8	—	—
1957	1,102	—	—	—	17	38	—	—
1962	2,778	—	—	—	65	78	—	—
1965	3,292	150	—	—	86	130	—	2
1970	4,351	201	—	—	—	—	—	—
1975	7,546	464	—	1,001	—	—	—	—
1978	9,581	675	—	1,436	—	—	—	—
1980	10,205	579	6,152	1,875	188	802	5	35
1985	11,668	704	7,055	2,593	369	848	137	39
1989	19,584	894	8,840	3,558	428	1,290	174	48
1990	19,808	930	9,112	3,517	394	1,166	200	44
1991	24,169	907	10,178	3,903	425	1,607	246	49
1992	25,807	1,104	11,071	4,233	431	1,786	330	55
1993	29,280	998	11,437	4,842	2,343	4,545	326	69

Source: *Guangdong tongji nianjian* (Statistical Yearbook of Guangdong), various years.

Table 5.4 Primary Energy Consumption and Composition in Guangdong

Year	Total Mtce*	Coal (%)	Oil (%)	Hydropower (%)
1985	24.47	45.1	41.9	13.0
1986	26.21	45.7	43.8	10.5
1987	28.80	49.0	41.3	9.7
1988	30.75	57.0	39.9	3.1
1989	35.98	57.5	35.5	7.0
1990	36.90	56.5	35.3	8.2
1991	41.62	59.5	35.0	5.5
1992	45.54	56.9	35.1	8.0
1993	49.84	58.3	33.0	8.7

Source: *Guangdong tongji nianjian 1994*, p. 277.
* Mtce stands for million tonnes of coal equivalent.

Energy supplies within the province have never been adequate to meet demand. About two-thirds of the energy used is imported from other regions of the country or imported from outside, including Hong Kong. Table 5.5 shows the pattern of energy imports since 1985.

Despite the rapid growth in energy demand in Guangdong, the level of consumption compared with most developed nations is still very low. Industrial sector consumption constitutes approximately 70% of the total, while transportation and domestic uses account for approximately 20%.

Table 5.5 Energy Production and Imports in Guangdong

(Unit: Mtce*)

Year	Energy production	Imported from provinces	Imported from abroad
1985	8.55	21.56	0.30
1986	8.64	20.91	2.31
1987	9.04	23.48	1.76
1988	10.02	26.16	1.66
1989	10.07	29.92	3.76
1990	10.10	29.55	4.74
1991	11.15	34.15	5.18
1992	14.53	33.82	10.46
1993	16.14	32.69	17.80

Source: *Guangdong tongji nianjian 1994*, p. 274.
* Mtce stands for million tonnes of coal equivalent.

This indicates that there is still tremendous potential for growth in energy demand, especially in the transportation and household sectors. Table 5.6 provides a comparison between Guangdong and China and selected higher income countries.

Table 5.6   Comparison of Energy Consumption and Composition

	Consumption (Mtce*)	Composition (%)			
		Transport	Industries	Household	Others
Guangdong (1993)	55.90	8.44	70.52	12.38	8.66
China (1994)	1,227.37	4.58	74.47	12.56	8.39
USA (1985)	1,281.26	34.70	30.60	31.20	3.40
UK (1985)	139.73	26.30	29.90	41.50	2.40
France (1985)	134.84	26.50	33.40	37.30	2.90
Italy (1985)	105.95	26.70	36.10	34.20	2.90
Japan (1985)	250.55	23.00	47.60	26.10	3.40

Sources: *Guangdong tongji nianjian 1994, China Statistical Yearbook 1995* and Wang Hanchen (ed.), *Daqi baohu yu nengyuan liyong* (Air Quality and Energy Usage) (Beijing: Zhongguo huanjing kexue chubanshe, 1992).
* Mtce stands for million tonnes of coal equivalent.

The future demand for energy in Guangdong will depend on a number of important factors:

1. the rate of economic growth which depends very much on the designated role of Guangdong in the national development programme;
2. the rate of increase of population and in the standard of living, resulting in increases in transport, commercial and household energy consumption; and
3. the planning and management of energy supply and demand by the Guangdong government.

The national strategic economic plan is targeted at doubling the gross national product (GNP) every ten years. However, considering just electricity demand, assuming that there will be steady economic growth similar to Hong Kong and that the level of energy demand gradually reaches the 1991 level of the territory over the next ten years, then Guangdong will need to increase its power production from the current 613 kWh per capita to 4,089 kWh per capita. Also, assuming the energy demand grows at the same rate as GNP (that is, doubling every ten years) energy demand in the decade to come will be 74 million tonnes of coal equivalent in 2001. The electricity requirement will be 263,290 million kWh in 2001.

Energy and Power Policies and Management

Shortages of energy are acute in Guangdong and have definitely constrained economic growth. Local media reports confirm this. For example, it was reported that demand outstripped supply by over 40% during the summer months, and the situation became desperate, with shortages idling about 50% of the province's industrial capacity.[3] Many factories can only work for a half-day and power cuts are common for domestic users. Most factories cope with the problem by installing their own diesel generators, but clearly, this does represent an inefficient use of energy resources. These shortages, as suggested here, relate to a very large extent to the specific characteristics of the energy situation, namely, the regional imbalance in supply and demand, inefficient use of energy and inappropriate energy pricing. In addition, the province is heavily dependent on coal and oil, energy-using technologies are in many cases old and of low efficiency, and the negative environmental impacts of energy use are substantial.

In tackling its energy problems, China faces the dilemma of determining an appropriate balance between market and central planning. A number of characteristics of the Chinese energy economy such as the high energy intensity in GNP, low household energy consumption, energy shortages in rural areas and disproportionate energy consumption by industry can be seen as the legacy of central planning.

Despite recent economic reforms, energy in China has continued to be allocated largely through administrative measures, with market forces playing only a minor role in energy distribution. The most important mechanism for determining allocations is the annual plan, which provides for most of the energy used by state enterprises and fixes allocations for commercial departments. Allocations result ultimately in the establishment of quotas for individual enterprises.

About half of China's coal is produced by the central government and is distributed through state planning; the other half is produced by local governments and collective mines and is distributed through market channels.[4] Pricing by government has distorted demand; the official price is only about half the market price. This induces excessive demand for government-produced coal. Demand may be reduced by up to 35% if the price is allowed to be raised to match the market price. The coal and oil markets established in Shanghai and Nanjing to a certain extent help the nation move in the right direction.[5]

Allowing energy prices to move upwards has at least three major benefits: (1) consumers, especially the energy intensive users, will be more cautious in energy consumption; (2) highly energy intensive products will become more expensive and demand for them should drop which in turn will force these products out of the market; (3) the financial return from power investment should improve.

Adjustments in energy prices are expected to meet strong opposition from various sectors with vested interests, including transportation, metallurgical and chemical industries. The two-tier price system developed in recent years may provide at least a partial solution here. For example, coal may now be sold at two different prices: at the set price within the limit of the production or consumption quota, and at the floating price for above quota production or consumption. The fixed price ensures that vested interests are being considered and the floating marginal price affects the behaviour of producers as well as consumers.

The same phenomenon happens in the power sector. Average electricity tariffs are well below long-run marginal costs. Special subsidized rates have been introduced from time to time to help new industrial and agricultural users during their initial years. These preferential rates, however, have seldom been revoked after the beneficiary firms become firmly established. In the centrally planned system, fixed capital costs have not been included in charges and the power sector as a whole has achieved satisfactory financial returns, despite the relatively low tariffs. These returns are, however, passed on to the central government with the plant management only retaining 23% for its own purposes. Before 1986, all power plants were financed, built and managed by the central government. The budget was very small — in the order of RMB100–200 million per year — which was only sufficient for maintaining the power stations. Consequently, many power plants are relatively small and old, the technology in use is outdated and inefficient with generating capability falling far short of demand.

Additional financial resources will have to be provided to finance much greater investment in power plants. This can be done through an increase in tariff revenues or an increase in state investment allocations, or both. An adjustment in the tariff structure will also have the potential benefit of encouraging conservation. This applies especially to the industrial sector, which accounts for over 70% of total power consumption.

Indeed, improvement of energy production technology as well as energy management will become crucial in the process of economic reform of Guangdong. However, these efforts will have little impact if energy continues to be wasted on the same scale. Energy conservation is therefore an essential element of a comprehensive energy policy.

The major policy guidelines for conservation, as published by the State Science and Technology Commission in August 1986 are:[6]

1. strengthen research and development work on conservation; develop and disseminate new technology, techniques, equipment and materials;
2. speed up retrofitting of energy conservation equipment; replace low efficiency, high consumption equipment;
3. design and popularize energy saving of buildings;
4. develop energy recovery systems, use waste industrial heat and combustible exhaust gases rationally; and
5. strengthen energy management; lay down energy saving rules and standards.

There have been some successes in certain aspects of energy conservation. Each year since 1980, through technical improvement and economic restructuring, energy intensity declined by 5.6% per year between 1980 and 1988. China saved the equivalent of 175 mtce of energy over the entire period, or 22 mtce per year.[7] All state enterprises have been required to install energy consumption metering equipment since 1985. In addition, industrial enterprises that consume more than 0.5 mtce per year must establish energy conservation units. An Office of Energy Conservation has been established to set standards of energy consumption for enterprises. Three main macro-economic factors appeared to be responsible for the improvement in energy efficiency: (a) energy conservation programmes; (b) improvements in macro-economic performance and (c) increases in energy prices.[8]

External Energy Relationships of Guangdong

The shortage of energy in Guangdong has prompted the local government as well as collective and private enterprises to explore various means to improve the supply situation. Measures adopted include buying electricity from Hong Kong as well as pursuing collaborative energy exploration and production projects with foreign investors.

The Power Sector

From the early 1980s, when the Shenzhen Special Economic Zone (SEZ) was established, Guangdong has been buying power from the China Light and Power Company (CLP) to support the development of the SEZ. The power supply to Shekou was commissioned in November 1986. The amount of electricity sold to Guangdong since 1987 is shown in Table 5.7.

Table 5.7 Power Supply to Guangdong from Hong Kong, 1987–1995

Year	1987	1988	1989	1990	1991	1992	1993	1994	1995
Shenzhen (million kWh)	1,300	1,121	1,631	1,386	2,220	4,020	—	—	—
Shekou (million kWh)	114	187	215	292	323	366	—	—	—
Guangdong (million HK$)	529	402	672	636	951	1,913	2,385	843	841

Source: China Light and Power Co. Ltd., *Annual Reports*, various years.

Buying electricity from Hong Kong has certainly helped the economic development of Shenzhen and Shekou in the short term. However, it has become a great burden for Guangdong to pay for the energy in hard currency. The Guangdong General Power Company Limited (GGPC) subsequently agreed in 1987 with CLP to pay part of the cost in the form of raw coal to be used in CLP's Castle Peak power station. Thus, coal is bartered for electricity. Obviously, long-term reliance on CLP may not be practical. This explains the severe drop in electricity purchased from Hong Kong since 1994. Building up Guangdong's own power production capacity must be accorded a high priority by the Guangdong govern- ment. One of the most effective ways to secure enough funding for constructing new power plants is to solicit financial support from foreign investors.

The first collaborative power production project was initiated by CLP in the early 1980s: the Daya Bay nuclear power plant. This is a joint project of the Hong Kong Nuclear Investment Company Limited, a company established by CLP and the Guangdong Nuclear Investment Company Limited. Hong Kong owns a 25% share and Guangdong the other 75%. It is a 2×900 MW PWR plant. The contract was signed in January 1985. Some 70% of the plant's output will be sold to Hong Kong in order to repay the huge bank loans. The first unit started operation in 1993. The success of this plant both technologically and financially has tempted the Guangdong authority to develop another nuclear plant, the location of which has still to be determined. Current verified uranium reserves in China are sufficient to sustain operation of 15,000 MW of PWRs for thirty years. At present there is only one 300 MW PWR power plant at Qinshan, Jiangsu province.[9]

The Daya Bay project requires the Guangdong authority to commit itself to shouldering a considerable foreign debt which the authority itself does not feel at all comfortable with. Gordon Wu's Hopewell Holdings Company Limited provided a more attractive package — a BOT (Build, Operate and Transfer) coal fired plant at Shajiao B in Shenzhen in 1986. This plant is a 2×350 MW station, costing US$3.8 billion and it became operational in 1988.[10] Following this project, Shajiao C (3×660 MW), estimated to cost US$7.8 billion, the Zhujiang thermal plant, costing US$2.3 billion (a joint project of the New World Company Limited and the Guangdong authority), Nanhai and Zhuhai power plants of the Cheung Kong Holdings follow suit.

Based on these experiences, the Chinese authorities have formulated a new set of rules for the power production industries which include:

1. allowing foreign investors to invest in domestic power production industries and providing them with preferential terms;
2. allowing the price of electricity to be adjusted according to market mechanism;
3. allowing profits earned by power production industries to be retained by them, thereby removing the requirement to remit a substantial portion to the central government authorities; and
4. establishing a power development fund, supported in part by a contribution from the power tax.

The Guangdong government is moving quickly to capitalize on these new measures. Goldman Sachs (Asia) Ltd., an American investment consultant, has been appointed to study the feasibility of selling equity in provincial power plants to foreign investors. The level of shares on sale will be between 25–35%.[11] This will have a great impact on the current energy management structure. If successful, this policy will help to bring the Chinese power sector in line with international regulations and practices. However, since most of the existing power plants in Guangdong are old and inefficient, it is doubtful whether these plants could attract the interest of foreign investors. In other words, if this level of foreign investment is to be achieved, there will be a growing number of new power plants.

Oil Developments

In March 1985, China announced that in order to speed up oil development, foreign participation in exploration work in ten southern provinces, including Guangdong, would be permitted. Many oil companies showed interest and about sixty odd delegations came to investigate. Unfortunately, the conditions in these fields were poor and as the oil price was dropping at the time, only one Australian company eventually signed a collaborative project. After three and a half years of work in Hainan Island, the contract was terminated because no commercially viable discoveries were made.

However, in 1990, Huizhou 21-1, the first offshore oil field in the Pearl River estuary, started production. It was jointly developed by Nanhai East Corporation, China National Offshore Oil Corporation and the ACT Group (formed by Agip [Overseas] of Italy, Chevron Overseas Petroleum and Texaco Petroleum Maats Chappij [Netherlands] BV of the United States). Another oil field, Huizhou 26-1, is being developed by the same consortium. The estimated development costs are US$240 million for oil field 21-1 and US$260 million for oil field 26-1. The oil reserves of 21-1 are put at 5.35 million tonnes and nearly double that figure of 26-1.[12]

The US-based Amoco Corporation also signed an agreement with the China National Offshore Oil Corporation to develop the country's largest offshore field, Liuqiong 11-1, south of the Pearl River Delta in February 1991.[13] The total investment was around US$500 million.

As a result of these developments, the Shenzhen government, together with the China Resource Corporation and the China Oil Refinery Corporation, decided to develop a refinery with a processing capacity of 3 million tonnes. The total development cost will be in the order of HK$600 million.[14]

Prospects

It is clear that the demand for energy in Guangdong is increasing rapidly and cannot at present be met. Central planning for energy has not been capable of responding to the changing situation brought about by economic reform, and shortcomings in planning and management have adversely impacted on economic development and growth. Policy changes, particularly those allowing foreign equity participation and the freeing of energy prices, have been introduced as part of the package of economic reforms. The current targets for foreign participation are for 25–35% foreign ownership in the power sector in Guangdong and up to 49% in oil production. Freeing energy prices to reach a market-determined level offers a chance to the energy industries to become profitable enterprises.

With this new policy in place, the development of the energy sector has rapidly gathered momentum over the last five years. The success of collaborative development projects like the Shajiao and Zhujiang thermal power plants, the Daya Bay nuclear power plant and oil production in the South China Sea, as well as the oil refinery in Shenzhen, has given the Guangdong authorities more confidence in soliciting foreign investors. When the anticipated level of foreign investment is achieved, Guangdong may be better equipped to tackle its energy problem. The demand will not only be met but energy management and control will be brought in line with international practices with the prospect of cleaner and more efficient use of energy.

Notes

1. Wu Zongxin and Wei Zhihong, "Policies to Promote Energy Conservation in China," *Energy Policy*, Vol. 19, No. 10 (1991), pp. 934–39.
2. *Eastern Express*, 4 May 1994.
3. *Hong Kong Standard*, 8 March 1992.
4. A. V. Desai, *Energy in China* (New York: Wiley Eastern Limited, 1990).
5. *Hong Kong Economic Journal*, 1 December 1992.
6. N. J. D. Lucas, J. Ambali, E. Chang, M. S. Forbes-Richarte and R. M. Shrestha, *Energy Policies in Asia: A Comparative Study* (New York: United Nations Publication, 1987).
7. See note 1.
8. Lin Xiannuan, *China's Energy Strategy: Economic Structure, Technological Choices, and Energy Consumption* (Westport, Connecticut: Praeger, 1996).
9. The World Bank, *China: The Energy Sector* (Washington D.C.: The World Bank, 1985).
10. Hong Kong Institute of Engineers and Electricite de France International, "Electricity Development in China: An Exclusive Interview with Gordon Wu," *Electric Focus*, No. 2 (1992).
11. *Hong Kong Economic Journal*, 9 November 1992.
12. *Hong Kong Standard*, 15 September 1990.
13. *South China Morning Post*, 18 February 1991.
14. *Hong Kong Economic Journal*, 9 April 1992.

6

Industry and Trade

Lau Pui-king

The development of Guangdong province after 1978 has been characterized by rapid growth in production, in export and in increases in the size and relative importance of industrial output and employment. The adoption of export-oriented economy has changed the relative importance of light industry, which suffered from the industrial policy set in the 1960s under the hypothetical threat of warfare. Accompanying the policy change, there was economic reform from the centrally planned economy to a market economy. The emergence of collective, private and foreign capital invested enterprises has accelerated the changes.

Businessmen who invest mainly in industrial processing in China tend to choose locations and forms of investment according to the freedom in management and preferential treatments granted. The establishment of Special Economic Zones (SEZs), coastal open cities, economic and technological development zones, bonded areas for imported goods, etc., has facilitated the provision of more attractive investment environments for investors and initiated economic reform and development.

The other force of development came from changes in ownership and management of enterprises under the improving competitive market environment. The increased weighting of output value and profitability of collective and private firms against state-owned enterprises gave strong support to enterprise reform in China. It has also expedited rural industrialization and urbanization of the province.

The national policy to expand export trade and to attract foreign capital through industrial processing, joint ventures and sole ownership initiated the changes in political, legal, economic and institutional structures which support the transition to a market economy. The protection of the domestic market from foreign competition in the past gave Chinese enterprises a chance to nurture and to earn monopolistic profits.

The differences in organization and management of foreign capital-invested firms have caused a significant impetus to enterprise reform in Guangdong. The setup of Chinese firms in Hong Kong with capital from Guangdong has also helped to bridge the emerging domestic market economy with the international economic environment.

Industry

Industrial Structure

Before 1949, the Guangdong economy was characterized by its richness in agricultural endowment, its craft industries, its historical external relations and its trading activities. Mao Zedong's economic policy has dominated the economic development of the province. Grain production was placed at top priority. Under the price control and procurement system, capital accumulation was not possible. In the thirty-five years before 1978, Guangdong remained a poor and backward province. Under the industrial policy which emphasized heavy industry, Guangdong established a number of state-owned enterprises such as iron and steel, petroleum and chemical, and textiles before the 1980s. The development of tertiary industry was suppressed, especially that related to foreign trade. The Canton Trade Fair being held twice a year was the major meeting point of China traders and the specialized trading companies of the Ministry of Foreign Economic Relations and Trade.

Aiming at the building of a socialist state modelled after the former Soviet Union, China, for thirty years after 1949, pushed through collectivization and increase in the weight of state-owned enterprises. At the latter stage of the Cultural Revolution, China claimed that 97% of the economy was collectivized or nationalized. Before the launch of the economic reform policy, Guangdong also followed the direction of developing agriculture and heavy industry. It was not surprising that the policy had not brought about economic prosperity, and the well-being of the people suffered.

During the First Five-year Plan, mechanical machinery was heavily invested. It surpassed the textile industry and became the largest industry in Guangzhou. It was intended that Guangzhou could be restructured from a commercial centre into a self-sufficient industrial base of southern China. To fulfil this objective, a group of heavy industries were built during the Great Leap Forward, such as iron and steel, metallurgy, chemical, coal, machinery, electrical, textile, etc. The steel industry was regarded as a key industry for development. Many collective industrial plants were nationalized to be state-owned enterprises. Rural labour was sent to the industrial plants to speed up industrial production. Yet, the movement did not bring about higher productivity but caused an increased burden in labour costs in the industrial sector. As a result, many state-owned enterprises suffered financial losses.

In 1962, China readjusted her economic policy and Guangdong re-emphasized the development of light industries and reversed her industrial structure in the order of agriculture, light and heavy industries. The under-employed labourers were sent to the countryside to reduce labour costs of state-owned enterprises in the cities. The readjustment was effective and many state-owned enterprises became profitable.

The Cultural Revolution in the mid-1960s brought the industrial sector of Guangdong into demise. Iron and steel was the key industry again. Guangdong was required to build a complete industrial system as the major sector in the economy. The authority of managers was challenged and the Chinese Communist Party (CCP) unit set up in the plant was in command with the support of workers and the army. Agricultural and industrial labour exchanged their posts for political purposes in the movement. Production ground to a halt and management was in chaos. In 1969, industrial production recovered again as the political situation was relatively stabilized. The trend could not last long because of the disruption caused by the rise of the Gang of Four. By 1976, the Chinese economy had almost collapsed in the political turmoil.

By the end of 1978, the Chinese government adopted economic reform and open policy and called for a reversal of the order of the industrial structure: agriculture came first, followed by light and heavy industry. Consumption was encouraged and the proportion of forced capital accumulation through price-control gradually relaxed.

The contracting system in the rural sector successfully increased productivity and released abundant labour from farming. This rural labour was channelled to develop industrial production, trading and services activities in their hometowns. These people were pioneers of manufacturing and services industries of the rural sector in Guangdong, leading to changes in the industrial structure of the economy. The stages of development are reflected by the relative importance of the primary, secondary and tertiary sectors in the composition of the gross domestic product (GDP) of Guangdong province (Table 6.1).

Collective ownership was encouraged in the economic reform and the development of small-sized private business was allowed in certain business areas. By the end of the 1980s, the gross output value of collective and private enterprises had surpassed that of state enterprises (Table 6.2).

The changes can be explained by the success in agricultural reform and the associated increase in household income level and strong purchasing power for consumer goods, such as garments, shoes and the like. The proportion of light industry in total industrial output has increased significantly from 57.3% in 1978 to 66.1% in 1994 in Guangdong.

The average annual growth rates of gross industrial output of

Table 6.1   **Percentage Composition of Gross Domestic Product of Guangdong**

Year	Primary	Secondary	Tertiary
1949	60.1	12.9	27.0
1952	48.7	22.7	28.6
1957	49.2	24.9	25.9
1962	42.9	32.0	25.1
1965	42.9	32.0	25.1
1970	39.3	39.4	21.3
1975	30.8	45.5	23.7
1978	29.9	46.4	23.7
1980	33.8	41.1	25.1
1985	31.1	40.8	28.1
1989	26.8	40.3	32.9
1990	26.1	39.9	34.0
1992	20.3	45.9	33.8
1994	16.4	50.5	33.1

Source: *Guangdong tongji nianjian 1995* (Statistical Yearbook of Guangdong 1995).

Table 6.2   **Gross Industrial Output and Ownership**

Year	Industry (%)		Ownership (%)				Gross output* (RMB million)
	Light	Heavy	State	Collective	Others (e.g. private)	Co-op, village	
1949	87.6	12.4	59.6	—	—	40.4	7.58
1952	87.6	12.4	69.4	0.9	—	30.6	14.95
1957	82.1	17.9	69.0	20.1	—	10.9	31.89
1962	76.7	23.3	71.9	22.9	—	5.3	39.64
1965	71.5	28.5	76.7	18.2	—	5.0	64.17
1970	64.8	35.2	75.8	20.7	—	3.4	104.46
1975	60.8	39.2	71.9	25.0	—	3.2	157.17
1978	57.3	42.7	67.8	26.1	—	6.1	199.65
1980	63.0	37.0	63.1	27.6	1.9	7.3	234.35
1985	67.5	32.5	52.5	30.5	4.6	12.4	505.08
1989	68.7	31.3	37.5	28.6	17.2	16.6	1221.90
1990	69.3	31.0	39.3	24.5	19.9	12.3	1430.80
1992	67.3	32.7	32.5	22.3	27.8	17.4	3352.80
1994	66.1	33.9	17.6	18.8	37.5	26.1	6219.87

Source: *Guangdong tongji nianjian 1995.*
* Gross output 1949–1970 at 1957 constant price; gross output 1975–1980 at 1970
  constant price; gross output 1985–1990 at 1980 constant price; gross output 1992–
  1994 at 1990 constant price.

Guangzhou in periods based on the breakdown of policy changes since 1949 are as follows:

1949–1959:   26.48%;
1959–1969:   3.62%;
1969–1979:   8.85%;
1979–1988:   13.42%; and
1989–1994:   20.77%.

The changes in the industrial structure and the correlative average annual growth rates of gross industrial output have taught the Chinese government a lesson. To speed up economic growth, there should be more economic freedom. It also showed that the economy has grown faster as industrial policy placed emphasis on light industry instead of heavy industry.

Industrial Policy under Economic Reform Programme

In July 1979, Guangdong and Fujian were granted "special policy and flexible measures" to go "one step ahead" of the other provinces in the reform programme and open policy. The objectives were to build a mixed economy with more freedom for local collectives and private enterprises. Under the budget constraint, it was unrealistic to rely on the central government to provide capital for development. In addition to domestic investment, Guangdong could utilize foreign capital in the forms of joint ventures, industrial processing and sole ownership by foreign investors to stimulate economic growth. In other words, Guangdong was given more autonomy to build an export-oriented economy which could respond to market changes.

The influx of industrial processing from Hong Kong in the early 1980s relieved the problem of unemployment arising from agricultural reform in Guangdong and brought about high income to the region. By the end of 1990, there were more than 13,000 firms using foreign capital, and employing more than three million workers in factories. Private enterprises also flourished under the relatively favourable environment. They were limited in number and scale through the control of licensing and tax assessment. Many of them had to disguise themselves as co-operatives or collective enterprises. As a result, the policy has changed the proportion of output between the planned and market sectors (Table 6.3).

In 1994, the industrial output value for state-owned, collective and

Table 6.3   Industrial Output Value by Ownership in Guangdong

Year	State-owned		Collective		Others	
	Number of establish-ments	Output (RMB million)	Number of establish-ments	Output (RMB million)	Number of establish-ments	Output (RMB million)
1978	6,034	13,541	15,178	5,215	—	1,209
1980	5,654	14,792	16,720	6,479	—	2,164
1985	5,717	26,513	17,768	15,428	394	8,567
1990	6,886	50,125	20,641	38,044	2,877	54,911
1992	6,927	108,863	20,587	74,930	4,654	93,120
1994	6,342	109,742	21,890	116,720	9,607	233,123

Source: *Guangdong tongji nianjian 1995.*

other enterprises were RMB110 billion, RMB117 billion and RMB233 billion, respectively. Total fixed capital investments in the three categories were RMB164 billion, RMB28 billion and RMB22 billion, respectively, in the same year. The state enterprises were heavily invested, yet the total output value of collective and private enterprises have out-stripped state enterprises.

Employment in the Industrial Sector

In 1994, total employment in the industrial sector accounted for 33.6% of the labour force, producing RMB214 billion of value-added, or about 50% of Guangdong's GDP (Tables 6.3 and 6.4). The growth of the industrial sector in terms of employment and output value in the years of economic reform signified the process of industrialization and urbanization in the province.

Table 6.4   Employment in Guangdong

Year	Primary (%)	Secondary (%)	Tertiary (%)	Total number of workers ('000)
1975	78.8	11.0	10.2	21,538.7
1980	70.6	16.8	12.5	23,677.8
1985	60.1	21.1	18.7	27,311.1
1990	52.7	24.9	22.4	31,181.0
1992	47.4	30.4	22.2	33,672.1
1994	42.3	33.6	24.1	34,931.5

Source: *Guangdong tongji nianjian, 1994 and 1995.*

The emergence of foreign and private enterprises also caused significant changes in the size and structure of the labour market in Guangdong. According to *Guangdong xiangzhen*,[1] employment in the urban industrial sector in 1990 was 3.3 million. State enterprises employed 1.8 million workers and the other 1.5 million worked for collective and private enterprises. Of the 22.7 million workers employed in the rural sector, about 6.6 million were engaged in industrial production in local non-state enterprises or joint ventures. About 1.2 million workers were imported labour from other provinces.

In 1994, there were 5.7 million and 4.9 million labourers engaged in the secondary and tertiary sectors, respectively, accounted for 42.5% of the 24.9 million rural labour force.

Location of Industry

Light industries such as food and beverage, electronic equipment, electrical machinery and textile products are mainly operating in the Pearl River Delta. Most of these products are exported. Proximity to Hong Kong is one of the major considerations in investment, especially for foreign investors. Industrial policy adopted by local authorities and the availability of infrastructure are important in the development of their industrial sector (Table 6.5).

The open-door strategy for development also favoured the Pearl River Delta and the coastal areas. The three SEZs in the province, namely Shenzhen, Zhuhai and Shantou are coastal cities. Other than the advantage in location, the local governments of these SEZs were granted more autonomy and investors enjoyed lower tax rates or tax exemptions. In order to attract foreign capital, local authorities have been competing in offering preferential treatment in areas bearing the names of Economic and Technology Development Zones, Bonded Areas of imported raw materials for processing and Free Trade Zones.

The objective of this strategy is to provide a better environment for economic take-off in these areas. When economic development has started, the local government will have better access to capital for the construction of infrastructure. In turn, the improved infrastructure will further attract more foreign and local industrial investment.

The strategy has been successful in initiating economic growth in the Pearl River Delta and the coastal areas. When local authorities are competing for more foreign investment, they have to be more efficient and

Table 6.5   Major Industries in Guangdong, 1994

Industry	Establishments		Output		Employment		Major concentration
	Number	%	RMB million	%	Number ('000)	%	
Electronic and communication equipment	1,631	4.3	62,157	13.5	269.8	7.7	Shenzhen
Electrical machinery and equipment	1,671	4.4	46,745	10.2	215.0	6.1	Foshan
Textiles	1,871	4.9	32,602	7.1	244.6	7.0	Jiangmen
Clothing & fibre products	3,536	9.3	27,340	5.9	298.6	8.5	Guangzhou
Non-metallic mineral products	2,939	7.8	25,255	5.5	249.7	7.1	Foshan
Chemical raw material and products	1,503	4.0	24,692	5.4	153.8	4.4	Guangzhou
Metal products	2,650	7.0	20,742	4.5	151.2	4.3	Foshan
Transportation equipment	1,233	3.3	19,007	4.1	118.0	3.4	Guangzhou
Plastic products	1,982	5.2	18,625	4.1	109.9	3.1	Foshan
Food processing	963	2.5	17,957	3.9	140.0	4.0	Zhanjiang
Others	17,860	47.3	164,484	35.8	1,562.6	44.4	—
Total	37,839	100.0	459,606	100.0	3,513.2	100.0	

Source: *Guangdong tongji nianjian 1995.*

thus reducing the transaction costs for investors in the negotiation of contract, the establishment of business organization and the operation in production.

The choice of investment location in China by foreign investors has been affected by the relaxation of regulatory control of the government. As local authorities compete for a better investment environment through deregulation, an institutional set-up for market economy has emerged gradually. Other than competition as an endogenous force for evolution, foreign capital-invested firms in Guangdong have become an exogenous force for reform in the process of transferring management knowhow to local Chinese management personnel.

Management of State-owned Enterprises

Guangdong started its experiment of enterprise reform in 1979 by giving more autonomy to the management in decision-making and paying bonus from retained excessive profits in 179 large and medium-sized enterprises. In 1980, eight enterprises started the experiment of a "tax-for-profit" scheme. Under such a scheme, an enterprise paid a certain amount of tax, which was agreed between the enterprise and its control unit. The excess profit was retained by the enterprise. In 1981, the management contracting system was widely adopted in the province.

State-owned enterprises implemented the "tax-for-profit" scheme as the second stage of reform in 1984. Many local governments implemented a management contracting system, accompanied by a mixture of permanent and contract labour systems, and a manager responsibility system fixing the term of appointment. By September 1984, 81.1% of the state enterprises within the budgetary sector had adopted the management responsibility system.[2] In the management responsibility system, profits in excess of the remitted profit target would be distributed among the enterprise, the government and the control unit.

The success of using a bonus system for incentive stimulation depends on the shares distributed among different parties and the formula for calculation. In the assignment of target, many followed a past-performance principle, which means those efficient enterprises would have a larger increment in remitted profits in the coming year and those with a poor performance would enjoy subsidies from the government budget. Yet, many of them have suffered from the burden of pension payment to retired workers or loss due to price control.

In order to improve performance of the state-owned enterprises, China has launched, in 1992, a nation-wide enterprise reform by separating state-owned enterprises from the bureaucracy and giving more autonomy to managers. New measures have been implemented in 1996 to overhaul the state-owned sector.

Large and Medium-sized State Enterprises

By the end of 1990, Guangdong had 697 large and medium-sized enterprises, which employed 761,600 workers and received RMB48 billion sales income. Yet, these state enterprises paid up to half of their total revenue to the government. In 1990, these enterprises recorded a 3.63% increase in revenue, much lower than the growth rate of the overall economy. Profits and tax submission had decreased by 22.97%. Among these enterprises, 36.45% of their accounts were in the red.[3] The inefficiency of the state enterprises was the result of institutional problems.

Firstly, many state enterprises committed the mistake of over-expansion. For example, Guangzhou Petrochemical Works, a petrochemical complex constructed in the 1970s, was expanded during the Seventh Five-year Plan with RMB1.4 billion bank loans. The debt had to be paid back within the next five years. Due to market fluctuation and tax increases, like many of these state enterprises, it encountered a very tight financial situation.

Guangzhou Weaving Mills, a state enterprise with over 8,000 workers, is another example. The plant was over-expanded in the 1980s. It was estimated that the capacity for textile production doubled what was required.

Secondly, many enterprises were set up in wrong locations and invested in wrong directions. They suffered from the previous industrial policy which assumed that strategic heavy industries could speed up economic growth and strategic locations should be selected for defence consideration. Guangzhou Petrochemical Works is located far away from a deep water port through which crude oil from northern China is shipped. The enterprise is planning to build a harbour in Shenzhen in order to import its crude oil directly so as to lessen the cost of transportation. Guangzhou Iron and Steel Mills, another huge state enterprise, has the same transportation problem for iron ore.

As a remedy to the mistaken investments in the past, these state enterprises seek to diversify their business with their retained profits and assets in activities such as restaurants, hotels and property development. Others seek to expand their production in the existing business by forming joint ventures with foreign investors.

Without a market for capital goods and the lack of flexibility in employment contract, enterprises which were over-invested during the economic boom failed to respond to market changes. These enterprises were plagued by cumulated stock and excess capital equipment. Yet, they have to pay for bank loans and wages for the workers who were under-employed. The losses turned into further subsidies from the government budget.

Another cause of economic inefficiency in state enterprises was market distortion under government controls, such as price and credit controls. The general manager of Guangzhou Iron and Steel Mills argued that if the price control on steel were relieved, its accounts would be in surplus instead of in the red. State enterprise managers also complained that state enterprises suffered from price increases and cancellation of a guaranteed supply of raw material for production. At the same time, their remittance in profits, various types of taxes and charges to the government and control units were increasing.

The state-ownership raised the principal-agency problem that various government departments become stewards and the plant management personnel become agents.[4] There are also conflicts of interest between the management and workers in the internal industrial organization. The management wants to fulfil the output target without taking the additional responsibility of commercial risks. Both managerial personnel and workers are averse to taking risks and prefer higher immediate bonuses, fringe benefits and a retirement scheme.

The accelerating profit and tax remission scheme based on past performance also failed to enhance performance of state enterprises. In the management contracting system, there was a mark-up on total profit of the previous year in the calculation of remitted profit and tax of the coming year. In some localities, both base figures and rates of increment were fixed to provide better incentives for the management and workers to improve productivity.

State enterprises in Guangdong were also caught by the "triangular debt" problem, or the debt chains. There are two main types of debt chains. The first type happened in the investment on infrastructure projects. During the period of austerity, without a financial market, many ongoing projects failed to meet the repayment schedule due to delay in completion. The second type was due to the lack of an institutional structure to enforce commercial contracts signed among enterprises. When a firm was in financial difficulties and breached the contract, there was no clause nor mechanism to protect the creditors, nor was there a contingency plan to keep the project on the move. Many of these debts have involved government departments at different levels and their state enterprises. People could only wait for a recovery of the economy.

The "triangular debt" problem of state enterprises in Guangdong, however, has not been too serious in comparison with those of other provinces. Firstly, the economy is export-oriented. Secondly, Guangdong has more informal channels access to the financial market. Thirdly, businessmen in Guangdong are more prudent and profit-oriented.

The adjustment for the improvement in management mechanism

through a shareholding system was proposed, discussed and implemented. Yet, so far there is no simple solution to the problem.

Horizontal Economic Integration

In 1984, China encouraged horizontal economic integration by forming consortia as a means to attain economies of scale, build up vertical integration, reduce risk by diversification, benefit from synergy and use financial resources more fruitfully. Most important of all, it could cut off the control of government bureaucracy and allow more autonomy for the enterprises. By the end of 1986, over 3,000 consortia were formed. They built up contractual links in different ways, and for different purposes, with firms in the same line of production or in diversified industries.

In a centrally planned economy, all enterprises are units of account instead of separate entities and all transactions are internally determined under the controlled units. Managers of state enterprises are bureaucrats who are risk-averse and aim at output maximization. The forming of consortia in China cannot be interpreted as a process of internalization in the literature of vertical integration, but rather a process of externalization under the economic reform programme.[5] Under the Chinese enterprise reform, the contract management system, the managerial responsibility system and the internal contract system turned state enterprises into semi-autonomous units within a planned hierarchy. Managers have to fulfil the remitted profit and tax target as well as output target. After price and market reforms, they lost the protection of raw material supply and guaranteed market channel. They have to perform as managers of firms under the market economy, i.e. minimization of production and transaction costs and maximization of profit. Yet, the market as an institution which provides both physical facilities, information channels and legal framework cannot be built in one day. It has to emerge gradually as a result of changes in institutions and organizations. The reform without a market environment left the business of state enterprises in uncertainty. As obligatory market contracting was not reliable, enterprises were keen to form groups which indicated contracting of various forms. Some of them arranged loose and short-term supply contract for raw materials, parts and products. Others tried to build up integration in production, marketing and financing. Contracts among members in the consortia provided substitution to state planning and distribution channels.

Another explanation of the rapid increase in the number of consortia was government policy. The central government emphasized that consortia should have more autonomy in decision-making. The controlled bureaucracy could not interfere in their business decisions. The management of consortia could have more freedom and preferential treatment in diversifying their business, thus spreading their risk in the volatile market environment.

Because of economies of scale, many of these consortia had lower average costs, diversified risk and higher profit, and played an important role in large projects such as property development and investment in infrastructure.

As the market environment changed, contractual relations among the firms had to be adjusted. In 1989, many of these consortia suffered from recession and many of them have since dissolved. Some of them have diversified their investment. They did not succeed in fulfilling the expectation of the Chinese leaders who would like to see conglomerates being built and their business competitive in the world market.

Township and Village Industries

In 1994, Guangdong had 1,457,500 rural enterprises, known as *xiang-zhen qiye* or township and village enterprises (TVEs).[6] Gross output has an average annual growth of 48% since 1990 and reached RMB352.6 billion (Table 6.6). In 1994, rural industrial output accounted for 44% of the total industrial output of Guangdong, which indicates the degree of in-dustrialization of the rural sector in the province (Table 6.7).

Of the gross output value, township and village owned enterprises produced 67.2% while private and co-operative owned enterprises produced 32.7% (Table 6.6). More than 6 million surplus rural workers joined the industrial sector. Because of the restriction on residential per-mits, migration to cities was limited. Yet, industrial labour in the rural area has doubled that in the urban area.

In 1990 about 16,700 of the TVEs were export-oriented, employing 1.42 million manufacturing workers in the rural areas. Their total export value reached RMB12,746 million and foreign exchange earning was US$2,674 million, or 25.3% of the total exports of Guangdong province. The contribution of foreign exchange earnings among domestic enterprises, intermediate processing and joint venture exports were 41%, 32% and 27%, respectively.

The market-oriented rural industrial sector has invested mainly in light

Table 6.6   Township and Village Enterprises in Guangdong, 1994

Ownership	Township	Village	Co-operative	Private	Total
No. of establishments	27.4	106.3	66.3	1,257.5	1,457.5
('000)	(1.9)	(7.3)	(4.5)	(86.3)	(100.0)
No. of employees	2,180.5	3,279.6	705.1	4,000.9	10,166.1
('000)	(21.4)	(32.3)	(6.9)	(39.4)	(100.0)
Total revenue	131.7	105.0	24.3	94.9	355.9
(RMB billion)	(37.0)	(29.5)	(6.8)	(26.7)	(100.0)
Gross output value	137.4	99.6	25.1	90.4	352.6
(RMB billion)	(39.0)	(28.2)	(7.1)	(25.6)	(100.0)

Source: *Guangdong tongji nianjian 1995.*
Note: Figures in brackets are percentages.

Table 6.7   Rural Economy of Guangdong, 1994

(Unit: RMB billion)

Gross output	Guangdong	Rural	%
Gross output	1,071.36	471.19	44.0
Gross industrial output	621.99	273.84	44.0

Source: *Guangdong tongji nianjian 1995.*

industries. The major products in terms of output value are electrical machinery (13.56%), non-metal mineral products (9.44%), clothing (8.62%), metal products (8.60%) and plastics (5.59%). There has been a trend of diversification over the past few years.

Property Rights and Management of TVEs

Most of the TVEs are under collective ownership. They are invested by the local district, county, town and village governments. Managers are mainly local people selected by the officials in charge. Most of them adopt a fixed contracting system. The enterprises are entitled to residual claims in the forms of bonuses, housing, expenses and capital for expansion and investment.

With limited support from the central government, Guangdong has successfully built a few large enterprises at the township level. The production of electrical appliances in Shunde is widely known. Refrigerators produce accounted for over 40% of China's domestic market. Production of electric fans also occupied more than half of the domestic and overseas markets. Many of these successful enterprises have adopted modern managerial technique. Under the import-substitution policy, they were given quotas for importing major body and parts for the processing and assembly of their products. The value added was reported to be about 10% of the product value. As income per capita in the Pearl River Delta increased, their sales went up dramatically. When the local market was saturated, markets in northern China were emerging and spreading.

These TVEs have also successfully improved their management. The general manager of an enterprise is given full responsibility and autonomy in decision-making on investment, employment of workers, distribution of retained profits, forming joint ventures with foreign investors and market development.

Similar to state enterprises, property rights in the TVEs are not clearly defined. Yet the relationship between the local authority and the firm is so close that the officials in charge can monitor the performance of the firm effectively. The supervisory officials share with the management the residual claims by appointing people whom they trust. As these enterprises grow in scale, the monitor costs increase and become ineffective.

Most of the workers in the TVEs are employed in contract term. It allows more flexibility in adjustment. In the survey of TVEs, it was found that those employing local workers adopted the same labour system as state enterprises. They provided housing, education and medical subsidies and amenities to employees, and the old pension system was implemented. In the future, they may face the same problems of state enterprises if the problem of property rights is not resolved.

Some rural enterprises have started to explore the possibility of setting up a shareholding system. The local government and other organizations will be major shareholders. They have to reach an agreement on how profits and responsibilities are shared. It is not an easy task, for example, to define property rights among shareholders for historical reasons. An enterprise owned by a local and a state enterprise received a piece of land free many years ago, but shareholders could dispute the sharing of the assets value developed on that piece of land.

Private Enterprises

Individual businesses (*getihu*) in Guangdong have emerged since 1984. In

1988, Interim Regulations Governing Private Enterprises in the PRC was implemented. The difference between an individual business and a private enterprise is the size of the firm in terms of the number of employees and requirements on registration, accounting and management systems, and taxation. These two make up the private economy of Guangdong.

In Guangdong, many private businessmen choose to register their enterprises as collective enterprises. In Foshan, there were 458 private enterprises registered as collective enterprises, which accounted for 32.2% of total TVEs in the area in 1988.[7] It is a common phenomenon in Guangdong for several reasons.

Firstly, individual business firms are required to pay average tax at RMB500 to RMB800, which is about 1% of sales revenue, while private enterprises have to pay RMB5,000 to RMB10,000, or 35% of total revenue as corporate income tax. Collective enterprises may enjoy two to three years of tax holidays.

Secondly, collective enterprises may avoid political risk since they are regarded as being in the socialist economic domain.

Thirdly, there is no restriction in the organization or management of collective enterprises. By contrast, private enterprises are under the strict supervision of government. They have to comply with regulations of the accounting system, the proportion of wage and reinvestment fund in distribution. Private enterprises also face difficulties in getting bank loans. Collective enterprises may receive preferential treatment in management charges in addition to tax remission. There are limitations on the number of workers employed in individual and private businesses. Collective enterprises are allowed flexibility in employing workers.

Many private enterprises in Guangdong accept orders for industrial processing from foreign investors. Registration as collective enterprises provides better credibility in negotiation with foreign investors. It is easier for collective enterprises to obtain import permits of raw material and equipment for industrial processing than private enterprises.

Local governments prefer to put private enterprises under collective ownership. It is politically secure in reporting to higher authority. Collective enterprises are more stable and easier to monitor.

If we count one-third of the collective enterprises as privately owned, the industrial output value of private enterprises reaches 59% of the total in Guangdong. This may serve as an indicator of the degree of privatization of the industrial sector of the economy.

The tax reform which aims at the elimination of preferential treatment and the plan to cut tariffs for imports may have significant impacts on the organization and management of collective and private enterprises in Guangdong.

Foreign Trade and Investment

Export Trade

The export data show that Guangdong has been very successful in expanding its exports, both by domestic firms and foreign investors since the open policy was adopted (Table 6.8). In the past twelve years, total exports and exports by firms with foreign capital, including export processing, compensation trade and *sanzi qiye* (three types of enterprises with foreign capital), have recorded annual growth in average by 19% and 47%, respectively. With the high growth rates in export trade, Guangdong has maintained trade surplus over the years. In 1994, exports by firms involved foreign capital reached US$32,029 million, which accounted for 68% of Guangdong's total exports.

Table 6.8   Foreign Trade of Guangdong

Year	Total export (US$ million)	Annual growth rate (%)	Export by foreign investors (US$ million)	Annual growth rate (%)	Total import (US$ million)	Annual growth rate (%)
1978	1,387.55	20.0	1.16	—	203.90	67.4
1980	2,194.72	29.0	88.98	—	356.12	46.6
1985	2,952.67	18.7	502.36	—	2,426.00	117.2
1986	4,290.00	45.3	752.00	49.7	2,625.00	8.2
1987	5,444.00	26.9	913.59	21.5	3,627.75	7.6
1988	7,483.83	37.5	1,605.10	75.7	5,110.18	40.9
1989	8,167.67	9.1	2,917.55	81.8	4,831.21	−9.0
1990	10,560.24	29.3	4,384.93	50.3	5,748.88	19.0
1991	13,687.87	29.6	6,222.26	41.9	8,510.09	48.0
1992	18,439.54	34.7	9,225.08	48.7	11,179.23	31.4
1993	20,419.00	10.7	11,324.12	22.36	14,843.00	32.7
	27,026.83*		16,793.76*		19,898.61*	
1994	46,992.70	73.9	32,029.20	90.72	34,270.25	72.2

Source: *Guangdong tongji nianjian*, various issues.
* Data after 1993 based on gross export value instead of processing fee for *sanlaiyibu* (compensation trade).

Hong Kong alone handled 83.3% of the US$46,992 million exports of Guangdong in 1994. Export value produced by domestic firms was US$14,963 million, or 31.8% of the total. That means Hong Kong investors handled all the products of industrial intermediate processing, compensation trade, and joint ventures plus 70% of outputs by domestic firms. In other words, domestic industrial and trading firms in Guangdong have limited access to international markets. Since Guangdong was given autonomy in foreign trade, exporting firms of the province and their branches in Hong Kong have been involved in transactions of 71.87% of its total exports. The major exporting cities are Guangzhou, Shenzhen, Shantou, Foshan, Jiangmen, Zhongshan, Zhuhai, Dongguan, Zhanjiang and Zhaoqing. They are either located in the Pearl River Delta or the SEZs which have close links with Hong Kong. The Pearl River Delta and the three SEZs account for 76% and 25.8% of total exports, respectively. Obviously, Hong Kong and Guangdong have integrated with each other in capital formation, production, marketing and exports of manufactured products.

Other markets for Guangdong's exports include the United States of America, Japan, Taiwan and Germany. Again, export markets are highly concentrated (Table 6.9).

Table 6.9   Domestic Exports by Major Countries and Regions

(Unit: US$ million)

Country/Region	1986	1988	1990	1992	1994
Hong Kong	2,954.61	5,724.84	8,543.10	15,558.25	39,159.30
USA	283.58	326.41	402.97	778.30	2,441.97
Japan	103.81	262.31	288.20	473.40	1,302.51
Taiwan	—	0.56	8.95	62.62	797.73
Germany	71.33	109.43	117.01	128.50	422.07
Macau	133.40	142.24	166.01	236.21	298.02
UK	33.11	63.05	46.15	110.65	252.34
Singapore	84.00	36.81	139.74	146.39	221.33
France	27.22	44.54	44.72	89.62	168.22
Australia	15.98	28.43	38.18	64.21	137.03

Source: *Guangdong tongji nianjian*, 1987–1995.

Forms of Foreign Investment

Foreign investment in the first ten years of economic reform and open policy had close links with the export trade. Yet, the domestic market was not open to foreign investors. The classification of foreign investments was related to contractual relations and choice of organization under all kinds of formal and informal constraints. Both Chinese and foreign parties would choose investment contracts which could reduce production and transaction costs, yielding higher economic rent under the over-regulated economic institutions. For example, an investor could choose leasing instead of constructing a plant in order to bypass the inefficiency of the bureaucracy and complication in negotiation (Table 6.10). The three types of enterprises with foreign capital (equity joint venture, contractual joint venture and sole foreign ownership) are over-stated in capital value and output,[8] and their significance in exchange earning and technology transfer, while compensation trade and industrial processing are under-stated. There is no proof that equity joint ventures are using higher technology than processing of manufacturing products by importing machinery and raw materials.

Table 6.10   Forms of Actualized Foreign Investment

(Unit: US$ million)

Form of investment	1985	1989	1990	1992	1994
External loans	289.60	1,075.91	441.32	1,157.21	1,983.21
Foreign direct investment	515.29	1,156.44	1,459.84	3,551.50	9,397.08
Equity JV	171.63	564.38	645.63	1,300.46	3,600.08
Contractual JV	335.15	425.32	453.15	1,376.94	3,694.60
Sole ownership	8.51	166.74	361.06	874.10	2,102.40
Other foreign investment	114.21	166.80	122.31	152.76	66.35
Compensation trade	30.56	71.69	69.11	91.31	25.04
Industrial processing	83.65	39.07	42.51	43.05	21.62
Leasing	—	56.04	10.69	18.40	19.69
Total investment	919.10	2,399.15	2,023.47	4,861.47	11,446.64

Sources: *Guangdongsheng duiwai jingji maoyi lüyou tongji ziliao* (see note 9 below).
                  Guangdong tongji nianjian, 1995.

Not until recently has a trend of investing in projects with longer term consideration and larger scale emerged. It reflects that there has been an improvement of the investment environment and people have more confidence in the economic reform and open policy. After 1992, China has moved to open the domestic market, including the tertiary sector for foreign investment. In the Pearl River Delta, property development has drawn billions of capital from Hong Kong since 1991. Many looked forward to the retail markets of the region. The diversification but not the form of investment would encourage the further transfer in technology and management knowledge.

Foreign Investment and the Domestic Economy

In 1994, US$6,764 million or 72% of US$9,397 million foreign capital was invested in manufacturing. Negotiated capital, however, has shifted to other sectors. As a result, only 49.4% was in manufacturing and the rest was in property and public utility (37.2%), commerce, restaurants and hotels, storage (6.9%), transport and communication (2.7%) and agriculture and fishery (1.5%). The change in direction of investment is the result of policy change regarding opening of the domestic market.

In 1990, a total of 5,218 enterprises with foreign investment were registered and 617,050 workers were employed. Enterprises of industrial intermediate processing and compensation trade reached 13,000 in the same year.[9]

Sources of foreign capital have been highly concentrated. About 82.6% of the actual investment capital came from Hong Kong, followed by Taiwan (5.6%), Macau (3.1%), USA (1.6%) and Japan (1.4%).

Since products manufactured by enterprises with foreign investment were not allowed to be sold in the domestic market until recently, the impact of foreign investment on the domestic market has been minimal. Yet, the employment structure has changed and people received higher incomes in the form of wage, service charge and economic rent paid by foreign firms. The changes brought about improvements in the standard of living, in consumption pattern and in the structure of the economy. Restrictions were imposed on firms in their nature of business, product variation, imports of raw materials and sales on the domestic market, especially for foreign firms. As a result, many state-owned and collective firms which have been granted exclusive rights to run protected business thus enjoyed the privilege of earning monopolistic profits. Since China adopted the strategy of joining World Trade Organization (WTO), the protective trade policy has been phasing out and replaced by a relatively open and competitive market environment. The move has provided new opportunities for foreign investors who are interested in tapping the China market.

Foreign investment has provided a great impetus for economic reforms in the province. Foreign investors choose locations which provide an environment with the lowest production and transaction costs. In order to compete with the neighbouring regions, Guangdong has to lower the transaction costs by improving its investment environment further. The development of bonded processing zones is an example. Investors may import processing material without tariff clearance. It has lowered the cost of working capital and simplified administrative procedure for foreign investors.

Conclusion

Guangdong is the province which has benefited most from the economic reform and open policy. With the influx of capital, mainly from Hong Kong, in the forms of industrial processing and joint ventures, the industrial and employment structures of the province have changed drastically. Most important of all, foreign investment has generated capital for domestic industrial growth, especially in the Pearl River Delta. The interaction of foreign investment as an exogenous factor and market reform as an endogenous factor in Guangdong, has materialized Deng Xiaoping's economic development objectives.

The spatial development of industrial production has led to the rapid economic transformation and urbanization of the rural area. As a result, domestic markets have emerged and become mature. The improved market environment has further made capital available for the development of infrastructure, the tertiary sector, and land and property markets. Industrialization in Guangdong is characterized by the growth of enterprises which are collectively or privately owned. Their output value has increased much faster than that of the state enterprises which have been struggling for higher productivity and economic efficiency, with all preferential treatments granted and more fixed capital investment from the government. It indicates that the success of economic reform comes from marketization and the emergence of a free enterprise system, not from the improvement of state-owned enterprises and economic planning.

Over the past sixteen years, foreign investment and trade have been highly correlated due to the policy of protectionism. The outward oriented economic activities have also served as a catalyst for economic growth and reform in Guangdong. If China resumes her membership in WTO under the conditions of reducing trade barriers and opening the domestic market for international market competition, further transformation of Guangdong's industrial structure and external trading pattern is foreseeable.

Notes

1. Guangdongsheng nongye weiyuanhui ji Guangzhoushi shehuikexueyuan (ed.), *Guangdong xiangzhen* (Guangdong Villages and Towns) (Guangzhou: Guangdong renmin chubanshe, 1990).
2. Guangdong gaige kaifang gaohuo lilun yantaohui lunwenji bianxuanzu (ed.), *Guangdong gaige kaifang yanjiu* (Research on Economic Reform and Opening in Guangdong) (Guangzhou: Guangdong renmin chubanshe, 1988), pp. 192–93.
3. Based on an unpublished report of Guangdong Provincial People's Congress, 1992.
4. David Granick, *Chinese State Enterprises* (Chicago: The University of Chicago Press, 1990), chapter 2.
5. A. Ben-Ner and E. Neuberger, "Towards an Economic Theory of the Firm in the Centrally Planned Economy," *Journal of Institutional and Theoretical Economics*, No. 144 (1988), pp. 839–48.
6. Guangdongsheng nongye weiyuanhui ji Guangzhoushi shehuikexueyuan (ed.), *Guangdong xiangzhen* (see note 1), p. 26.
7. Le Chaopei and Zheng Yanchao (eds.), *Guangdong siying jingji yanjiu* (Private Economy in Guangdong) (Beijing: Zhongguo jingji chubanshe, 1989), p. 164.
8. P. W. Liu, Y. W. Sung, Richard Y. C. Wong and P. K. Lau, *China's Economic Reform and Development Strategy of Pearl River Delta* (Hong Kong: Nanyang Commercial Bank Ltd., 1992), pp. 21–24.
9. Guangdongsheng tongjiju (ed.), *Guangdongsheng duiwai jingji maoyi lüyou tongji ziliao 1990* (Guangdong's External Economic, Trade and Tourism Statistical Data, 1990), p. 232; Zeng Muye (ed.), *Yanhai xinchao yu Guangdong gaige* (Coastal New Trend and Reform in Guangdong) (Guangzhou: Guangdong gaodeng jiaoyu chubanshe, 1989), p. 74.

7

Service Industries

Wong Kwan-yiu

Defining Service Industries

The term "service sector" is usually used synonymously with "tertiary sector," the latter being the term commonly employed in the Chinese context (*disan chanye*). However, there is no internationally agreed definition of what constitutes the service sector. According to the United Nations,[1] through its International Standard Industrial Classification (ISIC), the tertiary (service) sector includes "commerce; transport, storage and communication; finance, insurance, real estate and business services; community, social and personal services." All other activities not adequately defined are also included in the tertiary sector. At the same time, the European Economic Community, through its Nomenclature des Activités Économiques dans les Communautées Européennes (NACE), devised another classification which is also quite commonly adopted. The NACE's definition of the tertiary sector is: "wholesale and retail trade and restaurants and hotels; transport, storage and communication; finance, insurance, real estate and business services; community, social and personal services."[2] The two definitions have many similarities except that the section on commerce is more clearly defined in the NACE case. Although there is still argument on the identity and delimitation of the service industries, it is not intended to follow up the discussion in this chapter. A full coverage of the debate can be found in published works such as Channon,[3] Daniels[4] and Riddle.[5] Both the ISIC and NACE will be used as the basic references in defining service industries here.

In China, statistical data offered usually include the following activities as part of the tertiary sector: transport and communication; commercial and restaurant business; material supply and sale (wholesale and retail), storage, real estate, public services, consultative services; health, sports and social welfare services; education, cultural and broadcasting services; scientific research and technical services; finance and insurance; government and party institutions, social organizations; and geological survey.[6] This is a longer list than that adopted in the ISIC or NACE. For the convenience of analysis, the approach taken in this chapter would be to use the Chinese definition when the tertiary sector is viewed at the aggregate level, and when discussing its growth and assessing its contribution to the economy of Guangdong are made as a whole. When detailed discussion is focused on individual aspects of the service industries, some adjustments will be made with reference to the ISIC and NACE classifications. Also, in order to avoid duplications with other chapters, certain service activities have to be left out of the discussion. After taking all these things into consideration, full analyses will be applied only to the commercial, restaurant, wholesale and retail business as well as hotels and leisure activities (including tourism).

Service Sector and Economic Development: Some Basic Concepts

It is probably important in the first instance to point out a general misconception that the growth of the service sector is a "post-industrial" development.[7] The expansion of the service industries is often associated with "industrialized" economies, not knowing that the service sector is as important, or even more important, to developing countries. In the latter case, economic growth, as fuelled by the manufacturing sector, is very much dependent on service provision such as transport and communication, a stable financial and capital market and a literate and technology-conscious workforce. Riddle[8] has studied the role of services in economic development in countries at four different levels of development, based on per capita income categories used by the World Bank in its *World Development Report* (that is, low income; lower-middle income; upper-middle income; and industrialized countries). The result shows that "there is not a clear dichotomy between developing and industrialized countries regarding the size of service sector."[9] Some of the newly industrializing economies (NIEs) are found to have larger service sectors than those of the industrialized nations. In fact, internal differences among the higher income and among the lower income categories are equally obvious. However, what has emerged from the analysis of statistics is that the service sector is by far the largest economic sector in virtually all countries, in terms of its contribution to gross domestic product (GDP), but not necessarily in terms of employment. Table 7.1 shows the percentage of GDP and employment in the primary, secondary and tertiary sectors by development categories (that is, from low income to industrialized countries), based on data from the International Labour Office and the United Nations in 1981. By the early 1980s when China fully implemented its open policy, the general world trend that the service sector has become the most important contributor to GDP to countries of all development categories in general had been established. In terms of employment in service industries, though, the difference between the low income and the industrialized nations was still large. But given the labour intensive nature of many service industries and the ability of the service sector to absorb excess work force, the increase in employment would be quite rapid once the development pace was set. What is perhaps the most important feature that has come out of Riddle's study is that China is the only country among the eighty odd nations investigated whose service sector's contribution to GDP is less than 35%. In other words, at the beginning of the 1980s, China lagged behind almost all other nations in the world in the growth of its service sector, in relation to its role in the economic development of the country concerned. This makes the study of China's service industries under the current open economic policy more important and meaningful.

Table 7.1   Contribution to GDP and Employment (%) by Economic Sectors, 1981

Economic sector	Development categories			
	Low income	Lower-middle	Upper-middle	Industrialized
GDP				
Extractive sector	42	27	15	7
Manufacturing sector	10	16	21	27
Services sector	48	57	64	66
Employment				
Extractive sector	72	53	25	9
Manufacturing sector	10	14	22	24
Services sector	18	33	53	67

Source: D. I. Riddle, "The Role of the Service Sector in Economic Development" (see note 8 below), p. 87.

One of the reasons for the underdevelopment of service industries in China, and in some other less developed countries also, is that the service sector is not often the target of comprehensive development planning. Even if service sector infrastructures were in place, they were usually poorly maintained, leading to the deterioration of the services. In case the development funding is coming from outside, development priorities are dictated by the funding agencies. Until recently, the World Bank and other assistance agencies still subscribe to the notion that development goes progressively from agriculture to manufacturing, with service sector development left to a post-industrial stage.

It is also important at this juncture to make a distinction between private and public provision of services. This is because since the end of World War II, a notable world trend in the growth of the service sector has been a rapid expansion in public sector employment,[10] for example in central government, local authorities and public corporations. Such expansion is related to demographic changes, to rising standards in the provision of education, social and community services, and to the extension of governmental activities (such as participation in international trade blocs or defence arrangements). In developing countries, it may be necessary for the public sector, in the interests of providing appropriate infrastructural services and utilities, to take the bulk of the responsibility for large areas of social and economic life. The consequence is, as exemplified in the case of India, a doubling of employment in public administration between 1957 and 1971.[11] However, it must be noted that excessive development of the public sector (public administration) or excessive public sector control may lead to inefficiency. A lack of governmental support services can hinder economic development, but an inefficient bureaucracy can also create unnecessary barriers. That is why there is a growing trend towards the "privatization" of many service industries, such as in transport, health care and waste disposal.

One final point on the general concept of services development that requires some elaboration is the international trade in services. Past discussions have focused too much on merchandise trade to the neglect of the dynamic portions of services trade. This "invisible" trade in services includes such components as tourism, transport, investment income, agents' fees, consultancy work and insurance. It has been estimated that such services accounted for about one-third of world trade in 1980.[12] It is for this reason that these items are included in the present chapter. What seems to be a matter of concern is that service exports are characteristic of the high-growth developed countries, whereas excessive dependency on imported services is characteristic of the low-growth developing nations. It has, therefore, been observed by many scholars that "effective development planning must include a strengthening of both domestic and international service sector — to reduce relative dependency on imported services while providing incentives for services export."[13] This is exactly the problem that China has to face in the development of its service sector. Due attention should be given to the exploitation of sources of comparative advantage that developing countries possess such as their geographical locations and natural endowments (for transportation and tourism services). Furthermore, an efficient infrastructure system (including telecommunications facilities) can potentially induce a comparative advantage in facilitating trade and attracting further domestic and foreign investments.

Development of the Tertiary Sector in Guangdong

The growth of the tertiary sector in Guangdong, and in fact in China as a whole, was very much related to the adoption of the open policy and economic reform in China since 1979. However, it was not until 1984, when the central government issued directives to push the growth of the service sector that significant progress was made. Guangdong, being one of the "most open" and economically developed provinces in China, has witnessed a much faster rate of growth in its tertiary industries than the national average, both in terms of its contribution to GDP and employment. In 1988, for example, the service sector accounted for 23.2% of the total labour force and 31.7% of the GDP of Guangdong, compared with 18.1% and 25.7%, respectively, for the nation as a whole. Before an attempt is made to discuss the characteristics of tertiary development in Guangdong, a couple of points need to be noted. Firstly, data for the service industries are very sketchy in China. In this chapter, they are almost exclusively drawn from the *Guangdong tongji nianjian*,[14] and when comparison is made with the national figures, from the *Zhongguo tongji nianjian*.[15] In view of the significant growth in the service sector since the adoption of the open policy, the State Department has undertaken a nationwide survey of the tertiary sector in 1993, providing some useful data as of the end of 1992. Secondly, it is common in China to categorize service provision into four levels:

1st level: circulation (transport, communication, commerce, etc.)

2nd level: producer services (for serving the production sector, including finance and insurance)

3rd level: services for the upgrading of the scientific and cultural level and the quality of life of its people (including welfare provision)

4th level: public services (public administration).

The first two levels of provision are usually affected by market mechanism, the supply of which is dependent on demand and profitability. The provision of the other two categories of services are less reliant on market factors, but rather on social needs. They are usually less profitable endeavours and as can be expected, are given less attention in the early stages of development. This means that there will be obvious differential growth rates among the different segments of the tertiary sector, resulting in an unbalanced structure. Such a phenomenon is quite typical in the Guangdong case.

An analysis of the data on the development of the tertiary sector in Guangdong during the last decade or so reveals certain salient characteristics:

1. In many developing countries, the growth of the service sector is often associated with the shift of the labour force away from the primary sector as a result of declining agricultural activities. Service industries, many of which can be labour-intensive, are considered to be capable of absorbing the excess labour displaced from primary production. This apparently is not the case in Guangdong. Table 7.2 shows the annual growth rate of population, labour force and employment in various economic sectors in Guangdong between 1975 and 1988. The expansion in secondary and tertiary sector employment (8.55% and 8.17%, respectively) far exceeded the rate of decline in the primary sector (0.28%). In terms of absolute figures, the total labour force in Guangdong increased by 8.88 million during the same period. The tertiary sector grew by 4.41 million while the decline in the primary sector was only 0.64 million. This means that the development of the services sector, in terms of employment, was associated with the expansion of the labour force as a whole rather than with a shift of workers from the primary sector. A rough calculation would indicate that about 93% of the tertiary sector employment growth is attributable to the expansion of the labour force and about 6% to workers released from primary production.[16] Thus, the growth of the tertiary industries in Guangdong is not at the expense of the agricultural sector.

Table 7.2   Average Annual Growth Rate in Guangdong, 1975–1988

Population	+1.55%
Labour force	+2.50%
Primary sector employment	–0.28%
Secondary sector employment	+8.55%
Tertiary sector employment	+8.17%

2. The ability of the secondary and tertiary production activities to capitalize on the manpower expansion varies in different time periods. Before the opening up of the country, between 1975 and 1979, among the newly recruited non-agricultural labour force in

Guangdong, 73.6% went into secondary production and only 23.7% entered the service sector. This gives the tertiary sector an annual growth rate of 4.7%, compared with the 12.6% in the secondary sector. During these five years (1975–1979), total employment in the tertiary sector (new recruits plus existing work force) grew by only 1.3%. However, since 1979, the pace of development in the service industries surpassed that of manufacturing industries. Between 1979 and 1988, of the new increase in the non-agricultural labour force in Guangdong, 45.9% went to secondary production and 54.1% to tertiary production, giving an annual growth rate of 7.0% and 9.6%, respectively. Within these ten years, total tertiary employment increased by 10.3%. This is perhaps one important indication that the development of the service sector is not necessarily a "post-industrial" phenomenon. In the process of modernization and industrialization in Guangdong since 1979, the tertiary sector is advancing at a faster pace than the secondary sector.

3. As can be expected, there are differential growth rates in service industries in Guangdong. These can be analyzed according to three aspects: by different segments within the tertiary sector; by difference between the public and private sectors; and by difference between urban and rural areas. Within the tertiary sector, it is generally observed that the first and second level activities, which are usually services with profit potential, are growing at a faster rate than the third and fourth level activities which have to depend partially on government subvention. Table 7.3 shows the growth rates of different service industries and it is not surprising to find that the fastest growing sectors are finance and insurance as well as transport and communication. Education and welfare services are among the slower growing categories. The 1993 survey has indicated that between 1978 and 1992, second level activities (particularly finance and insurance) have recorded the highest growth, followed by fourth level activities. The other two categories have shown stagnant growth although first level activities are still currently the leading sector in the tertiary industries. It is also apparent that most of the services growth occurred within the private sector, with the urban private sector growing at an annual rate of 21.9%, compared with only 2.2% for the public sector. Differential growth between the urban and rural areas is also to be expected. Tertiary

Table 7.3   Differential Growth within the Tertiary Sector in Guangdong, 1983–1987

By service categories:		
Tertiary sector as a whole	+10.0%	
Finance and insurance	+12.0%	
Transport and communication	+10.2%	
Educational and welfare services	+5.1%	
Scientific research, technical services	+7.1%	
Government and party institutions	+8.2%	(1984–1987)
By public/private sectors:		
Public ownership (public sector)	+2.2%	
Urban collective ownership	+11.8%	
Urban private sector	+21.9%	
Rural sector	+3.6%	

industries are better developed in the cities mainly because the level of economic development is higher in the cities and thus the demand for producer and other services is greater. In Guangdong, its twenty-one cities, with only 11.8% of the land area and 23.6% of the population of the province, accounted for 73.9% of the GDP in services in 1994. On the other hand, the rural area and the small townships, representing 88.2% of the land area and 76.4% of the population, accounted for 26.1% of the GDP.

4. Guangdong is among the top provinces in China that have developed a prosperous tertiary sector. In terms of the percentage of total employment in service industries, Guangdong ranks fourth (with 30.9%), after Beijing (48.7%), Shanghai (37.9%) and Tianjin (34.1%), which are all higher than the national average of 24.6%. The reasons for a faster-than-average growth in the tertiary sector in Guangdong are: (1) the level of economic development in the province is higher than the national average and hence the need for various kinds of services is correspondingly greater; and (2) Guangdong is a net exporter of services which means that services generated in Guangdong (such as transport, communication, commerce and tourism) are supplying the needs of consumers outside the province. In recent years, the tertiary activities of Guangdong are advancing at such a pace that by 1994 (see Table 7.4) it has surpassed China's average figure in terms of employment distribution among the different tertiary activities and

Table 7.4   Employment Structure within the Tertiary Sector, 1994

Tertiary activity	% of total employment			
	Guangdong		China	
Transport and communication	15.9	(3.8)	13.2	(3.0)
Commerce, restaurant, wholesale, retail and storage	38.8	(9.4)	27.8	(6.4)
Real estate, public service, consultancy services	8.1	(2.0)	5.0	(1.1)
Health, sports and welfare services	4.5	(1.1)	3.1	(0.7)
Education, cultural and broadcasting	12.2	(2.9)	10.2	(2.3)
Scientific research and technical services	1.0	(0.3)	1.3	(0.3)
Finance and insurance	3.0	(0.7)	1.9	(0.4)
Government and party institutions, community groups	8.6	(2.1)	7.3	(1.7)
Geological survey	0.4	(0.1)	1.0	(0.2)
Others	7.4	(1.8)	29.4	(6.7)

Note: Figures in brackets indicate percentage share of total employment in all economic sectors.

the percentage employment of service industries to total labour force (except in the scientific research and technical service sector).

Overall, the expansion of the service sector in Guangdong has made impressive progress since 1979. The previous problem of insufficient supply of services has in many ways been alleviated. For instance, in 1979, every retail establishment and restaurant had to serve 709 and 48,644 people, respectively. With the expansion in the number of service units, the figures were drastically reduced to 96 and 980, respectively, in 1989. It is expected the pattern of growth during the past decade will be maintained, and Guangdong's tertiary sector will continue to expand ahead of most other provinces in China. Table 7.5 shows the short-term targets for the development of the services industries in Guangdong and China, according to the four levels of tertiary activities previously explained. It is paramount that third level activities (educational, cultural, scientific and technical services) should be given more weight and expanded at a faster rate. First level activities will remain as the leading sector, but growth of fourth level activities (particularly the public administration sector) should be kept under strict control so as not to repeat the experience of many developing countries in having a huge but inefficient bureaucracy.

Table 7.5 Short-term Target for the Development of the Tertiary Sector, Guangdong and China

	% of employment in tertiary sector	1st level activities	2nd level activities	3rd level activities	4th level activities	Others
1988 Actual						
Guangdong	23.3	10.4	1.8	3.3	1.9	5.9
China	18.1	7.8	1.6	3.8	1.8	3.0
1995 Target						
Guangdong	27.0	12.7	2.4	4.8	2.0	5.1
China	22.0	9.7	2.0	4.7	2.0	3.6

Note: 1995 actual figures not yet available at the time of writing.

Changing Role of the Service Sector in Guangdong's Economy

Guangdong has experienced rapid rates of economic growth since 1979, and with such development came notable structural changes in its economy. The relative roles played by the primary, secondary and tertiary sectors have shifted significantly during the past few decades. Prior to 1979, the tertiary sector never assumed any important position in Guangdong's economy. Its percentage share of GDP among all the economic sectors declined from 28.56% in 1952 to 25.92% in 1957 and slipped further to 23.68% in 1978, an all time low (Table 7.6). During the same period, there was a consistent and continuous growth in the secondary sector, particularly since 1957, when emphasis on economic development was placed on manufacturing production, especially in heavy industries. The secondary sector's share of GDP increased from 22.69% in 1952 to 24.9% in 1957 and then climbed sharply to 46.38% in 1978 and became the largest economic sector in Guangdong. The primary sector was, on the other hand, originally the most important sector in the economy, especially in the early years after the setting up of the communist regime when it accounted for almost half of the GDP (from 1952 to 1957). Since the 1960s, and particularly in the 1970s, the primary sector entered a track of sharp decline and its share of GDP dropped to less than 30% of the total in 1978, although it still maintained the second position among the economic sector, ahead of the tertiary industries.

Since 1979, with the adoption of a more open and pragmatic policy, there was another marked shift in the economic structure of Guangdong.

Table 7.6   Changes in Economic Structure in Guangdong, 1952–1994

	% of GDP		
	Primary sector	Secondary sector	Tertiary sector
1952	48.75	22.69	28.56
1957	49.18	24.90	25.92
1978	29.94	46.38	23.68
1988	27.90	40.37	31.73
1994	16.38	50.46	33.16

Between 1979 and 1994, the primary sector continued its downward trend and slipped to the lowest position among the economic sectors, accounting for only 16.38% of the GDP. The secondary sector still maintained its leading position, but with a more fluctuating growth. Its share of GDP dropped from 46.38% in 1978 to 40.37% in 1988, but increased again to 50.46% in 1994. The tertiary sector was the one which experienced the most noticeable rate of growth. It has now replaced the primary sector as the second most important economic sector in Guangdong, accounting for 33.16% of its GDP and 24.1% of total employment. The growth was obvious in almost all sectors of the service industries. Between 1979 and 1988, for example, the number of commercial establishments and restaurants increased by 12.7 times, retail sales grew by 6.4 times; the number of tourists rose 11 times while foreign exchange earnings jumped 17.3 times; and the amount of money deposited in banks increased 9.7 times.[17] Into the 1990s, the tertiary sector will continue its upward growth trend, although it is not expected to surpass the secondary sector, both in terms of GDP and number employed, even up to the beginning of the next century. However, the tertiary activities will provide very important support services for economic development in Guangdong as a whole. Expansion of the transport and communication network, for example, can improve the investment environment of the region. Tourism will remain a major source of foreign exchange earnings, but there is a need to explore new resources, upgrade the quality of service and improve the standard of management. Many of these "traditional" services, including trade and commerce, tourism, and technical services, need to be modernized, and at the same time, the service industries have to diversify into new areas in order to keep pace with the rate of economic development. For example, information services, advertising, consultancy and business services all have good growth potential.

In the following sections, two specific aspects of the tertiary activities in Guangdong will be selected for more thorough examination, namely, the commercial (including wholesale and retail) sector and the tourism sector.

Commercial Activities

Commercial activities in the Chinese context are usually referred to as "retailing of social commodities" (*shehui shangpin lingshou*) which includes the supply or provision of commodities, food and beverages (restaurants) and services. Guangdong, being one of the most open provinces in China, has witnessed the fastest growth in this section of the tertiary activities in recent years. For instance, in 1978, total retail sales in Guangdong ranked third among all the provinces in China. In 1981, it jumped to first place and has maintained its leading position until now. Furthermore, changes in the economic system and policy in China over the past forty odd years have been reflected in the changing nature of the commercial activities in Guangdong. One significant aspect is the relative contribution of state enterprises, collective or cooperative enterprises and private (individual) enterprises to the total amount of retail sales (Table 7.7). Prior to 1953, when the provincial or local governments were not active in the operation of retailing activities, over 85% of retail sales were in the hands of individual enterprises. The percentage was as high as 96% in 1950. Since the mid-1950s, it was the government's policy to speed up the development of state and cooperative enterprises in the commercial sector, resulting in almost a monopoly of such enterprises in the 1960s and 1970s. Shares of retail sales by these state and cooperative enterprises always accounted for over 90% of the total in these years. On the other hand, the importance of individual enterprises declined sharply. By 1978, retail sales by state and cooperative enterprises in Guangdong accounted for 96.2% of the total while individual enterprise sales dropped to only 0.43%. Such monopolistic control by the state generally lacks vitality and results in fairly slow growth. For example, between 1950 and 1978, total retail sales in Guangdong increased by only 6.9% per annum. If only the period 1958 to 1978 is considered, annual growth rate was 4.6%.

Since 1978, the Guangdong provincial government has adopted a new economic policy and a more positive attitude towards the reform of the "commodity circulation" system. The state monopoly of business enterprises was stopped and the market was revitalized. More attention was being paid to the development of collective and particularly individual

Table 7.7 Retail Sales According to Types of Ownership in Guangdong, 1952–1994

(Unit: RMB million)

Year	Total retail sales	State enterprises	Collective/cooperative enterprises	Individual enterprises	Joint enterprises	Farmer to non-farmer sales
1952	1,888	127	95	1,617	6	43
1957	3,048	846	762	211	1,114	115
1962	4,082	1,852	1,844	107	—	279
1965	4,019	2,134	1,724	52	—	109
1970	4,920	2,424	2,314	41	—	141
1975	6,673	3,500	2,912	20	—	241
1978	7,724	3,961	3,467	33	—	263
1980	11,747	5,698	5,269	120	13	647
1985	28,923	13,118	7,889	4,522	909	2,485
1990	66,736	25,905	12,726	18,112	1,995	7,998
1994	185,136	53,815	34,382	56,579	16,772	23,588
1978–1994 growth (%)	2,296.9	1,258.6	891.7	171,351.5	n.a.	8,868.8

	Total	State enterprises	Collective/cooperative enterprises	Individual enterprises	Others
No. of establishments in 1994	1,023,278	34,062	77,094	892,405	19,717
No. employed in 1994 ('000)	2,848.5	544.5	494.1	1,557.7	251.7

enterprises. Total retail sales in Guangdong in 1994 reached RMB185,136 million, an increase of 2,296.9% from 1978. Sales from individual enterprises grew phenomenally by 171,351% between these years. In 1994, the percentage share of total sales from state and cooperative enterprises has dropped to 47.6% while those from individual enterprises grew to 30.6%. In 1994, the number of retail establishments and number of service personnel employed were 1,023,278 and 2,848,471, respectively, in Guangdong, with the individual enterprises alone far outnumbering the state and cooperative enterprises: the former accounting for 87.2% of total establishments and 54.7% of the number employed. Such pattern of growth has not only reactivated the whole commercial activities but has also enlarged the range of commodity and service provisions. The increase in the number of retail establishments also means that there are more shopping opportunities and a higher retailing network. For Guangdong, there were only 13 retail establishments and 88 sales personnel per 10,000 population in 1978. In 1990, the figures grew to 141 establishments and 396 persons, respectively.

The consumption pattern of the people in Guangdong has also shown significant changes since the implementation of the new economic policy as reflected in the structural changes in the sales volume of basic retailing commodities between 1978 and 1994. Among the three major categories of retail business (food, clothing and household utilities) which together accounted for over 86% of total retail sales, both the food and clothing businesses have their proportion of total sales shrunk from 55.8% and 16.6% in 1978 to 52.6% and 11.8%, respectively, in 1994. On the other hand, sales of household utilities grew from 18.3% in 1978 to 21.9% in 1994. Even within these three categories, sales volumes have also shown marked changes among the different sub-items. In the food business, between 1978 and 1994, the proportion of sales of basic food grains dropped from 27% to 14.5% whereas sales in meat, poultry, eggs and aqua-products grew significantly from 17.6% to 41.5%. In the clothing business, the most noticeable change was in the drop in the sale of cotton clothing and the increase in wool and silk clothing and dresses. In household utilities, it is only to be expected that the largest increase in retail sales was in household electrical appliances.

In terms of the spatial distribution of retail sales volumes (Table 7.8), there is little doubt that Guangzhou outnumbered other areas. Retail business is also very active in the Special Economic Zones of Shenzhen and Shantou. The Pearl River Delta is also growing in its commercial

Table 7.8   Spatial Distribution of Retail Sales Volumes in Guangdong, 1994

	Total retail sales (RMB million)
Guangzhou	44,819
Shenzhen	22,114
Zhuhai	7,103
Shantou	9,105
Shaoguan	4,568
Heyuan	1,860
Meizhou	4,041
Weizhou	7,461
Chaozhou	2,733
Shanwei	3,573
Dongguan	6,718
Zhongshan	4,828
Jiangmen	10,400
Foshan	16,457
Yangjiang	3,180
Zhanjiang	10,017
Maoming	8,586
Zhaoqing	8,867
Qingyuan	3,973
Jieyang	4,733

activities, particularly in Foshan and Jiangmen, and so too is the city of Zhanjiang.

One special feature that deserves mention in the growth of commercial activities in Guangdong is the increasing number of markets (*jishi*) established since 1978. Before 1978, trading in markets was restricted and under control and was confined mainly to the rural areas with only very minimal sales volume. With the implementation of economic reform measures, the development of markets has become very active, both in the rural and urban areas. In 1994, there was a total of 4,266 markets in Guangdong, an increase of 147% from 1978. Among these markets, 27% were in cities while 73% were in the rural areas. Most of these (86%) were comprehensive markets selling a whole range of commodities, while the rest were specialized markets catering for particular types of commodities (such as different kinds of agricultural products or industrial products). Total retail sales in these markets in 1994 reached RMB77,926.66 million (of which 51% were in the urban areas) and this topped all the provinces in China. Over 60% of retail sales in the daily necessities of Guangdong people in meat, poultry, eggs, vegetables and aqua-products were handled in these markets, indicating the importance of this form of trading in Guangdong's retail scene.

Tourism

Before 1979, tourism in Guangdong was not active at all (with the number of people entering the province kept at a low level) and fluctuated greatly between years. In 1978, for example, the number of international visitors received in Guangdong was only 443,000, including 123,000 foreign visitors and 320,000 visitors from Hong Kong, Macau, Taiwan and countries where overseas Chinese reside.[18] Since 1979, Guangdong has not only attracted the interest of overseas visitors to see the latest conditions in China but has also opened up more cultural and scenic spots as well as established infrastructural provisions for tourism. Taking advantage of such a situation and its geographical location, Guangdong has, within a short period of time, developed a sound tourist system and it is now the leading province in China in terms of the number of tourists, number of people employed in the tourist industry, revenues received from tourism and the provision of facilities such as hotels. The number of international visitors received increased from 698,000 in 1979 to 6,108,300 in 1994, among which 17.6% were foreign visitors, 70.1% from Hong Kong and Macau, 8.4% from Taiwan and 3.9% were overseas Chinese.[19] It is important to note that the growth of domestic tourism is also keeping pace with international tourism. With economic prosperity, better income and higher living standards, growing numbers of domestic visitors from other provinces come to Guangdong for pleasure and business. The number of domestic visitors increased from 2.56 million in 1983 to 25.4 million in 1994 — a tenfold increase. Of the total number of tourists received by Guangdong in 1990, 19.4% were international visitors while 80.6% were domestic visitors.

The economic and social benefits derived from the development of tourism in Guangdong are vast, particularly in terms of the following respects:

1. The extent of economic gains from tourism has increased at a fast rate since 1978. In 1994, total revenue received from tourism

was RMB21,845.81 million (28 times that of 1978); total foreign exchange earned was US$1,144.46 million (91 times that of 1980); and the profit derived from the tourist industry was RMB1,344.02 million (189 times that of 1978).

2. Tourism development has accelerated the construction of hotels and other facilities or services associated with the tourist industry, oftentimes involving a substantial amount of foreign investment. For example, between 1978 and 1988, about US$1,200 million foreign capital had been injected into the hotel construction business. By 1994, there were 838 hotels in Guangdong for overseas visitors, with a total of 103,578 rooms and 214,715 beds. Among these, 750 hotels, 86,859 rooms and 179,854 beds were constructed since 1979. Some of these hotels also cater for domestic tourists. The occupancy rate of these hotels was about 63.5% in 1994. Apart from hotels, provision of tourist facilities has also resulted in the development of holiday villas, golf courses and amusement parks.

3. The development of tourism has also positive effects on the growth of related activities, particularly in the commercial sector (including restaurants, retailing, etc.), in the construction business and in the transportation and telecommunications sectors. More entry points to Guangdong have been opened and the transportation network (especially linkages with Hong Kong) has been expanded to cater for the increasing number of people entering the province.

4. The demand for tourism has also made possible the opening up of new tourism resources and more efficient utilization of existing ones. Since 1979, quite a number of tourists spots of scenic, cultural or historical value have been developed or upgraded. At the same time, tours for specific purposes have been organized, such as lychee tasting, health and rehabilitation and cycling. With these kinds of development, the tourist industry has generated new employment opportunities, and both the management and service standards of the tourist trade have been upgraded.

Like other economic activities, tourism development is quite unevenly distributed within Guangdong province. Table 7.9 shows the spatial distribution of tourism in Guangdong. As can be expected, most of the tourism provisions (hotels, for example) are located in Guangzhou and

Table 7.9 Spatial Distribution of the Tourist Industry in Guangdong, 1994

	Number of			No. of tourists received[a] (million)		Revenue (Total: RMB 21,845.81 million)	Foreign exchange earnings (Total: US$1,144.46 million)	Profit (Total: RMB 1,344.02 million)
	Hotels	Rooms	Beds					
Guangzhou	189	42,181	86,477	11.64	(2.03)	43.56%	25.5%	1,045.04
Shenzhen	209	22,952	46,024	5.60	(1.86)	22.49%	42.7%	450.31
Zhuhai	32	4,803	10,209	2.40	(0.42)	5.16%	10.3%	−107.90
Shantou	27	3,365	7,787	0.66	(0.13)	3.56%	5.9%	4.05
Shaoguan	29	2,334	4,978	0.68	(0.03)	0.67%	0.1%	−10.06
Heyuan	21	745	1,676	0.30	—[b]	0.29%	—[c]	−6.62
Meizhou	24	1,356	2,859	0.45	(0.02)	0.31%	0.4%	1.71
Weizhou	34	2,186	4,664	0.74	(0.09)	1.80%	0.3%	−72.70
Chaozhou	11	861	2,128	0.28	(0.03)	0.60%	0.4%	1.90
Shanwei	10	514	1,055	0.35	(0.05)	0.36%	0.1%	1.59
Dongguan	14	1,445	2,927	1.19	(0.44)	2.03%	0.4%	−1.50
Zhongshan	12	2,117	4,154	0.70	(0.30)	2.34%	2.0%	−18.89
Jiangmen	51	4,193	8,831	1.32	(0.21)	4.46%	2.4%	12.30
Foshan	38	3,325	7,157	1.09	(0.21)	5.10%	1.9%	9.97
Yangjiang	18	1,157	2,678	0.65	—[b]	0.21%	—[c]	2.18
Zhanjiang	16	2,291	4,038	0.53	(0.02)	1.73%	0.4%	14.53
Maoming	15	1,181	2,577	0.50	—[b]	0.69%	—[c]	2.17
Zhaoqing	43	3,433	7,566	1.08	(0.16)	2.94%	1.8%	7.68
Qingyuan	20	1,203	2,724	0.63	(0.04)	0.61%	0.1%	1.74
Jieyang	12	1,039	2,295	0.39	(0.02)	1.07%	0.3%	6.52
Yunfu	13	951	1,911	0.40	(0.06)	—[d]	—[c]	—[d]

Notes:
[a] Number of international tourists in parentheses.
[b] Number of international tourists less than 5,000.
[c] Less than 0.02%.
[d] Data included in Zhaoqing.

Shenzhen, and to a lesser extent in the Special Economic Zones of Zhuhai and Shantou, as well as in certain areas of the Pearl River Delta, particularly in Jiangmen, Foshan and Zhaoqing. The same pattern is observable in terms of the number of tourists (both international and domestic) and the amount of revenue received from tourism. In terms of foreign exchange earnings though, over 78% are confined to Guangzhou, Shenzhen and Zhuhai. Of particular concern is the profit generated from the tourist trade. Apart from Guangzhou and Shenzhen, the rest of Guangdong is not doing a flourishing tourist business at all, and many places are actually running at a loss. This probably indicates a need to improve the efficiency of the tourist business and to better utilize existing tourism resources.

Conclusion

Recent reports on the development of the geography of services[20] have indicated a continuing shift from the production of goods to the production of services in most world economies. It has also been observed that such structural shift towards services has been associated with growing interaction with other sectors of the economy. In the case of Guangdong, there is little doubt that the growth and dynamism of the service sector will be increasingly vital to the economic development of the province. The tertiary sector's contribution to the GDP of Guangdong has been continually set on an upward trend since the implementation of the open policy and economic reform. It now accounts for one-third of the GDP of the province. As remarked by Riddle, "focusing instead on 'servicization' would acknowledge the service sector appropriately as the crucial vehicle for economic growth. Not only is an efficient services infrastructure essential for the growth of other sectors of the economy, but the effective development of business or producer/intermediary services is vital to economic development."[21] However, there are certain problems that have emerged in the course of the development of service industries in Guangdong. One is the uneven resource allocation to different segments of the tertiary sector, particularly to the relative neglect of the third level services (that is, services for the upgrading of the scientific and cultural level and the quality of life of its people). These are usually less profitable or non-profitable services and are therefore less competitive for resources. Furthermore, it is difficult to attract foreign investment to these activities as in the case of the commercial, real estate or tourism segments. At the same time, certain services, such as consultancy, advertising or legal services, are less developed probably due to the lack of expertise. A more balanced development of the different segments of the service industry is therefore desirable.

The uneven spatial development of the tertiary sector is also a problem as most of the services in Guangdong are now confined to the urban areas. However, it would not be appropriate if services were blindly introduced into the rural area. Noting the relationship between service development and overall economic development, it is important that the promotion of services growth in the countryside should be coupled with adjustments to the underlying economic base.

It is also apparent that the efficiency of services provision has become a matter of concern. Apart from the lack of coordination in the development of services, the standard of services and the management skills are also less than satisfactory. What seems to be an appropriate action now for Guangdong is a more careful development planning that specifies the role of the service sector in the economy of the province and the allocation of resources to the different segments of the tertiary industry.

Notes

1. United Nations, Statistical Office (UNSO), *International Standard Industrial Classification of All Economic Activities*, Statistical Papers, Series M, No. 4, Rev. 2 (New York: UNSO, 1968).

2. Statistical Office of the European Communities (SOEC), *NACE: General Industrial Classification of Economic Activities within the European Communities* (Luxembourg: SOEC, 1970).

3. D. F. Channon, *The Service Industries* (London: Macmillan, 1978).

4. P. W. Daniels, *Service Industries: A Geographical Appraisal* (London and New York: Methuen, 1985), pp. 1–16.

5. D. I. Riddle, *Service-led Growth* (New York and London: Praeger, 1986).

6. Li Jiangfan, "Guangdong disan chanye de fazhan yu youhua" (The Development and Improvement of Tertiary Industries in Guangdong), *Jihua yu fazhan* (Planning and Development), March 1991, pp. 22–26.

7. See, for example, D. Bell, *The Coming of Post-industrial Society* (New York: Basic Books, 1973).

8. D. I. Riddle, "The Role of the Service Sector in Economic Development," in *The Emerging Service Economy*, edited by O. Giarini (Oxford: Pergamon Press, 1987), pp. 83–104.

9. Ibid., p. 84.

10. See, for example, A. Gartner, R. A. Nixon and F. Reissman (eds.), *Public*

Service Employment: An Analysis of Its History, Problems and Prospects (New York: Praeger, 1973).

11. H. Ezekiel and M. Pavaskar, *Services* (Delhi: Macmillan Co. of India, 1976).

12. Committee on Invisible Exports (CIE), *Annual Report, 1980–81* (London: CIE, 1981).

13. See note 8, p. 97.

14. Guangdongsheng tongjiju (ed.), *Guangdong tongji nianjian* (Statistical Yearbook of Guangdong), various years.

15. Guojia tongjiju (ed.), *Zhongguo tongji nianjian* (Statistical Yearbook of China), various years.

16. See note 6.

17. Ma Hong and Fang Weizhong (eds.), *Zhongguo diqu fazhan yu chanye zhengce* (Regional Development and Industrial Policy in China) (Beijing: Zhongguo caizheng jingji chubanshe, 1991).

18. The figures in this section refer to the number of tourists (whether international or domestic) received by the tourism system in Guangdong, and not the number of people entering or leaving Guangdong.

19. If the total number of overseas visitors entering Guangdong instead of the number of tourists received is considered, the figure for 1994 was 34,267,800, among which 4.0% were foreigners, 93.6% from Hong Kong and Macau, 2.2% from Taiwan and 0.2% were overseas Chinese.

20. See, for example, P. W. Daniels, "Some Perspectives on the Geography of Services," *Progress in Human Geography*, Vol. 15, No. 1(1991), pp. 37–46.

21. See note 8, p. 101.

8

Money, Banking and Finance

Tsang Shu-ki

Relative Achievements

One important feature of the Chinese economic experiment is that financial transformation has lagged behind the reform in the real sector. In this regard, Guangdong has been no exception.

Being one of the top growth areas in China, however, Guangdong still has witnessed some "above-average" development in money and banking in recent years. At the end of 1985, total bank deposits in the province amounted to 7.1% of the national total. The share increased to 9.8% in 1990 and 11.5% in 1994. Another indication is the monetization ratio (defined as bank deposits over GDP/GNP). For Guangdong, it was 54.9% in 1985, compared with the national ratio of 49.9%. In 1994, the province's ratio climbed to 81.1% while the national one rose to 65.3%. Within that period, therefore, the relative degree of "financial deepening" of Guangdong *vis-à-vis* the country as a whole moved up to 124% from 110%.

At the same time, the growth of bank lending has been less spectacular. Total bank loans in Guangdong represented 8.4% of the national total in both 1985 and 1990. Behind that phenomenon was a dramatic fall in the loan-deposit gap:[1] from 64.1% in 1985 to 11.0% in 1990 (Table 8.1). In April 1991, deposits exceeded loans in Guangdong's banking system

Table 8.1   Bank Deposits and Loans in Guangdong

(Unit: RMB100 million)

	1980	1985	1990	1994
Total deposits	103.10	303.70	1,141.19	3,385.67
Fiscal deposits	35.70	26.32	80.42	148.54
Enterprise deposits	24.29	130.91	418.50	1,419.77
Urban savings deposits	17.96	86.63	488.64	1,726.50
Rural deposits	15.58	39.11	104.16	18.22
Total loans	161.44	498.52	1,267.21	2,638.75
Working funds	117.04	349.36	1,006.54	2,005.31
Industrial	32.90	102.73	371.50	785.63
Commercial	84.14	240.47	551.16	763.50
State-owned, collective agricultural loans	13.03	35.88	82.27	n.a.
Fixed capital	0.57	n.a.	162.89	426.49

Source: *Guangdong tongji nianjian 1992*, Table 12–4; *Guangdong tongji nianjian 1995*, Table 12-4.

Note: The figures for 1980 include those of Hainan.

for the first time, producing a deposit-loan gap instead. The same feat occurred in the whole financial sector (including all non-bank financial institutions) in June 1991. In the banking system, the gap amounted to RMB9.583 billion, or 6.6% at the end of 1991. Deposits stayed above loans since then.[2] On the surface at least, this trend appears to be an indication that Guangdong has been able to finance an increasing portion of its development from a varying combination of enhanced saving, self finance, non-bank finance, inflow of funds from other provinces, foreign investments and external borrowing (largely from Hong Kong). The favourable financial as well as fiscal treatments given to the province by Beijing also have helped.

At a more micro-level, moreover, Guangdong has been pioneering some new forms of financial intermediation, with the stock market in Shenzhen being one of the outstanding examples. More radical plans for reforms are being nurtured after Deng Xiaoping's visit to the province in early 1992 and the confirmation of the goal of building a "socialist market economy" in the country by the Fourteenth Party Congress in October 1992. Guangdong again seems to be at the forefront of China's economic transformation.

These considerations do not imply that all is going well for the province. At both the macro- and micro-levels, various problems of inefficiency, structural imbalance and institutional mismatch have emerged. Although some of them may be, and have to be, resolved by the deepening of the reform and further growth in the economy, new problems will compound the remaining old ones if a great push towards radical transformation in the financial sector is implemented without careful design and coordination.

This chapter is organized as follows. The second section looks at the development of the financial sector in Guangdong in its historical context. The proliferation of financial institutions, instruments and markets is investigated in the third section, while the basic reasons for the achievements, including preferential treatments by the central government, are analyzed in the fourth section. The fifth section discusses the major problems in the financial system. Comments on its recent developments and future prospects are offered in the final section.

Four Stages and Three Levels of Financial Reforms

As Zhu Wanli, Chief of the Guangdong Branch of People's Bank points out,[3] the reform in banking and finance in the province can be divided into four stages, following broadly those of the whole economy:

1. 1979–1983: specialized banks were established and the branches of People's Bank of China were transformed into those of a central bank. The systems of funds and foreign exchange management were also changed.
2. 1984–1988: under the guidance of People's Bank, various financial institutions were set up, and different financial instruments issued. Financial markets started to emerge, mainly in the form of inter-bank short-term funds markets and markets for various types of bonds. Further improvements in the funds management system also took place.
3. 1989–1990: because of the nation-wide economic retrenchment, there was considerable backtracking in the financial reform. Quota management in credit was resorted to, in an effort to clamp down on over-investment and inflation.
4. 1991–now: further reforms at the macro- and micro-levels have re-emerged and are gathering momentum.

The financial reform in Guangdong has also been implemented at three levels:[4]

1. Shenzhen and Zhuhai: these two cities have been the foremost pioneers. As early as 1981, the Guangdong provincial authorities decided that the two cities should be experimental outposts for financial reforms, a decision that received formal State Council blessing in 1984.
2. Guangzhou and Jiangmen: in January 1986, the State Council listed Guangzhou as one of five experimental cities for financial reforms in the country, and Jiangmen as an experimental city for Guangdong.
3. In 1988, Chinese Communist Party (CCP) central leadership and the State Council decided that Guangdong should be an integrated experimental province, and major financial reforms were to be launched. The attempt was, however, delayed by the economic adjustment that started in 1989.

Development of Financial Institutions, Instruments and Markets

In a 1990 report, the World Bank commented that since 1986 the financial sector in China "has developed significantly, with a more diversified structure and a broader menu of financial instruments." Other than People's Bank of China, the World Bank classified China's financial institutions into six categories: (1) specialized banks; (2) universal banks; (3) development banks; (4) rural and urban credit cooperatives; (5) non-bank financial institutions (NBFIs) including trust and investment companies, insurance companies, finance companies, financial leasing companies, and securities companies; and (6) foreign deposit-taking institutions.[5]

All these forms of financial institutions have developed and proliferated in Guangdong and its special economic zones under the economic reform. Under People's Bank, there are the four specialized banks (Agricultural Bank, Industrial and Commercial Bank, Bank of China, and Construction Bank). Bank of Communication on the one hand and Guangdong Development Bank and Shenzhen Development Bank on the other are strong universal and commercial banks, respectively. The latter two, unlike Bank of Communication which operates on a nation-wide basis, are regional commercial banks whose activities are more restricted geographically as well as functionally. Another notable regional bank is China Merchant Bank, with its headquarters in Shekou. Its activities are, however, of the "universal" type. Here the development of banking institutions in Guangdong has gone beyond the 1990 classification of the World Bank. However, the four specialized banks have still maintained a relatively dominant position. At the end of 1993, they collected 88.1% of all RMB deposits and 84.3% of all foreign currency deposits in the province, while their aggregate shares in RMB loans and foreign currency loans were 88.5% and 83.8%, respectively.[6]

As to NBFIs, Guangdong International Trust and Investment Company (GITIC) is the leading international trust and investment company in the province. Its total assets in 1990, valued at RMB10.8 billion, was almost one-third of the consolidated assets of the famous national spearhead, China International Trust and Investment Company (CITIC).[7] In July 1988, GITIC also gave birth to a separate institution, Guangdong Overseas Chinese Investment Company, whose total assets increased by over ten times in three years. People's Insurance Company of China, on the other hand, has been having a very strong presence, as enriched citizens and enterprises become more susceptible to the idea of buying insurance. Since the start of the stock market in Shenzhen in 1988, securities companies have also been given a strong boost. With the province at the forefront of China's campaign to open up the economy, there were thirty-eight foreign (including Hong Kong) banks and representative offices in Guangdong at the end of 1993, more than any other province in China.

Overall, excluding foreign banks and representative offices, there was a total of 16,546 branches of financial institutions in the province by the end of 1990.[8] That would represent a "density" of 3,775 persons per financial branch.

With regard to financial instruments, it is reported that at the end of 1990, the total value of outstanding debt instruments in Guangdong (excluding Shenzhen) was RMB27.542 billion, of which 28.4% were national bonds, 47.4% financial bonds, and the remaining 24.2% enterprise bonds. Markets for the buying and selling of bonds emerged in 1986 in rather rudimentary forms in Shenzhen and Guangzhou. By June 1988, there were eight cities which organized secondary markets for national bonds and five brokerage companies.[9]

Guangdong began to experiment with the share-holding system in enterprise reform as early as 1986, while Shenzhen started its stock market in 1988. By the end of 1991, the Shenzhen SEZ had 136 stock-share companies, of which 17 were listed. The number of listed companies went up to 24 in 1992. Total trading volume also rose dramatically. It was RMB23 million in 1989; RMB1.76 billion in 1990; RMB3.508 billion in 1991[10] and RMB43.8 billion in 1992.[11]

Guangdong has also been the forerunner in a number of other financial instruments and services. The Zhuhai Branch of Bank of China was the first institution to launch the credit card business in 1985. Banks in Guangdong were also pioneers in accepting foreign currency deposits from citizens.

Preferential Policies towards Guangdong

The relatively greater development of the financial sector of Guangdong, in comparison with the rest of the country, has been due to a number of factors. First, of course, is the very high growth record of the province itself. Real economic growth averaged 14.5% per year between 1981 and 1994, compared with 9.4% for the country as a whole.[12] Per capita GDP in

Shenzhen and Guangzhou reached RMB7,938 and RMB6,464, respectively, in 1991, significantly above the national figure of per capita GNP of RMB1,714. It is well known in the economics literature that a high level of development is more conducive to the alleviation of financial repression and the emergence of financial services that cater for the accumulation of human capital and more sophisticated transaction and saving needs. Guangdong's high growth indeed owes a lot to its geographical proximity to Hong Kong, a factor which has been frequently commented upon. As an international financial centre itself, Hong Kong's influence on Guangdong however goes well beyond the exchange of goods and services. The "demonstration effect" is also very important.

Second, Guangdong's relative success in financial development has also been the result of preferential monetary and fiscal treatments that the central government has given to the province in the reform period so far. In the second section we mentioned that during different points in time Guangdong was often allowed to implement reform experiments in its financial sector, earlier than many other regions in the country. This policy has also been complemented by measures that have enabled the province to obtain sufficient funds for development. According to Zhu Wanli, at the beginning of the economic reform, the central government practised "special policies and flexible measures towards Guangdong, so as to let Guangdong move a step ahead."[13] The credit control policy adopted by People's Bank towards its Guangdong Branch in 1981, for example, was very lenient. On top of its loan-deposit gap in 1980, the gap was allowed to be increased by RMB400 million annually for three years,[14] with a mid-year temporary loan limit of RMB200 million. Moreover, short-term, medium and equipment loans were included in the *baogan* system. Zhu argues that these liberal policies increased the productive capabilities of Guangdong and paved the way for its robust growth in later years.

The fiscal *baogan* system imposed by the central government on Guangdong was also widely regarded as very favourable.[15] According to Lin Dengyun, the fiscal chief in Guangdong, a system of "fixed submission" (*ding'e shangjiao*) was practised in 1980–1987. As for 1988–1992, the contract delivery system was adopted and an annual increase rate of 9% was used to adjust the delivery upwards (*dizeng baogan*).[16] There were some intermittent reports of the amount of the fixed submissions in 1980–1987. The amount was RMB990 million in 1980,[17] RMB772.00 million in 1985, RMB778.08 million in 1986 and RMB778.00 million in 1987.[18] These looked very mild against the requirements imposed on other fiscal surplus regions or provinces such as Shanghai, Jiangsu and Zhejiang, which in 1985, for example, had to submit 74%, 61% and 45%, respectively, of the total fiscal revenue they collected to the central government.[19] Shanghai's submission rate was even increased to 76.46% in 1986 and 1987. This touched off strong dissent and in 1988 the central government backed down and changed the system to that of the "fixed submission quota" (*ding'e baogan*). The amount was set at RMB10.5 billion per year for a period of five years. As for Guangdong, given the system of *dizeng baogan*, the amount delivered in 1990 was reported to be RMB5.34 billion.[20] The province has apparently been left with ample funds for its development.[21]

Major Problems

Guangdong's financial development has had its own problems. First of all, given the preferential treatment and the inflow of funds from all sides, the efficiency of funds employment has lamentably not been high. An obvious symptom is related to the over-expansion of working capital. Between 1978 and 1988, the growth of working capital lending in the province increased at an average annual rate of 26.2%, which was 6.7% per year higher than the average GDP growth rate of 19.5% in the period. In 1988, the ratio of enterprises' self-owned working capital versus bank-financed working capital was estimated to be 1:9, after a secular trend of decline of the former in the reform years. Working capital lending in that year amounted to RMB109.102 billion. Hence the total pool of working funds available to enterprises in Guangdong was to the tune of RMB121.224 billion. Assuming an annual turnover rate of 2.5 times, the flow of short-term funds reached RMB303.061 billion in 1988. This however compared rather poorly with the GDP figure of RMB109.861 billion. Liang Guiquan et al. conclude that "these statistics demonstrate that the enterprises in the province acquired for themselves excessive working capital funds, definitely beyond the needs of practical economic development."[22] This view is echoed by Xie Yongping, who points out that in the 1980s working capital investment represented more than 10% of total investment in Guangdong, compared with the ratio of about 4% in South Korea and Taiwan in the same decade.[23] Xie argues that this reflects the low efficiency of funds utilization and investment in the province.

Secondly, the distribution of funding that has emerged, industry-wise as well as geographically, has also left much to be desired. With regard to industrial distribution, Liang et al. report that in the period of 1984–1988, lending to processing industries represented more than 75% of the total, while the ratio for basic industries was below 25% in all those years. In 1988, outstanding loans to the three core basic industries (energy, transport and communications) amounted to only RMB864 million, or merely 7.79% of total lending. This compared with the 10.42% share for the textile processing industries, 14.51% for the machinery processing industries, and 25.29% for the processing arm of light industries.[24] Han Houyuan et al., on the other hand, reveal that between 1984 and 1989, the Guangdong Branch of Industrial and Commercial Bank increased lending by RMB17.095 billion. Only RMB2.396 billion, or 14.02%, went to the basic industries. Most of the remaining loans were extended to the processing industries.[25]

The regional distribution of lending has also been uneven, showing a bias towards the Pearl River Delta, as Han Houyuan et al. argue, on the basis of the figures in Table 8.2.[26] The figures refer to the total amount of lending in Guangdong by People's Bank, the four specialized banks and the rural credit cooperatives. The Pearl River Delta has apparently fetched the lion's share of the lending increases, while the other coastal regions and the mountainous areas have been relatively neglected.

Thirdly, there is considerable doubt as to whether the bureaucratic structure and the administrative system in the province could catch up with the requirements of modern financial reforms without generating malpractice and economic disorder. The fiasco of the new share issues in Shenzhen in August 1992, which culminated in riots and a half-day closure of the stock exchange, is a case in point. Reports of corruption were widespread. Although the euphoria generated by acute excess demand for a limited

Table 8.2   Regional Distribution of Lending in Guangdong

(Unit: RMB100 million)

Region	1978		1989		1978–1989	
	Amount	%	Amount	%	Increase	% share
Pearl River Delta	62.14	57.9	864.45	68.7	802.31	69.7
Other coastal open regions	29.83	27.8	236.73	18.8	206.90	18.0
Mountainous areas	15.27	14.3	157.64	12.5	142.37	12.3
Total	107.24	100.0	1258.82	100.0	1151.58	100.0

Source: Han Houyuan et al., "Guangdong chanye jiegou tiaozheng yu jinrong tizhi gaige" (see note 25).

amount of shares was a main cause, the bodies involved in the process, including People's Bank, the Stock Exchange, the Industrial and Commercial Administrative Board and the Supervision Bureau were blamed for their mishandling of the situation.[27] Other commentators have pointed to problems in the share-holding system, the accounting standard and the regulatory framework, as well as the lack of reliable rating criteria and institutions.[28]

Recent Developments and Prospects

As mentioned above, the deposit-loan gap in Guangdong turned positive from April 1991 onwards, signifying an apparent abundance of funds that have been available. At the same time, currency in circulation also markedly increased. In the first nine months of 1992, cash receipts and payments in the provinces rose by 69% and 75.61%, respectively, over the same period in 1991. The result was a net issuance of currency to the tune of RMB2 billion, compared with the phenomenon of net withdrawal a year ago. Ren Hang attributes the seemingly contradictory situation to the "stock market fever" and the consumption boom, as well as the rapidly expanding private sector in the province, which uses a great deal more cash.[29]

Other than formally defining "socialist market economy" as the economic system into which China would transform itself, the Fourteenth Party Congress held in October 1992 also stressed the need to develop the service sectors in China, which have lagged behind.[30] The financial sector is an obvious priority to be promoted. In 1992, the number of approved share-holding enterprises in Guangdong increased by 109, and the volume of enterprise bonds and short-term debt instruments issued reached RMB7.95 billion, six times more than that in 1991. Over 160 financial institutions were newly set up, and four more foreign banks established branches in Guangzhou.[31] By the end of June 1994, the total number of share-holding enterprises reached 540.

It appears that many plans to reform and expand the financial sector in the province are being formulated. Shenzhen is certainly at the forefront of this trend. When interviewed, Wang Xiyi, Chief of the Shenzhen SEZ Branch of People's Bank said that he would try his best to obtain approval for the establishment of foreign exchange, gold and futures markets in the SEZ.[32] Other major efforts would include the modernization of the banking sector and the expansion of foreign participation in it. It is also reported that the Guangdong provincial government has plans to convert one-third of the large- and medium-sized state-owned enterprises into share-holding enterprises and open an exchange for "legal person shares" (*faren gu*).[33] Like Shenzhen, Guangzhou hopes to become a financial centre and set up its own foreign exchange, futures and gold markets, but no set time-frame is revealed.[34] The worry is, however, that if all these innovations are implemented in a rush, institutional confusion and serious operational problems may result.

As for the other major problems discussed in the above section, there is no guarantee that they can all be resolved in the future, although there are indications that some of them are changing for the better. The distribution of lending in the province seems to be rationalizing itself. A recent report points out approvingly that 60% of the total amount of loans in 1992 were extended to basic industries, enterprises of high efficiency, strong exporting capability and large sales volume, the mountainous areas and tertiary industries.[35] Unfortunately no further breakdown in the components of loans is given, rendering it impossible to gauge the actual extent of any real improvement made.

The problem can be observed from another angle. In 1978, the gross value of industrial and agricultural output of the Pearl River Delta constituted 32.7% of Guangdong's total. The share rose to 57.6% in 1990 and 68.7% in 1994. In contrast, the share of the mountainous areas, which constitute 60% of total land area and 40% of total population, declined from 16% to 13.4% during 1978–1990. Somewhat surprisingly, the ratio climbed back to 15.6% in 1994. Whether that was the result of a shift in government policy to alleviate inequality is an open question. Nevertheless, the per capita figures show an unambiguously rising inequality. Per capita GDP of the Pearl River Delta was RMB1,106.4 higher than that of the mountainous areas in 1985. The difference widened to RMB2,281.5 in 1990 and further to RMB12,500 in 1994. In the same period, the gap between the average per capita savings deposits rose from RMB548 to RMB2,254 and then to RMB3,135. One apparent cause of the imbalances may still have been the uneven allocation of resources.

Regional imbalance in Guangdong is related to the province's peculiar development path. As external linkage, in particular with Hong Kong, has been the major engine of growth, those areas that have poor endowments and unfavourable geographical locations have not been attractive to outside investors. The result is relatively low economic growth. On the other hand, because of very weak internal linkage within the province, the development of the rich areas has not significantly benefited the poorer areas, as both forward and backward linkage effects across different regions within the province have almost been absent.[36]

Given the ambitious plans of the province to economically catch up with the "four little dragons" of Asia in two decades, and the present emphasis on infrastructure-led growth,[37] there is a reasonably high possibility that the relative neglect of the basic industries, as witnessed in the 1980s, could be rectified. This may be caused by a deliberate policy change, because the lessons of the past decade have been learnt. It may also be an outcome of market forces, as sustained high growth would render infrastructural projects more attractive and profitable. Whether the regional distribution of funds would become more even is, however, a moot point. The extension of the transportation network could benefit remote regions and enhance their economic and, hence, funding prospect. Nevertheless, such an effect, if it turns out to be significant at all, would emerge only after a time lag.

A related problem is the possibility of balance-sheet fragility in the financial system. Inflow of funds from other provinces has apparently been a major, albeit certainly not the only, factor behind the emergence of the positive deposit-loan gap. These funds have been attracted by Guang-dong's rising economy, the booming stock and property markets, as well as its freer investment environment. In any case, the maturity structure of these funds remains an issue for concern. Should a great deal of them belong to short-term "hot money" which could easily be withdrawn due to cyclical or other factors, Guangdong's financial system would put itself at risk if it extends a large proportion of these funds as long-term loans.

One classic example of financial fragility is the province's foreign exchange imbalance. On the basis of customs statistics, Guangdong's exports totalled US$27.03 billion while imports amounted to US$19.90 billion in 1993, hence producing a trade surplus of US$7.13 billion. However, an article in *Guangdong jinrong* revealed that actual foreign exchange receipt from exports turned out to be only US$7 billion in the year whereas the actual usage of foreign exchange for imports was US$10.4 billion. In other words, a *deficit* of US$3.4 billion surfaced, and "had to be solved by going through the swap centres."[38] The deviation of the trade-related foreign exchange balance from the recorded trade balance is well known in China because of various forms of leakages and statistical discrepancies,[39] but the very low ratio of receipt from exports (only 26%), compared with the import utilization rate of 52%, was still striking.

The unpleasant reality is that Guangdong faces difficulties even in balancing its foreign exchange despite the superficial picture of huge capital inflow. To rectify this, Guangdong must do at least two things: (1) enhance the value added of its production; and (2) develop a more balanced industrial structure with a higher degree of internal linkage and coordination.

The Guangdong authorities have apparently been aware of these contradictions. A series of policy statements and measures was announced in the past few years, and the province has embarked on a new economic trajectory. An industrial policy has emerged, under which strategic industries including petro-chemical, automobile, electronics, metallurgy, construction material, textiles and drugs, etc. are targeted for promotion. On the other hand, a plan for regional division of labour with the province has also been nurtured, with the western region specializing in raw material, energy and heavy industries and the eastern region focusing on light and consumer goods industries. The centre, in particular Guangzhou, would spearhead the effort to develop services.[40]

The implementation of this newly emerging economic strategy requires more than just gestures. A more rational structuring of both industrial and locational patterns within the province, with a view to promoting internal linkage, division of labour and cooperation as well as technological upgrading, is needed. In the financial field, the task remains as how to ensure that this new development plan is facilitated as the banking system and the financial markets continue with the process of modernization. Efficiency is also a key issue. Both the providers and the users of funds need to undergo real changes in their mode of operation, if hard-earned money is not to be wasted.

Notes

1. The loan-deposit gap refers to the extent by which loans are greater than deposits. The reverse phenomenon is called the deposit-loan gap.
2. See Jin Zhong, "Yikao keji jinbu, tigao jingji xiaoyi — 1991 nian tou jiuge yue Guangdongsheng hongguan jingji yunxing qingkuang jianxi" (Rely on Technological Progress, Improve Economic Efficiency — The Macroeconomic Operational Situation in Guangdong Province in the First Nine Months of 1991), *Guangdong jinrong* (Guangdong Finance), No. 12 (1991), pp. 10–11, 55; Li Wenyang, "1992 nian Guangdongsheng huobi toufang xianxiang toushi" (An In-depth Analysis of the Money Issuing Phenomenon

in Guangdong Province in 1992), *Guangdong jinrong*, No. 12 (1992), pp. 11–12; "Guangdong jingji jinrong xingshi xichuwangwai" (Guangdong's Economic and Financial Situation Better than Expected), *Jinrong shibao* (Financial News), 28 January 1993, p. 1.

3. Zhu Wanli, "Shenhua jinrong gaige, cujin Guangdong jingji fazhan" (Deepen Financial Reform, Promote Guangdong's Economic Development), in *Gaige kaifang zai Guangdong — Xianzou yibu de shijian yu sikao* (Reform and Open Policies in Guangdong: Practice and Thinking One Step Ahead), edited by Lin Ruo et al. (Guangzhou: Guangdong gaodeng jiaoyu chubanshe, 1992), pp. 150–64.

4. Ibid.

5. World Bank, *China: Financial Sector Policies and Institutional Development*, World Bank Country Study (Washington, D.C.: World Bank, 1990).

6. Tsang Shu-ki, Liang Suizheng and Wang Zhenzhong, "Yinhang ji xindai" (Banking and Credit), in *Guangdong jingji touzi zonglan* (Encyclopedia on the Economy and Investment in Guangdong), edited by Lau Pui-king (Hong Kong: The Commercial Press, 1996), chapter 9.

7. Calculated from Zhongguo jinrong xuehui (ed.), *Zhongguo jinrong nianjian 1991* (Almanac of China's Finance and Banking) (Beijing: Zhongguo jinrong nianjian bianjibu, 1991), pp. 166, 223.

8. See note 3, p. 154.

9. Ibid., pp. 155–56.

10. Ibid., p. 156.

11. *Shenzhen tequ bao* (Shenzhen Special Zone Daily), 10 January 1993.

12. Guangdong's average real growth rate is calculated from the GDP index while that of the country as a whole is from the GNP index.

13. See note 3, p. 159.

14. According to one economist, Guangdong only used RMB700 million of the quota, saving RMB500 million of funds for the central government in 1981–1983. See Wang Zhuo, "Lun Guangdong shichang jingji tizhi jianshe zouxiang" (On the Direction of Guangdong's Construction of the Market Economic System) (paper presented at the China's Economic Development and Reform in the 1990s Conference, organized by the Chinese Culture Promotion Centre of Hong Kong and the Hong Kong Social Sciences Research Society, Hong Kong, 25–26 February 1993).

15. Although Guangdong itself does not necessarily think so, see *Yue–Gang xinxi bao* (Guangdong–Hong Kong Information Daily), 1 March 1992 for a contrary view.

16. Lin Dengyun, "Guangdong caizheng tizhi gaige de youyi changshi" (Beneficial Attempts of Fiscal System Reform in Guangdong), in *Gaige kaifang zai Guangdong* (see note 3), p. 139.

17. *Yue–Gang xinxi bao*, 1 March 1992.

18. World Bank, *China: Revenue Mobilization and Tax Policy*, World Bank Country Study (Washington, D.C.: World Bank, 1990), Table 3.3.
19. Ibid.
20. *Yue–Gang xinxi bao*, 1 March 1992.
21. A Shanghai researcher, Wang Zhan, points out that in the past decade, the amount which Shanghai had to submit to the central government was over RMB100 billion more than that by Guangdong. He argues that Shanghai's economic situation would have been very different if such an amount of money had been invested in the city. See *Ming Pao Daily News*, Hong Kong, 27 February 1993, p. 6.
22. Liang Guiquan et al., *Qifei di guiji: Guangdong jingji fazhan shizheng fenxi* (The Track of Rising Economy: A Sample Analysis of Guangdong's Economic Development) (Guangzhou: Guangdong renmin chubanshe, 1992), chapters 17, 18. A methodological note of caution should be made here. It is related to the issue of the monetization of the economy, under which money, self-owned or borrowed, is used in more spheres of economic activities, compared with the pre-reform period when various forms of barter and direct material allocations were practised. The degree of increased monetization in China during the reform years is difficult to gauge, but one available estimate pointed to a relatively mild change. See Tsang Shu-ki, "Controlling Money during Socialist Economic Reform: The Chinese Experience," *Economy and Society*, Vol. 19, No. 2 (May 1990), pp. 217–41. In general, monetization should have affected working capital calculations much less than fixed capital statistics (which need to adjust to the process of *bo gai dai* — the conversion of appropriations into loans). In any case, the analysis by Liang et al. of the situation in the year of 1988 alone, which is independent of the relative degree of monetization, serves as an alarming piece of *prima facie* evidence of financial inefficiency in Guangdong.
23. Xie Yongping, "Guangdong jinrongye zai 'zhui long' zhong de zuoyong" (The Functions of Finance in Guangdong's Effort to 'Catch up with the Dragons'), *Guangdong jinrong*, No. 10 (1992), pp. 5–7.
24. See note 22, p. 304.
25. Han Houyuan et al., "Guangdong chanye jiegou tiaozheng yu jinrong tizhi gaige" (Industrial Structural Adjustment and Financial System Reform in Guangdong), *Guangdong jinrong*, No. 1 (1991), pp. 8–10.
26. Ibid.
27. See "Bank May Shoulder Blame in Shenzhen," *South China Morning Post*, 14 August 1992.
28. See Lu Feng, "Zhongguo gushi liu da bingtai — Shenzhen fengbo de beihou xingsi" (The Six Types of Serious Sickness in China's Stock Market: Reflections on the Shenzhen Turmoil), *Hong Kong Economic Journal*, 14 August 1992; Wang Youjin, "Zhongguo gufenzhi de falu guifan" (The Legal

Framework of China's Share-holding System), *Hong Kong Economic Journal*, 27 August 1992.

29. Ren Hang, "Guangdongsheng huobi liutong xin bianhua" (New Changes in the Monetary Circulation of Guangdong Province), *Guangdong jinrong*, No. 11 (1992), pp. 4–5. Ren quotes the example of five peasant households which bid successfully the tender of a brick factory in Dongguan. They came up with RMB200,000 of cash from home in 45 minutes, without having to go to the bank!

30. For an analysis of the national economic trends after the Fourteenth Party Congress, see Tsang Shu-ki, "Dangqian Zhongguo jingji cunzai shenme wenti?" (What Problems Presently Exist in the Chinese Economy?), *Wide Angle*, December 1992, pp. 16–21. See also Chapter 7 of this volume.

31. *Jinrong shibao*, 28 January 1993.

32. *Shenzhen tequ bao*, 10 January 1993. A metal exchange is already in operation in Shenzhen.

33. *Ming Pao Daily News*, 15 February 1993, p. 7. Shares in a share-holding state enterprise in China are divided into three types: (1) state shares; (2) legal person (enterprise) shares; and (3) individual shares. Theoretically, only individual shares can be transferred or exchanged. However, in Beijing, an exchange system for legal person shares was set up in December 1990. It is called STAQ (Securities Trading Automated Quotations System). See CERD Consultants Limited, *Beijing gupiao shichang baogao 1992* (Report on the Beijing Stock Market 1992), Hong Kong, September 1992. It appears that Guangdong is trying to emulate that effort.

34. *Wen Wei Po*, 23 February 1993, p. 2. An integrated commodities exchange, the first of its kind in China, is scheduled to open in Guangzhou in August 1993. Spot and futures trading of agricultural products, rubber, petroleum, metal material, and construction material for participants within the country are to be included. See *Hong Kong Economic Journal*, 28 February 1992, p. 3.

35. *Jinrong shibao*, 28 January 1993.

36. For a discussion of the problems of imbalances in Guangdong's economic development, see Tsang Shu-ki, *The Economic Link-up of Guangdong and Hong Kong: Structural and Developmental Problems*, BRC Papers on China, CP95003 (Hong Kong: Business Research Centre, Hong Kong Baptist University, 1995).

37. Pronouncements and reports of these commitments abound. See for example, *Wen Wei Po*, 5 February 1993, p. 31.

38. Li Dan'er, "Jiusi jinrong gaige dui Guangdong jingji de yingxiang" (The Impact of the 1994 Financial Reform on the Guangdong Economy), *Guangdong jinrong* (Guangdong Finance), No. 6, 1994, pp. 4–6.

39. See, for example, Tsang Shu-ki, "Towards Full Convertibility? China's

Foreign Exchange Reform," *China Information*, Vol. IX, No. 1 (1994), pp. 1–41.

40. The major policy documents are compiled in Wang Dingchang (ed.), *2010 nian de Guangdong: Guihua ji zhanlüe yanjiu* (Guangdong in 2010: Planning and Strategic Studies) (Guangzhou: Guangdong renmin chubanshe, 1994).

9

Entrepreneurs Probing Uncertainty and Bounded Rationality

Maurice Brosseau

In the earlier version of this chapter, we had sought the meaning of entrepreneurship in the context of Guangdong's economic reform. The province's rising prosperity, especially in the Pearl River Delta, had been noted for its more than ten years of tenacity in the pursuit of economic gain. However, serious structural and administrative constraints affecting the behaviour of managers and private operators had led to the conclusion that the exercise of personal creativity had still been hampered.[1] Since then, in the wake of the 1992 decision to implement a (socialist) market economy, a new set of conditions — fiscal, financial and organizational — has further tested local administrators and managers, especially in regard to what theorists in and out of China have been considering one of the major reform objectives, the property regime in the non-agricultural economic sectors.

Ruling out generalized privatization, China's gradual economic transition has, in contrast to Eastern Europe, administratively kept the property question in relative abeyance while heading for a market economy. Whether the Chinese reform can be sustainable if managers and private enterprise owners are asked to take effective responsibility for economic decision without clear property and ownership guarantees, is the object of a debate, one purview of which can be found in the proceedings of a symposium on Victor Nee's "market transition" thesis reproduced in the January 1996 issue of the *American Journal of Sociology*. In the concluding summary, Ivan Szelenyi and Eric Kostello draw a picture of the experience of Eastern Europe as probably "the future of China": the two authors argue that the administrative and managerial relationships had not changed despite economic transformation; in contrast to Nee's thesis, there would be little chance "an alternative avenue of socio-economic mobility" could be created whereby a new stratum of entrepreneurs would displace the hitherto privileged party-state élites.[2]

This is so, of course, when one subscribes to the structuralist view proposed by Jean Oi that economic rationality and entrepreneurship in China be ascribed to energetic local government officials under "local state corporatism."[3] A kindred understanding can be drawn from Andrew Walder's study of management and administration in which he considers

---

This study was supported in part by a research grant from the South China Programme of the Hong Kong Institute of Asia Pacific Studies, The Chinese University of Hong Kong.

that China's economic reforms have decentralized administration with the result of a relatively successful bureaucratic enforcement of "hard budget constraints" on enterprises and the reaping of collective profits (albeit with assorted personal advantages).[4] At variance, Jean-Louis Rocca of France considers that Oi and Walder are mixing two different discourses, economic rationality and political motives. For Rocca, what Oi and Walder are looking at is not "true capital" but relationships, not "entrepreneurship" but managers acting as facilitators to administrative power,[5] a view of rationality "bounded" to political priorities also held by analysts of Chinese history.[6] David Wank, on the other hand, tries to bridge this gap by looking at the patronage of entrepreneurs by local administrators as a constructive function of an imperfect market.[7]

From the vantage point of analysts within China, the prolonged transition, if not leading to a dramatic change in stratification, has engendered a process of slowly nibbling away at the public assets.[8] With Fan Gang, recent financial difficulties have revealed a public ownership sector facing institutional breakdown, while it is confoundingly able to sustain a positive productivity performance.[9] Managers are preempting — in Fan's view, they usurp the right to — property regime change; and the state must oblige by admitting the bureaucracy's inability to monitor state assets and by sanctioning managers' competence.[10] Li Lulu, on the other hand, asserts on the basis of his analysis of survey data that Victor Nee's thesis of a shift in stratification may be in the process of partial realization as an increasing number of cadres are abandoning official careers for entrepreneurial ventures.[11]

The present inquiry contends that individual effort has been effecting change in unexpected ways, such as bringing about change in the established practices of economic administration. Entrepreneurship has been challenging from within the so-called Leninist fused system of bureaucratic politics and economic planning,[12] and it is pressing the unitary institution into a new transition that may enforce a solution to current difficulties (bargaining rather than market exchange, duplication of investments, soft budget constraints, loss of assets, rapid wage rise, corruption, etc.). Entrepreneurship has been gaining a margin of autonomy because its function is seen as a potential means to address the economic problems "according to economic premises and by economic means."[13] The changes in enterprises in the Guangdong economic context, especially after 1992, imply the tackling of the all-important question of property rights under the impact of the entrepreneurial function.

Basic Scenario

The case of China's development can be categorized as a learning curve in the development of a new form of leadership out of what Goldstein and others have called the "fused system." In the following pages, the emergence of entrepreneurship explains, for example, the need to reform the town-and-village enterprises (TVE) — so soon after their "creation" — and thus takes programmatic importance.

As expressed in many Chinese commentaries, it is an institutional reform (*gai zhi*), straining relations between the local government leadership and the enterprise management.[14] The history of the reforms shows the double opportunity to "fuse" the political leadership with the economic roles and the search for the ways to provide the enterprise and its manager a degree of autonomy. Entrepreneurship had been called upon from the very beginning of the reforms to build upon pragmatic experimentations, although no one in authority could guarantee that any of the innovative choices would become legitimate.

Guangdong, in this regard, proved demonstrative of the seriousness with which the practice of reforms would lead to both economic and political change taking place from *within*, thus promising validity, as postulated by Steven Goldstein.[15]

The data of Table 9.1, redrawn from a more elaborate macroeconomic depiction of growth in a study by a research centre at Zhongshan University in Guangzhou,[16] provide an impressive comparison of the rates of growth in the nation and in Guangdong; these statistics ascertain the "momentum" of the province's widely applauded performance. However, as many Guangdong analysts admit, numbers on gross domestic product, national income, and even total factor productivity indicators are mainly indicative of one's product; they are not revealing, as Fan Gang has insisted, the hidden costs which have shrunken the rate of profits going to the "owner," the local state, to be described in greater detail below.[17]

Much of the academic debate on the objectives and trajectory of the Chinese reforms hinges on the assumptions scholars hold about the Chinese Leninist regime as a "fused system," a monolithic ordering of command and a monopolistic articulation of the economy. A breach of the Leninist structure would presage the dislocation of the state and the dismemberment of the party.

Yet, as reviewed by Goldstein, after badly negotiated turns in the regime's history, quite a few policy concerns and choices — at the time

Table 9.1   Individual-average Indicators of Economic Development, 1993

Indicator	Pearl River Delta	Guangdong Province	Nation
GDP (RMB)	10,318.7	4,938.0	2,647.7
National income (RMB)	4,449.5	3,939.0	2,111.0
Fiscal income (RMB)	1,105.5	526.6	429.3
Total retail sale (RMB)	3,928.0	2,212.3	1,032.5
Use of foreign capital (US$)	289.9	146.7	31.0
Total export (US$)	786.4	310.2	77.5
Year-end savings (RMB)	6,452.3	2,847.8	1,247.5
Total investment (RMB)	5,128.3	2,476.4	998.1
Value-added by service sector (RMB)	2,727.6	1,176.1	715.9

Source: Zhongshan University Research Center of Pearl River Delta Economic Development and Management, *Zhujiang sanjaozhou jingji fazhan xin toushi* (New Perspective on the Economic Development of the Pearl River Delta) (Guangzhou: Zhongshan daxue chubanshe, 1995).

reasons for some of the polemics of the 1950s to the 1970s — crucially contributed to the present economic success for the very reason that the party had not stuck so staunchly to the Leninist fusion. One such obscure policy, the creation of the rural "five small plants," was to transform into or be the inspiration for the very successful collective and private TVEs of the 1980s and 1990s.[18] In institutional terms, the Chinese communists had been taking liberties, as in Eastern Europe.[19]

The economic reform momentum in the cities and rural towns of Guangdong had taken its roots largely in such ground, but not always for the enrichment of the population. Behind the often glamourized statistics, the perplexing dynamism led some commentators to depict the scene as more akin to dishevelled rough-and-tumble among political and administrative cadres than social-economic progress.[20]

Thus, it is worth asking what kind of entrepreneurship has been effective? More to the point, where has the entrepreneur made one's mark? A search for an explanation is the more significant, the more difficult has been the characterization of Guangdong development, especially since 1992, after elder Deng Xiaoping's dramatic visit (*nanxun*) to the province. It must have been quite unsettling for Guangdong leaders to be soon reminded by renowned economist Dong Fureng that their ersatz progressive model was running the risk of obsolescence,[21] "the squeezed layer in an economic sandwich,"[22] an aspiring economy not yet able to move up on its own to the next technological stage, in contrast to Hong Kong or Southeast Asian economies, for example, while being edged out of competition by newly emerging regions playing their comparative advantage of cheap land and abundant unskilled labour.

The incremental reforms had earmarked successful experiments in agricultural production and justified the town-and-village enterprises. The next step but less successful, the reform of the state-owned enterprise management system justifiably stood as one of the most important confutations of the "fused" system. Alongside the experiments with profit retention and a new tax system (*li gai shui*), dual-tier pricing and reduced planned obligations, the "contract responsibility system" in the late 1980s provided the occasion for the enunciation of an advanced role for managers, as well as for an extended debate on the meaning of entrepreneurship and innovative change. Up to 1992, the results were less than ideal: while the control once afforded by central planning had largely become non-determinant, the managers were still portrayed as reluctant or unable to gain autonomy, dependent on administrative counsel, "entangled in complex bargaining relationships," rather than motivated to the task of strategic management and raising efficiency.[23]

Yet, as Thomas Rawski noted, "China's reforms have taken the form of *enabling* measures that remove barriers to enterprise activity and permit new initiatives."[24] The intervention of the state, however intended, reflected such enabling of entrepreneurship to provide under guidance a range of possible pathways that would result in some suitable breakthrough (*tupo*), a suspect strategy frowned upon by many Chinese economists.

Chinese economic analysts, as represented by Zhang Weiying — and Fan Gang above — have taken a rather different view from their Western colleagues and have put the emphasis elsewhere, feeling that the treatment of the analytical favourite, "total factor productivity," had been of little solace. Rather than paying attention to such palpable progress that may have been achieved since 1978, Chinese researchers have been worrying about the reform of enterprise system, or "corporate governance." That is, whether managers' decision-making and operational autonomy, by the very reason that profits were being deflected for internal distribution rather than being divided between the state and the firm, were not dramatically demonstrating the need to recognize the time had come officially to move towards the redistribution of property.[25]

The quandary described by Zhang is that, under the terms of the reform transition, two frameworks or economic doctrines exist simultaneously: the first, the pre-reform, nominally "socialist doctrine" of ownership by the whole people, defining the state as principal agent with rights to the profit residual and the enterprise as a production unit under the dictate of the planners; the second, the "reform doctrine," which define the whole people as the owner, the state apparatus as a bond-holder entitled to a fixed return on capital and the enterprise management as the principal agent responsible for the property assets in return for the right to claim the profit residual. As Zhang Weiying indicates, during the transition, there are two legitimate principals competing with each other; and, under the "socialist doctrine," the economic bureau officials stand as sub-agents of the principal (the planners) in the enforcement of planning, while, under the "reform doctrine," the officials find themselves wearing two hats: as the reforms are aiming at the objective of gradually granting autonomy to managers, the state uses the bureaucrats as agents to monitor and control the learning process by managers, while the firm managers try to exercise and/or take advantage of their autonomy by seeking the assistance of bureaucrats to gain access and control of the residual. That is, the bureaucrats are using their advantageous mediating position "to eat both sides," optimizing their share of the economic rent.

Therein has lain one of the major sources of the uncertainty that has characterized the efforts of the variously interested actors experimenting with measures to find a rewarding protection of their interests during the transition to a new regime.

Without going into the details of Zhang Weiying's analytical explanations, suffice to say that the logic of the "reform doctrine" has painfully gained in clarity by pushing the limits of economic practice.[26] However, as said earlier, it has lacked a guarantee that any innovative choice — licit, illicit or marginal — would gain legitimacy by a decision of the party-state leadership. Decision making has been characterized by a limited capacity to follow a relatively open and systematic path, thus the need to bargain over goals and strategies, in other words, a form of sub-optimal calculation engrossed in "bounded rationality" and interdependency of choices.[27]

It also means that, for Chinese analysts, the logical priority is not whether there is a change in the stratification structure (as with Victor Nee) or whether the local government leadership proves "entrepreneurial" without the need to advance towards privatization or the clarification and separation of property rights (as with Jean Oi or Andrew Walder); the key question of the reform, its very logic, is indeed the highly intense pressure to redistribute property rights. In this endeavour, bargaining over contract terms, even the exercise of discretion by managers over profits and assets, become the core activity of the reform, because both types of activities energize the redistribution of élites.[28]

As seen earlier, the expansion of autonomy and decision-making to the public firms could not supply the analogue of the rural household responsibility system that had allowed substantive autonomy and quickly weaned the peasants from the commune. The manager remained dependent as long as there was no clear role delineation.

To this effect, by 1987, experiments with industrial management had progressed to the "manager responsibility system" further to formalize the division of powers: the manager had had to sign a formal contract with the authorized administrative supervisors (*zhuguan bumen*). In this respect, Guangdong had moved quickly to implement the new rules even to its TVEs under grassroots jurisdictions. Nationally, the contract system had been hailed, at first in analogy to the arrangement in agriculture with peasant households, as having achieved the same motivating and binding effect, the second benchmark (*licheng bei*) of the reform process.[29] It soon became apparent that it would incite fierce debates over its dangers and shortcomings.

Translated, the contract meant that the manager was gaining, in principle, an unprecedented control over plant finance and becoming, also in principle, accountable for profits and losses. Practically, there was no firm basis for, much less agreement on, the separation of powers although the contradiction of the state being both owner and regulator was widely recognized as detrimental to managerial autonomy and the maximization of the use of resources.[30] However, a fuller realization of autonomy, a clear delineation of socialist ownership, managerial authority and the marketization of enterprise assets were still being thwarted,[31] though financial reform was gaining ground with experiments with leasing, the creation of corporate holdings and share investment.[32]

The 1980s had been little different from earlier attempts from the 1950s onward when each attempt at reform had faced a similar pattern of officials' deviance to the detriment of policy implementation according to Wu Jinglian of the State Council's Research Centre for Development.[33] The major problem lay with the contract which required that the assets be clearly delineated in the document for responsibilities assigned to owner (in lieu of the general state, the bureau) and contractor. And, to evaluate the assets in the absence of a capital market and professional evaluators, the managers and plant directors were to be directly involved, resulting in systematic "leakage" (*liushi*) of state assets.[34]

The "Waves" of Reform

The process led by political administrators, as under Oi's "local state corporatism" or Walder's "hard budget constraints without privatization"[35] are both supportive of a grassroots reform administratively led, yet obviously failing to engage the whole economy and secure a unified market logic.

Pre-1978, the "fused" ethos, in Goldstein's terms,[36] commanding economic policy could be characterized as an urge to develop which had condoned the opening of a wide chasm between rural and urban economies. The rural leadership had been suffused by a "great leap" mentality of communes and production brigades (the towns and villages of post-1983) becoming self-reliant by developing their own implement and service industry. The latter had been further developed, in the wake of the Cultural Revolution, with the promotion of the "five small plants."[37]

Until about 1992, this ethos remained prevalent, tolerating after 1978 a relatively liberal reallocation of material rewards to the individual, party and non-party members alike, as Rocca would suggest. However, examples from several counties of Guangdong's Pearl River delta showed how the developments were steered to the advantage of the incumbent élite. If the Nanhai leaders had allowed in the early 1980s their grassroots leaders to redistribute all commune assets to the households and if two hundred or so kilometers south-west, Yangjiang county cadres had considered they had better let the peasant household keep ploughing the fields or go sea-fishing since state-owned and collective assets had been so meagre; by the early 1990s, their areas had become renowned for their quickly expanding private enterprise networks.[38]

Next door, however, Zhongshan or Shunde leaders had discerned the opportunity offered them to shape a course contrasting with the other regions. They coolly refrained from redistributing to households the (non-agricultural) productive assets, such as transport or factory equipments, having understood that there was soon to be a low-cost labour force displaced from agriculture in need of work; they appropriated all collective assets under exclusive county and town ownership. Shunde devised a strategy of industrialization aiming at creating large collectives; the area was to spawn majors in home appliances, such as Kelon, Meidi, Yuhua, Huabao, etc. Often edged on by Hong Kong kin and Macau compatriots looking for cheap labour and low-cost industrial rent for their increasingly squeezed establishments in their respective colony, the alert county cadres laid the foundations of the Guangdong reform economy to come.

The "second wave"

It was already becoming progressively evident on the eve of the 14th Party Congress in 1992 that the local Guangdong economy had been losing momentum. The major difficulties were the low quality of the work force (peasants recently released from the fields), the low level of technological endowment, the low level of managerial know-how, the lack of an enterprise normative framework, the age of the production equipment, the lack of investment in technical improvement, etc.

For the Chinese concerned, a "second wave of reform," or "reform deepening" (*shenhua gaige*), was needed to renew the undertaking started in 1978, with the "four modernizations."[39] Not obvious at first, the events of 1992 — Deng Xiaoping's visit to Guangdong as preamble to the "constitutional" breakthrough at the 14th Party Congress where the market supplanted the centralized economic planning order[40] — were to be epoch-making, both in positive and negative terms. The consequences, for Guangdong, were summarized in a hard hitting article in 1995; Yang Jisheng, chief-editor of *Jingji cankao bao* (Economic Information Daily), did not hide with his six reasons the dangers facing Guangdong's economic future:

— Preferential policies had lapsed as the focus of reform had shifted to the poor central and western regions. Light, processing industries were going to move away.

— The economic shift to the Yangtze river delta region, with Pudong at its core, provided attractive investment potentials, because of the broad economic strength, the advanced industrial base and the large financial backing and sophisticated strategies.

— The reforms now extended to the whole of China, no longer limiting foreign investors to the coast.

— The fiscal and financial reforms of 1993 would help Guangdong streamline its economy; but gone were the advantages of the previous tax responsibility system. City and county governments were being forced greatly to curtail investment.

— The early years of reform had allowed each county to seek and build itself up, protected from large-scale markets; the competition can no longer be informal; open competition risks much wasteful friction (*neihao*).

— The development of TVEs, however successful in the past, had now hit obstacles: internal management, labour relations, efficiency, and invest-ments had left a great void (*kongdong*) hiding behind successes, i.e., TVEs faced huge debts.

The author considered that Guangdong had already created for itself, on the base of labour-intensive processing for export, a solid economy from which to face the challenges.

By choosing Guangdong in 1992 as his rostrum to make his last major policy statement, Deng Xiaoping had proceeded to consolidate for the nation as a whole some of the structural advances realized there; however, the signal for new boldness in reform were interpreted at first as a renewed effort according to the old ways of expansion — a flurry of investments in new ventures, enterprise expansion, real estate speculation, etc. — a criticism already noted in the previous version of this chapter.[41] In quick order, the threatening rise of inflation, the cost of materials or the growing wage bills reminded the administrators that the threat of a boom-and-bust scenario could repeat its cycle. This time, however, the new strategy adopted by the state centre in mid-1993, new fiscal measures (taxation reform) and the reform of banking and financial controls, had a pressing meaning not lost on the local élite and administrators.

Provincial Data

Whatever the meaning of Guangdong leaders' 1995 visit to Shanghai "on pilgrimage" (*qujing*, to learn new ways), the local administrators could no longer skirt the issues of the nature of their enterprises. During the course of 1991 to 1994, while publicly owned enterprises (both state-owned, SOE, and collective-owned, COE, units) represented in numbers 72.1% of all industrial plants, their gross value of output were achieving only 48.5% of the total production, in contrast to the privately owned (various forms of private, including foreign-invested, industry) which numbered 27.9% but were accounting for the major part (51.5%) of output; of this remainder, 50.7% (up from 24.3% in 1990) was being taken up by the foreign-invested units.[42]

Even the great success of the TVEs was not without its problems. Guangdong by most measures was not even the most successful at it (see Table 9.2). Some Chinese researchers would not even consider the

Table 9.2 TVEs' Comparative Development in Leading Provinces, 1991

	Guang-dong	Hebei	Henan	Jiangsu	Liao-ning	Shan-dong	Zhe-jiang	Sichuan
Output (RMB billion)	79	51.6	51.4	152.7	41.6	115.1	92.6	—
Work force (million)	7.1	—	9.4	8.7	—	9.9	—	7.4

Source: Ma Rong, Wang Hansheng and Liu Shiding (eds.), *Zhongguo xiangzhen qiye de fazhan lishi yu yunxing jizhi* (The History of Chinese Town-and-village Enterprises' Development and Operational Mechanisms) (Beijing: Beijing daxue chubanshe, 1994), p. 17.

province's development in this regard a good example for valid regional comparison because of the strong influence of capital, managerial strategy and technical services coming from the Hong Kong and overseas Chinese.[43]

Guangdong could no longer boast of being the reform role model: a review made in 1994 indicated that the well-performing TVE units (apart from the foreign-invested) were a few large ones, while the great majority remained limited to the situation they had reached several years previously. In Foshan, one of the best performing areas with 18,000 TVEs, only 246 units could achieve a yearly production in excess of RMB10 million; the great majority were still rather small plants producing in the paltry range of RMB10,000 to RMB 1 million; and, many of the latter were really only family-led units with about 10 workers, typically in a small shop of about 200-300 square metres. Another study of the six major cities of the delta (excluding Shenzhen) found that, between 1988 to 1991, in most of these enterprises only RMB 944 million had been invested in technological improvement (7.37% of all capital investment); and, this, mainly by the few very large units, such as Kelon in Shunde. The greatest majority of the TVE units had kept pretty much as they had always been, using the same old machines and techniques, keeping high the rate of materials and energy consumption, and producing out-of-fashion products. In 1991 there had been officially 1,439 loss-making TVE units (out of about 120,000) in the Pearl River delta, 45.73% of all provincial units with a shortfall.[44] In other words, Guangdong's main organizational pride was broadly getting to be known in related circles to be on the decline.[45]

Although the aggregate statistics for the province were still remarkable, compared with some of the closest provincial competitors, there were other signs that were soon to come out.

The Private Entrepreneurial Function

Guangdong had quite a few private failures after early success had encouraged a sense of bravura: Yuhua Corporation in Shunde had been started by a peasant entrepreneur (Ou Jianquan) who had counted on his astuteness to establish his wealth and renown on sound equipment manufacture. Once successful, trust and credit had come his way, encouraging further diversification on market "intuition," such as engaging in steel butane containers and automobiles. Ou Jianquan's branching out could not, however, exchange quantity for quality or buy expertise out of operational size and soon faced collapse; the owner had failed to make research on the market and, symmetrically, to apprehend the changing needs of his organization. The corporate body ended "bankrupt, an empty shell."[46]

The case of Ou Jianquan says something about hubris but little about the prospects of private venturing in the socialist context. The glance provides the confirmation that much can be accomplished, and lost, within the fluid environment when the individual in pursuit of wealth meets head on with the institutional conditions.

Private enterprise in Guangdong has often been negatively described — an all-too-pervasive tendency of the official discourse[47] — as having energy but unreliable and almost built-in corrupting qualities in the pursuit of quick wealth. Spawning heroic projects, as in Shunde, is not enough. The entrepreneur still has to provide the equivalent of the risk-exploiting ability which stakes the ambient factors and seeks to harmonize them into long-term sustainability and growth from which society benefits. Highly suffused by the long-established political-ideological frame of mind, private entrepreneurship has been caught in the dilemma of the regime's. Is private capital going to be able to find its own space in relation to state ownership and the definition of its rights as against the state's? And, is private entrepreneurship going to achieve legitimacy in the eyes of the public? The answers vary.

First, private entrepreneurship is foremost a question of private property, or at least the protection and guarantee that non-state created property and its further growth are to be relatively inviolable. At present, the question is not only economic, it directly affects the ideological and organizational well-being of the Party. It is one thing for urban or rural officials to work on internal differentiation and create new institutions out of the public-owned sector. It is another question for private accumulation, having since the 7th National People's Congress (first session) of April 1988 gained protection by the amendment to the state constitution. Private ownership and capital formation can be engaged into, but constitutional protection has yet to move officially beyond "toleration" (*yunxu*), as offered in the amendment. After almost ten years, this amendment is still perceived by private operators to be only *quan yi zhi ji* (a calculated expediency) by a state under difficult political-economic circumstances ready to mobilize for a time as many "productive forces" as possible.[48] Full property rights granted to the private entrepreneur implies for the party-state more than the *de-fusion* of the Leninist system discussed by Steven Goldstein,[49] achieved in part by Shunde's property right experiment, as discussed below. The state has yet to find the formulation congruent with its ideological tradition that would grant private owners full "rights of exclusion" binding the state and other parties under law.[50]

The other key factor of private entrepreneurship, internal definition, in the present context is as old as China itself.

At this stage, private ownership may be gaining in efficiency, scope and size, but it is still relatively costly as manifested by private entrepreneurs' short-term goals, dilution of investment and kinship-based trust. Not to be forgotten, according to David Wank, is the lack of coherence, anaemic self-identity (individual and aggregate), the multiplication of cleavages responding to the variety of influences accentuated by diverse, high and low, officialdom which has developed scores of avenues to pursue localized and/or corrupt interests, as the previously normative planning framework has disappeared and the market structured by law and economic order has still to mature. Wank draws attention to the formerly unitary state seeing its cadre officialdom regrouping into various clusters, big or small, and of officials and entrepreneurs shifting away from the simpler patron-client to a "symbiotic" relationship in which valued goods are exchanged, following paths characterized as going from the grey, informal bestowing of advantage, to the plain illegal forms.[51]

The negative view is over-shadowed by Chinese analysts, such as Dai Jianzhong, who assimilate the Chinese private entrepreneurial stratum — in contra-distinction to Western bourgeois entrepreneurs who had quickly set their identity in contrast (conflict) with the nobility — with the almost perpetually dependent common people.[52]

Wank's entrepreneur is largely the profit-seeker who contributes little to the institutional evolution of the economic system, albeit to the refinement of the concept of clientelism, dependent or symbiotic; the model borrowed from Jean Oi's[53] and by intention seeking an institutional understanding of Chinese reform remains largely infertile. The "client," in Tables 9.3 and 9.4 drawn from Dai Jianzhong's work, has to fall back on relatives and friends to give one a hand, the latter being in many cases state officials or organization cadres.

This view of the Chinese entrepreneur examines an important but partial nature of the institution. In a graphic way, the descriptions have more to do with the attributes of clientelism or corruption than with the institutional questions which explain and sustain clientelism and corruption.

Thus, particularistic (familistic) attributes are primary features, understandably, considering the need for trust in the unfriendly environment. Yet, this is also portrayed by some entrepreneurs themselves as non conducive to good leadership and performance.

Table 9.3   Career Posting of Private Entrepreneur's Spouse

(Unit: %)

	Wife	Husband	Urban spouse	Rural spouse
Technician	7.0	14.4	8.2	3.6
Cadre	17.0	27.1	18.8	10.1
Worker	20.0	12.7	20.1	13.7
Salesperson	9.6	4.2	10.0	2.9
Military	0.1	0.0	0.1	0.0
Peasant	18.9	11.9	14.3	49.6
getihu	13.1	16.9	14.2	7.1
Other	14.2	12.7	14.3	12.9
Number	1,153	118	1,122	139

Source: Dai Jianzhong, "Zhongguo dalu siying qiye ji siying qiye zhu yanjiu" (Research on Mainland China's Private Enterprise and Private Entrepreneur), in *Frontiers of Social Indicators Research in Chinese Societies*, edited by Lau Siu-kai, Wan Po-san, Lee Ming-kwan and Wong Siu-lun (Hong Kong: Hong Kong Institute of Asia-Pacific Studies, The Chinese University of Hong Kong, 1996), p. 513.

Table 9.4   Career Posting of Private Entrepreneur's Relatives and Friends

(Unit: %)

	Relatives		Friends	
	Urban area	Rural area	Urban area	Rural area
Technician	13.2	6.4	17.5	12.9
Cadre	37.9	31.2	42.4	39.4
Worker	11.5	7.2	8.9	3.0
Salesperson	2.8	1.6	9.8	6.1
Military	8.3	0.8	1.4	0.8
Peasant	16.5	49.6	7.9	28.2
getihu	7.1	3.2	9.4	6.8
Other	2.8	0.0	2.9	2.3
Number	1,072	125	1,105	132

Source: As in Table 9.3.

Guangzhou's Private Entrepreneur

Guangdong had been, up to about 1992, nominally if not fully so in fact, one of the major leading jurisdictions of the reform process. Naturally, not all of Guangdong regions had been equally capable and motivated, in particular its far away and poorer mountainous regions which until today are largely the object of special help and the recipient of funds, expertise and technology transfers from the Pearl River delta pace-setters. More crucial to the overall reform momentum, Guangzhou as provincial capital should hold up its own and be one of the pace-setters by virtue of its being the political, administrative and, putatively, financial centre of the whole province. However, this has not been happening. To a large extent, Guangzhou has had to give Hong Kong the honour of being the "energy" centre of the Guangdong reform, Guangzhou having little chance of achieving qualitative upgrading.

In terms of private economic development, when other regions of the province and urban centres in the rest of the country have been taking steps to integrate the private sector within the socialist ownership structure, Guangzhou has been losing momentum to the worry of high officials and analysts.

The growth of the private economy has gained in importance for practical reasons, especially when the state- and collective-owned sectors have been showing unmistakable signs of a slow-down: however,

Guangzhou has been losing from the list of its own private operations at the very moment the city needs them most for its employment potential in the face of the reform and down-sizing of the public-owned enterprises.

In addition, when across the nation, in 1994, the creation of private enterprises (not counting the small-scale household *getihu* units) went up by 81.68% (14 provinces achieving a rate above 80%), Guangzhou's pace was 44.78%; in 1995, the national rate slowed down to about 30%, Guangzhou slumped to 16.36% (a respective drop of 62.5% and 63.5%). When elsewhere the rate of private working capital grew by 69.91% and employment by 26.77%, in Guangzhou the rates were 26.49% and 14.26%. On other indicators, Guangzhou equally showed a declining pattern: the number of private corporations (nation 8.84%, Guangzhou 8.59%), size of employees (nation 12.94, Guangzhou 10.57), proportion of the gross domestic product (nation 2.635%, Guangzhou 1.886%).

The deceleration has been happening more acutely in the last few years after the city had led the nation in this domain. It has been affecting not only the *siying* enterprises but also the *getihu* sector, prompting greater alarm, especially because, as Gao Yaohui of Guangzhou Administration of Industry and Commerce indicated,[54] the private enterprises' "major source of investment capital" has been the *getihu*; and, since the consumer market has been growing all over the country, particularly fertile area for *getihu* growth, about 33% in 1994 of them graduated to the level of enterprise (*siying qiye*). In terms of the economic reforms, the national consumer market and its infrastructure have been maturing, a quantitative growth feeding into qualitative change: operational scale, financial ability and diversification of services.

Guangzhou has been going in the other direction when jurisdictions across the country are debating ways to stimulate the increasingly useful private economy, to forge strategies to overcome weaknesses, such as the distrust of state policies most clearly symbolized by the tendency of private entrepreneurs at the sign of problems to de-register as private and re-register as collective (to "wear a red hat," or to *guakao*, literally "hang a [dependency] nameplate") and provide against the effect of policy changes (all too frequent in many locations) and to take advantage of biased (pro public-owned enterprise) policies or practices regarding bank financing, taxation rates, access to technical personnel, production factor inputs, sale services, etc.

Guangzhou municipal government realized the dysfunctional results of the bias and enacted in 1993 regulations to redefine private business;

from *getihu* to large private enterprises, all were to be characterized as fully fledged "market actors" (*zhuti*), in contrast to the previous categorization of "supplement" (*buchong*) to the erstwhile legitimate public-owned (state and collective) economy.[55] Unfortunately, the new language fell short of translating into practice as "backward" practices remained, in particular the *guakao*. The reason for it in Guangzhou had been the decision to allow the *guakao* as a means for neighbourhood committees and city districts to practise a form of "non-capitalization business" (*wuben shengyi*) whereby districts could raise their earnings from fees on enterprises without having to invest scarce funds into new establishments. The districts had been allowed to collect administrative fees from private entrepreneurs who would agree to relocate under *guakao* as "collective." An internally devised means officially to raise district earnings for investment and services on the basis of traditional planning norm had the perverse, though foreseeable, effect of weakening what was a dynamic engine of growth. To get private entrepreneurs under their wing, fierce competition had developed between districts — some had as many as 70% to 80% of their units as fake collectives, others not even bothering, getting their total income from *guakao* units — the latter often all too eager to get a protection that had the effect of confusing their rights to property, weakening their prospects for development and increasing regulatory problems attending to the self-definition as collective.

The New amidst the Old

Thus, in rural or urban jurisdictions, the "local state" has been faced with the need to alter its self-definition and with the need to avoid losing out to the sector of society which has been increasingly appreciative of the new market potential. For in Guangzhou and in other parts of Guangdong, private entrepreneurs (*getihu* operations, or formal *siying* organizations) have been learning from practice how to deal with bureaucracy.

As seen above, David Wank provided a categorization of private entrepreneurship and an analysis of its behaviour. He divided operators into three groups according to firm size or scale of operation, each group possessing a characteristic view of its style, survival strategy and habitual practice with regard to the political-administrative environment. The *getihu*, household-based (small retail, put-out production or small personal service) trade hiring less than eight workers, has no institutional anchoring outside the family, has few, and does not relish, links to the local state's officials and is quite completely at the mercy of the often predatory bureaucracy (Administration of Industry and Commerce, Tax Office, Public Security, etc.). At the next level, the private enterprise (*siying*) of small size (with more than eight employees but not many more) engages on a more stable and organized basis in small industrial, commercial and service production; it is a family-based, successful *getihu* which has made the daring qualitative jump to *siying*. By becoming a formal organization, it needs an associational link to give it official status, protection (without which, in the Chinese context, survival is near impossible and very unpleasant) and help from political-administrative entities (United Front organizations, such as the Civic Association of Private Industry and Commerce, Gong Shang Lian). The small operator keeps its distance from the Administration of Industy and Commerce (Gongshang Guanli Ju), formally in charge of implementing fiscal and supervisory regulations.[56] The third level is composed of the large private firm which has good relations with the bureaucracy and public-owned enterprises, often through family ties; it is quite fully institutionalized in the "local state" structure, supportive of the administrative *status quo*, engaging in the exchange of favours, taking on the regular gift, hush money or bribery and adding them to the operational transaction costs as a guarantee of growth.[57]

According to David Wank's view, the three levels of private entrepreneurship are, under the conditions he studied in the Xiamen of 1989–1990, somewhat coterminous but without internal linkages strong enough to presage the emergence of a "civil society" type of common interest, social cleavages among the three types of operation preempting cooperation. The larger firms are happy to establish clientelist relations with the bureaucracy for segmental and mutually profitable exchanges of favours, while the other two levels are largely inconsequential to the evolution of the political economy. What is the possible linkage that all three categories have with a traditional institutional set-up of habitual and informal relations under a commercialized environment not yet under market conditions that was to appear after 1992, further accentuated by the fiscal and banking reforms of 1993?

The latter conditions, we suggest, have occasioned a perceptible, though still faint, change of attitude among the two weakest segments which, as indicated above, have a clearer communality or continuity of interests as they are increasingly concerned about the operational cost of submitting to administrative discretion or predacity in exchange for the right to survival. As the supervisory state apparatus, and the "local state" itself, become more aware of the cost of their informal practices to their own financial progress under the market (private operators have been moving to different towns in the delta to avoid high taxes), the question then becomes what function do the entrepreneurs fulfil to bring about change in the traditional institution and to promote progress?

Picturesque Panyu

How do private entrepreneurs acquire their talent, create their productive organization and realize their institutional potential?

Quite a few Chinese commentators make the point that the private sector, taken as a whole, is the only economic category of actors which does not have a particular representative agency to stand on its behalf in centres of decision-making. Or, despite the growing portion of its contribution to the national economy (11.6% of national employment; 9.9% of enterprises [exclusive of *getihu*]; 38.4% of the operating capital; 19.5% of the gross productivity; 21.6% of operational income [exclusive of foreign enterprises]; 31.4% of retail trade; 19.9% of taxation) the private economy is still not part of the official macro-economic and administrative planning.[58] Operators are thus left to their own device to face difficulties without institutional protection. This view is easily understandable by reason of the historical conditions under socialism which attended to the rebirth of the private economy. Yet, what appears at first sight to be an impairment may in turn be considered a hidden advantage as the vulnerability of actors may motivate a prudential risk-taking because of the cost of having to get sectoral and administrative approval. The versatility of the TVEs has been explained in part by the very limited supervision to which it has been submitted, in contrast to the state-owned sector; the condition that does not hold for a private sector often discouraged, harassed or publicly criticized.

A different view may prevail in Panyu, the suburban area south of Guangzhou. Relatively small in territory and population, by the beginning of the economic reforms in the late 1970s, Panyu had faced a serious labour surplus problem as, apart from agriculture, there were few other avenues; moreover, the reform of agriculture was to mean the obvious displacement of a large number of young people who would not remain on the farm with the removal of job assignment under commune norms. For a total labour force of 363,998 in 1980, there were only 47,057 jobs in SOEs and 19,184 in collective organizations. When in 1988 labour outside agriculture outpaced, for the first time, the number of peasants (247,900 to 184,700), the credit had to go to the leaders of the early reform period who had encouraged the youth to start diversifying into various little ventures, the form of which at first had remained largely agricultural, such as commercial crops.[59]

From there grew rapidly a new "movement" that the local leadership was able to channel for several years according to their vision of what the market should be like and of the products that the consumer wanted. Officials offered some resources, but the young operators multiplied the assets or instruments on their own, even if in politically and administratively dependent position; in ways, the cadres were to admit later, they had not thought possible. The unfolding followed the path drawn by the "local state," but acumen and opportunity served the young entrepreneurs well. And, in the process, the young *getihu* and *siying* created for themselves a new social classification, a social cleavage with which the accredited pattern of stratification could no longer compete, to borrow an expression of sociologist Li Lulu commenting approvingly on Victor Nee's developing thesis of market-led transition in China.[60]

The beginning of the profound transition of Panyu, or its entrepreneurial breakthrough, took place with the decision in the mid-1980s to build a commercial centre (Yifa Bazaar) at the county seat (Shiqiao township) with shops and stalls to be made available to the *getihu* so as to better serve the community. The intention had been that rural produce sections would adjoin other stalls offering a panoply of domestic goods, ranging from clothing to hardware, from crockery to pharmacy, so as to create a sensibly balanced array of commonly sought products. In other words, a department store of a novel form was to run on a leasing or purchase basis for a large number of independent operators.

What had been planned, through administrative service to the *getihu* segment of the population, as a way to animate the traditional redistribution mechanisms took a life of its own that developed according to its own logic.[61] At the margin of the established retail market that the local leaders had already tinkered with in order to maximize the service to the struggling *getihu*, the entrepreneurial spirit found its way when some shop started selling home appliances and electronic equipment. The overwhelming popularity of the offering led to a rush by other operators in the bazaar to switch to the new products, and in no time the whole place turned into a one-type merchandise outlet. The great local success instilled in some of the entrepreneurs the notion of a potentially vast market in this line of products across the nation, which they grasped immediately spreading to the major cities. The opportunity and size of trade (RMB 250 million in 1993) let them become major importers and traders in the wholesale of foreign brand-names, often with exclusive licensing rights. Foreign distributors even came to Yifa Bazaar to set up shops in order to gauge the Chinese market in electronic appliances.

The young enlisted *getihu* of the early 1980s had broken open the boundaries of Panyu's market structure and had linked marketing with the Chinese hinterland and supplies from Hong Kong, Japan and Europe. Their success was to raise the quality of the economy of the whole county; the "peasant traders were to search for quality, offer high technology, assume trade risks, pursue high returns"; while a good number of small entrepreneurs would continue on the basis of family, the larger ones soon sought to raise the level of operation by hiring professional management and technical staff and by applying modern norms of strategic planning and information processing. The demonstration effect was to spread to other cities in Guangdong and major cities in China where the concept of specialized trading centres was to be replicated.

Like a growing wave, the transformation of Yifa Bazaar spawned a change in a whole number of other Panyu *getihu* which then transformed themselves into formal *siying* enterprises. The popularity and growth of the centre created its own problems as imitation reduced the chances of continued success among the fiercely competing outlets, especially in 1988–1989 when the austerity measures of the economic rectification and the aftermath of the Tian'anmen June 4th violence greatly depressed the new market. In a moment of remarkable reflection on their situation, the *getihu* realized the immature nature of their local economic practice. By what appear to have been a quite remarkable understanding, a process of diversification of ventures took place which answered the growing needs of the local economy nurtured by this unique market. The lodging, catering and entertainment industries developed in conjunction with the transport and communication industries serving the affluence of domestic and foreign traders who had been taking Panyu as a growing base of operation. Followed soon the creation of enterprises devoted to manufacturing, others to the development of high-technology. Some successful entrepreneur created other specialized trading centres in clothing, furniture, food produce. What had started as 600 specialized agricultural households (*zhuanye hu*) in 1978 had turned into 20,000 private enterprises by 1994.

The felicitous choice by the "local state" administration to lower the threat posed by unemployment was realized, not because of their acumen and mastery of the mechanisms, but because local entrepreneurs seized the opportunity to test the limit of the vision of convenience and transform the situation, going far beyond the original common sense solution.

In its benevolent choice of policy, the Panyu "local state" had set a path in 1978 that intended to nurture ability and creativity. The flowing together of the two forces of administration and entrepreneurship allowed the development of the "engine" of change that led to modern commercialization, industrialization, urbanization and agricultural modernization.

Shunde: The Pace-setter!

Although many territorial administrations have also proceeded with the reform of ownership, Shunde has become one of the most famous areas in Guangdong — even for the nation as a whole for that matter, along with Zhucheng in Shandong — to put into practice a daring experiment that would serve as example for others to follow, albeit with a slap or two on the wrist for offering to sell profitable enterprises to foreigners.[62]

Up to the beginning of the 1990s, Guangdong's privileged position by virtue of the special policies bestowed by the central government had allowed an apparently successful economic take-off without having to face the difficulty encountered by the Eastern Europe economies. The quite remarkable growth of the private sector was not in the spectrum as it had ostensibly, for certain revolutionary veterans, jeopardized the purity of the socialist domination.

The simple strategy in the province had allowed local governments, especially the county authorities, to take the lead. Shunde was such a county, under the prefectural authority of Foshan, which was to become with time in May 1992 a county municipality, the leadership of which was in 1993 to take the unusual step of transforming the whole administration as a first step of an in-depth reform of its economic structure. Difficulties had surfaced, indeed, with the realization that the TVE-based economy had drifted closely towards the stultified regime of state-owned enterprises. The choice for the collective enterprises (TVEs) had at first been effective in the 1980s as the prodigal manipulation of tax exemptions under the fiscal contract responsibility system could easily mobilize the local peasant population in need of jobs. The statistics for 1990 were indicative of the scale of investment that had taken place in the ten-year period (see Table 9.5).

Table 9.5   Growth of Guangdong's Township and Village Enterprises, 1980–1995
(No.: 10,000; Gross output[a]: RMB 100 million)

	1980	1985	1990	1994	1995	1994–1995 % change
Collect. town ent. (No.)	9.73	2.10	2.39	2.74	2.80	+2.2
Gross output	n.a.	77.22	309.22	1,255.82	1,599.59	+27.4
Collect vill. ent. (No.)	7.82	9.51	8.96	10.63	10.54	–0.8
Gross output	n.a.	55.88	176.37	915.51	1,272.66	+39.0
Priv. partnership (No.)	n.a.	4.84	5.88	6.63	6.26	–5.6
Gross output	n.a.	11.80	57.32	234.96	306.47	+30.4
Priv. household (*geti*) (No.)	n.a.	52.21	102.42	125.75	125.06	–0.5
Gross output	n.a.	29.95	187.43	844.40	1,259.52	+49.2

Source: *Guangdong tongji nianjian 1996* (Statistical Yearbook of Guangdong 1996)
(Beijing: Zhongguo tongji chubanshe, 1996), p. 168.
[a] Gross output value: 1985 according to 1980 value; other years, according to 1990 value.

Also in 1990, Shunde had 108 units each with over RMB 10 million of output; there were 28 corporations (*jituan gongsi*) which collectively produced for RMB 3,300 million of goods, accounting for 50% of all production (agricultural and industrial), or 72% of the industrial output. Altogether, there were 19,540 TVEs (of which 1,001 were strictly county and township "collective" property) with production technology of the early 1980s vintage, largely bought or transferred from Hong Kong, Taiwan and Japan. The funding for this type of purchase had officially been local, although a visiting scholar acknowledged the source to have been largely from "overseas" Chinese (Hong Kong, Macau or Taiwan).[63]

In about ten years, the county had passed from being an agricultural producer of rice, silk and sugar to an industrial fledgeling copying a labour-intensive technology and producing common home appliances, with a growing portion being exported. The successive leaderships had realized the aspiration of building a major base for advanced home and industrial products with more than RMB 10,000 million in capital assets of its own. Shunde had become one of the four "small tigers" of the Pearl River delta![64]

The secret of the local party-government leadership had been to seize the occasion in the early 1980s, and use the collective enterprises (the

Maoist "five small plants") as the starting base of an ambitious multiplication of projects for county-wide industrialization. According to elder economist Wang Zhuo, county leaders had from experience engaged, in rapid succession, to three major structural reorganizations of the governing system.

In 1984, they had decided to replace several offices overseeing agricultural and industrial production with an administrative Light Industry Corporation; the administrative corporation had been dismantled in 1987 for the creation of ten new corporations, each led by one large enterprise; in 1990, "endowed" with too many administrative duties, these had once more been reformed into eight major holding corporations, the hope being that the further distancing from the government would achieve the sought-after managerial autonomy and budget constraints.[65] The outline of a principal-agent system had been drawn.

However, by 1993 the finances of the municipality, had become threatened by imminent massive bankruptcies, despite the dramatic official statistics of growth and well-being (e.g., workers' average yearly income reaching RMB 7,000):[66]

— Of the more than 1,000 public-owned enterprises now in existence at the municipality and township levels, 259 TVEs had debts of RMB 820 million, some as old as the 1980s.

— Bank loans that could not be repaid totalled RMB 2,100 million.

— Worse still, of the 197 municipality-owned enterprises, officially with RMB 11,700 million in assets, only RMB 2,350 million were in fact accountable for, of which, once all obligations to retirement and welfare funds, unrecoverable losses and unpaid taxes had been added up, a mere RMB 710 million was left in the accounts.[67]

The convergence of looming disaster and central policy abandoning the economic planning order in favour of a (socialist) market economy required a drastic approach. There had been a grave and quite systematic erosion of state's assets that had strangely enough eluded all auditing exercises, administrative supervision and previous restructurings. The reform of corporate holdings had drawn an outline, but the key question, government ownership, had remained taboo, as Fan Gang would say. Needless to say, there was an urgent need to change the existing forms of financial control, to restructure ownership, the prevalent forms of which had been "obstructing further development and had become a major source of corruption."[68]

New forms of ownership seemed to be the answer, as both Western and Chinese authors were indicating, almost in the same terms of reference, that, with the success of the rural-agricultural reforms of the early 1980s, the meaning of property rights should also be devolved to the unit for its full utilization and development. However, up to 1993, because of the restraint shown towards the normative planning order, the radical (*da shoubi*) project in Shunde of a separation of the administration from the enterprise (*zheng qi fenkai*), which was to become more appropriately formulated as the separation of administration from capital (*zheng zi fenkai*), had still to be officially endorsed by the central authorities and backed up by law.[69]

Not only had collective enterprises operating under government ownership taken the administrative characters of the state-owned enterprises which they had out-competed in productivity a few years back, "they were now facing the possibility of being in turn dethroned by private enterprises!"[70] Indeed, private entrepreneurs — often, managers and skilled workers leaving specifically to compete with previous employers — had developed enterprises capable of producing equally sophisticated products, such as domestic appliances, that after all required a generally labour-intensive, easy-to-master technology; in terms of capacity and pricing, the private producers had been rapidly gaining on the tainted public units, as for example when several independent entrepreneurs were to band together and form their own Wanhe Corporation on the model of public-owned corporations, or when a deputy-manager moved out with associates to create eight autonomous units which would form an alliance frontally to challenge renowned Huada.[71]

Because the supervision of property rights had been unclear, the "local state" had lost control of investments, personnel income and the redistribution of profits, and the handling of the capital assets after the introduction in the late 1980s of the managerial responsibility contract. Managers had had a rather free hand as the fulfilment of the contract which was unenforceable by the bureaucrats and, in alliance with labour, had been eating out the profits, transferring assets to private use or failing to dispose of old equipment being left idle, because, under the planning institution, there had been no legitimate market to handle such transaction.

Merely with regard to the wage bill, the contract responsibility system of the late 1980s had specified that managers were entitled to a basic wage valued from 200% to 400% of the staff and workers' average wage. In alliance with labour, the incentive provided by the contract was not very appealing in itself — though played by workers in a *quid-pro-quo* meeting the managers' other wishes — as it would mean at most a yearly salary in the vicinity of RMB 30,000, generally insufficient to compete with private entrepreneurs'. More interesting, there was the ominous reversal of administrative fortune whereby relatively indispensable personnel, enticed earlier at high cost from large SOEs within or from outside Guangdong, were now asking for exorbitant salaries under the threat of "flying off" (*tiao cao*), either of accepting a rival offer or starting up lucrative private competition.

Symbolic of the transition, the direct link with the personnel and workers was officially kept and reinforced after the changes of 1993–1995, as can be seen in Table 9.6, suggesting that mutual dependency was being kept to encourage at least a semblance of income fairness, fostering solidarity. The familistic function of close relations (*renqing* or *tiexin jingying*), debated among political leaders and consultants, was retained in the very context of the change of property right adjustments, i.e., staff and workers being given preferential allotments of shares, a "rent" for peace and performance. Leaders had braved opposition, in such an unsettled time, to keep active the emotive ("sharing") dimension, even though the objective was to move towards the principal-agent (economic rational) relations.[72] It was not yet time, it was argued, within this still largely traditional context to set remuneration on an objective scale and cast off the link with past socialist morality.

If the "local state" élite felt, as represented by many an official commentator, that it had lost control of the managers, it could also be said that,

Table 9.6 **Manager's Salary Yield Formula on Taxes and Profits in Shunde**

Tax-profit/year	Enterprise rank	Manager's salary[a]
Below 1 million	Small enterprise	350%
1.1 to 3 million	Medium enterprise	400%
3.1 to 10 million	Large enterprise	450%
Above 10 million	Extra-large enterprise	500%

Source: Miao Guoliang, "Chuxian lunkuo de shehuizhuyi shichang jingji xin tizhi" (Preliminary Outline of the New Socialist Market Economic System), in *Jianshe you Zhongguo tese de shehuizhuyi daolu de tansuo* (Exploration in the Construction of a Socialist Road with Chinese Characteristics), edited by Liang Mu and Wu Guoxia (Beijing: Zhongyang dangxiao chubanshe, 1994), pp. 59–60.

[a] Of staff and workers' average wage.

under the contract system, the plant managers had overtaken the administrators' ability to administer information and their capacity to monitor the accounting. What government and academe had futilely considered the guarantee of managerial accountability had become the opportunity, at the "institutional boundary" as Wang Dingding would suggest,[73] for the managers "to become self-motivated" — in contrast to the previous structure of personnel administration which had geared them to a bureaucratic career. The contract had facilitated the conversion from *nomenklatura* careerist to entrepreneur since the contract had officially bestowed on them the legal responsibility of managing the state assets without adequate constraints — which had not been of their making. The responsibility contract had motivated them to "change their habitual patterns of thinking learned from previous socialization and modelled behaviour."[74] The contract had been a Schumpeterian external intervention that had led to the disequilibrium of the bureaucracy-built routine, which was dangerously sliding towards a "zero-profit" economy at the time of the dramatic intervention. Managers had been asked to create the new institutional framework of the socialist enterprise with Chinese characteristics; they had obliged in ways not contemplated by their administrative supervisors.

Out of the experience, the daring Shunde politicians devised a totally new strategy.

Administrative Reconstruction

For that purpose, the leadership newly put in place proceeded according to a tightly devised plan of operation, for it knew that the transformation would hit hard at the core of the administrative system that had hung on since before 1978. First, the unity and solidarity of the leadership were to be assured by making the respective heads of the government, the People's Congress and the Chinese People's Political Consultative Conference full members of the core party committee which was to have total and sole power over the whole process, avoiding thus the existence of any external (legitimate) "core" to be played against the party committee. Equally interesting, the committee assigned the various executive roles according to a unified division of labour whereby only one member for each sector would be accountable for each reform assignment to be completed, so as to minimize the possibility of bargaining over terms that the delegation to an executive sub-committee would have entailed.

Next, the party committee decided to attack the official and non-official *nomenklatura* and eliminate all functional administrative offices, all subordinate units and all technical sub-divisions, except for a few essential departments, such as the party organization department or the government finance office. Then, all commissions, executive offices and specialized sections with economic assignment created over the years were dismantled. The party departments were simplified into their simplest components, all government sub-sections recreated into streamlined offices (*ju*), where all offices were to be of equal ranking and under a unique leadership, respective to either the party or the government. All departments or offices were regrouped according to specific functions, eliminating in the process all overlapping. Moreover, all offices linked for their existence and sustenance on superior (external) jurisdictions were allowed to continue operation but strictly limited to linkage with their external superiors, devoid of authority to make any deal with the lower ranks within the territory.

The dismantled commissions, executive bureaux and economic offices were regrouped into three new *ju*: agricultural, industrial and trade development. All government *ju* had their power reduced and their function redefined in terms of macro-level coordination, supervision and service. Those that had had direct economic links with enterprises were separated from government, their administrative duties returned to the regrouped *ju* and their personnel reorganized into enterprises with exclusively economic objectives.

As a result, of the previous 56 party and government offices, only 29 remained; 125 sub-offices had been eliminated; 400 officials had been given jobs outside government. New rules of operation came into force whereby previous decisions that had had to obtain the approval of several offices and be sealed by a myriad of signatures (chops) would now need to obtain a single departmental approval.[75]

Enterprise Restructuration

The municipal leaders set out to create the basis of an ownership reform which involved a large number of investors who would buy into corporations and would restructure the assets that had been "carefully" evaluated for fixed capital, immaterial values, land, debts, receivables, obligations, etc. A new level of officially recognized ownership would be created according to the "outline" that had developed in the course of the 1980s and had to go beyond the abortive corporations (*jituan* or *jituan gongsi*). Thus, boards of trustees (unfortunately not identified, except for the objective of attracting private capital to buy voting shares into capital holding corporations) were being created and would take over.[76]

Three principles had been set ahead of this reform, which lasted from May 1993 to January 1995. First, the enterprises that faced the most competition and the highest risk (enterprises producing similar and common consumer products), had their ownership structure divided into shares open to as many investors as possible. The idea was to make the enterprises fully "public securities" under a board of trustees who would set enterprise policies and appoint the managers. Secondly, infrastructure and public utility enterprises would have the "state" as monopoly or majority shareholder with participation from the public; the state would remain the main managerial decision-maker, and management reset as a corporation. Thirdly, regarding the large, profitable and high-technology corporations "embodying the future economic policy designs of the administration," the state was to keep a strategic portion of investments while inviting other investors; the board of trustees was to sit non-cadre investors.

Though still hemmed in by superior political, ideological and administrative uncertainty as to the validity and licitness of such administrative innovation (selling high-value firms to foreign investors being rebuffed by Beijing), the protracted reforms resulted in the following structure of ownership:

> Public ownership comprised two parts, the municipality 61.2%, external public ownership, 1.2%. Local private investment amounted to 22.6% and foreign investment to 15%. The ratio of the division of share ownership ended providing 30% to the owner category, 30% to management cadres, and 40% to ordinary staff and workers. The leaders indicated that the lack of a sufficiently developed property market for enterprise assets had meant that Shunde investors could not master more liquidity; and, on some occasions, the punters had had to be given "extra incentives"![77]

Another angle of the reform was described as follows:

1) Of the previous state monopolies, the state kept the public utilities reorganized into public corporations; some secondary organizations became state majority shareholding corporations;

2) the familiar large consumer-product enterprises (Meidi, Kelon, Wanjiale, etc.) were reorganized as "modern limited trust corporations" with official

legal person shares (state) and public (Chinese and foreign) equities. Some were going to be prepared for listing on an appropriate stock exchange;

3) the reform allowed the reorganization of foreign joint ventures into new joint ventures. Some previously camouflaged as "foreign" capital (Chinese capital laundered through Hong Kong and Macau) became fully foreign-invested capital;

4) a great number of ordinary, medium-size enterprises had their assets divided into state shares and plant personnel (whole body or portion) shares; a number of enterprises was leased out to the personnel and the machinery assessed a distinct rent;

5) a large number of small plants with low value-added, labour intensive products were released to the personnel and formed into share-cooperative (*gufen hezuo zhi*) enterprises (personnel buy-out). The board of director-owners was formed into a kind of mass organization on the basis of "one person, one vote," not "one share, one vote," to avoid the possible concentration of shares into a few hands.[78]

6) debt-ridden units or with negligible income were sold at public auctions, at times whole, at times piece by piece; the state thus recuperated RMB 21 million of the estimated 24.07 million in assets.

At the end of the exercise, of the original 1,001 enterprises originally defined as municipality-owned, the state had kept monopoly ownership of 94 and majority ownership of 48; the state had a minority ownership in another 21. To managers and labour, 331 had been leased; another 235 had been reorganized into share-cooperative units, some with full participation, others with partial participation of labour. The remaining 23 had been auctioned off or dismantled and sold.[79]

Much of the liquid assets thus generated went into infrastructural investment funds, industrial modernization funds and labour insurance and retirement funds.

One of the major reasons the Shunde political leadership had to face the reorganization and sale of some of its cherished assets to local and foreign interests and create, as described above, an officially sanctioned ownership structure distinct from the local "state" apparatus was that the managers had been fully, though deviantly in the context, "entrepreneurial" in a quintessential way. Diverting profits by an unholy alliance with labour or surreptitious leakage of assets (especially at the occasion of assets evaluation, *chonggu* or *pinggu*) to private (oneself) hands[80] finally drew attention to the active or passive collusion of bureaucracy, or to the latter's incompetence at mastering economic information.

In the incorporated world that has developed in recent years, the official head of the board — the delegated "principal," also called the "legal person" (*faren*) — is supposed to be protecting the owner's rights (individual, collective, state) and set the strategy of development. However, as indicated in *Jingji guanli* of September 1996 — also suggested by other authors — the chief trustee remains highly handicapped; he may get into conflict with the manager-agent, the latter able to hold out against many recourses. Because the head trustee and the manager may hold roughly similar party-state administrative ranking, such obstinacy may be even condoned by administrative officials getting back at the new incumbents who are threatening the bureaucrats' domain, without much harm done to the manager's career. As long as the ownership constraints are not further clarified and enforced, the head trustee has little recourse over the nature of the relationship with the hired agent-manager.[81]

The nature and requirements of the new market economy have been addressed under the influence of the new type of managers who have been changing their view of career and interests. For quite some time now, the normative literature from policy-study groups under state administration has been trying to define the entrepreneur (manager) as a professional in the process of being differentiated, sometime in term of profession, sometime in terms of social class,[82] from the administrative colleagues. The abstract social differentiation concept may have become in Shunde a living reality, since the "local state" chose to separate, at least formally, the career paths of bureaucrats and managers. On the part of the managers, to use Wang Dingding's notion of institutional change, the interference brought into the system by the contract system in the late 1980s forced a change of practices which were honed over the following years into new "habits."[83] The spread of the habits to the rest of the territory became a force strong enough to define the stature and role of the managers, which in turn influenced the "local state" to react by transforming itself. To mark the notional change, the "local state" decided on the important substitution to be made to its own administrative institution by dismantling the owner-government — what Jean-Louis Rocca has called the "rational bureaucracy"[84] — creating a new intermediary ownership structure and creating the "principal-agent" relationship.

We still doubt the authenticity of the new trustee-principal; we are pretty sure that the manager-agent has found, defended and won one's own distinct identity.

In a true sense, the deviant entrepreneurship of Shunde's managers (pervasive in all of China) had affected within their limited sphere not only their own but related key institutions. As indicated earlier, Guangdong had in the 1980s become renowned for the tolerance of multiple ownership types, sometimes merely cohabiting, sometimes intimately cooperating; they had yet, until this Shunde event, remained ill-at-ease with each other, some clearly licit forms, others risky, even more disguised (private firms "wearing a red hat" as guarantee against political change, unfriendly taxation, for stable supply, etc.). From now on, may prevail a more complex environment whereby essentially mixed types (*hunhe xing*) of ownership will no longer differentiate the original sources of capital and become mutually supportive for new, unique, and ethically (ideologically) legitimate purposes: investment and profits.[85]

Conclusion

What can we draw from the foregoing review of the strategy of managers and private entrepreneurs who have forced the rather daring crossing over "the stones at the bottom of the river"?

Crucially, we have tried to follow the actors from within their own context, their own point of departure — warts and all — without paying too much attention to warts for it is the effort to move ahead and the steps taken that are important. No doubt, the manager-entrepreneur has imposed one's own imprint on the evolution of the industrial organization and has affected the evolution of the economic institution, despite attempts to make the manager or entrepreneur interchangeable with the bureaucrat. Specialization and relationship networks have, in different ways, smoothened the career path; this is institutionally path dependent from different perspectives.

The question of property rights in the Chinese reform context has had to face a major challenge. Wang Dingding has used the graphic formula of the two-faced coin whereby the two major aspects of the problem are inextricably linked. One face represents property, the other employment: the solution to the first can not be fully realized until the second has received satisfaction. Closely associated in policy-making, the two faces stand in contradiction as well, the expansion of private property being a serious threat to full realization of the other.[86] The Chinese state has chosen to promote — as a second thought? — private property to help solve unemployment, choosing to look at a relatively limited regime of private property as a positive-sum equation. Because of the nature of their economy (economies), the acceleration and expansion of market as an "exchange of property rights" may help ease both the tension generated by unclear property rights and the threat of unemployment.

Shunde early and on many occasions has been the object of interest in offical circles because of its experiments with administrative structure; it has contributed in part to the reform process by assuring the consolidation of public ownership and by creating highly successful large collective producers. It has as well been the location of epic contests between public-owned and maverick private operations which have to be some of the factors affecting the decisions to engage in a bit of Leninist de-fusion.

The experience of Shunde and Panyu, each with its particularities, is not necessarily "generalizable" to the whole of Guangdong. The qualified process in each of the two places is just indicative of the fermentation of forces of change within an institutional set-up, forces which no longer defer to established authority, since the agents of change, the entrepreneurs, are often members of the élite. Those who are not of the élite may show more deference in function of the need to maintain policy stability, create the legal order, supply or assure a streamlined supply of production materials and economic infrastructure; they carry on, even in "symbiotic clientelistic" relations with the privileged officialdom, with conscious reservation about their lack of a proper social status and the right to create their own professional links.[87] Li Lulu has suggested from a stratification perspective that the movement of cadres and skilled profes-sionals from bureaux and business offices into entrepreneurial roles denotes a complex use of assets, in part "system capital," the use of which is an effort spreading across the established élite to join the growing ranks of the new category of people, the entrepreneurial cleavage.[88]

When they have a remunerating path of development, they do use all the means (capitals) at their disposal, and, against Wank's argument, they sense the need for solidarity amidst self-interested diversity, reminding us of Granovetter's affirmation of the structured human relations which com-plement rational behaviour.[89]

The party-state is no longer the disciplinary monolith of the past. That the leadership has persisted in the pursuit of the reforms despite the clear perception of the threat to institutional purity is a gauge for the future reform development. The question is no longer the presence or even the relative growth of aberrations (abuse of power, corruption, the transaction of power for money); the more interesting objective is to understand how the Chinese actors use the assets of their institutional arrangements to create a new institutional set-up, from within.

Notes

1. Maurice Brosseau, "Entrepreneurs Probing Uncertainty," in *Guangdong — Survey of a Province Undergoing Rapid Change*, edited by Y. M. Yeung and David K. Y. Chu (Hong Kong: The Chinese University Press, 1994), pp. 175–206.

2. Ivan Szelenyi and Eric Kostello, "The Market Transition Debate: Toward a Synthesis," *American Journal of Sociology*, Vol. 101, No. 4 (January 1996), pp. 1082, 1094–95. Victor Nee first presented his view of Chinese development in "A Theory of Market Transition: From Redistribution to Market in State Socialism," *American Sociological Review*, Vol. 54 (October 1989), pp. 663–81.

3. Jean Oi, "The Role of the Local State in China's Transitional Economy," *The China Quarterly*, No. 144 (December 1995), pp. 1132–49.

4. Andrew Walder, "China's Transitional Economy: Interpreting Its Significance," *The China Quarterly*, No. 144 (December 1995), p. 977.

5. Jean-Louis Rocca, "L'entreprise, l'entrepreneur et le cadre: une approche de l'économie chinoise," *Les Etudes du CERI*, No. 14 (April 1996).

6. Jin Guantao, "Socialism and Tradition: The Formation and Development of Modern Chinese Political Culture," *The Journal of Contemporary China*, No. 3 (Summer 1993), pp. 3–17; Jin Guantao, "Zhongguo jin xian dai jingji lunli de bianqian: lun shehui zhuyi jingji lunli zai Zhongguo de lishi mingyun" (Economic Ethic Change in Modern and Contemporary China: On the Historical Fate in China of Socialist Economic Ethic), *Yazhou yanjiu* (Asia Research), No. 5 (May 1994), pp. 2–50; Susan Mann, "Brokers as Entrepreneurs in Pre-socialist China," *Comparative Study of Society and History*, Vol. 26 (1984), pp. 614–36; and Susan Mann, *Local Merchants and the Chinese Bureaucracy, 1750–1950* (Stanford: Stanford University Press, 1987).

7. David Wank, "Private Business, Bureaucracy, and Political Alliance in a Chinese City," *The Australian Journal of Chinese Affairs*, No. 33 (January 1995), pp. 55–71; David Wank, "Bureaucratic Patronage and Private Business: Changing Networks of Power in Urban China," in *The Waning of the Communist State*, edited by Andrew G. Walder (Berkeley: University of California Press, 1995), pp. 153–83.

8. Ping Chen, "China's Challenge to Economic Orthodoxy: Asian Reform as an Evolutionary Self-organizing Process," *China Economic Review*, Vol. 4, No. 2 (1993), pp. 137–42.

9. Fan Gang, "Lun dangqian guoyou qiye chanquan guanxi de gaige" (On the Current Reform of Property Relations of State-owned Enterprises), *Guangdong jingji* (Guangdong Economy), No. 1 (February 1995), pp. 34–36.

10. Fan Gang's position is different from the one held by many Western students

of Chinese reform who see the "privatization of state assets — that is, the creation of clear and legally enforceable property rights of the firm against the state — (as) the only way to remedy the problems associated with soft budgets and bargaining over financial terms" (emphasis added), Andrew Walder, "Corporate Organization and Local Government Property Rights in China," in *Changing Political Economies: Privatization in Post-Communist and Reformist Communist State*, edited by Vedat Milor (Boulder: Lynne Rienner Publishers, 1994), p. 53. Fan Gang and colleagues are proposing a clarification of ownership and property rights which does imply only, or mainly, a differentiation of functions within the already existing state owner-ship.

11. Li Lulu, "Siying qiye jia de shehui jiegou: lun siying qiye de fazhan jizhi" (Social Structure of Private Entrepreneurs: On the Development Mechanisms of Privately Managed Enterprises), in *Zhongguo siying jingji nianjian* (Chinese Privately Managed Economy Yearbook), edited by Zhang Xuwu, Li Ding and Xie Minggan (Beijing: Zhonghua gongshang lianhe chubanshe, 1996), pp. 100–108.

12. It has been defined as "a political system whose aim (is) industrialization and which (is) structured so that administration and planning ... take the place of the market ... (that is the) 'fusion of politics and economics,'" see Steven M. Goldstein, "China in Transition: The Political Foundations of Incremental Reform," *The China Quarterly*, No. 144 (December 1995), pp. 1106–07.

13. Li Peng so stated during an investigation tour of the northeast region, see *Xinbao* (Hong Kong Economic Journal), 22 August 1995, p. 11.

14. *Jingji ribao* (Economic Daily), 6 April 1996, p. 5.

15. Steven Goldstein, "China in Transition" (note 12), p. 1121.

16. Zhongshan University Research Center of Pearl River Delta Economic Development and Management, *Zhujiang sanjiaozhou jingji fazhan xin toushi* (New Perspective on the Economic Development of the Pearl River Delta) (Guangzhou: Zhongshan daxue chubanshe, 1995).

17. Fan Gang (note 9); Deng Weigen, "Zhuanxing zhong de Shunde: Zhongguo shichang jingji de chuxing" (Shunde under Transformation: Embrionic Form Of China's Market Economy), *Guangdong jingji* (Guangdong Economy), December 1995, pp. 6–9; Woo Wing Thye, Wan Hai, Yibiao Jin and Gang Fan, "How Successful Has Chinese Enterprise Been? Pitfalls in Opposite Biases and Focus," *Journal of Comparative Economics*, Vol. 18, No. 3 (June 1994), pp. 410–37.

18. Goldstein credits the forward-looking insight found in Christine Pui Wah Wong, "Rural Industrialization in the People's Republic of China: Lessons from the Cultural Revolution Decade," in *China Under the Four Modern-izations*, Part 1; Selected papers submitted to the Joint Economic Committee,

Congress of the United States (Washington, DC: US Government Printing Office, 1982), pp. 394–418.

19. Such deviance was to give credence to the emergence of a new social-economic stratum, ultimately to the recreation of some form of "civil society," see Dorothy J. Solinger, *China's Transition from Socialism: Statist Legacies and Market Reforms, 1980–1990* (Armonk, NY: M. E. Sharpe, 1993); about Eastern Europe, Ivan Szelenyi, *Socialist Entrepreneurs: Embourgeoisement in Rural Hungary* (Madison, WI: The University of Wisconsin Press, 1988) and Ivan Szelenyi and Balazs Szelenyi, "Why Socialism Failed: Toward a Theory of System Breakdown — Causes of Disintegration of East European State Socialism," *Theory and Society*, Vol. 23, No. 2 (April 1994), pp. 211–31.

20. Yan Changjiang, *Guangdong da liebian* (note 2).

21. Some businessman comparing the reforms in Guangdong and Shanghai referred to them as, respectively, the reform of a traditional and a modern economy.

22. Dong Fureng, "Zhujiang sanjiaozhou ying bimian chengwei 'sanmingzhi jingji' de jiaceng" (The Pearl River Delta Must Avoid Becoming the Squeezed Layer in an Economic Sandwich), *Nanfang jingji* (South China Economy), No. 2 (February 1996), pp. 5–6.

23. Barry Naughton, "Hierarchy and the Bargaining Economy: Government and Enterprise in the Reform Process," in *Bureaucracy, Politics and Decision-making in Post-Mao China*, edited by Kenneth G. Lieberthal and David M. Lampton (Berkeley: University of California Press, 1992), pp. 275–76; see also Du Haiyan and Zeng Hongliang, "Chengbao zhi xia de guoyou qiye zhidu fenxi" (Analysis of the State-owned Enterprise under the Responsibility Contract System), *Guanli shijie* (Administrative World), No. 1 (February 1991), pp. 158–65.

24. Thomas G. Raski, "Progress without Privatization: The Reform of China's State Industries," in *Changing Political Economies: Privatization in Post-Communist and Reforming Communist States*, edited by Vedat Milor (Boulder, CO: Lynne Rienner Publishers, 1994), p. 33 (emphasis in the original).

25. Zhang Weiying, *Decision Rights, Residual Claim and Performance: A Theory of How the Chinese State Enterprise Reform Works*, Working Paper Series No. 82, Department of Economics and Finance, City University of Hong Kong, 1996.

26. At least amongst academics and advisors to decision-makers.

27. James Bohman, "The Limits of Rational Choice Explanation," in *Rational Choice Theory: Advocacy and Critique*, edited by James Coleman and Thomas J. Fararo (Newbury Park: Sage Publications, 1992), p. 211.

28. Zhang Weiying, *Decision Rights, Residual Claim and Performance* (note 25), pp. 11–18, 22–23.

29. Tian Yingkui, "Jianli xiandai qiye zhidu de nandian yu duice" (Difficulty with Establishing a Modern Enterprise System and Counter-measures), *Guangdong jingji* (Guangdong Economy), No. 8 (August 1995), p. 34.

30. Liu Guoguang, "Zhongguo guoyouzhi jingji gaige de tansuo" (Probing the Economic Reform of Chinese State Ownership), *Zhongguo jingji tizhi gaige* (Chinese Economic System Reform), No. 11 (November 1990), pp. 6–9.

31. *Qiyejia banyuekan* (Entrepreneur Bimonthly), No. 4 (August 1988), p. 29.

32. *Zhongguo jingji tizhi gaige* (Reform of Chinese Economic System), No. 2 (February 1988), p. 55.

33. Tian Yingkui, "Jianli xiandai qiye zhidu" (note 27), p. 34.

34. Tian Yingkui, "Jianli xiandai qiye zhidu" (note 27), pp. 34–35.

35. Andrew G. Walder, "Local Governments as Industrial Firms: An Organizational Analysis of China's Transitional Economy," *American Journal of Sociology*, Vol. 101, No. 2 (September 1995), pp. 263–301.

36. Steven Goldstein, "China in Transition" (note 12).

37. For a short but detailed history of the development, see *Zhongguo xiangzhen qiye guanli baike quanshu* (Almanach of the Chinese Administration of Town and Village Enterprises) (Beijing: Nongye chubanshe, 1987), pp. 1–2.

38. Yuan Enzhen (ed.), *Zhongguo siying jingji: xianzhuang, fazhan yu pinggu* (China's Private Economy: Current State, Development and Assessment) (Shanghai: Shanghai renmin chubanshe, 1993), pp. 231–41.

39. The reasons for and the background to the sudden shift in political-economic definition can be found in the political upheavals taking place in the socialist world after 1989, a consideration which is beyond the scope of the present discussion.

40. Sheng Hong, "Chanquan jiegou gaige chuang yishi xintai jinqu" (The Reform of Property Rights Rushes Ideological Taboos), *Mingbao yuekan* (Ming Pao Monthly), No. 2 (February 1996), pp. 40–42.

41. See Maurice Brosseau, "Entrepreneurs Facing Uncertainty" (note 1), pp. 191–96.

42. *Nanfang jingji* (South China Economy), No. 12 (December 1995), pp. 5–6.

43. Ma Rong, Wang Hansheng and Liu Shiding (eds), *Zhongguo xiangzhen qiye de fazhan lishi yu yunxing jizhi* (The History of Chinese Town-and-village Enterprises' Development and Operational Mechanisms) (Beijing: Beijing daxue chubanshe, 1994), pp. 17–18.

44. Guo Zhenglin, "Zhengfu neng wei sanjiaozhou xiangzhen qiye zuo xie shenma" (What the Government Can Do for the TVEs of the Pearl River Delta), *Zhujiang sanjiaozhou jingji* (The Economy of the Pearl River Delta), No. 1 (January 1994), pp. 40–41.

45. Tan Jianguang, Tan Dongfang and Zhang Shaoshan, "Geti siying jingji fazhan yu qingnian congyezhe xintai bianhua" (Economic Development of the Household and Private Economy and Attitude Change among Young

Operators), *Guangzhou shehui* (Guangzhou Society), No. 1 (January 1996), pp. 29–30.

46. Xu Nantie, "Shunde: Xunzhao xin de fazhan fangshi" (Shunde: Looking for a New Development Pattern), *Guangzhou shehui* (Guangzhou Society), No. 5 (May 1995), p. 28.

47. Christopher E. Nevitt, "Private Business Associations in China: Evidence of Civil Society or Local State Power?" *The China Journal*, No. 36 (July 1996), pp. 25–43.

48. Yuan Enzhen, *Zhongguo siying jingji* (note 38)), pp. 219f.

49. Steven Goldstein, "China in Transition" (note 12), pp. 1106–08.

50. With the relativity and limitations that ownership rights carry even in the Western economies which are most staunchly supportive of private property in reality and symbolically; see Douglass North, *Structure and Change in Economic History* (New York and London: W. W. Norton and Co., 1981), pp. 21–24.

51. David Wank, "Private Business, Bureaucracy, and Political Alliance," (note 7).

52. Dai Jianzhong, "Zhongguo dalu siying qiye ji siying qiyezhu yanjiu" (Research on Chinese Mainland Private Enterprise and Entrepreneurs), *Frontiers of Social Indicators Research in Chinese Societies*, edited by Lau Siu-kai et al. (Hong Kong: Hong Kong Institute of Asia-Pacific Studies, The Chinese University of Hong Kong, 1996), pp. 512–14.

53. Jean C. Oi, "Communism and Clientelism: Rural Politics in China," *World Politics*, No. 2 (January 1985), pp. 238–66; Jean C. Oi, "The Fate of the Collective after the Commune," in *Chinese Society on the Eve of Tiananmen: The Impact of Reform*, edited by Deborah Davis and Ezra F. Vogel (Cambridge, MA: The Council on East Asian Studies, Harvard University, 1990), pp. 15–36.

54. Guo Yaohui, "Guangzhou shi siying jingji de yinyou" (Worries about Guangzhou City's Privately Managed Economy), *Gaige daobao* (Reform Reporter), Nos. 11 and 12 (November–December 1995), p. 58.

55. The city government was to go further in 1995 by establishing a safety mechanism to protect private entrepreneurs' legal rights to cover the period leading to the time the central government would clearly define in law the related private property protection. The city party committee devised administrative rules and proceeded with the drafting of a city law to protect these rights, see *Zhongguo siying jingji nianjian* (China Privately Managed Economy Yearbook) (Beijing: Zhongguo gongshang lianhe chubanshe, 1996), p. 140.

56. For a graphic rendering of the complex routines of social engagement required in the age-old, traditionally defined exercise of political power at the street level in the economic environment of the mainland urban

neighbourhood, see Ole Bruun, "Political Hierarchy and Private Entre- preneurship in a Chinese Neighborhood," in *The Waning of the Communist State*, edited by Andrew G. Walder (Berkeley: University of California Press, 1995), pp. 184–212.

57. David Wank, "Private Business, Bureaucracy, and Political Alliance" (Note 7), p. 68; an analogous explanation is provided for Taiwan's large enterprises which seek political links to help growth, see Ichiro Numazaki, "The Role of Personal Networks in the Making of Taiwan's *Guanxiqiye* (Related Enterprises)," in *Business Networks and Economic Development in East and Southeast Asia*, edited by Garry Hamilton (Hong Kong: Centre of Asian Studies, University of Hong Kong, 1991), pp. 77–93.

58. Li Xinxin, "Woguo fei gongyouzhi jingji fazhan de xianzhuang, wenti ji xuyao minque de zhengci jiexian (Status, Problems and Policy Limits in Need of Clarification Regarding Non-public Economic Development), *Jingji yanjiu ziliao* (Economic Research Documents), No. 8 (August 1996), p. 13.

59. Tan Jianguang et al., "Geti siying jingji fazhan" (note 45), p. 29.

60. Li Lulu, "Siying qiyejia de shehui jiegou" (note 11), p. 107.

61. For the logic of the economic reforms in China, see Wang Dingding, "Zhongguo gaige guocheng de luoji" (The Logic of China's Reform Process), *Xinbao caijing yuekan* (Hong Kong Economic Journal Monthly), No. 223 (October 1995), pp. 3–16.

62. Xu Nantie, "Shunde: xunzhao xin de fazhan fangshi" (note 46), p. 29.

63. Guan Yuqian, "You Zhongguo tese de shehui zhuyi xian — Shunde" (Shunde: A Socialist County with Chinese Characteristics), *Xinbao* (Hong Kong Economic Journal), 15 January 1992, p. 8.

64. The other three were Dongguan, Nanhai and Zhongshan.

65. Wang Zhuo, "Lishun guanxi, zhuanbian zhineng" (Harmonizing Relations, Transforming Functions), *Chuangye zhe* (Enterprisers), No. 12 (December 1992), p. 4

66. Xu Nantie, "Shunde: xunzhao xin de fazhan fangshi " (note 46), p. 27.

67. Deng Weigen, "Zhuanxing zhong de Shunde" (note 20), pp. 6–7.

68. Xu Nantie, "Shunde: xunzhao xin de fazhan fangshi" (note 46), p. 28.

69. Andrew Walder, "Markets and Inequality in Transitional Economies: Toward Testable Theories," *American Journal of Sociology*, Vol. 101, No. 4 (January 1996), pp. 1060–73; Xu Nantie, "Shunde: xunzhao xin de fazhan fanshi" (note 46), p. 29; Zhang Shuguang, "90 niandai de Zhongguo gaige he hongguan jingji" (The Chinese Reform of the 1990s and Macro Economics), *Jingji yanjiu* (Economic Research), No. 6 (June 1996), pp. 21–30.

70. Xu Nantie, "Shunde: xunzhao xin de fazhan fanshi" (note 46), p. 29.

71. Deng Weigen, "Zhuanxing zhong de Shunde" (note 20), p. 9.

72. Huang Xiqin and Huang Zhi, "Shunde chanquan gaige yu jingji zengzhang fangshi zhuanbian lilun yantao hui zongshu" (Summary of Conference on

Theory of Change and Shunde Property Rights Reform and Change in Economic Growth Method), *Nanfang jingji* (South China Economy), No. 1 (January 1996), p. 61.

73. Wang Dingding, "Zhidu chuangxin de yiban lilun" (General Theory of Institutional Innovation), *Jingji yanjiu* (Economic Research), No. 5 (May 1992), p. 75.

74. Ibid., p. 78.

75. Luo Shuling, "Shunde: shixing 'yige juece zhongxin'" (Shunde: Implementating a "One Policy-making Centre), *Banyuetan* (Forthnightly Talk, internal [*neibu*] circulation), No. 6 (June 1996), pp. 35–36.

76. The hierarchy of organizations to be thus created has been variously borrowed by the recent literature about the restructure of the SOEs: local governments are encouraged to set up a first level of state property ownership, a State (Public) Property Commission which is half administrative and half economic in nature overseeing the whole jurisdiction, then at the second level a State (Public) Property Office which has an economic objective or purpose over assets of a particular sector of production, and finally, at the third level, an Asset Management Corporation (*zichan jingying gongsi*) which in principle should be concerned principally about investment and returns on investment (analogous to a venture capital corporation in the West) for a narrower sector of several enterprises or just one major production corporation. See such policy prospects for Guangzhou in *Zhongguo jingji tizhi gaige nianjian 1995* (China Economic Systems Reform Yearbook 1995) (Beijing: Gaige chubanshe, 1995), pp. 152–54.

77. Huang Xiqin and Huang Zhi, "Shunde chanquan gaige" (note 72), pp. 60–61.

78. Some share-cooperatives in other parts of Guangdong have been created under high-powered and prolonged mobilization methods to enjoin a skeptical labour to subscribe to a share ownership that is not marketable and limited to the period of employment; the practice disguises a technique to engage workers' self-interests in order to assure labour discipline; see, Yu Yongbin and Liang Zhaowen, "Xijiang mingyue gonchao sheng" (Shines the Moon on West River, Rises the Labour Community), *Dang feng* (Party Style, Guangdong), No. 3 (March 1996), pp. 30–32.

79. Deng Weigen, "Zhuanxing zhong de Shunde" (note 20), pp. 7–8.

80. Under the control of the manager, the only competent and knowledgeable person around, assessment was distorted either by inflating property value (not discounting debts, workers' insurance funds, financial obligations, etc.) or by deflating the value (using either original or net price and concealing non-material assets, land, etc.). Under the managerial contract system, the criteria of managerial performance were based on the terms of asset evaluation; a biased (high or low) evaluation opened the way for the transfer

of state assets to private hands during the contract period, see Tian Yingkui, "Jianli xiandai qiye zhidu" (note 27), pp. 34–35.

81. *Jingji guanli*, No. 9 (September 1996), p. 22.

82. Martinelli, "Entrepreneurship and Management" (note 32), pp. 493–96.

83. "Habits" are one of the key elements whereby social practices become through learning the expression of norms representative of an institution; a change of habits (such as brought about by innovative entrepreneurial behaviour) earmarks "at the margin" change affecting an institution, see Wang Dingding, "Zhidu chuangxin de yiban lilun" (note 73), pp. 75–77.

84. Rocca, "L'entreprise, l'entrepreneur et le cadre" (note 5), p. 28.

85. See Sheng Hong, "Chanquan jiegou gaige" (note 40); Yu Chengzhi, "Shunde shi zhengti tuijin hunhe xing chanquan zhidu gaige de chuangju" (The Whole Shunde Municipality Pioneers the Promotion of the Mixed Property System), *Guangdong jingji* (Guangdong Economy), No. 7 (July 1995), pp. 34–38.

86. Wang Dingding, "Zhongguo gaige guocheng de luoji" (The Logic of China's Reform Process), *Xinbao caijing yuekan* (Hong Kong Economic Journal Monthly), No. 223 (October 1995), p. 5.

87. Yuan Enzhen, *Zhongguo siying jingji* (note 38), pp.194–95.

88. Li Lulu, "Siying qiyejia de shehui jiegou" (note 11), pp. 105–07.

89. Mark Granovetter, "Economic Action and Social Structure: The Problem of Embeddedness," *American Journal of Sociology*, Vol. 91, No. 3 (November 1985), pp. 481–510.

10

Education

Grace C. L. Mak

The development of education in contemporary Guangdong reflects largely that in the nation.[1] Current attempts at education reform have again been spurred by national imperatives. The Third Plenary Session of the Eleventh Central Committee of the Communist Party of China (hereafter CPC) held in 1978 set the stage for the reform of the Chinese economy. It also pronounced the role of education to be that of promoting the four modernizations. The next fifteen years saw changes in other social institutions to parallel those in the economy. In 1985 the CPC issued an edict on "Resolutions on Reform of the Education System," the essence of which was to encourage local initiatives in expanding and improving educational provision by shifting decision-making and financial responsibilities from the state government.[2] Another major move, the promulgation of the Compulsory Education Act in 1986, aimed at ensuring that every school-aged child received nine years of education.[3] Local governments then announced specifics of implementation modelled after state guidelines.[4] The national imperative has not been intended to produce a high degree of uniformity in education among provinces as before the reform era. Rather, diversity in provincial characteristics is recognized and has contributed to disparate responses to the call from the centre. Guangdong enjoys a special economic policy which allows it greater autonomy than the rest of the nation. This privilege is crucial in making Guangdong the wealthiest in China. Thus a common source of impetus from the state and particular conditions of the province interact to set the context for educational development in Guangdong in the current era.

Education's pivotal role in economic development is repeatedly spelled out in most documents from the state or Guangdong government since 1978 promoting change in education. Yet the causal relationship between education and development is not so straightforward. Some early researches argued that educational change was a consequence of social change. The rise of modern schooling in Britain has been a classic argument for this thesis.[5] In a cross-national study Curle found no relationship between educational expansion and average growth in per capita income in the five years since 1954.[6] Other studies suggested the contrary. McClelland maintained that Curle's conclusion needed more detailed study, for the latter had not taken into consideration the time-lag needed for education to contribute to development. He surveyed the relationship between the two in the period 1930–1960 and concluded that countries that invested more heavily in education tended to develop more rapidly.[7] This was a resonance to Denison's study which attributed a sizeable portion of economic growth in the US in 1930–1960 to increased education of the labour force.[8] Education was given a new role by proponents of the human capital theory who conceptualized it as a form of investment, a human capital, rather than as a social service.[9] Accordingly, investment in education would increase the productivity of workers and, in turn, total output. Studies of Japan and South Korea, two of the countries that have performed economic miracles, are exemplary of this tenet.[10] In the 1950s and 1960s, governments in many developing countries shared the faith in education as a prime mover in development and thus expanded their education systems significantly. However, educational development did not always bring about the desired results. Poverty has persisted in much of the developing world, and educated unemployment reiterates the scepticism in education.[11] Thus the causation between education and economic development is inconclusive. The complexity of the issue has long baffled scholars.[12]

Guangdong presents an interesting case in that an abrupt turn in state policy provided the motive force for economic development. (Although the term "economic development" appears in much of the literature on education in Guangdong, it actually refers to simple increase in wealth, often in terms of increasing GNP by x times by a certain year, i.e. economic growth, rather than economic development which involves processes of structural change.[13]) Some of the latent conditions for the boom in Guangdong had already been in place, not least being its proximity to investment from the outside, mainly Hong Kong. China has been engaged in the process of educational expansion since 1949, but the call for economic reform in 1978 gave education a spurt. Education is a means employed to fuel the take-off. However, although education is assumed desirable, in the wake of a multitude of employment opportunities, the worth of education as a requirement to enter the labour market has somewhat weakened. The nascent prosperity may have depressed social demand for educational provision. Thus Guangdong's experience begs reflection on what triggers economic development, how education is used to sustain it, a possible subsequent change in public response towards educational provision, and a new pattern of distribution of education and wealth among social groups and geographical areas.

The discussion in this chapter starts from the premise that the economic reform in Guangdong since 1978 has stimulated innovations in education. Such a relationship in fact has a history. Socialist China has often cast a rigid function on education to serve political and economic goals, as exemplified in the linkage between manpower needs and school preparation. The chapter focuses on an assessment of the strategies adopted to sustain and accelerate economic production in the current era. The full implementation of nine-year compulsory education and a new balance between vocational content and academic content in education constitute two of the major strategies to meet economic needs. Prefaced by a historical profile, the chapter examines the impetus behind the current change and the means to promote it. It then investigates into enrollment in and content of education which are high on the agenda of education reform in the province. The chapter will close with a review on how far the current reform departs or ironically continues from the past. Thus, rather than exploring the causation between education and development, the chapter takes a close look at the phenomena which emerged in the interactive process between the two.

Historical Background of Education in Guangdong, 1949–1978

Various accounts of educational development in Guangdong by mainland writers point to the weak base the province started from. Before the communists came to power, education was a scarcity and illiterates and semi-literates constituted close to 80% of the population.[14] After 1949, one of the priorities of the government was to extend education to those denied it before. This is manifested in numbers (see Table 10.1). The rates of increase peaked in the Great Leap Forward in 1958–1959, only to decline sharply in the next few years. A period of consolidation and stability followed. The brief calm was again interrupted during the Cultural Revolution, when schools and colleges were temporarily closed, and teaching was irregular when they reopened. Thus, in the late 1970s, Guangdong inherited a frail education system which had swayed from one extreme to another, each time mirroring shifts in the larger political scene. The disruptions aside, educational provision has witnessed an overall upward trend. The rate of increase over the last four decades is impressive, at about six times for primary education, twenty times for secondary education and seven times for higher education. Primary education has almost been universalized, with an enrollment rate of children seven to eleven years of age at 99.58% in 1994, which compared favourably with the national rate of 98.4%, although Guangzhou lagged behind Jiangsu and the mega-cities of Beijing and Shanghai (99.92% and 99.97%, respectively).[15]

Table 10.1 Enrollment Trends by Levels of Education in Guangdong, 1949–1993

Year	Primary education	Secondary education						Higher education
		Technical education	Teacher education	Worker education	General education	Vocational education	Total	
1949	1,345,626	4,447	12,606	—	122,056	—	139,109	12,953
1952	2,999,984	15,400	20,326	—	205,309	—	241,035	10,016
1957	3,435,209	17,500	18,431	—	413,968	—	449,899	14,600
1958	4,849,825	—	23,547	—	539,945	71,520	—	25,740
1959	5,127,706	—	27,078	—	630,523	64,975	—	34,820
1960	5,183,588	—	3,625	—	673,101	58,845	—	43,712
1962	4,815,925	8,200	15,824	—	474,280	13,959	512,263	35,241
1965	7,042,405	7,900	13,116	—	500,595	174,488	696,099	27,745
1970	5,210,932	400	15,784	—	2,365,481	—	2,381,665	5,800
1975	7,738,483	20,600	14,491	—	2,335,613	—	2,370,704	24,103
1978	7,430,209	23,388	13,044	—	3,133,188	—	3,169,620	30,705
1980	7,488,593	27,767	17,823	16,075	2,521,103	17,240	2,600,008	41,004
1985	6,712,468	42,288	22,606	14,463	2,364,548	115,166	2,559,071	69,897
1990	7,472,928	89,956	30,869	52,176	2,340,301	222,389	2,735,691	95,929
1991	7,789,333	92,198	31,654	56,338	2,382,765	214,169	2,777,124	92,655
1993	8,321,421	118,445	36,009	76,775	2,771,877	192,125	3,195,231	116,957

Source: Guangdongsheng tongjiju (ed.), *Guangdong tongji nianjian 1994* (see note 15 below), p. 396.

The expansion changed the distribution of school places among social groups. Education became accessible to the poor. Of the children enrolled in secondary and primary schools in 1952, 71% and 80%, respectively, came from worker and peasant families.[16] In 1959 the figures rose to 86% and 83%, respectively, and 52% for tertiary education.[17] However, disparity due to intra-provincial differential development persists. Established centres like Guangzhou lead the province and poor hilly areas are gravely restrained.

The current initiative in education can be interpreted as yet another spurt in development policy. Provincial leaders saw that to maintain and prolong the momentum of economic growth in Guangdong,[18] the labour force must be adequately educated. This was all the more imperative as two acute problems surfaced with prosperity: low numbers and quality of workers and professionals. In 1983 Guangdong produced graduates to fill only a quarter of some 40,000 positions for those with higher education attainment.[19] The shortage has been somewhat eased, with a current supply and demand ratio of 1:1.4.[20] But qualified people are still in demand. A quick solution is to recruit from other provinces.[21] As industry in Guangdong grows in sophistication and moves from labour-based to technology-based, the concern about labour quality intensifies.[22] The optimism in Guangdong's economic future was reinforced by Deng Xiaoping's tour in south China in early 1992 and approval of the shape which the economy was taking. Since then, the provincial government has been aspiring to be on a par with the newly industrialized countries in Asia.[23] Meanwhile, as China opens up more interior and coastal provinces after the Guangdong model, the competitive edge that Guangdong has been enjoying is scaling down. So Guangdong senses an urgency to speed up its own supply of talents.

As noted earlier, education for development is an explicit rationale behind new initiatives in education. The Guangdong provincial documents of 1983 and 1985, both responses to state initiatives, announce or reiterate this goal.[24] As in most similar documents, all levels and areas of education are covered. The priorities though are the implementation of nine-year universal basic education and increase in the proportion of vocational education relative to academic education at the secondary level; these measures are in fact replays of an old theme. Extending education to all has consistently been a declared goal of the Chinese communist government. For example, the First Five-year Plan (1953–1957) had among its priorities the implementation of mass education. A ten-year education for all children across the province by 1985 was one of the goals listed in a 1975 provincial document on educational planning.[25] The difference this time is that the priorities have a new mandate — to produce large numbers of workers with the appropriate skills required for current economic needs. Conditions favourable to the mandate and how it is achieved constitute the rest of this chapter.

Factors Conducive to Education Reform

The administration of education in contemporary China has been characterized by a high degree of centralization. However, there is growing awareness that the goals of education reform are unlikely to materialize if the provinces continue complying to rigid, standardized central directives that are insensitive to diverse local needs. The problem is apparent in a country of contrasts like China. Decentralization in educational provision and management is a strategy which distinguishes the current reform from previous ones. The state sets the general direction. The provinces supposedly enjoy greater flexibility than before in realizing it. They set provincial principles for different levels of local governments, each of which has its specific responsibilities and some autonomy over how to fulfil them. For example, basic education used to be provided for by the municipality and the county, whereas now the municipality, county, town and township are each responsible for running their own schools. Similarly, administration of institutions of higher education has extended from the state and province to the municipality and county. However, decentralization must be understood in relative terms. Although provinces enjoy more freedom, they nevertheless follow principles set at the top. Their subordinate position to the state remains, at least in theory. This is why provincial education documents look alike in spirit.

In practice the province is not as docile to the state as it appears on paper. Decentralization is in part an answer to the central government's difficulties in dealing with insufficient funding and ineffective management. When the one who controls the purse strings is short of funds, he will invite the recipient to devise ways to make up the difference. Growing financial strength then entitles the recipient to greater independence, which explains why local governments can increasingly afford to divert from central instruction. Decision-making power and ownership of funds therefore are two sides of the same coin. Decentralization has allowed Guangdong to change education in ways that are supposed to meet its needs better.

But contributions from various levels of government cannot cover all expenses especially because costs of living and salaries in Guangdong are among the top in the nation. Large portions of education budgets are spent on staffing, leaving little for other areas of need.[26] The tapping of new sources of finances permeates discussion on education.[27] Increase in allocations for education is dwarfed by actual needs. Between 1979 and 1988 educational expenditure in Guangdong surged 3.7 times.[28] Comparable national rates are 3.3 times.[29] Other statistics report similar growth. In the nation as a whole, education as a percentage of total government expenditure has almost doubled, from 8.4% in 1978 to 16.4% in 1988 and 16.9% in 1994.[30] But this is not enough to revitalize post-Cultural Revolution education. Also, when inflation is taken into consideration, expenditure on primary and secondary education actually dropped, e.g., 8.5% between 1986 and 1987, and that on higher education 1.7%.[31] When compared with the nation as a whole, Guangdong consistently budgeted a lower proportion of its GNP to education, at 2.16%, 1.9%, 1.84% and 1.59%, respectively, in 1980 and individual years in the period 1985–1987, when corresponding figures for the nation were 2.24%, 2.22%, 2.28% and 2.07%.[32] This was a mockery to the declared importance of education. Since education is gravely underfunded, new resources have to be explored. In the name of decentralization, local governments can impose different forms of education tax.[33] Another strategy is communist China's age-old tradition of mobilizing cadres and the masses to support government agenda. Reports like that of the cadres and people of Xinyi donating money to renovate crumbling school buildings are not new.[34] Already in the 1950s, local governments were encouraged to pool resources from parents and the community at large to make up for insufficient funding.[35] A new channel in the reform era is contribution from enterprises. Such contribution is reported to be increasingly significant.[36]

Budget concerns hit the student body directly. In higher education now there are two kinds of sponsorship. Students recruited under state quotas continue to enjoy free education. Those sponsored by their employers or by themselves (mostly their parents) are fee-paying.[37] The proportion of these two latter groups is significant, at 29% in 1991,[38] and up to 35% a year later.[39] For non-fee paying students, a stipend for students from poor families (*zhuxuejin*) and therefore an equalizer between social classes, is replaced by scholarships, selection for which is based on academic merit.[40] This signifies a change in the nature of educational provision which may have far-reaching implications. Free state education is gradually eroding away to hints of privatization. This applies not only to Shenzhen, a special economic zone which is licensed to stray from orthodox socialism, but to the province and indeed the nation as a whole. At lower levels of schooling, the kinds of fees schools impose on students challenge one's imagination. Some of them are tuition fees (for upper secondary school), miscellaneous fees (*zafei*), practice fees for technical subjects, textbooks, health examinations, student identity cards, graduation diplomas, water fees for swimming pools, oil fees for generation of electricity during blackouts — so many that the Guangzhou municipal government issued regulations on what fees are allowed.[41] Their proliferation suggests the inadequacy of the formal channel of funding as well as a phenomenon which contradicts the spirit of free universal education.

School personnel have been given the greenlight to generate earnings. Institutions of higher learning busy themselves with making money. They sell services and products and set up enterprises which may or may not relate to their academic expertise. With the excuse of integrating teaching, research and practice, they try to supplement salaries and institutional expenditure which the formal budget fails to accommodate. Primary and secondary schools join the endeavours. They set up small low-technology factories. Students take part in some kind of work-study programme and are paid a modest sum. The profits go to schools. Since 1978, more than 70% of primary and secondary schools have resumed this mode of alternative income.[42]

Guangdong's advantage also lies in its long history of emigration. Chinese abroad and in Hong Kong have all sorts of connections with their native places in Guangdong. Many wealthy businessmen donate large sums to schools.[43] Such donations constituted almost a quarter of funds pooled from various sources to supplement the sum earmarked by government.[44] It is similar for other provinces which have rich kin abroad, but Guangdong tops the nation in this aspect.

Against this backdrop of assets and strategies to develop education, how successful has the Guangdong experience been? The next two sections address this question.

Enrollment in Education

With primary education near universalization, Guangdong has raised its target to nine years. This section examines enrollment in different levels of education.

Primary and Secondary Education

China has done well relative to other countries of a comparable level of development in its provision of basic education. The current drive is economic. Provision of nine years of education is believed to be most cost-effective for society as a whole.[45] Interestingly, the impact of a policy measure informed by economic considerations is inherently egalitarian. Universal basic education can be assessed by the extent of implementation. The goal of province-wide implementation has been revised continuously. In 1988, it was postponed to the end of the century.[46] However, in 1994 only 84 counties, municipalities and districts, comprising 67% of the province's population, had implemented it,[47] making the end-of-the-century target overly optimistic. Guangdong officials recognize that there is much room for improvement in order for Guangdong to emerge as leader of the nation in universal basic education.[48]

The haste to expand universal basic education has bred many contradictions. The fees schools charge have made education a burden to the poor. Better-off parents can send their children to schools which charge more and are possibly better. So a school's discretion to charge fees as a measure to accelerate universal basic education may defeat the latter's titular principle. Another contradiction is that the boom which calls for more educated workers has also lured away school children. Educational attainment continues to determine one's occupational prospect if one opts for salaried employment in the state or collective sectors. Professional ranks tend to require educational qualifications.[49] However, education is no longer the single most important factor. Abundant opportunities in the labour market convey the message that one does not always need an education to earn a decent income. In the current structure of the labour market, individuals, often school dropouts who otherwise may have been scorned in the mainstream sectors, set up small businesses and earn far more than those hired in public sectors. There has been a rise in the proportion of small private business in the economy.[50] Such an increase in effect undermines the value of formal education as a preparation for employment. Education wastage has been a problem. Between 1985 and 1989, the province lost 1.12 million students, of whom 95% were from primary and lower secondary schools.[51] The loss appears related to uneven levels of development. In developed areas, like Foshan, where universal basic education is well in place, wastage tends to be low. In medium developed areas which have just tasted the sweet fruit of reform and therefore a new surge of jobs, e.g. Huidong, and poor regions where universal basic education has not made inroads, wastage is higher.[52] The majority of school dropouts are likely to be girls. Of the child labour in China reported in 1987, 85% was female.[53] These young people either chose or were made by adults to opt for waged employment. In Dongguan, which saw spectacular economic growth in the last decade, young women aged fifteen or so worked in factories rather than stayed in schools.[54] Because light industries which dot the towns and townships in the Pearl River Delta need large numbers of female workers, it is possible that there is more educational wastage among girls than boys. If such is the case, the impact of economic growth on girls may be mixed. Earnings from factory work may raise their status at home and in society, but limited education may also tie them to lower ranks. Another reason why basic education is not universalized is that it lacks strong enforcement. Many employers and parents who do not value education simply ignore its binding power.[55] Although some towns and townships stipulate regulations, e.g. adolescents who have not completed lower secondary school must not be hired,[56] their effectiveness is doubtful.

Any common goal in a province as diverse as Guangdong will have differential results. Universal basic education is successful in urban centres like Guangzhou, the newly developed areas in the Pearl River Delta, and Special Economic Zones like Shenzhen, where resources are more available.[57] For example, in 1989 Shenzhen reached a 100% enrollment for primary and junior secondary school aged children and a promotion rate at 85% to upper secondary schools, far higher than comparable provincial and national rates.[58] Conversely, poor hilly areas managed to universalize six-year basic education in 1985, but extension to nine years poses a challenge. This affects the performance of the entire province as these areas constitute 42% of the provincial population.[59]

The rigid assessment mechanism presents another problem. Excellence is measured in terms of promotion rates from one level of education to another, cumulating at the point of promotion from upper secondary school to university. Higher education is scarce in a society where only 3–5% of the age cohort had access to it as recently as the turn of the decade.[60] Teaching effort focuses on preparing students for examinations and parents choose schools that have produced high examination scores. This to the authorities is "anti-educational." Since the goal now is to curb student ambition at secondary education, the stress is on a balanced and relevant preparation of youths to be rank-and-file factory workers. The authorities repeatedly attack conventional assessment criteria. Yet precisely the same quantifiable assessment is employed in education. In report after report, success is described in promotion rates. In 1994, Guangdong had a primary enrollment rate of 99.58%, an annual retention rate of 98.92%, and a transition to lower secondary school rate at 91.8%.[61] The province is mainly concerned with meeting target numbers set by the nation. Without an alternative assessment scheme, the government is trapped in the very problem that it attacks. Within schools old habits die hard. They stream students by ability and run additional classes after school hoping to raise students' examination scores, all pointing to the prevalence of convention.[62]

A major setback to raising the quality of education is the inadequacy of teaching qualifications which has its roots in the Cultural Revolution, when the training prospective teachers received was scant for the jobs they were to enter. In China professionals aged 40 and above, mostly trained before the Cultural Revolution, tend to be the mainstay in their fields. The generation that follows generally does not demonstrate comparable ability. This discontinuity is found in the teaching force as well. In 1990, teachers aged 35 or below made up only about half of the entire force. Many of those in the group aged 40 or above will retire soon. The staggered profile is also seen in Guangdong.[63] Coupled with it is a drastic demand for expansion in education. Schools compromise by planting teachers in positions they may not be qualified for. In theory, training at degree-granting tertiary institutions prepares one for teaching in upper secondary school, non-degree tertiary for lower secondary school and upper secondary level for primary school. In 1994, 10% of primary teachers, 25% of lower secondary teachers and 46% of upper secondary teachers were still not qualified for their jobs.[64] Qualified teachers in poor areas have options of mobility and tend to move to wealthier areas, hence aggravating intra-provincial disparity. Another measure is to fill the positions with *minban* (managed by the people) teachers, who lack the required qualifications and are paid less. If qualifications are a sufficient indicator of teacher quality, compensatory training for teachers is a must. Multiple forms of in-service teacher education are launched. Normally in-service teacher education aims at enriching qualified teachers with new knowledge. In China this is more an aspiration than a reality. In-service teacher education is preoccupied with compensatory education for unqualified teachers.[65] When effective, these measures only partially solve the problem. More disturbing is the lack of attraction teaching has compared with other occupations. Before the reform era the gap between the salaries of teachers and those of other occupations was narrower than today. In the late 1980s teachers were at the lower end of the pay scale. In 1987 secondary school teachers made on average RMB1,198 a year and primary teachers RMB1,138, as compared with RMB1,767 for employees in the state-owned sector.[66] Since then, the government has introduced new measures to entice teachers, such as raising their salaries and providing subsidized housing, so that the teaching force has stabilized in the mid-1990s. *Minban* teachers made considerably less. New occupations, especially those in the private sector, tend to pay far better than teaching and often set less rigid requirements on academic qualifications. Low salaries breed a number of cousins: low status, brain drain and low quality of students recruited to teacher education. The loss of teachers to other occupations has become a crisis. It is especially acute among younger (aged 30–40) and better qualified teachers; thus prosperity in the labour market has aggravated teacher attrition. Government interference has not stopped teacher loss from reaching an alarming peak in 1992.[67] New teachers replace more in numerical than quality terms. In China as well as Guangdong, teacher training institutions have difficulty in recruiting bright students. It has always been so. Teachers colleges have never been among the most prestigious institutions. But never has it been so bad. Teachers colleges have devised a number of strategies to recruit students, not least being the lowering of admission scores. Students end up in teacher education for sundry reasons: insufficient examination scores to enroll in a field of their choice, rural students hoping to settle down in an urban school after graduation, or students from poor families who are attracted by a meal allowance which is not issued to their counterparts in other fields of studies.[68]

In short, one will miss the full picture of primary and secondary education in Guangdong if enrollment figures alone are considered. The gradual emergence of inequalities in education, the crisis within the teaching profession, the persistance of a conventional mentality among school personnel, and the competition between schools and the economy for young people during an initial stage of economic boom all point to the need for scrutiny of the subject.

Higher Education

Parallel to primary and secondary education, decentralization affects higher education. To maximize efficiency of investment in education, a new accounting system has been introduced since 1980. Each institution of higher learning is earmarked a lump sum. It has to seek ways to solicit additional revenues in the case of need and can decide what to do with surplus.[69]

Expansion in higher education is captured in the number of new institutions and enrollments. The former grew from 29 in 1978 to 47 in 1994.[70] Enrollment has also soared. China produced 3.25 million graduates from higher education in the decade since 1978, which exceeded the sum total of the three decades before.[71] Guangdong shared the progress, with enrollment at 137,458 in 1994,[72] as compared with 30,705 in 1978 (see Table 10.1). The geographical spread of tertiary institutions reflects shifting centres of action. Since the mid-1980s, municipalities have been encouraged to set up new institutions. On the eve of the communist takeover, of 20 institutions of higher education, 18 were in Guangzhou and 2 on Hainan.[73] Today 29 are in Guangzhou and 18 in the rest of Guangdong, many of which used to be rural.[74] Guangzhou maintains leadership status in the type and quality of higher education it offers. It houses prestigious comprehensive and specialized institutions. Nevertheless, such leadership is weakening. Although of a lower quality in general, the new centres offer training in specialized fields and at lower status, such as non-degree teacher training or other skill-oriented programmes. (The change in content of higher education is discussed in the next section.)

The most significant change has been in selection criteria. Before the reform era, admission to higher education in China either focused on academic performance or on family origin as criteria. Students fought for entrance and their fortune depended on the criterion in force. Now ideological emphasis is weakened by pragmatism. Students compete for high scores. It can be said that meritocracy prevails. However, multiple criteria apply. As discussed earlier, students with high scores are publicly supported, those with lower scores can still gain admission by paying fees. Incomprehensible though it may have seemed if it had happened before 1978, some students drop out from tertiary education, convinced that they can do without a university education. While they constitute a minority of the entire student population, that there is dropout at all is enough to alarm people to reconsider the meaning of higher education to the individual. This leads to concern about the "futility of studying," a popular attitude during the Cultural Revolution when academic knowledge was condemned. Today knowledge is not condemned, but it is not always rewarded. A higher education does not always pay off. Some students leave higher education to set up small businesses or to seek employment in joint ventures, which not only pay better but may also lead to emigration opportunities.[75] The meaning of "futility" differs somewhat from before. Some of the dropouts seek ways to study abroad. Studying is contextual. Students are not against studying per se. It is sought after when taking place abroad. Change in the status of knowledge has to be understood in the context of the current stage of development and employment structure. When the economy of Guangdong becomes more sophisticated and people equipped with relevant education are better rewarded, as in the newly industrialized countries of Asia, education may be more attractive. Besides, the gradual erosion of the job placement system for college and university graduates means that a higher education does not necessarily guarantee employment. However, reduced enthusiasm towards education is not consensual. Many students are enticed into employment, others insist on studying. Fee-paying private students are a good example. These are often serious students from intellectual families.[76] To them knowledge is worth acquiring, although like other students, their choice of field is dictated by the popularity of skills. In 1989, 80% of them were studying skills in demand, such as business studies, technology and foreign languages, whereas only 10% were in arts and 5% in pure science.[77]

Overall, although expansion in higher education has not attracted as much attention as that in primary and secondary education, it has changed in fundamental ways. The appearance of tertiary institutions in medium-sized cities has reduced geographical inequalities, yet the new selection criteria are likely to breed new inequalities among social classes. Development in higher education therefore takes opposite directions.

Content of Education

What to teach students is another major area of reform in education since 1978. The concern is the relative relevance of academic and vocational knowledge to the economy.[78] This is hardly new. Vocational content has always been heavy in Chinese higher education. The proportion of humanities and natural sciences, at 16% of the enrollment in higher education in 1949, gradually dwindled to 12% in 1983. Students in practical fields — engineering, medicine, teaching, etc. — represent the majority.[79] The issue now is to vocationalize secondary education and to introduce new vocational studies to tertiary education.[80] Traditionally, at the secondary level grammar education is "real" education and therefore superior to vocational education. Since 1980, quotas have been set and periodically revised to raise the ratio of vocational to grammar education. The latest goal is 50:50. More students are to be trained in more trades. The strategy is to encourage local governments to set up new vocational schools or to convert grammar schools to vocational ones. Whether vocational education is so effective in producing the right kind of workers for industry is debatable. In fact, studies conducted during the last 20 years have been increasingly sceptical of the efficacy of vocational education in economic development.[81] Contrary to the international tendency, China is pushing full steam for vocational education. In Guangdong the current concern is how vocational education is run, rather than the basic question of whether vocational education best meets economic needs. Again, numbers become a convenient yardstick to assess achievement. Reaching the magic 50:50 ratio is what local governments strive for, with much less attention to what is behind the figures. This is a major failure of the current reform.

The problem is threefold. From the start vocational secondary education is ill-conceived. Since nine years of education is believed to be most cost-effective for economic development, demand for more education must be curbed. The majority of students are encouraged to acquire medium-level skills and leave after secondary education, although they are reassured that they have a chance of going on to higher education if they so desire. As a mechanism to differentiate unfavourably, the appeal of vocational education is questionable. The second part of the problem is quality. Typically a vocational school in Guangdong lacks proper equipment and teachers. Students spend a few years learning rudimentary skills which they probably learn better on the shopfloor. Finding appropriate teachers is a dilemma. Often those who possess technical expertise lack teacher training, and are probably paid better in their trades. Teachers in vocational education tend to lag behind developments in their trades and what they teach becomes obsolete.[82] The dilemma in China is aggravated because of many new skills in demand. Amateurs lack both proper training and state-of-the-art knowledge to guide students. Teachers trained for conventional academic subjects may be transferred to an area of vocational education which overlaps with their hobbies. A music teacher may be asked to teach dressmaking, or a physics teacher machinery.[83] However, in a province as diverse as Guangdong, quality is not monolithic. Cities like Guangzhou have been more successful with vocational education.[84] The third part of the problem lies in the relevance of vocational education to rural economies and student aspirations. In theory, the goal of rural vocational education is to equip the population for rural development. However, the goal has proven elusive. Surplus labour in rural areas means that innovations, if sought, should be in advanced technology, which graduates from vocational schools are unlikely to be capable of introducing. Vocational education is ill-placed. The number of courses in agricultural production has been declining. In 1991, only about 20% of rural vocational schools still offered such courses.[85] On the other hand, courses which have less to do with agricultural development, namely, electronics and construction, have mushroomed to meet student demand. Students hope the possession of such skills will open their way to urban employment, whereas policy planners try to tie them to the land. So rural vocational education defeats its own purpose. The more successful it is, the more it steers away from rural goals. This has to do with student aspirations. Education is a possible vehicle to leave the countryside. Besides, some students aim at higher education and so prefer a grammar education. Failing that, they seek factory employment in Shenzhen or the delta. This example eloquently articulates a long-time phenomenon of superficial education reforms in China. Completion of tasks often means meeting the set quota. But the figures carry little meaning. In this sense local autonomy has not been used in a constructive way, and the present does not depart significantly from earlier decades.

Vocationalization also accelerates at the tertiary level, where it has met less resistance. The move takes two directions. First, existing comprehensive universities such as Zhongshan University in Guangzhou, which specialized in humanities and sciences before, introduced technological courses and management courses.[86] Second, and more extensively, "vocational universities" or polytechnics have been founded in recent years in newly developed municipalities like Jiangmen, Foshan, Shaoguan, Dongguan and Huizhou, which have prospered economically. Their quality may not match the term "university." In their haste to produce results, many of them were founded on existing facilities and resources. For example, Xijiang University was founded on Zhaoqing Specialized Teachers School and Huizhou University on the merge of two teachers institutes and a vocational institute.[87] Others, like Zhongkai Agricultural Technical College, was upgraded from a specialized secondary school.[88] Their standards waver. Faculty quality is a major concern. Most faculty members graduated from university in the 1950s and 1960s, when development emphasis in China was on heavy industry. Whether they adequately meet the demands of new technology in light industry deserves investigation. The short-cycle courses these institutions offer reflect the direction industries in Guangdong are heading. Examples are construction, communications, energy, light industries, food processing, finance, law, foreign languages and management studies.[89]

The demand for vocational skills also found expression in adult and non-formal education. In China this category includes literacy campaigns, on-the-job training in rural and urban settings, and non-formal higher education. Flexibility of this form of education engenders a significant complementary and compensatory cushion to the formal channel. For example, institutions of adult higher education and correspondence programmes offered by regular tertiary institutions mushroomed in the last decade and a half, so that enrollment reached 137,014 in 1994,[90] which was more than a sevenfold increase from 1978. The figures compare favourably with an enrollment of 137,458 in formal higher education in the same year. Although completion rate in the non-formal panel is lower and takes more years, its size convincingly argues for its importance in a newly developing economy. Another inexpensive route is the self-study programme. Participants study on their own and then take qualification examinations set by established universities in Guangzhou. It provides a second opportunity for those who are otherwise denied any higher education. Other non-formal courses like accounting, dressmaking, typing, English, and flower arrangement flourish. Many of their participants have already completed formal education. The numbers are considerable. In Guangzhou, 800,000 working people, or 44% of its total labour force, were in some kind of non-formal education in 1991.[91] This shows that Guangdong people are, after all, a learning people, although they revere academic knowledge less than before.

Conclusion

This chapter sets out to examine changes in education in Guangdong in the context of a nascent economic take-off in the 1970s. It argues that education alone does not trigger economic growth. Rather, education is used to mediate with economic reform policies to sustain and accelerate growth. The review suggests that the Guangdong experience offers a different perspective on the study of education and development. It takes as a cross-section the achievements and problems at a time of rapid expansion.

Increasing school places and restructuring the content of education form the major strategies of education's response to economic needs. The effectiveness of the strategies hinges on assessment criteria. Educational providers in Guangdong tend to measure progress in numerical terms. Thus, Guangdong's move towards universalization of basic education and raising the proportion of vocational content in education has been impressive. However, it has been argued that an assessment which does not probe into the contradictions hidden in the numbers, fails to be comprehensive. Though education wastage in Guangdong is not exceptionally higher than comparable international rates, the reasons behind it are qualitatively significant. They suggest that education, deemed a mover in development by planners, does not carry the same value for individual students and parents. Basic education does not significantly enhance the competitiveness of workers at a time of rudimentary but active boom, when the need for labour is large and the existing labour force of generally low calibre. The high enrollment rates thus gloss over the complexities of the value of education and, in turn, individuals' response to it. A similar phenomenon finds expression in higher education. Again, although the number of youth resisting higher education is far from a crisis, it does point to a rift between the official view and the individual's view on the function of higher education. It reflects that at this particular point of growth, some individuals opt for immediate monetary gains rather than long-term rewards that education may bring. These contradictions are sharpened by financial constraints. The latter are partially resolved through tapping resources from multiple channels and decentralizing management autonomy, but they still pose a barrier to educational expansion. Similarly, concealed in optimistic figures is a crisis in the nature of change in the content of secondary education. Educational personnel head towards an ever higher proportion of vocational education, not taking heed of the warning signals against it. The move continues in spite of poor implementation and conflicting use of vocational secondary education by planners and students.

On the other hand, some responses to the current needs of the economy have brought positive structural change which is probably not planned. The spread of tertiary institutions, albeit of less than excellent quality, away from the provincial centre of Guangzhou, presently reduces geographical disparities within the province. The proliferation of adult and non-formal courses point to an alternative route for employees to strengthen themselves while keeping their jobs.

At the height of Guangdong's economic spectacle, officials continue to declare their faith in education. That education enhances the quality of the labour force in general seems logical, but what it can and cannot do if and when Guangdong falls prey to recession is probably a question raised too early. The experience of some countries suggests that the faith in education may turn into scepticism at times of economic hardships. A more discernible worry for Guangdong is competition from Shanghai, which begins to enjoy similar policy privileges as Guangdong has been allowed in recent years.

Lastly, how innovative is the education reform? Measures are new in the context in which they are placed. Yet they are but a latest variation on a tradition in Guangdong. Aside from strategies, the goal of catching up with newly industrialized Asia parallels that of aspiring to catch up with Britain and America during the Great Leap Forward in the late 1950s.

Notes

1. For studies on education in contemporary China, see, e.g. C. T. Hu (ed.), *Chinese Education under Communism* (2nd ed.; New York: Teachers College Press, Columbia University, 1974); Julia Kwong, *Chinese Education in Transition* (Montreal: McGill-Queen's University Press, 1979); Ruth Hayhoe (ed.), *Contemporary Chinese Education* (London: Croom Helm, 1984); and John Hawkins, *Education and Social Change in the People's Republic of China* (New York: Praeger, 1983). Those which study Guangdong are Jonathan Unger, *Education under Mao* (New York: Columbia University Press, 1981); Stanley Rosen, *Red Guard Factionalism and the Cultural Revolution in Guangzhou (Canton)* (Boulder, Colorado: Westview Press, 1982); and Susan Shirk, *Competitive Comrades* (Berkeley: University of California Press, 1982).

2. "Zhonggong zhongyang guanyu jiaoyu tizhi gaige de jueding" (Resolutions of the Communist Party of China on Reform of the Education System) (May 1985) in *Zhongguo dangdai jiaoyu sichao 1949–1989* (Educational Thought in Contemporary China, 1949–1989), edited by Yuan Zhenguo (Shanghai: Sanlian shudian, 1991), pp. 398–406.

3. "Zhonghua renmin gongheguo yiwu jiaoyufa" (Compulsory Education Act of the People's Republic of China) (April 1986), ibid., pp. 410–11.

4. The provincial execution of central directives is illustrated in the chapters on each province in Zhongguo jiaoyu nianjian bianjibu (ed.), *Zhongguo jiaoyu nianjian 1989* (China Education Yearbook 1989) (Beijing: Renmin jiaoyu chubanshe, 1990). An example of local variation is "Zhuhaishi puji jiunian zhi yiwu jiaoyu shishi xize" (Detailed Regulations on the Implementation of Nine-year Universal Education in Zhuhai) discussed in "Jiaoyu shiye" (Education), *Zhuhai nianjian* (Zhuhai Yearbook) (Guangzhou: Guangdong renmin chubanshe, n.d.), pp. 205–12. A similar example is the Shantou

Special Economic Zone (SEZ). See Shantou jingji tequ nianjian bianji weiyuanhui (ed.), *Shantou jingji tequ nianjian, 1981–1989* (Shantou SEZ Yearbook 1981–1989) (Guangzhou: Guangdong renmin chubanshe, n.d.), pp. 319–23.

5. M. D. Shipman, *Education and Modernisation* (London: Faber & Faber, 1971).

6. Adam Curle, "Education, Politics and Development," *Comparative Education Review*, Vol. 7, No. 3 (1964), pp. 226–45.

7. David C. McClelland, "Does Education Accelerate Economic Growth?" in *Scientific Investigations in Comparative Education*, edited by M. A. Eckstein and H. J. Noah (London: Collier-Macmillan, 1969).

8. Edward Denison, *The Sources of Economic Growth in the United States and the Alternatives before Us* (New York: Committee for Economic Development, 1962).

9. For example, Theodore Schultz, "Investment in Human Capital," *American Economic Review*, Vol. 51 (1961), pp. 1–17; George Psacharopoulos and Maureen Woodhall, *Education for Development: An Analysis of Investment Choices* (New York: Published for the World Bank by Oxford University Press, 1985).

10. Ronald Dore, *Education in Tokugawa Japan* (Berkeley: University of California Press, 1965); Noel F. McGinn et al., *Education and Development in Korea* (Cambridge, M.A.: Council on East Asian Studies, Harvard University; distributed by Harvard University Press, 1980).

11. Hans N. Weiler, "Education and Development: From the Age of Innocence to the Age of Scepticism," *Comparative Education Review*, Vol. 14, No. 3 (1978), pp. 179–98; Rafael L. Irizarry, "Overeducation and Unemployment in the Third World: The Paradoxes of Dependent Industrialization," *Comparative Education Review*, Vol. 24 (1980), pp. 338–52.

12. The investigation is summarized in Ingemar Fagerlind and Lawrence J. Saha, *Education and National Development: A Comparative Perspective* (2nd ed.; New York: Pergamon, 1989), and Wadi D. Haddad et al., *Education and Development* (Washington D.C.: The World Bank, 1990).

13. For a discussion of the distinction between "economic growth" and "economic development," see Robert A. Flammang, "Economic Growth and Economic Development: Counterparts or Competitors?" *Economic Development and Cultural Change*, Vol. 28 (1979), pp. 47–61.

14. Guangdongsheng tongjiju (ed.), *Qianjin zhong de Guangdong: 1949–1988 nian Guangdong shehui jingji fazhan qingkuang* (Guangdong Marching Forward: Economic Development of Guangdong 1949–1988) (Hong Kong: Dadao wenhua, 1989), p. 202.

15. Zhonghua renmin gongheguo guojia jiaoyu weiyuanhui jihua jianshesi (ed.), *Zhongguo jiaoyu shiye tongji nianjian 1994* (Educational Statistical

Yearbook of China 1994) (Beijing: Renmin jiaoyu chubanshe, 1994), pp. 268–69; Guangdongsheng tongjiju (ed.), *Guangdong tongji nianjian 1994* (Statistical Yearbook of Guangdong 1994) (Beijing: Zhongguo tongji chubanshe, 1994). Also, in transition of primary six children to junior secondary school, Guang-zhou lags behind six major cities in China. See Li Zibiao et al., "Guangzhou zhongxue jiaoyu fazhan yu jingji shehui fazhan" (Development of Secondary Education and Socio-economic Development in Guangzhou), *Guangzhou jiaoyu* (Education in Guangzhou), No. 1(1988), p. 14.

16. See note 14.

17. Renmin jiaoyu chubanshe (ed.), *Jiaoyu shinian* (Ten Years of Education) (Beijing: Renmin jiaoyu chubanshe, 1960), pp. 155–62.

18. For the relative superiority of Guangdong over the nation in economic growth, see Xu Mingdi and Zhou Guoxian (eds.), *Zhujiang sanjiaozhou jiaoyu zhanlüe lun* (Educational Strategies of the Pearl River Delta) (Guangzhou: Guangdong gaodeng jiaoyu chubanshe, 1992), pp. 1–3.

19. *Guangdong jiaoyu nianjian 1986* (Guangdong Education Yearbook 1986) (Guangzhou: Guangdongsheng jiaoyuting Guangdong jiaoyu nianjian bian-jibu, 1986), p. 1.

20. *Guangzhou ribao*, 23 June 1992, p. 3.

21. The phenomenon is dubbed "kongque dongnan fei" — "peacocks flocking to the south-east," an allusion from a Chinese poem.

22. *Guangzhou ribao*, 8 June 1992, p. 2.

23. Xue Renzhi, "Zhuigan si xiaolong: Guangdong pujiao zuoshi de gousi" (Catching Up with the Four Little Dragons: Thoughts on Trends in Universal Basic Education in Guangdong), *Guangdong jiaoyu*, Nos. 7–8 (1992), p. 3.

24. See "Zhonggong Guangdongshengwei, Guangdongsheng renmin zhengfu guanyu nuli kaichuang wosheng jiaoyu shiye xin jumian de jueding" (Resolutions of the Guangdong Provincial Party Committee and the Guangdong People's Government on Innovations in Education in Guangdong) (March 1983) and "Zhonggong Guangdongshengwei, Guangdongsheng renmin zhengfu guanyu 'Zhonggong Zhongyang guanyu jiaoyu tizhi gaige de jueding' de yijian" (Comments by the Guangdong Provincial Party Committee and the Guangdong People's Government on the "Resolutions of the CPC on Reform of the Education System") (October 1985), in *Guangdong jiaoyu nianjian 1986* (see note 19), pp. 1–14. Problems that need to be attacked are summarized in Zhu Yuanxing, "Dui Guangdong shishi yiwu jiaoyufa de jianyi he yijian" (Suggestions and Comments on the Implementation of Nine-year Universal Education in Guangdong), *Jiaoyu luncong* (Forum on Education) No. 2 (1991), pp. 2–3, 6.

25. See note 19, pp. 23, 25.

26. *Guangzhou ribao*, 31 May 1992.
27. See note 19, p. 5; Chen Haotian, "Shenhua Guangzhou jiaoyu zhi wojian" (My View on Intensifying Education Reform in Guangzhou), *Guangzhou jiaoyu*, No. 6 (1988), pp. 33–34.
28. See note 14, p. 203.
29. Li Tieying, "Guanyu woguo jiaoyu gongzuo ruogan wenti de huibao" (Report on Some Questions Concerning Education in China), in *Zhongguo jiaoyu gongzuo de ruogan wenti* (Some Questions on Education in China), edited by Guowuyuan jiaoyu gongzuo yantao xiaozu bangongshi (Beijing: Renmin jiaoyu chubanshe, 1990), p. 28.
30. Calculated from Guojia tongjiju (ed.), *Zhongguo tongji nianjian 1991* (Statistical Yearbook of China 1991) (Beijing: Zhongguo tongji chubanshe, 1991), pp. 209, 217; and Guojia tongjiju (ed.), *Zhongguo tongji nianjian 1995* (Statistical Yearbook of China 1995) (Beijing: Zhongguo tongji chubanshe, 1995), pp. 215, 221.
31. Li Xiuhong et al., *Guangdong jiaoyu huanjing yu fazhan zhanlüe yanjiu* (A Study on the Strategies in Education and Development) (Guangzhou: Guangdong gaodeng jiaoyu chubanshe, 1992), p. 397.
32. Ibid., p. 393.
33. Dongguan, e.g. imposed an education tax on electricity consumption. See also note 18, p. 3.
34. *Yangcheng wanbao*, 31 March 1992, p. 1; note 18, p. 35.
35. See note 19, p. 56.
36. See note 18, p. 34.
37. *Zhongguo jiaoyu gongzuo de ruogan wenti* (see note 29), p. 69; note 19, p. 4; Shenzhen jiaoyu kexue yanjiusuo (ed.), *Shenzhen tequ jiaoyu yanjiu* (Research on Education in Shenzhen SEZ) (Wuhan: Wuhan daxue chubanshe, 1985), pp. 21–29.
38. Calculated from *Yangcheng wanbao*, 28 July 1991, p. 1.
39. *Guangzhou ribao*, 6 June 1992, p. 2.
40. See note 19, p. 4; *Shenzhen tequ jiaoyu yanjiu* (see note 37), pp. 4–12.
41. *Yangcheng wanbao*, 26 December 1991, p. 1.
42. *Zhongguo jiaoyu gongzuo de ruogan wenti* (see note 29), p. 31.
43. For example, between 1979 and 1985, Chinese from Hong Kong and abroad donated RMB2.4 billion to build and renovate school buildings. See note 19, pp. 16, 83, 124–25; and note 18, p. 35.
44. See note 31, p. 392.
45. For example, *Shenzhen tequ jiaoyu yanjiu* (note 37), pp. 60–66.
46. See note 19, p. 638.
47. Guangdong nianjian bianzuan weiyuanhui (ed.), *Guangdong nianjian 1995* (Guangdong Yearbook 1995) (Guangzhou: Guangdong nianjianshe, 1995), p. 572.

48. Xu Renzhi, "Renqing xingshi, ba jiaoxue gaige baishang zhongyao weizhi" (Know the Situation and Assign Priority to Reform in Teaching), *Guangdong jiaoyu*, Nos. 1–2 (1992), pp. 4–5.

49. The relationship is succinctly illustrated in Yang Guoyu (ed.), *Guangdongsheng wanhu chengzhen jumin jiating diaocha ziliao huibian 1990* (Report on the Survey of 10,000 Urban Families in Guangdong Province 1990) (Guangzhou: Guangdongsheng caizhengting et al., 1990).

50. Ibid., p. 2.

51. Li Ji, "Liushisheng yu diling fanzui" (School Dropouts and Youth Delinquency), *Guangdong jiaoyu*, Nos. 7–8 (1991), pp. 9–10.

52. Qian Daoyuan et al., "Guangdong yiwu jiaoyu jieduan xuesheng liushi, liuji wenti de yanjiu baogao" (Report on Student Dropout and Repetition in Universal Education in Guangdong), *Jiaoyu luncong*, No. 1 (1990), p. 15.

53. *Wen Wei Po*, 7 March 1987.

54. Guangdongsheng fulian xuanchuanbu et al., "Gaige kaifang gei nongcun jiating dailai de xin bianhua — Dongguan Dalang qu 130 hu jiating diaocha" (Change Brought by Reform and Opening up to the Rural Family — A Study of 130 Families in Dalang District, Municipality of Dongguan) (Unpublished paper, 1986).

55. Zhu Yuanxing, "Dui Guangdong shishi yiwu jiaoyufa de jianyi he yijian" (see note 24), p. 2.

56. Zhong Weikun, "Guangdongsheng shishi jiunian yiwu jiaoyu de huigu yu shexiang" (Review and Recommendations for the Implementation of Nine-year Universal Education in Guangdong), *Jiaoyu luncong*, No. 1 (1991), pp. 2–5.

57. For differential educational attainment of the population in selected regions in Guangdong, see Table 3.2.2 in *Guangdong jiaoyu nianjian 1992*, p. 132.

58. See note 31, p. 105.

59. Zhong Weikun et al., "Chuangzao tiaojian, tuijin wosheng shanqu yiwu jiaoyu" (Create Conditions to Promote Universal Education in Hilly Areas in Guangdong), *Guangdong jiaoyu*, No. 5 (1990), p. 5.

60. Fang Bao, "Jiji tuijin wosheng nongcun jiaoyu zhonghe gaige" (Actively Promote the Comprehensive Reform of Rural Education in Guangdong), *Guangdong jiaoyu*, Nos. 1–2 (1991), p. 3.

61. See note 47, p. 572.

62. He Qifen, "Nongcun zhongxue ying zenme ban?" (What Should Rural Secondary Schools Do?), *Guangdong jiaoyu*, No. 3 (1991), p. 7.

63. See note 19, pp. 5, 92; Peng Jieping, "Qingnian jiaoshi de xinli shiheng ji shudao" (Loss of Psychological Balance by Young Teachers and Ways to Deal with It), *Guangdong jiaoyu*, No. 9 (1991), p. 21.

64. See note 47, p. 571.

65. Chen Youhong, "Gaohao jiaoshi gangwei peixun zhi wojian" (My Views on

Improving In-service Teacher Education), *Guangdong jiaoyu*, No. 9 (1991), p. 22.

66. See note 31, p. 395.

67. *Yangcheng wanbao*, 15 March 1992, p. 1; Zeng Youhua et al., "Jiaoshi duiwu jianshe mianlin de wenti he duice" (Problems and Strategies Facing the Building of the Teaching Labour Force), *Guangdong jiaoyu*, No. 4 (1992), pp. 9–11.

68. Liang Xingyi, "Gaodeng shifan jiaoyu de kunjing yu chulu" (Problems and Outlook in Teacher Education at the Tertiary Level), *Guangzhou jiaoyu*, No. 1 (1989), pp. 23–25; Li Qiying, "Shenzhen jiaoyu xueyuan zhong shishen zhuanye shixiang zhuangkuang de diaocha baogao" (Report of a Survey on the Attitudes towards Teaching of Students of Teacher Education at Shenzhen College of Education) in *Shenzhen tequ jiaoyu yanjiu* (see note 37), pp. 172–76; Guojia jiaowei gaoxiao xueshengsi, "Shifan yuanxiao zhaosheng qingkuang diaocha" (Report on a Survey of Recruitment to Institutions of Teacher Education), *Jiaoyu yanjiu*, No. 8 (1990), pp. 68–72.

69. Ibid., p. 37.

70. Excluding four on Hainan, which later was elevated to the rank of province. *Guangdong tongji nianjian 1994* (see note 15), p. 397; *Guangdong nianjian 1995* (see note 47), p. 570.

71. Li Shiyun, "Cong shinian jiaoyu de chengjiu yu shiwu kan jinhou de gaige" (Prospects of Reform as Viewed from Ten Years of Achievement and Failure in Education), *Jinan jiaoyu*, No. 2 (1990), p. 15.

72. See note 47, p. 570.

73. See note 47, p. 1.

74. See note 47, p. 570; Guangzhou nianjian bianzuan weiyuanhui, (ed.), *Guangzhou nianjian 1995* (Guangzhou Yearbook 1995) (Guangzhou: Guangzhou nianjian chubanshe, 1995), p. 396.

75. Zeng Fanluo et al., "Xin de 'dushu wuyong lun' pingxi" (Critique of the New Version of "Futility of Studying"), *Zhongguo gaodeng jiaoyu*, No. 10 (1988), pp. 20–22.

76. *Guangming ribao*, 3 February 1989, p. 1.

77. Ibid.

78. Here vocational education refers in a narrow sense to an alternative type of secondary education, as distinguished from grammar education. Philip Foster argued that all education is vocational in that it prepares students for employment. See his "The Vocational School Fallacy in Development Planning," in *Education and Development*, edited by C. A. Anderson and M. J. Bowman (Chicago: Aldine, 1966).

79. Zhonghua renmin gongheguo guojia jiaoyu weiyuanhui jihua caiwusi, *Zhongguo jiaoyu chengjiu 1949–1983* (Achievements of Education in China 1949–1983) (Beijing: Renmin jiaoyu chubanshe, 1984), p. 62.

80. There are three main types of secondary vocational school — skilled workers schools, secondary technical schools, secondary vocational schools. The first operates under the Ministry of Labour and Personnel and the latter two under the State Education Commission. For a detailed analysis see Harold Noah and John Middleton, *China's Vocational and Technical Training* (Washington, D.C.: Population and Human Resources Department, The World Bank, 1988).

81. Haddad et al., *Education and Development* (see note 12), pp. 45–49.

82. R. B. Hobart, "Teacher Education for Vocational and Industrial Education," in *The International Encyclopaedia of Teaching and Teacher Education*, edited by M. J. Dunkin (New York: Pergamon, 1987), pp. 787–93.

83. Lin Songxing et al., "Zhuahao shizi peixun, tigao zhizhong zhiliang" (Improve Teaching Training and Raise the Quality of In-service Teaching), *Guangzhou jiaoyu*, No. 4 (1986), pp. 22–24.

84. Gan Mu, "Wei Guangdong nongcun zhiye zhongxue jiaoyu jinyan" (Advice on Vocational Education in Rural Areas), *Guangdong jiaoyu*, No. 5 (1991), p. 5.

85. Ibid., p. 6.

86. Li Xiuhong (ed.), *Guangdong gaodeng jiaoyu shinian gaige tansuo* (Reflections on a Decade of Reform in Higher Education in Guangdong) (Guangzhou: Guangdong gaodeng jiaoyu chubanshe, 1990), pp. 145–50.

87. Ibid., pp. 200, 216.

88. Ibid., p. 123.

89. See note 19, pp. 8, 10.

90. See note 47, p. 575.

91. *Yangcheng wanbao*, 29 November 1991, p. 1.; *Guangzhou ribao*, 3 March 1992, p. 2.

11

Changing Health Needs and Emerging Health Problems

Wong Tze-wai, Suzanne C. Ho and Ignatius T. S. Yu

Introduction

This chapter is divided into three sections. Section one describes the health and health care in China in general and the special features in Guangdong. The theme is the contrast between the province and the rest of China. It begins with a health profile and disease pattern, followed by a description of the health care system, with special reference to the organization of primary health care and its characteristics in urban and rural China. Statistics on health facilities and health manpower are presented. Health manpower training and development, and the role of traditional Chinese medicine are discussed. Section two deals with occupational health, i.e. health and health care for workers. Occupational health is of particular concern to Guangdong as industrial development is proceeding at a very rapid pace. This section starts with a general description of the occupational health policy and services in China. The occupational health conditions in different types of enterprises in Guangdong are then described and problems associated with the present path of industrialization are discussed. Section three deals with the existing problems confronting the fast growing elderly population in obtaining health care services, and also describes the challenges faced by the health care providers in meeting the needs and demands of this segment of the population.

Health and Health Care

Health Profile

After forty years of effort in promoting public health, most of the serious communicable diseases and endemic diseases in China are under control. The infant mortality rate in China was 34.98 per 1,000 livebirths in 1980, while the life expectancy at birth was 67.9 years.[1] These figures compare favourably with those in many developing countries. The weighted average infant mortality rate per 1,000 livebirths for 29 least developed countries was 160 and for 90 other developing countries was 94, while the life expectancy at birth was 45 years for the former group of countries and

The authors would like to thank Professor Zhou Jiongliang, Director, Institute of Preventive Medicine, Sun Yat-Sen University of Medical Sciences, Guangzhou, for his invaluable comments and advice on the manuscript, and for arranging meetings with relevant health officials and academics in Guangdong.

60 for the latter group. In 1993, the infant mortality rate fell further to 13.5/ 1,000 (in 36 major cities) and 21.5/1,000 (in 87 counties and villages in 14 provinces). In China per capita gross national product (GNP) in 1980 was US$214 with US$7.1 spent on health care, amounting to 3.3% of GNP, compared with a per capita GNP of US$170, US$1.7 per person on health care and 1% of GNP on health care in the 29 least developed countries and a per capita GNP of US$520, US$6.5 per person on health care and 1.2% of GNP on health care in 90 other developing countries. From 1989 to 1992, health care expenditure ranged from 2.27% to 2.45% of total national expenditure. In 1981, communicable diseases ranked the seventh major cause of death in China, while other chronic degenerative diseases and cancers were becoming more important. In 1993, communicable diseases ranked the ninth major cause of death in 87 counties but fell outside the top ten causes of death in 36 cities, while malignant neoplasms, cerebrovascular diseases, respiratory diseases and heart diseases were among the top five in cities and counties alike. This pattern of mortality represents a transition to that seen in developed countries.

In recent years, Guangdong has played a leading role in economic reform. This socio-economic change has been paralleled by changes in mortality and morbidity pattern. A disease surveillance and evaluation report in selected surveillance centres within Guangdong in 1990 showed that heart diseases topped the ten leading causes of death, with a death rate of 70.3 per 100,000, followed by malignant neoplasms (64.5), cerebrovascular diseases (56.4), respiratory diseases (42.9), accidents (28.6), infectious diseases (22.8), diseases of the digestive system (18.2), diseases of the urinary system (9.3), neonatal diseases (8.5) and endocrine diseases (3.9). Infectious diseases occupied the lowest rank among the two urban surveillance centres and the sixth in three rural surveillance centres.[2] From a population of 482,332 under the surveillance system, 11,582 cases of infectious diseases were notified. Diarrhoeal diseases, mumps and influenza were the most common infectious diseases. Viral hepatitis, pulmonary tuberculosis, typhoid fever, bacillary dysentery and gonorrhoea were important both in terms of incidence and health effects. Rarer but more dangerous diseases still existed, including rabies and Japanese encephalitis. Since the 1950s, much effort has been made in the nation-wide control of schistosomiasis, a dangerous parasitic disease endemic in central and southern China. While the goal of disease eradication appeared to have failed elsewhere, no cases have been reported in Guangdong in recent years. Malaria was hyper-endemic on Hainan Island, formerly a part of

Guangdong. Its incidence has declined even before Hainan was separated from Guangdong.[3] Communicable diseases covered by the World Health Organization Expanded Programme of Immunization, except for tuber-culosis, were rarely found, thanks to a high coverage rate of childhood immunization. Diphtheria and paralytic poliomyelitis were absent, while the incidences of whooping cough, measles and tetanus neonatorum were very low (0.21, 0.62 and 0.41/100,000, respectively). Today, the major task in communicable diseases control is the prevention of cholera, dengue fever and the acquired immunodeficiency syndrome (AIDS). According to a health behaviour survey, the smoking rate was 23.9% among city dwellers and 16.3% among rural residents in the province. The drinking (alcohol) rate, on the contrary, was higher among rural folk (11.1%) than city dwellers (5.2%). Though less common than in northern China, hyper-tension was still the most prevalent chronic disease. Endemic fluorosis is found in the Chaozhou and the Shantou area while endemic goitre is present in the northern mountainous part of Guangdong.

Health Care System

The health care system in China is centred on primary health care and disease prevention.[4] The target "Health for all by the year 2000" adopted by member countries at the World Health Assembly in 1977 was said to have originated from observations of the success of primary health care work in rural China by Dr. Mahler, the then Director General of the World Health Organization. "Health for all" refers to the availability of primary health care to all people, which the health planners aimed to achieve in Guangdong as early as in 1995. At village and township levels, the basic units of primary health care services in China are the health centres and village clinics. At the city level, there are health clinics in schools, mines, factories and other government institutes and health units of residents' committees. The target clientele of primary health care are population groups ranging from workers in factories, students in schools and employees of institutions to residents of villages, towns, cities, provinces and the whole country. A typical three-tier (i.e. county–township–village) health care network model is shown in Figure 11.1.

According to a national health service survey in 1985, county hospitals handled about 12% of patients in the county, while only 2% of patients required referrals to hospitals at higher (provincial) levels. Nearly 50% of patients were treated in village health stations (the first point of contact

Figure 11.1 A Typical Organizational Structure of Health Facilities from County to Village Level

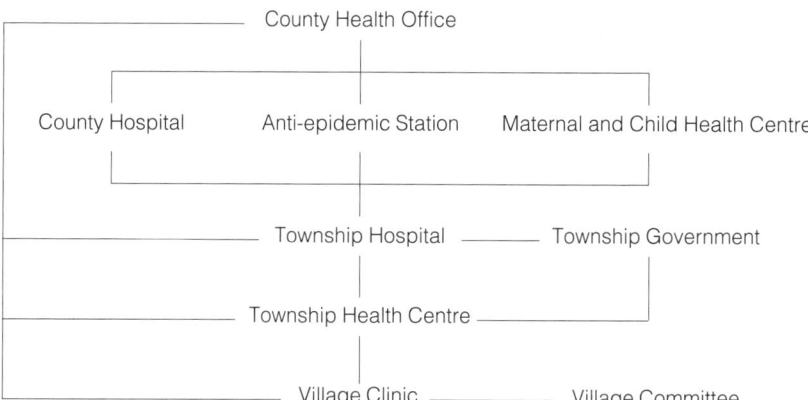

between the village population and the health care service), about 27% in township health centres and about 10% in township hospitals.

Health care in cities is organized at four levels, namely, city, district, street block (*jiedao*), and residential committee level. Health care organizations at the district level include district health and anti-epidemic stations, district people's hospitals, district maternal and child health centres and district specialist clinics, all of which are administratively under the district health bureau and professionally under the respective city health organizations. The area health centres are administratively under the respective area offices which, in turn, are under the district health bureau. Also under the area offices are the residential committees which are in charge of the residential committee (R/C) health units, usually staffed by part-time health workers. Professionally, R/C health units are supervised by the area health centres which, in turn, are under the district health organizations (Figure 11.2). Area health centres may be state-owned or collectively owned, their size and facilities depending on the catchment area, the size of the population they serve and the proximity to major hospitals. R/C health units are usually staffed by one to three health workers on a part-time basis, providing general health services such as immunization, treatment of minor ailments and health education. With the rise of industrial and other enterprises, many R/C health units have become health units serving their workforce rather than the residential community.

Figure 11.2   A Typical Organizational Structure of Primary Health Care Facilities at the City Level

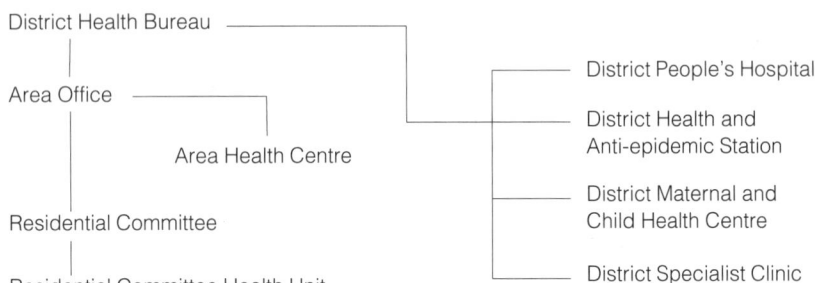

The main functions of the primary health care service in the cities include the following:

1. Medical examination, which can be divided into:
   (1) pre-employment examination of various workers, including army personnel, and pre-school examination of students;
   (2) periodic medical examination of workers, especially those in the food industry, catering workers, child care workers, employees in milk factories and water works units;
   (3) mass health examination, usually conducted in out-patient clinics or the community; and
   (4) personal health examination, usually in out-patient clinics or hospitals (where comprehensive medical examinations are carried out during a short period of hospital stay).

2. Disease screening and early treatment
   These are population based health activities, especially applicable to certain diseases such as hypertension and certain common malignancies and are generally regarded as the cornerstone of secondary prevention. Early detection of diseases through screening and timely treatment improve the effectiveness of therapy, reduce mortality and minimize complications resulting from the diseases.

3. Control of communicable diseases
   The major activities include disease surveillance, rapid exchange of epidemiological information on disease outbreaks, recognition of the source and cause of the outbreak, breaking the cycle of

transmission and protection of high risk individuals. A comprehensive immunization programme for infants and children is another important element of disease control.
4. Other areas of health activities
These include maternal and child health, food hygiene, school health and occupational health.

Primary health care in China is characterized by political commitment, community participation, a multi-disciplinary health care workforce and the promotion and integration of traditional Chinese medicine into the official health care system. As with other developing countries, the problems faced by the health administration in China are the scarcity of health resources and the vast need. Several types of health facilities co-exist, namely, state-run health facilities, "collective ownership" (owned by local governments and/ or other enterprises) and private health care. Health institutions at the county level and above are state-owned and administered, while township and village health facilities are "co-operative facilities" collectively owned by the local government, units of economic production or organizations, with self-sufficient financing, independent administration and accounting. At the village level, group and individual medical practices on a fee for service basis are available. Statistics in late 1985 showed that at the village level, collectively run health institutes constituted 39% of all health institutes while individual/group practices constituted 42%, indicating the growing importance of the non-state-run health enterprise.

At present, health expenditure is covered by five systems of health financing: government provision, workers' insurance, health insurance, co-operative insurance and the private, fee-for-service system. Private medical practice, considered to be an important supplement to the overall health system, was formally approved by the State Council in September 1980. The number of private practitioners, mostly in villages, has grown rapidly since then.

Statistics on Health Facilities and Manpower[5]

Statistics on health facilities throughout the past decades in Guangdong reflect major shifts in health policy. In 1950, there were 512 health institutions (all kinds) including 180 hospitals, and a total of 11,037 beds with 9,785 hospital beds. There were 40,455 health workers with 36,952 skilled health workers. The number of health institutions in 1952 was 1,500, a threefold increase, which again tripled in 1957 to 4,823, while the number of hospitals and hospital beds grew much more slowly, with an increase of 18% and 72%, respectively, in 1957 compared with the 1950 baseline. This trend marked an emphasis on the establishment of primary health care institutions rather than hospitals. The number of health institutions reached a peak in 1962, which again recorded a threefold increase from the 1957 figure to 13,783, while the number of hospitals and hospital beds doubled in the same period. The year 1970 saw a drastic 50% reduction of hospital institutions from 12,875 in 1965, while the number of hospitals and beds increased marginally. This represented a major cut which inevitably resulted from over-expansion. From then onwards, there was a steady increase in health institutions, hospitals, beds and skilled health manpower to the present. In 1993, there was a total of 8,572 health institutions, with 1,968 hospitals and 139,812 beds (2.12 per 1,000 population), 129,317 (1.96 per 1,000 population) of which were hospital beds. The bed occupancy rate for hospitals in Guangdong was 78.4% with a turnover of 19.1 and an average length of stay of 14.4 days. For county health centres, the corresponding figures were 47%, 34.7 and 4.8 days, respectively. There were 168 anti-epidemic stations and 66 maternal and child health centres. The health workforce totalled 267,432 with 211,874 being skilled health workers.

Health Manpower Training and Development[6]

Education came to a halt throughout the country during the Cultural Revolution and medical education was no exception. In 1968, various systems of medical training were established to fill the void, ranging from one- to three-year programmes, producing paramedicals and *xiyishi* (medical personnel with three years of Western medical training). Primary health care workers, often called "barefoot doctors," were trained with even shorter programmes and provided health care to the rural population.

The Sun Yat-sen University of Medical Sciences was among the first to restore medical education to a six-year programme in 1977, which by 1978 was followed by other medical schools in Guangdong and elsewhere.[7] A medical graduate then needed to spend three more years for a master's degree and another three years to complete a PhD programme. In view of the lengthy medical education, a shorter system of medical education, a five-year programme followed by a two-year master programme was established in 1989 and adopted on a nation-wide basis. The number of doctors professionally trained in Western medicine in Guangdong in

1978 was 20,088, with a 28.5% increase to 25,817 in 1980.[8] With economic reform and an increase in medical institutions, there was a steady increase in the number of medical doctors. By 1985, there was another 23.5% increase to 31,878. By 1990, the number reached 44,066, a 38.2% increase in five years. The 1991 figure stood at 44,806.

Despite the restoration of professional medical education, the number of *xiyishi*, continued to increase from 12,973 in 1978 to 14,523 in 1980. By 1990, the number had grown to 17,743. By 1993, there were 90,115 doctors (1.37 per 1,000 population), with 63,076 physicians (modern and traditional) or 0.96 per 1,000 population, a sixfold increase from 1950. A similar trend is observed for nurses, whose numbers grew from 21,783 in 1978 to 35,960 in 1991 and 56,248 in 1993 (0.85 per 1,000 population), a 30-fold increase since 1950. In 1985, there were 2,724 nursing professionals who had received university education. By 1990, the number grew by more than five times to 14,178. This reflects a higher demand for health personnel in Guangdong, as well as high quality, highly trained medical and nursing professionals. The mean number of skilled health care workers per 1,000 population in the province was 2.50 in 1978, compared to 3.14 in 1991 and 3.22 in 1993. The mean number of doctors per 1,000 population was 0.95 in 1978, compared to 1.31 in 1991 and 1.37 in 1993. By contrast, the number of nursing aids declined from 10,126 in 1978 to 7,439 in 1991, while the number of other primary health care workers decreased from 17,600 to 11,970 in the same period.

Traditional Chinese Medicine[9]

Traditional Chinese medicine is formally recognized as an integral part of the health care system in China. Tertiary education in Chinese medicine is available in Guangdong as in other provinces of China. The Guangzhou College of Traditional Chinese Medicine was a major national training institute for traditional Chinese doctors. Similar to their Western counterparts, shorter (three-year) training programmes at post-secondary levels are available, leading to *zhongyishi*. The number of traditional Chinese doctors (including *zhongyishi* and other traditional Chinese practitioners) in Guangdong has been steadily increasing from 14,863 in 1978 to 20,287 in 1990. Integration of Chinese and Western medicine is firmly entrenched in the national health policy and Guangdong is strategically placed to benefit from exchange education programmes with medical institutions in Hong Kong and other countries.

Occupational Health in Guangdong

China proclaims herself to be a workers' state and thus has put much emphasis on the welfare and protection of workers. Occupational health has all along been given high priority in China since the 1950s. As all enterprises were practically state-owned before the modernization and privatization process in the late 1970s and 1980s, the provision of occupational health services followed guidelines set down by the State Council. Basically every employee in industry was being covered by a medical scheme which usually included a pre-employment check up, periodic examinations and biological monitoring in addition to curative treatment for any medical problem.[10] For many workers, the curative medical benefit also covered their dependents and could be considered to be part of primary health care for a significant portion of the population.

In addition to the medical supervision of the workers, every enterprise was supposed to have monitoring programmes for the environment inside the workplace. In fact, according to the "three concurrent" policies[11] laid down by the State Council, design for occupational health and safety systems should be concurrent with the design of any new factory or production process; health and safety devices should be built concurrently with the construction of the factory or production process, and health and safety systems should be able to function concurrently when the production starts. This proactive preventive approach was considered to be very advanced and effective in reducing occupational health problems and accidents even by Western standards.

With this two-pronged approach to environmental improvement and medical monitoring of workers, the occupational health situation in China has much improved since the 1950s. Traditional chronic chemical poisoning (e.g. lead and mercury) has become less and less common.[12]

The above advantageous system is usually only possible in big enterprises because of the investment needed to provide the necessary health and safety facilities. This is almost universally true, but occupational health problems are more prevalent in small industries. In addition to the initiatives of enterprises, the Ministry of Health, Ministry of Labour and National Trade Union all have a role to play in the monitoring and promotion of occupational health in China.

The Guangdong Scene

Guangdong is ahead of the rest of China in terms of modernization and economic development. The traditional agriculture-based economy has given way to industrialization, and occupational health problems are progressively replacing agricultural or rural health problems in terms of numbers and importance. Small manufacturing industries bloomed with the economic development, especially within the Special Economic Zones around the Pearl River Delta. New enterprises are no longer state-owned. A significant proportion consists of joint ventures with foreign (largely Hong Kong) investment, while others are owned by townships or villages or have emerged as a result of individual effort and investment. As a result of these changes, the conventional preventive approach in occupational health becomes inapplicable in many instances. The following paragraphs will describe the occupational health situation in Guangdong, especially in the economically more advanced coastal areas.

State-owned Factories

The situation in state-owned enterprises basically remains the same. Big factories (like oil refineries) have their own employee hospitals inside the factory complex. These hospitals provide in-patient and out-patient services as well as accident and emergency services. All sorts of health problems, including occupational diseases and poisoning, will be attended to and workers as well as their families are entitled to utilize such services, basically free of charge. Employee hospitals can have more than 100 beds and are staffed by more than 100 doctors. Major specialties, such as surgery, internal medicine, occupational medicine, etc. are usually available. In addition to this central health care facility, many workshops inside big factories also have sanitation and first-aid stations that are able to offer front line health care services. These are under the direct leadership of the employee hospital.

Other than providing emergency and curative services, the employee hospital is also responsible for preventive aspects in occupational health.[13] This includes secondary preventive measures such as pre-employment and periodic medical examinations, including biological monitoring. Primary prevention is also emphasized and health educational programmes are organized regularly.

In some factories, the environmental monitoring task is also being taken up by the employee hospital or done in collaboration with or separately by an industrial hygiene division. Major occupational health hazards inside the workshops, such as noise, radiation, chemicals, are being monitored by standard equipment and methods. If the exposure levels to these hazards exceed national standards, procedures will be initiated to ameliorate the anomalies either by engineering and administrative methods, or by enforcing the use of personal protective equipment.

Smaller state-owned or collective-owned factories or enterprises may not have their own hospitals, but they usually provide similar services/benefits to their employees and their dependents by contracting them out to hospitals nearby.[14] Most factories usually fully reimburse their employees for the money spent on medical consultation and treatment (a kind of unlimited medical insurance coverage by the company), but more recently, with the awareness and emphasis on cost analysis for individual enterprises, some companies have already put a limit on the amount of medical benefit that can be claimed within one year by an individual worker.[15] Any expense above the limit will be borne by the worker himself. Industrial hygiene and environmental monitoring are also being contracted out to competent units in research institutes and universities.[16]

According to the information given by health care workers in state-owned enterprises, the occupational health situation in these enterprises is progressively improving and cases of chronic poisoning are rarely seen today although acute poisoning incidents still occur from time to time. Most occupational health problems seen nowadays are subclinical cases detected during routine surveillance programmes.[17]

Joint Ventures

The situation for enterprises established by foreign investment or owned privately is quite different from what was mentioned above. Many factories of the former category originated from Hong Kong. These are usually low-technology, manufacturing plants which are labour intensive and have been moved to Guangdong mainly because of the cheap labour cost there. Many of these "technology transfers" also brought with them the old production processes and out-dated machineries which often create an unhealthy and unsafe work environment as evidenced by the high industrial accident rates among manufacturing industries in the past in Hong Kong. Furthermore, these companies are often granted exemptions from labour policies and regulations in China and thus the occupational health condition can be quite appalling. Occupational health services are essentially non-existent, although limited medical benefits may still be provided by a limited number of factories. Unless any major accident occurs, the state and the local government have little reason to intervene. Factories established by investments from Macau and Taiwan are also quite common and the occupational health conditions inside these establishments are similar to those mentioned above.

A number of international/multinational companies have also started running factories in Guangdong. According to occupational health professionals dealing with such establishments,[18] the occupational health and safety conditions are usually much better than in other factories. They usually follow the occupational health practices in their parent companies and have good systems for medical surveillance and biological monitoring as well as paying much attention to primary preventive measures.

Township Industries

The privately owned enterprise and the township small industries are the most troublesome according to health workers in the field and this coincides with the conclusion of some surveys recently conducted in China.[19] Most of these are small-scale companies which cannot be expected to invest heavily in occupational health and safety matters. Others, though not small in terms of investment and profits generated, have very little idea about the importance of occupational health and safety. Clinic rooms are a rarity among these factories. The majority of them do not provide medical coverage for common diseases for their employees and a substantial proportion of them even evade the responsibility of paying for medical expenses incurred as a result of industrial injuries and occupational accidents.

Furthermore, many of these smaller companies work as sub-contractors for larger enterprises and the production processes involved may change from time to time and so will the working environment. The sub-contracting system sometimes creates ambiguity as to who is really the employer and is supposed to be responsible for the health and safety of the workers.[20] Some workers may sub-contract out small pieces of work for themselves or their families. Investments in occupational health and safety are often given the lowest priority under such circumstances. The condition is further aggravated by the fact that, unlike workers in state-owned enterprises who are often being assigned by the state and stay in their job for a very long period, there is a high proportion of migrant workers in the township industries.

Migrant Workers

Many of these migrant workers come from the rural areas of northern Guangdong or from other less well-off provinces where they are used to the hardships of life. They tend to be employed for the "dirty jobs" and in jobs that require heavy labour. There is a tendency for them to work in each job for a relatively short period of time, sometimes only a few months during the winter season, and then go back to their home county and engage in farming again. When they come to the township industry next time, they may work in an entirely different job for another factory. This high mobility of workers makes it very difficult to trace the relationship between work and health in these industries. Also, these migrant workers are so keen to earn money that they are willing to accept an unhealthy and unsafe working environment provided that the job is well-paid. Furthermore, since the job nature varies frequently, it would be very difficult for them to familiarize themselves with the health and safety practices of each job. Accidents and acute poisoning are common among them; the chronic health effects are not known yet because they are difficult to trace as no health record is kept. For the more well-established enterprises in the coastal districts, high mobility of workers is less of a problem. Many migrant workers from other provinces tend to stay for a period of two to three years before returning home. Quarters are usually provided for this group of workers by the factories, but the living environment of some of these quarters can be quite unsatisfactory.

Administrative Aspects

On the administrative side, monitoring of occupational health is the responsibility of the Health Bureau at the provincial, municipal and county levels. Most of the supervisory and monitoring programmes are conducted by the Health and Anti-epidemic Stations[21] which frequently have a team specializing in industrial hygiene and occupational health. They conduct inspections of workplaces and check on the records of industrial hygiene measurements and biological monitoring. Fines will be imposed on those factories that violate health and hygiene standards; advice and assistance will be offered in order to improve the situation. They will also investigate outbreaks of poisoning and keep records on occupational diseases.

A recent survey in China revealed that there is a critical lack of manpower for industrial hygiene supervision at the township level. Each industrial hygiene professional (most of them in fact have not attained post-secondary educational level) is responsible for the supervision of over one thousand factories and the occupational health services for over 20,000 workers.[22] Furthermore, equipment for hygiene monitoring is grossly lacking as a result of inadequate resources being put into occupational health at the county level. Needless to say, it is impossible to have a satisfactory outcome. With little initiative from the enterprises and inadequate supervision from the government, it is not surprising to find appalling occupational health conditions in township industries.

There are special centres for the treatment and follow-up of occupational diseases: the Guangdong Provincial Occupational Diseases Prevention and Treatment Centre (situated inside Guangzhou) and the Guangzhou Occupational Diseases Prevention and Treatment Centre. These two centres provide hospital beds for the treatment and convalescence of workers suffering from different types of occupational diseases. Workers suffering from chronic irreversible diseases, such as silicosis, can stay in a sanatorium-like environment for years as a sort of compensation and benefit. In addition to these two centres, many major hospitals, including teaching hospitals of the medical schools, also have a division of occupational diseases which provides inpatient treatment for acute and chronic poisoning as a result of occupational activities. They may also provide preventive occupational health services to industry on a fee-for-service contract basis.

The two occupational diseases prevention and treatment centres have very close links with the Health and Anti-epidemic Stations and provide back-up support for their work. Furthermore, the provincial centre is also a research institute for industrial hygiene and occupational diseases and has a strong team of researchers with experience in a wide range of disciplines related to occupational health, e.g. toxicologists, ventilation engineers etc.[23] They take on research tasks commissioned by the Ministry of Health or the State Council. In addition, the provincial centre also provides training courses and attachment opportunities for professionals in related fields.

Statistics of Occupational Diseases

A look at the statistics of occupational disease in Guangdong in 1991 revealed that only 508 cases were reported. Pneumoconiosis is the most commonly reported occupational disease (367) and poisoning (acute and chronic) accounted for 92 cases. For the pneumoconiosis, more than half were reported from the coal industry and were probably coal-miners pneumoconiosis or anthraco-silicosis. Shaoguan is the worst city accounting for about 43% of all reported occupational diseases in Guangdong with 177 cases of pneumoconiosis and 37 cases of poisoning. This might be related to the small coal mines and metal reclaiming and refinery workshops that are prevalent in that part of the province.

As with reports on occupational diseases in most places in other parts of the world, these figures are usually under-estimates of the true picture and really depend on the vigilance of the surveillance programmes that are in force. Thus, although the official figure showed that the township industry was responsible for only a very small proportion of the reported cases, a purposeful survey conducted in China by the Ministry of Health[24] on the occupational health situation of township industries in 15 provinces (including Guangdong) revealed a high prevalence of clinical and subclinical occupation diseases among the workers, which is seven times that of state-owned enterprises. A sub-standard working environment was also very common and over 60% of hygiene measurements with regard to dust, toxicants and noise exceeded national standards.

Health of the Elderly

Population Structure of the Elderly in China and Guangdong

The population in China increased from 602 to 1,032 million between the first census in 1953 and the third census in 1982. During these years, the elderly population aged 60 and above almost doubled from 41 to 79 million and the average life expectancy at birth increased from 35 to 69.[25]

In 1982, 7.6% of the population was aged 60 and above. The proportion will increase to 10% by 1995 and China can be considered as an aged society. The ageing of the population results from the decline in both the death as well as the birth rates. The crude death rate has gone down from 20 per 1,000 in 1949 to 6.3 per 1,000 in 1990 and the birth rate from 36–37.9 per 1,000 to 21–23 per 1,000 between 1975 and 1990. As in other countries, the male-to-female ratio decreases with age. The 1987 1% Whole Country Population Sample Survey showed that the ratio was 91.1 in the age group 60–69, and declined to 34.9 in the age group 80 and above. About one-quarter of the elderly men and one-half of the women lost their spouse after age 60.[26]

There are geographical variations in the distribution of the elderly population in China. A higher proportion of the aged population is found in cities and coastal areas compared to the inland and western parts of China.

Compared to the rest of China, Guangdong ranks seventh (with 8% of the population aged 60 and above) in population ageing, after Shanghai (11.5%), Beijing, Tianjin, Shandong, Jiangsu and Zhejiang (8.5–11%).[27] Guangdong is one of the most populated provinces. Between 1982 and 1987, the total population in Guangdong increased by 4.4 million. The yearly population growth rate is 1.59% during this period, while that for the elderly aged 60 and above is 3.77%. It is estimated that 10.2% of the population in Guangdong will be aged 60 and above by 1994 and 15% by 2020. The population ageing will be even faster in the urban districts like Guangzhou, Foshan, Jiangmen and Zhongshan.[28]

The average life expectancy of the population in Guangdong is also among the highest when compared with the rest of China. The 1982 Third Population Census showed that the life expectancy at birth in Shanghai was 72.91, Beijing 71.92 and Guangdong 71.29, as compared with 68.49 in Fujian and 60.73 in Yunan. It is among the aims of the "Health Care Development Plan of Guangdong" to increase the life expectancy of men to 72 and women to 74 by the year 2000.[29]

Health Problems in the Elderly

Generally there is an increase in chronic illnesses and disability with age. The mortality pattern has shifted from one of predominantly infectious diseases in the past to that of chronic diseases. The major causes of mortality in the aged are heart diseases, cerebral vascular diseases, cancer, respiratory diseases, digestive diseases and injuries. The most common conditions found in the elderly population include hypertension, chronic obstructive lung diseases, coronary heart disease, diabetes mellitus, rheumatoid arthritis, gall stone disease, cataract and gastric ulcer.[30] Data based on the recent retirement physical examinations of the cadres in Guangdong showed that 41.7% had some forms of disease conditions. A recent survey of the Guangzhou elderly also showed that two-thirds had two to three disease conditions. These data revealed that a high proportion of the elderly population in Guangdong is in need of health care support.[31]

Health Care Service for the Elderly

Although it is among the government's priorities to provide health care for the vulnerable groups — the old, the young, the poor and those residing in the mountain and border areas — the existing services face great difficulty in meeting the increasing needs of the fast growing elderly population. The concomitant increase in ill health with old age has placed increasing demand on the hospital and health care services. The percentage of beds occupied by the aged has increased substantially from 2.3% in the 1950s to 8.8% in the 1980s.[32]

At present, there are no comprehensive health care services specifically catering for this segment of the population. Basically, the Ministry of Public Health attempts to strengthen the three-tier health care system in the provision of health care for the aged. The delivery of health care in the urban areas is through the city-district/sub-district/street levels, and in the rural area through the county–township–village three-tier health care network. There is some attempt to give special consideration in clinic registration, doctor consultation and dispensary of drugs to the elderly.[33] However, such policies have not been widely adopted. There is also an acute shortage of hospital beds and few hospitals provide geriatric services and arrangement for convalescence and rehabilitation. Health care services for the aged are paid fully or partially from the retirement or insurance funds for retired workers. However, in the rural areas, the cost is mostly borne by the family.

The elderly in Guangdong encounter similar difficulties in obtaining clinical consultations, hospital care and rehabilitation services. The following sections will describe the existing health services and highlight some of the major difficulties in the delivery of such services in Guangdong.

Health Maintenance and Clinic Services[34]

A yearly physical check-up is available for special groups of workers aged 50 and above belonging to managerial level and above and academics belonging to associate professor level and above. Geriatric health maintenance clinics are set up in a few of the major hospitals such as the Guangdong Provincial People's Hospital and the Shenzhen People's Hospital. However, most of these services are by referral and are only known to a minority of the elderly population. The street, neighbourhood health stations and activity centres for old cadres may also provide some basic screening and preventive health care services. The check-up and screening provided may vary from very minimal basic measures to a more comprehensive check-up and many of these services are directed to certain selective groups of the aged.

Geriatric specialist clinics, mainly in the form of "expedient services" catering for the "high-ranking" elderly, are provided in some provincial hospitals. At present, there is little provision for consultation specifically catering for the elderly population in general. The need for clinical consultation is generally unmet. It is estimated that 280,000 of the old people in Guangzhou alone require clinical consultation. They also run into problems of transportation and getting family or other members to accompany them to the clinics. Many also have difficulties in coping with the complicated procedures in seeking such services. The problem of access to health care services is even more acute in rural areas where there is a general shortage of trained health manpower and medication.

Hospital Services

Only four hospitals in Guangdong can be considered as geriatric hospitals. The Guangzhou Geriatric Hospital is a joint establishment of the Department of Transport and the Guangzhou Municipality and has about one hundred beds. The Yi Shou Hospital is a private venture located in a Guangzhou suburban area with less than one hundred hospital beds. The Huangpu Hospital offers traditional Chinese medicine and has around fifty hospital beds. The Yuexiu Geriatric Hospital, opened in September 1992, is the only government geriatric hospital funded by the Ministry of Public Health and has forty-five hospital beds. Although special rooms for geriatric patients are available in the county and provincial hospitals, they are mainly reserved for the retired or elderly cadres belonging to the senior grades. A survey done in 1988–1989 in Guangzhou revealed that out of the 400,000 elderly population aged 60 and above, 2% would need hospital care. The existing hospital beds in Guangdong are far from being able to meet the hospital needs of the aged population. Moreover, the existing three-tier health care network seems to have broken down because of the recent admission policy of most hospitals which is based on the ability to pay for hospital fees rather than on referral. Attempts have been made to develop home-bed services in order to ease the shortage of hospital beds and partly overcome the difficulty in obtaining consultations.[35]

Rehabilitation Services

A national survey of disablement carried out in 1989 showed that among the disabled, 39.2% belonged to the age group 60 and above. The main categories of disablement are loss of vision or hearing, and limb disablement. Many of the common conditions and diseases such as stroke, musculoskeletal problems, coronary heart disease, chronic obstructive lung disease, fracture and cataract encountered in old age are also in need of rehabilitation. The purpose is to help the patients to function to the best of their capability and be able to lead a family and community life. There is a vast and increasing need of rehabilitation services for the elderly. At the moment, few convalescence and rehabilitation services can be provided to the discharged patients, and some may even have to be discharged early because of an acute shortage of hospital beds. The burden of their care generally falls on their family members who may have little training in their care. The development of home-bed and community-based rehabilitation services is some attempt to solve these problems. The Institute of Rehabilitation Medicine of Sun Yat-sen University of Medical Sciences is one of the World Health Organization collaborating Centres in Rehabilitation. The focus of their work is community-based and the aim is to retain those affected in the community. Sites have been selected in Guangzhou and Conghua for the community-based rehabilitation work. However, much more planning, work and resources are needed to meet the existing and future need for rehabilitation services for the fast growing elderly population.[36]

Health Insurance

Family resources constitute the major form of support for the elderly. Though elderly and nursing homes are available both in the cities and the villages, they mainly admit those without family members. Retired workers in the cities can partly rely on pension or insurance funds for payment of medical expenses. The scheme may range from total to partial or very minimal coverage. Some schemes will only pay for a pre-specified amount of health care cost. In the rural areas, though some well-off places such as Buji of Bao'an County provide full coverage of health costs for their residents, the majority of the rural elderly have to pay their medical fees from their own family resources. The provision of health care for the rural old people poses a great challenge to the health providers. A collective health care system in the villages whereby a yearly subscription is to be paid for the coverage of primary health care will probably be a major mechanism to be adopted.

Areas of Development

It is the aim to establish a comprehensive health care network for the elderly especially in the areas of prevention, early detection of diseases and rehabilitation. In order to meet these needs, emphasis of future development will be placed on community-based health care, to tap the existing community resources and to retain the elderly in community living as far as possible.

Yuexiu district of Guangzhou has been selected as an urban trial area for the development of a community-based health care project under the management of the Guangdong Provincial Institute of Geriatrics, the Guangdong Medical College Primary Health Care Research Unit, the Yuexiu District Primary Health Care and the Street Office. About 3,000 or 13% of the population in Yuexiu district are aged 60 and above. The aims of the five-year plan include, firstly, to prolong the average life expectancy of the population aged 60 and above by 0.5 to 1 year; secondly, to decrease the proportion of the elderly unable to carry out self-care by 5%; and thirdly, to reduce injury among the elderly by 0.1%. The health care unit will be based at the Street Health Station, and volunteer retired health workers will be recruited to carry out the basic health care activities and health education work. It is also planned to provide one to two years' training for the street health workers (one to two from each street) to carry out health education, home visits and some basic health care. It is also planned to provide a yearly health check for the old-old and a bi-yearly health check for the young-old. Health education will also be done by means of street posters, booklets and audio-visual programmes. As self-care forms a major component of health care for the individual, especially in old age, education will form a major component of health care. The main emphasis will be on the change of personal habits, e.g. stop smoking, reduce alcoholic drinks, balanced and nutritious dietary intake, adequate sleep and exercise, and weight maintenance. Neighbourhood activities will be organized to improve the mental and social health of the old people in the community. This community-based health care project for the elderly will also serve as a model trial area for the delivery of primary health care. It is also planned to select a rural district for such development work. Dongguan may be designated as one of the possible trial areas.[37]

Research on the Health of the Elderly

The Guangdong Geriatric Research Institute was established in 1978 and was one of the first such institutes established in China. It was upgraded to a provincial institute in 1982. The Association of Geriatric Medicine of the Chinese Medical Association was also formed in Guangdong in 1980.

Other geriatric research institutes have since been established in Shenzhen and Dongguan.

Besides basic research in pathology, genetics, biochemistry, immunology, bacteriology and blood flow pattern and change, past research emphasis has mostly been on hospital-based clinical research in the common chronic diseases such as cardiovascular and cerebral vascular diseases. Studies on the geographical distribution and characteristics of centenarians and the related environmental factors, the role of traditional medicine in "anti-ageing" and prolongation of life have also been popular research topics. Recent research activities have been extended to community-based studies such as the baseline survey on the health of the elderly population in specific geographical areas, dementia, quality of life, sexual satisfaction; research has also been done on physiological and anatomical parameters such as height, weight, blood pressure, etc. in the elderly. Research in behavioural and social aspects of ageing is now receiving increasing attention. However, better coordination in research activities seems to be necessary as repetition in research efforts is found among the various geriatric research institutes.[38]

Conclusion

With economic reform a number of significant changes have been noted. The development of township industries has led to an affluence of the populace unparalleled in the history of the PRC. There is an ever greater demand for a high-quality health service, in particular preventive health services such as antenatal checks for pregnant women and periodic medical examination (adults and school children alike). The low-quality health services offered by township health centres and village clinics are no longer satisfactory. There is a tendency for affluent village folks to utilize medical services directly at major provincial hospitals in big cities. The decreased utilization of township health centres and village clinics has also been attributed to the high medical fees charged for low-quality health care, resulting from the policy of reduced state subsidy and self-accountability of profit and loss for such organizations. There is an increasing tendency for the development of health care services as enterprises with financial automony. In this respect, Guangdong is well placed geographically and historically to benefit from capital investment by overseas Chinese, Taiwanese and Hong Kong and Macau residents. Examples of medical institutions established with major "overseas capital" are the Shantou Medical College and Hospital and the Shunde Hospital, both of which were financed by Hong Kong businessmen. In 1989, a research centre for cardiovascular disease was established in Guangzhou aided by a generous donation from Hong Kong. Another modern medical research centre was planned in Zhuhai in early 1992, with a target completion date in 1995. Many hospitals in Guangzhou and Shenzhen cater for Hong Kong and Macau residents besides the local population. These developments in Guangdong have brought about competition among the health care providers for quality service. While competition has its merits, an inevitable problem is the accompanying escalation of health care cost. Another important consequence of the rapid economic development of towns and villages in Guangdong is a fundamental change in the structure of the workforce, with a decline in the proportion of primary production workers and health care workers and a rise in the industrial and service sector. Environmental and industrial health problems have followed the development of township industry. Major industrial health problems are silicosis, asbestosis, lead poisoning, poisoning by benzene and other organic solvents, pesticide poisoning and noise-induced deafness. Occupational diseases and accidents and extensive environmental pollution have become important threats to the health of workers and the general population. This appears to be the rule during development in most other countries. How China, as a socialist country claiming to give top priority to the welfare of workers, is going to tackle this problem and prevent the onslaught of the evils of industrialization still waits to be seen.

The progressive increase in the elderly population places an unending demand on the health care services. The three major difficulties faced by the elderly in Guangdong, as in other parts of China, are the seeking of medical consultation, hospitalization and rehabilitation. The existing geriatric care mainly caters to the senior elderly cadres, and the extension of such services to the remaining elderly population seems to be limited. The three-tier health care system is also being diluted by the present open market economy and there is competition among hospitals to admit patients who are financially better off.

At present, there is no specialty of geriatrics medicine; the provision of such care is mostly incorporated in general medicine. Most of the health care staff are not trained in the treatment and care of geriatric patients. An overall planning for comprehensive primary, secondary and tertiary health care and manpower training is urgently needed to meet the tremendous task of improving and maintaining the health of the existing large and fast growing elderly population in Guangdong. This forms a major challenge to health care provision in the coming decades.

In conclusion, the rapid economic development in Guangdong has brought about unprecedented changes in the entire health care system and new health problems as well, especially those related to occupational health and elderly health. These problems will be escalated unless remedial measures are taken to rationalize the provision of health care, control health care cost and tackle the specific health problems exemplified in this chapter.

Notes

1. Guo Qing (ed.), *Chuji weisheng baojian* (Primary Health Care) (Guangzhou: Guangdong keji chubanshe, 1989).
2. Gao Zhongying et al., "Guangdongsheng 1990 nian jibing jiance dian ziliao pingjia" (Evaluation of Disease Surveillance Data in Guangdong Province in 1990), *Jibing jiance* (Disease Surveillance), Vol. 7, No. 1 (1992), pp. 8–12.
3. Zhou Jiongliang (Professor of Occupational Health and Toxicology and Director of Institute of Preventive Medicine, Sun Yat-sen University of Medical Sciences, Guangzhou), personal communication.
4. See note 1.
5. Guangdongsheng tongjiju (ed.), *Guangdong tongji nianjian 1994* (Statistical Yearbook of Guangdong 1994) (Beijing: Zhongguo tongji chubanshe, 1994); *Zhongguo weisheng nianjian* bianji weiyuanhui (ed.), *Zhongguo weisheng nianjian* 1988–1994 (Yearbook of Public Health in the People's Republic of China 1988–1994) (Beijing: Renmin weisheng chubanshe, 1988–1994).
6. See note 5.
7. Zhou Jiongliang, personal communication.
8. Guangdong nianjian bianzuan weiyuanhui (ed.), *Guangdong nianjian 1994* (Guangdong Yearbook 1994) (Guangzhou: Guangdong nianjianshe, 1994).
9. *Zhongguo weisheng nianjian*, 1988–1994 (see note 5).
10. H. K. Abrams, "Occupational Medicine in the People's Republic of China," *Journal of Occupational Medicine*, Vol. 22, No. 8 (1980), pp. 553–57.
11. Weishengbu weisheng jiandusi et al., "Xiangzhen gongye zhiye weisheng fuwu xuqiu yu duice" (The Needs and Strategies for Occupational Health Services for Township Industries), *Zhonghua laodong weisheng zhiyebing zazhi* (Chinese Journal of Industrial Hygiene and Occupational Diseases), Vol. 10, No. 4 (1992), pp. 193–201.
12. Zhou Jiongliang, personal communication.
13. E. C. Stein and M. B. Schenker, "Occupational Health in Developing Nations: The Case of China," *Preventive Medicine*, No. 18 (1989), pp. 532–40.

14. Wang Yanhua et al., "Da zhong xing qiye laodong weisheng yu zhiyebing de fangzhi guanli gongzuo" (Management Aspects of Industrial Hygiene and Occupational Disease Control in Large and Medium Size Enterprises), *Zhonghua laodong weisheng zhiyebing zazhi*, Vol. 10, No. 4 (1992), pp. 223–24.
15. Zhou Jiongliang, personal communication.
16. Ibid.
17. Jiang Chaoqiang, personal communication.
18. Zhou Jiongliang, personal communication.
19. See note 11.
20. Jiang Chaoqiang, personal communication.
21. Gu Xueji et al., Xiangzhen gongye zhiye weisheng fuwu, jiehe nongcun chuji weisheng baojian de tansuo (Exploring the Unification of Occupational Health Services in Township Industries with Primary Health Care in Villages), *Zhonghua laodong weisheng zhiyebing zazhi*, Vol. 10, No. 2 (1992), pp. 109–11.
22. See note 11.
23. B. D. Tang, personal communication.
24. See note 11.
25. Gu Xingyuan and Gong Youlong (eds.), *Shehui yixue* (Community Medicine) (Shanghai: Shanghai yike daxue chubanshe, 1991).
26. Guojia tongji ju renkou tongjisi (ed.), *1987 nian quanguo 1% renkou chouyang diaocha de zhuyao shuzi* (1987 1% Whole Country Population Sample Survey) (Beijing: Zhongguo tongji chubanshe, 1988).
27. Zeng Erkang, "Woguo laonianren dili fenbu guilü tedian de chubu yanjiu" (A Preliminary Study on the Characteristics of Geographic Distribution of the Aged in China) (paper presented at the seminar, The Increased Longevity: History and Future Dimensions, organized by Centre for Contemporary Asian Studies, The Chinese University of Hong Kong and Goethe College of Germany held in Hong Kong, November 1988).
28. Li Peixiong, *Lao you suo yi — Guanyu jiaqiang wosheng laonian yiliao baojian gongzuo de jianyi* (Health and Medical Care for the Aged — Proposals to Strengthen Geriatric Health Care in Guangdong Province) (Guangzhou: Guangdong-sheng laonian yixuehui, 1991).
29. See note 1.
30. Xu Taojun, "Guangdong laonian yixue yanjiu dongtai ji jianyi" (Activities and Proposals in Research in Geriatric Medicine in Guangdong) (Guangzhou: Guangdongsheng laonian yixue yanjiusuo, 1991).
31. Zhu Gaozhang (Vice-Director, Guangdong Provincial Institute of Geriatrics), personal communication.
32. See note 30.
33. See note 25.

34. Zhu Gaozhang, Zhou Jiongliang and Lu Weishan (Chief of Shenzhen Geriatrics Institute, Shenzhen), personal communications.
35. Ibid.; see also note 25.
36. See note 1.
37. Zhu Gaozhang, personal communication.
38. Ibid.; note 28; Lu Weishan, "Woguo sisheng sishi jian- kang laonianren wuxiang shengli cankaozhi de diaocha" (Studies on Five Physiological Parameters of the Healthy Elderly in Four Provinces and Four Cities in China), *Zhonghua laonian yixue zazhi* (China Journal of Geriatrics), No. 4 (1985), pp. 214–22.

12

Welfare Provisions

Eva B. C. Li

Introduction

In defining social welfare services, the Chinese government used to adopt a very narrow definition, covering only major responsibilities, and operating under the traditional concept of taking care of the old, the widowed, the handicapped and the orphaned. Hence, people generally have been accustomed to receiving minimal assistance from the government and a strong self-help spirit has thus developed. The growth of private charity, however, has been greatly influenced by religious philosophy, particularly Buddhism, so that, by being charitable to others in need, one can also hope to achieve a better life in the process of reincarnation. Persons in poverty, therefore, are considered as being in a situation of their own making, and thus must pull themselves out of their misery by their own efforts. The intent of this chapter is to trace the changes and developments in the approaches to welfare since the adoption of the open policy in China and to examine some of the social consequences of rapid economic development since 1978.

Social Security — 1985

The first adoption of any systematic writing on the concept of welfare appeared in a translation of a book published by the International Labour Office, entitled *Shehui baozhang jichu*, in 1989.[1] This translated version was adopted by Peking University as the basic text in a course on social security in the training of social workers. However, when the Communist Party's National Representatives Meeting passed in September 1985 the Seventh Five-year Plan, it spelled out clearly the national goal of the master plan in upgrading the standard of living for all. It adopted the idea that the components of social security in China should include social insurance, social relief, social welfare and privileged security.[2] It is therefore pertinent to examine these concepts and their contents as understood in China, which may have different interpretations in most Western societies.

"Social security" in China means the provision of support to all people in need and of due honorary recognition to brave men and women of the armed forces, dead or alive, and their descendants. The responsibility of providing social security is primarily rested on the shoulder of the government but "society" (denoting enterprises, voluntary associations and local communities) should also participate actively towards the same goal as supplementary actors. The government will concentrate on the formulation of policies and legal structure for the delivery of services but "society" will be involved in the implementation of such policies.[3] However, four components of the social security system designed to serve specific target groups and the coverage of different types of assistance, whether in cash or in kind, are listed as follows:[4]

Social Security System of China

1. Social insurance
   - old age insurance
   - medical insurance
   - maternity and birth insurance
   - accident and occupational disease insurance
   - handicapped insurance
   - widowed insurance
   - unemployment insurance.
2. Social relief
   - widow, orphan and handicapped relief
   - distressed family relief
   - unemployed or bankrupt relief
   - natural disasters relief.
3. Social welfare
   - residential institutions for orphans and elderly
   - welfare factories
   - rehabilitation and treatment centres for handicapped
   - communities services.
4. Privileged security
   - financial assistance on compassionate grounds dismissed on non-criminal grounds and dependants
   - privileged pension
   - retirement homes for honorary servicemen.

The approach in maintaining each component as well as its goals and functions, the target population and the qualification for application are entirely different as Table 12.1 shows.

In 1987, it was reported that a total of RMB624 billion for the whole nation had been spent on social security with a ratio of almost 5:1 between urban and rural districts. A breakdown of this amount according to the

Table 12.1   Comparison of Components of Social Security

Component	Sources of finance	Goals	Target population	Functions	Qualification
Social insurance	Workers, employers, government	Prevention	Insurants	Primary	Subscription record
Social relief	Government, society	To fight against poverty	All citizens	Needy	Means test, residence
Social welfare	Government, society	To provide services	All citizens	Needy	Residence
Privileged security	Government, society	To strengthen national defence	Servicemen and descendants	Special	Residence, service records

Source: Chen Liangjin, *Shehui baozhang jiaocheng* (see note 2 below), p. 155.

different components is shown in Table 12.2.[5] The total expenditure of RMB624 billion was derived from two major sources as shown in Table 12.3.

Having looked at the 1987 approximations, it is instructive to examine the four components in more detail.

"Social insurance" is the primary system which aims at providing financial assistance to any worker who is sick, unemployed, giving birth to and caring for her baby, handicapped at work, aged or when dead, to his or her dependants; so that no one will be faced with the crisis of no income, temporarily or permanently. This system is run on a contributory basis with participation from workers, employers, the community and the government. Since China is such a huge country, economic development and financial ability among the provinces and even within each province

Table 12.2   Social Security Expenditure, 1987

(Unit: RMB billion)

Social security component	Urban	Rural	Total
Overall expenditure	519	105	624
Social insurance and social welfare	511	72	583
Social relief	2	21	23
Privileged security	6	12	18

Note: The total expenditure of RMB624 billion was derived from two major sources as shown in Table 12.3.

Table 12.3   Sources of Income in Social Security, 1987

(Unit: RMB billion)

Source of income	Urban	Rural	Total
State-owned enterprises	422	21	443
Collectively owned enterprises	97	84	181
Grand total	519	105	624

Source: Chen Liangjin, *Shehui baozhang jiaocheng* (see note 2 below), p. 113.

may vary drastically. Consequently, the local community or provincial government is given flexibility in apportioning the contributory share of each concerned party. The entire process of the financial management of social insurance can be perceived in Figure 12.1.[6]

"Social relief" is designed as a right of every citizen to receive financial assistance in times of need in order to maintain a minimal standard of living. In fact, such a right is being spelled out in the Constitution of the

Figure 12.1   The Social Insurance Model

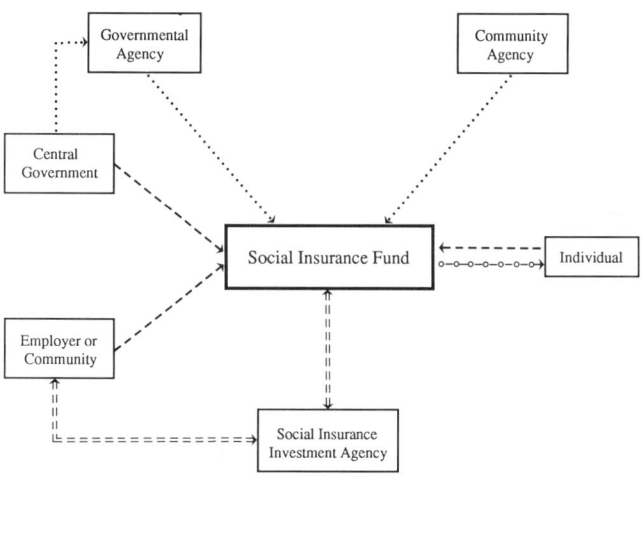

country, under Article 45, that every citizen when aged, sick or incapable of work can obtain financial or material assistance from the government. Hence it is not a charitable dole given by the government but the right of the citizen to claim the needed form of help. However, the need of the citizen must be proven, thus a means test is administered to ascertain the applicant's eligibility. It is also the philosophical assumption that such a practice must also reflect society's perception of social justice; that is, everyone should be able to receive fair compensation for a fair amount of work. In other words, no able-bodied person should receive subsidy instead of work as a personal preference, for it is not the aim of this system to promote or to nurture habitual relief recipients. Apart from helping people in real need, relief is normally provided to victims of natural disasters, handicapped persons without earning capacity, and "dropouts" of rapid economic and social change who could not keep pace with development because their traditional earning skills had become obsolete. As a market economy is gradually taking over the previous centrally guided economy, the gap between the newly rich and the poor appears to be widening as time goes by. People find themselves in increasing hardship unless some form of assistance, either price control of basic commodities or subsidies in basic items of living, or better still, opportunities for retraining to meet the demands of new technology, are provided. At the moment, the most significant programme in this relief system is the "five guaranteed programme" provided for the elderly and orphans, ensuring them of food, shelter, clothing, medical services and a decent funeral service for the elderly or educational opportunity for orphans. Another programme is the development of mutual co-operative saving funds, normally found in the rural districts so that members of the fund can borrow money free of interest or at extremely low rates in a time of emergency. At the national level a relief fund is being accumulated every year for natural disasters. Such a fund, though centrally administered, will be applicable to all provinces whenever the occasion arises.

"Social welfare" is designed by the central government to support its social policy and law in order to assure and to maintain a standard of living above the poverty line for all. This system provides five different types of services:

1. a temporary public assistance scheme for all in order to enable the recipients to adjust to new surroundings or situations;
2. a work-related scheme of help, known as occupational welfare, to

provide services such as nurseries or day-care centres managed by the work-unit, a staff canteen, a medical clinic, schooling for children of workers, a recreation centre and a tuck shop selling daily necessities at cost price;

3. locally instituted social services such as homes for the elderly or orphanages as well as asylums for mental patients;
4. sheltered workshops for all kinds of physically handicapped to be managed on a financially self-viable basis. Such workshops are operated by both normal and handicapped persons so that the latter's contact with the rest of society is facilitated in the operation of the business. Tax exemption on the profit of the enterprise is given by the government on the ratio between these two groups of employees; a higher rate is given if more handicapped workers are employed; and
5. a variety of services, whether recreational, medical, residential or personal, including match-making for the elderly or domestic helpers, are provided at the grassroots level for the young and the aged. As long as a demand for such a service is manifested, the local community will try to set it up. In short, the social welfare model can be simplified as in Table 12.4.

"Privileged security" is designed to give special privileges to both existing servicemen and their families, veterans and their families as well

Table 12.4   The Social Welfare Model

	Public assistance	Occupational welfare	Social services
Resource	– Government treasury	– Government treasury – Profit from enterprises – Labour union welfare fund	– Government treasury – Fund raised by community – Welfare enterprise
Management	– Governmental welfare agencies	– Administrative units of the enterprise – Local government – People's groups	– Ministry of Civil Affairs – Local government – People's groups
Fund utilization	– Directly	– Directly and indirectly	– Indirectly

Source: *Guangdong tongji nianjian 1992* (see note 16 below), p. 371.

as to the dependants of heros who gave up their lives for the country. The philosophy behind this scheme is not only the recognition of contribution but also as an incentive for youngsters to join the forces and stay with them. Apart from the regular forces, occasionally "voluntary" servicemen/women are called upon from the rural areas whenever the need arises. These "volunteers" are also entitled to similar privileges; for instance, such as their entitled plot of land will still be held under their names whilst enlisted and their families will receive a special cash allowance while the farm is temporarily one man/woman short for cultivation. This scheme offers death compensation to families of the deceased, handicapped compensation, retirement arrangement, and dismissal arrangement on non-personal violation of regulations such as cash compensation or arrangement of work in the community.

Situation in Guangdong

Social Insurance

In social insurance, Guangdong has been setting up pilot projects in various parts of the province. Shenzhen, after experimenting for about three years, finally adopted in August 1992 a temporary plan which covers a housing scheme, a retirement scheme and a medical scheme. Housing scheme is supported entirely by the employer based on an individual account basis, so that when a worker changes his job, the account will still exist under his name in the central provident fund for housing. The contribution from the employer in this respect is 13% of the worker's total monthly income. As far as the retirement scheme is concerned, the worker would contribute between 5% of his monthly wage (if it is less than RMB600 per month) to a maximum of 10% (if the wage is about RMB1,000 and above), whereas the employer would contribute 16% of the employee's total monthly income. With regard to medical insurance, the employer alone would shoulder all the responsibility by making a contribution of 8% of each worker's total monthly income to a central fund.[7] In another area, Jinghai, the farmers promote another method of medical insurance by putting part of the responsibility onto the shoulders of the people themselves. According to the ratio of contribution made by the village collectives and the individuals separately, the cost of medication and hospitalization is shared accordingly. For example, every farmer would contribute RMB5 per year into a medical fund, and the collective system would also make a greater share, then whenever the need arises, 60% of the total cost would be covered, while the rest would be taken up by the government.[8] In the province as a whole, social insurance system has made steady progress not only in the number of voluntary participation in unemployment insurance but also in old age insurance. In the *Guangdong tongji nianjian 1995* (Statistical Yearbook of Guangdong 1995), 4,180,000 workers have joined the unemployed scheme and a little more than 1,150,000 retirees have also participated in the old age insurance scheme.[9]

In the labour market, Guangdong has successfully achieved the free choice model rather than assignment of work by the authorities when one is old enough to work. The basic principle in such a move is that recruitment of workers should be made public, based on examination of some kinds, and the best performers would be employed.[10] People are also encouraged to choose their employment according to their interest and ability. In order to facilitate such a move, 1,100 manpower offices in 1994[11] have been established throughout the province assisting thereby over three million people in their search for work. Moreover, there are now about 123 training institutes engaging about three thousand teachers which have cumulatively trained over one million workers. In short, in 1994, the number of new recruits into the labour market was around 456,000 workers, and the unemployment rate was only 1.86% in the same year.[12] Since 1986, the provincial government has been able to raise RMB2.45 million for the "waiting-for-employment" insurance scheme.[13]

Social Welfare

Ever since 1978, Guangdong has gradually tried to implement this motto: social welfare services should be provided by society at the grassroots level.[14] The spirit of partnership in welfare provision is being influenced partly by changes in the nature of economic development in the nation. If people could be given the opportunity to function as entrepreneurs for economic gains, they could similarly act in the provision of welfare. Guangdong is an excellent example for illustration. Indeed, during the late 1980s, Guangdong achieved three distinct characteristics:[15]

1. welfare enterprises emerging from all levels of society;
2. development of joint ventures with overseas financing; and
3. improvement of technology in welfare enterprises.

1. Four administrative units in Guangdong will participate in the

provision of welfare enterprises, which means that cities, districts, "administrative streets" and villages and small towns will each try their best in such an endeavour. Such provision of welfare enterprises constitutes the primary base of service provision. From fewer than ten such projects in the late 1970s, the number had increased to about 1,116 in 1990, engaging 8,360 handicapped persons. From the official source of information, however, the picture is even more encouraging, as shown in Table 12.5.[16] The plausible differences may be explained by the fact that official statistics included everything under the term "social security" whereas unofficial figures indicated only those of welfare enterprises.

Table 12.5   Welfare Enterprises in Guangdong

Item	1980	1985	1990	1992	1994
	Number of projects				
Social security at the grassroots levels	—	—	5,210	9,138	2,886
Rural areas	—	—	225	581	1,050
Urban areas	—	—	4,985	8,557	1,836
	Number of persons				
Arrangement of physically handicapped persons in jobs	2,927	5,995	17,801	19,067	21,791
By the Ministry of Civil Affairs	2,927	3,627	4,649	5,189	5,506
By enterprises	—	2,368	13,152	13,878	16,285

Sources: *Guangdong tongji nianjian 1992*, p. 459; *Guangdong tongji nianjian 1994*, p. 416 and *Guangdong tongji nianjian 1995*, p. 468.

2. The inducement of capital from overseas for joint enterprises has also proved to be very successful. In 1989, fourteen cities within the province had 87 such joint projects almost to the extent of incorporating US$10 million, bringing in almost a net profit of US$20 million; and the trend of such activity can be seen from Table 12.6.

3. Intensive improvement of existing equipment and techniques did result in higher productivity throughout the province. Through different channels, the provincial government has been able to raise RMB40 million within the past few years for the purpose of modernizing the means of production, and as a result the assets of these assisted enterprises amounted to a little more than RMB2 billion. These types of projects cover electronic equipment, plastic industry, equipment for rehabilitation, paper products

Table 12.6   Contributions from Overseas Chinese and Those Living in Hong Kong and Macau

Item	1980	1985	1990	1992	1994
Value (in RMB million)					
Total	12,031	54,529	91,887	687,814	291,656
Social welfare	291	2,071	21,422	177,547	42,951
Health	997	2,303	10,453	39,154	32,007
Culture and education	4,081	8,133	24,695	100,570	55,350
Industry and agriculture	4,373	19,660	30,837	357,342	67,647
Tourism	1,338	4,948	2,480	4,309	167
Others	951	17,414	2,000	8,892	93,534
In percentage (%)					
Total	100	100	100	100	100
Social welfare	2.4	3.8	23.3	25.8	14.7
Health	8.3	4.2	11.4	5.7	11.0
Culture and education	33.9	14.9	26.9	14.6	19.0
Industry and agriculture	36.3	36.1	33.6	52.0	23.2
Tourism	11.1	9.1	2.7	0.6	0.1
Others	7.9	31.9	2.2	1.3	32.1

Sources: *Guangdong tongji nianjian 1992*, p. 371 and *Guangdong tongji nianjian 1995*, p. 378.

industry, food and drink materials production, arts and crafts, bamboo, wood and rattan industry, dresses and leather works, toys industry, traditional dyeing industry and common drugs wrapping. Almost 80% of all physically handicapped persons within the province have been gainfully employed in these enterprises. The blind have been specially trained as therapists using mainly the technique of massage in clinics. It is most encouraging to see the operation of "sheltered factories," as they are called in China, as business enterprises throughout the nation and the province for physically handicapped persons. The equivalent set-ups in Hong Kong and elsewhere, termed "sheltered workshops," are operated by non-governmental agencies mostly as welfare projects for both physically and mentally handicapped persons.

There are three major differences, however, between these two similar workplaces. The first distinction is that in China not all the people working in a sheltered factory are handicapped but a proportion of the workers are healthy people. Take the Dongqing Children's Garment Factory at Guangzhou as an example. This sheltered factory caters for people who are deaf and dumb and sign language is used among all workers for communication. Among the some three hundred workers, almost half of them are deaf and dumb and about another twenty or more are people in wheel chairs, while the remaining workers are healthy people. This factory is not only supplying children's clothing to other parts of the province but also to the rest of the nation through face-to-face negotiations and mail orders. Also, this factory operates a retail store for the local people, hence it is important that some staff members of the factory are able to travel and to communicate verbally with potential customers. Secondly, the central government is giving subsidies to such factories on a percentage basis by way of profit tax deduction according to the number of handicapped workers in the factory as well as subsidies in the provision of raw material needed for production. It is possible to be a self-financing business which provides not only wages for all workers but benefits in kind, such as housing, medical and nursery facilities to all workers as well as retirement benefits. Thirdly, all workers are paid on an equal basis according to work performance and degrees of responsibility, irrespective of being handicapped or not.

Social Relief

In December 1991, the provincial government of Guangdong decided in its Eighth Five-year Plan to adopt ten projects for the purpose of eliminating poverty in the mountain-districts, which have been notorious for their poverty stricken conditions. It must be borne in mind that the prosperous Pearl River Delta occupies only about 25% of the total area within the province whereas the mountain-districts comprises approximately 65%. As far as agricultural land is concerned, about 42% is found in these districts and the total population living in such poor districts accounts for about 40.8% of the provincial total.[17] It is obvious, therefore, that any effort to combat poverty in the province must be concentrated in these mountainous areas. Apart from constructing a viable infrastructure for development, modernizing farming methods is also indispensable in the projects. Furthermore, advanced technological skills were also introduced into such districts so that new strains of farm produce could be harvested.[18] High quality cash crops such as pomelo, lychee, passion fruit and tea have been introduced into the districts for obvious reasons. Scientific technology has also been intensively researched resulting in an asset of RMB2.8 billion during the years 1989–1990.[19] Among the twenty-five poor districts out of a total of forty-nine within the province, about four million farmers have gradually and successfully raised their standards of living. In March 1992, it was reported that the annual average personal income in such areas had increased to about RMB650 and about 1% of the people had achieved an annual income of RMB1,000.[20] Table 12.7 indicates approximately the financial involvement during the past ten years and more.

Table 12.7 Expenditure in Social Relief

(Unit: RMB million)

Social relief	1980	1985	1990	1992	1994
Social relief service	2,417	2,900	6,418	8,381	16,399
Natural disaster	2,015	4,643	2,679	4,322	7,561

Sources: *Guangdong tongji nianjian 1992*, p. 459; *Guangdong tongji nianjian 1994*, p. 416 and *Guangdong tongji nianjian 1995*, p. 468.

Privileged Security

The target population served by this type of service includes both existing servicemen as well as retired ones, those dismissed early on non-criminal grounds and their families. Descendants of deceased servicemen are also entitled to receive this service. For the retired group, institutional care is provided and for the handicapped group either cash allowances or retraining opportunities are provided. For the dismissed group including those who have decided to withdraw from the services, arrangement for employment is made. Table 12.8 indicates the situation in Guangdong for the past ten years or more.

Impacts of Economic Development

Economic development in the province has certainly brought about prosperity and improved standards of living to a small group of people, but it has also resulted in unintended side-effects of certain social ills, such as the re-emergence of prostitution and migrant labourers. It is interesting to note the changes in the status of women. The position of women has definitely changed remarkably, for better and for worse. In 1989, a committee was set up in April for the purpose of drafting a new law to protect the rights and position of women by the central government; the enactment took place in April 1992, and was known as the Law of the People's Republic of China on the Protection of Rights and Interests of Women.[21]

Table 12.8 Privileged Security in Guangdong

Item	1980	1985	1990	1992	1994
Total number of units	28	26	40	39	54
By Ministry of Civil Affairs	28	26	31	33	36
By collectives	—	—	9	6	18
Total number of consumers of service	697	1,149	1,556	1,737	1,952
By Ministry of Civil Affairs	697	1,139	1,515	1,696	1,732
By collectives	—	10	41	41	220
Total expenditure (RMB million)	1,404	4,686	12,250	14,939	24,851
By Ministry of Civil Affairs	1,404	2,319	5,941	7,156	12,136
By collectives	—	2,367	6,309	7,783	12,715

Note: Since the figures under the year "1990" in *Guangdong tongji nianjian 1992* are a misprint, the author has verified and counter-checked against that in *Guangdong tongji nianjian 1991* in order to make the correct presentation.

Sources: *Guangdong tongji nianjian 1991*, p. 423; *Guangdong tongji nianjian 1992*, p. 459; *Guangdong tongji nianjian 1994*, p. 416 and *Guangdong tongji nianjian 1995*, p. 468.

This law, no doubt, has given women strong self-confidence and reliance, which have increased further by the economic power that comes with employment. Divorce rate in the nation has also increased markedly. Divorces are often initiated by women, resulting in an increased number of broken families and juvenile delinquency. The re-emergence of prostitution, however, is also quite alarming. Reasons for taking up this occupation can probably be identified as follows:

1. A personal preference for materialistic enjoyment without the necessity of working. Almost 25% of the girls interviewed in a survey conducted in early 1992 in Guangzhou expressed such a tendency. In each transaction, the money derived ranged between RMB200 and RMB1,000. Some 54% of these girls originally acquired a meagre but steady income from other work, but they were not satisfied then with their consumption patterns. They turned to prostitution initially as a second job but changed later to full-time prostitutes.

2. Running away from home constituted the second reason, particularly those coming from poorer neighbouring provinces. Approximately 36% of the prostitutes found in Guangzhou belonged to this category. When they left home to search for work, they did

not think of prostitution as an occupation; it was only failing to find suitable jobs and being too ashamed to return home penniless, that tempted them to turn to prostitution.

3. A deteriorating social environment has also contributed to the revival of prostitution. A changed perception on the value of money, the influence of the drug trade, and the so-called freedom of sex have also permeated the social atmosphere in Guangzhou in recent years; in particular, the pursuit of brand-name goods. Lack of a proper sense of morality and responsibility, absence of a basic knowledge of sex education and the after-effects of a promiscuous sexual life, all have contributed to a view of prostitution as the easiest route to wealth.

4. Poor administrative management in general in hotels and bars is another major reason for the re-emergence of this trade. Some entrepreneurs assume that overseas businessmen coming to the country expect the provision of female companions as part of the deal; hence hotel managers pretend not to be aware of such activity.

5. Effectiveness in the rehabilitation of these girls when caught is not too successful. Once released and sent back to their place of origin, no supervision of any kind is carried out as a follow-up. Relapse cases are quite common.

When all the above factors occurred at the same time in a rapidly changing society, it could only be expected that the oldest profession of the world would reappear. In a socialist country, strict measures could no doubt be enforced to curb, if not to root out, the growth of the phenomenon via different channels. In my opinion, however, as a long-term measure, education, formal and informal, of women could be the ultimate solution to such a social problem. Even in correctional institutions, education rather than punishment should be emphasized.

Another phenomenon is that a high proportion of the migrant labour force coming into Guangdong from other provinces is female. Apart from being prostitutes, they are also employed in light industries or as domestic helpers. Such geographical mobility creates not only problems in Guangdong but also drastic changes in their own places of origin. Families may be broken up, marriage may only remain a dream for a lot of bachelors in the poorer places back home. Also, social security and order may be indirectly and adversely affected in Guangdong and elsewhere. It is suggested, therefore, that in order to curtail the ill social effects of economic development, the following points should be duly considered:

1. Education via mass media and adult education classes must be vigorously carried out emphasizing self-respect and dignity of women, who must also be encouraged to be strong enough to resist the temptation of yielding to materialism at the expense of personal integrity. It is enough to mention here that the All-China Women's Federation throughout the country, including Guangdong, has done a tremendous job in educating women through informal measures on their legal rights as stipulated in law. The said federation is also providing free legal advice to any woman who is ignorant or uncertain about her rights at home and at work, and even to get free legal counselling in court cases.

2. It is important that all persons involved in illegal solicitation of women for sale or prostitution must be severely punished. A similar approach must also be considered in treating the customers, whether they are local Chinese or people from overseas.

3. Now is also an appropriate time to review any loophole in existing regulations or laws so that a sense of social justice can be maintained in the sentences.

4. Inter-provincial cooperation in the issue of the migrant labour force, particularly female workers, must be closely coordinated and supervised. Should any of these girls wish to get married to a local man and settle down in their workplace, some kind of assistance or counselling might be organized for them by the All-China Women's Federation. It is vital to ascertain the eligibility of entering into a matrimonial relationship for both parties in order to avoid possible tragedies later on.

Conclusion

It is true that economic development since 1979 has brought prosperity to a small group of people in Guangdong, particularly along the coastal cities and the Special Economic Zones, but it also has brought along feelings of social injustice and a widening gap between the rich and the poor. When all enterprises were controlled and managed by the government, it was understandable that the nation would assume all responsibilities for assisting the poor and treating all alike. However, when joint-ventures with overseas finance is made possible, the question of shared responsibility in taking care of employees presents a new problem. China throughout these years has undertaken studies of different systems of social security in various countries and has arrived at the approach of providing assistance to its people to ensure a decent and rising standard of living.

Due to its geographical proximity to Hong Kong, Guangdong has reaped the fruits of economic reforms with only slight difficulties by receiving not only financial assistance and investment from Hong Kong but also personnel and technological assistance. Unfortunately, due to easy access via the mass media, Hong Kong has also exported its value systems and interpersonal relationship patterns to Guangdong, particularly to Guangzhou and Shenzhen. It is no surprise, therefore, that prostitution has reappeared. Juvenile behaviour was also patterned after the Hong Kong style in clothing, hair style and consumption behaviour, such as patronizing karaokes. The All-China Women's Federation, with all its divisional chapters throughout the province, has been most active in assisting women and families to cement their roots in upholding the traditional good values of society via their effort in self-education and in widening their vision of law and society. Part of their effort is concentrated in nurturing the next generation as well; hence a Children's Fund is being set up for research and services, such as provision of homes for abandoned children. Mobilization of unemployed youth as volunteers in homes for the aged is also organized. As far as the social security system is concerned, the central government in China takes full responsibility as a secondary source to guide and support the operation. A strong emphasis is stressed on social insurance rather than relief or welfare for the underlying philosophy is that: work is both a right and a duty of every citizen, and so no one is given the choice to be a welfare recipient rather than a worker, except those in real need or incapable of work. Temporary assistance is only a means rather than an end in helping the recipient to stand on his/her own feet again. Thus the emphasis on re-education or retraining is a vital supplement of the entire system. Undoubtedly, social problems of one kind or another will gradually be appearing as China is moving towards a market economy, but the desire and will to correct any social ill as a by-product is also evident. With the new developments occurring in Shanghai and its neighbouring districts, Guangdong's experience may provide an example with all its pros and cons, during the process.

Notes

1. Wang Gangyi and Wei Xinwu, *Shehui baozhang jichu* (Basics of Social Security) (Jilin: Jilin daxue chubanshe, 1989).

2. Chen Liangjin, *Shehui baozhang jiaocheng* (Social Security System of China) (Beijing: Zhishi chubanshe, 1990), p. 149.

3. Ibid., p. 5.

4. Ibid., p. 156.

5. Ibid., p. 113.

6. Ibid., p. 181.

7. *Wen Wei Po* (Hong Kong), 5 May 1992, p. 8.

8. Ibid.

9. Guangdongsheng tongjiju (ed.), *Guangdong tongji nianjian 1995* (Statistical Yearbook of Guangdong 1995) (Beijing: Zhongguo tongji chubanshe, 1995), p. 11.

10. *Wen Wei Po*, 2 July 1993, p. 17.

11. See note 9, p. 11.

12. Ibid.

13. A "waiting-for-employment" insurance scheme is very similar to the concept of unemployment scheme. The difference is that no contribution from the individual is required. Since no work is assigned by the authority, a school-leaver is waiting for employment (*daiye*) rather than unemployed (*shiye*, literally meaning loss of one's job) because he has never been employed.

14. Lu Woquan, "Wosheng fazhan chengshi shehui fuli shiye de jingyan" (The Experience of Developing Urban Social Welfare Services in Guangdong), *Minzheng* (Civil Affairs Forum), February 1990, pp. 8–10.

15. Guangdongsheng minzhengting chengfuchu, "Gaige kaifang cujin liao wosheng shehui fuli qishiye" (Modernization and the Promotion of the Development of Social Welfare Enterprises of Guangdong), *Minzheng*, February, 1990, p. 1.

16. Guangdongsheng tongjiju (ed.), *Guangdong tongji nianjian 1992* (Statistical Yearbook of Guangdong 1992) (Beijing: Zhongguo tongji chubanshe, 1992), p. 459.

17. *Wen Wei Po*, 27 January 1991, p. 14.

18. Ibid., 7 December 1991, p. 6.

19. Ibid., 27 January 1991, p. 14.

20. Ibid., 20 March 1992, p. 35.

21. Decree of the President of the People's Republic of China, No. 58. Zhonghua renmin gongheguo funu quanyi baozhangfa (Law of the People's Republic of China on the Protection of Rights and Interests of Women). Adopted at the Fifth Session of the Seventh National People's Congress on 3 April 1992.

13

Housing

Rebecca L. H. Chiu

Introduction

Before the 1980s, housing in China had been regarded as a component of state welfare that the government was responsible to supply to all, charging only nominal rents. In the rural sector, average peasants were allowed to keep their houses while those of the landlords and rich peasants were confiscated. In the urban sector, housing had been mainly constructed, rehabilitated, allocated, maintained and managed by the government through local municipal housing bureaux or work units by which the household heads were employed. Houses were allocated mainly according to seniority and rank at work. Over the years, due to the consumptive nature of the housing system in the socialist economy and the burgeoning population size, the Chinese government at different levels faced tremendous problems in providing sufficient and decent housing to the population. A series of housing reforms have thus been introduced since the early 1980s to alleviate the problems, following the adoption of more liberal economic policies in the country since 1978. Hitherto, Guangdong has been taking the lead in the housing reform experiment.

This chapter aims at providing an overview as well as a critical understanding of the current housing conditions and development in Guangdong. The objectives of this chapter are threefold: to survey the current housing conditions in Guangdong; to examine the content and the nature of housing reforms taking place in the province; and to evaluate recent housing developments in the leading cities of Shenzhen, Guangzhou and Zhuhai. As such, the emphasis of the chapter will necessarily be placed on the urban housing sector in which reforms have been more drastic and extensive compared with those in the rural housing sector.

Housing Conditions in Guangdong

Housing conditions in Guangdong have been significantly improved since 1978. Heavy investments have been channelled to the housing sector following the country's higher emphasis on raising living standards of the populace. As shown in Table 13.1, annual investment in housing increased from a meagre sum of RMB213 million in 1978 to more than RMB27,656 million in 1994. The drastic rate of increase (102%) between 1991 and 1992 could be due to Deng Xiaoping's tour to the south in the spring of 1992 confirming on the open policy. More specifically, housing investment made by state-owned enterprises increased more than 64 times

Table 13.1   Housing Investment in Guangdong in Selected Years after 1978

(Unit: RMB million)

Source of housing investment	1978	1980	1985	1991	1992	1994
State-owned enterprises	213[a]	554[a]	2,687	6,440	13,906	n.a.
Collectively-owned enterprises	n.a.	n.a.	273	719	2,113	n.a.
Individuals	n.a.	n.a.	2,555	5,107	8,712	n.a.
Total	213	554	5,515	12,266	24,731	27,656[b]

Sources: *Guangdong tongji nianjian*, various issues.
Notes: n.a. = Data not available in the 1994 and 1995 issues of *Guangdong tongji nianjian*.
      [a] The investment for redevelopment is not included as the data are not available. However, the investment should not have been significant in these early years of economic reform.
      [b] Investment for market housing only.

between 1978 and 1992 in gross terms. Investment by individuals, mostly rural households building houses for own use, was also sizeable, and was comparable to the investment made by state-owned enterprises between 1985 to 1991.

Correspondingly, the annual housing production also expanded exponentially over the same period, increasing from about 2 million sq m (approximately 27,857 units) in 1978 to 67 million sq m in 1994 (958,429 units) (Table 13.2). The increase was greater in the province as a whole (4.9 times) than in cities (3 times) between 1985 and 1994, implying that housing was developed at a higher speed in the rural areas than in the

Table 13.2   Housing Production in Guangdong in Selected Years after 1978

	1978	1985	1990	1991	1992	1994
Gross floor area completed ('000 m^2)						
Cities[a]	n.a.	7,816	6,241	7,181	11,390	23,750
Whole province	1,950	13,736	25,165	11,220	20,339	67,090
Estimated housing units completed[b]	27,857	196,229	359,500	160,285	290,561	958,429

Sources: *Guangdong tongji nianjian*, various issues.
Notes: [a] Include officially designated cities as stated in the *Guangdong tongji nianjian* of the respective years.
      [b] The average gross area of a housing unit is assumed to be 70 sq m.

urban centres. The trough in production in 1991 could have been due to the social movement in 1989, allowing for the lead time for construction. The production nevertheless picked up again in 1994, as a corollary of the upsurge in housing investment in 1992.

Apart from increasing the supply of housing, the large-scale investment in housing since the 1980s has also improved housing conditions in Guangdong markedly. This is evident in space standards and the provision of facilities and services.

Space Standards

According to sample surveys[1] conducted by the Guangdong Statistical Bureau over the years, the average living area[2] per capita in the urban areas had increased steadily from 3.2 sq m to 15.7 sq m between 1952 and 1994 (Table 13.3). The overall increase was about fivefold during the period, showing higher growth rates after 1978. Similarly, housing space standards in the rural areas had also been improved, albeit at a lower rate due to the larger base number.

Table 13.4 compares the average living area per capita across major cities in the province in 1994. It seems that cities like Dongguan, which has undergone rapid development recently, achieved the highest space standards (18.6 sq m per capita). In contrast, more built-up and older cities such as Guangzhou, Foshan, Shantou and Zhanjiang had lower space standards. As new cities, Shenzhen (13.6 sq m per capita) and Zhuhai (13.2 sq m per capita) scored highly because of the absence of a large slum area, relatively better urban planning and higher living standards.

Table 13.3   Average Per Capita Living Area in Guangdong in Selected Years, 1952–1994 (Sampled Surveys)

(Unit: sq m)

	1952	1957	1965	1978	1980	1985	1990	1994
Average per capita living area[a] in urban areas	3.2	4.2	5.1	5.5	6.4	8.6	12.1	15.7
Average per capita living area in rural areas	n.a.	n.a.	n.a.	8.7	10.5	14.9	17.4	20.5

Sources: *Guangdong tongji nianjian 1991*, p. 358; *Guangdong tongji nianjian 1992*, p. 402 and *Guangdong tongji nianjian 1995*, pp. 126 and 421.

Note: [a] See text for definition of living area.

Table 13.4 Average Per Capita Living Area in Major Cities in Guangdong, 1994

(Unit: sq m)

City	Average per capita living area
Guangzhou	9.3
Shenzhen	13.6
Zhuhai	13.2
Foshan	9.0
Dongguan	18.6
Shantou	10.8
Zhanjiang	8.6

Sources: *Zhuhai tongji nianjian 1995*, p. 332 and *Guangdong tongji nianjian 1995*, pp. 126–29.

Table 13.5 illustrates the improvements in housing space standards between 1985 and 1994. Apparently, homelessness has almost disappeared since 1990. The proportion of overcrowded and inconvenient households had also dropped from 12.4% in 1985 to 2.2% in 1994, and from 5.4% in 1985 to 2.1% in 1991, respectively. Similarly, the proportion of households with living space of 4 to 8 sq m per capita had decreased from 35.1% in 1985 to 13.1% in 1994. Conversely, the proportion of households with a living area more than 8 sq m per capita had increased from 46.7% in 1985 to 84.6% in 1994. Hence, by the mid-1990s, a major proportion of the Guangdong urbanities enjoyed a housing space standard higher than that of public housing tenants in the more developed neighbouring city of Hong Kong, the median gross housing area (inclusive of kitchen, bathroom, internal corridor and common area) of which was 8.3 sq m per capita in 1994.

A sampled household survey[3] conducted by the Statistical Bureau in 1991 further found that the average living area per household ranged from 41 sq m to 70 sq m. However, analyses of the survey findings indicated that space standards were not directly proportional to income levels, but were more directly associated with employment status. These findings reflected the nature of the housing allocation criteria which were mainly based on ranking and years of service at work. The average living area per capita was, however, found to be generally disproportionate to household size, i.e. smaller households tended to have a larger average living area per capita. It is unfortunate that similar analysis has not been conducted by the Statistical Bureau since 1993. Nonetheless, it was indicated that in 1994, the average living area per person varied from 4.4 sq m (Shanwei) to 18.7 sq m (Dongguan) among the cities of Guangdong.[4]

**Table 13.5   Housing Characteristics in Urban Guangdong, 1985–1994
(Sampled Surveys)**

	1985	1989	1990	1991	1992	1993	1994
Number of surveyed households	1,600	1,500	1,500	1,550	1,550	1,550	1,550
Homeless households	7 (0.4)	3 (0.2)	0	0	1 (0.1)	0	1 (0.1)
Overcrowded households[a]	199 (12.4)	105 (7.0)	75 (5.0)	52 (3.4)	7 (0.5)	20 (1.3)	34 (2.2)
Inconvenient households[b]	86 (5.4)	47 (3.1)	51 (3.4)	32 (2.1)	n.a.	n.a.	n.a.
Households with per capita living area of 4–6 sq m	276 (17.3)	112 (7.5)	110 (7.3)	86 (5.5)	41 (2.6)	49 (3.2)	69 (4.5)
Households with per capita living area of 6–8 sq m	285 (17.8)	190 (12.7)	170 (11.3)	147 (9.5)	64 (4.1)	100 (6.5)	134 (8.6)
Households with per capita living area above 8 sq m	747 (46.7)	1,043 (69.5)	1,094 (72.9)	1,233 (79.5)	1,437 (92.7)	1,381 (89.1)	1,312 (84.6)

Sources: *Guangdong tongji nianjian 1992*, p. 409 and *Guangdong tongji nianjian 1995*,
p. 418.
Notes: Figures in brackets are percentages.
[a] Overcrowded households refers to households with living area below 4 sq
m per capita.
[b] Inconvenient households refers to households with living area above 4 sq m
per capita but with three generations living in one room, or parents living with
children over 12 years old in one room, or adult siblings of opposite sex living
in one room.

Provision of Facilities and Services

Apart from the rise in space standards, statistics also show that more and
better facilities were provided inside the dwelling. As illustrated in Table
13.6, only three households within the sample were not supplied with tap
water in 1994, indicating that less than 0.2% of the urban population in
Guangdong needed to obtain water outside their dwellings. This compares
favourably with 3.6% in 1985. Furthermore, a majority of the households
(94.7%) enjoyed an independent water supply.

However, improvements in the provision of sanitary facilities were
less desirable. By 1994, only 77.3% of the sampled households lived in
dwellings with toilets and bathrooms, while 9.7% were in units without
any sanitary facilities and 8.2% were in units with toilets only. Fortunately,

Table 13.6 **Provision of Internal Household Facilities in Urban Guangdong in Selected Years, 1985–1994 (Sampled Surveys)**

	No. of households						
	1985	1987	1989	1991	1992	1993	1994
Water supply							
Without piped water	58	37	12	4	2	2	3
	(3.6)	(2.3)	(0.8)	(0.3)	(0.1)	(0.1)	(0.2)
Shared tap water	262	232	123	88	69	73	79
	(16.4)	(14.5)	(8.2)	(5.7)	(4.5)	(4.7)	(5.1)
Self-contained	1,273	1,327	1,362	1,458	1,478	1,475	1,467
	(79.9)	(83.1)	(90.9)	(94.1)	(95.4)	(95.2)	(94.7)
Sanitary facilities							
Without sanitary facilities	652	534	397	273	239	193	150
	(40.9)	(33.5)	(26.5)	(17.6)	(15.4)	(12.5)	(9.7)
Shared sanitary facilities	169	134	110	127	104	90	74
	(10.6)	(8.4)	(7.3)	(8.2)	(6.7)	(5.8)	(4.8)
With toilets but without bathrooms	220	252	270	238	138	100	127
	(13.8)	(15.8)	(18.0)	(15.4)	(8.9)	(6.5)	(8.2)
With toilets and bathrooms	552	676	720	912	1,068	1,167	1,198
	(34.7)	(42.4)	(48.1)	(58.8)	(68.9)	(75.3)	(77.3)
Kitchen							
Without kitchens	101	87	47	47	29	31	33
	(6.3)	(5.5)	(3.1)	(3.0)	(1.9)	(2.0)	(2.1)
Shared kitchens	168	131	88	71	58	58	45
	(10.5)	(8.2)	(5.9)	(4.6)	(3.7)	(3.7)	(2.9)
Self-contained	1,324	1,378	1,362	1,432	1,462	1,461	1,471
	(83.1)	(86.3)	(90.9)	(92.4)	(94.3)	(94.3)	(94.9)
Fuel Supply							
Coal	930	823	587	386	295	238	178
	(58.4)	(51.6)	(39.2)	(24.9)	(19.0)	(15.4)	(11.5)
Bottled gas	413	609	837	1,123	1,199	1,236	1,276
	(25.9)	(38.2)	(55.9)	(72.5)	(77.4)	(79.7)	(82.3)
Piped gas	0	0	7	0	25	39	74
	—	—	(0.5)	—	(1.6)	(2.5)	(4.8)
Others	250	164	66	41	30	37	21
	(15.7)	(10.3)	(4.4)	(2.6)	(1.9)	(2.4)	(1.4)
Total	1,593	1,596	1,497	1,550	1,550	1,550	1,550

Sources: *Guangdong tongji nianjian 1992*, p. 409 and *Guangdong tongji nianjian 1995*, p. 418.

Note: Figures in brackets are percentages.

an absolute majority of the households had their own kitchens by 1994, amounting to 94.9%. In the supply of fuel, the majority of the households had also shifted from using coal in 1985 (58.4%) to using bottled gas in 1994 (82.3%). This change certainly helped to keep the dwelling places cleaner and reduced air pollution. However, piped gas was limited to the very few (4.8%). Hence, while there was still room for improvement, such as the provision of independent toilets and bathrooms, Guangdong had gone quite a long way to improve facilities within the dwelling.

Initial improvements have also been accomplished in the provision of community services in the proximity. Since the 1980s, Guangdong has adopted a more comprehensive and integrated approach in housing planning and development. Instead of constructing individual blocks on an uncoordinated basis, both the housing bureaux and development companies developed new housing projects on a larger geographical scale with provision of community services such as schools, markets and shops. By the end of 1991, 290 housing districts with such facilities, taking up 44% of residential development in urban areas, had been completed.[5]

As a result of heavy investment injected into the housing sector since 1978, Guangdong has achieved a relatively high space standard. Further, most households have been equipped with an independent water supply and kitchen facilities. Sanitary facilities and fuel supply have also been improved but further upgrading is desirable. These improvements have nevertheless been costly, and were partially results of housing reforms that various local governments have introduced to further relieve housing problems.

Recent Housing Developments

The Need for Housing Reforms[6]

The introduction of housing reforms was necessitated by the extremely low rent-income ratio fostered by the welfare nature of housing in China. As shown in Table 13.7, tenure types of housing in urban Guangdong were dominated by public renting prior to 1994. Public tenancy, which charged very low rent, included renting directly from the housing bureaux and employers in the public sector, state- or collectively-owned enterprises. (Most enterprises are directly or indirectly state-owned or collectively owned). There was only a slight drop of about 4% in public tenancy between 1985 and 1991, however, it had contracted fast since then and ceased to be the dominant sector in 1994. Private tenancy had been insignificant and it continued to taper off. Conversely, the owner-occupier

Table 13.7   Tenure Types of Housing in Urban Guangdong, 1985–1994

Tenure type	No. of households						
	1985	1987	1989	1991	1992	1993	1994
Public tenancy	1,148	1,191	1,077	1,049	915	800	616
	(72.1)	(74.6)	(71.9)	(67.7)	(59.0)	(51.6)	(39.7)
Private tenancy	90	68	49	39	32	26	29
	(5.6)	(4.3)	(3.3)	(2.5)	(2.1)	(1.7)	(1.9)
Owner occupation	344	322	365	461	597	721	901
	(21.6)	(20.2)	(24.4)	(29.7)	(38.5)	(46.5)	(58.1)
Others	11	15	6	1	5	3	3
	(0.7)	(0.9)	(0.4)	(0.1)	(0.3)	(0.2)	(0.2)
Total	1,593	1,596	1,497	1,550	1,550	1,550	1.550

Sources: *Guangdong tongji nianjian 1992*, p. 409 and *Guangdong tongji nianjian 1995*, p. 418.
Note: Figures in brackets are percentages.

sector had expanded quickly since 1992 and became the major sector (58%) in 1994. These tenure changes were produced by the housing reforms implemented since the mid-1980s. The reforms were prompted by a number of reasons.

Rentals of public tenancy were very low and costed less than one *yuan* per capita before 1990 (Table 13.8). This was insufficient to cover maintenance and management costs, let alone construction costs. Whereas the average household income had almost increased fivefold between 1978 and 1991, the rental level had merely doubled. The discrepancy was even more phenomenal in absolute terms. Hence the rent-income ratio was almost negligible, only standing at 0.6% in 1991. Compared with other basic household consumption, housing expenditure was obviously on the low side. Even water and electricity costs had surpassed the rental level since 1985, not to mention other more costly items such as food and clothing (Table 13.8). Hence, the government found its investment in housing not only non-recoverable (e.g. in 1989, the national average rent was RMB0.13 which was only 6.5% of the full-cost rent), but was also inductive to further housing expenditure: for each additional housing unit it built, the government was responsible for its maintenance and management permanently. Thus, if the old housing policy were to remain, the snow-ball effect of its housing expenditure would render the government less and less able to afford new housing projects. The crux of the housing problem hence lay in the welfare nature, and in more specific terms, the low-rental policy of the housing system.

Table 13.8   Average Income and Expenditure Per Capita in Urban Guangdong in Selected Years, 1978–1994 (Sampled Surveys)

(Unit: RMB)

Monthly income and expenditure	1978	1985	1990	1991	1993	1994
Income	33.5	75.1	177.9	211.3	356.4	489.8
Expenditure						
Rent	0.5	0.6	1.0	1.2	1.7	5.9
Food	22.2	43.2	94.6	105.6	153.9	200.4
Clothing	3.0	5.2	11.4	14.5	22.3	29.2
Water & electricity	0.3	1.4	4.7	5.2	8.4	12.2
Others	7.5	24.7	66.2	84.8	170.1	242.1

Sources: Compiled from *Guangdong tongji nianjian 1992*, p. 402 and *Guangdong tongji nianjian 1995*, p. 409.

Note: Compared with tables of previous issues of *Guangdong tongji nianjian* containing results of the same surveys, tables in the 1995 issue provides figures of much greater value. It is believed that the figures have been adjusted to the 1994 prices.

The low-rental policy, which still operates to various extents in urban Guangdong, has engendered several problems. First, the rental was so low that not only construction cost was non-recoverable, it was insufficient to cover maintenance costs. Second, as the rental only consumed 0.6% of the average household income, the government argued that the low rental policy released income for the purchase of other consumer goods, thus heightening inflation. Building costs were inflated as a corollary, reducing the real value of housing investment.

Third, the very low rental level and the de facto life-long ownership enjoyed by the tenants had minimized their incentives to purchase their own homes. The low rental was generally held responsible for the government's inability to recover construction costs through housing sales. Fourth, the low-rental policy had led to over-consumption of housing. Because housing costs were almost negligible, households tended to manipulate their power to get hold of as much housing as possible: both in terms of size and the number of units.

There were other problems not directly related to the rental policy. A major one lay with the allocation system. As allocation was based on purely administrative grounds prior to the introduction of housing reforms, housing exchange motivated by financial returns was non-existent. The absence of a housing market in which consumers could trade housing freely had thus fostered a rigid housing system. The situation was further aggravated by the low rental policy which encouraged over-consumption. Wastage in the housing system was therefore allegedly high. The housing reforms started in Shekou (in Shenzhen Special Economic Zone) in 1980 and later spread to other parts of urban Guangdong have thus been attempting to address the above problems — at least some of them.

The Housing Reforms

The housing reforms are aimed at creating a sustainable housing system by commodifying the housing sector. Simply interpreted, housing commodification in China means to turn housing from a "free good" to a "subsidized good," and eventually to a "commodity," the price of which (i.e. either the rent or sale price) includes full costs and a profit margin. Thus, housing subsidy will be minimized. Commodification also implies the right of property possession, either fully or partially. The policy operates on the principle that housing consumers should be responsible for their own housing service which they could afford. Ultimately, the policy aims at turning government's dead-end spending in housing to be at least partially recoverable for further investment. It is also intended that the housing reforms absorb the huge pile of idle cash in the hands of urban citizens, thus invigorating the general economy.[7] The introduction of the reforms has not been smooth even in the more open cities such as Shenzhen and Guangzhou because it requires commensurate changes in the financial sector, the labour policy, the legal system, the political ideology and people's attitude. The reform measures introduced in Guangdong can be broadly classified into those related to production, consumption and allocation.

Production Reforms

Production reforms in Guangdong have primarily been involving the scale, structure and finance of production. In terms of scale, various levels of government in Guangdong have recently made a commitment to reduce the size of housing units in order to adjust to the affordability of both producers and consumers. For instance, the Shenzhen government was able to reduce the municipality's average flat size from 86 sq m in 1986 to 70 sq m in 1992. Another new trend of production is, as previously discussed, the construction of housing districts provided with more community facilities.

The major reform in the production structure is the increasing emphasis given to development companies. These companies operate under the auspices of the Ministry of Construction but are given a relatively high degree of financial autonomy. They lease land from the local governments by tender, auction, or negotiation. Land cost and other production costs are fully accounted for in the final housing price or rent which also includes a market profit margin. These companies were subject to profit tax in some cities and the appropriation of the profit with the government. However, they were free to allocate the net income for re-investment, staff bonuses or staff welfares.[8] In Shenzhen, for instance, the annual net income kept by the development companies in the years between 1989 and 1992 ranged from 36% to 96% of the gross profit.[9] Hence, the staff are made more conscious of the performance of the companies, and hence more demand-driven and efficient methods of housing production.

Houses built by these companies are mainly sold or rented to work units or enterprises not entitled to direct allocation from the government. Previously, these work units had to either directly build or supervise building projects in order to provide housing for their staff. Production efficiency was thus hampered as these enterprises had neither comparative advantage nor expertise in construction. The rapid growth of development companies, undeniably induced by the prospective profits and financial autonomy, has helped to redress the anomaly. In 1993, the investment and floor area output of the development companies dominated the housing sector, accounting for 95% and 84% of the respective municipal total.[10]

With regard to the provision of public housing, i.e. housing directly allocated by the housing bureaux or employers within the government bureaucracy, several new methods have recently been introduced. For instance, eligible work units in need of housing can request the housing bureaux to build houses for their staff if they raise sufficient construction funds. Upon completion of the project, housing is sold to the employees by their employers at full cost. As well, in cities such as Shenzhen and Guangzhou, the housing bureau sub-contracts building projects to development companies. In Guangzhou, individuals and work units can collaborate between and among themselves to finance housing projects. These new production methods in fact help to diversify the sources of production finance, which is indeed pivotal to the whole housing reform.

In view of the shortage in production finance, it is primarily important to allow more capital to fund housing projects. A radical approach is the permission for foreign capital to collaborate with development companies to provide market housing for domestic and overseas buyers. The most significant reform measure introduced, however, is the release of rental housing for purchase at sub-cost level, full cost level and market price level. The availability of *existing* housing for sale is particularly significant as not only does it release the government and the employing enterprises from maintenance burdens, it also turns dead money to active capital for future housing re-investment. To a lesser extent, the raising of the rents to sub-cost and full-cost levels also helps to increase income for housing providers. Hence, it is the commodification of housing and the availability of existing housing for sale that constitutes a new source of construction capital. Similar pricing and tenure reforms introduced to *newly completed* housing stock further facilitate the creation of a sustainable financial flow.

Another measure is the stipulation for housing tenants to pay a certain amount of rental deposits, ranging from RMB20 to RMB80 per sq m of living area. When the tenancy terminates, the principal and interest of the deposit will be refunded. This measure not only guarantees some maintenance funds, it also helps to raise the housing capital stock as tenancy tends to go on for a long time, if not a life time, in China. Similarly, the institution of a housing provident fund (discussed later) increases the revenue for housing construction.

Nonetheless, while the reforms raise construction funds, they also incur extra spending because the state and the work units need to provide a housing allowance to the staff and workers in order that they can afford the increased rentals and the housing price. Although there are controls on the total amount of allowance to be given (e.g. not to exceed 25% of the total basic wage payment in the case of Shenzhen), the government estimates that if the total housing stock is only commodified for renting, extra spending would be incurred. This would be due to exemption of rental increase in compassionate cases, the compulsory provision of housing allowance to all including house owners in some cities, and the decrease in profit tax from enterprises which deem the housing allowance provided to the staff as running costs of the enterprises. However, the government would have an additional income if all housing stocks were sold. This extra income would be created owing to the need of the buyers to use their own savings and monthly wages, in addition to the housing allowance, to pay off the housing price. Hence, the government regards it as expedient to emphasize home ownership in order to tap a genuine additional production fund. Consumption reforms have therefore been concurrently introduced to promote home purchase.

Consumption Reforms

The consumption reforms mainly aim at stimulating the incentive to buy by raising affordability and the willingness to buy. These include boosting purchasing power, instituting affordable payment methods and granting price concessions. Other important measures such as the enactment of property rights laws have also been introduced. Disincentives against over-consumption and speculation are also enacted as a corollary. The increase in purchasing power, however, is fundamental to the promotion of home ownership.

The basic means of raising the purchasing power of households in the initial years of the housing reform was to provide a housing allowance to employees in addition to their basic wages. This policy has in fact changed the housing component of the workers' remuneration packages from that of wages-in-kind to wages-in-cash. A survey in Shenzhen showed that the housing allowance had diminished the real rental increase to RMB20–30 which was considered to be acceptable.[11] In the case of home purchase, the net average monthly mortgage repayment ranged between RMB40 and RMB60 which was also regarded as within the affordability limit of the households.[12] Usually, if there was a surplus after paying for housing, the payees are free to use it for other consumption.

Another measure to boost affordability in the long term is the stipulation of a housing provident fund. Drawing on the spirit of the Central Provident Fund system of Singapore, the government requires employees and employers alike to contribute a certain proportion (currently 5% and expected to increase to 15% by the year 2000) of the gross wages to a fund designated for housing expenditure only. The fund is kept on individual accounts and is usable for home purchase, house building, and renting and renovation of private houses.

Other measures in boosting the incentive to buy are the introduction of affordable payment methods and the granting of price discounts. Payment by instalment in a maximum period of ten to fifteen years is usually permitted. Only a downpayment equivalent to 10% of the housing price is normally required and the monthly interest rate is fixed at 2% to 6% which is lower than the borrowing rate. A further price concession of 5% to 10% is granted if the housing price is paid off within five years. Another measure to quicken housing sale is the provision to increase the annual depreciation rate from 2% to 3% in the price determination of the existing housing stock if the purchase is conducted within a short period (e.g., one year) after the implementation of the reform programme.

Similarly, mortgage loans are available for the purchase of all other types of housing in Shenzhen and Guangzhou. Unlike the case in market economies, the terms of the mortgage loans extended by the banks are defined by the municipal government. As such, the repayment period, the downpayment requirement and the interest rate are similar to those of the instalment payment method.

Apart from improving affordability, the ensuring of property rights by law, the deliberate effort of the government to publicize the commodification ideology, and the escalating housing price implying a good profit prospect before mid-1993, have all helped to heighten the incentive to purchase housing property. Hence, the government needs to provide disincentives against over-consumption and speculation. One of the measures is the stipulation of price indices based on flat size. Shenzhen and Guangzhou have introduced an index system for newly-completed flats and it is applicable to all buyers regardless of rank at work. In Shenzhen, incremental indices are imposed on flats which are larger than the standard size of 65 sq m. For housing already occupied, these pricing indices do not apply but sitting tenants, when purchasing the existing units, would need to pay additional charges for the portion exceeding their entitlement according to their ranks at work. Resale restrictions, in contrast, are equally applied to newly completed and old housing stock. Owners of subsidized housing can only resell their housing units to the housing authority or their employers before the expiry of the resale restriction period (which is five years in Guangzhou), and they are not entitled to any repurchase of subsidized housing.[13] These restrictions are intended to deter speculation and to restrict the provision of a housing subsidy to those specified by government. Reforms in housing allocation have also enabled housing subsidies to be more cost-effective.

Allocation Reforms

The most significant reform introduced in allocation is certainly the establishment of a market pricing mechanism. In the past, all housing was allocated purely by administrative means. Alongside with the commodification process, the new rental and pricing methods exert a sorting out effect on the allocation priority and standard. The pricing indices and the additional charges levied on the ultra-standard housing area for both renting and purchase have effectively injected an economic element in the allocation of housing.

The economic element in public housing is, however, not quite a market factor as it is introduced administratively to deter over-consumption rather than being a direct outcome of the interplay of housing supply and demand. The market effect is nonetheless much more conspicuous in the pricing of flats supplied by development companies. Although the government, such as in the case of Guangzhou before 1992, only permitted a maximum profit margin of 8%, the disguised real profit always goes far beyond it.[14] In effect, a housing market led by the interplay of supply and demand has been in operation in urban Guangdong since the mid-1980s. Owing to various factors discussed later, the housing market situation was tight in the early 1990s, leading to phenomenal rises in prices.

As market housing becomes more expensive and hence unaffordable to individuals and work units, local governments have to provide fully or partially subsidized housing to work units which are not eligible for public housing. The new housing schemes of "small-profit housing" and "comfortable housing programme" have thus emerged since 1992. These types of housing are sold below the market price but cover full production costs. As the eligibility is usually limited to non-profit making and self-financing work units or enterprises patronized by the government, and the pricing is somewhat pegged to market prices, they represent a new allocation method based on a combination of administrative means, market forces and affordability. Hence, a more sophisticated allocation mechanism has been developed in Guangdong.

Thus, housing reforms in Guangdong have emphasized the reduction of government subsidy, the introduction of a market mechanism and the promotion of home ownership. Guangdong's Implementation Opinion on the State Council's Decision on the Deepening of Urban Housing System Reform announced in June 1995 intensifies the reform and re-confirmed the above reform direction. It extends the housing provident fund to all work units, requires all housing to be sold at full-cost price, and escalates rental increase aiming to achieve a rent-to-income ratio of 15% by the year 2000.[15]

The progress and performance of the housing reforms and the newly emerged housing market, however, vary in different cities and in Guangdong. Shenzhen has been by far in the lead, followed by Guangzhou and Zhuhai. The following will attempt to provide a preliminary examination of the recent housing developments taking place in these three cities.

Housing Reforms and Housing Markets in Shenzhen, Guangzhou and Zhuhai

Housing Reforms

As shown in Table 13.9, housing reform programmes were first introduced in the public housing sector in Shenzhen in June 1988, followed by Guangzhou in October 1989, and Zhuhai in April 1992. In 1992, the approximate proportions of the total housing stock in the public sector in Shenzhen and Guangzhou are 45% and 70%, respectively. By August

Table 13.9 Housing Reforms in Shenzhen, Guangzhou and Zhuhai

	Shenzhen	Guangzhou	Zhuhai
Commencement date	June 1988	October 1989	April 1992
Production reforms			
Reduction of flat size	✓	✓	✓
Construction of living districts	✓	✓	✓
Growth of development companies	✓	✓	✓
Collaboration between housing bureaux, work units and individuals	✓	✓	✗
Sale of existing housing	✓	✓	✓
Sale of new housing	✓	✓	✓
Commodification of rent	✓	✓	✗
Rental deposit	✗	✓	✗
Small-profit housing/comfortable housing programme	✓	✓	✓
Consumption reforms			
Housing allowance	✓	✗	✗
Payment by instalment	✓	✓	✓
Mortgage loans	✓	✓	✗
Price discounts	✓	✓	✓
Price and rental indices	✓	✓	✗
Housing superannuation scheme	✓	✓	✓
Resale restrictions	✓	✓	✓
Allocation reforms			
Market pricing mechanism	✓	✓	✓
Others			
Property laws	✓	✓	✓

Notes: The symbol ✓ represents the practice of a particular reform measure in the respective city; the symbol ✗ represents restricted implementation of the specified reform measure; and the symbol ✗ represents the non-existence of the particular reform measure.

1991, the reform policy had been implemented over 75% of Shenzhen's public housing stock which was subject to the reform scheme. Home ownership rate reached 68% in Shenzhen in 1993, and 82% in Zhuhai in 1994.[16]

There are more common features between Shenzhen and Guangzhou than between Zhuhai and the other two cities. Some major differences do exist between Shenzhen and Guangzhou, however. In rental commodification, Shenzhen raised the old rent to the sub-cost level (RMB2.6 per sq m) at the onset of the reform programme, whereas Guangzhou only began with RMB0.27 per sq m in 1989, and raised it to RMB0.5 per sq m in June 1992, and is scheduled to achieve the sub-cost level (RMB2.93 per sq m) by 1997. Reportedly, rental commodification in Zhuhai was not strictly implemented.[17] Furthermore, the institution of rental deposits for new tenancies and a housing provident fund (5% contribution from employers and employees) had only been introduced in Guangzhou by 1992, while small profit housing was only supplied in Shenzhen. However, both measures are now in operation in the two cities.

A major difference also lies in the provision of housing allowance. The Shenzhen government grants housing allowance to all income earners, fixed at 48% (increased to 56% in 1993) of the difference between the gross wages and basic living costs. In contrast, Guangzhou has stopped the payment of housing allowance altogether since June 1992. Prior to that, housing allowance was fixed at 40% of the rental paid by the households. When the rental was raised from RMB0.27 per sq m to RMB0.5 per sq m in June 1992, the government reviewed the affordability of the tenants and considered that the new rent was, in fact, set within the affordability limit of the tenants given their wage levels. Hence the provision of a housing allowance was removed. The abolition was sustained when the rental was increased to RMB1.0 per sq m in July 1995. Similar to the rental reform, the provision of a housing allowance has not been strictly implemented in Zhuhai.[18]

Finally, in the sale of existing housing to sitting tenants, seniority and rank of the tenants at work are major factors in the determination of housing price in Guangzhou and Zhuhai. However, they are not taken into account in the case of Shenzhen. The progress of housing sale also differs. A total of 68,249 units was sold by the end of 1993 in the Shenzhen Special Economic Zone, creating a revenue of RMB1.7 billion[19] (excluding payment in later instalments). In Guangzhou, a total of 203,500 units had been sold by the end of 1994, creating a total revenue of RMB1.706

billion[20] (again, excluding payment in later instalments). It was noted that 67% of the sales before November 1992 took place in 1992 following Deng Xiaoping's tour to the south earlier in the year. The visit should have exerted a similar impact in Shenzhen.

It can be inferred from the above that the average housing price per unit was RMB25,115 in Shenzhen and only RMB8,383 in Guangzhou, without accounting the inflation factor over time. In fact, the sale price was fixed at the sub-cost level of RMB490 per sq m in Shenzhen in 1992 but the price is set below the sub-cost level of RMB260 per sq m in Guangzhou. In some cases, senior cadres or staff could purchase their existing housing units at prices as low as RMB150 per sq m in 1992.[21]

Thus, a higher level of commodification and privatization has been achieved in Shenzhen than in Guangzhou. The continual provision of housing allowance in Shenzhen has nevertheless mitigated the financial gain of the reform. Given the higher sale price and the higher level of home ownership, it seems that Shenzhen, being more affluent, is closer to achieving the goals of the housing reform. The goals are, namely, to create a sustainable financial flow in housing so that more capital is made available for relieving the housing shortage problem. The provision of market housing by development companies is yet another important source to resolve the housing problem.

Housing Markets[22]

The housing market, which was first conceived in Guangdong, was triggered off by land reforms and public housing reforms introduced in the early 1980s. Land fees were first charged in Shenzhen according to a geographical scale in 1982, aiming at creating new capital for infrastructural development. Guangzhou followed suit in 1984. Tender and bidding were then introduced in Shenzhen in 1987 for the lease of land. Subsequently, China passed a series of land laws between 1988 and 1992 to legalize the purchase, sale and resale of land. Thus, a land market was being formed and it has led to the commodification of housing and the formation of housing markets in China.[23]

As the strategy for housing reforms in the public sector was commodification highlighting owner occupation, it has facilitated the commercial operation of development companies. Work units which purchase accommodation from the development companies for their staff are encouraged by the government to adopt similar commodification and home ownership policies in housing allocation. Given the continual economic development, the gradual enactment of property laws protecting property rights of both individuals and collective owners and permitting free trading of properties, and in view of the escalating housing prices signalling good investment prospects, the demands of market housing from work units and individuals increase rapidly, creating tight market conditions in the early 1990s. The permission for foreign investment to participate in the property markets for both internal and external buyers has further fuelled the booming property market.

Since their operation in the late 1980s, housing markets proliferated most rapidly first in southern China and later in Shanghai. In southern China, development has concentrated in Guangdong. It was reported that in 1991 alone, 7,286,500 sq m of market housing was completed and 79% was sold in the same year.[24] Within the province, property development is most rapid in Shenzhen, followed by Guangzhou and other major urban areas in the Pearl River Delta, such as Zhuhai, Huizhou, Zhongshan, Dongguan and Foshan.[25] Reportedly, all existing housing stock in Shenzhen and Guangzhou had been sold by April 1992 and the purchase of properties still under construction had been very competitive.[26] Resale markets have also been established in Shenzhen and Guangzhou, although the scale of operation is greater in the former.

Table 13.10 shows that except in 1989 and 1990 when the democratic movements exerted an adverse effect on the housing market, housing production and consumption in Shenzhen had been on the rise. The gross housing price and rent increased continually between 1986 and 1993, at the average rates of 32% and 20%, respectively. Due to the overspill effect from the Hong Kong property market in 1991 and Deng Xiaoping's tour to the south in early 1992, housing prices have doubled between the two years, ranging from RMB4,500 to RMB10,000 per sq m.[27] In an attempt to deflate the housing price, the Shenzhen government increases land supply and imposes capital gains tax. Furthermore, the government has stipulated that developers cannot apply to presell the housing units until one-quarter of the development project in terms of investment value has been completed.

Similarly, the Guangzhou government has also attempted to exercise control on the overheated housing market. Between 1989 and 1991 the government imposed controls on rent levels, sale price and the profit rate (8%) of development companies. However, the real transaction price, part of which was paid unofficially, was as high as five times the stipulated

Table 13.10 Housing Market Conditions in Shenzhen Municipality, 1986–1993

Year	Total housing stock ('000 m²)	Housing produc-tion ('000 m²)	Housing consump-tion ('000 m²)	Vacancy ('000 m²)	Vacancy rate (%)	Average price[a] (RMB/m²)	Average rent[a] (RMB/m²)
1986	3,361	974	453	175	5.2	1,068	16
1987	4,209	848	733	261	6.2	1,373	20
1988	5,497	1,288	1,082	135	2.5	1,678	22
1989	6,702	1,205	593	187	2.8	2,401	24
1990	7,510	808	546	188	2.5	3,264	27
1991	8,422	912	971	126	1.5	4,482	32
1992	9,782	1,360	1,158	n.a.	n.a.	6,822	49
1993	11,750	1,968	1,408	n.a.	n.a.	7,175	51

Sources: *Shenzhen fangdichan nianjian 1992*, p. 49 and *Shenzhen fangdichan nianjian 1994*, pp. 62, 83, 86 and 93.

Note: [a] Shenzhen Special Economic Zone only.

price.[28] The profit rate control was therefore removed in 1992. The average housing price in Guangzhou as a result skyrocketed from RMB800 per sq m in 1988 to RMB5,000–6,000 per sq m in November 1992. The Guangzhou government also prohibited commercial transaction of housing units which were still under construction, but sale and purchase still took place in the disguise of free gift.[29]

The housing markets in both Shenzhen and Guangzhou have, however, entered a bust period since mid-1993. Several reasons are accountable for the downturn. One of them is the over supply resulted from the completion of development projects commenced in previous years. Another is the unrealistically high price relative to income. The price-to-income ratios were found to be as high as 27 to 41. Work units obliged to provide housing to their staff also found the price unaffordable.[30] The main reason for the bust conditions is nevertheless the tightening of control by the Central Government in the aspects of finance provision for both consumption and production, property production mix, land supply and market regulation and management.[31] It is reported that vacancy has been escalating fast in Shenzhen: 1 million sq m in 1993, 3 million in 1994 and 4.5 million in 1995. The capital trapped in the vacant stock was estimated to be RMB50 billion.[32] Thus governments of both cities faced a different challenge in the past three years: how to tackle the problems ensued by a declining market. The measures subsequently introduced are, for example, institution of mortgage loans for local purchasers in Guangzhou, and permitting the resale of pre-completed units and the sale of the original internally consumed housing to external buyers in Shenzhen.[33] The most important solution which has a long lasting effect is, nevertheless, the enactment of essential legislations and the establishment of enforcing organizations to protect property rights and to legalize property transactions.[34]

Conclusion — A Preliminary Evaluation

It is undeniable that housing conditions in Guangdong have improved significantly since 1978, as reflected in the space standards and the provision of facilities and services. However, it has been argued that housing resources have not been efficiently utilized and hence the housing shortage problem is not effectively resolved. Thus, housing reforms in Guangdong emphasize the minimization of government subsidy, the commodification of the housing sector and the promotion of home ownership. Thus, on the productive side, development companies are allowed to multiply to dominate housing production. Flexible means are also devised by the government to collaborate with individuals, work units and development companies to expand the production of affordable housing. Additional production capital is also sought by introducing foreign capital, raising rents and selling the housing stock. These measures have undoubtedly raised the efficiency of the housing system in that resources are tapped additionally and they are more fully utilized, maintaining a higher rate of return. However, the effectiveness of these measures to create extra revenue is hampered by the affordability problem in two aspects. First, the need to provide housing allowance to residents has nullified or mitigated the financial gain generated by the commodification policy, unless the housing stock was dominantly sold. Second, the soaring price has rendered market housing unaffordable to many. The small-profit housing scheme introduced in Shenzhen and the comfortable housing programme in other cities at a later date, is yet to be expanded pending the amount of production resources manipulatable by the government.

On the consumptive side, the provision of housing allowances in cash, the institution of the housing provident fund and mortgage loans, and the payment of housing price by instalment are effective or potentially effective measures to promote affordable home ownership. They are also efficient in channelling household savings to the housing sector and transforming the household consumption pattern in favour of housing expenditure. Further, the indexing of rent and housing price are effective economic means to reduce wastage in the housing system.

The switch to the pricing mechanism as the major allocation method is certainly an efficient means to utilize housing resources and to minimize government subsidy. However, similar to and associated with the production reforms, it also faces affordability hurdles. Hence, it seems that on the whole, housing reforms in Guangdong, spearheaded by Shenzhen, are able to significantly enhance the efficiency of the housing system but their effectiveness is hindered by affordability. While the expansion of low cost housing schemes is the most plausible solution, it may also be necessary for the government to devise effective measures to regulate housing prices at an affordable level. If the Guangdong government has succeeded in establishing housing markets in the 1980s, and improving the legal environment in the early 1990s, their major task in the second half of the 1990s will be to institute appropriate intervention in the market to ensure that housing provision is affordable to work units and households.

Notes

1. The sampling methods used in the surveys are not delineated in the yearbooks. It is therefore impossible to estimate the accuracy and representativeness of the surveys. The results are hence regarded as only indicative of general housing conditions.

2. Living area is conventionally used as the measurement of housing area and is defined as the internal floor area of bedrooms and sitting rooms inside a dwelling unit. Kitchens, toilets and corridors are excluded. When included, it is termed as usage area.

3. Guangdong nianjian bianzuan weiyuanhui (ed.), *Guangdong nianjian 1991* (Guangdong Yearbook 1991) (Guangzhou: Guangdong renmin chubanshe, 1991), pp. 402–5.

4. Guangdongsheng tongjiju (ed.), *Guangdong tongji nianjian 1995* (Statistical Yearbook of Guangdong 1995) (Beijing: Zhongguo tongji chubanshe, 1995), pp. 126–29.

5. *Guangdong nianjian 1992* (see note 3), p. 62. The statistics are not updated in the later issues of the *Guangdong tongji nianjian*.

6. The term "housing reforms" in Chinese literature refers to reforms in the public housing sector only. It is, however, used in this chapter to include new policies and practices in non-public sector housing.

7. *Beijing Review*, 1–7 July 1991.

8. Fieldwork in Shenzhen, July 1992.

9. Shenzhen fangdichan nianjian bianji weiyuanhui (ed.), *Shenzhen fangdichan nianjian 1994* (Yearbook of Shenzhen Real Estate 1994) (Beijing: Renmin chubanshe, 1994), p. 62.

10. Rebecca L. H. Chiu, "Commodification in Guangzhou's Housing System: Analysis and Evaluation," *Third World Planning Review*, Vol. 17, No. 3 (1995), pp. 295–331.

11. Shenzhenshi zhufang zhidu gaige bangongshi (ed.), *Shenzhen jingji tequ zhufang zhidu gaige* (Housing System Reform in Shenzhen Special Economic Zone) (Shenzhen: Haitian chubanshe, 1992).

12. Ibid.

13. *Shenzhen fangdichan nianjian 1994* (see note 9) and fieldwork in Guangzhou, November 1992.

14. *Yangcheng wanbao* (Guangzhou), 3 August 1992.

15. *Ming Pao Daily News*, 10 June 1995.

16. See note 11, p. 149; Shenzhen jingji tequ nianjian bianji weiyuanhui (ed.), *Shenzhen jingji tequ nianjian 1994* (Shenzhen Special Economic Zone Yearbook 1994) (Shenzhen: Shenzhen tequ nianjianshe, 1994), p. 515; Zhuhaishi tongjiju (ed.), *Zhuhai tongji nianjian 1995* (Zhuhai Statistical Yearbook 1995) (Beijing: Zhongguo tongji chubanshe, 1995), p. 331.

17. Fieldwork in Zhuhai and Guangzhou, October and November 1992.

18. Ibid; *Zhuhai tequ bao*, 4 October 1994; and *Xinxi shibao*, 17 November 1994.

19. *Shenzhen jingji tequ nianjian 1994* (see note 16), p. 517.

20. Guangzhou nianjian bianzuan weiyuanhui (ed.), *Guangzhou nianjian 1995* (Guangzhou Yearbook 1995) (Guangzhou: Guangzhou nianjianshe, 1995), p. 162.

21. Fieldwork in Zhuhai and Guangzhou, October and November 1992.

22. The foreign segment of the housing market *per se* is not a subject for discussion for the purposes of this chapter. Nevertheless, its impacts on the domestic housing market are referred to.

23. Zhou Zhiping et al., *Zhongguo fangdichanye toushi* (Thorough Examination of China's Real Estate Development) (Hong Kong: Joint Publishing Company Limited, 1992), pp. 1–30.

24. *Guangzhou ribao*, 27 July 1992.

25. Although no official statistics are available, it is generally estimated that more than 50% of the new housing stock in these municipalities have been purchased by Hong Kong investors for speculation. Fieldwork in Zhuhai and the Pearl River Delta, October 1992 and January 1993.

26. *Guangzhou ribao*, 27 July 1992.

27. *Ming Pao Daily News*, 14 June 1992 and fieldwork in Shenzhen, July 1992.

28. *Ming Pao Daily News*, 6 October 1992.

29. Ibid.

30. Rebecca L. H. Chiu, "Housing Affordability in Shenzhen Special Economic Zone: A Forerunner of China's Housing Reform," *Housing Studies*, Vol. 11, No. 4 (1996), pp. 561–80.

31. *Shenzhen fangdichan nianjian 1994* (see note 9), p. 137.

32. *Ming Pao Daily News*, 29 April 1995.

33. *Shenzhen jingji tequ nianjian 1995* (see note 16), p. 256; and *Ming Pao Daily News*, 8 November 1995.

34. See note 10; and *Ming Pao Daily News*, 27 May 1995.

14

Transport and Communication

Luk Chiu-ming

This chapter is devoted to an analysis of the development of transport and communication of contemporary Guangdong. In addition, explanations of such developments and future forecasts will be offered.

Role of Transport and Communication in Economic Development

In considering the economic development of a region, two dimensions could be used. One is a vertical dimension which involves matters dealing with the economic structure of that region. Hence, organizational matters and economic policies have to be considered. Another dimension is a horizontal one which is concerned mainly with the distribution and circulation of economic production over space. Transport and communication are associated with the latter dimension which has a distinctive geographic expression. This will be the approach taken in this chapter.

Before moving further into the more theoretical aspects of the subject, a note of definition is in order. The twin terms "transport and communication" are, strictly speaking, two sides of one coin. They are component parts of discussions on transport studies under the general umbrella of economic geography. However, transport and communication are somewhat different. "Transport" in its conventional sense deals primarily with the actual transshipment of goods, services or people over land, on water, or in the air. It actually involves some sort of carrier. On the other hand, the term "communication" has a much wider meaning. It is usually concerned with the transmission of ideas over distant areas by means of specific networks in different forms. Examples may include postal service, fax, television, radio, etc. It is characterized by a large physical separation between the origin and destination of information transmitted. Hence, some may even equate "communication" with "telecommunications," although the latter has largely computer-related connotations.

At a general level, agricultural and industrial societies rely heavily on transport as a means to deliver goods, services and people over space. As one enters a post-industrial phase, the topic of communication begins to attract much wider attention. Nevertheless, the distinction is not always that clear-cut. As technology diffuses from developed to developing countries, communication development may coexist with transport development. The case of Guangdong province is one good example.

One general theme that transport and communication share is the result of space and time collapse with their development.[1] This promotes integration, whether one uses the word in the economic, social or political sense, when they are pursued. In earlier literature, the role of transport in economic development can be summarized as being a "necessary but not sufficient" interactor with development.[2] In other words, transport improvement is no longer seen as a catalytic agent in regional development, but only one of the elements which is responsible for enabling economic development to move forward.[3] Nevertheless, if a basic transport infrastructure is not provided, it cannot be argued that the region in question is approaching a state of economic take-off. In a sense, therefore, basic transport provision (in particular road, rail and water transport) should be a primary concern for any development planner. On the other hand, air transport can be treated as an advanced type of transport in the priority order of attention.

Compared to transport, communication seems to assume a higher status in the economic development of a particular region. Within the various types of communication being used in this Guangdong case study, they can be subdivided into basic and advanced types, too. Postal service, radio broadcasting, and to a certain extent, television, are considered the very basics in a modern society. In the advanced category, facsimile transmission and pager service are included. The latter includes the necessities in service-oriented sectors of an economy. From this perspective, communication development will assume greater importance as the basic transport and communication pattern have materialized. Table 14.1 identifies the typology used as the conceptual framework for this chapter.

Table 14.1 Typology Used as the Conceptual Framework of This Study

	Sub-category	Importance in development
Transport	Road, rail, water	Basic to facilitate circulation of items
	Air	Advanced type for rapid and costly transshipment
Communication	Postal service, radio broadcast, television	Basic importance to transmit ideas over distant areas
	Facsimile transmission, pager service	Advanced setup for instant transmission of information

Guangdong's Transport and Communication

In this section, Guangdong's transport and communication development will be dealt with individually. For each of the two broad categories, there will be divisions according to the various types identified. Two notes of caution are provided here. For the sake of convenience, all discussions in this chapter with regard to Guangdong will exclude Hong Kong and Macau.[4] Also, the various transport and communication types identified here are dictated by information availability.[5]

Transport Development

Road Transport

As one type of land transport, road construction is heavily determined by favourable geographic characteristics[6] (e.g. presence of lowlands) as well as by the level of economic development. Hence, roads will avoid steep slopes and mountainous areas and they will be denser in areas which are more developed. One would then hazard a guess that roads are concentrated in the Pearl River Delta, where Guangzhou is the hub.

Such a description is only a superficial one. Road transport development is far more complex than expected. First, roads can be subdivided into a hierarchy of classes; and each class may show different patterns of distribution. Second, the debate on whether roads bring forth development or development leads to road construction is often regarded as a "chicken or egg" issue. Third, road construction under a socialist setting like China may carry connotations in addressing the issue of regional imbalance, as the following paragraphs show.

Figure 14.1 shows the road network of Guangdong in the early 1990s.[7] For the sake of simplicity, only tar-surfaced and unsurfaced trunk roads are shown. In fact, when looking at *Zhongguo fensheng gonglu jiaotong dituji*, where all road types are depicted, there is not much to say except that accessibility to all counties in Guangdong is guaranteed. However, Figure 14.1 effectively demonstrates the fact that trunk road development has reached all corners of Guangdong. Especially with regard to tar-surfaced roads, extensions from the hub at Guangzhou to the north, east and west can clearly be seen. This is particularly noteworthy when one discovers the long-time spatial imbalance in rail transport distribution.

Without doubt, the Guangdong authorities have been trying hard to increase road accessibility (even low grade ones) as a basic step in integrating all parts of the province into its jurisdiction. This has been the past strategy. Current strategy has already shifted in two ways. One is the intensive upgrade programmes of its road system. In the strictest sense, Figure 14.1 does not capture the most recent upgrades, in particular the upgrades towards tar-surfaced trunk roads. Areas that might have already finished such upgrades include the portions from Shenzhen to Guangzhou, Guangzhou to Huizhou, and to a certain extent, Shantou's road connection northwards to Meizhou. According to a recent report, the full Guangzhou–Shantou trunk road network has already been completed to the Fujian border, shortening the travel time to only ten hours instead of thirteen.[8]

Another noteworthy shift in road construction is the heavy emphasis placed on highways. Dating back to 1987, Gordon Wu of the Hopewell Holdings in Hong Kong reached an agreement with Guangdong to construct a super-highway which runs astride the Pearl River Delta and connects the twin Special Economic Zones of Shenzhen and Zhuhai with Guangzhou, the provincial capital. The map inset in Figure 14.1 shows the original idea which consists of three phases, with the first one being completed in late 1993. The intriguing issues involved in this HK$8 billion

Figure 14.1   Road Network as of Early 1990s

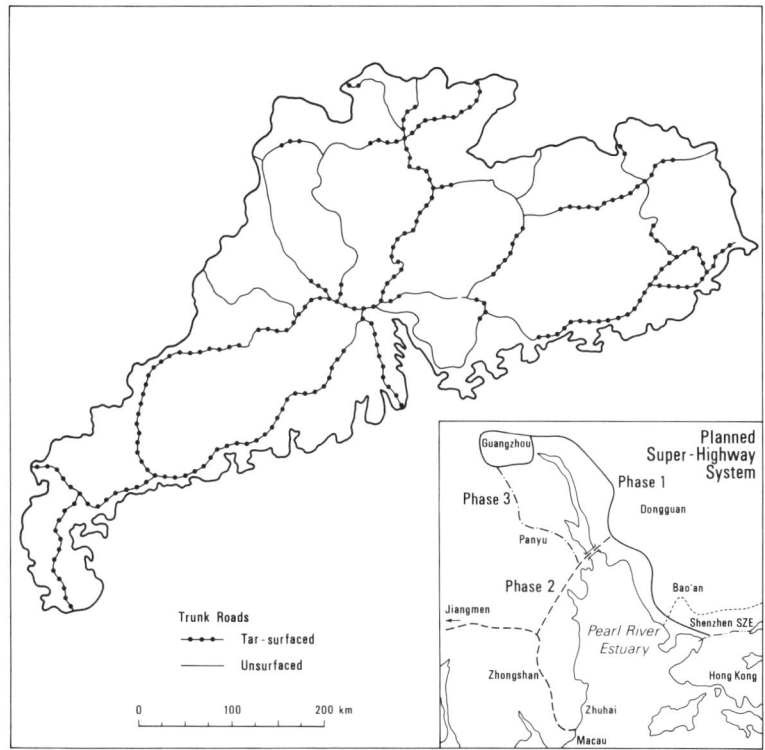

highway, being 302 km long with 6-lanes, are many. One possible explanation for its long delay may concern the tremendous difficulties in resumption of land along its way. Another could be a concern over insufficient demand to generate profits given the competition posed by other highways already under construction by other local authorities. Intense negotiations delay things even further. As reported in the local media, there is unease between the Guangdong authorities and the Hopewell Holdings over the long delay, and one indication of such unhappiness is the decision by Guangdong to construct a similar highway on its own that basically resembles the road plans in Phase 2 of the project.[9]

Guangdong's active plans in highway construction are crystal clear. Economic considerations are of utmost concern. The Pearl River Delta has already emerged as China's fastest growing economic region. Its further development has to be supported by a more efficient road system that ensures greater speed flows. So, trunk roads are no longer sufficient. Uninterrupted highways are needed to meet economic needs. By the end of 1995, Guangdong already possessed 84,563 km of highways. Major highways connect the following sets of cities: Shenzhen–Shantou, Foshan–Kaiping, Guangzhou–Shaoguan, Guangzhou–Zhaoqing, Guangzhou–Huizhou, etc.[10]

Rail Transport

Rail transport is distinctive in providing long-distance transfer of bulky goods or people in a relatively cheap way. However, it is constrained by topography. Nevertheless, rail construction is often regarded as an indicator of basic transport provision for interaction among areas beyond one's territory.

Figure 14.2 gives a picture of the rail network as of the mid-1990s.[11] If one is to concentrate on the existing rail system, two points stand out. One is the north–south running of the trunk route, which connects South China with its northern counterpart. To be specific, it constitutes the Beijing–Guangzhou rail, the main artery of north–south movement. For long periods of time since 1949, Guangdong only had this north–south route plus its westward extension to Sanshui. Up to the present moment, extensions from this trunk begin to bear fruit. To the west, the "terminus" has reached Yunfu; to the east, the rail service has extended to Huizhou[12] in 1992. The rail was further extended eastwards as the Guangzhou–Meizhou–Shantou line, constructed through the raise of bonds instead of

Figure 14.2 Rail Network in Guangdong, c.1995

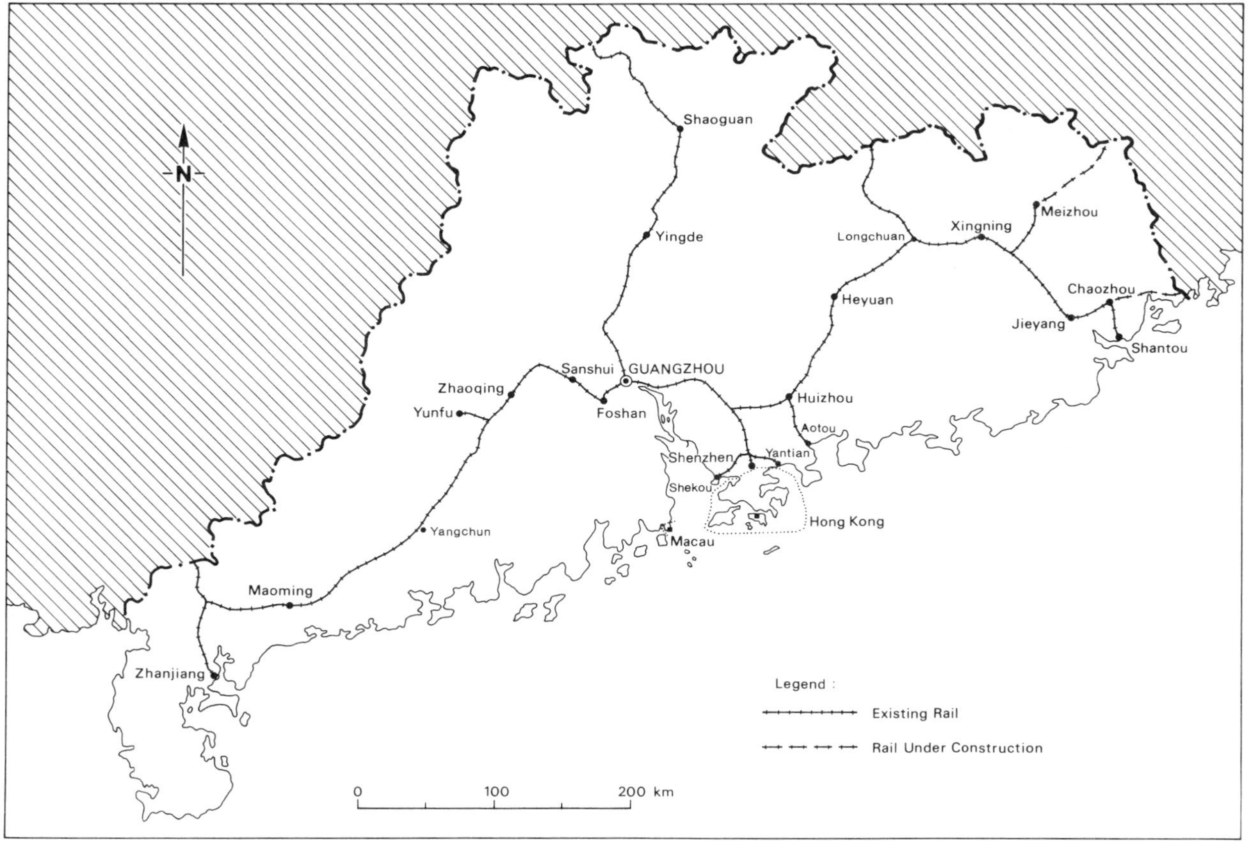

Legend :

Existing Rail

Rail Under Construction

N

0   100   200 km

Shantou

Chaozhou

Meizhou

Jieyang

Xingning

Longchuan

Heyuan

Huizhou

Aotou

Yantian

Hong Kong

Shenzhen

Shekou

Macau

Shaoguan

Yingde

Sanshui GUANGZHOU

Foshan

Zhaoqing

Yunfu

Yangchun

Maoming

Zhanjiang

sheer provincial investments. One must also be aware of the northward rail extensions from Longchuan. This forms the portion of the 2,536 km Jingjiu railway that connects Beijing and Jiulong (i.e. Kowloon), officially opened in 1996. Henceforth, this eastern rail subsystem of Guangdong has far more significance in the economic development of the area than it should be. Plans have been laid to develop specialized food wholesaling depots along that route to assist the realization of a commercial corridor along this Guangdong portion of the Jingjiu railway.[13] Needless to elaborate much, Hong Kong is connected to Shenzhen and Guangzhou by rail too. The popular Guangzhou–Hong Kong through-train service is one of the most heavily patronized services.

The second point relates to the rail routes in the far west. Maoming and Zhanjiang are the two important economic centres in western Guangdong. That rail system is in fact the terminal portion of the Guangxi system. By looking at this subsystem alone, economic considerations are very clear. Zhanjiang performs the role of an outport for goods of southwest China to be shipped overseas. Maoming's importance is derived from its shalestones, giving some oil production. Refined oil products have to be shipped out cheaply; hence rail is the ideal choice.

Before the present rail system appeared, the unbalanced situation has been much criticized for a long time. During periods like the Chinese New Year, tens of thousands of Hong Kong people cross the border to visit their relatives in Guangdong. In the absence of rail connections to the east and west, natives from these parts of Guangdong have no choice but to make long-distance travel by buses. This may take up to twenty hours of travel one-way. For those who are from Meixian (the county where Meizhou lies), bus travel is even more tiresome. They have to first go eastwards to Shantou before turning northwards. With the gradual economic development in both the west and the east, such undeveloped rail service cannot be tolerated any more.

Several points can be made with respect to the construction of such new rail routes. Guangdong's determination to address the issue of spatial imbalance in rail coverage can be clearly seen. After the extension was completed, all parts of Guangdong are accessible by rail. This facilitates the mass transshipment of goods and people all around the province. Second, the western extension is particularly significant to southwest China's future. To people in that part of China, past rail connection had to go through Hunan before reaching Guangdong. This new route strengthens and increases their contacts with Guangdong, possibly resulting in a lasting impact if Guangdong still propels itself as the engine of economic growth in south China. From the perspective of Guangzhou, such an extension helps to extend its hinterland, giving it even more opportunities to be the economic capital of the south.

A third issue has to do with the eastern route. Meizhou, as an important source of overseas Chinese, generates many contacts, perhaps to a similar degree as Shantou on the coast. Hence the rail runs not directly along the coast, but first towards the northeast. This is chiefly driven by consideration of overseas connections. As the system completes itself, direct travel to Shantou may use the coastal highways while travellers to Meizhou can go by rail.

Water Transport

Water transport exhibits different degrees of importance with respect to different regions. Figure 14.3 shows the current water transport situation in Guangdong.[14] It is clear that water transport can be subdivided into two types. One is internal water transport on rivers which offer navigable waterways. The other is sea transport which operates with deep seaports on Guangdong's coast or along its large river tributaries.

For internal waterways to be of use in transporting goods, they must be navigable all year. This implies a copious riverflow and sufficient water depth along its way. Hence, only this type of river is shown. In principle, there are only two large river systems. The first is the Pearl River system, involving the Bei, the Xi, and the Dong rivers which converge around Guangzhou. In the map, the Pearl River system is a large cluster of rivers which comes close together at the centre. One should also note that the distributaries of the Pearl River at its estuary have always been important waterways for the transshipment of agricultural and other produce of the delta. The second system is the Han River system on the east. As expected, that system renders invaluable assistance to the rise of the Han River Delta, also supporting the growth and development of large cities like Chaozhou and Shantou.

There are few long navigable rivers in western Guangdong, due to the lower rainfall there. However, good seaports are not absent in that area. In general, one can identify ports in Guangdong to be river ports or seaports, with the latter being further subdivided according to functions: they could be ports primarily devoted to fishing, like Tangjiang and Dianbai on the west, Shanwei on the east, or those for overseas shipping purposes. In

Figure 14.3   Water and Air Transport in Guangdong

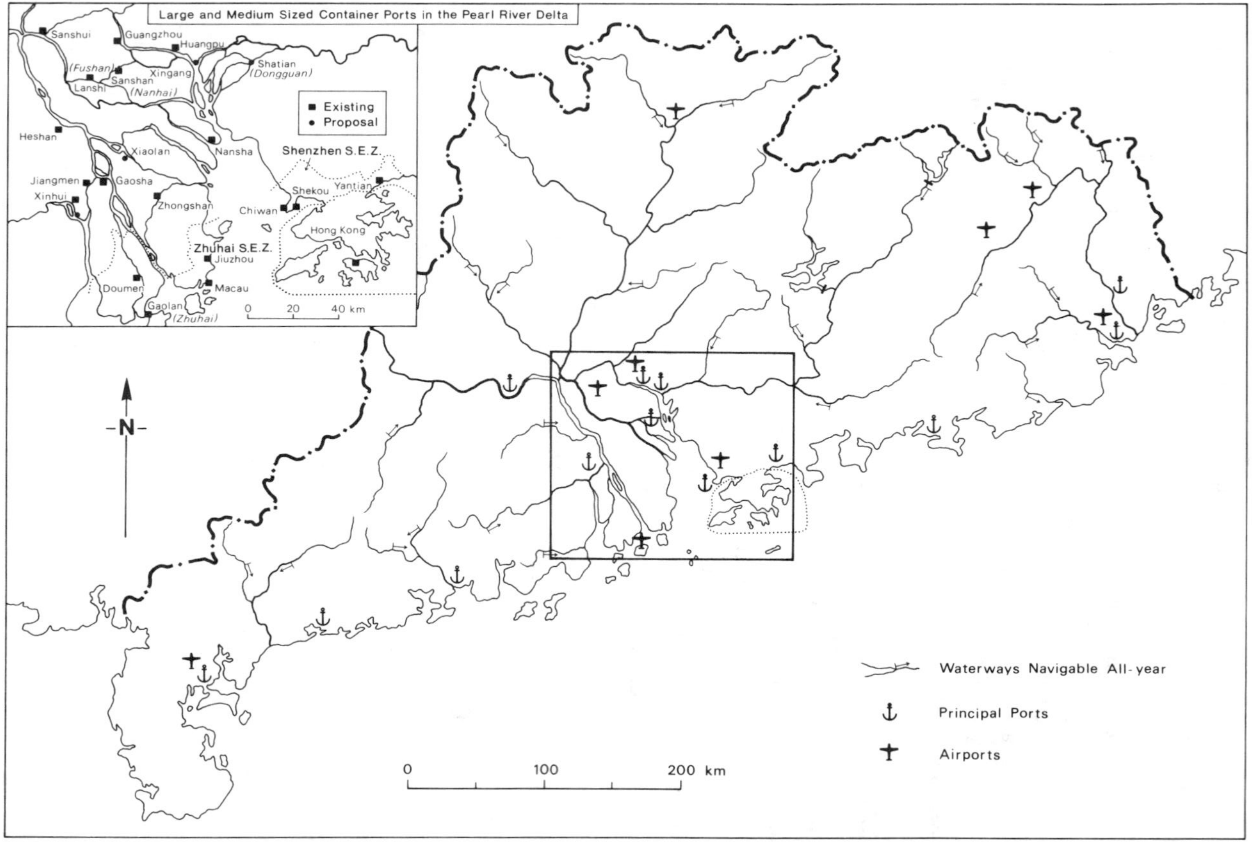

Large and Medium Sized Container Ports in the Pearl River Delta

Existing
Proposal

Shenzhen S.E.Z.

Zhuhai S.E.Z.

Sanshui
Guangzhou
Huangpu
(Fushan)
Sanshan
Xingang
(Nanhai)
Lanshi
Heshan
Xiaolan
Nansha
Shatian
(Dongguan)
Yantian
Shekou
Hong Kong
Chiwan
Zhongshan
Gaosha
Jiangmen
Jiuzhou
Macau
Xinhui
Doumen
Gaojian
(Zhuhai)

0   20   40 km

Waterways Navigable All-year

Principal Ports

Airports

N

0   100   200 km

terms of river ports, Zhaoqing on Xijiang, Rongqi and Jiangmen on the Pearl River, and Chaozhou on the Han River are more famous examples. Each is devoted to the handling of goods and passenger traffic which runs along its respective river system. Due to its location at the heart of the Pearl River Delta and its close proximity to Hong Kong, Rongqi has been rapidly developing as a passenger port for travellers going into the delta. This stimulates substantial development in its surrounding areas.

Guangdong's coastal location is not the only reason for the rise of its seaports. The other reason is the importance attached to overseas trade dating back to even the second century B.C. although the peak occurred during the Tang dynasty (A.D. 618–907). Currently, there are three clusters of seaports converging in the vicinity of Guangzhou (such as Huangpu and Nansha), Shenzhen (such as Shekou, Chiwan and Yantian) and Zhuhai (such as Jiuzhou and Gaolan), all located in the Pearl River Delta. Outside the Delta, more important seaports include Zhanjiang in the far west and Shantou in the far east.

During the open policy and reform period, the development of container ports, especially in the Pearl River Delta, has been phenomenal. Such growth was due to rapid growth of international trade (at the rate of around 15% per annum), which necessitates the efficient handling of goods via containerization. In the map inset of Figure 14.3, one can observe the dense clustering of large and medium container ports at the mouth of Pearl River. Usually, a container port is attached to an important city. For example, Jiangmen city itself is a port with Gaosha an additional container port to assist its development. For even larger municipalities, a cluster of container ports appear. A clear example is the set of three container ports located within the Shenzhen Special Economic Zone.

Air Transport

Air transport belongs to an "advanced" type of transport. Generally speaking, air transport is used to transfer selected types of goods which are costly and perishable. Another major use is for tourism which brings large economic benefits to the destination areas.

Figure 14.3 shows the system of airports in Guangdong. A total of eight can be identified. Without doubt, Guangzhou, the provincial capital, is not only the centre of aviation in Guangdong, but also the hub in south China. For a long period of time, Guangzhou's primacy was unchallenged. Any passenger who would fly elsewhere (within Guangdong or outside) must go through Guangzhou. In the years to come, Guangzhou likely remains one of the three national aviation hubs in China, after Beijing and Shanghai. Current plans for a new replacement airport for Guangzhou is underway. In 1991, Shenzhen's new airport started operation. It has direct flights to other parts of China, thus relieving much congestion in Guangzhou. By 1996, the newly operated Zhuhai international airport began to offer charter flights that serve overseas.

All other airports are "regional" ones within the area of Guangdong. In the west is Zhanjiang, the economic centre in that part of the province. In the north is Shaoguan. On the eastern coast is Shantou, where the third Special Economic Zone is located. These three airports serve principally their respective regions. One should also note the occurrence of two others in the northeast: Meizhou and Xinning. The predominance of overseas Chinese from the Meixian area explains the necessity for an airport there. On the other hand, the Xinning airport is somewhat difficult to justify.

Over the past few years, airport construction in the Pearl River Delta was a boom. The Zhuhai Special Economic Zone has its own international airport since Shenzhen has completed one. In terms of air transport infrastructure, brief mention is made here of the development of two other international airports in both Macau and Hong Kong. The former has started to offer scheduled flight services. The most well-known one is flights to Taiwan, offering a semi-direct link between both sides of the Taiwan Strait. The new Hong Kong airport will be operational by 1998, replacing the old Kai Tak Airport. Hence, within a diameter of some 50 km on the Pearl River estuary, there will be four international airports before the close of the twentieth century! It is not difficult to envisage a decrease in patronage for each airport, thus lowering their cost-efficiency. Also, the competition for air space within this small area, if improperly managed, could cause danger in air traffic. This will be likely to occur if the economy within the Pearl River Delta continues to prosper. Looked at from this perspective, it is an irony in planning for the delta.

Communication Development

Postal Service

As one type of communication, postal service is the most conventional and frequently used. Mail is sent out to destinations far away from the source. Hence, mail is an important means to send messages afar.

In China, the Ministry of Post and Communication is in charge of all matters with regard to postal service. While postal service is regarded as something commonplace in the West, Chinese data on this subject are highly lacking. Recently, some information on this subject began to be released so that some kind of analysis can be done.[15] However sketchy it may be, it represents the only available information.

Figure 14.4 shows express mail as an example of the extent of this service in Guangdong currently.[16] In this data source, delivery time is defined as the number of days needed to deliver mail among selected mail transfer offices. It is calculated from the *following day* after the letter has been deposited in the mail office (i.e. origin) until it is in the hands of the receivers (i.e. destination). In this example, there are altogether twelve offices to form the matrix of delivery times. Apparently, when origins and destinations are far away from these mail transfer offices, extra time should be added. Also, from the raw data matrix, entries in the lower and upper parts of the diagonal are not totally identical. Some hidden reasons must have existed which the publication cannot account for.

A cursory analysis of the three diagrams in Figure 14.4 clearly reveals the following. First of all, only a handful of large cities close to Guangzhou can enjoy the privilege of having a one-day service (aside from express mail delivery between points located in the same mail transfer office). In terms of physical straightline distance, Shenzhen is farthest away in that one-day service. Its status as a Special Economic Zone might explain why such a privilege exists. Second, a four-day delivery exists between Maoming and Shaoguan, probably due to the extremely tortuous transport connections between them.

Comparatively speaking, the two-day delivery is worth noting. While most connections make sense in terms of the duration required, quite a few others do not. These include connections between Meizhou and Shantou, Shenzhen and Huizhou, Jiangmen and Guangzhou, plus Zhanjiang and Maoming. Physical distances among them are relatively short, and yet they require the same two-day delivery time as between Zhanjiang and Guangzhou! This clearly shows an inconsistency, probably caused by differences in the development of fast and efficient transport connections.

A three-day delivery is by far the dominant pattern. Taking into consideration the size of Guangdong, this is understandable. However, from the perspective of express mail delivery, much improvement is anticipated.[17] For example, when more air and land transport is improved (with the addition of airports and highways), connection times should be shortened

Figure 14.4 Express Mail Delivery Time between Large Cities, 1992

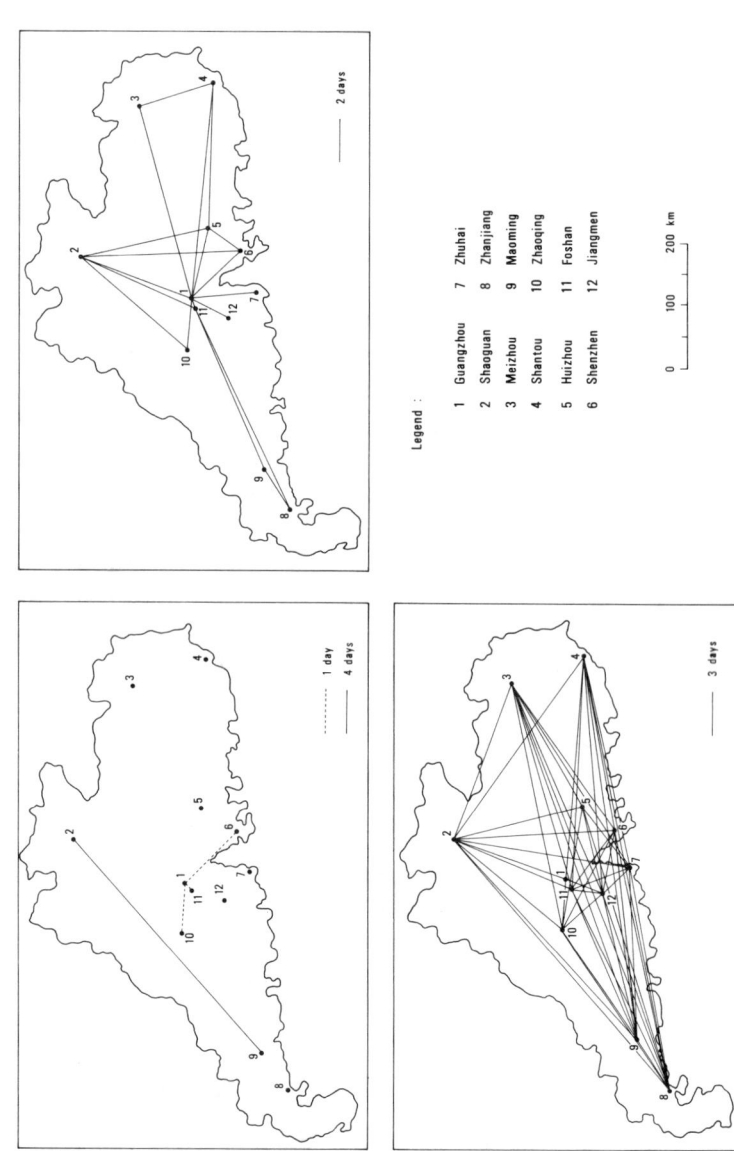

Legend :

1	Guangzhou	7	Zhuhai
2	Shaoguan	8	Zhanjiang
3	Meizhou	9	Maoming
4	Shantou	10	Zhaoqing
5	Huizhou	11	Foshan
6	Shenzhen	12	Jiangmen

—— 1 day
—— 4 days

—— 2 days

—— 3 days

0   100   200 km

within close proximity of such newly added items. Hence, it is logical to anticipate connection times within and between locations in the Pearl River Delta to be less than three days in the not-too-distant future.

Radio and Television Broadcasting

Broadcasting in the forms of radio and television is considered a basic communication medium in a modern society. In China, however, such a thing is considered to be quite sensitive, due to the fact that broadcasting, as one form of the media, has an important propaganda role for the Communist Party. Therefore, in the past, it was very difficult to gain access to related data and information with regard to Guangdong. Since 1978, information on broadcasting began to leak out from China. One important publication is *Zhongguo guangbo dianshi nianjian*.[18] Figure 14.5 shows data generated from the same source.

The primary objective in making Figure 14.5 is to show the extent of the spread of radio and television as forms of communication. Within a socialist setting like Guangdong, the role of disseminating Communist Party decisions and directives is paramount. While provincial set-ups can extend its coverage territory-wide, there is also a need to develop other subprovincial units to ensure effective communication between the government and the local people. Hence, the set-ups at the prefecture/city and county levels are also significant in how they reveal the importance attached to that area. In differentiating those set-ups between 1985 and 1989, one can observe the rapidity as well as any significant spatial preference or trend.

First of all, radio set-ups in 1985 were very much centred in large cities or important counties in the Pearl River Delta, plus in strategic points in the north, the west and the east. This was reasonable for effective control of the media in the early days. With regard to small set-ups, there were only a few in close proximity to those already in existence. Turning to those newly established set-ups in 1989, one observes an extension outwards from the Pearl River cluster. As a matter of fact, the expansion of radio at the county level was very rapid during the period 1985–1989. It began to occupy almost every county by 1989. The spread is easily observable as "infilling" of every empty space in Guangdong, leaving only a mere handful of counties unoccupied. In sum, the development strategy for radio broadcasting may be described as one of "selectivity followed by universality."

Figure 14.5 Developments in Broadcasting, 1985–1989

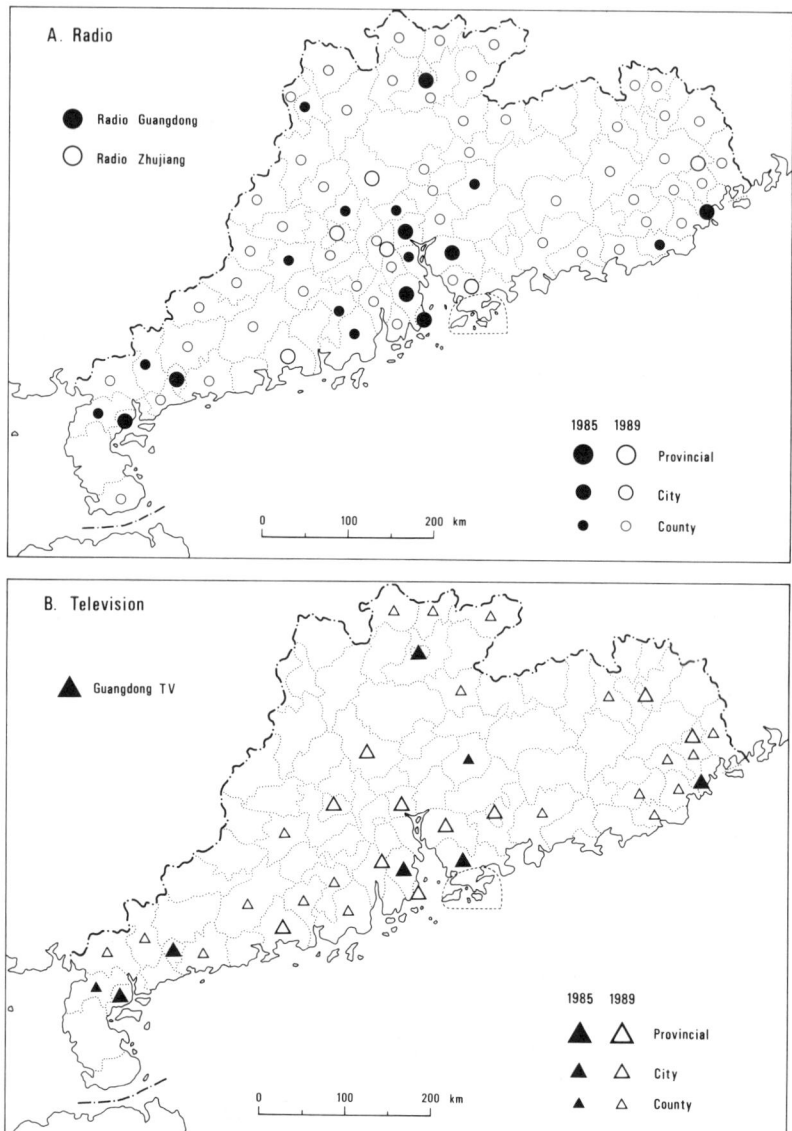

For television broadcasting, the picture is similar. In 1985, only important cities or counties possessed television set-ups. Clear consideration of spatial balance is revealed in their establishment. Hence, the Pearl River Delta is heavily populated by television set-ups, with major regional centres at the peripheries of Guangdong. The situation in 1989 was also one of out-diffusion of television stations. However, there were differences. First of all, not all counties were occupied to the extent of radio. This could be because of the much higher costs in establishing television stations. Second, new establishments in 1989 were either on the coast or somewhere along the northern border. There was an absence of new television stations at the centre, a point not easy to explain.

In sum, there are several points of note with regard to broadcasting in Guangdong. The hierarchy of stations for both radio and television is clearly distinguishable. Each has one or two stations which are responsible for the entire province. At the other extreme, those set-ups at the county level are much more widely dispersed. Second, a clear spatial preference can be seen as an attempt to achieve more spatial balance. Regional balance so cherished in socialist ideology is aptly expressed by looking at the locational strategy of the media.

Facsimile Transmission

Advance in communication technology over the last few years has been most rapid and revolutionary. At the very beginning, such developments were usually associated with interconnections among computers via modems over telephone lines. Later, the invention of the facsimile machine and its popularization revolutionized the means of transmitting ideas to distant areas. Several advantages of transmission via fax account for its rising popularity. First of all, unlike telephone, telex or cable, facsimile messages in image form can be transmitted directly to the receiver. If the hardware set-up is of a high quality, the receiver can actually receive an exact copy of the original. This is especially important if written documents are required. Second, facsimile transmission is fast, almost instantaneous. It is even faster than any express mail or international courier service. Especially in the commercial world where competition is so keen, facsimile transmission is indeed a must. Third, facsimile transmission is relatively cheap. As the price of a facsimile machine drops, the real cost is the length of time needed for transmission, i.e. the same cost as if making a long-distance telephone call. If the transmission is local, as in the case of Hong Kong, no telephone charge is made. This actually eliminates the cost of mailing or even hiring a messenger.

Since the opening of China in the late 1970s, many trading and commercial activities have been going on between Hong Kong and nearby areas of Guangdong. Gradually, businessmen on both sides began to realize the importance of having fast and efficient means of communication. Thus, facsimile transmission began to take a foothold. Due to the lack of related information on this issue, no one seems to have delved into it before.

Figure 14.6 attempts to show the spatial pattern of facsimile machine distribution in Guangdong for both 1991 and 1993.[19] The number of facsimile machines is a clear indication of established economic status. To be specific, an area which has good commercial links with the outside world will most likely possess facsimile machines. Since these installations have to rely on telephone lines, they will only be set up after an area has progressed to a certain level of economic development. Because of their importance in sustaining and generating commercial links, their distribution expresses the propelling force of economic growth, at least in the foreseeable future.

One can easily identify, for both years, the extreme concentration of facsimile machines in Guangzhou as well as Shenzhen. Each of them exceeds several hundreds. Also, there is a cluster in the delta area, with Shantou and Zhanjiang again standing out as regional foci. The "leaders" remain as "leaders" after two years of continuous growth. Scattered around Guangdong are counties with a few facsimile machines. As one would expect, high-tech products like facsimile machines exhibit a highly concentrated pattern.

When taking population into consideration, the number of fax machines per 100,000 people for the two years reveal some other interesting facts. The Pearl River Delta is consistently a core, with clear evidence of spatial spread outwards. However, this phenomenon is not observable for regional foci like Zhanjiang and Shantou. With regard to percentage growth in fax machines by counties, highest growth is registered at Nanhai and Chaozhou, both are neighbours to major municipalities. Again, this implies contagious spread outwards. With the only exception of Maoming (a negative growth), the vast majority of Guangdong counties experienced a zero growth over the 1991–1993 period.

In contrast to the distribution pattern of broadcasting which reflects governmental preference in spatial balance, the pattern in facsimile

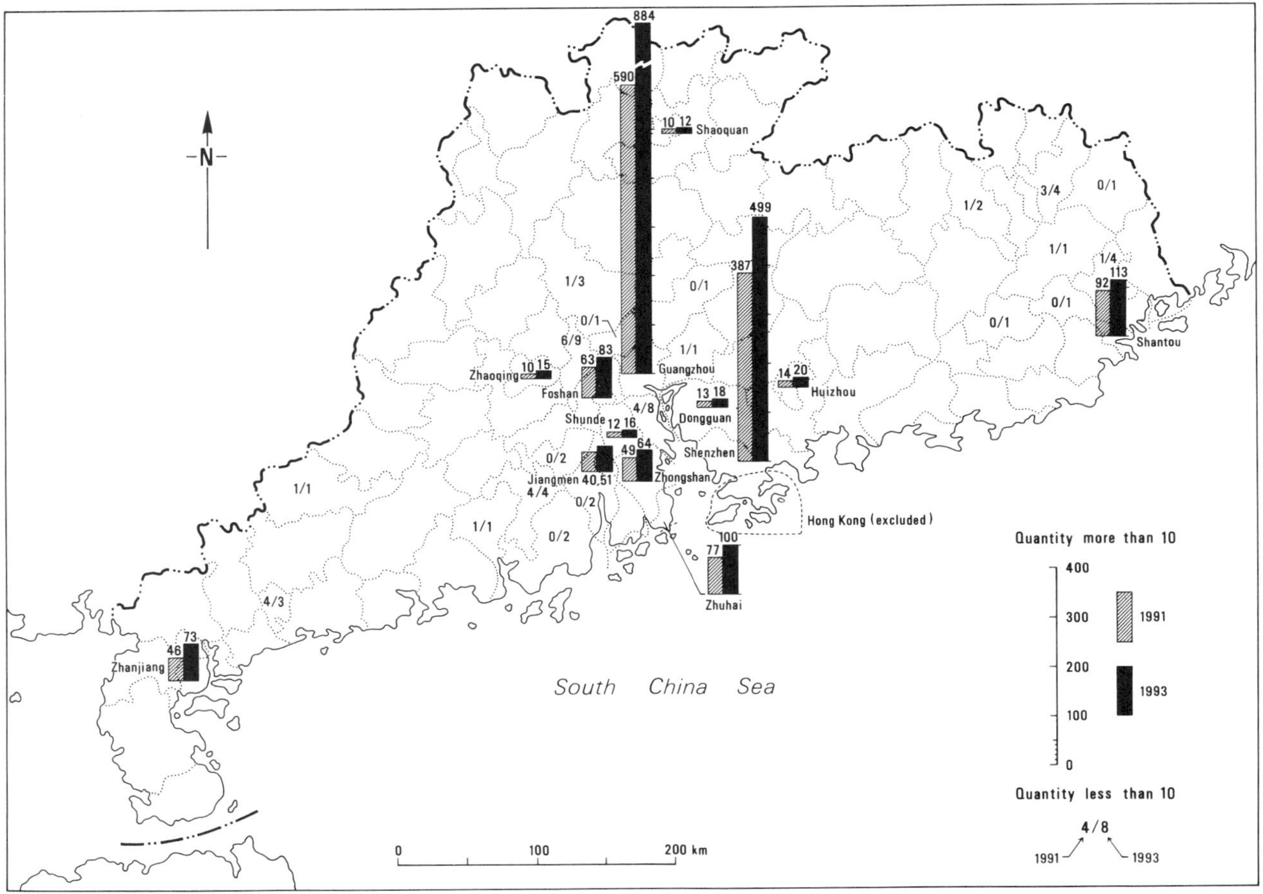

Figure 14.6 Distribution of Facsimile Machines in Guangdong, 1991 and 1993

machine distribution reveals the opposite trend. They are distributed according to free market forces. The more an area is developed, the more likely it will be to possess facsimile machines. Hence, the concentrated pattern perpetuates itself. Both hierarchical and contagious types of diffusion occur over the two time slices, a characteristic common in free market situations. Another important point to note is the tremendous influence of Hong Kong in this regard. As reported, for every 100 telephone lines in Hong Kong, 17 are devoted to facsimile usages.[20] This is second only to Japan (26 for every 100) in the whole world! As Guangdong's trade is heavily dominated by Hong Kong investors, this has a tremendous impact on related developments across the border. From the statistics gathered, among the 1,432 fax machines enumerated for Guangdong in 1991, 87.2% were located in the Pearl River Delta. The remaining 12.9% were spread out afar.

Pager Service

Like facsimile transmission, pager service is an advanced type of communication. Its rise is also due to the intense need for rapid and efficient communication as required in the commercial world. As Guangdong opens to the outside world in its search for capital and knowhow for modernization, the changing pattern of communication has to be accommodated.

Pager service is one kind of wireless transmission of information. However, information is only limited. Figure 14.7 depicts how the first newly established dual-frequency pager service operates.[21] Two individual sets of wireless stations are set up on either side of the Hong Kong-Guangdong border. Any person who wants to communicate with a pager subscriber can make a telephone call to the wireless station on his side. The station will then send out wireless messages (sometimes a beep or simple words) which can be received at the subscriber's pager. He can then call the station to receive the full message. For cross-border connections, the station can transmit such requests too.

This type of communication really depends on the development of strong signals to be transmitted through the air. As described in the promotion leaflet by ABC Communications, at present this service is available to certain places in the Pearl River Delta area such as Guangzhou, Zhongshan, Shenzhen, Jiangmen, Foshan, Dongguan, Shunde and Huizhou. Later on, the service will be extended to other parts of Guangdong, including counties like Shaoguan, Meixian, Heyuan, Chaozhou, Shanwei, Zhuhai,

Figure 14.7   A Schematic Representation of the Pager Service between Guangdong and Hong Kong

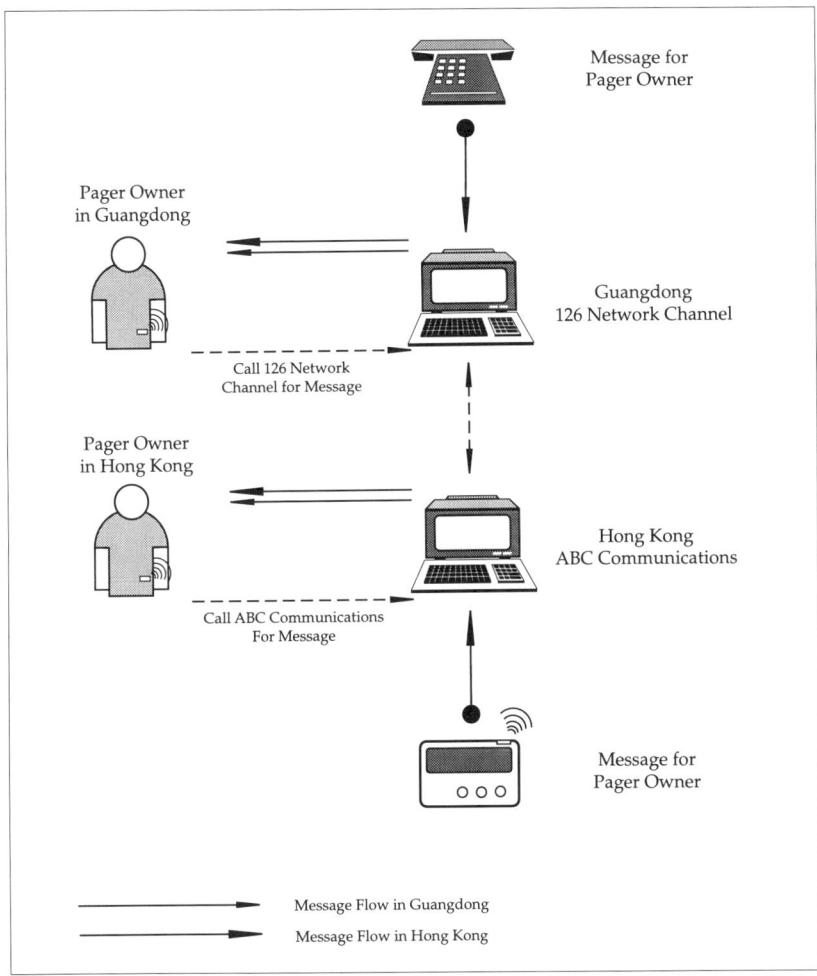

Yangjiang, Maoming and Zhanjiang. Hence, all parts of Guangdong will eventually be covered by this service.

Since pager service is half-financed by non-local investors, the commercial component is significant. Hence, a decision whether or not to offer pager service has much to do with economic development at a certain point which needs recognition. Judging from the present coverage, there is no doubt that the delta area receives foremost attention. These decisions are heavily influenced by trade connections with Hong Kong. From prospective coverage areas, they also reflect how overseas investors perceive the spatial structure of Guangdong's regional development. Undoubtedly, a trend of Hong Kong–Guangdong continued commercial links is assumed to take place in those areas mentioned.

Interpretation and Forecast

The analysis and interpretation above reflect the current status of transport and communication in Guangdong. In this section, several broad interpretations which are important to an overall understanding of transport and communication there will be offered. At the end, some forecasts will be made with reference to what was observable as of mid-1996.

One special point to note is Guangdong's increasing attention to developing communication at least on a par with transport. The change in technology is one reason for this change. Gone are the days when the main form of communication was letters mailed and received after days and weeks. As the standard of living rises, the demand for products or services involving high technology increases. The availability of facsimile machines and the pager service are typical examples of such a shift in preference. In order to stay competitive, any person in the business world has to be well informed on the spot. Without reliance on high technology applied in communication, there is no way to catch up with the larger society.

The Hong Kong factor has to be taken into account in the interpretation, too. While conventional transport needs were basically internal affairs of Guangdong, there is a general need to incorporate the factor of Hong Kong in the development of transport and communication in Guangdong. For highways and air transport, more and more consideration is now given to plan with Hong Kong in mind. Further development in communication in Guangdong really depends on the intensity of Hong Kong's participation. An example is the huge number of pager subscribers in Hong Kong (presently standing at around 900,000) which offers a tremendous impact on the further development of this service in Guangdong. While no figure on pager subscribers in Guangdong exists, there is an estimate of 180,000 in Shenzhen alone.[22] This indicates that the trend of having pager service in Guangdong is developing with great speed.

From the above analysis, it is clear that the socialist imprint of balanced spatial development still exists to the present day. The example of radio and television broadcasting is typical. The spatial layout and current extension of roads and railways follow a similar path. On the other hand, another trend is gaining momentum. To be specific, an economically strong Pearl River Delta is exerting a tremendous pressure on Guangdong to devote more of its attention to the further development of transport and communication. Further upgrading of Guangdong's infrastructure is fundamental to enhancing its likelihood of becoming the Fifth Little Dragon in Asia by the turn of this century.

One last important observation is the significant change in Guangdong's orientation towards economic construction under the umbrella of open policy. Three Special Economic Zones (Zhuhai, Shenzhen and Shantou) have become regional foci of intense growth, thus creating a great need for further development of transport and communication. The establishment of the Pearl River Delta Open Economic Zone is one step further in a concentration of efforts at the central part of Guangdong. Of course, one cannot neglect the historical inertia that explains Guangzhou's and the delta's prominence in economic strength. Nonetheless, the impetus as a result of the open policy is direct and forceful for Guangdong to realize its great achievements of the last decade or so.

A few words about the future. If we subscribe to the view that transport is basic, while communication is a catalyst, to economic development, then Guangdong is on its way to achieving the status of a modern society. One example is Guangzhou's increase its telephone digits from seven to eight in June 1996,[23] following a similar implementation in Hong Kong at the beginning of the same year. This effort arises out of a need to accommodate the ever-increasing demand in telephone communication. So far, the quality aspect of Guangdong's transport and communication has not been touched upon. As improvements in quantity are made, no doubt the quality question will come to the fore. A trend of more concern about higher quality can be envisaged in the not-too-distant future. In fact, some signs of this have come about. For example, the preference for highways, containerization development, double-tracking and electrification of rail, and the like. In terms of new communication, the opening up of Guangdong's market on cross-border digital mobile phones is high on the priority list.[24] Consequently, quality upgrades of Guangdong's existing transport and communication infrastructure will also be made.

Finally, Guangdong's future cannot be divorced from the return of the present colonies of Hong Kong and Macau to China in 1997 and 1999, respectively. Their present status as magnets of economic growth is widely known. As a consequence, transport and communication in the Pearl River Delta are actually responsive to the needs of Hong Kong and Macau. After their return to China, they will be Special Administrative Regions located along the coast of Guangdong. Although administratively separate, their interconnections with Guangdong will be even more intense than today. Hence, it is natural to predict the formation of an economic giant along the Pearl River estuary. It will possess the characteristics of a megalopolis with high density networks of transport and communication within. In fact, Guangdong has plans to develop an international telecommunications network which is compatible with the present configurations operating in Macau and Hong Kong. Within the Ninth Five-year Plan period, the plan is to more than double Guangdong's overseas telephone lines and interconnections with these two future Special Administration Regions.[25] As a consequence, the area now referred to as the Pearl River Delta will form an even larger regional development axis. This will exert a tremendous influence on the present peripheral areas to advance more rapidly in improving their transport and communication infrastructure.

Notes

1. This is the principal theme of a recent book on the geography of communications, see Stanley D. Brunn and Thomas R. Leinbach (eds.), *Collapsing Space and Time: Geographic Aspects of Communications and Information* (London: HarperCollinsAcademic, 1991).

2. Thomas R. Leinbach and Chia Lin Sien, "The Role of Transport in Development" in their *South-East Asian Transport: Issues in Development* (Oxford: Oxford University Press, 1989), p. 2.

3. Ibid.

4. Hong Kong has returned and Macau will return to China as Special Administrative Regions in the years 1997 and 1999, respectively.

5. All discussions in this chapter focus on the contemporary period with special reference to the late 1980s and early 1990s.

6. The geographic characteristics of Guangdong are provided in Chapter 18. Another good source of information is Wu Yuwen (ed.), *Guangdongsheng jingji dili* (Economic Geography of Guangdong Province) (Beijing: Xinhua chubanshe, 1986).

7. The best map I could find on the hierarchy of road types of Guangdong is provided in *Zhongguo fensheng gonglu jiaotong dituji* (Provincial Atlas on Road Transport in China) (Beijing: Zhongguo ditu chubanshe, 1990), map

23. In this atlas, six types of roads are identified. They are, namely, super-highways, tar-surfaced trunk roads, unsurfaced trunk roads, tar-surfaced ordinary roads, unsurfaced ordinary roads and simple roads. Figure 14.1 only portrays the two types of trunk roads.

8. *Ming Pao Daily News*, 26 October 1992.

9. *Hong Kong Economic Journal*, 6 and 26 October 1992.

10. *Ming Pao Daily News*, 11 April 1996.

11. Same source as Figure 14.1. See note 7.

12. Guangzhou–Huizhou rail freight started in July 1992 and its passenger service began in November of the same year. See *Ming Pao Daily News*, 25 October 1992.

13. *Ming Pao Daily News*, 3 November 1995.

14. Figure 14.3 is adapted from Wu Yuwen (ed.), *Guangdongsheng jingji dili* (see note 6), pp. 331, 368.

15. One encouraging fact is the publication on *Zhongguo youzheng bianma tuji* (Atlas of Chinese Postal Codes) (Harbin: Harbin ditu chubanshe, 1988) in which postal codes down to the township level are presented for each province. Another publication of note to analyze postal service is Lu Dingyi and Zhang Guangyu (eds.), *Youdian tongxin dili* (The Geography of Post and Communications) (Beijing: Renmin youdian chubanshe, 1992). Within this publication, analytic information on the hierarchy of postal routes and mail exchange offices is provided.

16. *Youzheng kuaijian yundi shixianbiao* (Tables on Express Mail Delivery Times) (Beijing: Youdianbu youzheng zongju, 1992), chapter on Guangdong. It is not for sale and only available over the counter in post offices.

17. This is particularly so when the normal delivery time matrix is considered. Most delivery takes four days. Hence, the difference between express and ordinary delivery is not significant at all.

18. *Zhongguo guangbo dianshi nianjian* (Yearbook on Chinese Radio Broadcast and Television) (Beijing: Beijing guangbo xueyuan chubanshe, various years).

19. Data were compiled from the 1992 and 1994 editions of *China Telex and Fax Directory* (Hong Kong: The China Phone Book Company Limited). The reliability of this publication is high. As indicated on its copyright page, all entries in the body of this directory are published free of charge. There is no reason for a commercial firm to leave itself out of this directory, given that a publication like this can upgrade one's visibility to existing and potential customers.

20. *Ming Pao Daily News*, 2 November 1992.

21. The first pager service is provided by the ABC Communications in Hong Kong and GTP (Guangdong) Telecom in Guangdong. Cross-border paging began in June 1992. See *South China Morning Post*, 27 June 1992.

22. *Sing Tao Jih Pao*, 27 June 1992.
23. *Ming Pao Daily News*, 28 November 1995.
24. See note 22.
25. *Ming Pao Daily News*, 2 April 1996.

15

Urban Development

Edward S. W. Woo

Introduction

In Guangdong, one does not need to go to Guangzhou — the provincial capital city (*shengcheng*) — to experience a new phase of urban development. In most market towns throughout the province, one can have already found evidence from thriving businesses which supply a great variety of goods and services, some of which were not even available in Guangzhou before the reform. These include shops selling imitation jewellery or hairdressing salons offering perms for men. The monotonous Maoist-style people's halls and local government offices enshrined as symbols of a town's development are replaced by varied landmarks of multi-storey buildings, housing, shops, restaurants, guesthouses, banks, commercial offices and residential units. Almost as much traffic in the form of vans, trucks and sedan cars rumbles in the main streets as did bicycle traffic, which was the predominant scene, before.

Intermediate cities are also developing rapidly. Those in the Pearl River Delta, especially Shenzhen and Zhuhai, the two Special Economic Zones (SEZs) set up since 1980, exhibit a great deal of physical resemblance to their neighbouring cosmopolitan city of Hong Kong. The booming business of manufacturing, construction, commerce and trade in many of these cities is comparable to those in Guangzhou and other major cities established before the reform. Table 15.1 compares the economic performance of the cities in Guangdong. The non-farm population there is also approaching or has surpassed that of the major cities.

At the same time, the primacy of Guangzhou and other major cities is generally declining. Many of their central functions are now shared by the intermediate cities and even market towns. To survive and grow, they are diversifying their functions and developing closer interaction with their hinterlands. In doing so, they undergo marked morphological changes. Hotels, office buildings, factories and general housing grow up at a remarkable speed on the sides of wider and better roads built to facilitate internal circulation and reinforce external links. Figure 15.1 shows the distribution of major urban centres in Guangdong.

The changing urban scene in Guangdong bears testimony to the economic reality of the province created by the reforms since 1978. Four aspects of the reforms and their consequences are particularly influential in producing the present pattern of urban development. Firstly, rural reforms served a dual function of encouraging circulation between urban centres and rural districts on one hand, and transferring surplus labour to urban

Table 15.1 Production and Population Statistics of Cities in Guangdong, 1994

City	Secondary production (RMB million)	Tertiary production (RMB million)	Non-farm population (million)
Major cities:			
Guangzhou	45,675	45,880	3.11
Shantou	7,901	8,977	0.71
Shaoguan	5,520	3,162	0.40
Huizhou	8,465	6,118	0.23
Jiangmen	13,985	9,470	0.29
Foshan	24,631	14,966	0.36
Zhanjiang	8,647	7,757	0.49
Maoming	9,195	6,330	0.24
Zhaoqing	7,633	5,032	0.27
Intermediate cities:			
Shenzhen	31,547	23,789	0.69
Zhuhai	9,074	6,591	0.30
Heyuan	1,219	1,300	0.12
Meizhou	4,095	3,071	0.17
Shanwei	2,013	2,170	0.14
Dongguan	8,213	5,245	0.34
Zhongshan	6,779	4,391	0.34
Yangjiang	2,547	2,543	0.25
Qingyuan	3,303	2,517	0.17
Chaozhou	3,709	2,512	0.23
Jieyang	6,493	4,127	0.17
Yunfu	5,429	2,624	0.21

Source: *Guangdong tongji nianjian 1995.*
Note: The non-farm populations are apparently under-estimated because of narrow official definition.

production on the other. Secondly, the promotion of township enterprise development enhanced the economic strengths of towns and induced migration to towns. Thirdly, endorsement of a diversified economy promoted the development of individual-run enterprises, which instilled vitality in secondary and tertiary production in cities and towns. Finally, to facilitate the implementation of the open policy, power was devolved from the central government to Guangdong. This allowed the province to formulate its urban policies to stimulate both foreign and domestic investment and trade.

Figure 15.1   Major Urban Centres in Guangdong

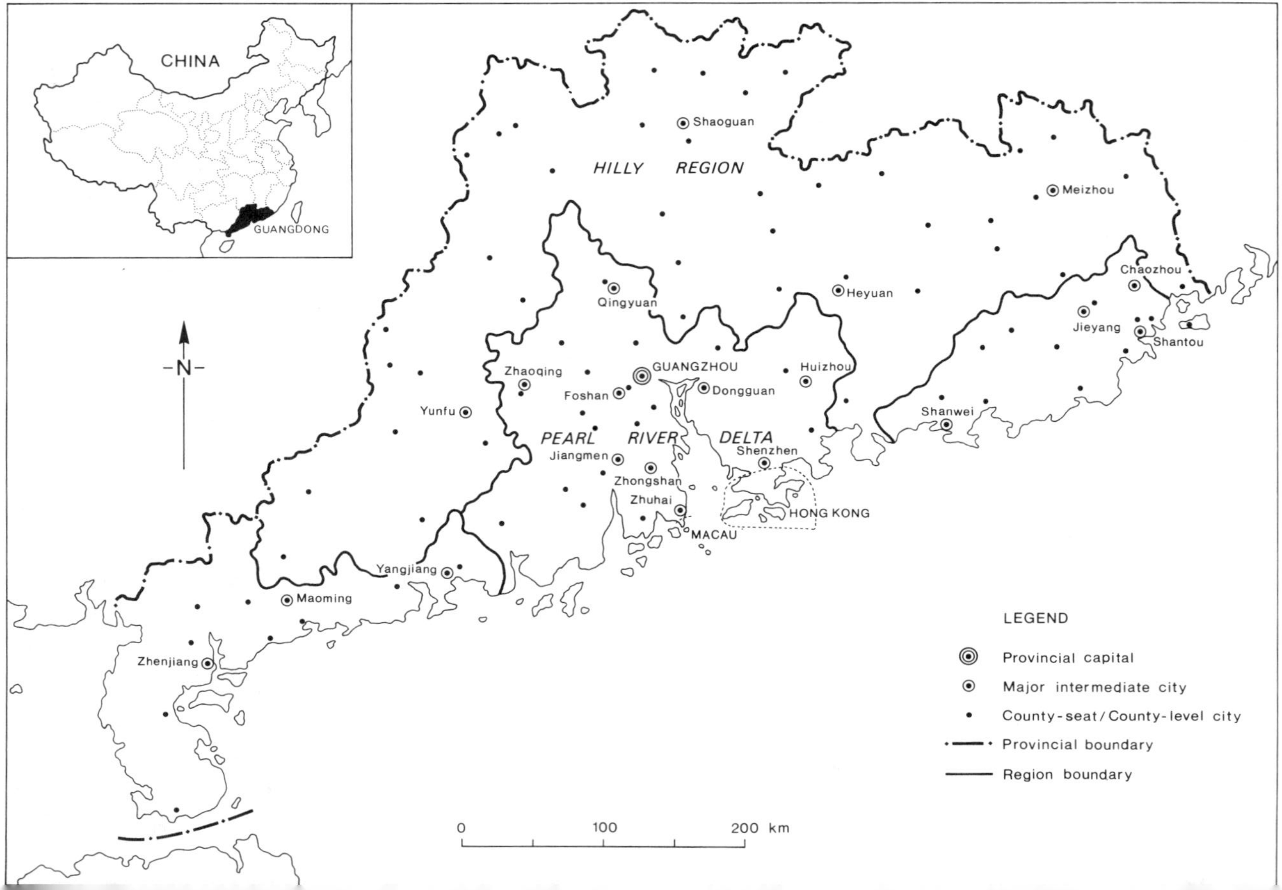

The purpose of this chapter is to examine the patterns and processes of Guangdong's urban development in the light of the factors outlined above. It will focus on three aspects of development — multiplication of urban centres, diversification of urban functions in major cities and emergence of urban regions. In the conclusion, a re-assessment of the inter-relations between urban development and economic progress will be presented, highlighting once again the major issues of urban development in the reform era.[1]

Urban Development in Retrospect

Guangdong experienced an early history of urban development. Its major cities such as Guangzhou, Shaoguan and Foshan were founded as urban settlement more than 1,300 years ago.[2] Towns sprang up to provide for the needs of the hinterland just as they did in other parts of the world. Up till 1949, Guangdong had 13.3% of its population living in towns and cities.[3] This rate was higher than the national average of 10.3% at that time. The higher level of urbanization matched well the higher level of economic development. In 1949, the per capita income of Guangdong of RMB88 was substantially higher than the national figure of RMB66. Much of Guangdong's higher economic performance was due to the better developed tertiary sector in the cities and traditional market towns.[4]

However, this trend took a sharp plunge under the Maoist regime. Urban development in Guangdong suffered partly due to an error in developmental strategy which overlooked the significance of market towns and rural-urban integration in economic development; and partly due to a bias in the defence strategy which regarded Guangdong as a "frontier" province which did not warrant large-scale capital construction.[5] These policies were opposed to the development of towns and cities. Within the three decades of the Maoist "experiment," the number of towns dwindled. The 1964 census showed there were 154 towns in Guangdong but the number fell to 132 in 1980, two years after the Maoist strategy was repealed by the pragmatists in the Communist Party. The overall level of urbanization also stagnated into the early years of the pragmatist reform.[6] In 1953, Guangdong's urbanization level of 13.2% was caught up by the national average and in 1982, its 18.6% even fell behind the national level of 20.6%.

The sluggishness of Guangdong's urban development in Mao's time was a reflection of the slow development of the province's economy. Two indicators of urban economic vitality showed that Guangdong fared less well than the national average. In the period 1949–1978, Guangdong's gross value of industrial output (GVIO) increased by only 26.2 times while the national average increased by 30.2 times. In the period 1952–1978, Guangdong's total value of retail sales rose by only 4.7 times while the national average rose by 5.6 times. These poor performances were both a cause and a result of the lower level of urban development in the province. Another indicator — gross value of agricultural output (GVAO) — which can reflect the ability of a region to sustain urban development also showed Guangdong's inferior position in the country. In the period 1949–1978, Guangdong recorded an increase of 4.7 times in GVAO while the national average recorded an increase of 5.4 times.

Development of Market Towns, Industrial Towns and Intermediate Cities

Under the pragmatist economic reforms, Guangdong's economy has gained remarkable progress. General prosperity has been experienced in the province at an unprecedented level. Deng Xiaoping's tour in Guangdong in early 1992 signified his satisfaction with the results the province had achieved under the reforms he initiated. In the period 1978– 1994, per capita income in Guangdong rose by 15.3 times while that of the nation rose by only 9.7 times. Equally remarkable is the growth in the number of towns which rose by almost eleven times in the same period.[7]

One reason behind the growth in the number of towns is the administrative reform in 1984 which dismantled the commune system and replaced it with civic town administration. Former communes were re-established as "administrative towns" (*jianzhizhen*) when they met the requirements laid down by the state.[8] This transformation dramatically raised the number of market towns in Guangdong from 268 in 1984 to 1,294 in 1989.[9] However, this does not explain the increase in urban activities and population in these towns which effected the transformation. Reasons have to be sought in other directions.

Market Towns

Since the early 1980s, the countryside of Guangdong has implemented a production responsibility system as a measure to boost rural productivity. This means that farmers, instead of receiving production orders from the commune or brigade and sharing their inputs and outputs with their fellow-farmers in the commune or brigade, are free to enter into contracts with the local government in terms of type and quantity of output. Besides having to satisfy a state quota which is still shared among them, farmers can sell the rest of their output in the free market for higher prices. This freedom in marketing is partly traded for the state's subsidies in input supplies. In other words, farmers have to look for and pay for their own. But even with increases in the costs of production thus incurred, farmers have generally regained their incentives in farming and the overall farm output level rises, especially in highly marketable outputs such as vegetables, fruits and poultry. This, in turn, stimulates trading — an essential ingredient of the market town economy. Not only is there an increase in the sale of foodstuffs in the agricultural trade market and in the sale of farm chemicals and farm equipment in the town's retail outlets, there is also an increasing sale of consumer goods and services such as catering and entertainment as farmers' demand increases with higher income. Table 15.2 shows the change in transactions in agricultural trade markets in the period 1980–1994. Among farm outputs traded, the biggest increase was recorded in poultry and eggs, aquatic products, vegetables and fruits. Both production and consumption of these items were discouraged prior to 1978.

Table 15.2 Transactions in Agricultural Trade Markets

	1980	1994	1980–1994 % change
Number of markets	1,891	4,266	226
in cities	104	1,149	1,105
in towns	1,787	3,117	174
Transaction volume by location (RMB million)	2,272	77,927	3,430
in cities	207	39,733	19,195
in towns	2,065	38,194	1,850
Transaction volume by category			
of grain and oil	218	5,594	2,566
of poultry and eggs	733	26,132	3,565
of aquatic products	147	9,733	6,621
of vegetables	120	5,910	4,925
of fruits	46	8,372	18,200
of pasture and feeds	122	608	498
of livestock	164	463	282

Source: *Guangdong nianjian 1995.*

The revival and boom of these "free markets" in towns and cities are associated with the slackening of state control on the supply of farm produce. Since the early 1980s, the state has gradually reduced the procurement of farm produce. In 1988, only 17.5% of the grains and 19.8% of the pigs produced in Guangdong were procured by the state. As state procurement prices are much lower than market prices, farmers have good reasons to prefer selling their outputs in the markets. Moreover, as the state procurement order drops, farmers can switch to productions which are more profitable. Local governments also help to develop local trade by building or rebuilding agricultural trade markets in towns. As traders generally need to pay for a business licence, encouraging retail trade means more revenue for local governments.

The boom in retailing as well as other non-farm economic activities in towns could alternatively be seen as a response to the state's quest for diversifying local economies and improving productivity in the country-side. Two state policies are extremely influential in these respects. One is the endorsement of individual-run business and the other is the promotion of township enterprises.

The existence of individual traders in rural towns was as old as the rural towns themselves. However, Mao's collectivization policy was effective in weeding out most of them from the market place and suppressing the business of the remainder. Since 1981, their status in the rural economy has been reinstated by the state which recognized that:

> in a rather long historical period, it is absolutely certain that mutliple economic ingredients and multiple forms of operation should co-exist.... Reviving and developing non-farm individual businesses in towns and cities is meaningful for developing production, vitalizing the market, satisfying needs of the people and increasing employment opportunities.[10]

Furthermore, it was recognized that "developing rural individual industrial and trade enterprises ought to benefit the building of small market towns."[11] These decisions of the party and the state give clearer directions for rebuilding the private sector, which was suppressed before.

In the 1980s, the number of individual-run trade and service enterprises in towns of Guangdong rose tremendously, from less than 14,000 in 1981 to over 350,000 in 1988.[12] Apart from operating in the "agricultural trade markets," many of them occupy the front of the town's buildings while the rear is used for residence. Apart from engaging in the trade of agricultural produce, many of them are involved in retail of manufactured goods such as household items and clothing. Many more are engaged in catering and services. Indeed, the nature and format of such a "free market" in towns are not much different from those in Western towns.

Industrial Satellite Towns

Guangdong's comparatively weaker industrial base was partly attributable to the deficiency in state investment. In the reform era, new measures were implemented by the state to arouse local enthusiasm in developing Guangdong's economy. Only a few months after the Communist Party had vowed to launch economic reforms in 1978, Guangdong was instructed by the state to formulate "special and flexible policies" in order to achieve the economic goals set down by the party. Consequently, several measures granted Guangdong more autonomy to allow it to chart its own development. These included the founding of three Special Economic Zones (SEZs) — at Shenzhen, Zhuhai and Shantou in the 1980s, the designation of Guangzhou and Zhanjiang as "open coastal cities" in 1984 and the demarcation of the Pearl River Delta Economic Open Region in 1985.

All these meant new frontiers for urban development in Guangdong. Besides the direct impact on the cities designated by these policies, many towns also opened up a new doorway of development as the provincial government demarcated them as "industrial satellite towns." In earlier times, Guangdong suffered from the lack of state investment on industrial development because of its "frontier" location. Few urban centres had substantial industrial development comparable to cities in north and northeast China, which also enjoyed a much higher level of urbanization. But in the reform era, such "frontier" location becomes invaluable for establishing an "external orientation" and attracting both domestic and foreign investment in industry. Among various regions, the Pearl River Delta benefits most from these policies because of its physical proximity — and cultural affinity to, Hong Kong — a world-class cosmopolitan centre known for its miraculous financial and industrial success. In the 1980s, 138 market towns in the delta region representing 56% of the total number of towns there obtained "industrial satellite town" status, which could enjoy a wide range of autonomy and institutional support to boost economic development.[13] These towns share a common characteristic, namely, that over 50% of their workforce is employed in industry. In some cases, such as Guizhou, Beijiao and Lunjiao towns in Shunde, the proportion may exceed 70%.[14]

The growth of industrial towns is also attributable to the state policy which promotes the development of township enterprises, particularly township industry. These non-farm businesses, formerly known as commune and brigade enterprises, were reorganized and expanded at the proposal in two state documents in 1979 and 1984.[15] According to these documents, both collectives (local authorities) and individuals in the countryside are encouraged to run non-farm enterprises as a means to improve local productivity, to increase household income and to boost local government revenue.[16] These enterprises are different from those before 1978 by their profit motive, and profitability is precisely the major cause behind their rapid boom in the 1980s. Table 15.3 shows the increase in township factories in Guangdong in 1978–1994. The growth in individual-run industries is the most substantial, and reasons for that have been outlined earlier. Most of these factories, especially those run by town authorities, are located in the town proper. Some occupy old buildings — such as ancestral halls — and general housing which is not constructed for industrial purposes. But some are newly built in specially prepared industrial zones on the outskirts of towns. Each industrial satellite town may have more than one industrial zone. Shadui, for instance, has four such zones.

Most of these factories are engaged in export-processing — a phenomenon created by the government's urge for "external orientation" as a developmental strategy. Hong Kong is the biggest client of and biggest investor in these factories. With the growth of these factories, the industrial towns have now shed most of their agricultural character and taken up a more specialized path of development. In 1994, the gross industrial output

Table 15.3   Township Factories in Guangdong, 1978–1994

	1978	1984	1994
All types	39,702	173,998	601,000
Town-run	9,846	11,170	90,599
Village-run	29,856	56,464	
Joint-household-run	—	16,342	510,401
Individual-run	—	90,022	

Sources: Guangdong Province Township Enterprise Management Bureau, internal documents; *Guangdong tongji nianjian 1995*; *Statistical Yearbook of China 1995*.
Note: No individual-run township factories were recorded in 1978.

value from the township factories in Guangdong amounted to RMB254,445 million, compared with RMB109,742 million from the state factories in cities.[17] Industry in these towns is surely no mere supplement to the provincial economy but is becoming a substantial component.

These industrial towns may or may not be located close to the cities and the level of industrialization has little direct relation to the distance from the city although some factories do have business connections with enterprises in the cities. The implication here is that the energy of development of these towns has come mainly from below — the efforts of local officials and peasants — rather than the municipal administration. Industrial output from these towns is distributed throughout the country and is not confined to outlets in cities in Guangdong alone. Export to Hong Kong and other foreign countries is increasing.

In general, industrialization is an important factor for the development of the town's economy. Each of the industrial satellite towns in the delta recorded over RMB5 million of industrial outputs in 1986 and many of them had over RMB10 million.[18] This is equivalent to six to ten times the value of agricultural output in the rural districts under their administration.

Construction Boom and Rural-Urban Migration in Towns

Non-industrial towns, especially those in the hilly regions, do not have the same industrial vigour as the industrial satellite towns. But in general, all the towns share a similar overall growth in their economy in the reform era and are characterized by two features of development — construction boom and rapid population growth.

Construction boom arises as demand for better housing increases. Stimulated by the rise in income, local people began to rebuild their houses which generally lacked maintenance or became non-functional. The increase in spending on house improvement or building by people in towns and villages is enormous. From an average of RMB14.99 per person in 1978, it rose to RMB163.33 in 1994. At the same time, as the finance of local governments improves, new offices are built. So are buildings for local state or collective enterprises. In town centres, it is not uncommon to find new houses and construction sites blending with worn-down old buildings mostly built in the early 1900s. But increasingly, new town quarters are also planned or developed to cope with rising needs.

A general boom is also found in the development of social amenities such as clinics and schools. These are expanded partly with local investments and partly with donations from overseas Chinese or compatriots in Hong Kong and Macau. In 1994, these donations in Guangdong amounted to almost RMB2.96 billion. Road construction in towns is also developing fast. New and wide concrete roads now crisscross most town centres and are extending by over half a kilometre per year in an average town. In the period 1985–1986, the built-up area in Guangdong towns increased by more than 10%.[19] This rate was faster than that of the cities.

The multiplication of economic activities in towns in Guangdong attracted a large number of peasants. The number of peasant-workers in township enterprises went up from 1.5 million in 1978 to 10.2 million in 1994. Indeed, the transferral of farm labour and the associated rural-urban migration is a key factor in the urban development in Guangdong's countryside. In the pre-reform period, this was suppressed by the rigid household registration system. Since then, the population policy has become more flexible. Peasants can now take up non-farm jobs or conduct trade in town and move to live in town. This increases the towns' population significantly. In Panyu, for example, the number of workers in town-run enterprises rose by 10% in the period 1987–1988. Its non-farm population — an indicator of urban population — also rose significantly by 6%, while the overall population rose by a less remarkable 2%. But many of the immigrants to town are not fully registered as towns' residents because of their household registration in the villages. In this way, the official figures of population growth in towns may not seem to be as large as they should be. Those workers or traders not fully registered are known as "population catering for their own grain supply" (*zili kouliang renkou*), which means they do not get subsidy on food prices obtained from state outlets as fully registered town people do.[20]

Nowadays, many towns in the delta accommodate migrants not only from the nearby countryside but also from the more difficult and less prosperous hilly regions of Guangdong, as well as from the less developed parts of Hunan, Sichuan and Jiangxi provinces. Such migration was induced primarily by the higher wages the delta region can offer. As most of these new immigrants are young and unmarried, they significantly modify the demographic structure in towns.

Intermediate Cities and County-level Cities

With the reforms in progress, some counties recorded distinctive growth in secondary and tertiary outputs as well as sizeable increases in non-farm population in their towns, particularly in the county seat. These were important criteria for the state to promote three counties — Zhongshan, Dongguan and Chaozhou — to cities in the first half of the 1980s. A new regulation issued by the State Council in 1986 laid down more precise requirements for transforming towns into cities.[21] Among them, population and economic production are two major concerns. In 1992, five more counties — Shunde, Panyu, Nanhai, Taishan and Xinhui — were upgraded to cities. Among the eight new cities, Zhongshan, Dongguan, Shunde, Nanhai, Panyu, Taishan and Xinhui are located in the Pearl River Delta. The first four are sometimes hailed as the "little tigers of Guangdong" for their dynamic economy and rapid rate of growth. Table 15.4 shows the per capita national income of these intermediate cities in the 1980s and the 1990s. They all approximated or exceeded the provincial average, except in the case of Taishan and Chaozhou.

The economic strength of these cities is not merely nucleated at the administrative centre or the former county-seat. Instead, there is a high degree of dispersion to industrial towns and market towns. Township enterprises, which are widely spread in the suburban or rural districts, are much more productive than state enterprises in the city proper. The administrative centres of some intermediate cities — such as Shiqi in Zhongshan and Guancheng in Dongguan — have a bustling economy. But in Shunde and Nanhai, industrial towns may surpass the administrative centre in terms of prosperity.

Table 15.4　Per Capita GDP of Selected Intermediate Cities in Guangdong

	1985 (RMB)	1994 (RMB)	1985–1994 % increase
Guangdong average	657	6,337	964
Zhongshan	1,110	10,571	952
Dongguan	1,086	10,960	1,011
Taishan	686	5,390	785
Xinhui	699	7,572	1,083
Shunde	1,126	12,925	1,147
Nanhai	1,314	13,801	1,050
Panyu	966	13,461	1,393
Chaozhou	460	3,720	808

Source:　*Guangdong tongji nianjian*, 1986, 1995.

New cities were also established in Guangdong in the reform era for the purpose of monitoring regional development. Qingyuan, Meizhou, Heyuan, Yangjiang and Shanwei were set up in the 1980s, merging counties under those names with some districts of neighbouring cities. The first three are located in northern Guangdong. They have a hilly environment, which does not favour development. Yangjiang and Shanwei are near the coast but their isolation and poor land transport also hinder development. However, the strategic position of these cities could rally economic development in their respective region and in themselves by soliciting more provincial or state investment and by integrating local efforts. Contrary to the "little tigers," these cities do not have a well-developed township enterprise sector. There are also no industrial satellite towns. Industrial output levels are significantly lower than in the other cities as shown in Table 15.5.

Despite the late development and difficult environment, the integrated efforts from above and below have now established a central urban district of reasonable scale in this second group of intermediate cities. New residential and commercial buildings spring up along newly-built concrete

Table 15.5   Gross Value of Industrial Output (GVIO) of Major Cities, 1994

	GVIO (RMB million)	As % of Guangdong
Guangdong total	459,585	100.0
Guangzhou	93,429	20.3
Shantou	17,542	3.8
Shaoguan	9,950	2.1
Huizhou	22,123	4.8
Jiangmen	44,963	9.7
Foshan	66,609	14.4
Zhanjiang	14,349	3.1
Maoming	11,111	2.4
Zhaoqing	27,101	5.8
Heyuan	1,840	0.4
Meizhou	6,478	1.4
Shanwei	1,571	0.3
Qingyuan	4,010	0.8
Chaozhou	4,720	1.0

Source: *Guangdong tongji nianjian 1995.*
Note: Excluding village enterprises.

roads. Also within the city are new industrial zones. Roads leading to other cities are expanded and improved, such as the National Highway 107, which links Qingyuan with Guangzhou. In particular, the development of railway transport has been given priority in these hilly regions for its efficiency. The Guangzhou–Meizhou–Shantou line, which will link up Heyuan and Meizhou with Guangzhou, and the Guangzhou–Maoming line, which will link up Yangjiang with Guangzhou, will become lifelines for these cities. With more convenient transport, the potential of these cities can further be exploited. Some export-processing industries characterizing the delta region are already dispersed to these cities because of their lower wages and adequate land supply.

Another group of intermediate cities was developed by policies which founded the SEZs. Intended primarily to effect the absorption of foreign investment and technology in the coastal region and to promote foreign trade, the SEZ policy laid the foundation for the development of Shantou, Shenzhen and Zhuhai. Except Shantou, which has been a major city, Shenzhen and Zhuhai were small border towns before the 1980s. With special arrangements made by the central and provincial governments, they were quickly transformed into modern cities.

Urban development there takes a more comprehensive and yet diverse approach than in the other intermediate cities. Foreign investment from other provinces in industry and commerce is a major factor which brought changes to these cities. In 1994, Shenzhen absorbed US$1,729 million of foreign investment and Zhuhai US$762 million, ranking second and fourth, respectively, among cities in Guangdong. Capital construction has proceeded rapidly. Shenzhen has set up six industrial and twenty-one residential districts. Zhuhai also has four industrial districts and its pattern of development is more or less similar to Shenzhen except on a smaller scale. The influx of workers from other provinces, which is encouraged by both the central and local authorities, is also a key factor for the rapid development in these cities. Most of the immigrants have come with their families and this contributes largely to the population growth. Transport in these cities is much improved. Not only are roads built to link up the various districts within the cities, they are also constructed to link up with other regions. Both of them have port facilities for external shipping. In fact, external transport with Hong Kong and Macau is extremely busy. Shenzhen now has three road check-points on its border with Hong Kong and Zhuhai has one with Macau. There are also two water-bound border check-points in each city. Both Shenzhen and Zhuhai now have an airport;

that of Zhuhai is publicized as the most modern in China. Air transport will play an important role in fostering more extensive linkages between these two cities and the rest of China, thus enhancing their status.

Transformation of Major Cities

Divergent Paths of Development

Of the twenty-two cities in Guangdong, nine have had a long history and were major cities in the province in the pre-reform period. They are Guangzhou, Shantou, Shaoguan, Huizhou, Jiangmen, Foshan, Zhanjiang, Maoming and Zhaoqing. Their development, however, had been much impeded by the former rigid strategy which over-emphasized their unitary administrative or industrial function. But in general, they can be differentiated into three categories: resource cities, port cities and historical cities.

Shaoguan and Maoming are resource cities. They are the only cities in Guangdong where the gross output value of heavy industry exceeds that of light industry. Situated close to the mountain resources in the northern hills, Shaoguan has been delegated an industrial centre for Guangdong by the state since the 1950s. The resources available include ferrous and non-ferrous metallic ores, coal and timber. They were mostly extracted and utilized by the large state or local-state enterprises. Shaoguan is also one of the major power production centres in Guangdong. Its electricity production is fed to the provincial power grid to serve other places and its industrial electricity consumption is only second to Guangzhou. This background has sustained the development of metallurgy, engineering and energy-production as Shaoguan's major industries. Maoming's rich reserve of oil shale was the primary factor for developing an oil industry in the city. In fact, the development of the whole city since the 1950s was based on the plan for an oil city for the energy-deficient south China. Subsequent development of other industries was based on its energy industry. Comparatively speaking, urban development in these two cities was given more emphasis than in other cities before 1978. Urban population growth was also more substantial, partly due to rural-urban migration and the transfer from other cities to support industrial development there.

Guangzhou, Jiangmen, Zhanjiang and Shantou are port cities. Guangzhou has served as an important port for foreign trade since the sixteenth century and Jiangmen, Shantou and Zhanjiang were founded ports in the nineteenth century. In the 1930s, Guangzhou and Shantou ranked among the top three biggest ports in China along with Shanghai. Their subsequent development in the pre-reform period, however, was impeded by the dwindling foreign trade. They were turned into administrative centres for the respective regions. The limited hinterland and poor overland transport had also hindered further development of some of these cities. Among the four cities, Jiangmen and Shantou are not yet served by railways. On the other hand, because of strategic reasons, Zhanjiang received a greater thrust in development. It has been a naval port in south China and an important seaport serving southwest China, which is accessible through the Laitang–Zhanjiang railway. In an attempt to serve the development of the interior of China in the 1960s and 1970s, the state poured substantial investment into Zhanjiang.

The other cities — Foshan, Huizhou and Zhaoqing are historical cities. Foshan has been known as one of China's four famous towns since the Ming dynasty (A.D. 1368–1644). It has had a well-established trade and manufacturing sector. Huizhou was an administrative city, where local governments had sat since the Song dynasty (A.D. 960–1125) and has been developed into the most important trading centre in the Dongjiang valley. Zhaoqing's development can even be traced back to the Han dynasty (106 B.C.–A.D. 220) as a local government seat. Both Huizhou and Zhaoqing had a much weaker industrial base than Foshan. Although the earlier policy required cities to set up their own industrial base, urban development in these two cities had not been thus stimulated. On the other hand, the scenic beauty of the lake districts in these two cities — Dinghu and Xinghu in Zhaoqing and the Xihu in Huizhou — attracted a great deal of tourism, even before 1978.

Convergence on a Similar Theme: Diversification

Development of these major cities in the reform era took divergent paths but was focused on one common theme: diversification of urban functions. Although many of the major cities were not founded as industrial centres, they have now acquired a reasonable industrial base. The gross industrial output value of the various major cities are shown in Table 15.5.

Within the industrial sector, there are three distinct features peculiar to the reform era. One is a high degree of diversification, another is the growing importance of the collective sector and the third is the dispersal of industry in the city. In Shaoguan, for instance, the output of the textile industry has now caught up with that of engineering and the output of pharmaceuticals has exceeded that of metallurgy. The collective industry sector is represented by enterprises managed by the Second Light Industrial Bureau and district and street factories in the city proper and township enterprises in the suburban districts. The output value of the collective industries in Shantou and Foshan exceeds that of the state or local-state sector. As the collective industries have proliferated into different parts of the city area, industrial distribution has become more diffused than before. Some of these cities have also set up special "economic development zones" to facilitate industrial development and to induce both local and foreign investment. They are shown in Table 15.6.

Together with reform in the industrial sector, the tertiary sector has also expanded in these cities. Retailing, catering, transport and services are increasingly generating more income and providing more employment. The nodal position of these cities is generally conducive to the development of trade. The performance of retail trade in the cities is shown in

Table 15.6   Economic Development Zones

Name	Set-up date
Chaozhou Economic Development Experimental Zone	1992–10
Chaozhou Yinfu Economic Development Experimental Zone	1992–10
Dongguan High-New-Tech Production Development Zone	1994–1
Foshan High-New-Tech Production Development Zone	1992–12
Guangzhou Economic and Technological Development Zone	1984–12
Guangzhou Tianhe High-New-Tech Production Development Zone	1991–3
Heyuan Poverty-Relief Economic Development Experimental Zone	1992–7
Huizhou City Yenzhou Haidao Development Experimental Zone	1993–12
Jiangmen City High-Tech Production Development Zone	1993–2
Meizhou Economic Development Experimental Zone	1992–10
Maoming City South Suburban Economic Development Zone	1992–12
Qingyuan Poverty-Relief Economic Development Experimental Zone	1991–9
Qiyang (Yuhu) Economic Development Experimental Zone	1992–8
Shantou High-New-Tech Production Development Experimental Zone	1993–7
Shanwei Honghaiwan Development Experimental Zone	1992–11
Weizhou Zhonghai High-New-Tech Production Development Zone	1992–12
Yangjiang Jinlandao Development Experimental Zone	1993–5
Yangjianggang Economic Development Experimental Zone	1993–8
Yunfu Lindu Economic Development Experimental Zone	1992–10
Zhanjiang Economic Development Zone	1984–11
Zhanjiang Shuidong Economic Development Experimental Zone	1992–6
Zhanjiang Donghaidao Economic Development Experimental Zone	1992–7
Zhuhai High-New-Tech Production Development Zone	1992–12

Source: *Guangdong nianjian 1995.*

Table 15.7. Note the predominance of the port cities, which are privileged by better transport development.

There are three specific aspects about the development of the trade sector in these cities. First is the emergence of individual-run enterprises, which are getting an increasing share of the business, just as in the market towns. This has led to a greater diversity of suppliers and abundance in supplies. This is particularly true regarding farm produce. Direct sales by the farmers in the cities amounted to a substantial portion of the total value of retail sales as Table 15.7 shows. Agricultural trade markets in the cities — averaging twenty-five in each city — are generally the venue for these retail transactions but roadside stalls and grocery shops are also quite popular. These market places are strongly supported by increases in farm output and by the growing urban demands which result not only from an increase of population but from rising household income.

Development of the trade sector or the tertiary sector in general also creates more employment opportunities for the city people. In Guangdong, over 5.2 million of the urban labourers are engaged in tertiary production. Among them, 80% are self-employed. Indeed, individual-run businesses are now infiltrating every corner of the city. All kinds of shops, restaurants, hair-salons and repair workshops can be found along the streets, together with temporary stalls and hawkers in the busy market districts. Sometimes, they pose serious problems of littering and blocking pedestrian traffic.

The development of one component of the tertiary sector — transport — in fact technically determines the development of other components.

Table 15.7 Total Value of Retail Sales (TVRS) in Major Cities, 1994

(Unit: RMB million)

	TVRS	Direct supply of farm outputs by peasants
Guangzhou	44,819	12,361
Shantou	9,105	3,736
Shaoguan	4,568	1,692
Huizhou	7,461	3,249
Foshan	16,457	5,169
Jiangmen	10,400	2,777
Zhanjiang	10,017	5,064
Maoming	8,586	3,565
Zhaoqing	8,867	3,217

Source: *Guangdong tongji nianjian 1995.*

Improvement in transport both within the cities and to and from the cities increases the flow of people and goods. Besides the bicycle, which is still a primary mode of transport in the cities, there is a substantial growth of motor-vehicles, especially vans which can be used for both passenger and cargo transport. In 1994, there were over 982,044 registered motor-cars in Guangdong, increasing from 240,000 in 1985. Many of them serve the city and its rural counties.

Improvement in transport also helps to promote tourism. Some of these cities have become tourist centres. Apart from Shantou and Jiangmen, all major cities are served by railways which form part of the national network. (Shantou is going to be linked with the national network with a Guangzhou–Meizhou–Shantou line which is under construction. Jiangmen, on the other hand, is a node on the proposed Guangzhou–Zhuhai line.) Except Zhaoqing and Jiangmen, all cities have an airport. The fact that airports in Guangzhou, Foshan, Zhanjiang and Shantou are served by both domestic and international flights further enhances the tourist potential of these cities. Development of tourism in the major cities is shown in Table 15.8. Guangzhou, privileged by its well established land, sea and air transport, gets the lion's share of the tourist business.

Besides the port cities, other major cities are also developing their water transport, making use of the waterways which pass through them. Shaoguan has a water-borne cargo transport link with Guangzhou and Hong Kong. Foshan has set up its container terminal at Lanshi and it has

Table 15.8　Revenue in Tourism in Major Cities, 1994

	Revenue (RMB million)
Guangzhou	9,516
Shantou	778
Shaoguan	145
Huizhou	393
Foshan	1,114
Jiangmen	974
Zhanjiang	377
Maoming	150
Zhaoqing	643

Source:　*Guangdong tongji nianjian 1995.*
Note:　In state-run/local government-run enterprises.

regular passenger ferry service to Hong Kong. Zhaoqing also enjoys external shipping facilities through Xijiang. It has scheduled cargo and passenger traffic to Hong Kong. Huizhou has river transport on Dongjiang.
Despite the limited navigability of the river, it still has 1.3 million tonnes
of water-borne freight traffic annually. Situated near the coast, Maoming is
developing port facilities at Shuidonggang, which is 24 km away.

Physical Growth, Problems and Solutions

The increase in economic activity in these cities and the growth of population proceeded hand in hand with progress in construction. The built-up
area in these cities expands and improves together with increase in social
amenities. Among the major cities, the port cities of Guangzhou, Shantou
and Zhanjiang have undergone a more vigorous construction boom,
averaging over 600,000 sq m of completed building per year. Indeed, these
port cities also have the largest residential areas. Guangzhou being the
provincial capital has the biggest built-up area as shown in Table 15.9. It is
also expanding physically much faster than other cities except Shantou,
where the SEZ is also rapidly growing. However, although Guangzhou has
the most extensive built-up area, the average living area of its population is
relatively limited. Because of the rapid growth of population, Guangzhou
has become a more crowded city than most of the others. The cause of the
rapid population growth is not so much natural increase, which is well

Table 15.9 Living Space in Major Cities, 1994

	Built-up area (sq km)	Residential area (million sq m)	Average living-area (sq m/person)
Guangzhou	216	29.04	9.34
Shantou	86	7.26	10.84
Shaoguan	34	2.06	5.15
Huizhou	23	2.41	10.95
Jiangmen	37	3.22	11.10
Foshan	29	3.32	8.97
Zhanjiang	57	4.19	8.55
Maoming	27	3.50	7.14
Zhaoqing	20	1.86	7.15

Source: *Guangdong tongji nianjian 1995.*
Note: Figures refer to that of city proper (*shiqu*).

controlled just as in other cites, but in-migration — people come to Guangzhou for a share of its prosperity or for reunion with family members after years of separation under the pre-reform policies. In fact, Guangzhou has been plagued by the so-called "blind-flow" problem in recent years. In the Spring Festival in 1992, over 350,000 people from other parts of Guangdong and from other provinces arrived in Guangzhou for job opportunities.[22]

Like other big cities in the world, Guangzhou is experiencing many kinds of urban problems apart from overcrowding. Traffic congestion and pollution are serious.[23] City officials are now responding positively to these problems. An underground mass transit railway and a second ring road are under construction. Residences and economic activities are being relocated to suburban districts such as Tianhe in the east, where a new railway station is located. Extensive construction is also underway in Henan district in the south which lies close to the new city of Panyu. The Haiyun Bridge, which spans the shores of the Pearl River in Guangzhou since 1990, has facilitated the commuters.

Guangzhou's development to the east and south not only reflects the availability of land in these districts but also the increasing link it has with the cities in those directions: Dongguan to the east and Panyu to the south are Guangzhou's rapidly industrializing neighbours. Development towards these two cities would facilitate greater economic interaction with them, and also with Shenzhen SEZ to the south of Dongguan.

Emergence of Urban Regions

Factors for Localized Development

Just as Guangzhou is growing towards Dongguan and Panyu, many cities and towns in the delta region are undergoing similar metamorphism. But before 1949, cities in Guangdong had little interaction among themselves and had not effectively diffused economic development to the towns surrounding them. This limited their expansion and the eventual development of urban regions. From the 1950s, the Maoist developmental strategy emphasized self-sufficiency and self-reliance other than interdependence and exchange. This balked the integration among the cities and towns. Free traffic of goods and people was severely restricted, and the administrative segregation of regions and districts limited the development of the city's sphere of influence.

Relatively speaking, the Pearl River Delta carries a denser cluster of towns and cities. However, the mere physical barrier of the numerous distributaries posed severe difficulties handicapping their interaction. For instance, Guangzhou and Panyu have a physical distance of only 15 km but motor transport took more than two hours to reach the other side. Bridging these waterways was completed only in 1990; and now, the time of road transport between the two cities is shortened to forty-five minutes.

Factors Encouraging Integration

The return to economic considerations in the reform era by and large lifted the administrative segregation of urban units. But more importantly, the greater attention given to investment in inter-urban transport is a prime factor encouraging interaction and integration. Panyu, for example, spent RMB289 million in the period 1987–1989 in bridge construction and road development. Now it is not only linked with Guangzhou in the north by the Dashi and Leqi Bridges, it is also linked with Shunde in the west by the Sanshan Bridge. From the centre of Panyu to that of Shunde, it takes less than half an hour by car. To the east, Panyu has a vehicular ferry service with Dongguan and a new Humen Bridge spanning the two cities across the Pearl River is now in service.[24] Better transport links help to knit major urban centres into a network. Along the trunk roads between the urban units in the Pearl River Delta, settlements sprang up on land converted from farmland. Many township factories specializing in export-processing for Hong Kong or Taiwan firms also found the convenience of ribbon location and mushroomed along the roadside. From the suburb of Guangzhou to Dongguan and all through to Shenzhen, the line of settlement is almost uninterrupted. Parallel development takes place from Guangzhou to Foshan, Nanhai, Shunde and then to Zhongshan and Zhuhai. Towns in other parts of the delta are also linked with the cities in a similar manner.

Transport between cities and towns is also greatly improved. Three factors are responsible for this. First, the former inward-looking self-sufficiency and self-reliance principles of rural development have been replaced by a dynamic outward-looking "external orientation" of local officials who understand better the relation between exchange and growth. As the local economies grow, town governments can afford greater spending on transport improvement. Second, with the increase in farm productivity, more foodstuffs and raw materials are available to meet increasing urban demands. At the same time, more goods and services are needed by the peasants who have become better off. This has been outlined earlier. Therefore, flows and exchanges within the hierarchy of cities, towns and villages increase. Third, the tide of rural industrialization necessitates better transport facilities. The growing number of industrial satellite towns in the delta region mentioned earlier illustrates the extent of this demand as many factories in these towns are engaged in subcontracting production for industries in cities or are producing for retail and export agencies in cities.

A unique feature of the development of urban regions in Guangdong is the limited involvement of state or provincial planning. Rather, the spontaneous efforts of the local people and the need of the local or regional economy have created the dynamics for development and this dynamism can increase as long as local needs multiply. The laws of economics rather than political goals now dominate urban development.

The Pearl River Urban Region

Against the background described above, the Pearl River Delta is being transformed into a large urban region with a distinctively higher density of urban centres: one in every 100 sq km, compared with one in every 135 sq km in average Guangdong and one in 195 sq km in the hilly region. Within this region of almost 44,300 sq km, the cluster of cities of Guangzhou, Foshan, Shunde, Nanhai and Panyu forms the core. On the periphery, there are Dongguan, Shenzhen, Zhuhai, Zhongshan and Jiangmen. Three cities lie on the outskirts of this urban region: Qingyuan, Zhaoqing and Huizhou. The hierarchy of urban centres in the delta region is shown in Figure 15.2.[25]

It must be noted that the impact of rail development on the urban region in the delta has been much smaller than the development of roads. Many more string settlements have sprung up along roads than along railways. This is due mainly to the greater flexibility and efficiency of road transport in effecting inter-urban interactions especially over short distances. However, it should also be recognized that rail development is able to bring more interactions over longer distances and help to generate a more extensive urban network. For instance, the extension of the railway from the delta region to Shaoguan in the north, to Maoming, Zhanjiang and Yangchun in the west and to Huizhou, Heyuan, Meizhou, Chaozhou and

Figure 15.2   Diagrammatic Representation of Major Nodes and Links in the Urban Region of the Pearl River Delta

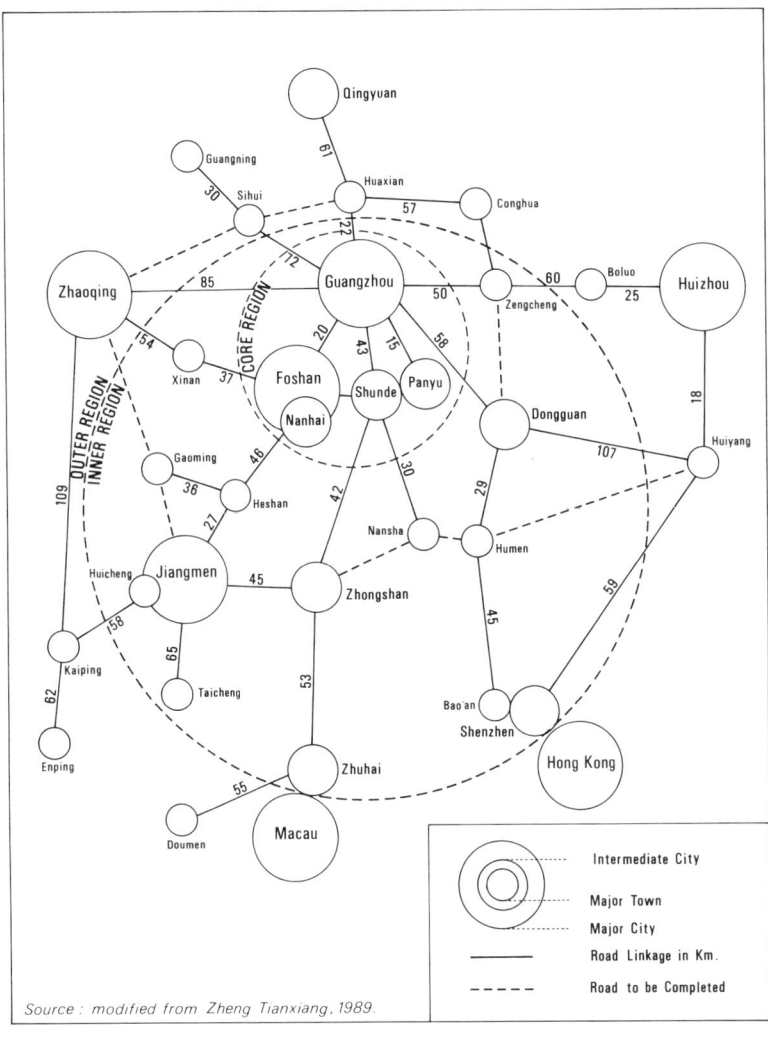

Source : modified from Zheng Tianxiang, 1989.

Source: Modified from Zheng Tianxiang, "The Spatial Relationships among Hong Kong, Macau and the Pearl River Delta Area" (see note 25).

Shantou in the east will be important in enhancing the central position of the core urban region centred at Guangzhou. Networking the cities can help to expand their hinterlands and promote their comparative advantage. This will, in turn, integrate and promote economic development in Guangdong as a whole.

Conclusion

Guangdong's urban development has a close relation to its economic development. As a heritage of the former development strategy, Guangdong's level of urban development ranked only eighteenth among the provinces of China in 1980, just as its low level of economic development. However, under the economic reforms, both Guangdong's economic development and urban development took a huge leap forward. Four aspects of economic development are particularly important for urban development in Guangdong: improvement of rural productivity, development of township enterprises, diversification of urban functions and development of transport.

Rural reforms improve rural productivity and increase the supply of foodstuffs, both essential in supporting the growth of urban population. The reforms stimulate the retail market and promote economic transaction in towns and cities. This helps to revitalize market towns. At the same time, a lot of rural labour can be transferred to non-farm production. Development of township enterprises is instrumental in absorbing the exodus of surplus labour from the farm sector and is an essential factor for developing industrial satellite towns.

Diversification of urban functions created new intermediate cities. These cities were set up by the state (and provincial government) with particular economic intentions or reasons. Shenzhen and Zhuhai were developed as enclaves for trying out capitalistic ways of production. Qingyuan, Heyuan and Meizhou were founded as regional centres to promote economic development of the backward hilly regions. Zhongshan, Dongguan, Shunde, Panyu, Nanhai and Chaozhou are hubs of economic activities and their economic progress accounts for them achieving city status.

Major cities in Guangdong had a comparatively slower rate of economic growth than some of the intermediate cities mainly because of factors such as increase in rural productivity and development of township enterprises, which were predominant in the latter but did not gain the same momentum in the former. But major cities generally have a more diversified economy and their development is favoured by either the presence of good port facilities or rail and air transport or both. They also have a reasonable industrial base. Among them, Guangzhou, Foshan and Shantou have a more developed light industry sector, while Shaoguan, Maoming and Zhanjiang have a more developed heavy industry sector. Zhaoqing and

Huizhou have more tourist resources and trade potential. Nevertheless, all the major cities now emphasize diversification and are putting an increasing investment on construction of both infrastructure and housing. They also focus on the transport development which could enhance their "external orientation."

"External orientation" generally means relationships developed with localities in both Guangdong and other provinces, as well as overseas. Hong Kong, though not a model followed by all the urban centres in Guangdong, is a catalyst for urban development in the province, especially in the Pearl River Delta. This has resulted in the creation of an extensive urban region there with conspicuous ribbon development along the artery roads. Many of these urban centres are engaged in export-processing for Hong Kong business firms.

Urban development is the key to the economic development in Guangdong, and conversely, without the economic motive, urban development is difficult to sustain. As economic development is more widespread in the province, the number and size of urban centres also grow. This has the effect of further diffusing and enhancing development. Through the improvement in transport and increase in the flow of people and goods, a more integrated urban network is being set up in Guangdong, centred around the provincial capital and the Pearl River Delta and linked up with the other major cities, intermediate cities and towns. Although the primacy of Guangzhou is decreasing to a certain extent, its gravity of attraction is increasing. As the economy of Guangdong is further shifting rapidly towards the secondary and tertiary sectors, it is not difficult to envisage more vigorous urban development in the future. In this respect, Guangdong perhaps needs to plan ahead to ensure a more rational distribution of urban centres and/or urban functions so as to enhance economic efficiency.

Notes

1. The definition of "urban" in this chapter will follow the Chinese notions of "city" (*chengshi*) and "town" (*chengzhen*). For a more detailed discussion, see Chan Kam Wing and Xu Xueqiang, "Urban Population Growth and Urbanization in China Since 1949: Reconstructing a Baseline," *The China Quarterly*, No. 104 (1985), pp. 583–613.

2. Zhu Yuncheng (ed.), *Zhongguo renkou: Guangdong fence* (Population in China: Guangdong Volume) (Beijing: Zhongguo caizheng jingji chubanshe, 1988), p. 208.

3. Ibid.

4. If Guangdong's per capita gross value of agricultural and industrial output, which calculates only agricultural and industrial production, is taken into account instead, its performance would fall behind the national average. See Guojia tongjiju (ed.), *Zhongguo tongji nianjian 1986* (Chinese Statistical Yearbook 1986), pp. 31, 40, 71; Guangdong nianjian bianzuan weiyuanhui (ed.), *Guangdong nianjian 1990* (Guangdong Yearbook 1990) (Guangzhou: Guangdong renmin chubanshe, 1990), p. 534.

5. Xu Xueqiang et al., *Zhujiang sanjiaozhou de fazhan yu chengshihua* (Development and Urbanization in Pearl River Delta) (Guangzhou: Zhongshan daxue chubanshe, 1988), p. 85; Liu Qi and Wei Qingquan, *Guangdongsheng dili* (Geography of Guangdong Province) (Guangzhou: Zhongshan daxue chubanshe, 1988), p. 199; Zhu Yuncheng (ed.), *Zhongguo renkou: Guangdong fence* (note 2), p. 209.

6. Urbanization level is taken to mean the percentage of overall population living in towns and cities. Caution has to be exercised over the Chinese definitions. See note 1; also Zhu Yuncheng (ed.), *Zhongguo renkou: Guangdong fence* (note 2), p. 209.

7. Figures since 1989 exclude towns in Hainan Province, which was part of Guangdong before 1988.

8. Lo Chor Pang, "Population Change and Urban Development in the Pearl River Delta: Spatial Policy Implications," *Asian Geography*, Vol. 8, Nos. 1, 2 (1989), pp. 11–34.

9. Guangdongsheng tongjiju (ed.), *Guangdongsheng shi de xian gaikuang* (General Conditions of Guangdong's Cities, Regions and Counties) (Guangzhou: n.p., 1985); Guangdongsheng minzhengting and Guangdongsheng ditu chubanshe (ed.), *Guangdongsheng zhengqu tuce* (Administrative Atlas of Guangdong Province) (Guangzhou: Ditu chubanshe, 1989).

10. Guowuyuan, *Guowuyuan guanyu chengzhen feinongye geti jingji ruogan zhengceshang guiding* (State Council's Several Policy Regulations Concerning Non-farm Individual Economies in Towns), 7 July 1981.

11. Guowuyuan, *Guowuyuan guanyu nongcun geti gongshangye de ruogan guiding* (State Council's Several Regulations Concerning Rural Individual Industry and Commerce), 17 April 1984.

12. Yu Hongjun and Ning Yuemin, *Chengshi dili gailun* (An Introduction to Urban Geography) (Hefei: Anhui kexue jishu chubanshe 1983), p. 148.

13. Guangdongsheng tongjiju, internal document. Apart from the Pearl River Delta, fifteen towns in the suburbs of Maoming and Zhanjiang were also designated industrial satellite towns. See *Guangdong nianjian 1990*.

14. Shunde renmen zhengfu, *Shundexian zhenban gongye* (Township Industry of Shunde County) (1987).

15. Zhonggong zhongyang yu guowuyuan, "*Zhuanfa nongmuyuyebu he*

budangzhu 'Guanyu kaichuang shedui qiye xinjumian de baogao' de tongzhi (Notification on Relaying Ministry of Agriculture and Its Party Branch's "Report Concerning the Creation of a New Situation for Commune and Brigade Enterprises"), *De tongji*, 1 March 1984; Guowuyuan, *"Guanyu fazhan shedui qiye ruogan wenti de guiding"* (Regulations on Several Issues Concerning the Development of Commune and Brigade Enterprises), *De tongji*, 3 July 1979.

16. Edward Woo, "The Development of Local Economies in Guangdong: Lessons from the 'Little Tigers,'" in *New Imperatives for East Asia and Southeast Asia*, edited by East Asian Educational Association (Hong Kong, 1991), pp. 57–78.

17. *Statistical Yearbook of Guangdong, 1995; Statistical Yearbook of China, 1995.*

18. Guangdongsheng tongjiju, internal document.

19. Ibid.

20. Some workers in town are not registered even as "zili kouliang renkou" for various reasons. They are known as "temporary residents" or "black market residents."

21. *Singtao Evening Post*, 15 February 1992.

22. Ibid.

23. *Wen Wei Po*, 13 March 1992 and 18 May 1992.

24. *Wen Wei Po*, 3 May 1997.

25. See also Zheng Tianxiang, "The Spatial Relationships among Hong Kong, Macau and the Pearl River Delta Area," *Asian Geographer*, Vol. 8, Nos. 1, 2 (1989), pp. 89–102.

16

Changes in the Legal System

Susan Finder

Guangdong has been at the forefront of China's post-1979 economic reforms, opening to the outside world and experiencing social changes. In this period, Guangdong has created a unique position within China's legal system and undertaken important legal reforms. At the same time, economic and social changes have created new challenges and stresses on the province's legal institutions. This chapter will examine some significant changes in the province's legislative, judicial and law enforcement organs.

Guangdong and Legislative Reforms

An important aspect of the post-1979 reforms has been to give Guangdong a unique position in the Chinese legislative system. The People's Republic of China (PRC) has a unitary legislative system, in which the national legislature, the National People's Congress (NPC), wields supreme legislative power. Part of the decentralization of power under the reform policies has involved granting increased law-making powers to provincial people's congresses and their standing committees.

The 1982 Constitution empowers provincial people's congresses (and their standing committees) to enact legislation entitled local regulations (*difangxing fagui*). National law does not give provincial people's congresses exclusive authority over any legislative area but rather allows them to legislate to implement or supplement national laws or administrative regulations or to deal with specific local problems. Their enactments may not contravene the Constitution, national laws (enacted by the NPC or its standing committee), or administrative regulations issued by the State Council. Among the post-1979 reforms has been the passage of national law which gives Guangdong and Shenzhen unique legislative authority. Shenzhen is no longer unique in its legislative authority as national law has given similar authority to the Xiamen Special Economic Zone (SEZ).

In 1981, a resolution of the NPC Standing Committee gave the Guangdong and Fujian People's Congress and their standing committees increased legislative power to formulate separate economic regulations for their SEZs in the light of their specific conditions and actual needs.[1] Regulations drafted by governments or legislatures of the SEZ's had to be submitted to the provincial congress (or its standing committee) for approval to achieve the status of local regulations.

In line with the role of Guangdong, particularly the Shenzhen SEZ as China's "window to the outside world," many of the economic regulations adopted by the Guangdong congress have been significant in providing a legal foundation for China's transition to a market economy. Some regulations have been "pilot-studies" for national legislation. In early 1984, for example, the Guangdong Provincial Congress adopted the Shenzhen SEZ foreign-related contract regulations. Those regulations provided drafts of national legislation with real-world experience which assisted them in the drafting of the National Foreign Economic Contracts Law. Some important provisions on commercial law, such as the 1993 Shenzhen SEZ Enterprise Bankruptcy Regulations, are without counterparts in national law. Legislation drafted in the Shenzhen SEZ, particularly in the areas of commercial law and land use, has borrowed from provisions from Hong Kong law.

While some Shenzhen provisions were submitted to the Guangdong People's Congress for approval, other regulations have remained in the form of documents issued by the SEZ people's government, because the provisions were "too radical" for the Guangdong congress to accept. People's governments at the provincial level, provincial capital cities, and large cities approved by the State Council are empowered to enact local administrative measures entitled local government rules (*difang zhengfu guize*), within the limits of national law and State Council administrative rules and regulations. Government authorities at the lower levels, such as those of the Shenzhen municipal government, lack such authority, which left Shenzhen documents in a "legal limbo."

The Shenzhen authorities pressured Beijing for the authority to enact local regulations. In the spring of 1989, the NPC authorized its standing committee to grant the Shenzhen SEZ the power to enact local regulations, in apparent violation of Art. 100 of the Constitution, which gives such authority to the people's congresses of provinces and directly administered municipalities. The delegation of authority was conditional on the SEZ establishing a people's congress. The proposal to grant the Shenzhen SEZ power to enact local regulations came under heavy criticism by some NPC delegates, who abstained and voted against the proposal. In late 1990 the Shenzhen People's Congress and its standing committee were established.

In July of 1992, the NPC Standing Committee granted the Shenzhen SEZ the power to enact local regulations. Similar authority was given to the Xiamen SEZ in 1994. Shenzhen has speeded the pace of promulgating market-oriented legislation, especially by drawing on the legislative experiences of Hong Kong and other jurisdictions.

There remains a gap between the promulgation of legislation and its enforcement. This has been especially dramatic in the area of fire safety. Although Guangdong Province has adopted a number of regulations on fire safety, a series of fires in industrial premises and a budget hotel in Shenzhen have highlighted deficiencies in the enforcement of fire safety standards in Shenzhen.

Civil Dispute Resolution

One of the most important, but least noticed, legal changes in Guangdong has been the creation of institutions to resolve civil, particularly commercial, disputes. Guangdong has witnessed an exponential growth in the number of commercial disputes, a by-product of the province's dramatic economic changes. These commercial disputes include disputes between domestic Chinese companies, between foreign and domestic companies, and between individual private businesses. The growth in commercial disputes is linked with the greater financial independence of state-owned companies, the growth of the private sector and the large-scale growth of foreign-invested companies.

The explosion in commercial disputes in the last ten years has pushed Guangdong to the forefront in China, in establishing new institutions to resolve commercial disputes. The new institutions include an international arbitration commission, a specialized maritime court and specialized commercial divisions within the local courts.

Arbitration: The Shenzhen Commission of the China International Economic and Trade Arbitration Commission

The China International Economic and Trade Arbitration Commission (CIETAC) of the China Council for the Promotion of International Trade (CCPIT) is the only institution in China that arbitrates foreign trade and investment disputes. Chinese law does not require Chinese companies to arbitrate disputes in China, but the Ministry of Foreign Trade and Economic Cooperation encourages Chinese organizations to do so. CIETAC was established in 1956 with its headquarters in Beijing. In 1984, CIETAC established its first branch in Shenzhen, known as the China International Economic and Trade Arbitration Commission, Shenzhen Commission (Shenzhen Commission). The Shenzhen Commission was established to provide greater convenience to parties in Chinese foreign trade and investment disputes, many of whom are located either in Hong Kong or in southern China.

Under the auspices of the Shenzhen Commission, trade, investment and other international commercial disputes are settled through arbitration. Like other international arbitration organizations, the Shenzhen Commission accepts cases only if the parties have a written agreement to submit their disputes to arbitration. Contracting parties may specify by contract or in a supplementary agreement that they want to submit their disputes to arbitration in Shenzhen.[2] If their arbitration agreement does not so specify, but does provide for arbitration by CIETAC, CIETAC rules provide that the claimant shall decide the place in which the dispute shall be arbitrated.[3]

According to CIETAC arbitration rules, arbitration proceedings held in Chinese, are closed to the public and arbitral awards are final. The rules provide that cases are heard by panels of three arbitrators, one selected by each disputing party from CIETAC's list of arbitrators. The third arbitrator may be chosen jointly by the two parties or the parties may delegate authority to appoint the third arbitrator to the Chairman of the Arbitration Commission. If the parties fail to choose a third arbitrator, the Chairman of the Arbitration Commission shall appoint the third arbitrator.[4] Arbitrators, however, do not represent either party.

Until October 1994, the Shenzhen and Beijing Commissions had separate panels of arbitrators. The panel of the Shenzhen Commission included several Hong Kong lawyers even before the Commission in Beijing included foreign and Hong Kong lawyers on its list. A unified list of CIETAC arbitrators was released in 1994. It includes Hong Kong and foreign arbitrators, as well as mainland arbitrators. According to the CIETAC arbitration rules, parties may designate agents to represent them in arbitration proceedings who may be either foreign or Chinese citizens, but need not be lawyers. Parties usually designate lawyers because competent representation at an arbitration proceeding involves knowledge of international trade or investment law. In an increasing number of cases, Hong Kong lawyers have appeared on behalf of their clients in Shenzhen Commission arbitration proceedings. As of July, 1996, the Shenzhen Commission had arbitrated over 790 international trade, joint venture and other international commercial disputes. Most of these were disputes between Hong Kong and Chinese companies. In recent years the number of disputes arbitrated by the Commission has escalated rapidly, going from 57 cases in 1993 to 146 in 1994 and 147 in 1995.

CIETAC arbitration may apply foreign law to a dispute if the contract so specifies or choice of law rules so indicates, unless otherwise provided by law. Chinese joint venture law, for example, requires that Chinese law be the law of PRC joint venture contracts. In reality, many Chinese foreign trade contracts fail to specify the law of the contract and CIETAC arbitration generally applies Chinese law, supplemented by international practice. Because Chinese commercial law is relatively undeveloped, CIETAC arbitrators often run into difficulties in applying Chinese law because of the lack of specificity in some Chinese legislation and because the contractual documentation used by the parties is inadequate. The latter is a particular problem in disputes between Hong Kong and PRC parties because the parties expect that their disputes will be settled informally, rather than through legal proceedings.

Unlike courts, arbitral organizations such as CIETAC lack the authority to enforce their awards. If a party fails to execute an arbitral award, the other party must apply to a court for enforcement. In China, a party seeking to enforce a CIETAC award may apply to the intermediate people's court in which the defendant's place of business or property is located. Some parties seeking to enforce CIETAC awards have encountered difficulties because of "judicial local protectionism," the tendency of local courts protecting local enterprises. Because China acceded to the 1958 United Nations Convention on the Recognition and Enforcement of Arbitral Awards (generally known as the New York Convention) in 1987, arbitral awards of the Shenzhen Commission can be enforced in Hong Kong, or other jurisdictions which have acceded to the New York Convention. Thus far, over twenty Shenzhen Commission arbitral awards have been enforced through the Hong Kong courts. The New York Convention ceased to be applicable between the mainland and Hong Kong as of 1 July 1997. As of this writing, there is no mechanism in place for the mutual enforcement of arbitral awards after the return of Hong Kong to China, although the issue was discussed by the Sino-British Joint Liaison Group and has now been left for the SAR Government.

Among the Hong Kong and foreign legal community, CIETAC arbitration is held in generally good repute. Giving foreign (and Hong Kong) parties confidence in the fairness of CIETAC proceedings is the inclusion of several Hong Kong and foreign lawyers on CIETAC's panel of arbitrators and the fact that non-PRC lawyers may represent clients in arbitral proceedings. The mainland arbitrators on the CIETAC panel of arbitrators generally number among the country's experts in international commercial law. There has been some criticism within the international legal community of the requirement in the CIETAC arbitration rules that parties are limited in their choice of arbitrators to those approved by CIETAC. Although CIETAC arbitration has not been entirely without problems, there have been relatively few improprieties and little or no interference from Chinese government authorities. Parties have found greater difficulties when seeking to enforce CIETAC awards in the mainland courts. In response to this problem, in the fall of 1995, the Supreme People's Court issued a circular requiring approval of higher courts for the refusal to enforce a CIETAC (or foreign) arbitral award. It remains to be seen whether this circular will facilitate the enforcement of CIETAC awards in China.

Domestic Arbitration Commissions (Rider 1)

The PRC Arbitration Law which came into force in 1995, provided for the establishment of local Arbitration Commissions throughout China, intended to replace the economic contract arbitration commissions under the auspices of the State Administration of Industry and Commerce. The law was intended to make major changes in the domestic arbitration system by separating domestic arbitration from government administration and thereby diminishing the influence of local government in the dispute resolution process.

However, the Arbitration Law provides that the local people's governments to organize the establishment of the Arbitration Commissions, including funding. It is understood that some local governments are encouraging their affiliated companies to include arbitration clauses designating the local Arbitration Commission in their standard contracts. Although the domestic Arbitration Commissions have only been established for a short time, old problems of lack of competence and political interference have not entirely disappeared. According to anecdotal information, staff in some local Arbitration Commissions as well as some local arbitrators are unfamiliar with arbitration.

Parties have the freedom to choose the Arbitration Commission which is to have jurisdiction over any disputes, regardless of location. This is aimed at breaking down the influence of local protectionism.

An arbitration clause or subsequent arbitration agreement must be concluded for an Arbitration Commission to have jurisdiction, unless the contract contains a reference to the now defunct economic contract arbitration commissions. Parties are allowed to designate arbitrators for their tribunal from a panel of arbitrators selected by the Commission in question. Some Hong Kong solicitors have been named to the Shenzhen Arbitration Commission.

It is understood that nationally, approximately 120 Arbitration Commissions have been established, including ones in Shenzhen and Guangzhou. As of late 1996, the Shenzhen Arbitration Commission had accepted 45 cases.

The primary focus of the Arbitration Commissions work is arbitration of disputes between Chinese entities. However, in 1996 the domestic Arbitration Commissions were authorized to accept foreign-related cases, although this decision has been criticised in China by some for its questionable legal basis. However, it is understood that the Shenzhen Arbitration Commission, among others, has already accepted a number of foreign-related cases.

The foreign business community should be aware that it is not certain that foreign lawyers may appear before the domestic Arbitration Commissions. An additional disadvantage is that the choice of arbitrators is more limited than before CIETAC. In addition it is unresolved question whether an award made by a domestic arbitration tribunal convening a foreign related case would be enforceable in the usual way in a New York Convention country.

Foreign businessmen, especially those unfamiliar with legal matters, may easily confuse the Beijing, Shanghai, or Shenzhen Arbitration Commissions, which are domestic Arbitration Commissions, when they intend their contracts to refer to CIETAC's head commission in Beijing and its sub-commissions in Shanghai and Shenzhen.

The Courts

The economic changes in Guangdong have been accompanied by an explosion in commercial disputes, both international and domestic. In most of these disputes, the parties have failed to conclude agreements to submit their disputes to arbitration. Therefore, the increase in commercial disputes has caused the Guangdong courts to be inundated with commercial cases. The explosion of commercial litigation in Guangdong has forced the province to be in the forefront in China, in the creation of institutions within the courts to resolve new types and a large number of commercial cases.

Like all Chinese provinces, Guangdong has a three-tier court system, including a provincial Higher People's Court, located in Guangzhou, approximately twenty intermediate people's courts, located in municipalities and rural prefectures, and 120 basic level people's courts, established in rural county seats and urban districts. In addition, Guangdong has a specialized Maritime Court which hears maritime cases in the first instance.

Guangzhou Maritime Court

One of the important legal reforms in Guangdong in the post-1979 period is the establishment of the Guangzhou Maritime Court. Unlike other legal systems which have had specialized courts to hear maritime (admiralty) cases for hundreds of years, China did not establish such courts until 1984. The establishment of maritime courts in China is a product of the post-1979 economic reforms. During this period, China has expanded its ocean-going fleet exponentially. There has been a great increase in traffic by foreign vessels to Chinese ports. The increase in Chinese maritime traffic has meant a jump in both the number of contractual disputes involving maritime trade and tort claims arising from maritime collisions.

In the period 1979–1984, an increasing number of maritime cases were heard in local courts in China. The local courts are poorly prepared to hear such cases, which require a knowledge of specialized areas of law and often, technical aspects of shipping. Although China has had a specialized international maritime arbitration commission since 1958, it cannot arbitrate cases which lack arbitration agreements.[5] The number of maritime cases in which the parties did not conclude arbitration agreements rose in the period 1979–1984. Therefore, in 1984, the Standing Committee of the National People's Congress passed a law authorizing the Supreme People's Court to establish maritime courts in several coastal ports.[6] The law limits the jurisdiction of maritime courts to maritime tort and contract cases and does not include criminal or civil matters. Immediately thereafter, the Supreme People's Court established maritime courts in five ports, including Guangzhou.[7] The number of maritime courts has subsequently been expanded to nine.

A maritime court was established in Guangzhou because of the heavy maritime traffic on the Pearl River and in the South China Sea. The territorial jurisdiction of the Guangzhou Maritime Court originally extended from Guangxi to the Guangdong border with Fujian, including Hainan, thus including the busy ports of Huangpu, Shantou, Shekou and Guangzhou.[8] In 1990, a maritime court was established in Haikou, reducing the territorial jurisdiction of the court.[9] The number of cases filed in the Guangzhou court has remained about the same, indicating that the number of maritime cases arising from the jurisdiction of the court has increased.[10]

According to sources in the Guangzhou Maritime Court, approximately 70% of the cases that the court hears involve domestic parties, while 30% involve foreign parties or a transaction or collision involving Chinese parties abroad. The Guangzhou Maritime Court is one of the busiest in China, hearing over 100 cases per year. About 50% of the judges on the court are university law graduates, while the other 50% have a maritime background and subsequently received legal training. Like all Chinese judges, they lack long-term tenure. In practice, there is relatively little personnel turnover in the Guangzhou Maritime Court. The cases that the court hears are generally complex, with relatively large sums of money in dispute. Appeals from the Guangzhou Maritime Court are heard by the Guangdong Higher People's Court. Unlike the local courts, which are funded by local governments, the Guangzhou Maritime Court is funded by the Ministry of Communications.

The major problem that has handicapped the Guangzhou Maritime Court is inadequate substantive and procedural law. This problem is not unique to Guangzhou, but rather is common to all maritime courts. Although maritime courts were established in 1984, for many years the courts had to decide cases despite a dearth of procedural and substantive provisions. In the area of procedural law, for example, initially Chinese maritime courts lacked the power to order the arrest of ships before a claim was filed. Because the 1982 Civil Procedure Law omitted such provisions, the Supreme People's Court issued a legal interpretation to give maritime courts such authority. In the area of substantive law, Chinese contract law lacks provisions on maritime charter agreements, for example. It is only since the Standing Committee of the National People's Congress promulgated the Maritime Commerce Law in late 1992 that the Chinese maritime courts have had a more complete body of law on which to rely.

The Guangdong Courts

As mentioned above, the Guangdong court system includes a provincial Higher People's Court, located in Guangzhou, approximately twenty intermediate people's courts, and 120 basic level people's courts. The economic changes in Guangdong have been accompanied by an explosion in civil litigation. The major (and virtually unreported) change in the Guangdong legal system is that the courts have had to make significant structural changes to cope with a vastly increased caseload which primarily involves civil, rather than criminal, cases.

Contrary to popular impressions both in China and abroad, most cases heard in the Guangdong courts are *not* criminal cases, rather they are civil disputes (see Appendix). In 1993, for example, approximately 75,000 civil cases and 40,800 economic cases were tried in the Guangdong courts, in comparison with 19,000 criminal cases.[11] Chinese practice classifies civil cases into "economic cases," involving contract or tort actions in which at least one disputing party is a corporate organization, and "civil cases," in which the disputing parties are individuals.

Guangdong courts have had to cope with a skyrocketing increase in the number and variety of commercial cases. First-instance economic (commercial) cases soared from 19,000 cases in 1986 to over 40,000 cases in 1993. Civil cases, including contract and tort disputes between individuals, real estate and family law cases rose from approximately 56,000 cases to 75,000 in the same period. The number of foreign-related (involving non-PRC parties) cases doubled between 1986 and 1990. Real-estate cases heard in the courts quadrupled in a matter of three years.

To cope with its heavier and more complex caseload, the Guangdong courts have taken the lead in initiating court reforms in the area of civil dispute resolution. These reforms have involved the establishment of special court divisions to adjudicate foreign-related commercial disputes, real-estate cases and centres for the mediation of commercial disputes.

Guangdong leads the country in the number of foreign-related economic cases. In 1991, for example, of the 644 foreign-related (cases involving Hong Kong, Taiwan, Macau, or foreign) commercial disputes heard in the Chinese courts,[12] 455 were heard in Guangdong. As mentioned above, the number of foreign-related economic cases doubled between 1986 and 1991. The sharp increase in international commercial cases has led several courts in Guangdong to establish separate divisions to hear foreign-related economic cases, among them are the Shenzhen Municipal Intermediate Court and the provincial Higher People's Court. The purpose of creating a separate division is to create a corps of judges who have some familiarity with international commercial and investment law. Courts in other parts of the country with significant international trade and investment activity, such as Beijing and Shanghai, have followed

Shenzhen's example. With the increasing economic integration of southern China with Hong Kong and Taiwan, the caseload of the foreign-related economic divisions in Guangdong can be expected to rise.

The Guangdong courts have also led the nation in the creation of separate divisions to hear real estate cases. One of the important legal reforms of recent years in China has been the commercialization of land rights. Guangdong has led China in the sale of land rights to both foreigners and domestic Chinese. Disputes over sales or leasing of land rights and other real property, including residential and commercial properties, have escalated from 12,000 in 1986 to 64,000 in 1991. The statistics for recent years can be expected to be far higher, with the rapid increase of Guangdong property transactions and the collapse of the real estate market in the Pearl River Delta. To deal with the increasing number of real estate cases, the Shenzhen and Guangzhou Municipal Intermediate Courts in 1989 established real estate divisions, to try cases involving corporate bodies or individuals. Again, some courts in other parts of China have done the same, learning from Guangdong's example.

The third innovation of the Guangdong courts is the establishment of mediation centres for economic disputes. The first centre was established within the Shenzhen Municipal Intermediate Court. If both parties to a case are willing and the court has jurisdiction, they can submit their commercial dispute to a mediation centre. The mediation centres handle both domestic and foreign-related commercial disputes. In general, one judge works with the parties to work out a mediated settlement. Mediation centres are not bound by the procedural provisions of the civil procedure law.

Both litigants and courts have found advantages in mediation centres. There are several reasons why litigants often prefer to submit their disputes to mediation centres rather than have a court hearing. In mediation, because the proceedings are not conducted according to the procedures in the civil procedure law, they are less formal and more flexible. Parties are generally able to reach a mediation agreement faster than if their case were heard in either of the economic divisions. Such a mediation agreement is given equal legal authority with a court judgment or ruling. Moreover, resolving a business dispute through a mediation centre enables disputing parties to achieve a settlement while not disclosing illegal conduct that would otherwise be revealed in the course of litigation.

Courts favour mediation centres because the centres enable them to resolve a greater number of cases more quickly. Courts prefer to resolve as many cases as possible because it enhances their prestige, with litigants, higher levels of courts, local legislatures and other local authorities. Chinese courts are required to report the number of cases accepted and resolved both to higher levels of courts (ultimately to the Supreme People's Courts) and to the local legislature. Courts also favour mediation centres because court fees assessed by such centres are the same as in normal civil litigation, a percentage of the amount of money in dispute.

The problems faced by the Guangdong courts in resolving civil disputes are not peculiar to the province. There are several major problems. Courts, especially those in Guangdong, often find themselves in the unenviable position of trying to decide cases with few legal provisions to apply. Because Guangdong is in the forefront of Chinese economic reforms, frequently commercial disputes occur before legislation has been promulgated. In 1992, for example, the Shenzhen courts had to decide several disputes over stock ownership, in the face of a virtual legal vacuum. This problem is connected with the rapidity of economic change in China and the slow pace of legislation.

A second problem faced by the Guangdong courts is common to Chinese courts nationally. Although increasingly complex commercial litigation requires well-trained judges, a substantial number of Guangdong judges lack university legal training. The better trained judges tend to be found in the Intermediate Court in Shenzhen, the Guangzhou Intermediate Court and the Provincial Higher People's Court. The Guangdong court system runs training courses aimed at giving judicial personnel a *dazhuan* (three-year post-secondary) degree and many courts seek to recruit university law graduates.

A problem facing the Guangdong courts, but not confined to Guangdong, is the enforcement of civil judgments, both within China and abroad. The reasons for each are different. Although by law, legally effective judgments, rulings and other legal documents are enforceable anywhere in the country, in fact courts in other localities frequently delay or refuse to enforce judgments against local persons or enterprises. This phenomenon is popularly known as "local protectionism." The reasons are complex, and are connected with the complex organizational and personal ties between the local courts, government and enterprises. An increasing problem for Guangdong courts is that they may issue judgments against Hong Kong, Macau, Taiwan or foreign defendants but decisions of Chinese courts generally cannot be enforced beyond China's borders. The issue of the recognition and enforcement of civil judgments is politically sensitive. China lacks judicial assistance agreements with Hong Kong, Macau,

Taiwan as well as most nations. It means that Guangdong courts can only enforce their decisions against non-domestic Chinese natural or legal persons if they or their assets are located in China.

A problem faced by the courts in Guangdong, as elsewhere in the country, is that the lack of judicial tenure and dependence of local courts on funding from local governments makes local courts susceptible to pressure from local government officials. The general trend, however, is that local officials are involving themselves less in court operations.

Corruption in the judiciary is a significant problem, but is a problem not confined to the judiciary, or to Guangdong. It can be safely said that corruption in the courts is not a problem confined to one particular division. Factors encouraging judicial corruption include low judicial salaries coupled with inadequate social prestige, the permissibility under Chinese law of parties (or their counsel) meeting with judges outside the courtroom and the permissibility of judicial investigation of cases.

Punishment of Criminal Conduct

The profound changes since 1979 in the Guangdong economy and in Guangdong society have seen significant changes, as well as an overall increase, in the criminal cases heard in the province. This is the area of the law that concerns Party and government authorities most, as well as ordinary citizens.

In the past ten years, there have been dramatic changes in Guangdong criminal cases. The most significant changes include a skyrocketing number of narcotics cases, smuggling cases, commercial crimes, and prostitution-related offences as well as the internationalization of criminal activity in Guangdong.

In recent years, there has been a large increase in narcotics cases in Guangdong. Guangdong is an important transit point in the drug trade between the Golden Triangle, Yunnan Province and Hong Kong. By all reports, Hong Kong triad groups are involved in this lucrative export trade. In recent years, both Hong Kong and domestic Chinese citizens have been caught trying to smuggle narcotics out of China, but these cases probably represent a small fraction of the overall narcotics business. Under Chinese law, persons caught smuggling a minimum of 50 grams of heroin may be sentenced to death. The Guangdong courts have executed a number of Hong Kong citizens for narcotics offences.[13]

With rapidly rising incomes in Guangdong, there is also an increasing amount of drugs consumption within the province. The increase in the number of drugs cases led the provincial higher court to undertake a study of drugs consumption in the province. It found narcotics consumption was concentrated in Guangzhou, Shenzhen, Zhuhai and Zhongshan.[14] Although penalties in China for narcotics offences are severe, it does not seem to deter the growing number of persons who are looking to make easy money from the sale of narcotics. In a recently reported case in Shenzhen,[15] for example, a Shandong native transported over one kilogram of opium from his home province to sell in Shenzhen, but he and his three associates were caught by the Shenzhen police when making the sale. The Shandong native was sentenced to fifteen years, while his assistants received ten or four year sentences.

The number of smuggling cases in Guangdong have increased significantly, although only a tiny fraction of offenders are caught by either the Hong Kong or Chinese authorities. It is widely believed that there is significant involvement by Chinese authorities in cross-border smuggling. At least one Hong Kong official has been punished for involvement in cross-border smuggling. Punishment for smuggling offences includes the death penalty. Smugglers, however, are attracted by the large profits to be made by importing goods and evading high customs duties.

Guangdong has seen a flourishing of commercial crimes, including corruption, fraud and embezzlement. Corruption in Guangdong (and the rest of China) has flourished under an economic system which gives significant authority to officials with little checks and balances, and draws a fuzzy line between government and business and which controls the movement of persons within and outside China. An increase in fraud and embezzlement has accompanied the growth of the Guangdong economy.

The "world's oldest profession" is again flourishing in today's Guangdong. Prostitutes work out of all classes of hotels, karaoke lounges and nightclubs. For the most part, however, prostitution-related offences are not dealt with by the courts. Prostitutes and their customers are generally penalized by the police. Under Chinese law, offenders (prostitutes and their customers) can be punished by public security organs through procedures that do not require court trial, such as the Security Administration Punishment Act and "Shelter for Re-education." In 1991, over 5,000 persons were sent to "Shelter for Re-education" centres in Guangdong.[16]

One side-effect of the open policy is that those persons from outside

China are increasingly involved in criminal activity in the province, particularly Hong Kong and Macau residents. Along with legitimate Hong Kong businesses, illegal (i.e. triad) businesses have extended their operations into southern China. Hong Kong triad groups import "cheap labour" from the mainland to work for them in Hong Kong. There has also been an increase in the number of crimes whose victims are non-PRC citizens. Such crimes have ranged from kidnapping to murder. In 1992, for example, a Taiwanese businessman was murdered by a disgruntled former employee.

Another development in the area of criminal law is the re-emergence of traditional crimes, such as road banditry. Bandits prey on the main trade routes, such as Guangzhou–Shenzhen and Shantou–Guangzhou.[17] The Guangdong courts revealed that in 1990, one-third of all criminals sentenced to death for this crime were sentenced in Guangdong.[18]

Criminal law is an area of special concern to national and local authorities in China. Like politicians everywhere, when the central (and provincial) authorities perceive that "law and order" is being threatened by spiralling crime rates, they try to do something about it. Criminal law enforcement, therefore, has the closest ties with changes in Party policies. On a regular basis, Party authorities initiate anti-crime movements to focus criminal law enforcement on particular crimes. Party directives may direct the court, public security and procuratorial officials to cooperate to "punish quickly and severely" those convicted of the targeted crimes (though within the flexible restrictions of the criminal law). For example in 1992 and 1993, Guangdong provincial authorities targeted drugs, prostitution, women and children selling and forcing women into prostitution as the objects of a "seven evils" campaign. An effect of the anti-crime movements is that punishment for crimes may vary, depending on whether the crime is among those targeted.

Criminal convictions in Guangdong, as elsewhere in China, do not include what would be classified as minor crimes (misdemeanors), such as prostitution, petty theft and minor assaults. Such offences are not generally punished under the criminal law, but rather under various administrative sanctions administered by the public security authorities.

Conclusion

The changes in the Guangdong legal system can be evaluated briefly as follows. The overall importance of courts and arbitration organizations in

Guangdong is increasing, because a transition to an international and market-driven economy means that the increasing number of commercial disputes are resolved through the courts or arbitration rather than through administrative means. Like all Chinese courts, the Guangdong courts operate under the leadership of the Communist Party. In reality, operation of economic divisions is generally less affected by changes in political policies. Although economic divisions of courts may occasionally be requested to co-operate with other authorities in the implementation of Party policies, such as the late 1989 rectification of companies, most issues with which civil and economic divisions are involved are not connected with politics. The operation of criminal divisions, for example, is more subject to changes in Party policy, such as the implementation of various anti-crime movements.

There is a clear trend towards greater specialization, such as the establishment of an international arbitration organization and specialized commercial divisions within the courts. The greater functional specialization of the courts is leading to greater independence of the courts (relatively speaking) from government and Party authorities, because there are an increasing number of cases in which technical legal knowledge is necessary for resolution. An overall increase in the quality of the judiciary in Guangdong can be detected as a greater number of law graduates recruited into judiciary and training programmes are implemented for the former military officers and other judicial officials with little or no legal background.

The Guangdong legal system has made substantial improvements in a few short years, although it faces many of the problems plaguing Chinese legal institutions. The 1997 reunification of Hong Kong with China means additional legal problems, as the legal infrastructure regarding interaction of the mainland and Hong Kong legal systems, as of this point, is virtually lacking.

Appendix

Listed below are statistics on cases in the Guangdong courts: economic, civil, and criminal cases.[19]

Guangdong Economic Cases 1986–1991, 1993

Case categories	1986	1987	1988	1989	1990	1991	1993
First-instance cases received	19,099	22,675	23,047	35,195	36,146	36,674	40,799
First-instance cases resolved	14,722	18,139	—	30,134	29,847	31,530	35,441
Foreign cases resolved	161	122	141	222	322 (467 nationally)	455	612
Maritime cases resolved	—	103	107	—	88	108	—
Rural contracts	—	1,211	—	—	1,227	1,683	734
Bank loan contracts	—	—	—	8,345	—	—	—
Economic contracts	—	—	20,135	—	—	—	—
Compensation claims	—	—	60	—	—	—	—

Guangdong Civil Cases 1986–1991, 1993

Case categories	1986	1987	1988	1989	1990	1991	1993
Family law	—	27,075	26,948	—	24,935 (divor.)	27,807	27,616
Obligations	—	15,340	16,512	—	20,704	64,550*	15,308
Housing/real estate	—	12,329	9,486	48,717	—	—	—
Compensation (torts)	—	4,042	4,096	—	—	—	2,844
Inheritance	—	1,065	1,186	—	—	—	—
Intell. property	—	5	60	79	—	—	99
Total 1st instance	56,475	64,240	62,953	73,915	75,113 (and 2nd instance)	—	75,000
Labour	—	—	—	—	544	—	—

Note: * Extrapolated, due to misprint in original.

Guangdong Criminal Cases 1986–1991, 1993

Case categories	1986	1987	1988	1989	1990	1991	1993
First-instance cases received	12,800	14,543	14,835	16,276	20,574 (1st and 2nd instance)	20,579	18,879
First-instance cases resolved	12,200	13,973	14,081	—	19,814	—	18,174
Appeals received	2,400+	2,694	2,451	2,460	—	—	—
Appeals resolved	2,200	2,455	2,230	2,259	—	—	—
Less than 5 years sentence	—	62.4%	61.1%	—	—	—	55.7%
5 years sentence and greater	—	37.1%	37.5%	—	12,116 (48.6%)	11,630 (47.3%)	77.2%

Notes

1. Resolution of the Standing Committee of the National People's Congress authorizing the People's Congresses of Guangdong and Fujian provinces and their Standing Committees to formulate separate economic regulations for their respective Special Economic Zones (26 November, 1981), *The Laws of the People's Republic of China (1979–1982)* (Beijing: Foreign Languages Press, 1987), p. 255.

2. Article 12, China International Economic and Trade Arbitration Commission Arbitration Rules, October, 1995.

3. Ibid.

4. Ibid., Article 24.

5. In 1958 a Maritime Arbitration Commission was established under the aegis of the China Council for the Promotion of International Trade, which arbitrates maritime disputes. See the decision of the State Council of the People's Republic of China concerning the Establishment of a Maritime Arbitration within the CCPIT, 21 November 1958, *Laws and Regulations of the People's Republic of China Governing Foreign-related Matters (1949–1990)*, Vol. 3 (Beijing: China Legal System Publishing House, 1991), p. 1909.

6. See the decision of the Standing Committee of the National People's Congress on the Establishment of Maritime Courts in Coastal Port Cities (14 November 1984), *The Laws of the People's Republic of China (1983–1986)*, p. 151.

7. "Zuigao renmin fayuan guanyu sheli haishi fayuan jige wenti de jueding"

(Decision of the Supreme People's Court Concerning Some Issues Regarding the Establishment of Maritime Courts), *Zuigao renmin fayuan gongbao* (Gazette of the Supreme People's Court), No. 1 (1985), p. 5.

8. Ibid.

9. "Zuigao renmin fayuan guanyu sheli Haikou, Xiamen haishi fayuan de jueding" (Decision of the Supreme People's Court Concerning the Establishment of Maritime Courts in Haikou and Xiamen), *Zuigao renmin fayuan gongbao*, No. 1 (1990), p. 24.

10. See Appendix, Guangdong Economic Cases 1986–1991 (Table).

11. *Guangdong nianjian* 1994 (Guangdong Yearbook 1994) (Guangzhou: Guangdong renmin chubanshe, 1994), p. 175.

12. *Zhongguo falü nianjian 1992* (China Law Yearbook 1992) (Beijing: Zhongguo falü nianjianshe, 1992), p. 855.

13. See "China Executes Traffickets," *South China Morning Post*, 27 June 1992, p. 1.

14. "Dangqian Guangdong xidu qingkuang de diaocha" (Investigation of Drugs Consumption in Guangdong), *Renmin sifa* (People's Justice), No. 11 (1991), pp. 31–32.

15. *Yanli daji xingshi fanzui huodong anli xuanbian* (Selection of Cases for the Severe Strike at Crime Movement), 17, poster edited by Shenzhen sifaju and Louhuqu sifaju (Shenzhen Municipal and Louhu District Justice Bureaux), 26 June 1992.

16. *Guangdong nianjian 1991*, p. 184. "Shelter for Re-education" centers have been set up in Guangzhou, Shenzhen, Zhenjiang, Foshan, Zhongshan, Dongguan, Shaoguan, Qingyuan, Chiaozhou and other cities. Persons can be detained for six months to two years. *Quanguo renmin daibiao dahui changwu weiyuanhui guanyu yanjin maiyin piaochang de jueding* (Decision of the Standing Committee of the National People's Congress Concerning the Strict Prohibition of Prostitution and Patronization of Prostitutes), 4 September 1991.

17. "Guangdong Suffers as Raids Soar," *Sunday Morning Post*, 16 March 1992, p. 3.

18. *Guangdong nianjian 1991* (Guangdong Yearbook 1991) (Guangzhou: Guangdong renmin chubanshe, 1991), p. 192.

19. Compiled from *Guangdong nianjian*, 1987–1991, 1993 (see note 18). Categorization and reporting of cases vary from year to year. If numbers are absent from the tables, it is an indication that no reporting was given in that category.

17

Population Mobility

Li Si-ming and Siu Yat-ming

The Regional Economy of Guangdong and Its Implications for Population Migration

Guangdong is the major beneficiary of China's open and reform policy launched since 1978. The provincial economy has been experiencing phenomenal growth. The economic growth, however, is spatially uneven. A core-periphery relationship has been in existence for centuries.[1] More specifically, the Pearl River Delta, with its rich alluvial soils and a highly developed network of waterways, has been for many years the most prosperous and economically most advanced region of the province.

Figure 17.1 shows the distribution of per capita gross domestic product (GDP) of Guangdong by counties and cities in 1989.[2] It can be seen that the south-central part of the province, i.e. the Pearl River Delta in the broader sense, constitutes a distinct core in the provincial economy, with the cities of Guangzhou, Shenzhen and Zhuhai being the centres of a tripartite regional system. Bordering this core region and extending westward along the Xi River to include the city of Zhaoqing and along the coastline towards the southwest to include the cities of Maoming and Zhanjiang, lies an intermediate zone. The eastern, northeastern and northwestern parts of the province, which include the city of Meizhou and the counties of Lianxian, Huaji, Wuhua, Xingning and Dabu, have the lowest per capita GDP, thus constituting the province's periphery. Note that the gradation used in the map is in the logarithmic scale. The difference among counties in terms of per capita GDP is very large indeed.

Rapid industrialization and the existence of large gaps in development both within the province and between the province and other parts of the country have brought about an unprecendented shift in labour force composition and massive population migration. The introduction of the household responsibility system in the agricultural sector in the early 1980s and the gradual relaxation of the household registry (*hukou* system), which has been in place since 1958 and which acts as an highly effective barrier separating the urban from the rural, also contribute significantly to the migration flow.[3] Of course, the increase in labour mobility and population migration are not restricted to Guangdong. The Sunan region and the

This research is supported in part by Hong Kong Baptist University, Research Grant FRG 90/91–II–19. The authors would like to thank Bosco Tsang of the Department of Geography, Hong Kong Baptist University, for the original map work.

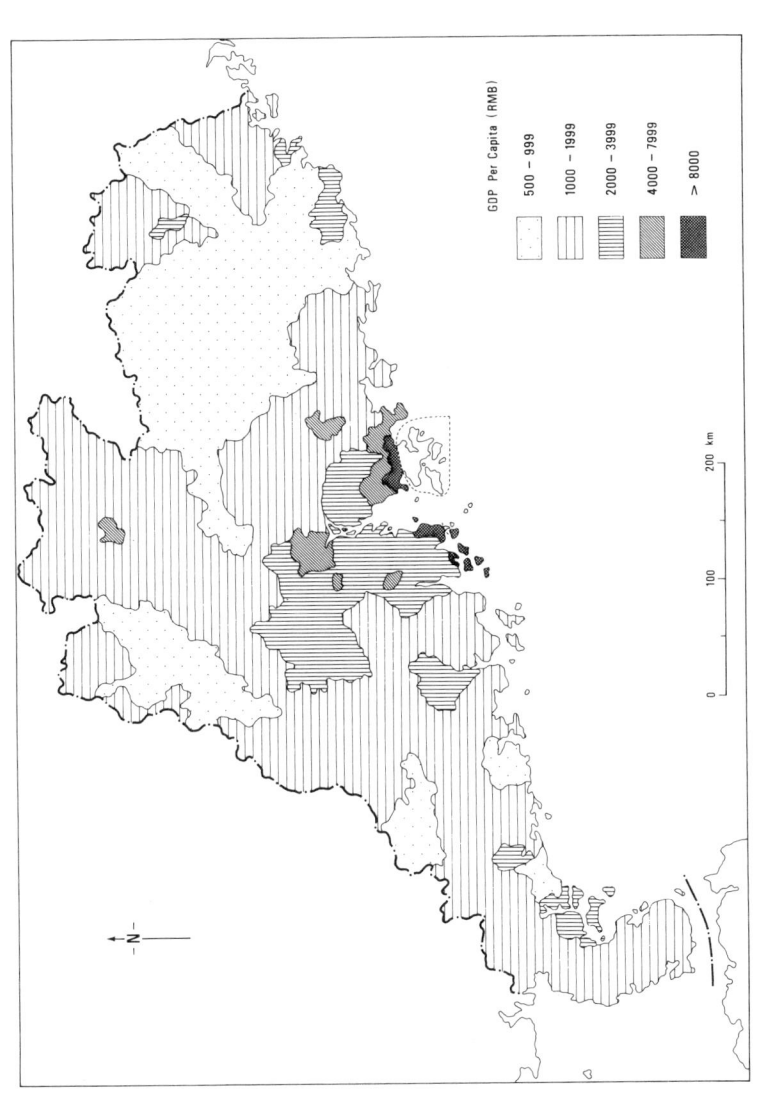

Figure 17.1 GDP Per Capita in Guangdong, 1989

GDP Per Capita (RMB)

500 – 999
1000 – 1999
2000 – 3999
4000 – 7999
> 8000

N

0   100   200 km

large cities in the coastal areas, in particular, are also recipients of large influxes of migrant workers. But certainly it is in Guangdong that the impacts of labour shift and population migration are most apparent.

The importance of this shift in labour force composition and massive migrant flow is being increasingly recognized by scholars in and outside China and by the authorities. A number of studies have been conducted to unravel this process of population flow both within and beyond the province. These include, *inter alia*, studies on labour mobility and urbanization in the Pearl River Delta,[4] a study of migrant workers in the Shenzhen Special Economic Zone,[5] a large-scale survey on population migration in 74 cities and towns across the country (which include Guangzhou, Zhaoqing, Zhuhai and Longjiang in Guangdong) in 1987 by the Population Research Institute of the Chinese Academy of Social Science,[6] and a series of studies on the "mobile" or "floating" population (*liudong renkou*) in large cities (which include Guangzhou) organized by the Institute of Urban and Rural Construction and Economic Research of the Department of Construction of the Chinese Government in 1989 and 1990.[7] The State Statistical Bureau also included in its 1% Sample Population Survey conducted in 1987, the 1990 Population Census and the 1995 1% Sample Population Survey an extensive array of questions on population migration. The information released to date, together with the findings of the earlier studies, is sufficient to depict a more or less complete picture of population migration and shift in the labour force in Guangdong and in other parts of the country. Some of these findings will be reported below.

Interpreting Migration Statistics in Chinese Literature

Population migration and mobility carry a plethora of meanings in the Chinese literature on the subject. To some, the term "migration" refers to a change in the official residence (*hukou*) under the household registry system across municipal, county or other administrative boundaries.[8] This, in effect, represents a *de jure* definition of migration and is the view taken by the State Statistical Bureau when it compiles the annual statistical yearbooks. To others, migration refers to a change in the permanent place of residence, whether this involves a change in the official residential status or not.[9] This represents a *de facto* definition of population migration and is the most commonly used yardstick for measuring migration flow internationally. Interestingly, the State Statistical Bureau also adopted this view in the conduct of the 1987 and 1995 1% Sample Population Surveys and the

1990 Population Census. In addition to population migration, the Chinese literature also pays increasing attention to what is called the mobile or floating population (*liudong renkou*). Again, different authors seem to have used the term in different ways. Some refer to all people on move, whether this involves a short-term visit or a more permanent change in residence. Others refer only to those engaged in short-term moves. Still others, from a legalistic point of view, refer to all those who have moved out of their official place of residence but have been unable to establish *hukou* in the place of destination.[10] Because of this, care has to be taken in interpreting the official statistics and findings of individual studies.

Scale of Migration in Guangdong

The 1987 and 1995 1% Sample Population Surveys and the 1990 Population Census have provided the most comprehensive sets of data on the migration process to date. According to the 1990 Population Census, the resident population of a given county or city includes those whose normal place of residence is in that county or city, regardless of whether the persons concerned have established official residence (*hukou*) in it or not. People who have moved out of their official residence for less than one year and have not established *hukou* in the place of destination are still considered to be part of the resident population in their former place of residence.[11] The migrant population refers to those whose permanent residence at the date of census, i.e. 1 July 1990, was different from that five years before on 1 July 1985. Similar definitions were used in the 1987 and 1995 1% Sample Population Surveys. Of course, the respective dates used to measure migration were 1 July 1987 and 1 July 1982 and 1 October 1990 and 1 October 1995. However, instead of using one full year as the cut-off point for delineating migration without corresponding change in *hukou*, both the 1987 and 1995 1% Sample Population Surveys considered six-month residence as sufficient for resident population classification. Because of the special definition of resident population adopted, as far as migration which did not involve a change in official residence was concerned, the 1990 Population Census, in effect, measured only those who had moved out of their former residence in the four-year period between 1 July 1985 and 1 July 1989; and the 1987 and 1995 surveys only measured those who moved out in the four-and-a-half-year period between 1 July 1982 and 1 January 1987 and between 1 April 1991 and 1 October 1995. Another difference between the 1990 Population Census and the 1987 1%

Sample Population Survey is that while in the former case only moves crossing city or county boundaries were enumerated, in the latter case moves across township (in rural areas) or city district (in urban areas) boundaries were also included. Thus, in comparison with the 1987 and 1995 1% Sample Population Surveys, the figures reported in the 1990 Population Census under represent the incidence of migration in China, especially for short distance moves.

Table 17.1 reveals the size of the migrant population in the five-year (four years for migration not involving a change of *hukou*) period prior to 1987, 1990 and 1995, respectively, for the entire nation and Guangdong as reported in the official enumerations. In the latter case, adjustments have been made to exclude Hainan Island, which was granted the provincial status in 1988, from the tabulations. In all three periods, the migrant population in China numbered approximately 30 million, representing slightly less than 3% of the total population. Largely because of the difference in the definitions adopted, the number of intra-provincial moves

Table 17.1   Size of In-migration in China, 1987 and 1990

	From other provinces	From within province	Total
1995			
Nation	10,660,600	22,569,200	33,229,800
Guangdong	1,946,900	2,142,700	4,089,600
1990			
Nation	10,836,260	23,004,350	33,840,610
Guangdong	1,165,330	2,522,990	3,688,320
1987			
Nation	6,312,100	24,220,500	30,532,600
Guangdong	258,800	1,961,000	2,219,800

Sources: Guowuyuan renkou pucha bangongshi (ed.), *Zhongguo 1987 nian 1% renkou chouyang diaocha ziliao, quanguo fengce*, p. 24; *Zhongguo 1987 nian 1% renkou chouyang diaocha ziliao, Guangdongsheng fengce*, p. 196; *Zhongguo 1990 nian renkou pucha 10% chouyang ziliao* (see note 11 below), pp. 682–83. Quanguo renkou chouyang bangongshi (ed.), 1995 Quanguo 1% rankou chouyang diaocha ziliao, quanguo fengce, pp. 540–541.

Notes: For the definition of migration, please see text. The 1987 national sample data given in the sources below were multiplied by 100 (sampling rate was 1:100) and the 1987 Guangdong data were multiplied by 120.5 (sampling rate was 0.83:100) to obtain estimates of the respective migrant populations. Correspondingly, the 1990 data was multiplied by 10 to obtain the 1990 estimates.

reported by the 1990 Population Census was slightly less than that given by the 1987 1% Sample Population Survey. There was, however, a substantial increase in inter-provincial migration between 1987 and 1990: from 6.31 million to 10.84 million. This increase in population mobility apparently has slowed down in recent years. The relative size of the migration flow in Guangdong was much larger than that of the nation as a whole. A total of 2.22 million migrants were recorded in the 1987 survey, representing some 3.8% of the province's population. In the 1990 Population Census, the number of migrants had increased to 3.69 million, accounting for 5.8% of the province's population. Despite the change in definition, moves within the province continued to show an increase in the 1990 Population Census over the 1987 survey: from 1.96 million to 2.52 million. But it was the long distance inter-provincial moves towards Guangdong which had shown the largest increase. The 1990 Population Census put the number of in-migrants to the province at 1.16 million, which may be compared with that of 0.26 million given in the 1987 survey. In fact, more than 10% of all inter-provincial migration in China in the five years leading to the 1990 Population Census were heading for Guangdong. Despite the slow down registered for the nation as a whole, in-migration from other provinces to Guangdong continued to show a significant increase in the 1995 survey. Up to 18% of all inter-provincial moves recorded in the latest national enumeration were bounded for Guangdong.

The 1990 Population Census statistics only measure moves between counties or cities. Moves within a given county such as from a small village to the county seat are excluded. Given that the migration propensity is an inverse function of distance, the size of such migration flows must be very large. In 1984, the Chinese government allowed, for the first time since 1958, peasants who could take care of their own grain needs, i.e. who did not have to rely on the state for the provision of subsidized grain supply, to establish *hukou* in county seats and in small towns. These peasants are called *zili kouliang hu*. As of 1990, there was a total of 983,000 people who had taken up residence in towns and county seats under this policy.[12] Of course, the size of the *zili kouliang hu* does not measure the full extent of migration within the county. But even this is sufficient to illustrate the scale of such migration flows.

It may be noted that moves involving a change in *hukou* account for only a very small percentage of the total. Most moves recorded are not officially sanctioned: out of the 3.69 million moves recorded in the 1990 Population Census, at least 3.29 million or 89.3% did not involve a change in *hukou*.[13] The 1990 Population Census was conducted in the midst of a three-year consolidation of the economy, which had put a brake on infrastructure developments across the nation and which had brought about much lower rates of growth. A sizeable number of township enterprises, especially those in the more remote parts of the country, closed down. Many migrant construction and factory workers were sent home. The massive migration flows towards and within Guangdong as reported by the Census were indeed remarkable in the light of the rather unfavourable national economic climate.

As was pointed out above, the migration statistics reported do not include those who have moved out of their official residence for less than one year but have not yet established official residence in the place of destination. It is difficult to establish the size of this migrant or mobile population. A post-census survey was conducted in a number of cities specifically for this.[14] Unfortunately, a full report on the survey findings has yet to be published. Only piecemeal information has been released to date. For example, a total of 281,000 residents who were labelled "population unfit for census enumeration" was reported in the *Shenzhen tongji nianjian*.[15] Presumably, these people belong to this category of migrants. Also, Peng reported that 270,200 such residents were identified in the post-census survey in Dongguan.[16]

Prior to the conducting of the census, there was a large-scale study of mobile population in the large cities conducted by Li and Hu which provided further information on the scale of population movement in China. For the city of Guangzhou, the size of the mobile population since 1979 was reported as follows:[17]

Year	Mobile Population
1979	235,000
1984	500,000
1986	800,000
1987	1,145,000
1988	1,170,000
1989	914,200

The mobile population above refers to all those who had not established official residence in Guangzhou. These included not only the migrants but also people engaged in short visits. A rather sharp decline was recorded in 1989 amidst the 4 June Incident and the three-year consolidation. A sample survey established that 29.0% of the mobile population had stayed 1–5 years, 24.3% 0.5–1 year, 17.2% 1–6 months; and the rest less than 1 month.[18] Assuming those who had stayed for one month or more to be *de facto* migrants, the size of the migrant population of Guangzhou in 1989 as given by this study, excluding those who had their *hukou* changed, was in the region of 645,000. Of these, 380,000 had stayed in the city for less than one year. In comparison, the total population of Guangzhou as given by the 1990 Population Census was 3.95 million.[19] Of course, because of the mobile nature of this segment of the population, the accuracy of the survey statistics may not be very high. Indeed, the 1990 Population Census put the portion who had stayed 1–5 years at 388,000, as compared with only 265,000 implied by the Li and Hu study cited earlier.

The 1995 1% Sample Population Survey gives a total of 6.05 million people whose normal place of residence was in Guangdong but whose hukou was not. The fact that this figure is larger than the total number of in-migrants to the province over the five-year period 1990–1995 indicates that many of the "temporary" migrants who moved to Guangdong in the earlier period were still in the province more than five years later. Yet they still could not establish official residence in their newly adopted home.

It is beyond doubt that the migration flow is enormous and is even larger than the census statistics might suggest. The great majority of these migrants have not established official residence in their place of destination. Their stay is legally dubious. The impact of such massive and most often unsanctioned migration flows on such issues as the local labour market, urban service delivery and social security is just beginning to be understood.

The Pattern of Migration Flow

Detailed tabulations from the 1995 1% Sample Population Survey are not available. The following discussions are based on earlier national enumerations. The 1990 Population Census provides rather detailed information on the pattern of migration flow. Table 17.2 shows the migration data in terms of a 4 × 4 matrix, using settlement type as the basis of classification for origin and destination. Figure 17.2 shows the magnitude and direction of the inter-provincial flows with respect to the province of origin. Detailed information on the direction of inter-county/city moves within Guangdong is not available. But the place of origin can be inferred from the item "people who have moved out of their official place of residence for more than one year but have not established *hukou* elsewhere" which is reported in *Guangdongsheng disici renkou pucha*

Table 17.2 Migration Flows by Settlement Type in Guangdong, 1985–1990

Origin	Destination							
	Cities		Towns		Counties		Province	
	Total	Male%	Total	Male%	Total	Male%	Total	Male%
	Inward inter-provincial migration							
Cities	16,913	58.14	2,912	62.74	1,033	83.74	20,858	60.05
Towns	5,540	50.02	4,348	52.02	568	63.03	10,456	51.56
Counties	43,952	45.31	34,348	40.87	6,919	53.23	85,219	44.16
Province	66,405	48.97	41,608	43.57	8,520	57.58	116,533	47.67
	Intra-provincial migration							
Cities	17,749	60.41	5,015	69.53	1,666	95.44	24,430	64.88
Towns	36,511	57.57	13,225	56.02	2,651	83.14	52,387	57.79
Counties	110,022	54.46	53,094	48.61	12,366	70.27	175,482	53.80
Province	164,282	55.82	71,334	50.95	16,683	74.82	252,299	55.55

Source: *Zhongguo 1990 nian renkou pucha 10% chouyang ziliao*, pp. 678–79. To obtain an estimate of the population, multiply N by 10. The same applies to Table 17.3.

Figure 17.2   Inflows of Migrants in Guangdong, 1985–1990

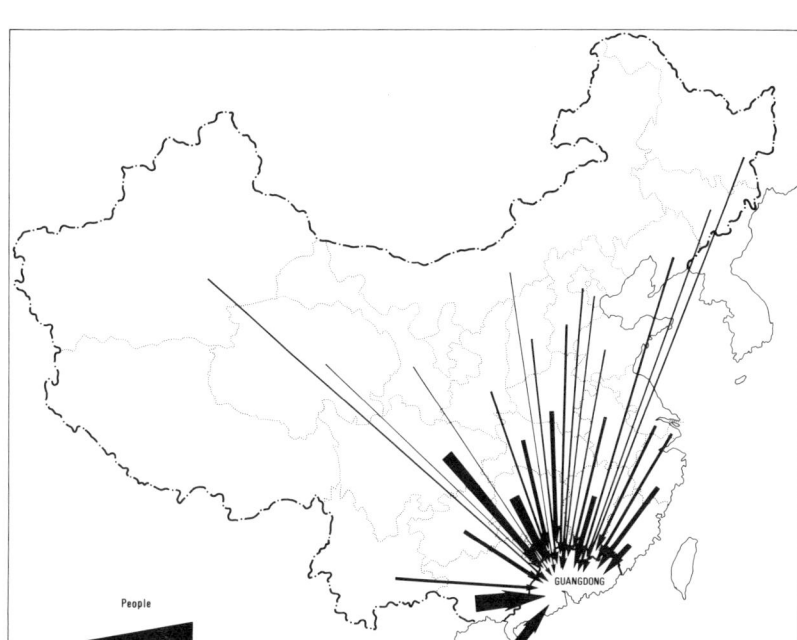

shougong huizong ziliao.[20] Table 17.3 shows the size of this population by *shi* (city). Also full information on the place of destination within the province for both the in-migrants and the intra-provincial migrants is not available, but can be inferred from the items "people who have resided in the county/city for more than one year but their *hukou* is elsewhere" and "people who have resided in the county/city for less than one year but have moved out of their official residence for more than one year." Figure 17.3 gives the size of these populations, using the greater *shi* as the basis of enumeration.

From Table 17.2, it can be seen that the great majority of moves were originated from the rural counties: 73.1% in respect to inter-provincial moves and 69.4% in respect to intra-provincial moves. On the other hand, the main recipients were the cities and towns: for inter-provincial moves, 57.0% headed for cities and 35.7% headed for towns; for intra-provincial moves, the corresponding figures were 64.9% and 28.2%, respectively. As a result of this mainstream rural-to-urban migration, and as a result of

Table 17.3   Population Who Have Moved out for More than One Year but Whose *Hukou* **Remains at the Place of Origin: Guangdong, 1990**

Place of origin	Number moved out		
	Male	Female	Total
Guangzhou			
Municipal region	49,899	42,821	92,720
City proper	16,309	10,782	27,091
Shaoguan			
Municipal region	46,199	37,985	84,184
City proper	7,813	6,027	13,840
Shenzhen			
Municipal region	7,687	7,810	15,497
City proper	669	487	1,156
Zhuhai			
Municipal region	7,924	7,723	15,647
City proper	987	993	1,980
Shantou			
Municipal region	179,641	137,305	316,946
City proper	3,309	2,735	6,044
Foshan			
Municipal region	27,617	26,930	54,547
City proper	5,864	4,270	10,134
Jiangmen			
Municipal region	79,773	65,974	145,747
Huizhou			
Municipal region	53,516	59,169	112,685
City proper	4,673	4,056	8,729
Meizhou			
Municipal region	185,015	127,455	312,470
City proper	4,861	4,405	9,266
Shanwei			
Municipal region	47,852	35,061	82,913
City proper	2,283	1,919	4,202
Heyuan			
Municipal region	128,741	105,960	234,701
City proper	30,958	28,398	59,356
Yangjiang			
Municipal region	62,172	45,340	107,512
City proper	22,252	13,315	35,567
Qingyuan			
Municipal region	71,492	74,354	145,846
City proper	28,357	26,303	54,660
Dongguan	5,934	3,695	9,629
Zhongshan	4,905	5,068	9,973
Chaozhou	13,309	10,241	23,550

Source: *Guangdongsheng disici renkou pucha shougong huizong ziliao* (see note 13 below), p. 30–40.

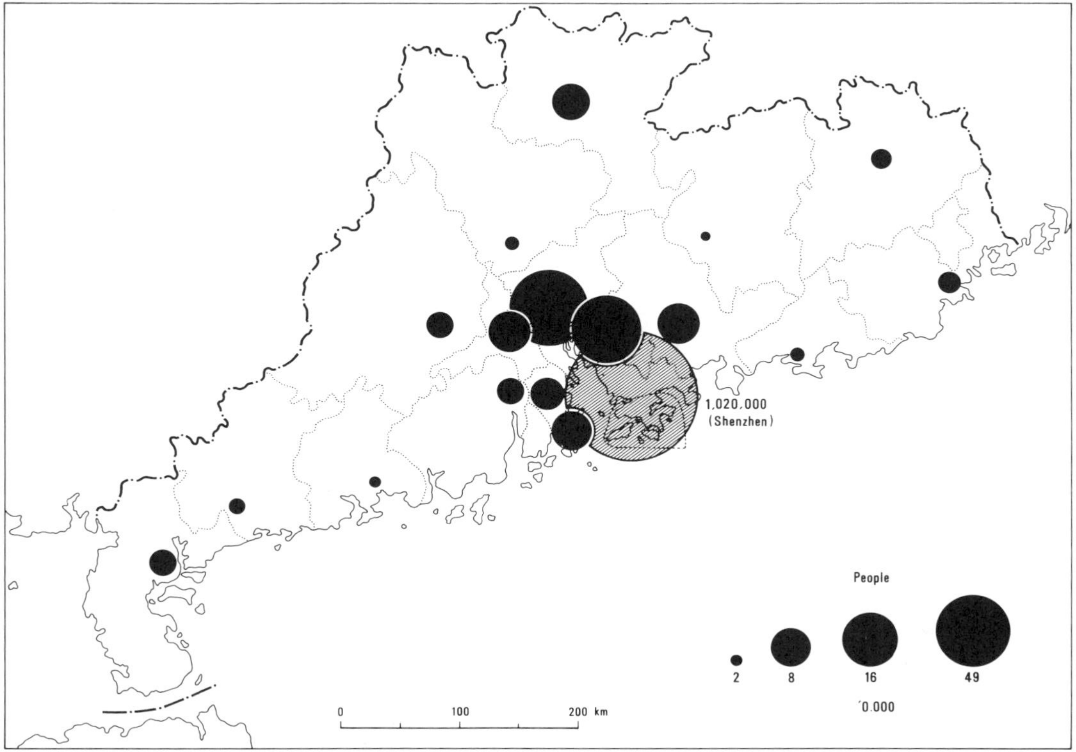

Figure 17.3 Distribution of Resident Population Whose Normal Place of Residence is Different from the Official One in Guangdong

industrial and urban developments in some of the former rural areas and the consequential changes in the status of the local administrative units (for example, from *xiang* [village] to *zhen* [town], and from *xian* [county] to *shi* [city]), particularly in the Pearl River Delta, the number of urban dwellers more than doubled between the 1982 Population Census and the 1990 Population Census: from 10.34 million to 23.13 million. The share of urban population or the rate of urbanization also increased from 19.3% to 36.8%. In comparison, the national rate of urbanization stood at 21.1% and 26.4% in 1982 and 1990, respectively.[21]

Figure 17.2 shows that most of the in-migrants to Guangdong came from the neighbouring provinces: out of the 1.17 million in-migrants reported in the 1990 Population Census, 366,000 came from Guangxi; 208,000 from Hunan; 84,000 from Hainan; 57,000 from Jiangxi and 50,000 from Fujian. But there was also a large inflow of 119,000 from Sichuan. Distance and population size alone seem to account for a large portion of the variance of the inter-provincial flow data. With the exception of Fujian, all the other provinces mentioned are laggards in the reform era.

From Table 17.3, it can be seen that within Guangdong, the major origins of migrants are the greater *shi* or municipal regions located in the mountainous "periphery." The Shantou municipal region, which contains such laggard counties as Jieyang, Jiexi and Puning, for example, sent out at least 317,000 migrants. (Migrants who moved with their *hukou* were not included in these head counts.) Also, the Meizhou municipal region, which contains the low income counties of Wuhua, Dabu and Xingning, sent out at least 312,000 migrants. Next comes the Heyuan municipal region which sent out at least 235,000 migrants. The municipal regions of Qingyuan, with at least 146,000 out-migrants, Huizhou (which contains the mountainous counties of Huidong and Boluo), with at least 113,000 out-migrants, and Yangjiang, with at least 108,000 out-migrants, are also important sources of migration out-flow.

As may be expected, the majority of the migrants ended up in the Pearl River Delta region (Figure 17.3). The major recipients include the municipal regions/cities of Shenzhen, with a minimum intake of 1.02 million (again, moves with a change in *hukou* are not included), Guangzhou with 489,000, Dongguan with 439,000, Foshan with 277,000, Zhuhai with 160,000, Huizhou with 136,000 and Shaoguan with 133,000. With the exception of Shaoguan, which was a centre of heavy industry even before the reform era, all the other municipal regions are in the delta region.

Moreover, it is the eastern part of the delta, i.e. Dongguan and Shenzhen, which exerts the greatest gravitational pull. This occurs despite the fact that cities and counties on both sides of the Pearl River estuary enjoy very similar levels of economic development. Perhaps the difference in industrial development strategies adopted contributes partly to the difference in the scale of migration inflow. Dongguan and Bao'an (in Shenzhen municipal region, incorporated into Shenzhen city proper in 1992) capitalize on their proximity to Hong Kong and concentrate on developing out-processing industries which, by nature, are highly labour intensive. Shunde (in Foshan municipal region) and Zhongshan, however, tend to specialize in home appliances and machinery which are more capital intensive.[22]

Within each of the municipal regions, it is the city proper that receives the great majority of the migrants. For example, in the case of Guangzhou, 83.8% went to the city proper; and in Zhuhai, 81.7%. Shenzhen and Foshan are the exceptions. In Shenzhen, both the city proper and Bao'an County received large numbers of migrants. In Foshan, in addition to the city proper, the prosperous counties of Nanhai and Shunde (which have been granted *shi* or city status subsequent to the conducting of the 1990 Population Census) are also major recipients of migration flow.

The 1990 Population Census tabulations to date have not contained county- or city-specific information about the migration process. But a previous study of industrial workers in Huadong of Huaxian County and Shajin of Bao'an County showed that the migratory path exhibits a high degree of directional bias.[23] In particular, migrant workers to Huadong, which in many respects is a satellite town of Guangzhou, invariably came from areas to the north, including northern Guangdong, Hunan and Jiangxi; whereas in the case of Shajin, most migrant workers came from the eastern and western parts of the province and from Guangxi and Fujian. Very few were from the northern part of Guangdong. It appeared that Guangzhou and Foshan act as important intervening opportunities, deterring migrant workers from moving to the smaller towns to the south.[24] Such a directional bias was not apparent from Wu's study of migrant workers in Shenzhen, however. This suggests that such intervening opportunities may not be sufficient to detract the migrants from moving to the Special Economic Zone and other destinations with large drawing powers.

As a result of the massive migration flow, almost every major city in the delta had registered a significant increase in population between the two census years, 1982 and 1990. The population in the city proper of

Guangzhou increased from 3.15 million to 3.93 million, in Shenzhen from 114,000 to 875,000, in Zhuhai from 133,000 to 334,000, in Foshan from 286,000 to 429,000, in Dongguan (granted *shi* status in 1984) from 1.15 million to 1.74 million, and in Zhongshan (granted *shi* status in 1984) from 1.02 million to 1.24 million. To this list, we may add the highly industrialized counties and lately cities of Nanhai (from 820,000 to 1.02 million), Shunde (from 808,000 to 965,000) and Panyu (from 670,000 to 785,000), and the county of Bao'an which has just been incorporated into Shenzhen proper (from 238,000 to 792,000).[25] Of course, Hong Kong and Macau are located in the delta's vicinity. The picture is clear. A megalopolis of a world order is fast taking shape in the delta. Unfortunately, to date, little effort has been made by the relevant bodies to coordinate this development.

Composition of the Migrant Population

Sex Composition

The 1990 Population Census showed that females accounted for a slightly larger percentage of inter-provincial moves to Guangdong whereas males accounted for a slightly larger share of intra-provincial moves. In both instances, however, the proportion of females was much larger for moves originated from rural areas than from cities and towns. Also, almost as a kernel to the above, males accounted for a much larger share of moves destined for rural areas than for cities and towns (Table 17.2).

The above refers to the entire migrant population. If we restrict ourselves to those aged 15 or above and in the work force, however, the picture is slightly different. According to the 1990 Population Census, 54.3% of the migrant workers from within Guangdong and 46.1% from outside Guangdong were females. A somewhat larger proportion workers moving out of the rural counties were females: 56.9% for intra-provincial moves and 52.3% for inter-provincial moves.[26] Previous studies which were conducted in a mainly factory environment had reported similar shares of females in the migrant population.[27] The migrant work force, especially the portion from the rural counties, is very much biased towards the female.

Age Composition and Marital Status

The official publications on the 1990 Population Census to date have not provided detailed information about the age distribution of the migrant population for Guangdong. But there are tabulations of data on Guangzhou. These tabulations show that the migrant population is very young. Out of the 639,826 in-migrants recorded (which includes all moves, whether they involved a change of residence or not), 154,196 (24.1%) were in the 10–19 age group and 324,348 (50.7%) in the 20–29 age group.[28] Also, Peng reported that among the mobile population, i.e. migrants without *hukou*, in Dongguan, Shenzhen and Zhuhai, 86.1%, 73.5% and 61.0%, respectively, were in the 15–29 age group.[29]

Smaller-scale studies conducted by individual scholars and research institutes yielded similar findings. For example, the Population Research Institute's study which covers all migrants, regardless of the date of establishing residence in the place of destination, reported that 57.3% of the migrant population in Guangzhou was in the 15–29 age group.[30] The survey on the mobile population in Guangzhou which focused on those without official residence status established that "youth," however defined, accounts for 87.6% of the mobile population. The Shajin study of industrial workers, the majority of whom were migrants, found that the mean age for males was 23.7 years and for females was 20.4 years. In another study, it was reported that over 90% of the "mobile population" in Bao'an were in the 17–22 age group.[31]

Regarding marital status, the 1990 Population Census showed that singles accounted for 59.4% of intra-provincial moves and 61.1% of inter-provincial moves. Studies conducted in a largely factory environment showed even higher percentages of singles. For example, in the Shajin and Huadong study referred to earlier, 88.6% and 66.2% of the sampled respondents were unmarried.[32] Also, a survey of migrant factory workers in Changping of Dongguan County and Guizhou of Shunde County reported similarly high percentages of singles.[33]

Education Attainment

In the absence of data on education attainment of the migrant population from the 1990 Population Census, the 1987 1% Sample Population Survey data have been utilized. Table 17.4 presents the migration data for both inter- and intra-provincial moves, cross-classified according to the type of settlement at place of destination and education attainment. There appears to be a gradation of education attainment in respect to the urban-rural continuum. It can be seen that migrants moving to the rural counties had

Table 17.4   Education Attainment of Migrants Aged 12 or Above in Guangdong, 1987

			Intra-provincial migration				
From	U Grad	U Student	S High	J High	Primary	Illit	Total
				To cities			
Cities	76	0	146	106	45	8	381
Towns	38	9	233	220	89	18	607
Counties	30	6	518	1,429	889	819	3,691
Total	144	15	897	1,755	1,023	845	4,679
%	3.08	0.32	19.17	37.51	21.86	18.06	—
				To towns			
Cities	21	0	80	35	26	6	168
Towns	26	8	490	561	268	64	1,417
Counties	12	2	831	2,145	1,334	330	4,654
Total	59	10	1,401	2,741	1,628	400	6,239
%	0.95	0.16	22.46	43.93	26.09	6.41	—
				To counties			
Cities	2	2	32	37	68	20	161
Towns	10	2	183	251	375	83	904
Counties	2	0	241	987	1,230	286	2,746
Total	14	4	456	1,275	1,673	389	3,811
%	0.37	0.10	11.97	33.46	43.90	10.21	—
			Inter-provincial migration				
From	U Grad	U Student	S High	J High	Primary	Illit	Total
				To cities			
Cities	91	6	152	92	32	14	387
Towns	6	2	18	31	7	1	65
Counties	8	0	53	132	69	14	276
Total	105	8	223	255	108	29	728
%	14.42	1.10	30.63	35.03	14.84	3.98	—

		Inter-provincial migration (cont'd)					
From	U Grad	U Student	S High	J High	Primary	Illit	Total
			To towns				
Cities	3	0	49	49	39	5	145
Towns	0	0	26	19	8	3	56
Counties	5	1	35	135	59	18	253
Total	8	1	110	203	106	26	454
%	1.76	0.22	24.23	44.71	23.35	5.73	—
			To counties				
Cities	0	0	11	7	16	14	48
Towns	2	0	4	11	11	0	28
Counties	0	0	38	231	279	116	664
Total	2	0	53	249	306	130	740
%	0.27	0.00	7.16	33.65	41.35	17.57	—

Source: *Zhongguo 1987 nian 1% renkou chouyang diaocha ziliao, Guangdongsheng fengce*, pp. 566–69.

Note: U Grad = University Graduates; U Student = Students in University; S High = Senior High; J High = Junior High; Primary = Primary Education; Illit = Il-literates.

very little education: for both inter- and intra-provincial moves, more than 50% had only primary education or less; and very few had senior high education or above (about 12% for intra-provincial migrants and 7% for inter-provincial migrants). Migrants to the towns had slightly better education: in both inter- and intra-provincial samples, some 45% of them had junior high education; also, some 22-24% had senior high education. The major difference between the inter- and intra-provincial groups lies in the city-ward migration. Whereas intra-provincial migration to the cities generally involved people with rather low levels of education attainment, quite a large portion of the in-migrants from outside the province had university (15.5%) and senior high (30.6%) education. This is reasonable as the scale of inter-provincial migration was much smaller in 1987, and as the building of Shenzhen, Zhuhai and Shantou Special Economic Zones required the transfer of a substantial high-status/high-skill work force from elsewhere in the country to Guangdong. In fact, in the 74 cities migration study, it was found that in both Guangzhou and Zhuhai, the migrant population (which includes all incomers regardless of the date of entry), on average, had higher education attainment than the locals.[34]

Occupation Status

As for occupation status, the data below are from the 1990 Population Census (Table 17.5). It is evident that the great majority of the migrant workers was engaged in productive and transport works: 58.5% for males and 60.6% for females in the case of intra-provincial migration, and 66.7% for males and 64.5% for females in the case of inter-provincial migration. As for comparison, the corresponding figures from the 1987 1% Sample Population Survey were 39.0%, 41.1%, 47.3% and 28.6%, respectively. Rather surprisingly, there was also quite a large proportion of the migrants who took up jobs in the agricultural sector. This was especially the case with the females: in regard to intra-provincial migration, 15.7% of the female migrants were engaged in agricultural activities; and in regard to inter-provincial migration, the proportion of the female migrants engaging in agricultural works was even larger, at 20.2%. Not surprisingly, the bulk of these agricultural workers came from rural areas. With the continual shift of the local labour force from the agricultural sector to the industrial and service sectors, the prosperous delta needed to import labour to work in the paddy fields and fish ponds to meet the state production quota and to maintain growth in agricultural output. The 1990 Population Census data clearly testify to this.

The development of industry and tertiary activities not only requires the input of productive workers but also professional and technical, managerial and clerical workers. Together, these three latter categories accounted for 13.6% of the intra-provincial and 19.2% of the inter-provincial male migrant workers in the 1990 Population Census for Guangdong. In fact, more than half of the male migrant workers coming from the cities (46.2% for intra-provincial migrants and 61.3% of the inter-provincial migrants) belonged to these groups. The 1990 Population Census data also showed that a much smaller proportion of female migrants was employed in the higher status jobs than male: only 7.4% for female migrants from within Guangdong and 7.8% from outside Guangdong belonged to the above-mentioned categories.

Reasons for Migration

Table 17.6 shows the 1990 Population Census migration data for

Table 17.5   Occupation Status of Migrants Aged 15 or Above in Guangdong, 1990

	From cities		From towns		From counties		Total	
	Male	Female	Male	Female	Male	Female	Male	Female
Inter-provincial migrants								
Provincial total	100,533	57,841	40,296	37,703	368,475	487,161	509,304	582,705
Professional and technical	36.96%	44.07%	12.36%	11.47%	1.40%	0.80%	9.28%	5.79%
Managerial	11.50%	3.37%	4.42%	0.43%	0.47%	0.03%	2.96%	0.38%
Clerical	12.83%	11.22%	16.44%	3.22%	4.35%	0.33%	6.98%	1.60%
Commerce	6.25%	6.23%	4.92%	4.27%	2.24%	1.02%	3.24%	1.74%
Service	2.78%	9.15%	4.80%	10.84%	4.18%	5.02%	3.95%	5.81%
Agricultural	0.93%	1.06%	4.91%	7.00%	8.80%	23.45%	6.94%	20.16%
Productive and transport	28.75%	24.90%	52.16%	62.78%	78.57%	69.36%	66.65%	64.52%
Intra-provincial migrants								
Provincial total	105,363	54,479	195,482	152,200	794,656	730,792	1,095,501	937,471
Professional and technical	26.13%	34.67%	9.92%	12.41%	2.61%	1.88%	6.18%	5.50%
Managerial	7.50%	1.84%	4.35%	0.50%	0.99%	0.08%	2.22%	0.25%
Clerical	12.59%	9.49%	8.97%	3.65%	3.34%	0.67%	5.24%	1.67%
Commerce	8.72%	9.21%	11.71%	8.61%	10.58%	5.42%	10.60%	6.16%
Service	5.48%	14.43%	7.33%	14.12%	7.14%	8.99%	7.01%	10.14%
Agricultural	2.27%	1.54%	5.37%	4.62%	12.54%	19.00%	10.27%	15.65%
Productive and transport	37.31%	28.83%	52.35%	56.09%	62.80%	63.96%	58.48%	60.64%

Source: Guowuyuan renkou pucha bangonshi (ed.), *Zhongguo 1990 nian renkou pucha ziliao*, Vol. 4, pp. 364–415.

Table 17.6   Reasons for Migration in Guangdong and China, 1985–1990

	Inter-provincial migration			
Reasons for migration	China	%	Guangdong	%
Total	11,065,361	100.00	1,257,508	100.00
Job transfer	1,666,745	15.06	132,574	10.54
Job assignment	500,904	4.53	35,830	2.85
Job search and trade	3,259,570	29.46	772,047	61.39
Study and training	927,482	8.38	27,841	2.21
Relatives and friends	1,149,585	10.39	23,549	1.87
Retirement	163,764	1.48	7,085	0.56
Dependents	1,201,823	10.86	86,034	6.84
Marriage	1,511,857	13.66	124,991	9.94
Others	683,631	6.18	47,557	3.78
	Intra-provincial migration			
Reasons for migration	China	%	Guangdong	%
Total	23,025,734	100.00	2,671,046	100.00
Job transfer	2,379,728	10.34	177,986	6.66
Job assignment	1,553,473	6.75	76,751	2.87
Job search and trade	5,302,947	23.03	1,534,014	57.43
Study and training	3,211,636	13.95	171,090	6.41
Relatives and friends	2,206,274	9.58	115,544	4.33
Retirement	369,519	1.60	20,057	0.75
Dependents	2,355,888	10.23	216,450	8.10
Marriage	3,241,164	14.08	161,991	6.06
Others	2,405,105	10.45	197,163	7.38

Source: Guowuyuan renkou pucha bangonshi (ed.), *Zhongguo 1990 nian renkou pucha ziliao*, Vol. 4, pp. 452–91.

Guangdong and for China according to reasons for migration. For comparison, the 1987 1% Sample Population Survey data are also included in Table 17.7. These tables clearly show that:

1. in comparison with the nation as a whole, Guangdong in 1990 had a much larger proportion of migrant population who migrated in search of better jobs and to engage in commercial trades. In fact, more than half of the Guangdong migrants,

Table 17.7   Reasons for Migration in Guangdong, 1982–1987

Reasons for migration	Intra-provincial	%	Inter-provincial	%
Total	16,276	100.00	2,148	100.00
Job transfer	1,743	10.71	398	18.53
Job assignment	696	4.28	57	2.65
Joh search and trade	4,014	24.66	399	18.58
Study and training	96	0.59	7	0.33
Relatives and friends	1,915	11.77	189	8.80
Retirement	458	2.81	32	1.49
Dependents	3,149	19.35	388	18.06
Marriage	3,040	18.68	578	26.91
Others	1,165	7.16	100	4.66

Source: *Zhongguo 1987 nian 1% renkou chouyang diaocha ziliao, Guangdongsheng fengce*, pp. 548–53.

including those who moved within the province and the in-migrants, moved out of their former residence for this reason, as compared with only one-quarter for the nation as a whole; and

2. in comparison with the 1987 data, the 1990 Population Census data showed that there was a large increase in migration in Guangdong in the latter part of the 1980s because of "job search and trade": from 24.7% to 57.5% for intra-provincial moves and from 18.6% to 61.4% for inter-provincial moves. Correspondingly, the proportion who moved because they were dependents showed a substantial decline: from 19.4% to 8.1% for intra-provincial moves and from 18.1% to 6.8% for inter-provincial moves. The proportion due to job transfer also experienced quite a large decline. For intra-provincial moves, this proportion decreased from 10.7% to 6.7%; for inter-provincial moves, the decrease was from 18.5% to 10.5%. These shifts in general correspond to the gradual relaxation of state controls, including the transition from a "command economy" in which job assignments and job transfers are all prerogatives of the state to a more market-oriented economy in which the "laws of value" prevail. The extent of these shifts also demonstrates that much had happened in the late 1980s and that frequent data updating is needed to monitor Guangdong's fast changing migration scene.

Summary and Conclusion

From the foregoing analysis, it is clear that migration in Guangdong is massive and the speed of development is unprecedented. Including those who have taken up residence in the place of destination for less than one year, migrants now account for more than 10% of the province's population. The Special Economic Zones of Shenzhen and Zhuhai are, of course, composed of migrants. But even in places like Dongguan and Bao'an, favourite locations for setting up out-processing factories by Hong Kong's manufacturers,[35] migrants still account for almost one-half of the total population. The size of the migrant population in Guangzhou and other parts of the delta is also large.

Given the rate of economic growth in Guangdong in general and in the delta in particular, and given the increasing ineffectiveness of the household registry system as a means to control migration flow, the growth and scale of migration to and within Guangdong are to be expected. The fact that quite a sizeable number of female migrants have taken up jobs in the agricultural sector at the place of destination suggests that the transformation of the labour force could be a stepwise process. It is the local labour force in the economically more advanced regions which first transforms itself from agriculture-based to industry- and tertiary-based activities. The vacancies that this shift creates are filled by farmers, largely female, from the poorer counties within and outside Guangdong. Of course, development in the industrial sector and, to a lesser extent, the tertiary sector has been so fast that new jobs in these sectors cannot be filled by the local labour force alone. Import of labour is thus necessary. The 1990 Population Census showed that such labour importations are enormous. The implied flow from a low productivity region to a high productivity region, of course, means an increase in the gross domestic product. Also, this helps to solve the labour surplus problems in the lagging regions. Moreover, the remittance (one estimate puts this at RMB1,000 per migrant worker in the Pearl River Delta[36]) and the new ideas that the migrant workers bring back to their home villages are of some importance in diffusing the growth process from the core to the periphery.[37] One may argue that unrestricted labour import depresses the local wage levels. But it is mainly cheap labour that attracts foreign investment in Guangdong.

Certainly, the size of the migrant population is an issue of concern. It is natural that such a large in-flow of population exerts substantial pressure on the local governments, especially in terms of housing, transport, health care and urban service delivery. Squatting, for example, has become a common feature in the major cities in the delta. There is evidence that in large cities such as Guangzhou, the migrant population tends to concentrate in the inner city areas, thus aggravating the problem of extreme overcrowdedness.[38] The implications of the migration flow for China's urban housing reforms and the impacts on the embryonic urban housing market are poorly understood. Also, family planning, to which the Chinese planners attach much importance, is difficult to enforce among the migrant population.[39] Furthermore, there have been allegations that the increased population mobility is responsible for increase in crime rates.[40] The experience of the Lunar New Year in 1989 is something to be remembered. Hundreds of thousands of migrant workers (one estimate puts the number at 1.5 million[41]) flooded the Guangzhou Railway Station and took the authorities by surprise. The Chinese press called them *mengliu* or "blind population flow." Many migrants had used up all their money and still could not find a job. Large numbers were stranded and slept on open ground in front of the railway station for weeks. Some had to beg for subsistence. Many were later sent back to their hometowns or villages by force. Such a scene has, to a lesser extent, repeated itself in subsequent Chinese new years, although the authorities are now more prepared for it. But, by and large, migration has taken place in an orderly fashion. It is indeed remarkable that most localities in the delta still appear to be able to cope with such large in-flows of population in so short a time.

The future is likely to be more problematic, however. So far, the economy of the delta has been booming. The adverse effects of the 4 June Incident proved to be short-lived. But as the region's economy is increasingly tied to the world economy, cyclical fluctuations will become more pronounced. Recessions in the United States, Europe and Japan will sooner or later have repercussions in the delta. What will happen to the migrant workers in the case of widespread layoffs and bankruptcies is something entirely unknown. But one thing is certain. Conflicts between locals and the recent in-migrants are bound to become more apparent, and this will have serious implications for social stability. Even if the economy is robust and continues to exhibit high growth rates, the fact that the bulk of the migration has taken place without a corresponding change in official residence could be a destabilizing factor. Only temporary residence is given to migrant workers. To date, planning at the local level mostly does not seem to take these migrants into account. The housing, health care and education needs of the migrants are limited as long as most of them are singles and young. But as the young migrant workers grow older, they will get married and give birth to children. Some of the female workers may go back to their home villages, but many more will stay. Will the local authorities be able and willing to treat them as anybody else and provide them with services that local residents enjoy, thereby risking the attraction of an even greater in-flow of migrants? If not, does it mean that the migrants' offsprings will be deprived of such basic civic rights as health care and schooling? In a large sense, then, the local authorities in the delta are at a crossroads, despite the region's prosperity.

Notes

1. Luk Chiu-ming, "Zhujiang Delta in Guangdong's Regional Development," *Asian Geographer*, Vol. 8 (1989), pp. 117–32; Frank Leeming, "The Pearl River Delta, Hong Kong and the Guangdong Hinterland," *Asian Geographer*, Vol. 8 (1989), pp. 151–64.
2. Guangdongsheng tongjiju (ed.), *Guangdong tongji nianjian 1990* (Statistical Yearbook of Guangdong 1990) (Beijing: Zhongguo tongji chubanshe, 1990).
3. Roger C. K. Chan, "Challenges to Urban Areas: The Floating Population," in *China Review 1991*, edited by Kuan Hsin-chi and Maurice Brosseau (Hong Kong: The Chinese University Press, 1991), pp. 12.1–12.21; Dorothy J. Solinger, *China's Transients and the State: A Form of Civil Society?* (Hong Kong: Hong Kong Institute of Asia-Pacific Studies, The Chinese University of Hong Kong, 1991).
4. Li Si-ming, "Labour Mobility, Migration and Urbanization in the Pearl River Delta Area," *Asian Geographer*, Vol. 8 (1989), pp. 35–60. Li Si-ming, Yu Fu-lai, Liu Qi and Zheng Xiangzhang, "Renli touzi, renkou liudong yu chengshihua: Zhujiang sanjiaozhou ge'an yanjiu" (Human Capital Investment, Population Mobility and Urbanization: A Study of the Pearl River Delta), in *Zhujiang sanjiaozhou ji Gang Ao diqu de shehui jingji fazhan* (Socio-Economic Development in the Pearl River Delta and Hong Kong and Macau), edited by Tang Shu-hung and Woo Tun-oy (Hong Kong: Hong Kong Baptist College, 1990), pp. 125–40; Xu Xueqiang and Li Si-ming, "China's Open Door Policy and Urbanization in the Pearl River Delta Region," *International Journal of Urban and Regional Research*, Vol. 14 (1990), pp. 49–69.
5. Wu Chong-tong, "The Special Economic Zones and the Development of the Zhujiang Delta Area," *Asian Geographer*, Vol. 8 (1989), pp. 71–88.
6. Zhongguo shehui kexueyuan renkou yanjiusuo (ed.), *Zhongguo renkou qianyi yu chengshihua yanjiu* (A Study on Population Migration and Urbanization in China) (Beijing: Beijing jingji xueyuan chubanshe, 1989).

7. Li Mengbai and Hu Xin (eds.), *Liudong renkou dui dachengshi fazhan de yingxiang ji duice* (The Impacts of the Mobile Population on Big Cities and Policy Response) (Beijing: Beijing jingji chubanshe, 1991).

8. Zhang Qingwu, "Guanyu renkou qianyi yu liudong renkou gainian wenti (The Conceptual Issues in Population Migration and the Mobile Population), *Renkou yanjiu* (Population Research), No. 3 (1988), pp. 17–18.

9. Liu Zhen, "Renkou lilun jiaocheng" (Lectures on Population Theory) (Beijing: Xinhua shudian, 1986); Zhongguo shehui kexueyuan renkou yanjiusuo (ed.), *Zhongguo renkou qianyi yu chengshihua yanjiu* (see note 6), p. 49.

10. Wu Ruijun, "Guanyu liudong renkou hanyi de tansuo" (An Investigation into the Meaning of the Mobile Population), *Renkou yu jingji* (Population and Economy), No. 3 (1990), pp. 27, 53–55; Li and Hu (eds.), *Liudong renkou* (see note 7).

11. Guowuyuan renkou pucha bangongshi, guojia tongjiju renkou tongjishi (eds.), *Zhongguo 1990 nian renkou pucha 10% chouyang ziliao* (The 1990 Population Census: 10% Sample Statistics) (Beijing: Zhongguo tongji chubanshe, 1991), pp. 681–82.

12. Guangdongsheng tongjiju (ed.), *Guangdongsheng tongji nianjian 1990* (see note 2), p. 113.

13. Guangdongsheng renkou pucha bangongshi (ed.), *Guangdongsheng disici renkou pucha shougong huizong ziliao* (The Fourth Population Census: Manual Tabulations for Guangdong Province) (Beijing: Zhongguo tongji chubanshe, 1991), p. 7.

14. Peng Faqiang, "Guangdong liudong renkou xiankuang" (The Mobile Population in Guangdong), *Nanfang renkou* (Southern Population), No. 3 (1989), pp. 23, 24–27.

15. Shenzhenshi tongjiju (ed.), *Shenzhen tongji nianjian 1991* (Statistical Yearbook of Shenzhen 1991) (Beijing: Zhongguo tongji chubanshe, 1991).

16. See note 14, p. 193.

17. See note 7, p. 192.

18. Ibid., p. 193.

19. See note 13, pp. 30–31.

20. Ibid., p. 31.

21. Ibid., p. 7; Guojia tongjiju (ed.), *Zhongguo tongji nianjian 1991* (Statistical Yearbook of China 1991) (Beijing: Zhongguo tongji chubanshe, 1991).

22. Li Si-ming, "China's Open Policy and Regional Development: An Explanatory Account with Special Reference to Guangdong Province," Hong Kong Baptist College, Faculty of Social Science, Working Paper Series, No. 9102 (1991), p. 14.

23. Li Si-ming, "Labour Mobility, Migration and Urbanization in the Pearl River Delta Area" (see note 4), p. 45.

24. See note 5.
25. See note 13, pp. 24–28.
26. Guangdongsheng tongjiju, Guangdongsheng renkou pucha bangongshi (eds.), *Zhongguo 1987 nian 1% renkou chouyang diaocha ziliao, Guangdongsheng fengce* (The 1987 China's 1% Population Sample Survey Statistics: Guangdong Province) (Beijing: Zhongguo tongji chubanshe, 1988).
27. Li Si-ming et al., "Renli touzi, renkou liudong yu chengshihua" (see note 4); Li Si-ming, "Labour Mobility, Migration and Urbanization" (see note 4); Liao Shitong and Liao Shitian, "Guangdongsheng renkou liudong qushi ji qi daoxiang" (The Trend of Population Movement and Its Implications), *Zhongguo renkou kexue* (China's Population Science), Vol. 6 (1989), pp. 7–25.
28. Beijing Shi, Tianjin Shi, Shanghai Shi, Guangzhou Shi renkou pucha bangongshi (eds.), *Jing, Jin, Hu, Sui renkou ziliao duibi* (Beijing, Tianjin, Shanghai and Guangzhou: Comparison of Population Information) (Beijing: Zhongguo tongji chubanshe, 1991), p. 146.
29. See note 14.
30. Deng Ying, "Guangzhou shiqu renkou qianyi he liudong de diaocha fenxi" (A Survey on Population Migration and Mobility in Guangzhou City Proper), in *Zhongguo renkou qianyi yu chengshihua yanjiu* (see note 6), pp. 401–11.
31. *Zhongguo renkou bao* (China Population News), 16 September 1990.
32. Li Si-ming, "Labour Mobility, Migration and Urbanization" (see note 4), p. 45.
33. Li Si-ming et al., "Renli touzi, renkou liudong yu chengshihua" (see note 4), p. 136.
34. Liao Shitong, "Zhuhai jingji tequ renkou qianyi de tedian ji dui qianyi zhengce de pingjia" (The Features of Population Migration in the Zhuhai Special Economic Zone and A Critique of Migration Policies), in *Zhongguo renkou qianyi yu chengshihua yanjiu* (see note 6), pp. 412–22.
35. Victor F. S. Sit, "Hong Kong's New Industrial Partnership with the Pearl River Delta," *Asian Geographer*, Vol. 8 (1989), pp. 103–16.
36. Li Zhi, "Cong Zhujiang sanjiaozhou kan liudong renkou" (An Examination of the Mobile Population from the Pearl River Delta Perspective) (paper presented at the Zhujiang sanjiaozhou fazhan yu jianshe Zhongguo tese shehuizhuyi yantaohui [Development in the Pearl River Delta and the Construction of Chinese Socialism Conference] held in Dongguan on 28–30 August 1992).
37. Liao and Liao, "Guangdongsheng renkou liudong qushi ji qi daoxiang" (see note 27); Li Zhi, ibid.
38. Tu Lizhong, "Chengshi liudong renkou wenti de lilun tantao he duice jianyi" (A Theoretical Investigation of the Urban Mobile Population Problem and

Recommendations for Policy Response), *Zhongshan daxue xuebao (Zhongshan University Academic Journal, Philosophy and Social Sciences Section)*, No. 3 (1990), pp. 1–9.
39. See note 37.
40. See notes 7 and 36.
41. Anthony G. O. Yeh, K. C. Lam, K. Y. Wong and S. M. Li, "Spatial Development in the Pearl River Delta: Development Issues and Research Agenda," *Asian Geographer*, Vol. 8 (1989), pp. 1–10.

18

The Environment

R. J. Neller and K. C. Lam

> Economic development and sound environmental management are comple-
> mentary aspects of the same agenda. Without adequate environmental protec-
> tion, development will be undermined; without development, environmental
> protection will fail.[1]

This statement highlights the false dichotomy of development and environment, and is particularly relevant to this discussion of the changing character of Guangdong's environment. Guangdong is one of the, if not *the*, most
rapidly developing regions in the world, with double digit growth rates, a
booming industrial base, rapid urbanization, rising living standards and
accelerated consumer spending. Unfortunately, severe environmental
degradation is also apparent in many parts of the province. Potable water is
becoming a scarce resource as pollution, salinization and high nitrate
levels diminish existing supplies, whilst urban watercourses are more like
open sewers. The erosion of hill slopes is still widespread and urban air
quality continues to deteriorate. To what extent, then, are the province's
natural resources being depleted, undervalued or overexploited? To what
degree is this economic growth real and sustainable, and what are the costs
to human welfare of environmental degradation?

Intriguing as these issues are, they are nevertheless beyond the scope
of this paper. Nor do the authors wish to provide an overview of environmental degradation in Guangdong, which would by necessity be somewhat
superficial. Instead, the authors seek to pursue a limited number of issues
so as to illustrate certain general or underlying principles regarding the
assessment and management of environmental problems in Guangdong.
This discussion is also largely limited to issues pertaining to the Pearl
River Delta region. This is not to suggest that issues outside the delta are
unimportant — indeed issues such as soil erosion and marine exploitation are intriguing topics. Rather, the Pearl River Delta is both a fragile
environment and the focal point of urban and industrial development.
Before proceeding in this direction, however, a brief overview of the
physical landscape is warranted.

Physical Landscape

For the most part the province consists of fluvially dissected, rolling to
rugged hill country, with more mountainous country to the north and
northeast. Only 23% of the province can be classified as plains: the
major areas including the Pearl River and Han River Deltas, the Leizhou

peninsula and coastal plains surrounding Zhanjiang, and the karst plains and plateaux to the north and northeast.

The province forms part of the Palaeozoic and Mesozoic geosynclinal fold zone encircling the Yangzi massif. Intense folding and faulting during the early Palaeozoic produced a series of mountain ranges aligned northeast-southwest, inducing a rectilinear drainage pattern within the East River and parts of the North River and Han River drainage basins. Regional metamorphism at this time produced a basement of quartzite, schist, gneiss and migmatite that is extensively exposed in the southern half of the province. Mesozoic intrusive rocks, principally coarse crystalline granite and monzonite granite, are widely spread across the province, whilst to the north and northeast, mesozoic sediments and smaller outcrops of Jurassic-Cretaceous volcanics and volcanic-sedimentary deposits are also found.

Within the East River and Han River basins to the northeast, intensely folded quartzite, schist and other metamorphic rocks are common, as are gneiss and granite. Rugged ranges, steep sided and sharp crested, interspersed with upland plateaux (1,000 m), provide a landscape of contrasts. In northern Guangdong, within the North River basin, the scenic red beds comprising very thick, sub-horizontal strata of shale, sandstone, conglomerate and breccia, are extensively exposed. Karst hill lands with high water storage capacities are also common. To the south, the Leizhou peninsula and the adjacent coastal plains are one of the few large expanses of relatively flat land/gently rolling hills, with a maximum elevation of 272 m. Lower Pliocene basalt covers the southern half of the peninsula whilst Pleistocene alluvial and marine deposits cover the northern, leading to moderate to high water storage capacities throughout the peninsula. Across the remainder of the southern part of the province are large exposures of the previously mentioned metamorphic rocks, granites and smaller outcrops of volcanic-sedimentary rocks.

Because of tectonic activity the province is richly endowed with geothermal waters, concentrated along the numerous major faults. These weak alkaline-natrium waters are rich in carbonates and of moderate to high temperature.

The province is largely drained by three tributaries of the Pearl River (Zhujiang), comprising the East River (Dongjiang), the North River (Beijiang) and the West River (Xijiang). The Pearl River is China's second largest river in terms of discharge, yet the extensive alluvial plains typical of the rivers in the north of China are absent along the tributaries of the

Pearl River. Instead these rivers pass through narrower confined valleys. Only the southwestern and northeastern parts of the province are not drained by tributaries of the Pearl River. The Han River drains much of the mountainous region of northeast Guangdong, whilst smaller rivers such as the To River and Lien River drain the northeastern coastal plains. These latter three rivers converge near the coast to provide deltaic environments that replicate on a much smaller scale the Pearl River Delta. To the south-west numerous shorter streams drain the Leizhou peninsula and adjacent coastal plains.

The southern part of the province experiences a tropical monsoon climate with long, hot and humid summers and cooler, drier winters. The northern parts are more sub-tropical monsoon, though this difference essentially refers to the cooler winter more so than the minor differences in the summer temperatures or precipitation, the latter averaging 1,500–1,800 mm per annum across the province.

Because Guangdong is characterized by hilly relief, and a sub-tropical monsoon climate (high rainfall erosivity) and a deep weathering mantle (high soil erodibility), there is a severe erosion potential over much of the province. Thirty-six of the 76 counties are extensively eroded and in three of these (Loding, Wuhua and Deqing) erosion affects over 50% of the county. The majority of these eroded areas are located in the remote hilly areas as well as in the upper courses of the river systems. Whilst most severe in the deeply weathered granite areas, erosion is also common in areas underlain by sandstone and calcareous shales.

Pearl River Delta

Because of its favourable physical characteristics (flat, fertile land, abundant fresh water, access to the sea), the Pearl River Delta has been the focal point of development within the province. But it is also a unique and fragile resource, for which reason it has also been the subject of environmental concern. Indeed, numerous internationally funded conferences have recently targeted this region.[2]

The Pearl River receives waters from an area of approximately 425,700 km^2, principally through the East River, North River and West River tributaries. Annual flows approximate 300–325 billion cu m which are concentrated in the six months between April and September (80% of total flow). These waters are discharged through eight major outlets to the sea, another hundred or so major interconnecting channels and a host of minor distributary channels, many of which were probably human-made (Figure 18.1). Of the eight main channels, four (Humen, Jiao Men, Hongqi Men and Heng Men) discharge into Lingding Yang Bay and the remaining (Yamen, Hutiao Men, Modao Men and Jiti Men) discharge to the south.

The delta is a late Pleistocene-Holocene sedimentary depositional system covering approximately 10,000 km². The collation of thousands of years of Chinese literature has been used to demonstrate the manner of delta growth and as late as the tenth century it was apparent that the ranges between Zhongshan and Macau were still islands.[3] The Pearl River Delta is a bayhead delta set against a backdrop of numerous rocky islands (at least 80 near to shore), and so is unlike most other major deltas in the world, both in plan and relief. Because these offshore islands reduce the energy of incoming waves and because of the limited tidal range, the basic structure of the delta is controlled more by fluvial processes than the tide or wave regimes. Only the Yamen and Humen outlets are dominated by tidal influences. Therefore, it is the high variability in runoff, the fine grained sediment size, the low silt/water ratio and other hydrologic characteristics that control the deposition of sediments.[4]

Between 71 and 88 million tons of suspended sediments are annually delivered to the estuary, a depositional rate that is estimated to advance the delta front seawards by about 50–120 m per year. The extensive mud flats that have developed are heavily utilized and require an extensive system of sea dykes for protection. Approximately 2,000 km of dykes protect about 187,000 ha.[5] The Modao Men outlet currently transports most sediment (23 million tons, largely input from the West River) whilst the Jiaomen, Hongqi Men and Heng Men also discharge heavy loads into western Lingding Yang Bay, and as such these are the two most rapidly growing parts of the delta. Only the Humen outlet has a relatively stable channel bed.[6]

Economic losses due to flooding and waterlogging are increasing due to urban encroachment and intensified agricultural practices.[7] The large variation in annual precipitation, the possibility of typhoons and the presence of a tidal estuary, with a lack of natural lakes or major water storages and an elevated river bed, combine to provide a high potential for flooding. Extensive flooding in 1983 was due to the coincidence of a high tide with flood runoff, whilst Guangzhou was flooded twenty-seven times between 1964 and 1990.[8]

From a geomorphic perspective, the delta is not stable and, because of

Figure 18.1   The Fluvial Environment in the Pearl River Delta Region

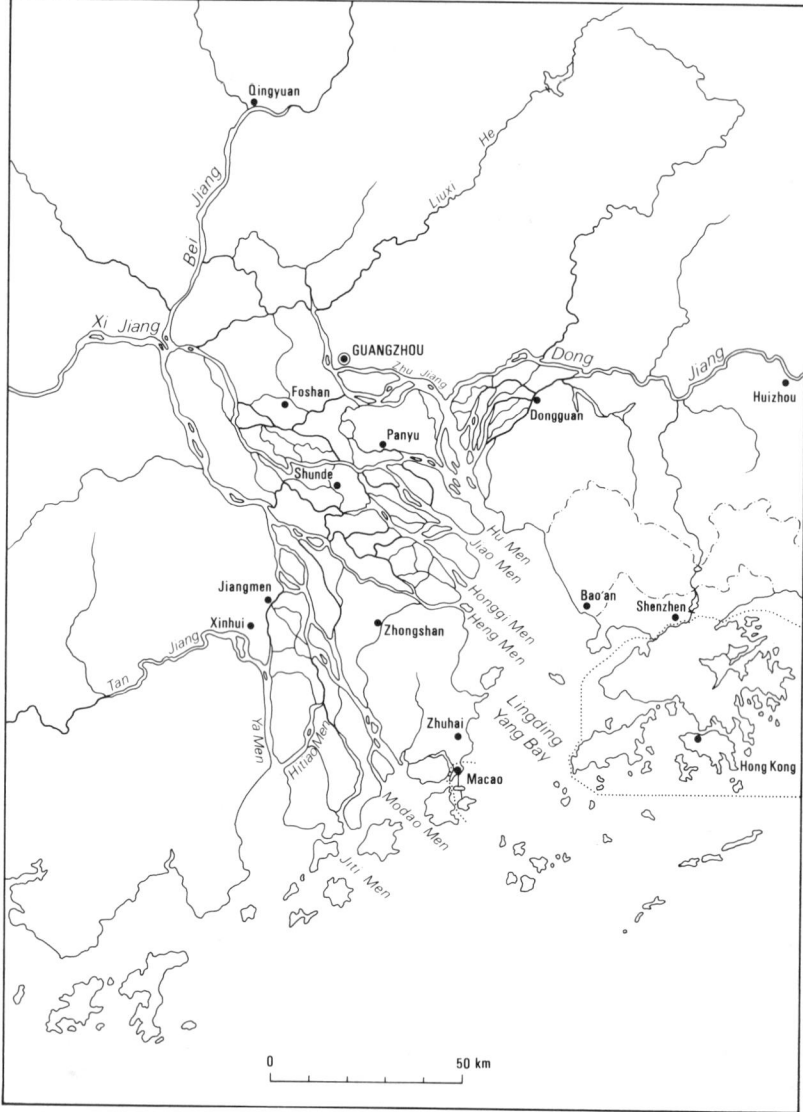

high rates of sedimentation, channels are constantly changing, flow is disrupted and navigation hindered. Moreover, human activities have dramatically altered the hydrodynamics of these channels, as evidenced by the geomorphic changes to the Shapa tidal inlet in recent years.[9] As previously mentioned, much of the area is also dependent upon embankments for flood protection, and drainage is an important issue. Furthermore, local subsidence leads to the drowning of parts of the delta. A comprehensive statement of the geomorphic and hydraulic problems of each of the eight main outlets has recently been provided.[10]

In concluding this overview of the physical landscape, those characteristics that are pertinent to the following discussion on environmental management are summarized. In this respect, perhaps the most significant point is that much of the province is essentially part of a large single catchment, characterized by source areas (upland regions), transport zones (albeit often poorly developed) and a large depositional sink (lowland delta). The coastal deltaic environment is the receiving end for waters, sediments and pollutants generated elsewhere in the province, but is also the focus of residential and industrial development and an increasing demand for natural resources such as fresh water. There is also a long coastal interface. The potential for conflicting land use is quite clear: problems of pollution of estuarine waters, urban encroachment of prime agricultural lands and exploitation of marine resources are all evident within this province.

Degradation of the Physical Environment

Perspectives

Discussions of environmental degradation and reconstruction in China are bound to arouse a variety of opinions, as the publication of *The Bad Earth: Environmental Degradation in China* demonstrated.[11] The devastation wrought by people in China is immense, and in some respects is intensifying: the Ministry of Water Conservancy, for example, announced in November 1992, that 3.67 million km^2 now suffer from some form of soil, water or wind erosion, a significant increase over previously published government statistics.[12] But the reconstruction effort is also immense, lending support to those who argue that China is making significant improvements in environmental management, and to those who, for whatever reason, attempt to downplay the seriousness of the situation.

The "signals" emerging from Guangdong are as conflicting as those from the rest of China. Following a survey of major Chinese cities in 1992, the National Environmental Protection Agency (NEPA) ranked Guangzhou second in its attempts to develop environmental protection and treatment strategies, whilst Guangdong has been rated as one of the top six provinces in terms of retaining its "ecological condition." Nevertheless, a recent inspection of Guangdong by a State Environmental Protection Commission team reported that there were insufficient mechanisms conducive to environmental protection, pollution technology was under-utilized and funding for environmental protection was insufficient.[13] Moreover, the water quality of the Pearl River, which receives up to 2 million tonnes of industrial waste and domestic sewage annually, was described as "comparatively serious" by NEPA in its 1990 communiqué on the environment.

Guangdong has experienced rapid economic growth over the last decade as a result of China's open policy and economic reform. Such growth provides both revenue and access to technologies for more effective environmental control, but at the same time creates problems of a nature and extent not yet experienced in other parts of China. This conflict between opportunity and uncertainty/inexperience can partly be placed in perspective by comparing aspects of industrial waste management in Guangdong in 1985 and 1994 (Table 18.1). In 1985 Guangdong's treatment of industrial liquid and solid wastes was proportionally better than the national average, whereas in 1994 its performance was about equivalent to the national average. Guangdong has not maintained its earlier lead in the treatment of industrial wastes, though its rapid development and booming economy have provided an opportunity to exceed national standards of achievement.

The rapid growth of Guangdong was initiated by foreign investment and as such the state has little influence on the rate of growth, nor on the type or mix of industries. In 1990, 64% of foreign investment came from Hong Kong. Indeed, Hong Kong has become the marketing outlet for Guangdong's manufacturing base. Nevertheless, the pattern of foreign investment is gradually changing with an increasing portion of money channelled to direct investment or joint investment projects.

The last decade has also seen a rapid proliferation of industries in the rural towns and townships in Guangdong. Measured in terms of industrial output, two-thirds of the rural enterprises in Guangdong are located in the Pearl River Delta. The remaining one-third are located around Chaozhou, Shantou and Zhanjiang. These rural township enterprises are welcomed by both the people and the government because they help to keep the population in the countryside and provide an alternative manner of economic support. Rural enterprises also facilitate infrastructural development such as communication and transport. One of the major side effects of this has been that prime agricultural lands have been levelled or reclaimed to provide land for immediate and anticipated urban development.

Table 18.1 Changing Character of Industrial Waste Treatment Effectiveness in Guangdong, 1985–1994

	Liquid effluent	Solid wastes
1985		
Provincial total (million tons)		
— all origins	2,053	—
— industrial origin	1,333	15.8
% Industrial waste treated	43.6 (22.1)	43.3 (19.5)
% Compliance industrial waste	40.4 (38.3)	—
% Compliance treated industrial waste	42.8 (56.7)	—
1994		
Provincial total (million tons)		
— all origins	3,372	—
— industrial origin	1,315	14.6
% Industrial waste treated	94.6 (92.1)	24.7 (28.5)
% Compliance industrial waste	54.7 (55.5)	—
% Compliance treated industrial waste	30.7 (23.9)	—

Sources: *Guangdong tongji nianjian 1988* and *Guangdong tongji nianjian 1992.*
        Zhongguo tongji nianjian 1986 and *Zhongguo tongji nianjian 1992.*
Note: Figures in brackets are national averages.

Unfortunately, this mode of economic growth inhibits comprehensive planning and adversely affects environmental quality, and environmental management tends to become reactive rather than proactive.

Chinese Environmental Protection Law

First promulgated in 1979, the Chinese Environmental Protection Law (Draft) outlined the principles of environmental protection on a national basis. These principles were subsequently translated into three major policy instruments in the early 1980s: the Three-Synchronization System, Environmental Impact Assessments System and an Effluent Charging System. The former two are protective measures, and remain the cornerstone of the Chinese Environmental Protection Law. The Three-Synchronization System is designed to minimize the cost of pollution control (both to the enterprise and to society) by incorporating control measures at the design, construction and operation stages. The Environmental Impact Assessments System is an economic measure which serves to redirect resources for pollution control and provide a major source of revenue for the control authorities. Since the emergence of a national environmental policy in the 1980s is well documented by Wu, no attempt is made to expand upon this early development of environmental legislation.[14]

Implementation of these policies was not without difficulty and, towards the end of the 1980s, Chinese environmental managers realized that these three instruments had not performed as expected. In response to this, five additional administrative measures were introduced in 1989.[15] Of particular concern was the effluent charging system (based on concentrations rather than total discharge control), which was replaced by a discharge permit system. Additional measures included an environmental evaluation system for major cities, environmental evaluation and auditing for enterprises, collective treatment systems for industrial cities, and new target dates for the elimination of existing major emission sources.

Recognizing that the stimulus for economic growth in the coastal cities of China was led by foreign investment, the State Council issued directives (in 1986) on environmental management in such "open" areas that explicitly discouraged the introduction of polluting industries into China. For those industries that were likely to produce pollutants, attention was to be given to pollution control and the Three-Synchronization System was to be strictly implemented. This was followed in 1991 by a notice of tightened control for the transfer of harmful substances into the country.

In addition to targeting foreign investment, NEPA has recently emphasized that city administrators should be more responsible for promoting urban environmental management.[16] They have developed a national environmental evaluation scheme for major cities, provided additional state funding for central treatment facilities and developed an evaluation scheme for state enterprises.

In spite of these regulatory developments, a number of problems remain. There is a lack of specific regulation and administrative procedures (the principles, but not the means, are provided), there is an underdeveloped legal system (difficulty of sanction in cases of non-compliance) and there exists an informal power base (avoidance of work to rule). Moreover, the effluent charge rates for foreign investments remains too low. Some of these issues will be developed in later sections.

Provincial Departmental Organization and Responsibilities

Figure 18.2 illustrates the hierarchy of the environmental protection machinery in China in 1992. It is a highly complex, multi-organizational hierarchy within which there is no one single policy and control authority (political decentralization)! For example, front line control is achieved by the environmental protection units in large and medium enterprises and environmental protection units in small enterprises/enterprises in towns. Large and medium enterprises are under the control of the county and city administrations and their environmental bureaux, though they are at the same time answerable to a variety of ministries at the state and Province/Autonomous Regions/Central State-administered Municipalities (PAM) government levels. Moreover, the structure is such that large and medium enterprises located in the counties are not subject to the control of the county environmental protection offices. The Guangdong government receives its environmental directives from NEPA, the executive branch of the State Environmental Protection Commission. One of the most important aspects of this relationship is that the central government determines the "principles, policies, decrees, and standards for environmental quality; and ... put(s) forward proposals for planning requirements. The concrete tasks of inspection and supervision are left to be carried out by organizations at (other) various levels."[17] The provincial governments are nevertheless permitted to set standards higher than those determined by the state or to include water quality parameters not otherwise issued by the state.[18]

In some respects this appears to be a sensible solution to the physical and ecological diversity and the large size of China, and Wong and Chan observed that decentralized implementation of authority should be more attuned to local problems.[19] Unfortunately, decentralized authority leads to a lack of uniformity in standards and implementation procedures, which are exploitable. Moreover, pollutants have no respect for administrative boundaries.

Translating policies into practical terms by local governments is seen by many as administratively clumsy. It requires a high level of technical, economic and planning competence at the local level which is not readily forthcoming from other, perhaps more relevant, authorities. Moreover, there is no assurance that financial resources will be provided by national or provincial agencies and indeed most county environmental protection offices are financially dependent on effluent charges. It is not surprising that in 1990 the Shenzhen Environmental Protection Office assessed only 80% of all projects that needed scrutiny, whilst Bao'an County achieved only 66% scrutiny in 1989. Nevertheless, in an economy where counties strive against each other for the fastest possible economic growth, we need to recognize that these counties are themselves unwilling to relegate

Figure 18.2 Environmental Protection Machinery in China, 1992

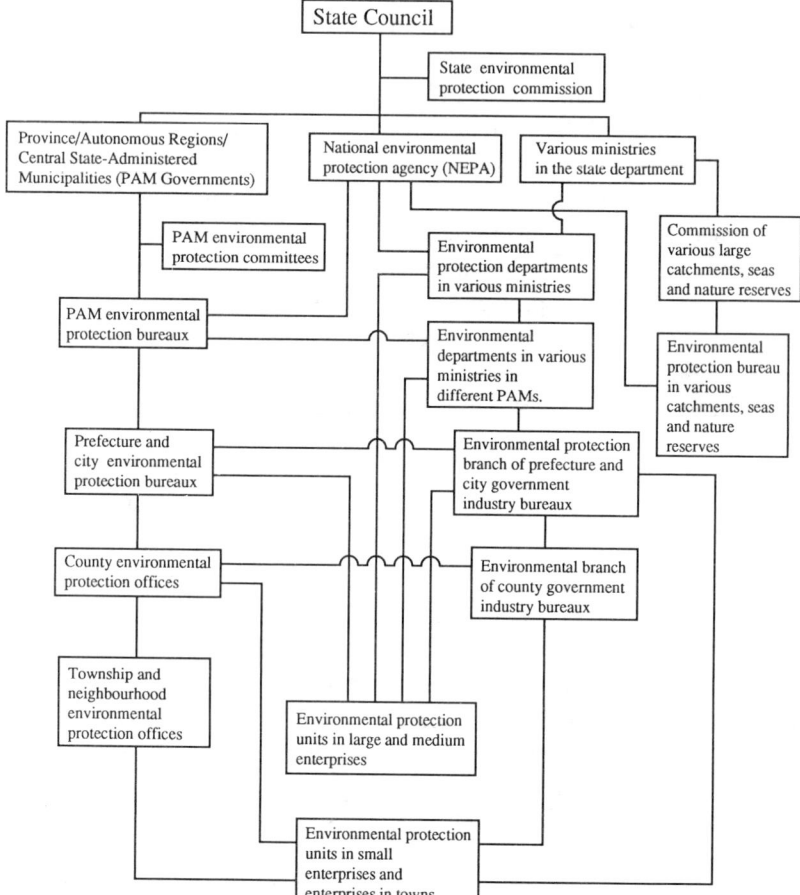

planning power to other authorities further up the hierarchy. The directives and regulations of Shunde County, which is acclaimed as a model of county environmental management, highlights the high level of administrative competence required at the county level as a result of this approach. The county is required to draft regulations and decrees in response to national and provincial directives and to draft its own socioeconomic master plan.

In other cases, the state policies are themselves ambiguous and/or open to interpretation. The Marine Environmental Protection Law, when passed in 1982, specified that coastal developments required environmental impact statements, but did not specify how or under what conditions such assessments should be made.[20] In addition, Fan notes that specific regulations concerning control matters should be determined by the coastal provincial governments, but the majority had not done so six years after the legislation had become effective; he also notes a lack of supportive clauses or regulations in other legislation pertaining to the marine environment.[21] It is also difficult to see how certain guidelines on standards for waste (such as no pathogens from industrial wastewaters or domestic sewage, and no floating material), specified by the State Oceanic Administration as baseline marine water quality standards, can be attained.

The provincial, regional, municipal and county environmental protection departments are supplemented by an array of other more specialist agencies. Using the waters of the Pearl River Delta as an example, the previously mentioned State Oceanic Administration incorporates a marine monitoring centre and a department of environmental protection and supervision. But other "players" include the Guangdong Coastal Area Investigation Department, the Pearl River Water Resources Commission (under the auspices of the Water Resources Commission), the Pearl River Basin Water Resources Protection Bureau (under the auspices of the Ministry of Water Resources and NEPA), the Guangdong Provincial Waterway Bureau and a host of other hydrologic, navigation and research agencies. The functions of these agencies are not always well defined and a lack of co-ordination leads to conflicting demands for scarce resources. For example, the Pearl River Water Resources Commission undertakes seismic investigations within Lingding Yang Bay and works on sea dykes for coastal protection, functions that would perhaps be more effectively managed by the coastal and marine agencies.

In the following sections, the effectiveness of these institutions and their policies are examined in a number of issues, including the dispersal of industry in the Pearl River Delta region and aspects of water and air pollution. As mentioned earlier, this choice of issues does not imply that these are the most important, or indeed the only issues worth examining. Rather, they illustrate certain general principles that we wish to develop.

Dispersal of Industry

Within the province, and particularly within the Special Economic Zones (SEZs), industrial production is perceived as the means by which economic activity can be stimulated. Although originally confined to a few SEZs and industrial estates, the dispersal of industry from larger urban centres to satellite towns and rural areas has proceeded at a rapid rate within the Pearl River Delta. This pattern of dispersal, though encouraged throughout the province, has essentially flourished within the delta region.

The growth of industries outside major cities has been encouraged by the state as a means of controlling the expansion of larger cities (reduced rural-urban migration) and of distributing society's productive forces. "The construction of small cities and towns shows that it is easier to manage the environment when cities are integrated with rural areas, when industry is combined with agriculture ..."[22]

However, it is widely believed that polluting industries are taking advantage of this decentralization policy and the failure to rapidly implement environmental management within these newly developing regions. It is believed that polluting industries have gradually moved from Hong Kong to the SEZs and then to neighbouring counties and smaller towns.[23] For example, of the 60 tanneries forced out of business in Hong Kong in the late 1970s, 8 moved to Shenzhen and 30 to the adjoining Bao'an County. Moreover, a survey undertaken in 1983 indicated that only 30% of the production lines established since the inception of the SEZ in 1979 were using state-of-the-art technologies, whilst another 30% were using outdated production technologies.[24] The latter are less efficient in energy and resource use and are prone to generate more pollutants.

Within the province, the percentage of township enterprises considered as polluting averaged 11% in 1990. By comparison, within Bao'an County 17% of foreign investment projects were classified as polluting (1986–1990), within Zhuhai the percentage of polluting industries rose from 30% pre-1988 to 68% in 1988–1989, and in Zhongshan 40% were classified as polluting (1987–1989). These data suggest that polluting industries are infiltrating different parts of the province.

The lack of uniformity in the implementation of industrial environmental policies pertaining to foreign investment, as noted above, is in part responsible for this relocation of polluting industries. In the 1980s, Hong Kong witnessed a period of environmental awakening, culminating in the implementation of more stringent control measures and the promulgation of several environmental legislations. In Guangdong, the environmental protection machinery was not established at the same time in various parts of the province, giving rise to a situation that could be exploited by investors. The machinery was generally set up earlier in the major cities and SEZs than in the counties and rural townships. For example, an Environmental Protection Office was set up in Shenzhen in 1980, but similar offices were not established until as late as 1986 in most counties. The regulations for environmental impact statements were promulgated in Shenzhen in 1983, but were only introduced into Shunde County in 1986. The tightening up of environmental control in Shenzhen has thus resulted in the re-establishment of polluting industries in the nearby Bao'an County: there are, for example, at least one hundred electroplating shops in Bao'an County. Ma anticipated that with the tightening of environmental control in Bao'an, polluting industries will gradually relocate to Huizhou.[25]

Differences in the implementation of policies are also reflected in the financial resources allocated to environmental control. For example, environmental spending accounted for less than 0.4% of total investment in rural townships in Bao'an County as compared to 2.7% in Shunde.

The fundamental policy of decentralization/dispersal of industries is, from an environmental perspective, fraught with problems:

1. The decentralization of industry does not necessarily remove industrial pollution but may simply redistribute it. The decentralization of industry must be accompanied by improvements in production and management strategies and the implementation of advanced pollution control measures, but there is evidence that this is not always occurring. Although the pollutant concentrations (per unit area) may not be as high as those in large urban agglomerations, they are nevertheless spread in a more insidious manner over the province.

2. Dispersal of industry does not allow industry or the community to enjoy the benefits of a collective waste treatment strategy or the economy of scale that a collective system offers. Advanced methods of pollution control can be expensive and industry should be encouraged to undertake collective control measures and alternative methods of waste management, e.g. recycling. This is best achieved with industrial agglomeration.

3. The monitoring of pollution is made more difficult because of its dispersed nature. The cost of effectively monitoring a larger area with scattered and/or isolated point sources is relatively high, and this places an undue reliance upon industrial ethics and self monitoring.

4. There is an insufficient number of trained personnel capable of

assessing environmental damage and enforcing local legislation. Combine this with an increase in the area of possible exposure to contaminants, cross-county pollution transport, i.e. downstream effects, and a variety of county and municipal legislations, then the task of pollution control officers is made more difficult.

5. Contamination of agricultural production is occurring. Indeed numerous farmers are known to use the income generated from the sale of their contaminated products to purchase the same products from uncontaminated regions for their own consumption.

The issue is further complicated by a reluctance of local community leaders and land managers to rigorously enforce environmental legislations that might deter industrial investment. After all, the per capita output of those engaged in rural township enterprises was 9.1 times greater than that of those in agriculture in 1988.[26] Moreover, certain industries, such as electroplating, bleaching and textile, chemical, paper making, tannery and food processing, are willing to relocate in these more remote regions so as to avoid the more stringent controls required in the larger cities.

Some of the possible effects of this on the environment become apparent when variations in the level of waste treatment in different parts of the province are examined (Table 18.2). This survey covers nineteen cities, which have been divided into four groups. The major cities include Guangzhou and Maoming, the latter being a petro-chemical industrial city. The satellite cities referred to those which have emerged over the last decade in the Pearl River Delta whilst the small cities are those which are scattered over other parts of the province. Finally there are the three SEZs.

The SEZs have done relatively poorly in terms of the control of liquid and gaseous pollutants. This is unexpected, because being newly developed areas, SEZs should be more amenable to environmental planning and pollution control. This may reflect the informal power structure in environmental protection machinery, a point to be addressed later. Regarding liquid effluents, there is evidence that environmental control in the major cities is more stringent than in the satellite cities and other small cities. However, this may also be indicative of the relocation of the more polluting industries away from the major urban areas. In the wake of a deteriorating aquatic environment, environmental managers need to reconsider the existing parochial approach to water quality management. The fact that water pollutants do not respect administrative boundaries should

Table 18.2   Levels of Treatment of Industrial Waste in Guangdong

(Unit: %)

	Liquid effluent		Gaseous emission		Ash & part.		Solid wastes	
	1989	1991	1989	1991	1989	1991	1989	1991
Major cities	44.9	62.5	56.8	29.3	72.4	90.9	14.3	15.2
Satellite cities	23.5	35.1	93.1	90.6	85.1	80.1	67.9	57.7
Small cities	22.6	33.5	67.9	71.8	76.4	84.0	11.6	42.6
SEZs	17.6	31.8	37.3	57.8	81.3	80.1	N.A.	25.0
Provincial average	33.2	48.1	67.3	54.4	75.6	89.0	28.5	33.7
National average	29.2	58.5	63.8	63.0	68.5	81.1	12.3	21.7

Sources: *Zhongguo chengshi tongji nianjian 1990* and *Zhongguo chengshi tongji nianjian 1992.*

Note: Major cities: Guangzhou and Maoming; Satellite cities: Foshan, Jiangmen, Huizhou, Zhongshan, Dongguan, Qingyuan; Small cities: Zhanjiang, Shaoguan, Zhaoqing, Chaozhou, Meizhou, Shanwei, Heyuan, Yangjiang SEZs: Shenzhen, Zhuhai, Shantou.

be recognized; the formulation of a comprehensive approach is urgently needed.

The data regarding air pollutants is intriguing. It appears that air pollution in the satellite and small cities is under tighter control than in the major cities, a pattern converse to that of water pollution control. However, it most likely reflects the much higher traffic volume (and hence vehicular emissions) and the greater number of major emission sources (power stations, petro-chemical complexes) in the major cities, where the treatment of gaseous emissions over this period has slipped dramatically. Many of the latter have been there for some time and are not receptive to change and/or control.

Both water and air pollution will be examined in more detail in the following sections. The essential point, however, is that the dispersal of industry to smaller urban centres may not necessarily lead to a reduction in provincial pollution levels, but rather to its redistribution throughout the province. This so-called "irrational" redistribution of industry in villages and townships is believed to have led to serious water pollution throughout the delta region.[27]

Quality of Pearl River Delta Waters

The quality of the waters of the Pearl River is, according to the surveys of the National Environmental Protection Agency, generally good.[28] Nevertheless, certain lower reaches of the river are seriously polluted, posing health risks to the population and problems of water supply. There are three main sources of water pollution in the delta region: untreated domestic sewage, industrial wastewaters and rural non-point pollution. The major pollutants derived from these activities are organic matter, ammoniacal and nitrite nitrogen, and suspended sediments, resulting in deoxygenation of water courses and offensive smells, and eutrophication of the estuary (evidenced by increasing incidence of red tides). In practice, however, it is difficult to identify discrete sources, particularly untreated domestic and industrial liquid sources which are sometimes discharged into river systems via combined urban wastewaters.

Clearly the city of Guangzhou is a major source of water pollution within the Pearl River Delta. Furthermore, an analysis of five major cities in the delta reveals that about 59% of the total urban wastewaters are industrial in origin and the remaining 41% municipal wastewaters.[29] Over the period 1986–1989, industrial wastewater volumes rose only 11% whilst municipal wastewaters increased 31%, reflecting rapid urban development. This, in turn, places an increasing burden of organic pollution on the river systems due to inadequate treatment facilities.

Over the same period, there has been rapid development in agricultural practices within the delta. An increase in intensive livestock production and an increasing reliance on chemical fertilizers and pesticides/ herbicides is apparent, with chemical fertilizer application increasing by 40% between 1986 and 1989. This also increases organic pollution loadings within the delta and the adjacent estuary due to mitigation measures rarely being adopted.

The most polluted stretch of water is the Jiangmen section of the West River, which maintains this status in both the wet and dry seasons and whose offending characteristics include high biochemical oxygen demand, mercury, petroleum, dissolved oxygen and phenol, reflecting a strong influence of domestic and industrial wastes from Xinhui County and Jiangmen City.[30] In particular, the Jiangmen Xinghua Paper Factory, the Jiangmen Sugar Plant and the Kaiping Nitrogenous Fertilizer Factory account for 20% of the total wastewaters.[31] The Yamen outlet is thus the most severely affected part of the estuary. The total inorganic N and chemical oxygen demand concentrations at the Yamen outlet are the highest in the Zhujiang estuary, whilst the level of dissolved oxygen is the lowest. There is little difference in the seasonal pattern of organic N (wet and dry seasons) suggesting both point and non-point sources.

The Humen outlet is also severely polluted because of wastewater inputs from Guangzhou. The soluble P concentrations are the highest in the Pearl River estuary and the relative importance of organic pollution in the drier season suggests predominantly point-source pollution (untreated domestic waste). Both the Humen and the Yamen are tide dominated (low runoff) outlets to the estuary and as such do not have strong flushing capabilities. Regional wastewater treatment priorities should therefore reflect this hydrologic feature of the delta.

The most polluted stretch of river running through an urban area is clearly the Shenzhen River, whose average pollution index is four times higher than the next most polluted waterway in the delta. Particularly offending characteristics are its ammonia-nitrogen and petroleum contents, high biochemical oxygen demand and low dissolved oxygen levels, which indicate both untreated domestic and industrial waste. Other urban channels elsewhere in the Pearl River Delta are also heavily polluted and all are graded IV or above according to the National Environmental Quality Standard for Surface Waters.[32]

There has been relatively more success in the treatment of industrial wastewaters than of municipal wastewaters, in part because industrial effluent discharges are under legislative control whilst domestic sewage is not. Approximately 54% of industrial wastewaters and 6% of municipal wastewaters are treated,[33] and it seems unlikely that the target of 30% treatment of municipal wastewaters by the year 2000 will be achieved, particularly given the need to install expensive sewage treatment plants.

Air Pollution

The increasing trend of gaseous emissions in the province has become a matter of great concern recently. The total emission increased by as much as 119% during the period from 1989 to 1994. Among the air pollutants, nitrogen oxides and carbon monoxide exhibit the highest rate of increase. In 1994, the level of nitrogen oxides was in fact so high that Guangzhou ranked third in the national survey of urban air pollution in a country notorious for its urban air pollution problems, preceded only by Urumqi and Dalian, both major industrial cities.[34]

As expected, air pollution is more of a problem in the cities than in the countryside. Moreover, air pollution due to vehicular pollution is considered a problem in both the older cities such as Guangzhou[35] and the newer cities such as Shenzhen.[36] Research by Qin indicated that although vehicular emissions accounted for only 68% and 22% of the total carbon monoxide and nitrogen oxides emissions in Guangzhou, respectively, its contribution to the ground level pollution in Guangzhou is significantly higher, accounting for 87% and 67% of the carbon monoxide and nitrogen oxides measured at the street level.[37] With the vehicle population in Guangzhou increasing at a rate of about 25% a year and the continuing use of leaded petrol, urban air pollution problems are expected to deteriorate rapidly in years to come.

Figures 18.3 and 18.4 show the trend of air pollution in Maoming and Guangzhou, two of the largest cities in Guangdong. It can be seen that the levels of SO_2 and Total Suspended Particulates in Guangzhou have remained largely unchanged. The levels of nitrogen oxides and carbon monoxide, however, are rising, indicating an increase in vehicular emissions. During the 1980s the number of heavy and light vehicles in Guangzhou increased by 2.4 and 12.3 fold, respectively. In fact, in 1988 the annual average concentrations of nitrogen oxides and carbon monoxide in Guangzhou were 0.11 mg.m^3 and 3.18 mg.m^3, respectively, whilst the environmental standards were 0.1 and 4.0 mg.m^3, respectively for a mixed commercial and residential area. Clearly there is no room for further deterioration.

In Maoming phenol levels remained largely unchanged between 1976 and 1986, whereas SO_2 levels decreased dramatically. Levels of SO_2 and NO_x are in compliance with the relevant air quality objectives. However, levels of volatile phenols and non-methylene hydrocarbon exceed the relevant standards by 40% and 100%, respectively, indicating the seriousness of industrial pollution in the city.[38]

As a consequence of the elevated levels of air pollutants, acid rain is also a problem in Guangzhou, with pH values less than 4 monitored at a number of stations in the Pearl River Delta area.[39] This can be attributed to the increase in high level emissions of sulphur dioxide by power stations in the area. With the commissioning of an increasing number of power stations in Hong Kong and the Pearl River Delta, acid rain may become more frequent.

A number of concerns about future air quality in the province have been raised. Firstly, within the urban areas, the increasing levels of

Figure 18.3 Air Quality Trend, Maoming

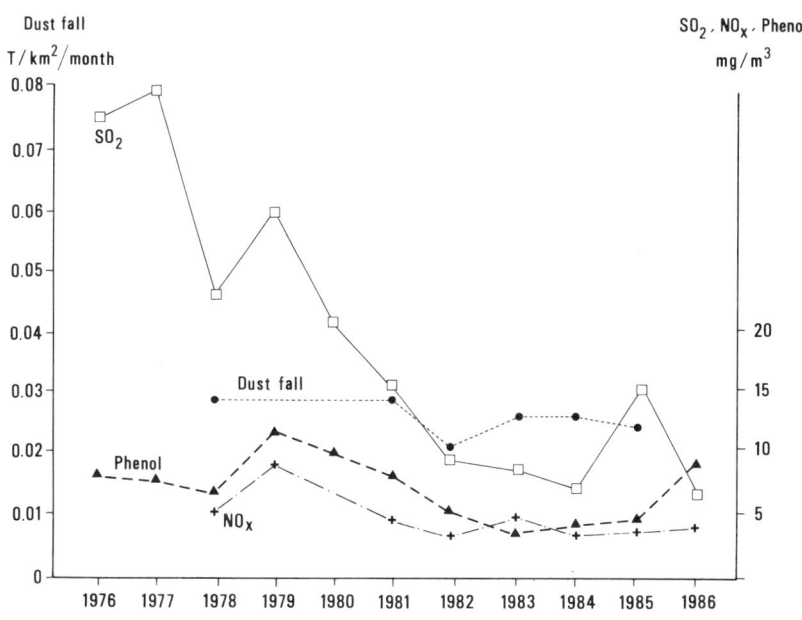

Source: Chen Xingeng and Deng Xiaosong, *Maomingshi huanjing yingxiang pingjia he huanjing guihua yanjiu* (see note 38 below).

nitrogen oxides are likely to continue as a result of the escalating vehicle population, increasing affluence and the opening up of more traffic links with Hong Kong. Secondly, the dispersal of industry is likely to promote a shift in both vehicle emission and industrial emission across the delta. Finally, the incidence of acid rain is likely to increase.

A Failure to Implement

The preceding discussion has identified a number of problem areas in environmental management in Guangdong: lack of uniformity of enforcement, relatively high percentage of non-compliance, and the relocation of polluting industries from SEZs to rural towns and townships.

These problems do not stem from the lack of detailed environmental legislations and standards. They are instead the result of a failure to implement the regulations and decrees that have been promulgated. It is also not

Figure 18.4   Air Quality Trend, Guangzhou

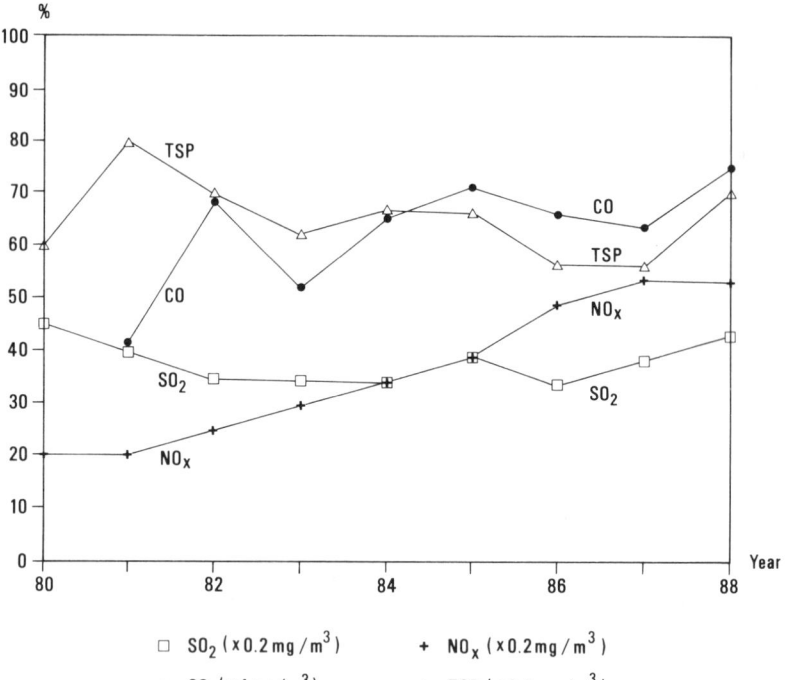

Source: Y. J. Qin, "Ground Level Air Pollution in Urban Area of Guangzhou" (see note 35
          below).

that the authorities in Guangdong set less stringent standards (indeed many
are more stringent than those in the developed world), but that there is less
efficient machinery for their enforcement. Implementation is difficult and
expensive, but unless legislation is equitably and rigorously enforced, control units empowered with authority, and economic development linked
with environmental protection, environmental planning will have negligible impacts. In short, implementation is the most critical component of
environmental management.

The failure to implement at a provincial level is due in part to an
understanding that economic growth must not be hindered by environmental policy. Wong and Chan observed that officials of the Guangdong
Environmental Protection Bureau believed that environmental and

developmental objectives were interdependent, but had a low sense of policy legitimacy and were unclear of their task definition.[40] This, they argue, was because provincial policy must be consistent with the national mandate, which clearly argues for the co-ordination of environmental policy with economic growth.

For policy to be implemented, there needs to be a sympathetic institutional set-up. Unfortunately, in Guangdong, environmental management is frustrated by a number of institutional factors: a fragmented bureaucracy, an informal power base, low public environmental awareness and an ethos that puts economy and development ahead of environmental quality and sound resource management.

The problems arising from a fragmented bureaucracy have been discussed earlier and will not be reiterated here, other than to emphasize the point that agencies which are low in the hierarchy are charged with the responsibility of enforcement, yet are not provided with the necessary resources. They have neither the staff nor the expertise to deal with complex environmental issues. Indeed, the majority of environmental protection professionals lack technical training.[41]

The administrative procedures for implementing policies are not well established, allowing the informal power base that exists to significantly undermine authority. At present no single authority is powerful enough to impose on another, or to make it conform to a proclaimed policy, and this leads to a lack of uniformity in the enforcement of environmental policies and regulations.

A high level of public awareness would assist the work of control authorities by providing public sanction and scrutiny of emission sources. An aware public may also assist authorities to target potential or frequent offenders and to prioritize work. Unfortunately, the level of environmental awareness in Guangdong is rather low, and there is no genuine desire by environmental protection bureaucrats to involve the public in decision making. Instead, government staff view themselves as interventionists.[42]

Finally, under the current political and economic climate, each administrative unit desires to be self-sufficient. It is not surprising, then, that those counties further removed from the growth poles shape a development approach that places economy ahead of environmental protection. A large proportion of Guangdong's environmental protection professionals also perceive economic growth as China's most pressing need,[43] and though the two objectives are not mutually exclusive, the provincial environmental policy directives are clearly couched in terms that promote economic growth.

Environmental management at the county level is also frustrated by a lack of technical expertise. The intentions of the Three-Synchronization System are highly admirable, but such a system requires a team of knowledgeable and competent staff, capable of assessing the suitability of treatment systems for different industries. Indeed, the Shenzhen Environmental Protection Office estimates that only 15% of all investment projects have been subject to post-audit. For this reason, few of the treatment systems function properly, and though sanction measures for failing to maintain such equipment are available, the penalties are not high.

Conclusion and Discussion

Although economic growth within the province has provided resources and technologies for better environmental management, this has not been realized and there remains much room for improvement. Nevertheless, there are no rapid nor painless solutions to the problems outlined in the preceding sections. Moreover, recommendations for improvement must recognize that economic growth is a priority and that a decentralized administrative structure is preferred by the authorities.

It is because of this emphasis on economic growth that there is an urgent need to reassess growth indicators and to incorporate into these statistics the depreciation of human and natural resources (particularly the degradation of shared renewable resources). A preliminary study of another of the world's growth regions, that of Mexico, revealed that the depletion of natural resources required a downward adjustment of the gross national product by 7%, whilst the avoidance of environmental degradation was equivalent to another 7%.[44] Although preliminary, these statistics are quite sobering. Guangdong is not well endowed with natural resources and relies heavily upon those available, particularly within the Pearl River Delta. For this reason, better auditing of these resources is particularly important. In the absence of such auditing, policy-makers can be misled by growth statistics.

The state government recognized the important role of foreign investment in environmental management in 1986, but despite directives issued then, there remains a need to further tighten foreign investment policy. This policy needs to explicitly state the restrictions on industry and the type and scale of development that warrants environmental impact assessments, and it requires a more streamlined endorsement procedure. The environmental measures so agreed should become part of the contract between the investor and the state with provision for non-compliance. Ideally the investor should provide a brief statement of possible environmental impacts and pollution abatement measures at the project proposal stage. These potential impacts would then be clarified at the feasibility stage with an environmental impact statement that followed the national guidelines for environmental impact assessments. The pollution control and abatement measures agreed to between the state and the investor should then be tested prior to the commencement of production by the relevant environmental protection agency.

There is an urgent need for integrated catchment management and/or improved co-ordination amongst the various departments dealing with environmental matters, incorporating agriculture, forestry, soil erosion, flood protection, water supply and so on. The liberalization and decentralization of the decision-making process by the central government and the lack of technical and legal expertise at the county level, places greater emphasis on the provincial government to accept responsibility for environmental management. There does exist a management committee for the Pearl River, but a provincial environmental ministry that straddles departmental boundaries and allocates resources commensurate with responsibilities would be more useful.

At a more general level, provincial strategic planning aimed at delineating growth areas and environmentally sensitive regions where industrial/urban development is closely scrutinized or discouraged is also needed. Such a plan should also provide guidelines for counties or townships that have not yet drafted master plans.

Despite significant improvements in the discharge permit system, there remains room for further improvement. For example, permits should be dependent upon the assimilative capacity of the region as determined by strategic planning. Moreover, foreign investors are somewhat insensitive to the current rates of charging.

Finally, the integration of the three rapidly developing regions of Guangdong, Hong Kong and Macau by the turn of the century requires more environmental protection cooperation efforts than currently exist. All three regions are part of the same major drainage system, as a consequence of which the two city-states of Hong Kong and Macau are the receivers of Guangdong's waste, particularly liquid waste, whilst Hong Kong may, in turn, adversely affect the region with its high sulphur dioxide emissions.

The increasing expenditure by the Hong Kong government in improving its own waters may be offset in part by the deteriorating waters of the Pearl River. The Hong Kong and Guangdong Environmental Protection Liaison Group, led on the Hong Kong side by the Secretary for Planning, Environment and Lands, meets annually and has initiated numerous studies pertaining to cross-border issues. The monitoring exercise of Deep Bay has, for example, been recently completed. Other offshore studies are underway, as are studies on sewage disposal and treatment systems. Despite increasing participation such as this, much more is needed. Wan and Zhang, for example, have recommended the establishment of joint research and monitoring projects, a regional fund for water protection and joint training programmes.[45] More importantly, the establishment of a co-ordinating organization responsible for drafting joint policies, long-term programmes, laws and regulations is recommended.

Notes

1. The World Bank, *World Development Report, 1992: Development and the Environment* (Oxford: Oxford University Press, 1992), p.25.

2. International Conference on the Pearl River Estuary in the Surrounding Area of Macau, October 1992; and the International Workshop on the Development of Strategies for Pollution Control in the Pearl River Delta, Guangdong and Hong Kong, held in Hong Kong, February 1993.

3. J. Huang, "Changes in the Deltas of the Major Rivers of China in Historical Periods," in *The Evolution of the East Asian Environment* (Occasional Papers and Monographs, No. 59), edited by R. O. Whyte, T. N. Chiu, C. K. Leung and C. L. So (Hong Kong: Centre of Asian Studies, University of Hong Kong, 1983), pp. 320–28.

4. Y. Z. Long and C. L. Huo, "The Characteristics of Sedimentation in Late Quaternary in the Pearl River Delta," in *Report of the 2nd Marine Geological Investigation Brigade* (Guangzhou: Ministry of Geology and Mineral Resources, 1988), p. 52.

5. Y. S. Chen, W. J. Zhu and M. X. Jian, "Design and Construction of Sea Dike Projects in the Pearl River Estuary Region" (paper presented at the International Conference on the Pearl River Estuary in the Surrounding Area of Macau, held in Macau, October 1992).

6. Y. M. Weng and Z. Y. Dong, "Improvement and Development of Pearl River Estuary" (paper presented at the International Conference on the Pearl River Estuary in the Surrounding Area of Macau, held in Macau, October 1992).

7. Zhang Shengcai, "Zhujiang sanjiaozhou honglao zaihai yu fangzhi chutan" (A Preliminary Study of Flood Disaster in the Zhujiang Delta and Its Control), *Redai dili* (Tropical Geography), Vol. 12, No. 4 (1992), pp. 329–34.

8. Ibid.

9. Q. M. Zhang, T. S. Lu, H. T. Zhao and X. S. Chen, "Contemporary Geomorphic Evolution of the Entrance of Shapa Tidal Channel, Guangdong," *Redai haiyang* (Tropical Ocean), Vol. 9, No. 4 (1990), pp. 45–52.

10. See note 6.

11. V. Smil, *The Bad Earth: Environmental Degradation in China* (New York: M.E. Sharpe, 1984).

12. Anonymous, *China Environment News*, December 1992.

13. Anonymous, *China Environment News*, January 1992.

14. Z. J. Wu, "The Origins of Environmental Management in China," in *Learning from China Development and Environment in Third World Countries*, edited by B. Glaeser (London: Allen and Unwin, 1987), pp. 111–19.

15. Qu Geping, "Nuli kaituo Zhongguo tese de huanjing baohu daolu" (Setting a New Path of Environmental Protection That is Appropriate for China), *Huanjing baohu* (Environmental Protection), No. 7 (1989), pp. 8–18.

16. Qu Geping, "1992 nian huanjing baohu gongzuo de gongzuo yu renwu" (The Major Tasks of Environmental Protection in 1992), *Huanjing baohu*, No. 3 (1992), pp. 5–8.

17. See note 14.

18. B. H. Qiang, "Water Environmental Management of Pearl River Delta in Guangdong Province" (paper presented at the International Workshop on the Development of Strategies for Pollution Control in the Pearl River Delta, Guangdong and Hong Kong, held in Hong Kong, February 1993).

19. K. K. Wong and H. S. Chan, *Environmental Attitudes and Concerns of the Environmental Protection Bureaucrats in Guangzhou, People's Republic of China: Implications for Environmental Policy Implementation* (Hong Kong Baptist College Working Paper, No. 9101) (Hong Kong: Faculty of Social Sciences, Hong Kong Baptist College, 1991).

20. Z. J. Fan, "Marine Pollution Legislation in China: Retrospect and Prospect," *Marine Pollution Bulletin*, Vol. 20, No. 7 (1989), pp. 333–35.

21. Ibid.

22. See note 14.

23. Ma Xiaoling, "Lun Guangdong yanhai kaifangqu jingji fazhan yu huanjing guanli" (Economic Growth and Environmental Management in the Coastal Open Areas of Guangdong), in *Huanan huanjing kexue yanjiusuo baogao* (South China Institute of Environmental Sciences Report) (memographed, 1992).

24. Ma Xiaoling, "Shewai qiye xiangmu huanjing zhengce yanjiu" (Environmental Policy Studies for Foreign Investment Projects in China), in *Huanan huanjing kexue yanjiusuo baogao* (memographed, 1990).

25. Ibid.

26. See note 23.

27. W. G. Liang, "Guangzhou's Foul Pearl River," *China Environment News*, December 1992, pp. 4–5.

28. Guojia huanjing baohuju, "Zhongguo huanjing zhuangkuang gongbao" (Environmental Situation in China), *Huanjing baohu*, No. 7 (1990), pp. 2–4; No. 8 (1991), pp. 2–4; No. 7 (1992), pp. 2–5.

29. X. Y. Liu and F. R. Lin, "The Present Conditions and Change Tendencies of Water Quality in Pearl River Estuary" (paper presented at the International Conference on the Pearl River Estuary in the Surrounding Area of Macau, held in Macau, October 1992).

30. B. Lue and Y. Zhai, "The Monitoring and Evaluation of the Pollutants in the Water Environment in the Pearl River Delta" (paper presented at the International Workshop on the Development of Strategies for Pollution Control in the Pearl River Delta, Guangzhou and Hong Kong, held in Hong Kong, February 1993).

31. Ibid.

32. Ibid.

33. See note 29.

34. See note 28.

35. Y. J. Qin, "Ground Level Air Pollution in Urban Area of Guangzhou," in *Proceedings: One Day Seminar on Ground Level Air Pollution in Urban Environment, 10th April, 1991* (Hong Kong: Hong Kong Polytechnic, Dept. of Civic & Structural Engineering, 1991).

36. Y. L. Tang, S. I. Hsu and K. C. Lam, "Dispersion of Vehicle Exhaust Gases and Photochemical Oxidants around Buildings in the Shenzhen Special Economic Zone," *Asian Environment*, Vol. 7, No. 3 (1985), pp. 30–37.

37. See note 35.

38. Chen Xingeng and Deng Xiaosong, *Maomingshi huanjing yingxiang pingjia he huanjing guihua yanjiu* (Environmental Assessment and Environmental Planning of Maoming) (Guangzhou: Zhongshan daxue chubanshe, 1988).

39. K. F. Xu and J. M. Hao, "Woguo suanyu xianzhuang tedian ji duice chuyi" (Characteristics of Acid Rain in China and Primary Considerations for Strategies), *Huanjing kexue* (Environmental Science), No. 11 (1990), pp. 61–66.

40. See note 19.

41. Ibid.

42. Ibid.

43. Ibid.

44. See note 1.
45. Z. Z. Wan and J. X. Zhang, "Strategies for Water Environmental Protection in the Pearl River Delta Region" (paper presented at the International Workshop on the Development of Strategies for Pollution Control in the Pearl River Delta, Guangzhou and Hong Kong, held in Hong Kong, February 1993).

19

History

Lau Yee-cheung

The Guangdong Region and Its Early Development

Around 100,000 years ago the Guangdong region, known as Nanyue, Baiyue and Lingnan in the history of China, was inhabited by man. It had already had contact with the north during the Spring and Autumn Period (770–476 B.C.). During the latter part of the Warring States Period (475–221 B.C.), the Han people started migrating to the region from the north, resulting in the gradual integration of the migrants and the native Yue people through interaction. Subsequently, the three major dialects spoken in today's Guangdong, namely Cantonese, Teochew and Hakka, were developed at different periods in its history. It was during the time of the First Emperor of Qin (221–210 B.C.) that closer ties between the region and North China were forged. The emperor was instrumental in incorporating it into the mainstream of Chinese history. For instance, he moved people there and built the Lingqu canal linking the region with the north. Subsequently, relatively advanced technology was introduced there, thus bringing about improvement to its agriculture and handicrafts. Gradually, the Guangdong region and China proper merged into one in terms of culture and ethnicity.

During the four hundred years or so of the West and East Han dynasties (206 B.C.–A.D. 8 and A.D. 25–220, respectively), the region's population grew rapidly, partly due to the relative peace and stability then (Table 19.1). People migrated in great numbers to the south both in the West–East Han transition years (A.D. 8–24) and the final years of the East Han. They went to the south along the coast by sea as well as the usual land route. In addition, followers and descendants of the officials who had taken up residence in the region and soldiers who had stayed behind also added to its growing population.[1]

Together, immigrants and the native Yue people transformed the Guangdong region into a rapidly developing one by building walled cities and roads and introducing iron wares and advanced agricultural technology. The introduction of Han culture there led to the change of its social institutions. The great historian Sima Qian (145–86 c. B.C.) compared the region favourably with the rich Yangzi River Delta area, adding that it was no longer a frontier outpost. Indeed, by his time the Guangdong region had become a major part of the national economy. Its cultural and scholarly activities also developed steadily.[2] For instance, two pioneer Guangdong scholars, Chen Qin and his son Chen Yuan, left behind them Guangdong's earliest works on Confucian learning.[3]

Table 19.1 Population of the Guangdong Region (Including Guangxi)

Period	Nanhai	Changwu	Yulin	Hebu	Guiyang	Total
West Han	94,253	146,160	71,162	78,980	156,488	547,043
East Han	250,282	466,975	81,409*	86,617	501,403	1,386,686
Growth rate %	166	220	114*	10	220	153

Sources: He Weiding, "Lun Dong Han shiqi Lingnan shehui de chubu fengjianhua" (see note 2 below), pp. 67–73; Xian Jianmin, "Handai dui Lingnan de jingji zhengce" (see note 10 below), pp. 32–38; Tong Shiheng, *Lidai jiangyu xingshitu* (A Historical Atlas of China) (Taibei: Guangwen shuju, 1982).

Note: * Estimate.

In the Tang dynasty (618–907), more administrative districts were created in the region as population increased, though people concentrated in today's Shaoguan area, the valley of the North River and the West River in contrast to the present day population distribution (Table 19.2 and Figure 19.1). Mining, textiles, shipbuilding, paper manufacturing, the

Table 19.2 Density of Population of the Various Guangdong Districts in the Tang Dynasty, 618–907

Above 3 households per km^2
  1. Lianxian, Lianshan, Yangshan
  2. Dianbai, Maoming
  3. Yangchun
  4. Xinxing, Yunfu

2–3 households per km^2
  1. Luoding
  2. Huazhou
  3. Deqing, Yunfu, Yunan
  4. Shaoguan, Qujiang, Ruyuan, Sixing, Lechang, Nanxiung, Renhua, Wengyuan

1–2 households per km^2
  1. Fengkaixian
  2. Yangjiang, Enping
  3. Lianjiang, Zhanjiang
  4. Guangzhou (including today's Pearl River Delta municipalities and adjacent areas)

Below 1 household per km^2
  1. Huizhou, Huiyang, Huidong, Zijin, Bolo, Xinfeng, Heyuan, Haifeng, Lufeng, Xingning, Wuhua
  2. Chaozhou (including today's Chaozhou and Shantou municipalities and most of Meizhou municipality)

Source: Xu Junming and Xu Xiaomei, "Shilun Tangdai zai Guangdong de renwen dili gaikuang" (see note 4 below), pp. 113–19.

Figure 19.1   Concentration Areas of Guangdong's Population

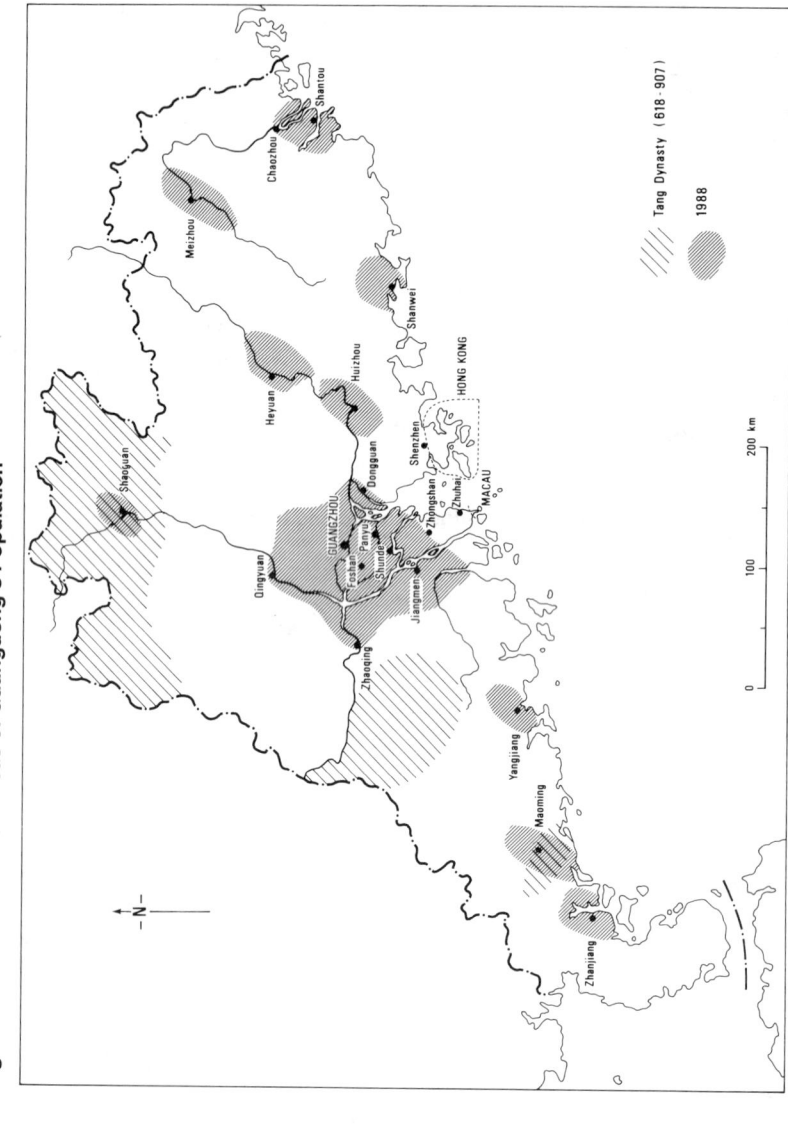

Sources: Xu Junming and Xu Xiaomei, "Shilun Tangdai zai Guangdong de renwen dili gaikuang" (see note 4), pp. 113–19; Guangdongsheng tongjiu (ed.), *Qianjingzhong de Guangdong: 1949–1989 nian Guangdong shehui jingji fazhan qingkuang* (Guangdong on the Move: The Social and Economic Development of Guangdong, 1949–1989) (Hong Kong: Dadao wenhua, 1989), p. 112.

porcelain industry, wine brewing, as well as agriculture further developed then. Bamboo, rattan, fruit, vegetables, wheat, rice, sugar cane and tea were also grown increasingly.

Foreign trade also developed in Guangzhou, Chaozhou and Enzhou, with Guangzhou as the most bustling port city. In Guangzhou, contacts with foreign ideas like Buddhism and Islam became frequent and temples erected then still exist today. Both the Buddhist monks and Islamic teachers arrived there whereas Chinese monks like Jianzhen (688–763) travelled to Japan from Guangzhou.[4] Early in the Tang dynasty Guangzhou still served as a destination for exiled court officials like Han Yu (768–824), Liu Yuxi (772–842), and Li Deyu (787–849) among others. By the end of the Tang and the beginning of the Song (960–1279), Guangdong had emerged as a relatively wealthy region. For instance, the Song's first emperor, Zhao Kuangyin (927–976), decided to conquer it in 971 largely out of economic considerations.[5] He followed up the conquest with a sensible policy in governing the region, thus having successfully brought about the subsequent social and economic growth there.

Guangdong experienced rapid growth in riverine and oceanic trade during the Tang, Song and Yuan periods (618–1368). Market towns and metropolises shot up along the navigational routes. The region's water transport network had an intrinsic relationship with its social and economic growth. Indeed, the region's prosperity from the Tang up until the Ming (1368–1644) was to a considerable degree due to its water transport network and maritime trade.[6] During this period the transport routes, river works, port facilities, shipbuilding and navigational knowledge all experienced growth. Also, both the number of passengers and the volume of goods carried by its vessels increased by leaps and bounds.

Guangdong's link with Central and North China was greatly enhanced when a new pass through the Dayu Mountain Range was opened up in 716 under the direction of Zhang Jiuling (673–740), the famous high court official in the Tang from Qujiang, Shaozhou. Thereafter, its North River and neighbouring Jiangxi's Gan River was linked up with the Great Canal to the north. The new link facilitated the movement of both goods and people between Guangdong and the north, thus furthering the region's integration with China proper. The Dayu Pass enhanced Guangdong's social and economic development in the Ming and Qing (1644–1912). By the Ming–Qing transition years, economically the province came under five sub-regions, namely, the Pearl River Delta, East, North, and West Guangdong and Hainan Island, with Foshan, Chaozhou, Shaozhou,

Haikang and Qiongzhou as respective sub-regional centres.[7] A sophisticated water transport network with the Pearl River waterways as the main
artery took shape in the province by the early Qing dynasty. Then its ships
sailed as far as to the North China coast. Consequently, the Pearl River
Delta enjoyed prosperity with a booming foreign trade, thus lifting itself
from the previous subsistence level of economy. Guangzhou, endowed
with a water transport network, had become the economic centre of South
China in the sixteenth and seventeenth centuries.

Guangdong enjoyed the longest coastline among China's maritime
provinces with its ships sailing from Guangzhou up to Fujian and Zhejiang
no later than the second century B.C. By the time of Emperor Wu of the
Han (140–87 B.C.), trade routes to as far as Malacca were opened up.
On the foundation of the Tang development, maritime transport in the
Song and Yuan dynasties further progressed and it was accompanied by
advanced commerce and handicrafts. However, beginning with the Ming
dynasty, restrictions or a total ban on maritime travel and trade drastically
weakened the region's links with the outside world. They also seriously
disrupted Guangdong's once flourishing foreign trade.

In 1685 Emperor Kangxi (1662–1722) of the Qing dynasty lifted the
ban on maritime activities, and foreign trade was allowed in Guangzhou,
Xiamen, Ningbo and Shanghai. In 1757 Emperor Qianlong (1736–1795)
ordered the closing of three of them, leaving Guangzhou as the sole trading
port of China for about one hundred years until the end of the Opium War
(1839–1842). Qianlong's single port policy turned Guangzhou into an
immensely prosperous centre for foreign trade. In Guangdong the oceanic
trade was mostly conducted by the Teochew-speaking people, whereas the
riverine trade and transport were largely in the hands of those speaking
Cantonese. However, the Guangdong merchants no longer controlled the
Southeast Asian trade as before, partly due to European expansion into the
East.[8]

After the end of the Opium War, Shantou in the Han River Delta
began enjoying foreign trade as a treaty port and was known for its sugar
export, accounting for the largest share in China. Due to its water transport
network, cotton textiles and handicrafts, Shantou's commerce developed
considerably. As for West and North Guangdong and Hainan Island, they
lagged behind both the Pearl River and Han River deltas with their lack of
water transport network and accompanying facilities.[9]

Indeed, Guangdong's social and economic growth owed a great deal to
its natural water transport network and sophisticated riverine and coastal

navigation system. As a result, trade and commerce grew, transforming the region's traditional economy into a multifaceted one. Its agriculture was supplemented with both domestic and foreign trade, whereas its handicrafts and agricultural products served as the main commodities. Many market towns located mostly in the vicinities of the water transport network subsequently emerged.

Agriculture

Sound policy in administering the region adopted by the government in the Han era led to the rapid growth of its economy and population.[10] It improved the irrigation system, transport network and agricultural technology. It also protected small farmers, enabling them to achieve self-sufficiency by offering them relief and tax exemption at times of hardship. During the lengthy period of disunion after the fall of the East Han, agricultural technology in the region nonetheless experienced advances in both ploughshare-making and the irrigation system.

In the Sui–Tang era, soil enrichment and expansion of cultivated land brought quantity of rice production to new heights. Besides, fisheries grew as the number of fish ponds increased. In the Song dynasty the Pearl River Delta emerged as an important agricultural region due to its increasing cultivated land and manpower. The Han River Delta to the east also developed into a significant agricultural area. In addition, more cultivated land was opened up in the Leizhou peninsula and the Nanxiong and Huizhou areas because of an improved irrigation system. Double-cropping cultivation became more widely practised. As agricultural productivity increased, for the first time Guangdong exported rice to other provinces like Guangxi and Zhejiang, and to Lin'an, capital of the South Song dynasty (1127–1279). In addition, wheat was also planted and economic crops increased. All this paved the way for Guangdong's future economic growth. Though disruption occurred in the Song–Yuan dynastic transition, by the mid-Yuan (1304 A.D.) Guangdong's population returned to the level of the early South Song. As more dykes were built and irrigation works conducted, more cultivated land was subsequently opened up.[11]

During the Ming dynasty Guangdong's agriculture moved forward steadfastly, thus making the province a leading economy in China. Its growth was evidenced by the irrigation works conducted then, twice that of the Song and Yuan projects put together, and by the area of cultivated land which increased by 9,683,000 *mu*, or 41%. Technological innovations like the advanced irrigation peddles, together with the extensive application of iron instruments and intensive farming boosted the importance of agriculture to a new height. In addition, triple-cropping farming, having earlier been introduced in Hainan Island, was introduced to the rest of the province as well. The adoption of rotation farming further helped in yielding greater harvests. As a result of these developments, the rice production increased sharply. Agricultural advances thus paved the way for Guangdong's economy diverting into commerce.[12]

Guangdong witnessed increase in both population and cultivated land in the six hundred years or so from 1368 to 1949 (Tables 19.3 and 19.4). Chaos and disorder in the Ming–Qing transition years soon gave way to agricultural recovery and sustained growth especially in the high Qing period. Steadily increasing agricultural yields enabled the province to experience subsequent development in handicrafts, commerce and foreign trade.[13]

Table 19.3   Population of Guangdong and China, 1381–1948

(Unit: million)

Year	Guangdong	Growth rate %	Index (1381=100)	China	Growth rate %	Guangdong's % of national total
1381	3.1	—	100	59.9	—	5.2
1491	1.8	−41.9	58	53.3	−11.0	3.4
1578	2.0	+11.1	65	61.0	+14.4	3.3
1636	2.4	+20.0	77	58.6	−3.9	4.1
1661	3.2	+33.3	103	61.6	+5.1	5.2
1762	6.8	112.5	219	200.5	+225.5	3.4
1820	21.1	210.3	681	353.4	+76.3	6.0
1850	27.7	+31.3	894	429.9	+21.6	6.4
1875	29.1	+5.1	939	322.7	−24.9	9.0
1911	28.6	−1.7	923	377.1	+16.9	7.6
1938	28.6	0	923	479.1 (1936)	+27.0	6.0
1948	26.1	−8.7	842	454.9 (1947)	−5.1	5.7

Sources: Ping-ti Ho, *Studies on the Population of China, 1368–1953* (Cambridge, Mass.: Harvard University Press, 1959), pp. 86, 94–95; Situ Shangji, "Ming–Qing he Minguo shidai Guangdong renkou he gengdi de lishi bianhua" (see note 13 below), pp. 64–72.

Table 19.4   Cultivated Land in Guangdong and China, 1387–1949

(Unit: Million *mu*)

Year	Guangdong	Growth rate %	Index (1387=100)	China	Guangdong's % of national total
1387	23.1	—	100	850.8 (1393)	2.7
1536	25.0	+8.2	109	—	—
1600	32.4	+29.6	140	1,161.9 (1602)	2.8
1632	32.1	−0.9	139	405.7 (1645)	7.9
1661	24.4	−24.0	109	549.4	4.4
1764	31.6	+29.5	138	741.5 (1766)	4.3
1820	32.5	+2.8	141	—	—
1873	39.8	+22.5	173	819.5	4.9
1893	40.2	+1.0	175	—	—
1913	40.2	0	175	—	—
1932	42.5	+5.7	184	1,248.8	3.4
1949	46.5	+9.4	202	—	—

Sources: Ping-ti Ho, *Studies on the Population of China, 1368–1953* (see Table 19.3, source note), p. 102; Situ Shangji, "Ming–Qing he Minguo shidai Guangdong renkou he gengdi de lishi bianhua" (see note 13 below), pp. 64–72.

Note: 1 *mu* is equivalent to 1/6 acre.

Industry and Mining

In the Qin and Han periods, handicrafts and industries like steel casting were in existence in the Guangdong region. Importing iron ore from the neighbouring Changsha, Hunan, and skilled smiths from Central and North China, the steel industry began to take shape and people attained considerable knowledge about steel manufacturing.[14] The Han government's encouragement of the steel industry led to the manufacturing of metal wares in the region. In the Ming, agricultural growth enabled both the development of handicrafts and market towns in the rural area of the province. One also saw female playing an active role in economic crop farming, raising silk-worms and reeling silk.[15]

Guangdong's shipbuilding industry enjoyed a long history with Guangzhou, Chaozhou and Gaozhou as the centres. The industry could be traced back to the Qin, as evidenced by the discovery of a large ruined dockyard in Guangzhou dating to the time of the Qin's unification of China. Various kinds and sizes of ships were made serving both seafaring and riverine navigation. Shipbuilding technology made steady progress during subsequent times. In the Qing, large-size battleships with twin masts and sixteen oars, equipped with movable cannons, were built.[16]

Guangdong began to export silk from its then leading ports, Xuwen and Hepu, around the West Han dynasty. For centuries the silk industry remained an important sector of Guangdong's economy. Mechanization of silk production began in 1874 when Chen Qiyuan (1834–1903), an intellectual turned entrepreneur, introduced the French production method to the Chinese silk industry.[17] Cotton was brought to the region from India no later than the Song and cotton textiles experienced rapid development in the Yuan dynasty (1279–1368). In the Ming and Qing, Guangdong also imported cotton from the lower Yangzi River valley, where dry weather suited the crop better.[18]

Guangdong's sugar refining industry can be traced back to the East Han dynasty and fine sugar had been manufactured around the sixth century. In the Ming and Qing, its sugar industry experienced remarkable growth with the acreage of sugar cane plantation almost equal to that of rice paddies in the Pearl River Delta. Its refineries produced various kinds of sugar catering for both domestic and foreign consumption. Guangdong's wine brewing industry also began in the East Han and, with all kinds of fruits produced and a great number of springs found in the region, various kinds of wine were brewed. In addition, dried fruit was counted among Guangdong's major food processing industries.[19]

It was recorded that a certain alarm clock had been produced in China before the Song though its technology was subsequently lost. Chinese people only learned how to make clocks again after the Portuguese brought them to Macau in the late Ming. Spectacles were also introduced to the Chinese at this time and crystal instead of glass was applied as material for manufacturing. Ivory sculpture, first produced in the region around the Han dynasty, also developed into an important industry. Guangzhou and its neighbouring area had developed various industries for almost 2,000 years with shipbuilding among the first of them. It became a great marketplace because of its abundant industrial goods and its links with the outside world. Foreign goods shipped there were brought to inner China through both the land and water transport network, thus furthering the city as a centre of both internal and foreign trade.[20] In addition, Shantou served as another major port city in Guangdong during the nineteenth and early twentieth centuries.

Porcelain manufacturing began in the Tang with many kilns unearthed dating to that period. Historically famous Shiwan kilns in Foshan now continue producing magnificent works because of the rich porcelain soil. The salt industry had also been significant in the region though the government monopoly policy always pushed the salt price to an artificial height.[21] In Guangdong copper refining had been in existence in Yangchun County in the West Han. Later, the discovery of bronze drums in west Guangdong indicated advanced technology of copper mining and casting in the region in ancient times. Silver mining was engaged in both Dongguan County and North Guangdong. Many pagodas, tombs and sculptures made of either iron or bronze were dated between the Tang and Song.[22] Mining in the Song also prospered with some twenty kinds of ruined sites unearthed. Foshan in the late Ming and early Qing emerged as an important town famous for producing iron wares making use of the iron ore mined in Yunfu County.

Commerce and Trade

By the early Qing, Guangdong merchants had traded far and wide, both in and out of the province and abroad. In internal trade the West, East and North Rivers served as the links between Guangdong and the neighbouring provinces. Foreign trade boomed during the Ming and Qing dynasties as Guangzhou became the leading port of China, whereas Chaozhou emerged as the trade centre of the province itself. In the early Qing, Guangdong's booming handicrafts and commercialization of agricultural products led to the rise of its commerce. With merchants from Guangzhou and Chaozhou as the most prominent ones, Guangdong merchants' activities expanded rapidly in the province and subsequently into the rest of the country.[23] The Chaozhou merchants even traded as far as in Southeast Asia. The merchants from other provinces also merged in Guangzhou in the early Qing giving rise to its bustling trade activities. In 1757 the port city became the sole place where Western merchants could trade in China, turning it into an exceptionally busy trade centre. Subsequently, the Meiguan Pass bordering the province and Jiangxi, through which goods from other provinces found their way to Guangzhou and foreign goods theirs to inner China, emerged as the busiest transit centre during the so-called single-port period.

Due to both busy internal and foreign trade, Guangzhou since the Tang had developed into an international commercial city. Great amounts of silver imported to Guangzhou from overseas were mostly used to purchase goods produced in the province. Basically, the city's development was in line with its trade activities. Also, in the Ming and Qing a prototype capitalist-labour relationship seemed to have emerged in the city's economy. All in all, movement of goods in and out of the province and abroad led to the rise of Guangzhou as a highly metropolitan port city in the Ming and Qing era.[24] On the other hand, Foshan, with its position as the place where goods from all over China concentrated, also received merchants from throughout the country. Especially, the merchants from both Shaanxi and Shanxi were among the most active in Guangzhou, profited greatly from the trade. Merchants from the same province formed respective associations in Foshan to look after their own interests while away from native province. As a result, they turned Foshan into a truly commercial town in pre-Opium War Guangdong.[25]

The merchants in Foshan, from all over China as they were, further promoted the circulating network of commodities and increased business capital investment there. New management ideas evolved as they exchanged their respective business experiences and practices. However, though having made great profits, Foshan merchants seldom reinvested sufficient capital back into their enterprises. Instead, they kept the wealth for their children, building ancestral halls and purchasing land. Others would purchase official titles to elevate their social and political status, sponsor local religious activities, or simply take the wealth back to their native provinces for those who came from outside Guangdong. Consequently, Foshan merchants, just as merchants elsewhere in China, suffered from instability both in their own community and business capital, typical of traditional Chinese merchants.[26]

By the mid-Qing, Foshan had emerged as another trade centre of the province other than Guangzhou. Since the introduction of the single-port policy in 1757, it became both the receiving and delivering centre of goods passing through the Meiguan Pass in both directions. Guangzhou and Foshan were then the dual trade centres of the province and the country at large (Figure 19.2). To the former, foreign goods were imported and goods from the rest of the country to be exported were brought. In the latter, goods brought from other provinces to be consumed in Guangdong were concentrated. That Foshan had emerged as another trade centre alongside with Guangzhou was also due to its solid industrial base, namely handicrafts, porcelains and steel casting. It therefore had its own products to sell and this alone turned it into a busy marketplace. In addition, the single-port

Figure 19.2   Guangdong's Duo-Centres of Trade in the Qing Dynasty: Guangzhou and Foshan

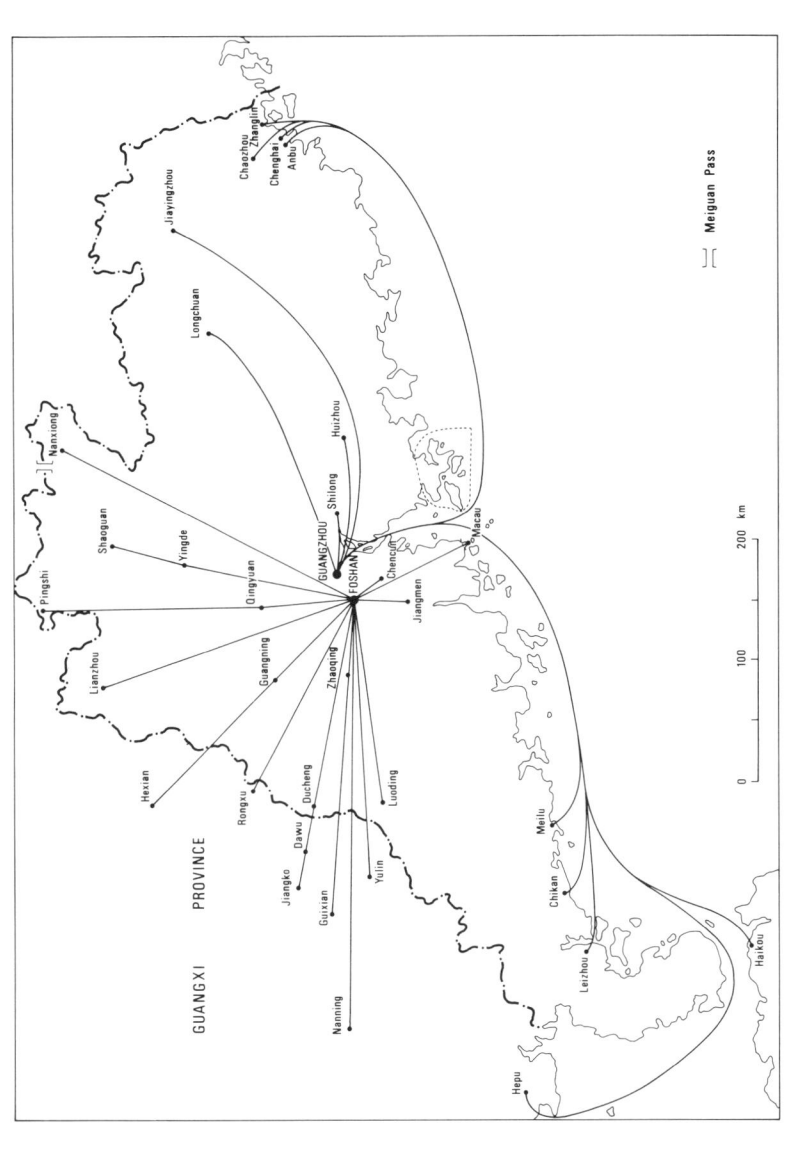

Source: Luo Yixing, "Qingdai qianqi Lingnan eryuan zhongxin shichang shuo" (see note 27), pp. 82–92.

policy that made the Meiguan Pass the all-important transit centre of goods from both South and North China, turned Foshan into the most easily accessible place for goods to be concentrated and delivered. However, after the Opium War no longer were goods brought through the Meiguan Pass, for the goods produced to the north of Guangdong were exported direct from Shanghai, one of the five treaty ports after the Opium War. Foshan as an important trade centre has declined considerably ever since.[27]

Guangdong and the Shaping of Modern China

The province witnessed the first attempts to strengthen China *vis-à-vis* the West in the midst of the Opium War. High officials like Lin Zexu (1785–1850), while serving as the imperial commissioner in Guangzhou at that time, was among the first to adopt Western technology in modern China. One of his close associates, Liang Tingnan (1796–1861), noted for his sophisticated knowledge about coastal defense strategy, also produced a number of impressive historical works on such subjects as Guangdong's customs office, the Opium War and the local history of his home district, Shunde, among others.[28]

Zhu Ciqi (1807–1881) of Jiujiang, Nanhai, an eminent scholar and an early champion of the statecraft ideas, was a great teacher imbued with patriotism in the face of foreign aggression during his time. One of his students, Kang Youwei (1858–1927), who later led a national salvation movement, no doubt due to his influence. Zou Boqi (1819–1869), a pioneer modern Chinese scientist, was noted for his advanced knowledge in optics, astrology and mathematics among other scientific fields. An eminent cartographer, he also devised a photographic process in 1844 independent of the French inventor Louis Jacques Mande Daguerre (1789–1851), who devised his own six years later.

The famous engineer, Wen Zishao (1834–1907), served as the first director of the Guangzhou Arsenal founded in 1874. Under his leadership it produced guns, cannons and gunboats of fairly high quality. Modern Guangdong also produced illustrious lawyers and diplomats like Wu Tingfang (1842–1922), who in 1880 was appointed the first Chinese Legislative Councillor of Hong Kong. Since 1882 he served in the Chinese government promoting its legal reform and, after the 1911 Revolution, assisted Sun Yat-sen with his reconstruction endeavour for China. Zhang Zujun (b. 1879), a pioneer female physician, championed for Chinese women's rights and equality through education and training.[29]

Guangdong and its people played a major role in modern Chinese political life. During the hundred years between 1850 and 1949, Guangdong was a fertile ground for both reform and revolution. In the closing months of 1850 Hong Xiuquan (1814–1864) of Hua County near Guangzhou and his followers were making final preparations for the Taiping Rebellion, which almost toppled the Qing dynasty. During one of his many attempts at the Civil Service examination held in Guangzhou, Hong received a Christian tract entitled *Quanshi liangyan*, or Good Words Exhorting the Age by Liang Afa (1789–1855), the first Chinese Protestant pastor and also a native of Guangdong. Hong and Feng Yunshan (*c*.1815–1852), also of Hua County and among Hong's earliest followers, organized the God Worshippers' Society in 1843. It later became the core of the anti-Qing movement lasting for fourteen years (1851–1864). The movement, originating in Guangdong with Hong and Feng as first leaders, developed into a formidable force in the neighbouring Guangxi whereto many Hakkas had previously migrated from Guangdong. The God Worshippers' Society had been very successful in recruiting the Hakkas, who became the backbone of the movement especially at its initial stage. Though eventually the Taiping movement failed, its legacy for future revolutionaries was far-reaching.

Thirty years after the Taiping movement, Dr. Sun Yat-sen (1866–1925), who had previously admired the Taiping heroes, launched the Republican revolution which succeeded in overthrowing the Qing in 1912. Sun and many of his early followers also came from Guangdong or were overseas Chinese of the Guangdong origin. Indeed, for the first decade of the Sun-led movement, fellow Guangdongese provided both most of the manpower and financial support. His right-hand men like Hu Hanmin (1879–1936), Liao Zhongkai (1877–1925), Zhu Zhixin (1885–1920) and Wang Jingwei (1883–1944) were some examples. In 1905, ten years after Sun made the first armed attempt to topple the Qing, the Guangdongese joined forces with the Hunanese and the Zhejiangese revolutionary societies to form the China United League, that finally brought down the last monarchy in China's extended imperial era in 1912.

A parallel movement, aimed at rejuvenating China through reform, was led by another two fellow Guangdongese, namely Kang Youwei and his student Liang Qichao (1873–1929). What they actually attempted to accomplish was to bring the half-century long reform endeavour to its seemingly logical conclusion. For more than half a century since the Opium War, concerned Chinese intellectuals had pushed for some sort of changes in Chinese political institutions in order to strengthen and enrich their country. Early in 1895, when China was being defeated in her war with Japan over Korea, Kang and Liang led a joint petition by the metropolitan examination candidates, who then gathered in Beijing sitting for the examination. They demanded political reform among other things in their petition. It turned out to be the beginning step for Kang and Liang's larger reform design of three years later. In 1898 they were able to enlist Emperor Guangxu's (1875–1908) support for their reform endeavour. Among their priorities was to streamline the bureaucracy by clearly defining lines of responsibility for each government office and its staff.

The reform movement could have been successful had it not been for Empress Dowager Cixi's (1835–1908) intervention and her fear of the Manchus losing their grip of political power to the Han Chinese. The Manchus, who ruled China since the mid-seventeenth century, were ever suspicious of the reform undertaken by mostly Han Chinese. Indeed, for the 268 years of the Qing rule the Manchus' suspicion of Han people had never disappeared. Their fear of losing power thus prompted them to crush the reform in a coup in September 1898. In retrospect, it turned out that the coup actually signalled the beginning of the end of the Qing's mandate to rule, for in less than fifteen years' time it was overthrown by a revolutionary movement.

During the early republican period Guangdong again served as fertile ground for still more revolutionary upheavals. For after 1917, Sun Yat-sen, with a stronghold in Guangdong and especially in Guangzhou, led another revolution aimed at toppling the warlord-controlled regime in Beijing. In 1924 the Guomindang under Sun's leadership joined hands with the newly founded Communist Party of China in their common endeavour to bring China out of the chaos resulting from imperialism and usurpation of power by the warlords. In Guangdong the allied revolutionary movement gathered momentum by building a solid base in the province. In the summer of 1926, slightly more than a year after Sun's death, the revolutionary troops charged north from Guangzhou and Guangdong in the heroic expedition against the warlords' armies. They defeated their enemies one after another in the provinces along the Yangzi and Yellow River valleys. In two years' time they swept their way into Beijing, then capital of the warlord-controlled regime. In 1928 China became nominally unified again.

It is evident that Guangdong had played a significant role in modern

Chinese history. It had been able to do so for the following three reasons:
(1) With its early contacts with the outside world, having enabled it to
come to terms with the West ahead of other provinces, it had always
pioneered social and political changes for the rest of the country. (2) It had
been able to produce illustrious personages who led both reform and
revolution. and (3) For the above two reasons, it had emerged as a fertile
ground for endeavours aimed at bringing about critically needed changes
to the *status quo.*[30]

Over the past two millennia Guangdong has developed from a frontier
outpost to the hub of China's new cultural life towards the closing years of
the twentieth century. To learn from Guangdong is now the vogue
throughout China. It remains to be seen if Guangdong will once again
provide the impetus for an all-round progressive movement in the country
as it did in the early decades of the twentieth century.

Notes

1. Lu Mingzhong, "Hanzu nanqian yu Lingnan Baiyue diqu de zaoqi kaifa"
   (Southward Movement of the Han Ethnic Group and the Early Development
   of the Guangdong Region), *Zhongguoshi yanjiu* (Study of Chinese History),
   No. 4 (1984), pp. 17–19.

2. Ibid., p. 21 and p. 24; He Weiding, "Lun Dong Han shiqi Lingnan shehui de
   chubu fengjianhua" (On the Early Feudalization of the Guangdong Region
   Society in the East Han), *Guangdong shehui kexue* (Guangdong Social
   Sciences), No. 1 (1986), pp. 71–73. According to one Dunhuang document,
   the Guangdong region was still not yet developed in the early Tang. See Cao
   Luning, "Cong Dunhuang wenshu kan Tangdai de Lingnan" (The
   Guangdong Region as Seen from the Dunhuang Documents), *Guangdong
   shehui kexue*, No. 4 (1988), p. 64.

3. Wang Tingkui, "Lingnan zuizao de jingxuejia — Chen Qin, Chen Yuan"
   (The Earliest Guangdong Region Scholars Chen Qin and Chen Yuan),
   Guangzhou yanjiu (Study of Guangdong), No. 6 (1986) pp. 69–70.

4. Xu Junming and Xu Xiaomei, "Shilun Tangdai zai Guangdong de renwen
   dili gaikuang" (On the General Condition of Guangdong's Human Geography in the Tang Dynasty), *Lingnan wenshi* (Literature and History of
   Lingnan), No. 1 (1985), p. 118.

5. Gu Jichen, "Lun Song Taizu tongyi Lingnan" (On Emperor Song Taizu's
   Unification of the Guangdong Region), *Guangdong shehui kexue*, No. 2
   (1990), p. 3.

6. Ye Xian'en, "Guangdong gudai shuishang jiaotong yunshu de jige wenti"

(On the Several Issues Concerning Water Transportation in Ancient Guang-dong), *Guangdong shehui kexue*, No. 1 (1988), p. 99.

7. Ibid., p. 104.

8. Ye Xian'en, "Ming–Qing Guangdong shuiyun yingyun zuzhi yu diyuan guanxi" (Operations, Organizations and Geographical Relations of Guang-dong's Water Transportation in the Ming and Qing dynasties), *Guangdong shehui kexue*, No. 4 (1989), p. 71; and "Qingdai Guangdong shuiyun yu shehui jingji" (Water Transportation and Socio-economy of Guangdong in the Qing dynasty), *Zhongguo shehui jingjishi yanjiu* (Study of the Chinese Social and Economic History), No. 4 (1987), pp. 58–59.

9. Ye Xian'en, "Qingdai Guangdong shuiyun yu shehui jingji" (see note 8), pp. 60–62.

10. Xian Jianmin, "Handai dui Lingnan de jingji zhengce" (Han's Economic Policy towards the Guangdong Region), *Jinan xuebao* (Journal of Jinan University), No. 4 (1989), p. 35.

11. Jiang Zuyuan and Fang Zhiqin (eds.), *Jianming Guangdongshi* (An Outline History of Guangdong) (Guangzhou: Guangdong renmin chubenshe, 1987), pp. 86, 103, 136–42, 163–67.

12. Jiang Zuyuan, "Mingdai Guangdong nongye de feiyue fazhan" (On the Rapid Growth of Guangdong's Agriculture in the Ming dynasty), *Guangdong shehui kexue*, No. 4 (1985), pp. 27, 29, 32.

13. Situ Shangji, "Ming–Qing he Minguo shidai Guangdong renkou he gengdi de lishi bianhua" (The Historical Changes of the Population and Cultivated Land in Guangdong during the Ming, Qing and Republican Periods), *Zhongshan daxue yanjiusheng xuekan* (Postgraduate Journal of Zhongshan University), No. 2 (1980), pp. 64–65; Chen Qihan, "Qingdai Guangdong nongye de huifu he fazhan" (Recovery and Growth of Guangdong's Agricul-ture in the Qing dynasty), *Guangdong shehui kexue*, No. 1 (1987), pp. 64–70.

14. Xian Jianmin, "Handai Lingnan de qingtongye he yetieye" (On the Bronze and Iron-casting Industries of the Guangdong Region in the Han dynasty), *Jinan xuebao* , No. 3 (1988), p. 53.

15. See note 10, p. 37 and note 12, pp. 78–79.

16. Xu Junming and Guo Peizhong, "Gudai Guangzhou ji qi fujin diqu de shougongye" (Handicrafts of the Ancient Guangzhou and Its Adjacent Areas), *Lishi dili* (Historical Geography), No. 1 (1981), pp. 170–71.

17. Wang Jiajian, "Guangdong de jiqi saosi gongye yu jindai Zhongguo diyici fanjiqi fengchao" (The Mechanization of the Guangdong's Silk Industry and the First Anti-machinery Unrest in Modern China), *Shihuo yuekan* (Economic History Monthly), Vol. 15, Nos. 3–4 (1985), p. 122.

18. See note 16, p. 172.

19. Ibid., p. 173.

20. Ibid., pp. 177–78.

21. Wang Xiaohe, "Qingdai liang Guang yanqu siyan chutan" (A Preliminary Examination on the Salt Smuggling in Guangdong and Guangxi in the Qing dynasty), *Lishi dang'an* (Historical Archives), No. 4 (1986), pp. 47–48.

22. See note 16, p. 175.

23. Li Hua, "Qingchao qianqi Guangdong de shangye yu shangren" (The Merchants and the Commerce of Guangdong in the Early Qing dynasty), *Xueshu yanjiu* (Learning and Research), No. 2 (1982), pp. 39–44.

24. Liu Zhiwei, "Ming–Qing shiqi Guangzhou chengshi jingji de tese" (On the Characteristics of the Guangzhou's Urban Economy in the Ming and Qing dynasties), *Guangzhou yanjiu* (Guangzhou Research), No. 1 (1986), pp. 63–65.

25. Jiang Zuyuan, "Qingdai Foshan shangren de goucheng ji qi dui shangye de yingxiang" (The Composition of the Foshan Merchants and Their Influences on Commerce in the Qing dynasty), *Guangzhou yanjiu*, No. 8 (1987), pp. 54–55.

26. Ibid., pp. 56–57.

27. Luo Yixing, "Qingdai qianqi Lingnan eryuan zhongxin shichang shuo" (Duo-centres of the Guangdong Region Marketplace in the Early Qing dynasty), *Guangdong shehui kexue*, No. 4 (1987), p. 24; and David Faure, "What Made Foshan a Town? The Evolution of Rural-Urban Identities in Ming–Qing China," *Late Imperial China*, Vol. 11, No. 2 (December, 1990), pp. 1–31.

28. Chen Huaxin, "Aiguo lishixuejia Liang Tingnan" (On the Patriotic Historian Liang Tingnan), *Guangzhou yanjiu*, No. 4 (1987), pp. 52–55; "Aiguo sixiangjia Zhu Ciqi" (Patriotic Thinker Zhu Ciqi), *Guangzhou yanjiu*, No. 7 (1986), pp. 69–70; and "Jindai Guangdong diyiwei kexuejia Zou Boqi" (Modern Guangdong's First Scientist Zou Boqi), *Guangzhou yanjiu*, No. 3 (1986), pp. 49–50.

29. Wang Tingkui, "Guangdong jindai guan jun gongye de changshizhe Wen Zishao" (The Pioneer-founder of Guangdong's Modern Government Arsenal Industry Wen Zishao), *Guangzhou yanjiu*, No. 8 (1986), pp. 69–70; Zhang Yunqiao, *Wu Tingfang yu Qingmo zhengzhi gaige* (Wu Tingfang and the Political Reform in the Late Qing dynasty) (Taibei: Lianjing chuban shiye gongsi, 1987); Jiang Yongjing, *Hu Hanmin xiansheng nianpu* (A Chronological Biography of Mr. Hu Hanmin) (Taibei: Zhongguo Guomindang dangshi weiyuanhui, 1978), p. 28.

30. Dai Aisheng, "Jindai Guangzhou diqu rencai beichu de yuanyin chutan" (A Preliminary Investigation into Why the Guangzhou Region Has Produced Numerous Talented People in the Modern Time), *Guangdong shehui kexue*, No. 2 (1986), pp. 102–106.

20

Synthesis of Economic Reforms and Open Policy

David K. Y. Chu

Introduction

In 1979, the PRC initiated three special economic zones (SEZs) in Shenzhen, Zhuhai and Shantou in Guangdong. Since then, these three SEZs have become the foci of economic reforms and the barometers of the openness of China. Initially, the SEZs were meant to carry out the following three objectives: (1) to observe and to understand capitalism at work and to follow the trend of modern economic development in the capitalist world; (2) to test different policies, especially those connected with various economic systems, by using the special zones as laboratories; and (3) to acquire modern technology and management methods.[1] Implicitly, they might also serve as buffer stations for integrating overseas Chinese and their financial capital with socialist China. Other factors like job creation, stimulating the local economy and building new cities and towns are secondary to the primary national objectives. The significance of the SEZs is therefore strategical, national and international.

To a certain extent Guangdong is fortunate to be the host province of the three SEZs. This not only signifies that Guangdong is the most open province of China but, necessarily, one step ahead in economic reforms among the provinces. Indeed, the experience and lessons learned in these zones have been most useful to the host province in promoting new or similar economic reform measures for other parts of the province. Many facets of these measures which have been discussed in the foregoing chapters will only be cross-referenced but not repeated here. The purpose of this chapter is to synthesize Guangdong's experience of economic reforms and open policy by highlighting the experience, problems and prospects of Guangdong's SEZs. The SEZs have been regarded as the cornerstone of China's economic reforms and open policies and can serve as the most representative models with which to understand Guangdong's economic reforms and open policy.

History and Geography of the Special Economic Zones

The Chinese special economic zone system is now seventeen years old. It was incepted under the Regulations on the Special Economic Zones of

The research assistance of L. S. Fung funded by University Polytechnic Grant Committee (UPGC) Research Grant No. HKU 5/91 in compilation of the data for the various tables of this chapter is much appreciated.

Guangdong Province in August 1980. The preparatory work for these zones, however, started much earlier. In late 1978, the idea of "special zones" that differed from the mainstream to undertake special tasks was getting popular among open-minded party leaders. In March 1979, Bao'an County and Zhuhai County were granted municipality status at the semi-prefectural level. In retrospect, one can interpret this as an early sign of designating these frontier counties for special tasks. On 5 July 1979, the central government announced that the provinces of Guangdong and Fujian would be allowed to practise special foreign economic policies and to experiment with "special export zones" in Shenzhen, Zhuhai, Shantou and Xiamen. Their official size and status were subsequently formalized in the Regulations in 1980.

Their current sizes vary to a great extent from what were assigned in 1980 (Table 20.1), except the Shenzhen SEZ to which a total of 327.5 sq km was designated in 1980 and its size has remained unchanged (Figure 20.1). In 1993 Bao'an County was redivided into two districts and annexed into the Shenzhen Municipal administration, with the original SEZ customs and immigration checkpoints function as before. The Zhuhai SEZ was only 6.81 sq km in 1980. Later, it was expanded to 15.16 sq km in 1983 and then 121 sq km in 1988 (Figure 20.2). Likewise, the Shantou SEZ has undergone three stages of expansion. Initially it was the smallest, only 1.6 sq km. In 1984, it became 52.6 sq km and in 1991 it was expanded to 234 sq km (Figure 20.3).

Frequent changes of boundary and areal size of the SEZs per se war-

Table 20.1   The Sizes of Guangdong's SEZs, 1980–1994

(Unit: km^2)

Year	Shenzhen SEZ	Zhuhai SEZ	Shantou SEZ
1980–1982	327.5	6.81	1.6
1983	327.5	15.16[a]	1.6
1984–1987	327.5	15.16	52.6[c]
1988–1990	327.5	121.00[b]	52.6
1991–1994	327.5	121.00	234.0[d]

Sources: *Shenzhen jingji tequ nianjian*, various years; *Zhuhai nianjian*, various years; *Shantou jingji tequ nianjian 1989*, pp. 527, 530; *Ming Pao Daily News*, 2 November 1991.

Notes: [a] From June 1983.
  [b] From April 1988.
  [c] From November 1984.
  [d] From November 1991.

Figure 20.1   The Special Economic Zone of Shenzhen

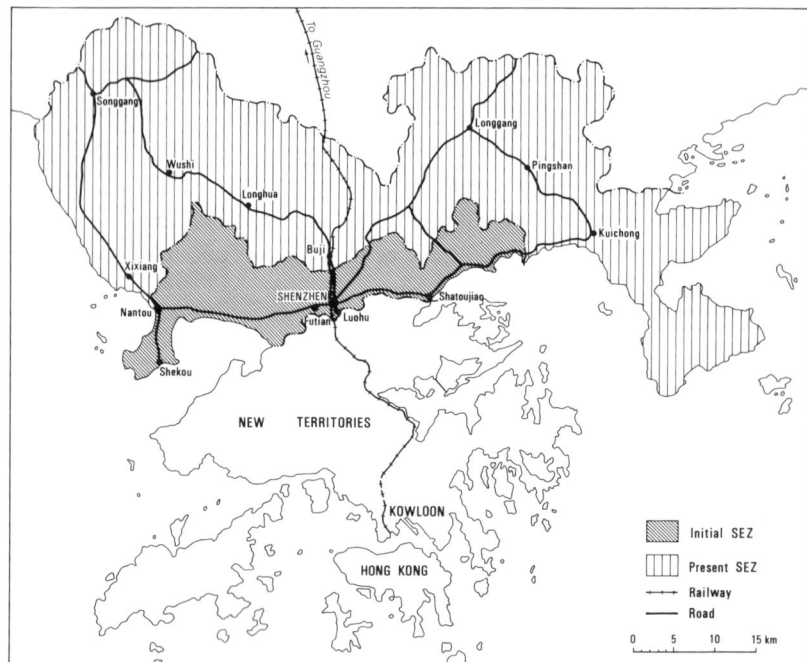

rant scepticism. It could be due to their unexpected success that they have
had to expand to cope with the situation. Or their initial sizes were simply
too small for them to function properly, and they had to expand before they
could fulfil their assigned tasks. Another reason is that changes in their
purposes called for changes in their areal size.[2] No matter what the real
reason is behind the frequent changes in their size, it is important to note
that statistics of the SEZs are sometimes not readily comparable because of
their varying sizes and coverage. Interpretation of SEZ statistics must be
undertaken with extreme care.

Policy Incentives for Foreign Investment

To attain the objectives mentioned earlier, the success of the SEZs in
Guangdong depends very much on their ability to attract foreign investors
who have management skills, new technology, capital, and external market
links that China finds unfamiliar but wanting in reforming its rigid central-
planning economic system. A set of preferential treatments to foreign

Figure 20.2   The Special Economic Zone of Zhuhai

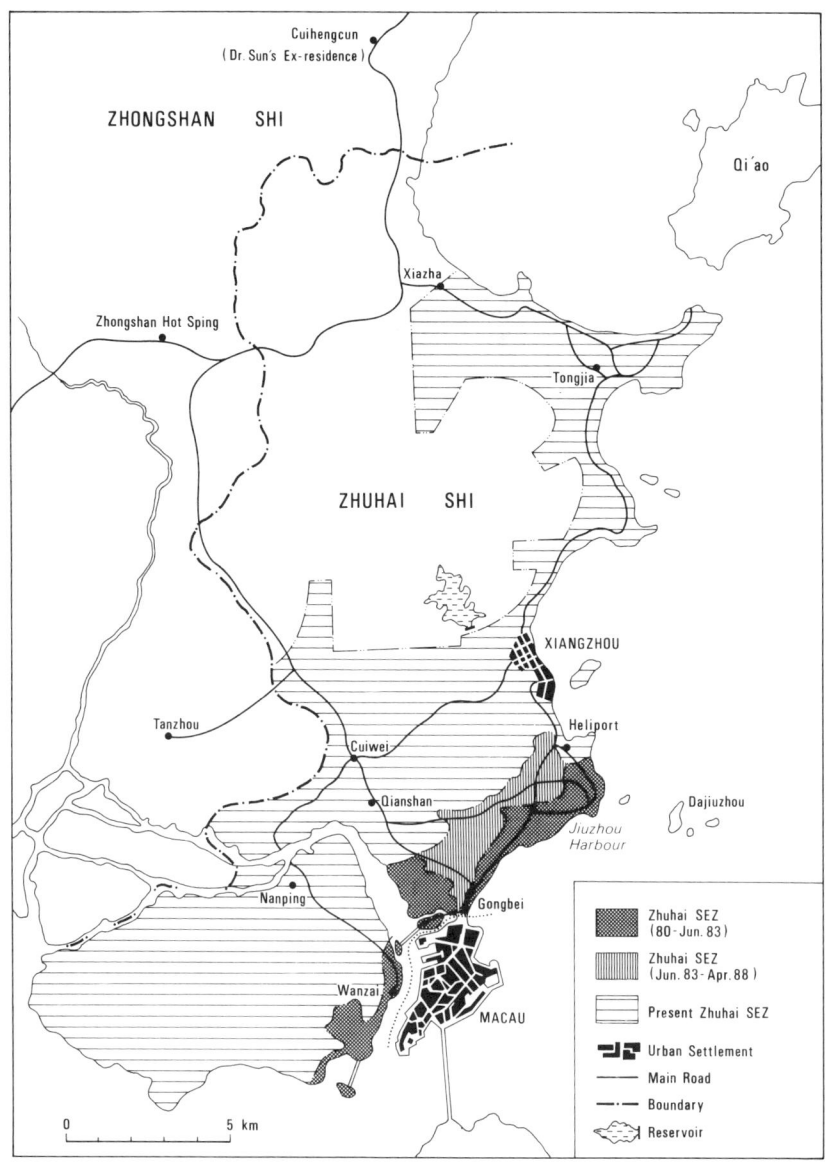

Figure 20.3   The Special Economic Zone of Shantou

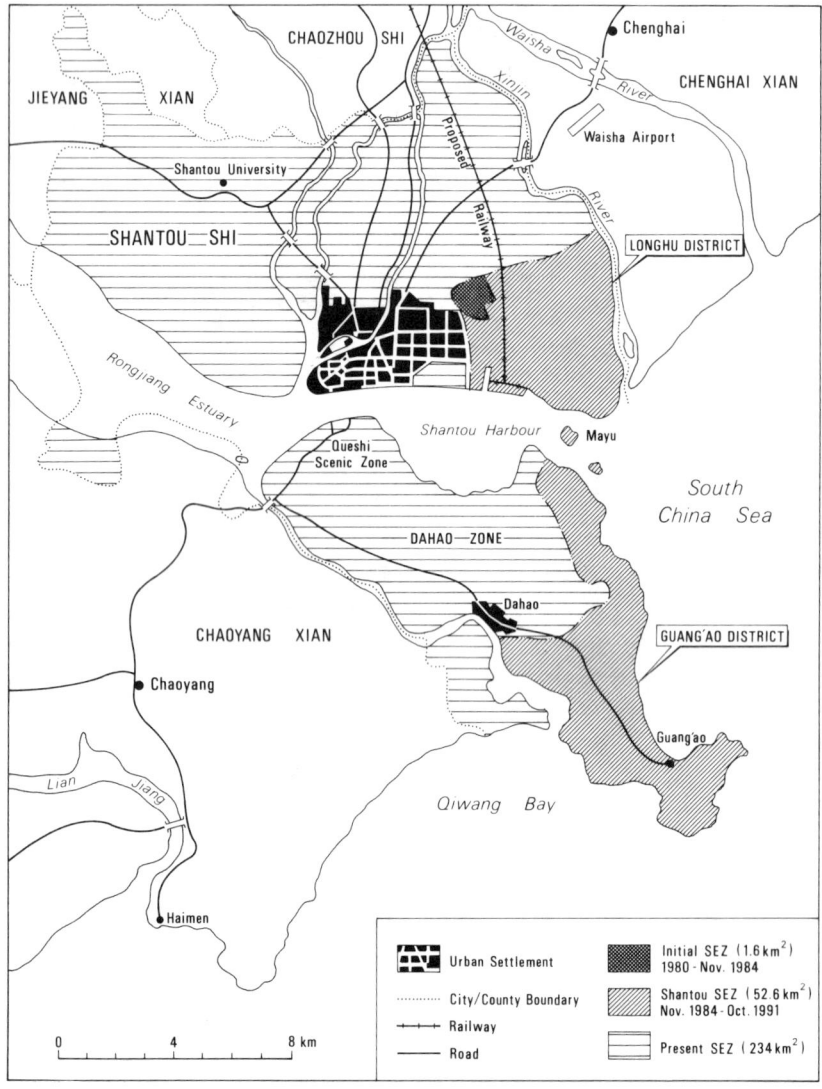

investors was offered as the most notable policy innovation in the early stage of SEZs. This included a 15% corporate tax rate, 1–3 years tax holidays in general but 5 years for investment over US$5 million, repatriation of corporate profit, personal income after tax, and repatriation of investment capital after completion of contract. Customs duties are free for import on raw materials and intermediate goods, and no export taxes are levied for items that are eventually exported from the SEZs. Sales in the inland market are allowed but restricted to certain percentages. These preferential treatments were first available in the SEZs, but no sooner were they implemented than in part or in entirety they were also available to some selected cities of China, making the SEZs less special and less attractive to foreign investors.[3]

In fact, the package of preferential treatments in the SEZs is necessary but definitely not sufficient to attract foreign investors. The number of contracts signed (Table 20.2), the volume of contractual foreign investment (Table 20.3), and the volume of realized foreign investment (Table 20.4) are good indicators that the attraction of the SEZs to the foreign investors varies whilst packages of preferential treatments have remained

Table 20.2 Number of Signed Contracts for Foreign Investment in the SEZs, 1980–1994

Year	Shenzhen SEZ	Zhuhai SEZ	Shantou SEZ
1980	142	—	—
1981	318	—	—
1982	357	—	—
1983	739	10	15
1984	550	97	28
1985	605	117	109
1986	190	45	16
1987	298	170	120
1988	622	290	260
1989	620	268	238
1990	602	386	174
1991	734	536	273
1992	1,077	669	668
1993	2,231	752	736
1994	1,503	503	394

Sources: *Shenzhen jingji tequ nianjian*, various years, and *Guangdong tongji nianjian*, various years.

Table 20.3   Contracted Volume of Foreign Investment in the Guangdong SEZs, 1980–1994

(Unit: US$ '000)

Year	Shenzhen SEZ	Zhuhai SEZ	Shantou SEZ
1980	218,810	—	—
1981	857,050	—	—
1982	175,740	—	—
1983	287,870	44,310	6,590
1984	575,640	97,360	28,610
1985	974,850	130,510	16,650
1986	495,810	28,610	12,020
1987	622,910	98,270	35,640
1988	430,650	277,440	72,800
1989	399,510	207,150	143,190
1990	516,010	282,940	147,850
1991	893,230	532,630	233,360
1992	1,824,150	1,217,240	895,990
1993	3,775,750	1,501,570	799,850
1994	2,070,600	1,125,390	971,050

Sources: *Shenzhen jingji tequ nianjian*, various years, and *Guangdong tongji nianjian*, various years.

Table 20.4   Actualized Foreign Investment, 1980–1994

(Unit: US$ '0000)

Year	Shenzhen SEZ	Zhuhai SEZ	Shantou SEZ
1980	2,657	—	—
1981	9,756	—	—
1982	6,690	—	—
1983	11,841	2,607	154
1984	20,663	11,054	787
1985	32,427	7,313	785
1986	48,401	3,915	1,178
1987	39,380	5,656	2,270
1988	41,439	20,220	3,440
1989	43,411	15,885	6,971
1990	47,654	9,605	8,368
1991	51,252	15,660	12,380
1992	58,582	30,033	23,629
1993	111,444	52,058	51,575
1994	110,783	67,239	41,841

Sources: *Shenzhen jingji tequ nianjian*, various years, and *Guangdong tongji nianjian*, various years.

more or less unchanged. Of late many of these preferential treatments have been withdrawn and there are few signs that the SEZs have lost their attractions afterall. Therefore other factors like infrastructural improvement might be more important.[4]

Institutional Reforms and Formation of Markets

China's SEZs were planned to be under separate administrative and political tutelage from the outset. The primary reason for this is to reduce official red-tape to a minimum. An SEZ office was created under the Ministry of Foreign Economic Relations and Trade (MOFERT) of the State Council for maintaining constant contact with other authorities in the central government and their subordinates. This extra-ministerial status for the SEZs has rendered certain political independence to the SEZs although operationally they are under the leadership of the provincial government — the Provincial Administrative Commission for the SEZs. As a token to the relative significance of the Shenzhen SEZ, its party secretary has also been one of the governors of the provincial government since 1981. This does not apply to the other two SEZs of Guangdong. The administrative arrangement, together with the relative autonomous legal and financial status of the SEZs, thus complicate the central–provincial relations of Guangdong.[5]

Internally, the key organizational unit in each SEZ is the SEZ Development Company. The company is a government planning and development enterprise but at the same time an official bureau to negotiate with foreign investors. It is also responsible for the development of infrastructure and land allotment to all enterprises, and subsequently real estate development. The separation of ownership and land-use rights, with the latter transferrable upon payment of fees, was pioneered by these SEZ development companies, a practice soon adopted elsewhere in Guangdong and then in other parts of China. A land market is thus formed. Sales of flats to locals by domestic enterprises and local governments create a domestic real estate market side by side with the foreign related real estate market (see Chapter 13).

To help and regulate the recruitment of workers in the foreign related enterprises, the SEZ Labour Services Company was formed. This is the starting point of a labour market in China. The practice of contracted labour, started with foreign related enterprise, has been widely adopted by domestic enterprises. Bonus and other material rewards soon dwarf the nominal salaries of workers so that they start accepting a high salary and low fringe benefit wage structure. Changes in the consumption pattern also occur. Rise in living standards is commonplace but the need for social insurance (see Chapter 12) and health care (see Chapter 11) also arises because fringe benefits associated with employment, especially the joint-venture and foreign wholly-owned subsidiaries, only cover the contractual periods and are seldom extended beyond the expiration of contract period. A new concept of social insurance is thus necessary.

Well before the advent of the land and the real estate market was the relief of price control on food staples and other consumer goods. The relaxation of food prices since 1 November 1984 did not diminish the agricultural output of the SEZs. On the contrary, it boosted the output to a new level and farming was practised more intensively. The primary production of SEZs led the other parts of Guangdong in terms of specialization, technological level and market commercial orientation (see Chapter 4). Capital goods and commodities from other provinces at negotiable prices helped to transform the SEZs into the biggest trading centres of China. The circulation of Hong Kong currency aided such development, so much so that the SEZ market has become a proxy to an international market. The flooding of imported consumer goods in the SEZs and the selling of these imported goods to inland China at a premium contributed to the severe trade deficit in the mid-1980s. At one time, almost all of the local state departments and enterprises were engaged in trade. Nevertheless a flourishing retail trade plus a booming tourist services sector, both overseas and domestic, are being witnessed in the SEZs. The success of the SEZs to a certain extent highlights the development of the tertiary activities of Guangdong as discussed in Chapter 7.

Institutional transformation of the SEZs is not complete without financial reforms and the development of a workable legal framework. New banks and financial institutions are established, including those under joint venture arrangement. The SEZs have been outposts for financial reforms although the SEZ currencies were not issued after protracted discussions. The setting up of regional banks is undoubtedly a great contribution from the SEZs to the national financial reforms (see Chapter 8). Enterprises formed under equity share-holding is the commonest format for joint ventures. Domestic enterprises that are formed jointly between SEZs and inland enterprises are equity share companies and perhaps the most fertile ground for development of entrepreneurship in the PRC setting (see Chapter 9). It is not surprising that Shenzhen SEZ has one of China's first two stock exchanges. Equally not surprising is the immaturity of the Shenzhen stock exchange system,[6] which resulted in a civic disorder on 10 August 1992.

Undoubtedly, it is a long road from the setting up of SEZs to the current relatively workable legal system. The SEZ is the laboratory for experimenting economic laws, especially foreign related economic laws. Starting from 1981, Shenzhen SEZ has a greater legislative power and autonomy to enact laws and local regulations (see Chapter 16). However law enforcement and public order in the SEZs are still problematic given the complicated structure of law enforcement bodies, limited resources, a long coastline and ever growing populations.

Infrastructural Improvement

The relative backwardness of the SEZs of Guangdong in 1980 meant that an enormous initial infrastructure investment was required.[7] Without this, the obstacles to the realization of the objectives were simply insurmountable. Throughout the past thirteen years, massive efforts have been put into the so-called "seven links and one levelling" projects in the SEZs. These include linkages of road, rail, shipping, air transport, water supply, electricity supply, telecommunications and levelling of land.

Remarkable improvement has been made to road links between Shenzhen and Hong Kong, Shenzhen and Guangzhou, Zhuhai and Guangzhou, Shantou and Guangzhou since 1980 (see Chapter 14). Previously, only low class road was available and vehicular ferries were employed to cross the major rivers and their distributaries. Unsurfaced roads have now been surfaced and upgraded. Bridges, many of which are tolled, have been built for easy and smooth crossing of rivers. Under construction are the first phase of the Hong Kong–Guangzhou high-speed expressway and the Shantou–Shenzhen expressway. On their completion the SEZs will be very well connected with their surrounding counties and other major cities in the Pearl River Delta by road. Internally a massive road construction programme is underway to link together the functional areas in the SEZs. Traffic congestion at bottlenecks is inevitable as this is commonplace to all fast developing cities.

Rail development for the SEZs lags behind road development. Only Shenzhen is connected by rail. However, rail communication will eventually be available to all three SEZs as many railways are now under construction or in an active planning stage. The railway between Shenzhen and Guangzhou has been upgraded by high-speed train, cutting journey time to one hour from the previous three hours. In addition, Shenzhen is now planning its mass transit railway.

Water transport is important to all three SEZs (Table 20.5). Zhuhai and Shantou both strive to have their own ports which will provide vital scheduled links between them and Hong Kong, especially when land transport is inadequate. Their container terminals are, however, too shallow and small for trunk line container vessels, but they are good enough for feeder vessels. The ports in the Shenzhen SEZ are of two categories. Shekou port is similar to the ports in Zhuhai and Shantou SEZs. The container terminals in Chiwan and of Shekou Peninsula are purpose-built, capable of diverting some container traffic from Hong Kong. Yantian port, especially now under Hong Kong management expertise, has great potential but needs a decade or two to complete. Golan port in west Zhuhai municipality is of a similar status as Yantian port. Both of them are bulk cargo ports with some general-cum-container cargo facilities, depending on market conditions.

Table 20.5   Cargo Throughput at the SEZ-related Ports, 1980–1994

(Unit: '000 tonnes)

Year	Shenzhen SEZ	Zhuhai SEZ	Shantou SEZ
1980	296	—	—
1981	393	—	—
1982	842	—	—
1983	1,200	—	—
1984	2,070	—	—
1985	3,260	—	20
1986	3,060	—	110
1987	4,850	900	140
1988	7,340	1,310	190
1989	9,560	1,650	160
1990	11,860	1,910	280
1991	14,140	2,570	320
1992	17,300	3,290	5,910
1993	25,410	3,430	8,640
1994	30,020	11,570	7,080

Sources: *Shenzhen jingji tequ nianjian*, various years; *Guangdong nianjian*, 1989, 1990 and 1991, and *Guangdong tongji nianjian*, various years.

Development of air links to the SEZs is easier said than done. Shantou's domestic airport is made to take the Boeing 737 after having been conferred the SEZ status, but not much improvement has been made. Zhuhai wanted to build its own airport but was turned down initially by the central government, which supported Macau airport instead. However, Zhuhai at last got its own way by having an airport at Sanzao. Shenzhen completed the first phase of its Huangtian airport and set up scheduled regular domestic flights. Since 1993, Huangtian airport has been used by Singapore Airlines and subsequently by many others, first for freight and then for passengers to supplement their flights to Hong Kong. Although it is less convenient, Huangtian airport has generally been regarded as a useful supplement to the Hong Kong international airport.

A fresh water supply is important to all cities. The SEZs are important industrial centres. Zhuhai gets its fresh water from the upper reaches of the distributaries of the Pearl River with relative convenience. Shantou, especially the southern portion which has been designated a petrochemical industrial district, requires a large supply of fresh water. Tapping fresh water from distant rivers is an unenviable task. Shenzhen is on the route of the East River–Hong Kong water transfer works. Initially, it had little problem with a fresh water supply. In the long run, Shenzhen has to compete for fresh water with Hong Kong because the East River water might not be enough for the two cities with their millions of inhabitants.[8]

Shenzhen is fortunate to have the opportunity of buying electricity directly from Hong Kong although Hong Kong is only a secondary source of supply after the Guangdong electricity network (see Chapter 5). Its electricity stoppages have more to do with technical problems than availability. Electricity shortage in Shantou is acute and would only be solved by constructing huge thermal generation plants along the seashore using coal shipments from north China. Zhuhai depends entirely on the Guangdong network for its supply of electricity without relying on Macau at present. Its shortage of electricity affects its tourism and industrial plants. A solution to Zhuhai's electricity supply problem is to construct large thermal plants in the Golan port zone, with coal being shipped in from China and overseas by coal carriers.

Remarkable progress is being seen in telecommunications in Guangdong. Shantou now has the capacity to operate 153,000 telephones — a 50-fold increase in comparison with the year 1978. By comparison, Zhuhai has 51 km of optical fibres and a capacity for 2,000 long distant telephone exchanges and 4,000 domestic telephone exchanges simultaneously.

Shenzhen is not only the best equipped with telephones, with 161,600 telephones already installed; facsimile machines and mobile telephones are also popular (see Chapter 14). Preparation of sites for urban development requires considerable engineering work. Progress is evidenced by the mushrooming of skyscrapers and standard factory buildings.

In order to undertake the projects mentioned above, enormous total capital construction investment is required (Table 20.6). It is an undeniable fact that the SEZs have not received much direct financial support from the central government coffers. Instead, local accumulation has been achieved through land sales and retained profits; and investment from outside the zone — from Guangdong, other provinces and the central ministerial enterprises — accounts for the lion's share of the capital construction expenditure.[9]

Table 20.6   Capital Construction Expenditure, 1980–1994

(Unit: RMB '000)

Year	Shenzhen SEZ	Zhuhai SEZ*	Shantou SEZ
1980	112,940	30,000	—
1981	265,080	65,000	2,910
1982	586,730	105,000	5,490
1983	836,420	136,000	19,220
1984	1,555,730	340,000	45,370
1985	2,601,080	765,770	110,070
1986	1,847,590	682,450	126,870
1987	2,047,020	790,010	198,210
1988	3,383,190	943,180	416,130
1989	4,233,700	845,000	453,000
1990	4,874,890	1,102,000	493,130
1991	6,521,480	1,019,260	798,080
1992	7,337,510	3,178,730	1,564,190
1993	12,221,460	4,546,000	3,148,270
1994	11,004,630	6,533,350	2,262,760

Note: * Figures for Zhuhai from 1980 to 1984 refer to the entire Zhuhai Municipality, figures from 1985 to 1888 are those by the state sectors in Zhuhai urban areas. Only after 1989 are the figures for Zhuhai SEZ.

Sources: *Shenzhen jingji tequ nianjian*, various years; *Zhuhai nianjian*, 1983, 1986, 1988 and 1990; *Shantou jingji tequ nianjian 1989; Guangdong tongji nianjian*, various years.

Changes in Urban and Demographic Structures

A direct outcome of foreign capital participation, institutional reform and infrastructural improvement is the emergence of a new million-inhabitant city just to the northern border of Hong Kong and a new urban hierarchy in Guangdong (see Chapter 15). Shenzhen is the second most important city in Guangdong and a contender in many spheres. Zhuhai SEZ is less populated with less than 350,000 permanent residents and about 100,000 temporary residents. Shantou SEZ after enlargement has over a million people. The rapid rate of population growth (Table 20.7) is a direct result of increasing fluidity and mobility of population throughout the province (see Chapter 17). As a result, Shenzhen has felt, with a total population well over one and a half million in 1994, enormous pressure in housing and other urban facilities.

Table 20.7 Population Growth of Guangdong's SEZs, 1980–1994

Year	Shenzhen SEZ		Zhuhai SEZ	Shantou SEZ
	Permanent	Temporary	Permanent	Permanent
1980	84,100	—	—	—
1981	98,300	—	—	—
1982	128,600	—	—	—
1983	165,000	—	12,500	—
1984	191,400	146,100	12,400	18,253
1985	231,900	237,900	15,900	23,700
1986	257,400	231,300	20,100	25,000
1987	286,900	312,700	21,400	27,300
1988	321,900	462,100	190,700	50,200
1989	362,000	664,900	216,000	52,800
1990	395,200	614,500	265,700	57,300
1991	432,100	765,900	278,600	91,000*
1992	472,800	—	292,000	894,000
1993	521,400	668,000	309,200	914,800
1994	565,200	910,100	331,000	1,015,200

Note: * By annexing the urban districts, Shantou SEZ had over 787,000 people in 1991.

Sources: *Shenzhen jingji tequ nianjian*, various years. For Zhuhai SEZ, data for 1983–1988 from *Guangdong nianjian*, 1987–1989; for 1989–1991, from *Guangdong tongji nianjian*, 1990–1992. For Shantou SEZ, data for 1984 from *Shantou jingji tequ nianjian 1989;* for 1985–1990, from *Guangdong nianjian*, 1987–1991; for 1991 onwards, from *Guangdong tongji nianjian*, various years.

Nevertheless, the rapid growth of population in the SEZs makes the process of rapid industrialization easier. Like Guangdong itself, export-led industrialization is a major means of economic development in the SEZs (see Chapter 6). Since 1990, for example, about 60% of Shenzhen's industrial output has been exported. This has been a remarkable improvement in comparison with the mid-1980s. Since 1984, the increase in local industrial export has enhanced the overall export performance of the SEZs as evidenced by their export figures (Table 20.8).

Table 20.9 shows the industrial structure of the SEZs by their output. Shenzhen and Zhuhai have a very high proportion of their industrial output made up of electronics. Other light industries make up the rest. Heavy industries only account for a small but increasing proportion. For example, in 1991 light industries in Shenzhen SEZ account for 74% versus heavy industries of 26% but in 1994 the ratio has become 56.9% and 43.1%, respectively. Technological transfer, dependent on whether only high technology is counted, is real. Without technological transfer, the electronic

Table 20.8   Export Trade of Guangdong's SEZs, 1984–1995

(Unit: US$ '000)

Year	Shenzhen SEZ	Growth rate (%)	Zhuhai SEZ	Growth rate (%)	Shantou SEZ	Growth rate (%)
1984	265,000*	—	11,000	—	4,490	—
1985	527,000	—	23,000	109.1	55,900	1,145.0
1986	643,000	22.0	17,000	–26.1	73,580	31.6
1987	1,297,000	101.7	260,000	1,429.4	178,010	141.9
1988	1,672,000	28.9	404,000	55.4	298,160	67.5
1989	1,905,000	13.9	343,000	–15.1	299,000	0.3
1990	2,572,740	35.1	456,340	33.1	419,500	40.3
1991	2,679,920	4.1	627,000	37.4	584,710	39.4
1992	4,787,280	78.6	829,370	32.3	1,434,500	145.3
1993	5,768,270	20.5	949,720	14.5	1,498,330	4.4
1994	8,881,750	54.0	1,461,700	53.9	1,779,300	18.8
1995	9,633,460	8.5	2,115,280	44.7	2,076,190	16.7

Sources: For Shenzhen SEZ, data for 1985–1988 from *Guangdong nianjian*, 1987–1989; for 1989–1995, from *Guangdong tongji nianjian*, 1990–1996. For Zhuhai SEZ, data for 1984–1988 from *Guangdong nianjian*, 1987–1989; for 1989–1995, from *Guangdong tongji nianjian*, 1990–1996. For Shantou SEZ, data for 1984–1988 from *Shantou jingji tequ nianjian 1989;* for 1989–1995, from *Guangdong tongji nianjian*, 1990–1996.

Note: * Export trade figure of Shenzhen in 1984 refers to both the SEZ and Bao'an Xian; SEZ figures are cited from 1985 to 1995.

Table 20.9 Value of Production by Major Types of Industries in the Three SEZs at 1990 Constant Prices

(Unit: RMB '000)

Type of Industry	Shenzhen SEZ	Percentage share	Zhuhai SEZ	Percentage share	Shantou SEZ	Percentage share
Electronics	27,192,860	50.04	4,085,830	20.29	1,265,710	9.54
Chemical & pharmaceutical	5,079,350	9.35	5,742,300	28.51	1,835,820	13.84
Textiles & clothing	4,028,880	7.41	1,533,380	7.61	2,816,110	21.23
Mechanical & machinery	3,862,790	7.11	4,177,050	20.74	2,036,580	15.35
Food & beverages	3,693,620	6.80	746,820	3.71	806,740	6.08
Metal & metal products	2,557,440	4.71	505,240	2.50	290,790	2.19
Plastics	1,235,420	2.27	745,360	3.70	1,844,240	13.90
Paper & printing	1,177,020	2.17	471,170	2.33	674,780	5.09
Building materials & nonmetallic products	1,136,480	2.09	548,680	2.72	171,830	1.30
Others	4,376,750	8.05	1,585,140	7.87	1,523,790	11.49
Total	54,340,610	100.00	20,140,970	100.00	13,266,390	100.00

Sources: *Shenzhen tongji nianjian 1995*, pp. 84–85; *Zhuhai tongji nianjian 1995*, pp. 108–9; *Shantoushi tongji nianjian 1995*, pp. 94–95.

industry will be very difficult to establish. More important perhaps is the adoption of Western practices in management and work discipline on the shop floor. Along with production concepts and techniques, social behaviour, leisure and consumer patterns of SEZ residents also get closer to the outside world. In terms of ownership, the large number of non-state-owned industrial enterprises also signifies that the SEZs are genuinely the meeting points of a socialist centrally planned economy and a capitalist market economy (see Chapter 6).

Concluding Remarks

Whilst it is hard to get a unanimous agreement on whether the SEZs of Guangdong have fulfilled all the primary objectives in serving regional and national interests, it will be difficult not to acknowledge their contribution to the local economy. The rapid rise of the gross domestic product (GDP) and GDP per capita is the best indicator. Other than a slight fall in 1986 and 1987, the underlying trend is an upward one. With GDP per capita in Shenzhen, for example, approaching RMB17,800 in 1994 (approx. US$1,800),[10] the SEZs are virtually the wealthiest areas in Guangdong. The biggest problem now facing the SEZs relates to the fact that the degree of openness of other parts of China is now getting very close to, if not greater than, that of the SEZs. Reforms of the rigid socialist centrally planned system that once were pioneered by the SEZs, are widely adopted in other parts of China. Under the umbrella term of "market socialism," many parts of China choose to experiment with more innovative reforms and are even less bound by formalism. The success of the Pearl River Delta counties in attracting commissioned intermediate processing and compensation trade, in fostering rural and village industries and in developing inland domestic markets shows that formalism is a big threat to economic development. After seventeen years, the SEZs are apparently complacent about their success and formalism is unavoidably getting into their thinking as much as into their daily practices.

There is a grain of truth in the assertion that many innovative measures of the SEZs, and to a lesser degree of Guangdong, originated from Hong Kong. Based on this logic, an unkind comment has it that the SEZs are getting assimilated by Hong Kong, Guangdong is getting assimilated by the SEZs and China is getting assimilated by Guangdong. As such, the relationship between Hong Kong and Mainland China is a most unfortunate one. Under the "one country, two systems" design, they should be different and maintain their own uniqueness. The SEZs should be more innovative than simply learning from Hong Kong or simply being the windows of China to observe the outside world. The historical role of SEZs is nearing an end and they have to redefine their functions and seek new roles in the coming years. Shenzhen, for example, is now considering the new task of integration with Hong Kong after China's resumption of Hong Kong's sovereignty in 1997. Presumably, this will be similar to Zhuhai when Macau reverts to China's rule in 1999. However, they are becoming modern, international, urban centres or are unwillingly becoming the industrial backyards of the nearby world cities or regional controlling points, their choices will be dictated by situations rather than by the subjective desires of the governors or planners of the SEZs. With the return of Hong Kong to China in 1997 and Macau in 1999, the Special Administrative Regions are and will remain the most "special" in China. Their "special" status will dwarf the efforts of all other special zones in their march towards market and institutional reforms and opening to the outside world. Similarly, the future of Guangdong cannot rely solely on being one step ahead of the other provinces. Instead, the economic future of Guangdong relies on strengthening its existing economic foundation and improving its relatively weak links (see especially Chapter 3) whilst the political and social future of Guangdong relies on the careful handling of central–provincial relations (see especially Chapter 2), and the improving of social and educational infrastructures (see especially Chapter 10). In between the other parts of China and the world-class Hong Kong, there should be enough room for Guangdong and its SEZs to contribute.

Notes

1. *Wen Wei Po*, 6 March 1981 and later, but for very much similar discussion by officials, see *Shenzhen tequ bao* (Shenzhen Special Zone Daily), 20 November 1990.

2. The author has discussed this issue in an earlier paper; see D. K. Y. Chu, "The Special Economic Zones and the Problems of Territorial Containment," in *China Special Economic Zones*, edited by Y. C. Jao and C. K. Leung (Hong Kong: Oxford University Press, 1986), pp. 21–38.

3. All technological and economic zones of the coastal open cities and their adjacent areas award some of these preferential treatments. Pudong of Shanghai could offer more. See Yue-man Yeung and Xu-wei Hu (eds.),

China's Coastal Cities: Catalysts for Modernization (Honolulu: University of Hawaii Press, 1992), p. 330.

4. Wang Huijiong et al. (eds.), *Zhongguo de touzi huanjing* (Investment Climate in China: Problems and Prospects) (Beijing: Zhongguo guowuyuan jingji jishu shehui fazhan yanjiu zhongxin kexingxing yanjiu zhuantizu; Hong Kong: Jing–Gang xueshu jiaoliu zhongxin, 1987), p. 389.

5. See G. T. Crane, *The Political Economy of China's Special Economic Zones* (Armonk, New York: M. E. Sharpe, 1990), p. 204.

6. Wang Peiyuan, "Guanyu Shenzhen gupiao shichang de jige wenti" (Some Issues Concerning the Stock Market in Shenzhen), *Shenzhen daxue xuebao* (Journal of Shenzhen University), No. 4 (1991), pp. 77–82.

7. Yue-man Yeung, "Infrastructural Development — The South China Experience," *Occasional Paper*, No. 118 (Hong Kong: Department of Geography, The Chinese University of Hong Kong, 1993), and see also Chapter 14.

8. Zhong Gongfu and Xu Zice (eds.), *Zhongguo jingji tequ dili yanjiu* (Research on China's Special Economic Zones' Geography) (Guangzhou: Guangdong renmen chubanshe, 1983), p. 245.

9. The efficiency of the capital construction investment is a controversial issue. One comment is that foreign capital only makes up a very small portion and Mayor Liang Xiang admitted in 1985 that only 20% was foreign capital and the rest was Chinese, see *Jingji ribao*, 11 December 1985. On infrastructure, P. W. Liu et al. also pointed out that SEZs and the Pearl River Delta, as a whole, have too many ports and airports, but not enough roads and electricity generation plants, so that the capital construction expenditure of the region has not been wisely spent. See P. W. Liu et al., *Zhongguo gaige kaifang yu Zhujiang sanjiaozhou de jingji fazhan: Yanjiu baogao* (China's Reform and Open Policy and Pearl River Delta's Economic Development: Research Report) (Hong Kong: Nanyang Commercial Bank, 1992), p. 142.

10. The figure refers to Shenzhen municipality.

Contributors

Y. M. YEUNG is Professor of Geography, Director of the Hong Kong Institute of Asia-Pacific Studies and Head of Shaw College at The Chinese University of Hong Kong. His wide-ranging research interests have recently focused on China's coastal cities, South China, globalization and Asian cities. He has published extensively, including *China's Coastal Cities* (1992), *Urban and Regional Development in China* (1993), *Pacific Asia in the 21st Century* (1993), *Emerging World Cities in Pacific Asia* (1996), *Global Change and the Commonwealth* (1996) and *Shanghai* (1996).

DAVID K. Y. CHU obtained his PhD from the London School of Economics and is Professor in the Department of Geography at The Chinese University of Hong Kong. He has published many articles and book chapters on the port of Hong Kong and China's special economic zones.

MAURICE BROSSEAU is Research Officer of the Hong Kong Institute of Asia-Pacific Studies at The Chinese University of Hong Kong. His basic interests are the evolution of institutions resulting from the systemic reforms of the Chinese economy and the relationship between local administration, organizations and individuals. In recent years, he has been investigating the emergence and functional development of entrepreneurship in the transitional environment of the Pearl River Delta. In the past several years, he has been co-editor of the annual publication *China Review*, by The Chinese University Press.

CHAU KWAI-CHEONG is Associate Professor in Biogeography, Soil Geography and Resource Managemennt in the Department of Geography at The Chinese University of Hong Kong. He obtained his PhD in forestry at the Australian National University. His areas of interest are soil amelioration, agroforestry and biological resource management.

PETER T. Y. CHEUNG is Associate Professor in the Department of Politics and Public Administration at the University of Hong Kong. He holds a PhD in political science from the University of Washington, Seattle and serves on the editorial committee of the journal, *Provincial China*. He has published on the political and economic development of South China. His latest work includes *Provincial Strategies for Economic Reform in Post-Mao China* (forthcoming, co-edited with

Jae Ho Chung and Zhimin Lin). His current research interests are concerned with the pattern of economic reform in Guangdong, development strategies of Guangzhou, Shanghai and Tianjin and external relations of China's provinces.

REBECCA L. H. CHIU is Associate Professor in the Centre of Urban Planning and Environmental Management at the University of Hong Kong. She specializes in housing education and housing studies. Among her research activities on various housing systems, she has conducted consultancy work on housing reforms in China for planning and international organizations.

SUSAN FINDER is a lawyer with the international law firm Freshfields. She is a graduate of the Harvard Law School and has an LL.M. from Columbia Law School. Her practice includes a variety of PRC investment matters, including the establishment of joint ventures and wholly-owned foreign enterprises, as well as advising on Chinese foreign exchange and other regulations. Before joining Freshfields, she taught Chinese law for several years at the City Polytechnic of Hong Kong (now City University). She has previously conducted research in the Law Department of Peking University and the Institute of State and Law, USSR (now Russian) Academy of Sciences and has also served as resident liaison and legal specialist in Kazakhstan, on behalf of the American Bar Association.

PETER HILLS is Professor and Director of the Centre of Urban Planning and Environmental Management at the University of Hong Kong. His major research interests relate to the analysis of energy-environment issues and energy planning in developing countries. He has published numerous books and papers on these topics and has acted as a consultant on energy issues to the International Labour Office, the Asian Development Bank, the United Nations Development Programme and other international bodies.

SUZANNE C. HO is Professor in the Department of Community and Family Medicine, The Chinese University of Hong Kong. She graduated from the University of California (Berkeley), obtained her Master of Public Health from Columbia University and PhD from the National University of Singapore. She was elected Fellow of American College of Epidemiology in 1992. Dr. Ho has served as adviser on epidemiological research to WHO Collaborating Centres in Research in Human Reproduction in China on many occasions. Her major research interests lie in the study of degenerative diseases and ageing and has been the Principal Investigator in a number of population based health research projects.

HUNG WING-TAT is Associate Professor in The Hong Kong Polytechnic University. He worked extensively in the construction and environmental fields before joining the University. His main research interest lies in transport energy consumption and environmental matters. He is now a member of the Working Committee on the trial management and operation of liquefied petroleum gas taxis established within the Hong Kong Government. He has been a District Board member for over ten years. He is also an Executive Committee member of the Conservancy Association, the oldest environmental group in Hong Kong.

PAUL C. K. KWONG, formerly Lecturer in Sociology at The Chinese University of Hong Kong, is with City University of Hong Kong Press. He holds a doctoral degree from Harvard University and specializes in family demography in Chinese populations. He co-edited *The Other Hong Kong Report 1992* and compiled its four-year index in *Hong Kong Trends, 1989–92*.

K. C. LAM is Professor in Geography and Programme Director of the Centre for Environmental Studies at The Chinese University of Hong Kong. Educated in Hong Kong, he undertook a PhD programme in catchment studies at the University of New England, Australia. Dr. Lam has considerable field research experience in southern China, ranging from environmental planning issues in special economic zones to land degradation and ecosystem rehabilitation problems in the remote and hilly parts of Guangdong.

LAU PUI-KING is Associate Professor and Associate Head of the Department of Business Studies, Co-ordinator for Training of the China Business Centre of the Hong Kong Polytechnic University. A graduate of The Chinese University of Hong Kong and California State University, she has specialized in the study of the Chinese economy, particularly Chinese state enterprises and joint ventures and economic reform in Guangdong. She has been an appointed Hong Kong representative to the Guangdong Provincial People's Congress since 1988.

LAU YEE-CHEUNG is Associate Professor in the Department of History at The Chinese University of Hong Kong and President of the International Association of Hakka Studies. His research interests have focused on the Hakka, local history of South China, including Hong Kong and Republican China. He has published *China Embarking on the Road to Modernization* (1995) and *Lineage and Popular Culture Among the Hakka* (1996).

EVA B. C. LI is former Senior Lecturer in Social Work at The Chinese University of Hong Kong. She has written extensively on various aspects of welfare services in China such as community development, changing status and roles of women and implications of the open policy on welfare and social work education.

LI SI-MING is currently Professor and Head of the Department of Geography, Hong Kong Baptist University. He holds a PhD in Geography from Queen's University, Canada. His major research interests are in urban and economic geography. Currently he is undertaking a research project on China's emerging housing market and its implications for the country's urban spatial structure. His recent publications include the edited volumes *The Other Hong Kong Report 1996* (co-edited with Nyaw Mee Kau) and *Perspectives on China's Regional Economy* (co-edited with Tang Wing-shing, Chiang Lan-hung and Jou Su-ching), and a number of research papers on urban-related issues in Hong Kong and mainland China published in international refereed journals.

LUK CHIU-MING holds a doctorate in geography from the University of Minnesota, USA. His major research interest lies in the regional development of China, Guangdong in particular. Lately, his research interests have extended to the study of the impact of high technology on regional development and issues associated with the advent of the information age. He is currently a Research Associate with the Joint Centre for Asia Pacific Studies at University of Toronto–York University, Canada.

GRACE C. L. MAK is Associate Professor in Comparative Education and Sociology of Education at the Faculty of Education, The Chinese University of Hong Kong. She has published numerous articles on women's education and education and development in China and in Hong Kong.

TOYOJIRO MARUYA is Senior Researcher at the Institute of Developing Economies, Tokyo, Japan. He is also Research Associate of the Centre of Asian Studies of the University of Hong Kong. His major interest is in the economic development of China, especially South China. He is the author of numerous articles on the South China and Hong Kong economy.

R. J. NELLER is Lecturer in the Faculty of Science at the Sunshine Coast University in Queensland, Australia. He obtained his Ph.D. from the University of New England after investigating the impact of urban development on fluvial systems. Since that time he has continued to research in the field of environmental geomorphology (including both fluvial and coastal research) in Australia, Peru, Finland and, for the past nine years, in Hong Kong.

SIU YAT-MING is Associate Professor of Sociology at Hong Kong Baptist University. His major research interests are in fertility and population mobility in China. He is currently conducting research on residential mobility in Beijing. He has published articles on China's population issues such as fertility and population mobility in books and journals.

TSANG SHU-KI is Professor of Economics at Hong Kong Baptist University. He holds a PhD degree from the University of Manchester. Before joining the academia in 1985, he had worked in the financial field. He has published four books on Hong Kong and China and a number of journal articles and book chapters on comparative economics, econometric modelling, monetary economics and the Chinese economy. Presently, he is a member of the New Airport Consultative Committee, the Consumer Council, the Energy Advisory Committee and the Transport Advisory Committee as well as a part-time member of the Central Policy Unit of the Hong Kong SAR Government.

WONG KWAN-YIU is Professor in Geography at The Chinese University of

Hong Kong. His main research interests are perception studies, urban and industrial geography and the economic geography of China. He has edited three books on China's modernization and the Shenzhen Special Economic Zone.

WONG TZE-WAI, Professor, Department of Community and Family Medicine, The Chinese University of Hong Kong, obtained an MBBS degree in the University of Hong Kong and an MSc (Public Health) degree in the National University of Singapore. He is Fellow of Australasian Faculty of Occupational Medicine and Member of Faculty of Public Health Medicine, United Kingdom. His research experience includes infectious, chronic and occupational diseases, environmental health, accidents and health services research, with over 60 scientific publications.

EDWARD S. W. WOO obtained his PhD from the University of Leeds. His research focuses on rural and urban development, and the growth of the non-state enterprises in China. He has taught China geography courses at the University of Hong Kong and the University of British Columbia. His recent research interest also includes Chinese immigrant issues in Canada. He has served as an administrator in the 4th World Chinese Entrepreneurs Convention and the APEC Conference held in Vancouver, 1997.

IGNATIUS T. S. YU is Associate Professor in the Department of Community and Family Medicine, The Chinese University of Hong Kong. He graduated from the Medical Faculty of the University of Hong Kong in 1978 and obtained a Master of Public Health degree from the University of Texas in 1983. Elected a Fellow of the Australian College of Occupational Medicine in 1986, he is currently Chairman of the Hong Kong Society of Occupational Medicine. He was recently appointed an Honorary Member of the Executive Committee of the Guangdong Preventive Medical Association.

Name Index

Amended index based on one prepared by Paul C. K. Kwong

Subject Index

Amended index based on one prepared by Paul C. K. Kwong